Reviews of *Unlocking the Ivory Tower*

Appealing to both academics and business leaders, **Eric Ball and Joe LiPuma not only provide the reader with grounded insight into a selection of themes that are critical to business success, but offer a valuable resource in bridging the worlds of academia and business.** *Unlocking the Ivory Tower* demonstrates how management research is relevant, and can be accessible to firms, in a very straightforward and concise manner.
> **–Rickie A. Moore, Past Chair of the Management Consulting Division, Academy of Management**

Ball and LiPuma do **an impressive job of collecting and illuminating important business research in a wide range of areas. Even better, they translate that research into practical takeaways for managers.**
> **–Steven N. Kaplan, Neubauer Family Distinguished Service Professor of Entrepreneurship and Finance University of Chicago Booth School of Business**

Peter Drucker taught us that in today's rapidly changing world, people "have to be prepared to live and work simultaneously in two cultures—that of 'the intellectual,' who focuses on words and ideas, and that of the 'manager,' who focuses on people and work." *Unlocking the Ivory Tower* **bridges those often-alien cultures beautifully, and in doing so it stands as a major contribution.**
> **–Rick Wartzman, Director of the Drucker Institute**

Unlocking the Ivory Tower is an excellent resource for business managers looking to make critical decisions based on best practices. The book represents a valuable summary of management research in key fields. Not only do Ball and LiPuma survey the literature past and present, but they inform what kind of research agendas can have the biggest real-world impact outside of the university environment. **Their book should be required reading for both students and faculty in business schools globally.**
> **–Audrey MacLean, Venture Investor, Consulting Professor, Stanford University, and Chairman, Coraid**

Ideas truly make the world go round. Given this impact, business leaders need to be able to ground their decision-making with state-of-the-art insights. Eric Ball and Joe LiPuma make this eminently possible through their **wide-ranging and thoughtful compendium of leading management research** on topics such as finance, strategy, entrepreneurship, leadership, and ⟨…⟩ ir work **allows a business leader to harne**⟨…⟩ s to offer to create real-world professional ⟨…⟩
> **–Mark Zupan, Dean of** ⟨…⟩ **School of Business at** ⟨…⟩

This book offers practical guidelines for clear thinking and informed decision-making distilled from the best business research. **Eric and Joe masterfully remove the academic clutter, bringing into focus simple yet powerful frameworks for thinking clearly and making informed business decisions.**
>—Clint Korver, Cofounder of Ulu Ventures and Partner at Crescendo Ventures

Too often, academic research lacks relevance to real-world business problems, or its most relevant lessons do not come to the attention of the people who can apply them. *Unlocking the Ivory Tower* **is a valuable bridge between academic findings and the people who can most benefit from them.** It delves into a variety of classical and recent works from the major academic fields and critically evaluates their relevance. (The annotated table of contents is an unexpected treat, too, providing an overview of a variety of important concepts.) Along the way, Ball and LiPuma also educate the reader about the evolution of each field, providing a rare—and fun—dose of intellectual history.
>—Noam Wasserman, Harvard Business School, author of *The Founder's Dilemmas: Anticipating and Avoiding the Pitfalls That Can Sink a Startup*

When academic management research and operational business management look at each other, there is often a sizeable gap. Based on their own practice and variety of experience, Eric Ball and Joe LiPuma bring us a powerful and insightful view on essential themes such as leadership, international business, organization, and processes. *Unlocking the Ivory Tower* **demonstrates how the academic and business worlds can efficiently get together to generate added value.**
>—Dominique Carouge, Vice President Administration and Management at Sanofi, Member of the Global Leadership Team

Imagine the greatest business thinkers in the world, all combined in a single classroom. Eric Ball and Joe LiPuma have written a monumental work that surveys the world of cutting-edge management thinking and makes it easy to grasp. **This is no ordinary business book: it is both a useful tool for practitioners and a powerful exploration of the workings of organizations, entrepreneurship, innovation, and finance.** This book is like an MBA and Ph.D. in one, guided by the hand of two highly experienced experts. *Unlocking the Ivory Tower* is a gift to the world, and it is a strongly recommended read for executives, investors, entrepreneurs, and others who seek to build successful businesses.
>—Victor Hwang, Cofounder of T2 Venture Capital, coauthor of *The Rainforest: The Secret to Building the Next Silicon Valley*

Unlocking the Ivory Tower:

How Management Research Can Transform Your Business

Eric R. Ball, PhD & Joseph A. LiPuma, DBA

Edited by Anna F. Doherty & Leslie F. Peters

Under no circumstances shall any of the information provided herein be construed as investment advice of any kind.

Unlocking the Ivory Tower:
How Management Research Can Transform Your Business
Eric R. Ball, Ph.D. and Joseph A. LiPuma, D.B.A.

Published by Kauffman Fellows Press
855 El Camino Real, Suite 12, Palo Alto, CA 94301, United States
www.kauffmanfellows.org

Library of Congress Control Number: 2012949781
ISBN-13: 978-0-9883807-0-7
Printed in the United States of America

Editing and design by Together Editing & Design
www.togetherediting.com

First Edition: October 2012
9 8 7 6 5 4 3 2 1

Cover images were taken for our use: University of Michigan Burton Tower photograph by Rob Hess 2012, used with permission; Oracle headquarters building photograph by Sheryl Axline 2012, approved for use by Oracle.

ACKNOWLEDGEMENTS

Eric would like to acknowledge just some of the people who made this effort possible:

- Phil Wickham and the Kauffman Fellows team who had the confidence to make this the first book published under the new Kauffman Fellows Press imprint.

- My graduate school classmates at the University of Rochester and the Drucker-Ito School of Management, who made the journey its own reward.

- The faculty and staff at the Drucker-Ito School, who carry forward Peter Drucker's unique legacy of straddling the academic and corporate worlds. Don Griesinger and Jay Prag have sustained the doctoral program over two decades. Richard Smith supported my academic interest while I was holding down a corporate career, and Rick Wartzman provided invaluable support in the development of this book.

- The very effective executive team at Oracle, particularly Safra Catz, for approving and supporting this project.

- Our tireless editors, Anna Doherty and Leslie Peters.

- All those who took the time to read and comment on early drafts, including Scott Page and Justin Rockefeller. The work improved from their comments.

- My sons Spencer and Carter, who look forward to my spending more of my weekends outside of my home office.

- My parents, who always wanted me to get a good education.

- My co-author Joe LiPuma, who shared long hours to bring this project from inception to finish, with dedication, insight, and humor.

- And finally, my wife and partner Sheryl Axline, who makes everything possible.

Joe also acknowledges the many people who helped make this book happen:

- The doctoral faculty and students at Boston University's Graduate School of Management 2002–2007 for their access to much of the literature we examine in this book.

- Josh Lerner and Scott Shane for leading seminars that explore some of the intersections of these various literatures.

- Anita McGahan, Jeff Furman, and Isin Guler for guiding my deep exploration into academic literature during my dissertation research.

- The International MBA students at EMLYON, who helped me realize how important a book like this could be to developing managers.

- My co-author Eric Ball, who provided the idea and impetus to carry this forward during times when it might have been easier to let it go.

- Anna Doherty and Leslie Peters, whose editing skills humbled me and led us to a better book.
- EMLYON for financial support of manuscript editing.
- Lucca and Ercole, my two boys, who keep me balanced and remind me why I do what I do.
- And mostly, Mary Roark, whose family support during the book's development kept our lives afloat, whose insight led us to the final name for the book, and whose belief in me made this happen.

All errors remain ours.

CONTENTS
THESIS SUMMARIES BY SECTION

Strategy is the long-term direction and scope of an organization as that organization pursues advantage through its configuration of resources, to meet the needs of markets and to fulfill stakeholder expectations (Johnson and Scholes 2006). Corporate strategy addresses which business a corporation will participate in, and business strategy focuses on how a particular business competes within its industry.

There are five competitive forces whose collective strength determines the ultimate profit potential in an industry: threat of new entrants, bargaining power of suppliers, bargaining power of buyers, threat of substitutes, and rivalry among existing firms. Managers can use these frameworks to determine the fit of their firm to the industry.

A transaction cost is a cost of coordination incurred in making an economic exchange, including search and information costs, bargaining costs, and enforcement costs. Costs associated with market transactions sometimes favor in-house production (i.e., hierarchies) and sometimes favor contracts (i.e., markets).

Strategies that are not based on resources are unlikely to succeed. Firms have different resource endowments, and it takes time and money to change these endowments. In addition, competitive market dynamics ensure that a firm will always be up against the best in whatever market it chooses to compete.

4. ORGANIZATION AND PROCESSES 169

Organizational design is the alignment of structure, process, rewards, metrics, and talent with the strategy of the business. In this chapter, we describe what has (and has not) been established to promote organizational effectiveness.

All companies—even new companies in new industries—must consider the global
environment in which they operate. Key international business literature addresses
dimensions such as theories of multinational enterprises, international political
economy, multinational management, and culture. These dimensions provide
managers with tools and concepts needed for growing beyond national borders.

Understanding the reasons, processes, and outcomes associated with
multinational business has been aided by recent development of theories of
the multinational enterprise (MNE). Such theories address international
operations and the control-based forms of multinationals, product
lifecycles, stage theories of inter**national**ization, and the eclectic theory
based on ownership, location, and **internal**ization advantages.

Internationalization is intended to provide companies with competitive
advantages, and companies take various approaches to their foreign market
entry and expansion in the context of broader economic, political, and
business activities. Knowledge acquisition and internalization are key to
multinational corporate evolution.

The environment in which MNEs operate affects—and is affected by—the
MNEs. As economic actors, MNEs affect other companies, the labor force,
technological and overall economic growth in their host countries. As
political actors, MNEs may influence the political environment in these
countries in ways that can be inconsistent with the political aims of the
corporate headquarters.

MNEs, as HQ and subsidiary units, affect the environments in which they
operate (both politically and economically). In this context, MNE managers
must determine how to structure the activities between headquarters and
subsidiary. How should the structure map to the firm's strategy and
learning, and the market needs of the industry globally and locally?

In the international context, corporate culture mixes with national culture
and becomes even more central to organizational performance. Culture
affects foreign market entry mode, multinational management, and
international negotiations.

Contexts for innovation vary based on location, industry, and country. We look
here at how innovation diffuses or spreads and thus how current technology such
as the web and social media might affect the adoption of innovative outputs. It is
essential that managers understand the contexts for innovation at the firm,
industry, and country levels in creating and managing innovation strategies.

Ideas, information, invention, and innovation are related, and require the
innovator's investment to extract returns. The economics related to perfect
markets and the market for information may lead to underinvestment in
innovative activities, thwarting invention and subsequent economic growth.
Managers must develop strategies and policies to promote innovative
company cultures and practices.

Economic theory may not be the best for explaining the birth, growth, and
death of firms. Innovation associated with venture emergence and growth
is path-dependent: the history of the entrepreneur and of the company
matter. Despite societal variance in creative individuals and economic
growth, innovation and industry lifecycles follow standard patterns, the
knowledge of which can aid strategic decision-making.

Innovation and innovative competition may vary based on the size and
position of the firm and the nature of the industry. Innovation may be
driven by industry incumbents, entrants, or by users. Protecting proprietary
information is key for innovators, as getting the value from innovation
motivates innovative activities.

Governments can play a role in the creation of environments conducive to
innovation, entrepreneurship, and economic growth. Governmental actions
can facilitate the development of systems of innovation, but may be less
important than the actions of entrepreneurs.

Agents are not rational, and markets are not efficient. People exhibit persistent and significant cognitive biases in how they process information, assess risk, and make investment decisions. These biases are consistent enough across people to be predictable.

Ensure everyone lives the mission. Be action-oriented and driven by results. Know who your customers are. Define performance concretely and keep score on yourself. Allocate your own life, make yourself a leader by focusing on what you want to be remembered for. Develop your strengths, not your weaknesses.

People are bounded in the time they take to make decisions, their rationality, their awareness, and their ethicality. Individuals tend to take cognitive shortcuts which result in mis-estimating risk and probability and making suboptimal or inconsistent decisions, even when the stakes are high. Understanding these tendencies can enable us to make better decisions, and to better evaluate decisions made by others.

Marketing is inseparable from strategy. The market orientation of a business determines its performance. Such orientation is facilitated by management's response to customer needs, higher interdepartmental connectedness, and decentralized decision-making. Consumers' cognitively biased tendency to engage in mental accounting has implications for marketers seeking to influence consumer behavior.

A complex adaptive social system consists of interdependent, interacting agents whose micro behavior responds to macro patterns they produce, resulting in a system which evolves. Computational modeling tools are well-suited to such systems. A variety of social phenomena (e.g., political, financial, economic, and natural behaviors) appear to be better understood using this perspective.

Tables & Figures

6. INNOVATION

7. FINANCE

INTRODUCTION

We have each spent a fair amount of time in both the academic and business worlds, which turns out to be unusual. From our perspective, with feet firmly in both spheres, the lack of contact between the two is remarkable but understandable.

University faculty do not often write for a real-world audience, which is why universities are often referred to as "the ivory tower," conjuring up an image of an impenetrable fortress where academic knowledge resides. When professors do write for a broad audience, they sometimes spoon-feed a simplified version of their work. Business schools primarily reward faculty who produce peer-reviewed academic journal articles, for which the primary audience is other academics. When faculty provide consulting for businesses, or when they do write for a broader audience, they often focus on a single idea coming from their own research. In our view, this often results in an article from a good practitioner-oriented journal (like the *Harvard Business Review*) being unnecessarily stretched into a full-length book containing a plenitude of anecdotes.

On the other side of this apparent divide, executives respect academic thinking but feel it doesn't really apply to them. They often view business research as overly theoretical and removed from their rough-and-tumble daily challenges. In addition, businesspeople generally lack the time to read through a vast amount of management research, much of which is physically and linguistically inaccessible, to glean the small fraction that could be useful in running their business.

The overall result is that the two environments exist as separate countries, communicating infrequently in any substantial way. This is the situation we would like to change.

MOTIVATION FOR THIS BOOK

We believe that management is a discipline that can be learned from study, and we see a large and diverse body of academic management research that has practical, actionable implications to help in managing a business today. In this book we have compiled and condensed some of the most relevant sources for each of several major components of business literature: strategy, entrepreneurship, leadership, organizational theory, international business, innovation, finance, decision-making, and other topics. In each area, our objective is to identify scholarly articles or books with relevance to a practicing executive and distill each of those sources into a brief summary while preserving the message of the original thinker. We also provide some context regarding how each contribution fits into the rest of the field and discuss how it might be applied in a business environment.

The result is a rather dense book that provides the basis for understanding major schools of thought in primary management fields. We see our role as interpreters—Eric's wife has dubbed our effort "CliffsNotes for Executives."[1]

Our primary audience is executives: the range of knowledge required by corporate managers requires an expanding breadth of concepts and skills. However, this book also appeals to educators and graduate students in business globally who may want a reference guide to academic contributions in major fields. Although much of the source material included here is covered in master's and doctoral programs, there are relatively few textbooks covering major contributions across fields. We stress the relevance of the content over an interest in providing original insights of our own, and in that sense are not unlike the authors of a textbook.

Finally, this book is intended for a global audience. In some parts of the world, many people are interested in learning about advanced management concepts and ways to apply them but lack access to schools or suitable programs.[2] Our hope is that this book may serve as a single reference for managers in areas without access to broader instruction.

HOW TO USE THIS BOOK

This book is intended as a useful reference for managers grappling with real business decisions in today's complex environment. The table of contents provides detail about the content of each chapter and section, through a

---

[1] By necessity, this is a non-exhaustive set of literature. Other excellent work exists, and the omission of a source does not imply its lack of applicability. We welcome the inevitable dialogues about what should have been included—and indeed, what should be included in the next edition.

[2] Business schools from Europe and North America are slowly establishing programs in China, for instance, but the quality and economics of these programs may not be sustainable as they are based on either foreign faculty with little experience or Western faculty "air-lifted" in for teaching.

synthesis of the thesis statement(s) of the source(s) summarized in the section. With these descriptions, readers can identify the chapters and sections most useful in addressing their practical concerns.

Each chapter focuses on a specific field of research and is divided into sections categorizing the various contributions in that field. Within each section, we provide a short takeaway (thesis) and a summary of one—or several—key sources (articles or books). Underlined sources (author names) indicate that the source is summarized in our book, so those who are interested can easily read more about that source.

At the end of each section we discuss the sources, including the relevance of the work to practitioners, which elements we agree with and find fault with, and the implications for managers in applying the concepts in the workplace. We also describe work that has been spawned by the key source(s).

A note about the summaries: although we have distilled some long articles and books into a handful of pages, we have tried to retain the spirit of the original language and the flow of that thinker. As a result, the summaries sometimes contain a fair amount of the original jargon and terminology; in some cases, this may be more worthwhile for students than for executives. We ask readers to bear with us and to feel free to skip ahead to the discussion of the managerial implications without tracing the development of the models.

We hope you enjoy the book.

Eric and Joe
Menlo Park, California and Lyon, France
October 2012

STRATEGY

Strategy has been studied and applied for thousands of years; many managers still read *The Art of War* written by the Chinese military leader Sun Tzu in the 6th century BCE. However, the systematic analysis of strategy in a corporate context is a much newer phenomenon, with only a handful of notable articles written prior to the 1960s.

Academics studying strategy ask questions like, "Why do some firms perform better than others?" and "Does firm success come more from careful planning or adroit reaction to market events?" Johnson and Scholes (2006) define *strategy* as the long-term direction and scope of an organization as that organization pursues advantage through its configuration of resources, to meet the needs of markets and to fulfill stakeholder expectations. As a management field, strategy is sometimes divided into two categories: *corporate strategy* addressing which businesses a corporation will participate in, and *business strategy* focusing on how a particular business competes within its industry. It is corporate strategy when GE determines which businesses it will engage in (e.g., jet engines, home appliances, broadcasting, leasing), and it is business strategy when the jet engine division determines how it will compete with other manufacturers like Rolls-Royce. Other than Porter's work on corporate strategy in the 1970s and 1980s, most of the work described in this chapter aligns toward business strategy.

The material covered in this chapter represents a small but significant subset of the history of strategy research. Herbert Simon, though not covered in this chapter, was an early great scholar in the field of business. His work was not limited to what we today call strategy, but his first book *Administrative Behavior* (1947) contained many practical insights including the notion of bounded rationality in decision-making, rather than the perfectly rational agent assumed in classical economics.

In the 1960s several authors introduced the strategic management concepts of mission statement, distinctive competence, and strengths and weaknesses.[1] Scholars developed these concepts and started applying what they observed in practice to research. The Boston Consulting Group (Bruce Henderson 1968, 1970) developed the idea of the experience curve, and Bruce Scott looked at diversification and firm performance (McArthur and Scott 1969). Work at Harvard extended the SWOT (strengths, weaknesses, opportunities, and threats) analysis into a framework of a firm in terms of its strengths and weaknesses, industry-economic-technical opportunities and threats, the personal values of implementers, and broader societal expectations.[2]

Also at Harvard, Michael Porter was a dominant author in the 1980s who linked social sciences and practical issues in managing a firm. He adapted an existing model of how industry structure can impact strategy which in turn can drive performance, developing a new industrial organization framework where structure is both a cause and an effect of strategy. Porter's impact is still felt today from his books *Competitive Strategy* (1980), *Competitive Advantage* (1985), and *The Competitive Advantage of Nations* (1990). These titles reflected the contribution of economics in the 1980s to the strategic management field in terms of how firms should position themselves in their environment, and are reviewed in Section 1.

Several articles appeared in the 1970s and 1980s debating the relative merits of strategy focused on institutional economics. Oliver Williamson at Stanford had explored the economic implications of transaction costs in the 1970s, and we describe in Section 2 how in the 1980s he applied this to strategy to explain differing forms of organization (Williamson and Ouchi 1981a). In a similar vein, Jensen and Meckling (1976) showed how, when ownership and management are separated (as in a large corporation), the owners and managers may have differing incentives. These misaligned incentives create agency costs which can drive organizations to respond in ways to limit managerial discretion. This work in transaction costs and agency costs generated disagreement over whether some assumptions made by scholars regarding self-serving behavior, and by managers about their employees, could be either prudent or self-fulfilling.[3]

In the same era, Birger Wernerfelt initiated the analysis of firms based on their differing resources (rather than their differing products) in his 1984 paper "A Resource-Based View of the Firm." He developed economic tools for analyzing a firm's resource position in order to identify appropriate strategic positions. *Resources* could be any source of strength or weakness, including both tangible and intangible assets available to that firm. This article led to a new

---

[1] See Selznick (1957), Chandler (1962), Andrews (1965), and Ansoff (1965).
[2] See Boston Consulting Group (1968, 1970) and Learned, Christensen, Andrews, and Guth (1969).
[3] See, e.g., Ghoshal and Moran (1996), and Moran and Ghoshal (1996).

school of research within strategy regarding how to deploy and develop unique resources to build a sustainable competitive advantage.[4] This school is described in Section 3.

C. K. Prahalad and Gary Hamel made significant contributions in the 1990s in their analysis of firms in terms of core competencies and strategic intent.[5] This work is summarized in Section 4. More recent work extends such competencies frameworks to capabilities-driven strategy.[6]

Also in the 1990s, several authors introduced the economic concept of *game theory* as a way of looking at strategic competition. Game theory attempts to describe behavior in strategic situations in which an individual's success in making choices depends on the choices of others. A notable application of this thinking to management is in a 1995 article by Brandenburger and Nalebuff summarized in Section 5. In Section 6, we highlight a timeless debate between whether strategic value comes from planning or from savvy reactions to external events, through competing explanations for the high degree of success of a single firm, Honda (Mintzberg, Pascale, Goold, and Rumelt 1996). In Section 7, we review how, as information technology accelerated the speed of decision-making in business in the 1990s, strategy analysis addressing the temporary nature of strategic advantage became increasingly relevant. D'Aveni (1994) stated that sustained competitive advantage is no longer a realistic goal, and established a framework in which competition is defined as building a series of temporary advantages over time. Since the late 1990s, there has been an increased focus in the literature on social capital and its value. We review one such contribution, from Nahapiet and Ghoshal (1998), in some detail.[7]

One of the larger disconnects between academic observers and corporate practitioners is in the area of mergers. Various studies since the mid-1980s, described in Section 8, have shown that the majority of acquisitions fail to add value for the acquiring company in either the short or long term. Several explanations have been offered (besides the obvious possible motivation of empire-building), but none are considered compelling, so that the continued popularity of acquisitions as a growth instrument is considered a puzzle in the academic community. This section presents some of these possible explanations (e.g., those listed by Cording, Christmann, and Bourgeois 2002), and then we offer our own view regarding what factors can help "beat the odds" in identifying and executing successful acquisitions.

---

[4] Subsequent authors include Dierckx and Cool (1989), Barney (1991), Amit and Shoemaker (1993), and Hall (1993).

[5] See Hamel and Prahalad (1989, 1994) and Prahalad and Hamel (1990); see also Hamel (1991, 1996), and Lado and Wilson (1995).

[6] Recent work in capabilities-driven strategy is described in Banerji, Leinwand, and Mainardi (2009).

[7] See also Ahuja (2000) and Burt (2000).

Stewart Myers used the term *real options* in 1977 to describe why companies might find value in leaving some of their debt capacity unutilized to take advantage of future opportunities. Subsequent work applied the tools of financial valuation to corporate investment. The concept of real options caught traction in the business world, and several authors developed guides for practitioners. One of these authors, described in Section 9, is Luehrman (1998), who demonstrated how the concept can inform the development of strategy.

Strategic planning often involves quantifying possible different future states of the environment and organizational outcomes. In Section 10, Davis-Floyd (1998) describes how Shell has taken the novel approach of fleshing out stories rather than numbers and found it to be an effective way to stimulate managers' thinking about how to plan and react to new developments.

Of course, success requires more than strategy formulation—execution is critical. Some recent work evaluates how successful companies differentiate themselves in how they act on their strategy. Clarifying who owns decisions and ensuring the proper flow of information are both key (Neilson, Martin, and Powers 2008). This is the focus of the last section in this chapter, Section 11.

Among the many contributions with constructive implications for the study of strategy, several are worth reading more to understand the academic development of strategy than to meet our objective of strategic insights of practical value. For instance, Godfrey and Hill (1995) noted that unobservable constructs (e.g., opportunism) lie at the core of influential strategy theories and described the debate between *positivists*, who hold that we can only use such unobservables to make predictions, and *realists*, who believe that good theory can provide knowledge about unobservables. Camerer (1985) provided an accurate, entertaining, and somewhat biting critique of the strategy literature, highlighting several pitfalls of even the most popular works: circular definitions (strategy as a means with a strategic objective as an end), a failure to test models stringently (to see that their predictions are not just better than nothing but also better than competing theories), and the pitfalls of inductive reasoning (e.g., developing general rules from specific cases). These articles are highly recommended for scholars and a good reminder to keep a skeptical eye, but may be less useful to businesspeople simply looking for tools to assist in positioning their firms; therefore they are not included here.

1. MICHAEL PORTER'S COMPETITIVE FORCES

Michael Porter is one of the best known strategy scholars, and the frameworks he described in multiple articles (and that are collected in his 1980 and 1985 books) remain part of the vocabulary of both academics and practitioners today.

These strategy frameworks are a central component of an industrial economics-based view of strategy.[8]

MICHAEL PORTER
Competitive Strategy (1980), Chapters 1–2. This material is revisited in Michael Porter, *Competitive Advantage* (1985), Chapter 1.

Thesis: There are five competitive forces whose collective strength determines the ultimate profit potential in an industry: threat of new entrants, bargaining power of suppliers, bargaining power of buyers, threat of substitutes, and rivalry among existing firms. Managers can use these frameworks to determine the fit of their firm to the industry.

Porter begins with a framework of the determinants of competitive intensity and then moves on to outline generic competitive strategies. There are five structural determinants of the intensity of competition. The collective strength of these forces determines the ultimate profit-potential in the industry, and the primary goal for a business unit is to find a position in the industry where it can best defend itself against these forces (or use them to its advantage).

Threat of New Entrants
- **Barriers to entry by competitors.** Economies of scale, product differentiation, capital requirements, switching costs, access to distribution channels, cost advantages independent of scale, and government policy are potential barriers to entry that competitors can introduce.
- **Expected retaliation.** If existing competitors are expected to respond forcefully against a new entrant, entry may be deterred.
- **The entry-deterring price.** If current price levels are too high, entrants are incented.
- **Properties of entry barriers.** Entry barriers can change as conditions change. Proprietary technology or high capital-investment requirements are two common barriers; as one fades in importance, another may become increasingly important. Some firms may possess resources that allow them to overcome barriers more inexpensively.
- **Experience and scale as entry barriers.** Experience is helpful, but an experience deficit can be overcome by hiring employees away from the

[8] Industrial Organization (IO) deals with how industries evolve and are organized. There are several textbooks available on the broad subject of IO, such as the recent text provided by Pepall, Richards, and Norman (2008).

first-mover firm. New entrants can even have an advantage if they can buy the latest equipment or use newer methods, unencumbered by past investment.

Intensity of Rivalry Among Existing Competitors
Rivalry occurs when one or more competitors feels the pressure or sees the opportunity to improve position. Firms are mutually dependent, and the intensity of rivalry increases when any of the following conditions exist:

- numerous or equally balanced competitors,
- slow industry growth,
- high fixed or storage costs,
- lack of differentiation or switching costs (making it easier for customers to defect),
- capacity augmented in large increments,
- diverse competitors,
- high strategic stakes,
- high exit barriers or entry barriers, and
- shifting rivalry.

Pressure From Substitute Products
Substitutes limit the industry's potential returns by placing a ceiling on prices that can be profitably charged. *Substitute products* are those that can perform the same functions.

Bargaining Power of Buyers
Buyers compete by forcing decreasing prices, bargaining for higher quality, and playing competitors against each other at the expense of industry profitability.

Bargaining Power of Suppliers
The conditions giving suppliers power tend to mirror those making buyers powerful.

Porter allows for discrete factors that can impact a company's competitive position, acting through these factors. Government can impact a company's or competitors' positions based on its role as a buyer or seller, or in setting regulations setting limits on competitors, buyers, or suppliers. Complements can also influence the demand for an industry's product. In a later book, Porter clarifies that, like government, complements do not represent a sixth force but rather affect profitability through the fundamental five forces (Porter 2008).

Once the firm conducts a structural analysis of the forces affecting competition and their underlying causes, the firm can identify its strengths and weaknesses. It can then create a defensible position against the five competitive forces:

- **Positioning.** The company takes the structure of the industry as a given and matches the company's strengths and weaknesses to it.
- **Influencing the balance.** The company can take the offensive by identifying key factors driving competition in this industry and thus locating places where action can yield the highest payoff.
- **Exploiting change.** Trends in the evolution of the industry are not as important as whether they affect the structural sources of competition.
- **Diversification strategy.** Structural analysis can identify the business' potential and valuable types of relatedness in diversification.

In Chapter 2, Porter turns to describing three generic competitive strategies.

Overall Cost Leadership
This strategy requires the aggressive construction of efficient-scale facilities, the pursuit of continuous cost reductions over time with manufacturing experience, implementation of tight overhead controls, and avoidance of marginal customer accounts. This cost-based approach gives the firm defenses against rivalry because it can earn returns at lower prices. Cost leadership also defends against powerful buyers (who can demand low prices) and sellers/suppliers (who may have a monopoly position that allows them to charge high prices). Such cost leadership can also provide a barrier to entry by other potential competitors if based on scale economies.

Differentiation
To use differentiation, a business creates an offering that is perceived throughout the industry as unique—a design or brand image, features, customer service, or other dimension. This strategy is a viable approach for earning above-average returns by defending against the five competitive forces.

Focus
Focus on a particular buyer group, product line segment, or geography rests on the premise that the firm can serve its narrow target more effectively or efficiently than broader competitors. This focus can come from low-cost or high-differentiation with its target market, or both. This approach implies limitations on the level of achievable market share.

Porter's chapter also addresses other requirements of his three generic strategies, the danger of being stuck in the middle, and the risks of each generic strategy.

Discussion and Implications

 Porter's framework is useful in evaluating the rise and fall of companies; for example, Eric worked at AT&T in the 1980s and 1990s when it was an $80 billion monolith. Porter's framework for competitive intensity offers ready explanations for both AT&T's dominance for most of the century and its decline since the 1980s. For decades, AT&T had been protected by strong barriers to entry: the large-scale costs to a competitor of building out a telecom network, the economies of scale of having the largest network in the world, and of course, government policy that granted the company a monopoly in providing phone service until 1984. Deregulation removed the primary barrier to entry. As new entrants crowded the field and transmission capacity increased by factors of magnitude to accommodate data, voice transmission became so commoditized and inexpensive that voice-over-IP vendors could offer it for free. By 2005, AT&T was a fraction of its former self and was absorbed into one of its former subsidiaries, SBC.

Telecommunications also provides an example of pressure from substitute products, in the form of mobile phones. In the United States, mobile phone providers did not have to earn a return on a network in rural areas (as AT&T did with its landline network), and could therefore provide an alternative to landlines for urban customers. Many developing countries skipped building expensive landline telecom networks and leapfrogged directly to sophisticated mobile networks.

Airlines provide another example of competitive intensity ramping up after deregulation, as well as being representative of the three generic competitive strategies. Southwest represents an airline that emphasizes overall cost leadership, using only one type of aircraft and keeping costs and fares low. Virgin America competes on a differentiated basis, based on a brand image crafted on its iconic founder Richard Branson. Midwest Express, until it became part of Frontier in 2011, pursued a focused approach in two ways: with a geographic focus on Wisconsin and the Midwest, and with its signature service making every seat a business-class seat.

Porter has been criticized for his "checklist approach." In particular, his framework reveals factors that can be relevant in considering one's competitive position, but does not address questions of the relative importance of different factors. For example, if you have low rivalry among competitors but face strong bargaining power from your suppliers, can you determine which of these factors will dominate? The broadness of the categories makes it a challenge to empirically determine which factors are more (versus less) critical in producing competitive intensity, or which competitive strategy is most likely to generate consistent profitability.

Our own view is that the framework itself does retain usefulness in ensuring that the CEO or strategist considers all the players and their potential influences on the value chain. It is productive to draw up a list of the five structural determinants of competitive intensity in your sector, and further, to list the various factors influencing each determinant. We suggest categorizing these according to what you can and cannot change, and using this list to help drive an understanding of the profit potential of your business. It is also worth thinking in terms of your own competitive strategy (cost leadership, differentiation, focus) and how it compares to that of your current and potential competitors. Regardless of one's view about Porter, we believe that the very popularity of his framework provides a common vocabulary for communicating strategy to others inside and outside a company.

In a later article ("What Is Strategy?" 1996), Porter makes additional points worth remembering. First, operational effectiveness, while important, is not strategy. In addition, strategy is unique for a given firm, requires tradeoffs to be explicitly made, and is based on fit for a particular company.

2. THE INSTITUTIONAL ECONOMICS APPROACH

Williamson and Ouchi's (1981a) institutional economics approach recognizes the reciprocal relationship between economics and organization theory. Their article (described below) builds on related work by Williamson on the role of transaction costs (see Williamson 1975, 1981).

OLIVER WILLIAMSON AND WILLIAM OUCHI
"The Markets and Hierarchies Program of Research: Origins, Implications, and Prospects" (1981a), in A. H. Van de Ven and W. F. Joyce (editors), *Perspectives on Organizational Design and Behavior.*

Thesis: A *transaction cost* is a cost of coordination incurred in making an economic exchange, including search and information costs, bargaining costs, and enforcement costs. Costs associated with market transactions sometimes favor in-house production (i.e., hierarchies) and sometimes favor contracts (i.e., markets).

The first section covers the origins of their approach. Humans are not perfectly optimizing agents but rather are *boundedly rational*, meaning that they have finite computational ability to determine perfect solutions; essentially, people do the best they can in a limited period of time for any given decision. In addition, the authors argue that people are often *opportunistic* ("self-interest seeking with guile," p. 351). That is, people are interested primarily in the returns to them as individuals from a course of action (rather than the impact of that action on others).

The second section introduces and justifies Williamson and Ouchi's conceptual framework, with its assumptions of bounded rationality and opportunism. With neither assumption, it would be possible to design a single contract covering in advance what each person will do in any possible scenario. If just opportunism is absent, it would be possible to address agents' limited ability to foresee possible outcomes by negotiating successive adaptations of a contract so that both sides gain the benefits of the contract. Where there are recurring transactions in the face of uncertainty, the authors show that an internal organization is well-suited to determine what actions each agent should take. The basic point of this framework is that the relationships central to an organization will limit bad behavior, because a single organization will not take advantage of itself.

In their third section they describe how this simple framework can explain many observed phenomena. Specific examples include the degree of vertical integration of companies, the specifics of contract law, the use of transaction cost by marketers, comparative economic systems, and even family law.

In the fourth section, the authors show that where autonomous contracting is costly and hazardous, internal governance will arise. Organizational structures include the following:

- **Vertical integration.** The authors observe vertical integration (single ownership of different parts of the supply chain) by U.S. manufacturers. Such integration can also help explain the multidivisional form of corporate governance, not in terms of removing executives from routine operations as Chandler (1962) proposed, but in terms of how managing businesses on a combined basis creates diseconomies from overhead costs, inter-dependencies, and the pursuit of subgoals at the expense of primary goals.

- **Bureaucracies and clans.** The authors address what management style is needed in the now-common multidivisional enterprise. What form of contracting should prevail inside the organization? *Hard (bureaucratic) contracting* relies on sanctions, whereas *soft (clan) contracting* relies more on social controls (e.g., reputation or peer pressure to do the right thing).

- **Other organizational design traditions.** Rather than looking at explanations that depend on the exercise of power (e.g., Pfeffer 1981), the authors recommend looking for efficiency-based explanations for the form that organizations take.

The authors finish by describing a research agenda for institutional economics. Any problem that can be cast as a contracting problem can be examined in terms of markets versus hierarchies. One can then compare alternative modes to each other rather than to some impossible frictionless ideal.

Discussion and Implications

 This transaction cost work is representative of the institutional economics perspective, which is different from the industrial economics framework in Porter's work. A transaction cost framework allows for the possibility that not all agents have the same objective that they can pursue in an optimal manner, and it traces out the implications if some boundedly rational people act in their own narrow self-interest rather than the firm's interest.

Williamson and Ouchi's approach begins with the question of why individual employees arrange themselves in firms in the first place, rather than interacting as individual contractors. Basically, they say it would involve complex negotiations and follow-up for individuals to construct the contracts needed to sell their services one at a time. Some employees could sell their output on a daily basis, while others might contract to undertake a project but simply pocket the money without producing the work. Arranging into organizations simplifies the contract and allows for internal fiat to ensure that work gets done. Similar considerations can provide for different types of relationships and organization. A company might buy a supplier (vertical integration) to get around differing incentives between the company and the supplier.

This approach suggests that part of the strategic role of senior management in any organization is to evaluate the form of organization. Will you use employees or contractors? Will you outsource whole functions (e.g., manufacturing, human resources)? Will you buy suppliers? Executives should consider what incentives each arrangement creates among the participants.

An interesting development over the past decade has been the growth of freelancing sites that facilitate the process of hiring remote contractors, by using information technology to connect firms to contractors and providing means for the contractors to demonstrate their quality and work ethic in advance. Such sites include oDesk, Elance, Vworker, Freelancer.com, Guru, and others.

It is worth mentioning here the similarity between this article and Jensen and Meckling's (1976) work in finance. Their landmark article explained the ownership structure of the firm as an institution designed to limit agency costs and considered that the objectives of senior management (agents) and shareholders (owners) will not always coincide. Managers wanting to maximize their own utility (rather than the value of the firm) may undertake suboptimal courses of action: making investment decisions tilted toward the short-term, failing to promote talented managers who threaten their positions, or taking expensive perquisites. In order to prevent employers from reducing managers' pay due to these expected costs, it becomes in the manager-agent's own interest to devise a contract that limits such conflicts.

Transaction costs and agency costs are at the heart of the institutional economics perspective on strategy. Both recognize that organizations are full of individuals who may not all be motivated solely by maximizing their employer's value.

Some strategy scholars are highly critical of the institutional economics approach, which has sparked meaningful debate regarding the implications for structuring and managing an organization. The following summarizes some contributions on both sides of this discussion, presented in chronological order.

- **C. Perrow (1981).** Bounded rationality and opportunism should act within a firm as well as outside, so it is not clear why these elements should lead to internalizing the conflicts within one organization. Williamson (1975) had argued that some problems are mitigated in the multidivisional form of company, but Perrow finds the examples unpersuasive. Perrow also disagrees with the efficiency explanation for the shift from markets to hierarchies, arguing that control rather than efficiency is the issue. He concludes that markets do not always work but are better for people than being in a hierarchy, saying that fiat is not better than negotiations for settling disputes if you are the one being fiated. In an unusual back-and-forth debate within the same publication, Williamson and Ouchi (1981b) accuse Perrow of having a romantic view of communal efforts and ignoring the reality that peer groups have limits driven by transaction costs.

- **Fowell (1990).** Fowell finds the choice between markets and hierarchies described by Williamson and Ouchi to be incomplete. Network forms of organization with reciprocal patterns of communication and exchange are a viable pattern of organization. Such networks are unlike either markets or hierarchies. Some arrangements may increase transaction costs but in return provide concrete benefits or intangible assets, which are more valuable.

- **Zajac and Olsen (1993).** It is possible to examine strategies between organizations from the standpoint of transactional value rather than transaction cost. The cost perspective (of Williamson and Ouchi) ignores the interdependence between partners, and neglects process issues. Zajac and Olsen propose a framework of joint value maximization in which the risk of exploitation is only one of many elements to consider in maximizing the cooperative opportunity.

- **Ghoshal and Moran (1996).** This article develops an argument that Williamson's (and Ouchi's) prescriptions are not only wrong but dangerous. Organizations are not mere substitutes for markets in structuring transactions—they also possess unique advantages for governing certain kinds of activities using a different logic than that of the market. Ultimately, Ghoshal and Moran see opportunism as a self-fulfilling prophecy. Fiat does not just increase the cost of opportunistic behavior, it also creates a negative feeling for the organization and ultimately leads to more opportunism (perhaps in other forms not addressed by that fiat). Basically, the authors say that employees will behave however management expects them to behave.[9]

In another point-counterpoint debate, Williamson (1996) responds that nothing but a frank examination of opportunism will enable us to mitigate its hazard. He suggests we avoid contractual naïveté and identify and mitigate potential hazards. His main message is to give and receive credible commitments: "Rather than assume that promises are self-enforcing, contract as mere promise unsupported by credible commitments is perceived to pose hazards" (p. 56). Moran and Goshal (1996) reply that markets and firms are very different kinds of institutions, and each must implement its own logic.

To locate ourselves in this debate, we find some support for both views in our experience. A more structured organization can mitigate some opportunism, but it is possible to go too far in constraining employee freedom such that employees live up (or down) to the implied set of expectations. Further, a company that limits decision-making will develop managers who do not make decisions, and there are limits to the number of decisions that can be made in the executive suite. For example, a company Eric has worked for requires CEO approval for every hire in a company of 100,000 employees, and tight spending limits such that even VPs cannot spend more than $25,000 on their own authority. In our view, such a restrictive spending approach leads managers to focus more on getting approvals from lesser-informed senior managers than on evaluating for themselves if a hire or an expenditure is needed. We find more opportunism in dominant companies than in competitive ones, perhaps because in dominant companies a given cost is lower relative to the overall profit of the company.

Culture can also play a role. In a contained environment like Silicon Valley or New York City, employees and companies have unique reputations that go beyond their current situation and help limit their opportunistic actions. eBay

---

[9] Others assert that, by teaching theories which assume managers are self-seeking, we are in fact instructing managers to behave that way. In a *Harvard BusinessReview* blog comment to a post by Steve Kaplan, Patnaik (2009) states:

> We didn't just teach students that economists view people as self-serving with guile. We taught students that they should be self-serving with guile if they wanted to do well in our classes. And we taught them the 'soft skills' they needed to get really good at it. That's a perfect model for a world where business leaders are chosen by internal competition, and the most aggressive sumbitch gets to the top.

In the same blog, Kaplan (2009) points out that past MBA students oversaw a long period of increased living standards, and existing MBA students have a higher social awareness than ever before. Our own view is that economists and management researchers should first strive to understand the world as it is, without worrying about whether revealing opportunistic behavior teaches students to act that way—and only then take up the cause of how to encourage better behavior.

has built reputation into its business model, where they post buyer and seller feedback from prior transactions, and experience surprisingly little truly opportunistic behavior.

3. THE RESOURCE-BASED VIEW OF THE FIRM

This section analyzes firms from the perspective of what resources they possess rather than what products they offer. Birger Wernerfelt (1984) wrote one of the early articles reframing strategy in this manner, and triggered significant work by other academics extending the framework.

BIRGER WERNERFELT
"The Resource-Based Theory of the Firm" (1984), *Strategic Management Journal.*

Thesis: Strategies that are not based on resources are unlikely to succeed, for two reasons. Firms have different resource endowments, and it takes time and money to change these endowments. In addition, competitive market dynamics ensure that a firm will always be up against the best in whatever market it chooses to compete.

Resources can be defined as anything that represents a strength or weakness within a given firm. Wernerfelt uses the concepts of resource position-barriers and resource product-matrices, in analogy to earlier work about *entry barriers* (which make it hard for competitors to produce similar products) and growth-share matrices. From this perspective, strategy involves striking a balance between exploiting existing resources and developing new ones. An acquisition represents the purchase of a bundle of resources in a highly imperfect market.

In the first section, examining firms in terms of resources leads to different strategic insights, especially with respect to diversified firms. A firm can identify resources that may lead to higher profits and then establish resource position-barriers.

In the next section, Wernerfelt models the link between resources and profitability.

- **General effects.** Production of a firm-specific resource by a monopoly will lessen returns available to users of that resource. If products resulting from a resource can be sold only in *monopsonistic markets* (i.e., markets with a limited number of buyers), that also will lessen returns from a resource. Returns are impacted by the availability of substitute resources.

- **First-mover advantages—Resource position-barriers.** An entry barrier without a resource position-barrier leaves the firm vulnerable to diversifying entrants, whereas a resource position-barrier without an entry barrier leaves the firm unable to exploit the barrier. One can identify types of resources that can lead to high profits. First-mover advantages should yield high returns in markets where the resource in question is dominating (later acquirers of this resource are impacted adversely compared to earlier acquirers of that resource).

- **Attractive resources.** It is possible to identify classes of resources for which resource position-barriers can be erected. Examples include production experience, machine capacity, customer loyalty, or technological leads.

- **Mergers and acquisitions.** With dissimilar firms, an acquisition can be seen as the purchase of a bundle of resources in a highly imperfect market. If the resource purchased is rare, the owner can charge more for it (or, in Wernerfelt's terms, the market imperfections can be maximized, which is another way of saying that resources can be leveraged through diversification). Here, it is optimal to build on one's most unusual resource position.

In the third section, the author develops an example of dynamic resource management and presents a resource-product matrix providing a way to visualize the tradeoff between exploiting resources the firm already possesses versus developing new resources. The use of a single resource in several businesses is the diversification pattern most often considered in business policy. Often it is better to develop the resource in one market and then enter other markets from a stronger position (i.e., *sequential entry*). The balance between existing and new resources is in theory the same as managing a product portfolio, but the two frameworks highlight different growth avenues.

Wernerfelt recommends thinking of resources as stepping stones. In managing a resource portfolio, candidates for product or resource diversification must be evaluated in terms of both their short-term effects and long-term capacity to serve as an intermediate step to further expansion (e.g., developing skills in chips prior to entering the computer industry).

Related Literature

The idea of analyzing a firm as a broad set of resources goes back at least as far as Penrose (1959), but this 1984 paper by Wernerfelt launched what can be considered its own school of thought within the strategy field. Several authors added to the framework over subsequent years, and the most relevant enhancements are as follows.

Dierckx and Cool (1989)

This article emphasizes that a key dimension of strategy is making choices about expenditures to accumulate nontradeable resources. The amount of a resource possessed at a certain point in time is termed a *stock*, while the activities contributing to that stock represent the resource *flow*. Flows can be adjusted instantaneously but stocks cannot. Think of a bathtub full of cold water: one can quickly adjust the temperature of incoming water, but it still takes time to make the water in the tub warm. The value of nontradeable assets decreases over time so the stock must be continually replenished, such that critical resources are accumulated rather than acquired in *factor markets* (i.e., markets where resource inputs are purchased).

The sustainability of a firm's asset position hinges on how easily assets can be substituted or imitated. Imitability is linked to the following characteristics of the process of asset accumulation:

- **Time-compression diseconomies.** Maintaining a given rate of R&D spending over a particular time interval is likely to yield more than spending twice as much money over half as much time.
- **Asset-mass efficiencies.** Firms that already have some stock of R&D knowledge are in a better position to make breakthroughs than those firms starting from scratch or from a very low level.
- **Interconnectedness of asset stocks.** Increments depend not just on the level of stock but also on the levels of stocks of other assets (e.g., to the extent that developments originate in customer suggestions, it may be harder for firms without a service network to develop technological know-how).
- **Asset erosion.** R&D know-how depreciates over time from obsolescence, in the absence of maintenance expenditures.
- **Causal ambiguity.** Asset accumulation may be unpredictable and lumpy (e.g., R&D in the pharmaceutical industry often produces no results for an extended time and then a sudden "jackpot"). Success factors are often ambiguous and therefore hard to imitate.

Asset stocks may be vulnerable to substitution by different assets that render them obsolete. For example, Canon designed copiers that do not require service, substituting superior design for Xerox's extensive service network. "Asset stocks are strategic to the extent they are nontradeable, nonimitable, and nonsubstitutable" (p. 1510).

Barney (1991)

This article examines the link between firm resources and sustained competitive advantage, and suggests four empirical indicators of the potential of resources to generate such advantage:

- **Value.** A resource cannot generate advantage unless it has significant value.

- **Rareness.** The resource must be rare as well as valuable (these are distinct, even though value often accompanies rareness).
- **Imitability.** The extent to which a resource can be imitated can depend on unique historical conditions, causal ambiguity, and social complexity.
- **Substitutability.** The resource should not be easily substitutable, so that the advantage cannot be easily gained from another resource.

Barney assumes that strategic resources are heterogeneously distributed across firms and that differences are stable over time. This variance in resource endowment stands in contrast to Porter's (1980) early work, which focused on a firm's opportunities and threats assuming that firms within the industry are identical in terms of their resources and potential strategies. Barney argues that the link between resources and advantage lies in a resource-based view (RBV) of the firm, with resources that differ across firms and are only imperfectly mobile. In this view, the differing resource endowments among firms are crucial to sustaining competitive advantage. In Porter's defense, his 1985 work did introduce a "value chain" to help managers isolate firm-specific attributes, but even there, such differences do not get nearly the emphasis as in these resource-based strategy articles.

Barney differs also from Dierckx and Cool (1989), who argue that a resource providing an advantage cannot be traded, arguing that strategic factor markets do exist for such resources. Some later authors (e.g., Chi 1994) examine how such trading may function.

Amit and Schoemaker (1993)

This article builds on the view of the firm as a bundle of both resources and capabilities, whose economic rents can be appropriated by the firm (where *rents* are the difference between the cost of these resources and what can be charged for them). *Capabilities* are defined as invisible assets and the firm's ability to deploy resources using organizational processes to a desired end. Firms are expected to differ in the resources and capabilities they control because of resource–market imperfections and discretionary management decisions about how resources are developed and deployed. This asymmetry can itself be a source of sustainable economic rent (i.e., continuing profits).

The authors focus on the linkages between industry analysis framework, the resource-based view of the firm, behavioral decision biases, and organizational implementation issues. Rent is shown to stem from imperfect decisions to develop and deploy resources made by boundedly rational managers who face uncertainty, complexity, and conflict within their own firms. One of the more interesting aspects of this analysis is that it explicitly ties the notion of managers' bounded rationality to strategic assets. Firms have differing levels of bias in how they make decisions, and thus, differing ability to imitate resources or optimize their use.

Hall (1993)

This article focuses specifically on the role of intangible resources in business strategy and evaluates how to identify intangible sources of sustainable competitive advantage. Such advantage results from the possession of relevant capability differentials. *Intangible resources* may be classified as either assets or competencies to include intellectual property, reputation, skills, and culture. Regulatory and positional capabilities are derived from intangible assets, whereas functional and cultural abilities derive from competencies. The author devises a framework linking intangible resources to capabilities and uses this framework as a basis for a new way of identifying the relative contribution of various intangible resources to competitive advantage. He also applies the technique to six organizations in the form of case studies.

Peteraf (1993)

This author synthesizes various resource-based view (RBV) models and identifies common strands. Four conditions must be met for competitive advantage:

- **Resource heterogeneity.** The production resources and capabilities must be different across firms.
- *Ex post* **(after the fact) limits to competition.** After a firm gains superior position and starts earning rents, there must be forces that prevent new competitors from coming in and taking those same profits. Having resources that are hard to imitate, and hard to substitute for, can be critical sources of such limits.
- **Imperfect resource mobility.** Resources are immobile if they cannot be traded, or partially mobile if they are somewhat specialized to the firm.
- *Ex ante* **(preexisting) limits to competition.** Prior to a firm's establishing a superior resource position, there must be limited competition for that position.

The author also shows how this model can be applied at the level of a single business strategy (how to position one's business) or at the level of corporate strategy (how to choose which businesses to be in).

Collis and Montgomery (1995)

This *Harvard Business Review* (HBR) article provides a good summary of the resource-based view.[10] This perspective combines the internal analysis of phenomena with the external analysis of prior approaches, and acknowledges the vastly differing collections of physical and intangible assets and capabilities

---

[10] The same authors provide a longer explanation in the 2005 second edition of their book *Corporate Strategy: A Resource-Based Approach.*

at different companies. The authors provide a concise checklist of what makes a resource valuable:

- Is it hard to copy?
- Does it depreciate slowly?
- Who captures the value?
- Can it be "trumped" by a different resource?

They also make the important point that practitioners need to disaggregate vacuous statements of core competence—a core competence is not "consumer marketing skills" but rather what specific and discrete skills your company possesses. The article gives case studies of companies who have upgraded their resources (e.g., Intel, AT&T, Nucor), and warns of three common mistakes in leveraging resources:

- overestimating the internal transferability of assets or capabilities,
- overestimating the ability to compete in profitable industries (which typically look attractive precisely because of entry barriers), and
- assuming that leveraging a generic resource (e.g., lean manufacturing) will be a major source of advantage in a new market environment.

Crook, Ketchen, Combs, and Todd (2008)

This meta-analysis reviews 125 empirical studies (covering 29,000 organizations) that have examined the link between organizations possessing strategic resources and performance. They find a positive link, which increases in strength for organizations meeting specific criteria for valuable resources and for those performance measures that are not impacted by potential value appropriation. The authors conclude that identifying, developing, and distributing value from strategic resources should therefore be a primary consideration for scholars and managers.

Discussion and Implications

 From the mid-1980s to mid-1990s, the resource-based view came to hold a central place in academic discussions of what drives value and profitability for companies. Collis and Montgomery describe examples of how companies can upgrade their resources: Intel added new resources by inserting a new brand name "Intel Inside" to their resource base, while Nucor moved into a structurally more attractive industry by transitioning from low-margin downstream business like steel joists to differentiated upstream business like thick-slab cast-steel sheets. In each example, the company thought about how to extract more value from its existing set of skills.

Even with the popularity of this resource-based view of strategy, it also has some significant limits and shortcomings that have been identified in the literature.

- **Unobservable constructs.** A core proposition of the resource-based view is that the more unobservable a resource, the harder it is to imitate, and so the more sustainable will be its resulting competitive advantage. Any theory based on unobservable factors is subject to reasonable criticism. Positivists (e.g., Godfrey and Hill 1995) argue that one cannot test if such a theory is "true" but can only test predictions that might hold if that theory were true. Under this point of view, there is not much to learn about these unobservable constructs from applying resource-based theory.

- **Identification, concreteness, and generality.** Ghemawat (1991) identifies issues with the concept of key success factors that also apply to resources. First, the issue of identification: there may be many resources as well as interactions that impact a firm's success. Second, the issue of concreteness: there may be ambiguity about causality. Third, the issue of generality: to be strategic, resources must be undervalued, and it is challenging to determine their value.

- **The resource-based view has a poorly defined chain of causality.** Michael Porter (2008) raises a number of concerns about resource-based theory. First, the chain of causality making certain resources into valuable strategic assets is poorly defined, and needs to be unraveled to evaluate the theory. Second, resources are not in themselves valuable; they are only valuable because they enable activities that create advantages in particular markets. Third, advantage also derives from separate sources (scale, sharing across activities, integration, etc.). Finally, the real source of advantage may be managerial choice rather than resources. So-called resources yield rent only to the extent that past managerial choices assemble resources in unique ways, combine them, pursue new market positions, or create resources internally.

- **The resource-based view disregards products.** This view does not directly consider the attributes of a firm's products. In addition, it ignores the fact that competitive success may depend on having the right products available at the right time, as well as the threat of substitute products.

- **The resource-based view may be circular.** Katherine Connor (1994) argues that RBV researchers have not shown how an entrepreneur can determine appropriate inputs to generate rents. A resource-based approach may not address issues of opportunism and control that can impact strategy execution. The resource view risks becoming tautological (circular) unless it can distinguish among different levels of resources. When everything is viewed as resource, then we can say that whatever created the advantage must have been a resource, and the theory loses any explanatory power.

The view ignores the degree of influence that the environment has on a firm. Eisenhardt and Martin (2000) counter Connor's view and argue that resources are based on dynamic capabilities consisting of specific strategic and organizational processes (best practices) that are neither vague nor tautological.

Teece, Pisano, and Shuen (1997) develop an extension of the resource perspective they call the dynamic capabilities approach. *Dynamic* reflects the capacity to renew competencies to match changing business environments, and *capabilities* emphasizes the role of management in adapting, integrating, and reconfiguring internal and external organizational skills/resources/ competencies to match the requirements of a changing environment. To be strategic, a capability must be honed to a user need, unique, and difficult to replicate. A capability is a way of getting things done which cannot be accomplished merely by using prices to coordinate activity. Three classes of factors can help determine a firm's capabilities:

- **Processes.** Processes have three roles in an organization, namely coordination and integration, learning, and reconfiguration and transformation.
- **Positions.** Strategic posture is determined not just by a firm's processes but also by its specific assets (e.g., specialized equipment, knowledge assets, reputational and relational assets).
- **Paths.** The strategic journeys of firms are path-dependent, and current position is often shaped by the path traveled thus far. Investment history matters. How fast a firm can proceed also depends on the technological opportunities that lie before it. The possible evolutionary path may be quite narrow and require assessment in terms of these opportunities and constraints imposed by processes, positions, and paths.

Rents can only be generated to the extent they are based on skills that are difficult to imitate. The three authors view this framework as easier to operationalize for practitioners than much of the earlier work in strategy.

Despite the limitations expressed above, the resource-based view has generated a lot of attention and does suggest some useful questions for practitioners to ask themselves regarding what unique assets their organization possesses and how can those assets best be deployed for sustainable advantage. Eric's experience at the leading enterprise software company (Oracle) embodies this resource view. Software code is an almost pure example of intellectual property. If one can write truly useful software that helps businesses function more efficiently, the value is high, the software is unique, and it is often hard to imitate the functionality in another way. Once written, the marginal cost of delivering to new customers is essentially zero (which also drives economies of scale, making larger software firms more profitable), while the pricing can be driven by the value created for the customer. The resource-based view is an academic theory that goes reasonably far toward describing the profitability of certain businesses.

4. STRATEGIC CAPABILITIES

In this section, we summarize two sources by the same co-authors (one on core competence and one on strategic intent, developed at almost the same time), before proceeding to the Discussion and Implications. Collectively, these two articles are foundational examples of a branch of the strategy literature referred to as the *strategic intent* or *capabilities perspective* within a resource-based view of the firm.

C. K. PRAHALAD and GARY HAMEL
"The Core Competence of the Corporation" (1990), *Harvard Business Review*.

Thesis: Executives are now judged on their ability to identify, cultivate, and exploit the core competencies that make growth possible.

Principles of management are in need of reform. To the extent that Japan's ascent in the 1980s came at the expense of Western firms, Western executives must assume responsibility for their competitive decline. Executives used to be judged on their ability to restructure and de-layer their corporations, but now they need to focus on the competencies that enable growth. In so doing, they are rethinking the concept of the corporation.

The critical task for management is to create an organization capable of infusing products with irresistible functionality. A prominent example of a company developing core competence is NEC, which seized on the convergence of computing and communications to enable it to compete in multiple businesses. NEC did not need to develop new ideas, but rather found it quicker and cheaper to use foreign technology, soon surpassing GTE.

In exploring the roots of competitive advantage, there is an important distinction between viewing a corporation as a portfolio of companies and viewing it as a portfolio of businesses. In the short run, competitiveness derives from the price–performance attributes of existing products; in the long run, it derives from an ability to build, at lower cost and faster speed, the core competencies that spawn unanticipated products. Core competence concerns organization of work and delivery of value, applies in services as in manufacturing, and involves commitment to working across organizational boundaries. Competencies are the glue binding the businesses and the engine for new business development. Management trapped in the strategic business unit (SBU) mindset, viewing the company as merely a collection of discrete businesses, almost inevitably find their individual businesses dependent on external sources for critical components. These components are the physical embodiments of competencies. A successful organization must learn to coordinate diverse production skills and integrate multiple technology streams.

This view of the company as a portfolio of competencies can be seen in many case examples. Honda developed a specific competence in engines, starting with lawn mowers and snow blowers and then growing into motorcycles and eventually cars and trucks. Casio built expertise with display systems that allowed it to compete in calculators, laptops, and car dashboards. Sony leveraged its skill at miniaturization. Citi invested in an operating system enabling it to participate in world markets 24 hours a day. 3M's knowledge of sticky tape took it to the diverse businesses of post-it notes, magnetic tape, and photography.

Cultivating core competence does not mean outspending rivals on R&D, nor does it mean sharing costs among SBUs, nor vertically integrating. To develop core competence, an organization needs to take an inventory of skills and seek to apply them in nontraditional ways.

There are at least three tests for identifying a core competence:

- Does it provide potential access to a wide variety of markets?
- Does it make a significant contribution to the perceived customer benefits of the end product?
- Is it difficult for competitors to imitate?

A complex harmonization of technologies and skills should be challenging to emulate.

Prahalad and Hamel warn that one cannot "rent out" through outsourcing the embedded skills that give rise to the next generation of competitive products. Outsourcing can provide a shortcut, but typically contributes little to building the skills necessary to sustain product leadership.

A company can also lose by forgoing opportunities to establish competencies that are evolving in existing businesses. One lesson is that the cost of losing a core competence cannot be wholly calculated in advance. A second lesson is that since competencies are built through a long process of continuous improvement, a company that has failed to invest will find it difficult to enter an emerging market as other than simply a distribution channel. One cannot get off the train, walk to the next station, and then reboard.

Core products are the physical embodiments of one or more core competencies, the components or subassemblies that actually contribute to end product value. It is important to distinguish between core competencies, core products, and end products because competition is played out by different rules with different stakes at each level.

- At the level of competencies, the goal is to build leadership in the design and development of a particular class of product functionality.
- To sustain leadership in competencies, companies maximize their manufacturing share in core products to generate the revenue and market feedback that determine the pace at which competencies can be extended.
- A dominant position in core products allows a company to shape the evolution of applications and end markets, leading to economies of scale and scope.

The authors also decry the tyranny of the strategic business unit, stating that it is better to view the company as a portfolio of competencies rather than of business units. U.S. companies generally have the technical resources to build competencies but often lack the vision and administrative means for assembling resources spread across multiple businesses. Among the three planes on which battles for global leadership are waged (core competence, core products, and end products), a corporation must keep accurate track of whether it is winning or losing on each plane. If a corporation is winning the competencies race, it will almost certainly outpace rivals in new business development. If it is winning the race for manufacturing share in core products, it will likely outpace rivals in improving product features and in price–performance ratio. In the race for global brand dominance, companies like 3M, Black & Decker, Canon, Honda, NEC, and Citi have built global brand umbrellas by proliferating products out of their core competencies.

There are three important traps to avoid falling into:

- **Underinvestment in developing core competencies and products.** When the organization is viewed as a multiplicity of SBUs, no single business feels responsible for maintaining a viable position in core products nor for justifying the investment to build leadership in a core competence.
- **Imprisoned resources.** The people who embody the competence are often seen as the sole property of the business in which they grew up. Benefits depend on velocity of circulation as well as the size of the stock held. When people who carry the competencies do not get assigned to the new opportunities, their skills atrophy. SBU managers who compete for cash in the budgeting process typically do not compete for the more precious asset that is people.
- **Bounded innovation.** If competencies are not recognized, individual SBUs will pursue only those incremental innovation opportunities that are close at hand. Conceiving of the corporation in terms of competencies widens the domain of innovation.

In order to develop strategic architectures, executives should recognize that the fragmentation of competencies becomes inevitable when a diversified company's information systems, communication patterns, career paths, managerial rewards, and processes of strategy development do not transcend business-unit lines. A strategic architecture can provide a roadmap for dramatically reducing the investment needed to secure market leadership. Such an architecture asks if each new market opportunity exploits or adds to the core competencies and makes resource allocation priorities transparent to the entire organization. In short, strategic architecture yields a definition of the company and the markets served, revealing the broad direction of the corporation without giving away every step.

To ensure that competence-carriers are not held hostage by an SBU, business units should bid for core competencies in the same way they bid for capital. These are corporate resources and may be allocated by corporate management. It is also worth ensuring that reward systems and career paths do not focus only on the results of a single product-line. Here are other ways to wean employees from the idea they belong to any one particular business:

- introduce a planned rotation program for early-career managers;
- bring together competence carriers from across the corporation to trade ideas;
- encourage these carriers to discover new market opportunities, and make the competencies the wellspring of new business development; and
- require top management to add value by enunciating the strategic architecture that guides the process of acquiring competencies.

GARY HAMEL and C. K. PRAHALAD
"Strategic Intent" (1989), *Harvard Business Review.*

Thesis: It is not resources but rather *resourcefulness* that drives success, and the resourcefulness of a company can be stimulated by choosing ambitious goals that are clearly beyond a firm's existing capabilities.

Like Porter, Hamel and Prahalad evaluate the key strategic choices made by a firm. However, where Porter focuses on the constraints placed on choices by the external environment, these authors suggest a more proactive approach in creating advantages that existing conditions do not offer.

Too many companies expend energy just to reproduce the cost/quality advantages of their competitors, in an endless game of catch-up. Traditional competitor-analysis has focused on existing resources rather than on *resourcefulness*, which represents the speed at which new competitive advantages are being built. However, taking a snapshot of a moving car will not tell you where it is going, or how fast.

Companies that have risen to global leadership since the 1990s began with ambitions totally out of proportion to their existing resources and capabilities, creating a passion for winning that can be dubbed *strategic intent*. Such intent couples a management process to ambition, captures the essence of winning, and is stable over time. Strategic intent also motivates by communicating the value of the target, identifying a target deserving of personal effort and commitment. In the automotive market, the Ford Motor Company recognized that a concrete objective like market share or efficiency motivated employees more than "shareholder value," and so showed workers videos of Mazda's most efficient plant.

Strategic intent is clear about ends and flexible about means, leaving room for improvisation. It implies a meaningful stretch for the organization, forcing the organization to be inventive since closing such a large gap between resources and ambitions will require a series of quantum leaps. Managers should view the goal as a marathon to be run in 400-meter sprints, and can present corporate challenges that specify the next "hill" within the longer race.

Companies must manage scarce resources to take on better-financed rivals, and change the game in ways that disadvantage incumbents. There are four approaches to competitive innovation:

- **Build layers of advantage.** Build a base to dominate in other businesses. For example, Japanese television makers used low labor costs developed in making black-and-white TVs to go into making other products.
- **Search for loose bricks.** Stake out your competitor's underdefended territory by finding the part of the value chain where each competitor is vulnerable (on the low-end, high-end, as supplier, etc.). Honda identified low-end motorcycles as an uncontested market. While selling 50cc bikes in the United States, it raced bigger ones in Europe and amassed the design and technical skills it needed to dominate the entire business.
- **Change the terms of engagement.** Refuse to accept the frontrunners' definition of industry and segment boundaries. While Xerox built a wide range of copiers, Canon standardized to reduce costs. Canon also sold rather than leased, and marketed to end users rather than to purchasing departments. Xerox's structure (a national sales force dedicated to leasing to corporate procurement officials) became a barrier to retaliation. Competitive innovation is like judo in using the larger competitor's weight against it; an incumbent's greatest weakness is its belief in accepted practice.

- **Compete through collaboration.** Collaborate and win without fighting through licensing, outsourcing agreements, and joint ventures. Japanese firms like Fujitsu hijacked the development efforts of potential rivals by manufacturing next-generation products for Western companies (including Siemens and Amdahl) that cut their own R&D.

Existing theories of strategy can lead to a competitive "pathology of surrender" (p. 71). Can the essence of Western strategic thought be reduced to five competitive forces, eight rules for excellence, or three generic strategies? Such paradigms can become self-fulfilling. If you know a competitor is managing by the portfolio concept, it is possible for you to predict just how much share has to be lost before the CEO puts the unit on his "sell" list. Measuring performance based on return-on-investment can lead to "denominator management" because investment is easier to control than sales, which can create a downward spiral.

In a traditional approach, corporate executives craft strategy for business-unit managers to execute, which the authors argue disenfranchises employees and results in a code of silence where problems are not aired. Creative strategies are seldom the result of an annual planning ritual allowing for only incremental improvement. Consistency is better derived from clearly-articulated strategic intent than from top-down plans. The challenge is to enfranchise employees to invent the means to accomplish ambitious ends.

Discussion and Implications

It is critical for every organization to know the source of its ability to add value. Apple developed into one of the world's most valuable companies, not just for one round of good technical products, but rather from product innovation and an understanding of how people interact with technology.

Although the term *core competence* is now a common part of most executives' vocabularies, it is too often used simply as a synonym for "what the company is good at" rather than understood within the strategic framework provided by Prahalad and Hamel. The core competence articles summarized here tend to emphasize coordination issues in corporations with multiple SBUs, but the lessons apply also to companies that remain at the single business stage.

It is also worth emphasizing that companies who thrive do not necessarily have the best product planning, but rather build the skills that allow them to capitalize on unanticipated products. Honda developed skills in making small, efficient engines for lawn mowers and motorcycles, which put them in position to exploit the sudden demand for smaller and more fuel-efficient cars in the 1970s—a combination of competence and serendipity. Speed is crucial, and the developments since these articles were written (through the internet and other forms of instant communication with suppliers and customers) make this observation even more relevant today.

Among other benefits, understanding the source of a company's growth and value allows a more-informed identification of the individuals within the company who embody the core competence. Apple has shown that it is not just competent engineers who should be retained, but also those engineers who make it easier for non-engineers to use their product. The authors here provide human resources (HR) as well as strategy prescriptions, particularly in their recommendation to have business units bid for internal talent in the same manner they bid for capital in the budgeting process.

Several legitimate limitations of this framework have been identified by other researchers.

- Some later authors (e.g., Campbell, Goold, and Alexander 1995) provide a valid criticism that this framework may be hard to operationalize, given the lack of reliable analytical tools with which to identify one's own competencies. It may be difficult to identify or agree on competencies, and a competency may not always translate into a competitive advantage.

- Banerji, Leinwand, and Mainardi (2009) find the competency framework insufficient, and propose that capabilities establish a foundation for competing: "Capabilities are the interconnected people, knowledge, systems, tools, and processes that establish a company's right to win in a given industry or business" (p. 7). In their view, capabilities are non-obvious, explicitly precise, very small in number, capable of scaling to the full customer base, and distinctive. In their framework, Frito-Lay's capability is not distribution or marketing but more specifically the ability to serve small stores on several continents; Apple depends on product innovation and an understanding of how people interact with technology; and Dell utilizes rapid delivery, low-priced customization, and customer service. This focus on capabilities leads to evaluating portfolios not in terms of financial performance but rather according to the coherence of the capabilities required to manage them together. These authors argue for cutting down to a coherent set of businesses to enable subsequent growth.

Prahalad and Hamel start with a premise that long-term success will not result exclusively from exploiting existing resources or advantages, because these can be copied; sustainable advantage results from rapid adaptation, and adaptation in turn results from the ability to learn. This premise makes a number of assumptions. It requires that change is possible and that change can be rationally guided toward the best interests of the firm. It does not address issues at the core of agency theory in that it does not consider self-serving behavior among different members of the organization. Finally, it requires that adaptations be complex enough to hinder duplication by competitors, yet understandable enough for the relevant managers within the firm to grasp and execute.[11] These limitations reinforce our view that the strategic intent framework is not a complete story for business strategy.

In our own view, despite these valid limitations, the strategic intent framework still makes several key incremental and useful points:

- To achieve great things, resourcefulness matters more than resources.
- Goals should be completely disproportionate to your starting point.
- You can use a larger competitor's weight and existing investments against it. These insights have become more salient, and progress swifter, since the articles were written. Microsoft and Apple took 23 and 31 years to go from their founding in the mid-1970s to a $100 billion market cap. Cisco took 14 years from 1984 to accomplish the same feat, Google took 7 years from 1998, and Facebook took 8 years from 2004. All four companies started with few resources and ambitious goals. Microsoft and Apple took on large and established competitors, like IBM, and out-innovated them.

Today, even the newest and smallest startups mostly start with the premise that they will change the world. This is not hubris; it is realistic, possible, and useful to hold such ambition. As Larry Page said at Michigan's commencement in 2009,

> I think it is often easier to make progress on mega-ambitious dreams. I know that sounds completely nuts. But, since no one else is crazy enough to do it, you have little competition. There are so few people this crazy that I feel like I know them all by first name. They all travel as if they are pack dogs and stick to each other like glue. The best people want to work the big challenges....What is the one sentence summary of how you change the world? Always work hard on something uncomfortably exciting!

Economists have separately observed that countries behave like companies in that there is little correlation between a country's resources and its wealth. In fact, there are many African economies rich in resources that remain mired in poverty, while wealthy nations like the United States and Japan contain relatively little in the way of exploitable resources. This appears to be another example where resourcefulness matters more than starting conditions.

---

[11] Some later work challenges these assumptions: Peter Senge (2006, building on an earlier 1990 edition) questions whether change is possible in most organizations, suggesting that most managers share a number of "learning disabilities" that prevent them from seeing the full complexity of problems and opportunities that they are addressing. Jeff Pfeffer (1993) takes a more cynical view that managers will use any change process to further their own agenda, which may or may not align with the goals of the organization. This self-dealing will frustrate learning. Of course, the fact that these barriers to adaptation exist would reinforce Hamel and Prahalad's contention that those companies which do adapt are challenging to imitate and therefore may sustain any competitive advantage.

We believe that this view is more applicable over time as the pace of change accelerates, and within sectors that experience more rapid change (e.g., technology firms). All advantages are temporary. For example, in 1999, technology leader Sun had a $200+ billion market cap. Ten years later, Eric worked on the Oracle team that purchased Sun for only $5.6 billion (Oracle 2009). Cisco went public in 1990 and a decade later had the largest market cap in the world, over half a trillion dollars (another decade later, it was worth less than one sixth of that value).[12] In Silicon Valley, the slogan appears to be "adapt or die"—regardless of how strong you already are.

In a smaller but broader article entitled "Strategy as Revolution," Hamel (1996) delineates ten principles that we agree can liberate a company's revolutionary spirit. They can also keep strategy from becoming a bureaucratic annual exercise and ensure that a company is keeping strategy as a key, value-added, and fresh activity.

- Strategic planning, as typically practiced, is not strategic. Too often the process is a simple ritual.
- Strategy making must be subversive.
- Bottlenecks are at the top.
- Revolutionaries exist in each company.
- Engagement is the problem, not change.
- Strategy must be democratic.
- Anyone can be an activist.
- Perspective is worth 50 IQ points.
- Top-down and bottom-up are *not* the choices.
- You cannot see the end from the beginning.

5. Game Theory

Since the 1940s, game theory has arisen as a branch of economics. Many theorists examine how to optimize play within a particular game. In this section, we emphasize the work of Brandenburger and Nalebuff, who investigate instead how to design the most profitable game (i.e., writing the rules instead of following them). This article represented a useful adaptation of game theory to inform practicing corporate strategists.

---

[12] Market capitalization figures from Yahoo! Finance.

ADAM BRANDENBURGER and BARRY NALEBUFF
"The Right Game: Using Game Theory to Shape Strategy"
(1995), *Harvard Business Review.*

Thesis: It is more rewarding and profitable to shape the game you play rather than to play the game you find. Maximizing payoffs requires evaluating both win-win as well as win-lose opportunities versus other players in your space. Having a unique product is optional, but creating the right game is essential to building the best long-term position.

Brandenburger and Nalebuff use game theory to help understand the complex nature of competitive behavior between organizations. Traditional game theorists (such as von Neumann and Morgenstern, 1944) calculate how to win a given game.[13] Brandenburger and Nalebuff instead adopt a meta-game approach of designing the right game—that is, shaping the game you play. In business it is possible to create non-zero-sum games without traditional winners and losers; for example, Intel and Microsoft seek the same customers but have enjoyed mutual success. Also, unlike most games that have set rules, most of the action in business actually derives from changing the game.

One example is that of General Motors's introduction in 1992 of a new credit card allowing holders to apply 5% of their charges toward the price of a new car, up to a $3500 limit. They had the most successful credit-card launch in history. The director of the program explained that the card helps GM take market share from other carmakers in a traditional win-lose manner, but that it also changes the game. By replacing other incentives GM had offered, the net effect was to raise the price that a non-cardholder (e.g., someone planning to buy a Ford) would pay for a GM car. The program thus allows Ford to raise its own prices, and GM to raise its prices without losing customers to Ford, resulting in a win-win dynamic between GM and Ford.

The authors introduce the term *coopetition*, which captures relationships that have both cooperative and competitive elements. In this environment, success comes from exploring win-win as well as win-lose opportunities.

---

[13] Von Neumann and Morgenstern (1944) distinguish between games with and without explicit rules. When players interact according to specific rules of engagement, a player must forecast his or her opponent's reaction to any action, looking far forward and then reasoning backward to identify the optimal choice. In a game without understood rules, a player's added value is the difference between the value that can be created without his presence and the value with him participating. In this less-structured environment, in general a player cannot extract more value than he or she adds.

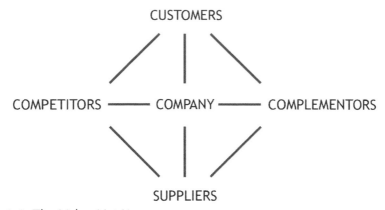

Figure 1-1. The Value Net.[14]

    They introduce the "value net" as a schematic map designed to represent the players and their interdependencies. Interactions take place along a vertical dimension: the company's customers and suppliers. Interactions also take place along a separate horizontal dimension: players with whom the company interacts but does not transact, termed *substitutors* or *competitors*, and *complementors*. *Substitutors* are alternative players from whom customers may purchase products or to whom suppliers may sell their resources. *Complementors* are players from whom customers buy complementary products or to whom suppliers sell complementary resources. One player can occupy more than one role simultaneously. Drawing and understanding this value net is an important first step in evaluating how to change your company's game.

    The second step is identifying all the elements of the game: players, added values, rules, tactics, and scope (abbreviated as PARTS). Changing the game involves changing one or more of these elements. Rules determine how the game is played by limiting the possible reactions to any action; to analyze the effect of a rule, you must look forward and reason backward. Games are linked across space and over time. You can expand the scope of a game by creating linkages to other games, or shrink it by severing linkages. Either approach can work to your benefit.

    The importance of complementors is in creating industry value, which then must be divided up. The key to maximizing your share is to increase your organization's own complement's added value while simultaneously trying to limit the added value of another player's complement. This can be done by differentiating your complement and restricting its supply while trying to commoditize another player's complement through greater competition and the creation of excess supply. Reducing the value of a complementary product will ensure that greater profit can be appropriated by your product.

---

[14] Used with permission from Brandenburger and Nalebuff, *Co-Opetition* (1997, p. 17).

Changing the game can be challenging, as there are five common traps that this framework can help you recognize and avoid:

- Trap #1: Accepting the game you're in. It's more rewarding to be a game-maker than a game-taker.
- Trap #2: Thinking that changing the game must come at the expense of others. Adopting a coopetition mindset enables you to look for both win-win and win-lose strategies, with ultimately more upside for your organization.
- Trap #3: Focusing solely on products only you can provide. Being unique is not a prerequisite for success.
- Trap #4: Failing to see the whole game.
- Trap #5: Failing to think methodically about changing the game.

Finally, it is important to recognize there is no one "master stroke." Altering the rules is an ongoing process, and others will be trying to change the game at the same time.

Discussion and Implications

 Additional examples of coopetition (both unsuccessful and successful) are easy to find. In the early 1990s, AT&T had a communications division selling long-distance service, and a separate network systems division selling telecom hardware to other providers of long-distance service. Many of the network-systems customers did not want to help their biggest competitor become more profitable, and AT&T eventually addressed this conflict by splitting into three separate companies in 1995. Today, Oracle has a dominant share in database software, and a #2 overall position in applications software to SAP.[15] Yet SAP remains the single biggest reseller of Oracle database. SAP wins because some customers want Oracle database and SAP applications; Oracle wins by having its biggest competitor help it sell product.

An expanded discussion of these useful concepts is provided by the same authors in their book *Co-Opetition* (1997). Some readers[16] have difficulty seeing how the game theory described by Brandenburger and Nalebuff differs from intuition. Many of the examples given may seem more like the direct application of common sense than the application of game theory. We think that the book and its examples do provide a set of questions which can help lead to common-sense solutions. For example, what strategies can help one's own firm and

---

[15] Data for database market share from Gartner Group (2012), data for applications share from Gartner Group (2011).

[16] E.g., the book review by Barbara Presley-Noble of the *New York Times*, available from www.strategy-business.com.

competitors in the industry at the same time? What are the competitor's weaknesses that can be used against them in "competitive judo"?

The article summarized here represents an effective use of rather basic game-theoretic thinking to shape strategy. We would go so far as to say that the single highest-value use of an executive's time is to think outside the traditional win-lose box and consider ways that the company can create win-win scenarios with existing and potential competitors, suppliers, and vendors. In addition, evaluate how to use competitors' strengths against them.

There is a saying, often attributed to Peter Drucker, that "the best way to predict the future is to create it." Don't accept the environment your business finds itself in today—create the environment that places your company in the strongest position, regardless of whether this helps or comes at the expense of other players in your value chain.

6. LEARNING VERSUS PLANNING

In this section, we review an article that summarizes a debate between those who view good strategy as "solid proactive planning" and those who see it essentially as "nimble reacting to new events."

HENRY MINTZBERG, RICHARD PASCALE, MICHAEL GOOLD, and RICHARD RUMELT
"The Honda Effect Revisited" (1996), *California Management Review.*

Thesis: The authors debate each other as to whether competitive advantage is arrived at through a systematic implementation of carefully thought-out strategy (planning) or through an often disjointed series of reactions to external events (learning).

This article is a point-counterpoint debate among the four authors (writing separately in succession) about the relative competitive value of planning versus learning. Mintzberg and Pascale begin the discussion by describing the impact of a 1984 article by Pascale describing two potential explanations of Honda's incredible success.

The Boston Consulting Group in 1975 prepared a 120-page report for the British government which ascribed Britain's decline in market share in motorcycles in large part to scale economy disadvantages that had been exploited in a purposeful and disciplined manner by Japanese competitors including Honda.

Pascale defines *strategy* as a noun representing the process of selecting opportunities and markets, and making deliberate resource decisions. He describes how BCG's analysis reflects the fact that strategy embodies an implicit model of how organizations should be guided and therefore preconfigures thinking. The formulation of strategy by BCG is assumed to be driven by senior management in a top-down manner, influenced by empirical models, and associated with a laborious planning process.

What created interest, and a lot of justified criticism toward both academics and consultants, was a set of interviews with six executives at Honda that Pascale conducted and described in his 1984 article. Honda's managers described nothing like the strategy that BCG said they implemented over a long period of time. Rather, the Honda executives ascribed their success to a willingness to experiment and learn from mistakes in the design process. These interviews revealed an emergent (i.e., haphazard) evolution of Honda's approach, and a gain in market share more from a combination of serendipity and astute reactions to external events than to a well-designed master plan. In layman's terms, the managers said they had essentially made it up as they went along, but paid attention and adapted based on the data they saw as they proceeded.[17]

Pascale writes,

> Western consultants, academics, and executives express a preference for oversimplifications of reality and cognitively linear explanations of events... We tend to impute coherence and purposive rationality to events when the opposite may be closer to the truth. (p. 89)

We would add that such oversimplification overlooks the process of adaptation and learning. The Japanese pursue continuous dialogue and what in hindsight is "strategy" actually evolves, so that strategy ends up defined as "all the things necessary for the successful functioning of the organization as an adaptive mechanism" (p. 90). Mintzberg sums up this scorecard simply as "Learning 1, Planning 0" (p. 92).

One of the authors of the original BCG report, Michael Goold, responds in this article that management researchers need to offer better prescriptions to corporate managers than "try something, see if it works and learn from your experience" (p. 94). He acknowledges a need for adaptation and reaction but concludes that "Planning 1, Learning 1, is surely a fairer reflection of the contribution of both sides" (p. 95).

Mintzberg replies that the BCG report implies that locking yourself in your office to do clever analysis is the key to competitive success. In his view, you are

---

[17] Prahalad and Hamel (1990) also use Honda's success as an example of their own theory. Honda coupled outsized ambition and resourcefulness to their core competence of designing small engines (for lawnmowers, motorcycles, and small cars).

better off selling your car and riding around on a bicycle observing your environment—the value is in what may appear in a planning analysis to be a nonstarter.

Goold says that it is unclear that either Pascale and Mintzberg's advice (to test new approaches and see what works), or Rumelt's advice (to just concentrate on how to build a better motorcycle engine) would have been any more helpful to Britain's response to its declining market share in motorcycles. He argues that BCG's advice to Britain recognizes the importance of relative cost, experience, and market share as reflected in the recommendation that Britain build share in targeted segments of the market to achieve viability. He acknowledges that BCG's analytical approach is better for testing strategies than for generating new ones, and criticizes the emergent approach as silent on how to choose between competing possible strategies.

Rumelt offers that the Honda experience supports various, very different views of strategy. BCG can point to the cost advantage from exploiting scale, Pascale can cite early scale driven by better product design and Honda's success in the U.S. market from experimentation, and Prahalad and Hamel couple Honda's success in motorcycles with its success in cars and characterize both in terms of core skills.

Rumelt concludes that the emergent school is right about good process being non-linear, and the design school is also right about the reality of scale, experience, and competencies providing strong forces that are not easily countered. His view is that strategy is more often imputed than observed and is frankly an overrated element of business success.

> If you know how to design great motorcycle engines, I can teach you all you need to know about strategy in a few days. If you have a Ph.D. in strategy, years of labor are unlikely to give you ability to design great new motorcycle engines. (p. 110)

Pascale gets the last word in this debate between strategic thinking and strategic learning. He offers five hypotheses about organizational agility:

- Agility is itself a core competence and important source of strategic, competitive advantage.
- Agility resides primarily in what an organization is *being* rather than doing.
- Four key dimensions define how an organization is being: power, identity, contention, and learning.
- The enduring nature of being derives from qualities that are socialized into an organization. Examples from Honda include office design, "waigaya" (a pattern of interaction that makes it acceptable to use straight talk regardless of rank), the three tribes (dividing Honda into R&D, process engineering, and manufacturing/marketing to ensure that manufacturing and marketing do not overwhelm the other functions), and the selection of Honda's CEO from its R&D community.

- These mechanisms of social engineering represent concrete organizational disciplines (e.g., discomfort with the status quo, managing from the future, straight talk, harnessing adversity).

The four authors conclude that there may be a partial revolution in the field of strategy, and that revolutions begin with an assault on language. For example, Hamel and Prahalad contribute the concepts of stretch (ambitious goals) and strategic intent to the language of the field.

Discussion and Implications

For those who view academics and strategy consultants as out-of-touch with the practical realities of how business is run, it may be fun to read the interviews with the Honda managers who were sent to the U.S. motorcycle market and who describe themselves as being unfamiliar with U.S. culture, having very limited resources, and starting with a haphazard process akin to "let's try some things and see what works." These Honda managers embody Prahalad and Hamel's contention (agreed on by the Google founders) that resourcefulness paired with ambitious goals yields the greatest outcomes. These interviews provide a stark contrast to the image painted by the well-paid consultants at BCG of these same Honda managers as wise men with a master plan.

This debate is reminiscent of an unverified story we have heard about a commencement address given by a Fortune 500 CEO who told the graduates that perhaps 1% of his success came from planning and 99% came from reacting faster than others to unexpected events. We agree that agility is an important component to organizational success, as reflected by the fact that (at the time of this writing) there are 210 books on the subject of agility listed in the business and investing section of www.amazon.com. Of course, the key is not merely to be nimble but also to engage in active learning, so that each step forward and backward generates takeaways about how to move closer to your ambitious goal.

However, we are also partial to the maxim that "luck favors the prepared." In any given year, the organizations that succeed are usually ones that have previously succeeded. We see this in consistently top-rated college football teams like the University of Michigan or Southern California, or in successful companies like General Electric. Success still attracts the talent that creates future success. If we are starting a new organization, a disciplined analysis of what has worked in similar groups in the past appears to be a good place to begin, even though reacting to new events will always certainly be critical to the organization's long-term success.

7. Sustainable Competitive Advantage and Social Capital

In this section, we summarize two sources investigating the foundations for sustainable competitive advantage. D'Aveni (1994) argues that all advantages are temporary rather than sustainable over long periods, while Nahapiet and Ghoshal (1998) focus on how firms now utilize social capital to sustain an advantage.

RICHARD D'AVENI
Hypercompetition (1994), Chapters 1–7.

Thesis: Strong competitive positions are temporary, and competition is defined as the process of building a series of new temporary advantages over time.

The strategy articles discussed above recognize that many advantages are temporary, to the extent that they can be copied by competitors. Hamel and Prahalad (1989) focus on adaptability and resourcefulness as the key to maintaining a competitive advantage. D'Aveni similarly acknowledges the temporary nature of a strong competitive position, and defines competition as a process of building a series of temporary advantages. Here, we focus on a particular section of his book that defines *escalation ladders* as the sequence of moves and countermoves that help explain how competition evolves over time.

D'Aveni argues that competitive advantage is typically no longer sustainable over the long term, so companies must maneuver and continually pursue temporary advantage. Several forces are contributing to this new era: customer changes (including fragmenting tastes), rapid technological change, falling geographic and industry boundaries as markets globalize, and deep pockets among competitors arising from giant, global alliances in many industries.

Despite these forces, long-term industry dominance may still be possible, by mastering the art of dynamically repositioning oneself in four key areas. D'Aveni identifies four escalation ladders and examines them within the context of the dynamic rivalry between Coke and Pepsi:

- **Cost and quality.** Each shift in the definition of quality provided an opportunity to renew the battle between Coke and Pepsi on a new playing field. Price and quality continue to be central factors in competition, though they are becoming less powerful as the perceived quality and cost structures converge on an ultimate value point.

- **Timing and know-how.** The most fundamental knowledge in the soft drink industry is how to invent a formula with a taste customers like and package it in a desirable manner. As the number of tastes expanded, each new product focused on a narrower niche while making bottling more expensive. This product growth and packaging variety may have led Coke and Pepsi to some cannibalization of their own products. Each taste and packaging innovation is now quickly copied by competitors.

- **Stronghold creation.** The key to creating and controlling a geographic stronghold in soft drinks is distribution. Both Coke and Pepsi initially granted bottling franchises based on geographic regions. Franchisees had exclusive marketing rights in their territory but had to agree not to sell competitor products. Pepsi attacked Coke's fountain stronghold by acquiring fast-food chains (e.g., Taco Bell and Pizza Hut). Coke argued to regulators that Pepsi was a competitor of these chains, and the FTC tried to weaken the exclusive territorial agreements of both companies' franchise networks after labeling them anticompetitive. New entrants now have access to an array of distribution partners, lowering entry barriers. Going forward, growth will continue to be higher outside the United States, and the key to stronghold creation for Coke and Pepsi will be who controls near-term markets in newly industrializing nations and long-term markets in high-population countries.

- **Deep pockets.** Coke initially used its resources to drive out other competitors, including appearing in court to defend its brand name and also engaging in heavy advertising. Coke used its cash to vertically integrate, getting into the bottling and distribution business, and focused on exploiting economies of scale in making and distributing cola. Pepsi recognized that Coke's deep pockets and rigid approach made Coke less flexible, and Pepsi used this inflexibility to its advantage in introducing a larger bottle for the same price.

This intense competition, labeled *hypercompetition*, keeps all players moving quickly from advantage to advantage and trying to seize the initiative in each of these four arenas. New products (like Diet Coke) are imitated quickly, and success often comes at the expense of existing product sales (e.g., Tab and regular Coke). While Pepsi used a largely offensive strategy, Coke as the market leader responded more defensively to first moves by Pepsi or other players.

D'Aveni concludes that in the long run, winners must play offense in all four arenas in order to stay one step ahead of the their competitors and thereby maintain the initiative. In his book, he also applies this four-lens analysis to the competition in laser printing between HP and Compaq prior to their merger.

In this pursuit of a series of only temporary advantages, D'Aveni identifies several sets of challenges to management:

- The pace of maneuvering can be described as hyperactive.

- Competitive moves can be erratic (characterized by occasional large movement).
- Moves can also be evolutionary (slow, continuous movement).
- Competition can be temporarily dormant, remaining inactive for a definite interval.
- Competition can be arrested, with no changes occurring and none foreseen.

D'Aveni also offers a new set of guidelines (which he calls a new set of seven *S*s[18]) for generating market disruption:

- **Stakeholder satisfaction.** Companies need to satisfy their customers and employees.
- **Strategic soothsaying.** Firms should establish a process for seeking out new predictions of what customers will want in the future.
- **Speed.** Speed is critical to respond to advantages and respond to counterattacks.
- **Surprise.** Companies should seek the ability to stun a competitor and build up a superior position before a possible counterattack. While IBM tried to dominate the PC market with its sales force and brand name, Dell created a successful direct mail and toll-free sales and distribution model that grabbed market share quickly.
- **Signals.** Verbal announcement of strategic intent can manipulate the future moves of rivals.
- **Shifting the market rules.** Changing the rules can disrupt competitors. Gillette introduced its Sensor disposable razor and transformed the market from a focus solely on convenience and price to an additional focus on premium quality.
- **Simultaneous or sequential thrusts.** A company can use several moves (e.g., a series of product announcements or concerted geographic market entries) to mislead a competitor.

JANINE NAHAPIET and SUMANTRA GHOSHAL
"Social Capital, Intellectual Capital, and the Organizational Advantage" (1998), *Academy of Management Review*.

Thesis: Networks of relationships represent a valuable resource. The interaction of this relationship capital and intellectual capital underpins organizational advantage.

---

[18] D'Aveni is here contrasting his list to an older set of seven *S*s developed by McKinsey (strategy, systems, structure, skills, style, staff, and shared values), described in Waterman, Peters, and Phillips (1980).

This is one of several articles since the late 1990s focusing on the application of social capital theory to a firm's ability to sustain competitive advantage. A central proposition is that networks of relationships constitute a valuable resource. As for the resource-based view, the focus is more on value creation than appropriation. Nahapiet and Ghoshal combine a focus on social capital with that of intellectual capital, proposing that advantage comes from their interaction.

Social capital is defined as the sum of the actual and potential resources embedded within, available through, and derived from the network of relationships possessed by an individual or social unit (i.e., company). In exploring the role of social capital in creating intellectual capital, one must consider three forms of social capital:

- **Structural.** Social capital concerns the properties of the social system and network of relations as a whole, and refers to the overall pattern of connections.
- **Relational.** Social capital also describes the kind of personal relationships people have developed with each other over their history of interactions.
- **Cognitive.** Those resources provide shared representations, interpretations, and systems of meaning among parties.

Each of these forms constitutes an aspect of the social structure and facilitates the actions of individuals within the structure. Social capital increases the efficiency of action and encourages cooperative behavior, thereby facilitating innovation.

Intellectual capital refers to the knowledge and knowing capability of an organization, and represents both a valuable resource and a capability for action based in knowledge. Knowledge can be tacit or explicit, individual or social. Knowledge is created through combination (combining elements previously unconnected) and exchange (where resources are held by different parties, exchange is necessary for combination).

There are four conditions that must hold for combination and exchange to occur:

- the opportunity exists to make the combination or exchange,
- parties expect the combination to create value,
- those involved are motivated (i.e., believe their engagement will be worthwhile), and
- the capability to combine experience exists.

Social capital theory offers a valuable perspective for explaining the creation of intellectual capital. Each of the three forms of social capital influence the four conditions for exchange and combination.

- **Structural.** Network ties provide access to resources (i.e., "who you know" affects "what you know"). These information benefits can occur in the form of *access* (receiving a piece of valuable information and knowing who could use it), *timing* (the ability of personal contacts to provide information sooner than it becomes available to others), or *referrals* (processes providing information to people in the network). Even if ties provide the channel for such information transmission, the overall network configuration constitutes a separate, important facet of social capital that impacts the development of intellectual capital. In addition, organizations created for one purpose may provide valuable resources for another (e.g., transfer of trust from a family or religious affiliation into a work situation).

- **Cognitive.** Communication (i.e., exchange and combination) requires sharing context between the parties, which can happen through the existence of shared language or through the sharing of collective narratives.

- **Relational.** This form of social capital influences three of the conditions for exchange and combination: access to the parties, anticipation of value through exchange, and the motivation of parties to engage in knowledge creation. *Trust* (the belief that one will find appropriate the results of another's intended action) secures dialogue. Higher levels of trust open access to people for intellectual capital and increase anticipation of exchange value. Trust fosters cooperation that itself breeds trust, which can lead to the development of generalized norms of cooperation. Obligations can also represent a commitment to act cooperatively. Identification, where individuals see themselves as one with other parties, increases the realization of exchange opportunities.

Nahapiet and Ghoshal build a theory of the firm expressed not in a market-failure framework (as with Williamson and Ouchi 1981a) but rather grounded in the concept of organizational advantage, with the special capabilities of organizations for creating and transferring knowledge as a central element. This advantage-based theory rests on two core arguments:

- **Organizations as institutional settings are conducive to developing social capital.** Social capital is jointly owned, and so is concerned with resources within structures of social exchange. As such, the development of social capital is significantly affected by factors shaping the evolution of social relationships: time, interaction, interdependence, and closure. All of these are more characteristic of internal organization than of market organization.

- **The co-evolution of social and intellectual capital underpins organizational advantage.** Social capital is created and sustained through exchange and enables such exchange to take place. Since both social and intellectual capital derive their significance from social relationships, their evolutionary paths are likely to be interrelated.

These arguments are consistent with resource-based theory, in which value is derived from rareness, durability, imperfect imitability, and nontradability. Evidence for the suggestion that firms with particular configurations of social capital are likely to be more successful at developing intellectual capital can be found in the observation that knowledge-intensive firms invest heavily in physical facilities that encourage strong ties.[19]

Nahapiet and Ghoshal identify several limitations in their own approach:

- Norms were assumed to be positive, without allowing for the possibility that certain norms may be negative.
- The cost involved in creating and maintaining some forms of social capital was not included.
- Dimensions of social capital were considered separately, when the interrelationships may be of greatest interest.
- They have focused on the creation rather than diffusion of intellectual capital.
- Knowledge was assumed to be the foundation of organizational advantage, but the analysis suggests that networks may underpin advantage.
- Their thesis about the relationship of social to intellectual capital was developed within only one type of boundary, the firm.

Discussion and Implications

D'Aveni's use of Coke versus Pepsi provides a good example of a hypercompetitive environment requiring serial moves and adaptations, such as matching each other's taste and packaging innovations. The "cola wars" also highlight the competitive judo analogy described by Hamel and Prahalad (1989), when Pepsi confronted Coke's advantage with restaurants serving fountain drinks by acquiring chains of restaurants itself (e.g., Taco Bell and Pizza Hut).

It is arguably not a profound insight that the pace of competition has increased, but the implications are significant in most industries today, and D'Aveni provides a relevant framework for executives to assess how they will act and react in such an environment. In a similar vein, Grantham, Ware, and Williamson (2007) discuss how to reduce fixed costs and institutionalize innovation to react faster to changing market conditions.

---

[19] This point was made strongly by Steve Jobs in his 2011 biography by Walter Isaacson. Jobs designed new buildings at Pixar to physically drive employees together, to the point of wanting to locate the only restrooms in the center atrium to maximize random encounters.

In the late 1990s, Eric worked at Cisco Systems, which had the catchphrase "the internet changes everything." It became fashionable to assume that all existing theories of business and strategy were obsolete. We do not think that web tools change the fundamentals of strategy, but they do allow strategy to be executed, and reacted to, at a faster pace. This only increases the relevance of insights about the temporary nature of competitive advantage and the critical importance of speed in execution described by D'Aveni.

We see the primary value of D'Aveni's framework as encouraging executives to bring their analysis up one level. If all competitive advantages are temporary, rather than thinking about how to get a competitive advantage, you should think about the process you will use to generate a series of competitive advantages, some of which you cannot yet see. This thinking will go beyond strategy into hiring, retention, and the fabric of the culture you build within your organization.

In Nahapiet and Ghoshal's framework, social capital comes from the network of relationships that an individual or group of individuals possess. This concept is not new; board members and employees have always been hired based on who they know as well as on what they know. But the authors make a contribution by explicitly incorporating this social value into a model of strategy in a way that makes it more straightforward for executives to identify sources of value from their relationships. Existing rolodexes are worth money, and innovative companies work to build and strengthen ongoing relationships. Such companies also create their physical facilities in a way that promotes interaction.

We agree with the authors that who the organization knows will impact what it knows, and that the interaction between who and what is known is a primary source of organizational value. A company that already has relationships with its potential customers and partners can more readily apply the information they have into profitable products. Furthermore, this ability represents a reason for the firm to exist: rather than have a web of independent contractors, the institutional setting of the company develops social capital and also intellectual capital.

There is a revolution underway in how people and companies build and exploit their social relationships. This social capital framework is prescient, as it was written before Facebook made a business model out of helping individuals connect with each other more easily, and then monetizing access to those individuals while they manage their personal relationships. People tend to use sites like LinkedIn for their professional relationships, which has changed how companies recruit new employees. Social networking is an entire new industry built on social capital, which is also having a significant impact on how companies in other industries do business.

Two other noteworthy social capital contributions come from Ahuja (2000; see Chapter 6, Section 4) and Burt (2000). Ahuja develops a theoretical framework that relates a firm's innovation output to three aspects of its ego network: direct ties, indirect ties, and structural holes (meaning disconnections between a firm's partners). Both direct and indirect ties have a positive impact on innovation but disconnections between partners can have either a positive or negative influence. Burt describes social capital as a metaphor and suggests that researchers focus on the network mechanisms responsible for social capital effects. He surveys empirical evidence showing that social capital is primarily a function of providing brokerage across disconnections between firms (as opposed to providing closure within a network) and suggests that these two leading network mechanisms (closure and structural holes) are complementary. Closure can facilitate the value of brokerage; structural holes can be a source of added value, but network closure can be essential in realizing the value contained in the holes/disconnections.

Although the consideration of social capital can be viewed as an extension of the resource-based view, there has been enough separate analysis since 2000 to view this as a unique academic perspective. We expect the increasing importance in social capital in the real world to be analyzed and reflected on an ongoing basis in the academic literature.

8. MERGERS AND ACQUISITIONS

One specific area within strategy of interest to business practitioners is that of mergers and acquisitions. Though there has been a large number of research studies devoted to describing and explaining M&A activity, it is an area in which we find that no specific article dominates. Therefore, we do not describe particular articles in depth but rather summarize a larger body of research in this section.

Do Mergers Create Value?

The primary driver of academic research in M&A is the question of why companies engage in so much of it, when relatively few benefits to shareholders have been documented. The estimated failure rate for acquisitions is high. Porter (1987) looked at 33 large companies from 1950-1986 and found most had divested more acquisitions than they kept. He concludes that "the corporate strategies of most companies have dissipated instead of creating shareholder value" (p. 285). Schoenberg (2006) found that 44% of acquisitions are later rated by the acquiring managers as not having met their financial objectives (p. 364).[20] Schoenberg finds approximately similar failure rates using different criteria for success, including the post-acquisition cumulative abnormal

---

[20] Huang and Kleiner (2004) are even more downbeat, asserting that no more than 23% of acquisitions even earn their cost of capital (p. 54).

returns of acquirers, subsequent divestment of acquired companies, and expert assessments of acquisition success. Other studies, using varying measures, produce estimated failure rates over 80% for acquisitions in general (Marks 1997, p. 272) and 83% for cross-border acquisitions (KPMG 1999, p. 2).

Although target company shareholders receive a premium for their shares, the consensus is that acquiring companies on average experience negative stock-price impact in both the short and long run. Only 35% of acquirers experience a stock price increase on the announcement date (per Sirower 1997, p. 146, who provides a survey of studies measuring immediate stock price reaction). A good survey of 22 studies of long-term acquirer stock performance is found in Agrawal and Jaffe (2000), who conclude that on balance these studies, particularly since 1992, show "strong evidence of abnormal under-performance following mergers" (p. 50). They consider several explanations and find the evidence does not support the premise that the market reacts only slowly to the news of the merger, nor that the market initially overvalues acquisitions resulting in higher earnings per share. They do find support that stock-financed acquisitions underperform more than cash-financed acquisitions, and that acquisitions by firms with a good reputation may become overvalued initially so that subsequent performance is lesser. Some literature suggests that acquisitions of companies in related businesses should outperform unrelated ones, but even this hypothesis has not been consistently upheld in empirical testing (for a discussion, see King, Dalton, Daily and Covin 2004).

Why Are Mergers So Popular?

Given that most acquisitions fail, both from the standpoint that few acquired businesses remain in the acquirer's portfolio 5-10 years later and from the standpoint of the acquirer's long-run stock performance, the natural question is why do mergers remain so popular? It is not to acquire talent; 70% of target-firm executives leave within five years (Krug and Aguilera 2005, p. 126). Cording, Christmann, and Bourgeois (2002) describe and assesses a number of explanations that have been offered and rejected, along with the associated implications for managers.

Overpayment
Prices for targets are often assumed to be set like prices for goods, where they are bid up to their fair value. However, Sirower (1997) argues that price may have little to do with value and encourages buyers to assume that zero synergies can be realized. Executives describe frequent breakdown in due diligence (Haspeslaugh and Jemison 1991), which can come from fragmented perspectives when acquirer staff lack both a broad and detailed understanding of the target (Jemison and Sitkin 1986). The impact of such breakdowns can be

amplified by the building of momentum to complete a deal. The implication for executives is to use a high discount rate in valuing future synergies.

Agency Conflicts

- Investment banker compensation depends on the amount paid (Kesner, Shapiro, and Sharma 1994). It may be beneficial to restructure the agreement with the bankers so that their fees are not linear with the size of the deal.
- Acquiring-firm CEO compensation depends on the firm's size (Schmidt and Fowler 1990), so the Board needs to control for this motivation for the CEO to over-acquire.
- Acquiring firms controlled by owners have better stock performance than those controlled by managers (Kroll, Wright, Toombs, and Leavell 1997).

CEO Hubris

Does exaggerated self-confidence lead to poor acquisition decisions? Hayward and Hambrick (1997) developed a measure of CEO overconfidence and found a strong correlation with the size of the premiums paid for target companies. Boards must remain aware of this tendency of firms with overconfident CEOs to overpay for acquisition targets.

Top Management Alignment

Shanley and Correa (1992) posit that if perceived and actual agreement between the two management teams is higher, then post-acquisition performance should improve. Walsh (1988) shows that conflict leads to high turnover among target executives and loss of the intellectual resource they represent. Having management teams with different functional backgrounds helps post-acquisition performance (Krishnan, Miller, and Judge 1997). Successful integration requires paying attention to the interaction dynamics of the teams and managing to minimize conflict and unwanted departures of target executives.

Experience

Haleblian and Finkelstein (1999) argue that the *experience curve* (measuring the relationship between experience and ability to understand the acquisition dynamics) is U-shaped. Inexperienced acquirers interpret events as unique; somewhat experienced acquirers are dangerous, as they may perceive events as similar to their past situations when they are not; and very experienced acquirers learn to discriminate between target environments. The lesson is to learn from experience but not to overgeneralize one's own limited experience.

Impact on Target Employees

Acquired employees undergo a significant life change, and can respond in productivity-lowering ways. Buono and Bowditch (1989) argue that an open, participative approach can lessen this dynamic. Managers should recognize that employee emotions are part of the equation.

Conflicting Corporate Cultures
The target may have various sources of cultural difference from the acquirer, including national culture (if its headquarters is in a different country) and organizational culture. The resulting differences in implicit assumptions can hinder performance. Chatterjee, Lubatkin, and Weber (1992) find a negative correlation between perceived cultural difference and stock market gains to the acquiring firms. The integration plan should be based on an understanding of national and organizational cultural differences.

The Integration Process
Haspeslagh and Jemison (1991) discuss barriers to capability transfer. In particular, capability transfer is impaired if management cannot adjust its approach based on new information, if value creation for the shareholders is perceived to come at the expense of the target employees, and if the combined firm cannot provide the right combination of institutional and interpersonal leadership. It is important to identify the resources and capabilities of both target and acquirer, to be transferred to the other.

Cording et al. also suggest that applying a resource-based view to M&A can lead to improvements in valuing target company resources in combination with acquirer resources, and in post-merger integration. We would add that the key here is to avoid the common empty overuse of the concept of synergies in favor of identifying what core resources and capabilities are being combined.

Keys to Identifying Attractive Merger Candidates

Why do some companies appear to be good at mergers despite this general climate of disappointing returns? The academic literature appears to offer little help in identifying the common ingredients of successful merger programs. Eric's personal experience at Cisco and Oracle leaves us convinced that it is possible to beat the baseline odds indicating that over half of mergers fail. Our personal view regarding some of the factors supporting that success follows.

Dedicated Business-Development Team
Although successful merger integration requires the participation of everyone in the company, having a dedicated M&A team helps in identifying targets, coordinating detailed full-time due diligence investigations, and ensuring that periodic debriefs occur to isolate what worked and what should change in the processes of identifying targets and integrating them.

Industry Structure

Industries that have a high level of fixed costs and low level of marginal costs, like telecommunications and software, have economies of scale that amplify the impact of genuine synergy. In software, for example, we see a strong correlation between size and profitability: for the years 1998–2005, the largest four software vendors grew revenues by a constant annual growth rate of 19.2% annually while the next 76 largest vendors grew by only 7.9% annually, and for 2005 the largest four were up by over 10% while the others were collectively flat (Goldman Sachs 2005, p. 44). Larger companies also had more than double the operating margin on average relative to small software companies. The ability to spread fixed costs like R&D over a larger base helps ensure that the largest vendors remain the most profitable, and increases the probability that acquisition will help rather than hurt profitability.

It also helps to be in a sector where customers are actively seeking fewer partners. This is the case in software, where customers have become less inclined to pay consultants to connect several distinct best-of-breed tools, but rather want to limit the number of vendors to a handful that can be actively managed.

Common Technology

Although much of the academic literature focuses on whether the acquirer and target are in related industries, we think the key is whether the technical people who create the product at each company speak a similar language. Oracle looks for targets employing software built using common technologies (e.g., Java, Oracle Forms) on compatible architectures (e.g., Oracle Database).

Overlapping Customer Base

It helps if customers know the products from both companies. This overlap can be thought of as a basic form of social capital.

Keys to Successfully Integrating Mergers

Based on our experience working with acquisitive companies, there are four key ingredients we believe are common to successful examples of merger integration.

- **Speed.** We believe that speed is the single most underappreciated factor in successful M&A. Huang and Kleiner (2004) find that productivity may be reduced by up to 50% in the 4-8 months following a merger (p. 54). Our view is that ambiguity is the most toxic element in any acquisition; when target employees do not know their job status, they do not execute effectively. Many acquirers take it slowly to allow the two cultures to get used to each other—but the exact opposite is called for. Oracle moves very quickly; every department presents a 100-day integration plan on the date of close, and the bulk of the integration is actually accomplished within that timeframe. Target employees know their job status within two weeks after the change-in-control date. Moving this quickly can create mistakes, but these are outweighed by minimizing the period where target employees do not know how they fit in. Within six months, it is often not possible to tell which Oracle employees are legacy and which are from the most recent acquisition.

- **Clear communication.** Employees want clarity. It does not help to use euphemisms, create job-allocation councils, or declare a "merger of equals" when it is usually one company dominating the other. Clear, plain-English communication kills misinformation and provides employees the ability to know if they have a job, what that job is, and whether it is one they want. Everyone can move on with their lives.

- **Focus and escalation.** Integration must be a part of every manager's job at a successful acquirer. Each executive must keep detailed track of progress and escalate quickly when problems arise. Senior management must dedicate a high fraction of their time to merger issues in the weeks following a large acquisition.

- **Measurement.** For companies making a habit of acquiring companies, it is vital to measure every element possible so that merger integration can become a core competency. Oracle takes measurement of multiple metrics: the percent of target employees offered a job who accept, the amount of time it takes to complete 100% of legal entity merges, the disposition of target real estate and facilities, and the migration of IT. Trends tell a story. Candid internal debriefs between acquisitions help ensure that the right questions become part of due diligence to avoid repeating the same mistakes.

In short, the literature shows that mergers are popular despite the lack of evidence that they (on average) create value. Our personal experience leads us to believe that disciplined and self-aware executives can beat the odds. But it is good to first know what the baseline odds are, and to have a very specific awareness of what you are doing differently to achieve a better result.

9. REAL OPTIONS

Existing methods of choosing among strategic alternatives often assume that a fixed course of action will be followed over time. In this section, we examine how analyzing business strategies as chains of real options can enable better strategic decision-making.

TIMOTHY LUEHRMAN
"Strategy as a Portfolio of Real Options" (1998), *Harvard Business
Review.*

Thesis: Specifically identifying the real options created by projects or strategies
can improve decisions about the sequence and timing of strategic investments.

Luehrman starts by pointing out that the financial tool most used
to estimate the value of strategy—discounted cash flow—
assumes executives will follow a predetermined plan regardless of
how events unfold. A better approach would incorporate the
uncertainty inherent in business and active decision-making, and options deliver
that insight. Business strategies can be analyzed as chains of real options and
can inform strategy with valuation analysis at the time of formulation, and not
as an after-the-fact exercise.

This article is a follow-up to "Investment Opportunities as Real Options:
Getting Started on the Numbers" from the July–August 1998 issue of *HBR.*
Luehrman's first article covered how to generate an estimate of option value for
a particular project. This article extends his framework to explore how options
can improve decisions about the sequence and timing of strategic investments.

In the first section, he provides a gardening metaphor of options as
tomatoes. Gardeners have to manage a portfolio of tomatoes: those that are
ripe and can be picked today, those that are bad and should not be picked, and
those in between with varying prospects (unripe ones that may improve, unripe
ones that may get eaten by squirrels, etc.). Passive gardeners just pick the ripe
tomatoes on the last day of the season. Active gardeners monitor the tomatoes
and influence the variables (water, sunlight, time) that determine their value.

The second section provides a brief tour of option space. Luehrman defines
two option-value metrics:

- *Value-to-cost* contains the standard net present value (NPV) of an investment
  plus the time value of being able to defer that investment. If this metric is
  between zero and one, worth is below cost; if greater than one, worth is
  above cost.

- *Volatility* depends on variance per period of asset returns, and time to
  expiration.

Any investment option can be plotted on a graph of these two metrics. The
resulting graph can be separated into three categories: never, later, and now.

- **Never.** If the ratio of value-to-cost is low and volatility is also low,
  investment is unlikely to yield value. "Invest never" when volatility is low,
  and "probably never" when volatility is medium.

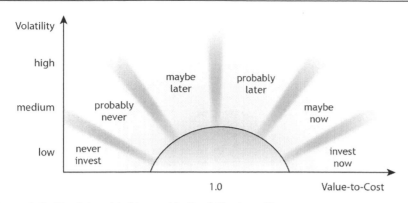

Figure 1-2. Decision-Making with Real Options.[21]

- **Later.** If volatility is high, investing later has more of chance to be profitable. Invest "maybe later" if value-to-cost is low and "probably later" if value-to-cost is high.
- **Now.** If value-to-cost is high, investing now is wise. "Invest now" if volatility is low, and "maybe now" if volatility is medium.

Luehrman then explores the decision of when to "harvest." Six projects with the same NPV can have different time and volatility profiles that then generate different values for their value-to-cost and volatility metrics. Assuming that one project falls into each region described above, the value of this portfolio of six projects can far exceed that estimated by conventional discounted cash flow analysis (in one example, by a factor of more than three). Instead of accepting two projects and rejecting four (as in a standard net-present-value decision framework), this options framework would cause the project manager maker to accept one now, reject one now, and wait for more information about prospects for the other four.

This framework leads to a dynamic decision-making approach. Over time, options tend to lose value because volatility decreases and value-to-cost tends to decrease, though good luck and active management can act in the opposite direction to add value. Evaluating a project as an option creates more to analyze but also instructs regarding what to analyze as well as providing a visual interpretation.

There are spillover effects whereby one option impacts another (e.g., adding a feature to one product may reduce the length of time a subsequent decision can be deferred). *Strategies* are series of options explicitly designed to affect one another.

Nests of options can be used to represent a sequence of contingencies designed into a business. For example, an option to expand production of a

---

[21] Authors' image; data from Luehrman (1998).

product is acquired only if the option to introduce that product in the first place is exercised, so the value of the introduction decision includes the value of both introducing the product and the value of the option to later expand its production. Changes in the environment (e.g., competitor response, changes in risk) can impact the value of multiple options, sometimes in the same direction and sometimes in opposite directions.

Like gardening, using options to think strategically is a skill that can be learned and that improves with practice. Options analysis lies at the intersection of strategy and finance. For finance to play a role in strategy, it must contribute interpretive analysis of sequences of decisions while they are still hypothetical.

Discussion and Implications

 A *real option* is the right (but not obligation) to undertake a business initiative over some period of time. As an example, consider an electric utility company that can build an oil plant, build a natural gas plant, or pay more to build a plant that can burn either fuel. The third alternative involves paying now to have the real option (flexibility) later to use whatever fuel turns out to be cheaper in the future.

The use of the term "real options" goes back at least as far as 1977, when Stewart Myers wrote his paper "Determinants of Corporate Borrowing" in the *Journal of Financial Economics*. Myers observed that bankruptcy costs are not strong enough to balance out the tax advantage of debt, so if these were actually the primary two opposing forces (as earlier finance papers since Modigliani and Miller had argued), the United States should see much higher borrowing rates. He explained lower borrowing in terms of the value of retaining financial slack to allow the company to take advantage of future, unknown investment opportunities. Therefore, "part of the value of the firm is accounted for by the present value of options to make further investments on possibly favorable terms" (p. 148).

Subsequent work used the tools of financial option valuation (such as Black-Scholes) to value corporate investment opportunities. Luehrman's paper uses this academic work to provide a guide to practitioners (the audience of *HBR*) for thinking in terms that allow financial concepts to inform strategic planning. In fact, in very few areas has academic research been followed by so much interest from practitioners, with a flood of "how-to" books coming to market (including Amram and Kulatilaka 1999; Trigeorgis 1998; and Copeland and Antikarov 2001). Amram and Kulatilaka highlight the particular value of the approach for investments made in stages with uncertain returns and the possibility of learning between stages.

While the insight that there is value to being in a position to make future investments is undoubtedly useful to strategic planners, real options frameworks have received legitimate criticism. Adam Borison (2003) finds that suggestions for implementation contain "a variety of contradictory approaches" (p. 2) that are rarely acknowledged. He notes that financial options theory assumes assets that are freely traded, an assumption that may not hold in a real environment. He catalogs five real options valuation frameworks, shows how they can lead to different investment conclusions, and classifies them according to their quality of results and ease of use. Fink (2001) points out that the flaw is not the complexity of real options analysis "but the fact that it ignores the psychological and political realities of capital investments" (p. 1) by wrongly assuming that companies possess the discipline to end a project without delay if the initial investment does not pan out.

Our own view is that a real options framework is essential to identify various alternatives to any large investment of capital, while agreeing with Kulatilaka (in Fink 2001) that real options analysis may be more useful in conceptualizing projects than in evaluating them. Where it is used to evaluate projects, we think an integrated approach that acknowledges and incorporates both market- and firm-specific sources of risk is valuable—an approach laid out by Smith and Nau (1995). We agree with Borison (2003) that this approach may be harder to implement but gives better results.

10. SCENARIO ANALYSIS

In this section, we present a case for a less quantitative approach to strategy. Creating and telling stories can help strategists identify different possible futures, and craft approaches for pursuing more valuable outcomes.

ROBBIE DAVIS-FLOYD
"Storying Corporate Futures: The Shell Scenarios" (1998), in G. Marcus (editor), *Corporate Futures*.

Thesis: Financial projections are an incomplete form of planning for the future. Scenarios in the form of stories are a valuable tool for evaluating different possible futures.

Davis-Floyd tells the story of Dr. Betty Flowers, a professor of English at the University of Texas who was approached by Shell in 1992 to serve as editor for myths they were consciously creating. These deliberate stories about the future were backed by research data collected by their team of 20 economists globally who had developed the scenarios over the prior three years. The point was to teach Shell managers to think causally, to see every event as located in a story, and to make business decisions based on where that story would lead if allowed to play out. Pierre Wack was the retired head of the division at Shell, who himself described their process in a working paper at Harvard Business School that was adapted into two *HBR* articles in 1985.

Shell planners had started using scenarios in the early 1970s, and initially developed scenarios that simply quantified alternative outcomes (e.g., will oil be $20 or $40 a barrel in one year?), but found these did not offer a basis for managers to exercise their judgment. So, they developed a new planning tool based on the following.

- **Predetermined elements.** These include forces that appear almost inevitable. For example, oil owners in the Middle East could not find investments that would appreciate faster than the oil in their own ground, particularly if oil production were limited to keep the price high. Therefore, subsequent low production and high prices were viewed as "baked in." For a gardening company, a predetermined planning element was the Baby Boom that would lead to more households and increased demand for gardening tools.

- **Uncertainties.** Uncertainties, as the name suggests, include variables which could take different values. Uncertainties could take the form of policy solutions by consumer countries such as price freezes, inaction, and so on.

The resulting scenarios were framed to highlight the temporary nature of the status quo, which depended on (a) oil producers depleting their reserves at a rate that did not optimize their own profits, and (b) the absence of war in the Mideast.

Shell positioned itself to handle the subsequent dramatic rise in oil prices in the 1970s better than many of its competitors. The same unit showed a scenario where discovery of new fields outside of OPEC in the 1980s could lead to a dramatic fall in the price of oil, which is exactly what happened. Shell rose from the 14th- to 2nd-biggest oil multinational during the 1980s (p. 144).

The Shell planners started with the premise that economic forces are complex and interdependent, and decisions must be made in a global rather than local context. They hired an English professor to translate economic scenarios into stories so that managers could be presented with alternative, fleshed-out visions of the future and decide which would be more likely.

One specific area of interest for the company was the future of South Africa, which at the time was under pressure worldwide to end its system of racial apartheid. The team developed four stories to describe how things might evolve there.

- **The ostrich scenario.** A South African government does not want to face realities. The international community moves on to other causes, the government becomes repressive, capital and skills leave, and the economy stagnates.

- **The lame duck scenario.** a decade-long transition in power incapacitates the government and leads to economic uncertainty for South Africa.
- **The Icarus scenario.** A popularly elected new government tries to do too much too soon. This government overspends and overborrows, the economy collapses, and the poor end up worse off than under apartheid.
- **The flight of the flamingoes.** A decisive political settlement results in good government and sustainable growth (flamingoes take off slowly, fly high, and stay together).

Shell used stories like these in workshops for their managers, and in fact patented the process of these workshops for developing managers who more consciously think about how to react to possible futures, and about the impact of their own decisions on framing those futures.

Discussion and Implications

 Story-based scenarios are useful for conceptualizing and evaluating different possible outcomes for any organization. It often seems dry to generate specific forecasts to answer questions like, "What will U.S. gross domestic product be next year?" or "Will Google grow its revenues by 5% or 10% next year?". In addition, business plans are notoriously inaccurate—companies struggle to forecast the next quarter or year, much less beyond that. However, many capital investments must be made well in advance of their payoff. The pace of change has also accelerated; the lifespan of the average S&P 500 company has fallen from 75 years in 1938 to 15 years in 2005 (Hagel 2010, para. 10). Corporate leaders must adapt faster, and spend more time envisioning what is predetermined and uncertain in their business environment. In order to start a forecast, it is helpful to first consider broad scenarios (stories) that could lead to different outcomes (e.g., positive or negative change).

One caution that we perceive with storytelling is the common tendency of individuals to mistake plausibility for probability. In Chapter 8, we explore how research in cognitive bias has demonstrated that people tend to overstate the probability of concrete, visualized scenarios—even assigning a higher probability to a vivid scenario than to a broader group of scenarios of which the vivid story is merely a subset.[22] This concern does not eliminate the usefulness

---

[22] In one example, Tversky and Kahneman (1983) asked diplomats to give a probability that the United States would suspend diplomatic relations with the Soviet Union in 1983. They then asked for the probability of a scenario in which Russia invades Poland, resulting in a suspension of U.S.-Soviet relations in the same year. The second question was assigned an average probability over three times that of the broader first question, despite the fact that

of storytelling for brainstorming potential outcomes, but motivates caution in assigning probabilities to specific scenarios.

11. STRATEGY EXECUTION

Even a perfectly formulated strategy is worthless unless it is executed. In this section, we focus on how companies can overcome barriers to the successful implementation of the strategies they develop.

 GARY NEILSON, KARLA MARTIN, and ELIZABETH POWERS
"The Secrets to Successful Strategy Execution" (2008), *Harvard Business Review*.

Thesis: Making it clear who owns decisions and ensuring that information flows to where it's needed are the key levers for successful execution of strategic initiatives.

 Most companies struggle with strategy implementation; Neilson et al. examined successful companies to identify commonalities in how they overcome barriers to execution. They conclude that failure stems from an overreliance on structural changes (e.g., reorganization), while successful companies focus on two stronger levers:

- **Clarifying decision rights**. The firm specifies who owns each decision and who must provide input.
- **Ensuring that information flows where it's needed**. The firm evaluates multiple ways to channel environmental information to headquarters and across organizations. For example, move managers laterally in order to build the networks required for the cross-unit collaboration that is critical to any new strategic approach.

Only after a company has tackled these two levers do the authors recommend altering organizational structure and realigning incentives to support those moves.

Neilson et al. constructed a list of 17 traits corresponding to one of the above building blocks for execution. They developed a profile tool and collected data from thousands of profiles to arrive at the following rank ordering of the impact of each trait on an organization's ability to execute:

---

the second scenario is obviously a subset of the first (p. 308). This inconsistency is referred to as a *conjunction fallacy*, which leads to tension between statisticians and storytellers.

1. Everyone has a good idea of the decisions and actions for which they are responsible.
2. Important information about the competitive environment gets to HQ quickly.
3. Decisions are rarely second-guessed once they are made.
4. Information flows freely across organizational boundaries.
5. Field and line employees have the information needed to understand the impact to profits of their day-to-day choices.
6. Line managers have access to metrics related to the key drivers of their business.
7. Managers up the line get involved in operating decisions.
8. Conflicting messages are rarely sent to the market.
9. The performance-appraisal process differentiates among high, adequate, and low performers.
10. The ability to deliver on commitments strongly influences advancement and pay.
11. The organizational culture can be described more as "persuade and cajole" than "command and control."
12. The primary role of corporate staff is to support rather than audit business units.
13. Promotions can be lateral moves.
14. Fast-track employees can expect promotions more frequently than every three years.
15. Middle managers on average have five or more direct reports.
16. If a division has a good year while the firm has a bad year, the division head still gets a bonus.
17. There are many other motivators besides pay to do a good job.

Discussion and Implications

 In Section 6 of this chapter, Honda managers demonstrated that learning may take a company further than formal strategic planning. This article makes the additional common-sense argument that successful companies must not only formulate well-reasoned strategy but also effectively execute the intended result. Announcing a reorganization is not strategy—implementing the new structure and collecting data to ensure it has realigned activities in the intended manner does represent strategic action.

Another effective tool for converting a business strategy into a plan of action is provided by Osterwalder and Pigneur in a useful handbook entitled *Business Model Generation* (2010), which the authors wrote with crowd-sourced contributions by 470 creators from around the world. This handbook develops a "business model canvas" (p. 12) that provides a means to visualize a company's business model. This template takes nine building blocks of a business model (customer segments, value propositions, channels, customer relationships, revenue streams, key resources, key activities, key partnerships, and cost structure) and encourages entrepreneurs to diagram how they fit together in pictures as well as in words.

A frequent shortcoming of studies in strategy is to develop a "laundry list" of factors that help drive strategy without addressing which are more important, or which will dominate when the factors point toward conflicting outcomes. Neilson et al. avoided that pitfall by collecting data on multiple organizational traits to see which had a larger and smaller contribution to the ability of an organization to execute. Top scorers were well-understood responsibility, data flows to headquarters and across organizational boundaries, and lack of second-guessing of decisions. We characterize these factors as *accountability*.

Rogers and Blenko (2006) similarly warn that ambiguity in accountability for decisions is a frequent source of strategic stalls, and Isaacson (2011) gives much credit for Apple's performance to the relentless culture of accountability instilled by its founder Steve Jobs. Accountability and information are more important than organizational structure, though an appropriate structure and set of incentives are important reinforcing mechanisms.

FURTHER READING

If you're interested in reading more on the topics discussed in this chapter, here are some sources to get you started. We do not offer this as a comprehensive or exhaustive list, but rather have selected well-regarded or significant works that space did not permit us to include in the main discussion.

1. MICHAEL PORTER'S COMPETITIVE FORCES

Magretta, Joan. 2011. *Understanding Michael Porter: The Essential Guide to Competition and Strategy*. Cambridge, Harvard University Press.

Porter, Michael. 1991. "Towards a Dynamic Theory of Strategy." *Strategic Management Journal* 12(S2), 95–117.

Porter, Michael. 2008. *On Competition: Updated and Expanded Edition*. Cambridge, Harvard Business Review Press.

2. THE INSTITUTIONAL ECONOMICS APPROACH

Besanko, David, David Dranove, Mark Shanley, and Scott Shaefer. 2009. *The Economics of Strategy*, 5th edition. Hoboken, Wiley.

Jensen, Michael. 2001. *Foundations of Organizational Strategy*. Cambridge, Harvard University Press.

3. THE RESOURCE-BASED VIEW OF THE FIRM

King, Adelaide. 2007. "Disentangling Interfirm and Intrafirm Causal Ambiguity: A Conceptual Model of Causal Ambiguity and Sustainable Competitive Advantage." *Academy of Management Review* 32(1), 156–178.

Mahoney, Joseph and J. Rajendran Pandian. 1992. "The Resource-Based View Within the Conversation of Strategic Management." *Strategic Management Journal* 13(5), 363–380.

4. STRATEGIC CAPABILITIES

Grant, Robert. 2010. *Contemporary Strategy Analysis: Concepts, Techniques, Applications*, 7th edition. Hoboken, Wiley.

Lynch, Richard, John Diezemann, and James Dowling. 2003. *The Capable Company: Building the Capabilities that Make Strategy Work*. New York, Wiley-Blackwell.

Makadok, Richard. 2001. "Toward a Synthesis of the Resource-Based View and Dynamic-Capability Views of Rent Creation." *Strategic Management Journal* 22(5), 387–401.

Merrifield, Ric, Jack Calhoun, and Dennis Stevens. 2008. "The Next Revolution in Productivity." *Harvard Business Review* 86(June), 72–80.

Teece, David. 2007. "Explicating Dynamic Capabilities: The Nature and Microfoundations of (Sustainable) Enterprise Performance." *Strategic Management Journal* 28(13), 1319–1350.

5. GAME THEORY

Dixit, Avinash and Barry Nalebuff. 2008. *The Art of Strategy: A Game Theorist's Guide to Success in Business and Life*. New York, Norton.

Straffin, Philip. 1996. *Game Theory and Strategy*. Washington, Mathematical Association of America.

6. LEARNING VERSUS PLANNING

Mintzberg, Henry. 1978. "Patterns in Strategy Formation." *Management Science* 24(9), 934–948.

Mintzberg, Henry. 2008. *Tracking Strategies: Toward a General Theory of Strategy Formation*. New York, Oxford University Press.

7. SUSTAINABLE COMPETITIVE ADVANTAGE AND SOCIAL CAPITAL

Adler, Paul and Seok-Woo Kwon. 2002. "Social Capital: Prospects for a New Concept." *Academy of Management Review* 27(1), 17–40.

Coleman, James. "Social Capital in the Creation of Human Capital." *American Journal of Sociology* 94, S95–S120.

Reagans, Ray and Ezra Zuckerman. 2001. "Networks, Diversity and Productivity: The Social Capital of R&D Teams." *Organization Science* 12(4), 502–517.

8. MERGERS AND ACQUISITIONS

Buono, Anthony, James Bowditch, and John Lewis. 1985. "When Cultures Collide: The Anatomy of a Merger." In P. Buckley and P. Ghauri (editors), *International Mergers and Acquisitions: A Reader*. 2002. London, Cengage Learning EMEA. pp. 307–323.

Depamphilis, Donald. 2011. *Mergers, Acquisitions, and Other Restructuring Activities: An Integrated Approach to Processes, Tools, Cases, and Solutions*, 6th edition. New York, Academic Press.

Lees, Stan. 2003. *Global Acquisitions: Strategic Integration and the Human Factor*. New York, Palgrave Macmillan.

Rosenbaum, Joshua and Joshua Pearl. 2009. *Investment Banking: Valuation, Leveraged Buyouts, and Mergers & Acquisitions*. Hoboken, Wiley.

Schoenberg, Richard. 2000. "The Influence of Cultural Compatibility Within Cross-Border Acquisitions: A Review." *Advances in Mergers and Acquisitions* 1(1), 43–59.

Straub, Thomas. 2007. *Reasons for Frequent Failure in Mergers and Acquisitions: A Comprehensive Analysis*. Wiesbaden, Deutscher Universitats-Verlag.

9. REAL OPTIONS

Collan, Mikael and Jani Kinnunen. 2011. "A Procedure for the Rapid Pre-Acquisition Screening of Target Companies Using the Pay-off Method for Real Option Valuation." *Journal of Real Options and Strategy* 4, 117–141.

Copeland, Thomas and Peter Tufano. 2004. "A Real-World Way to Manage Real Options." *Harvard Business Review* 82(March), 90–99.

Damodaran, Aswath. 2008. "The Promise and Peril of Real Options." NYU Working Paper. http://www.stern.nyu.edu/~adamodar/pdfiles/papers/realopt.pdf.

Merton, Robert. 1997. "Applications of Option-Pricing Theory: Twenty-Five Years Later." Nobel lecture reprinted in *American Economic Review* 88, 323–349.

Smit, Han and Lenos Trigeorgis. 2004. *Strategic Investment: Real Options and Games*. Princeton, Princeton University Press.

10. SCENARIO ANALYSIS

Cornelius, Peter, Alexander Van de Putte, and Mattia Romani. 2005. "Three Decades of Scenario Planning in Shell." *California Management Review* 48, 92–109.

Schoemaker, Paul. 1995. "Scenario Planning: A Tool for Strategic Thinking." *Sloan Management Review* 36, 25–40.

Schoemaker, Paul. 1998. "Twenty Common Pitfalls in Scenario Planning." In L. Fahey and R. Randall (editors), *Learning from the Future*. Hoboken, Wiley. pp. 422–431.

11. STRATEGY EXECUTION

Bossidy, Larry and Ram Charan. 2002. *Execution: The Discipline of Getting Things Done*. New York, Crown Business.

Dranove, David and Sonia Marciano. 2005. *Kellogg on Strategy: Concepts, Tools, and Frameworks for Practitioners*. Hoboken, Wiley.

Kaplan, Robert and David Norton. 2008. *The Execution Premium: Linking Strategy to Operations for Competitive Advantage*. Cambridge, Harvard Business School Press.

Rumelt, Richard. 2011. *Good Strategy, Bad Strategy: The Difference and Why It Matters*. New York, Crown Business.

WORKS CITED

Agrawal, Anup and Jeffrey Jaffe. 2000. "The Post Merger Performance Puzzle." In C. Cooper and A. Gregory (editors), *Advances in Mergers and Acquisitions*. Stamford, JAI Press. pp. 119–156.

Ahuja, Gautam. 2000. "Collaboration Networks, Structural Holes, and Innovation: A Longitudinal Study." *Administrative Science Quarterly* 45, 425–455.

Amit, Raffi and Paul Shoemaker. 1993. "Strategic Assets and Organizational Rent." *Strategic Management Journal* 14(1), 33–46.

Amram, Marth and Nalim Kulatilaka. 1999. *Real Options: Managing Strategic Investment in an Uncertain World*. Cambridge, Harvard Business School Press.

Andrews, Kenneth. 1965. *The Concept of Corporate Strategy*. Homewood, Dow Jones-Irwin.

Ansoff, Igor. 1965. *Corporate Strategy: An Analytic Approach to Business Policy for Growth and Expansion*. New York, McGraw-Hill.

Banerji, Shameet, Paul Leinwand, and Cesare Mainardi. 2009. *Cut Costs + Grow Stronger*. Cambridge, Harvard Business School Press.

Barney, Jay. 1991. "Firm Resources and Sustained Competitive Advantage." *Journal of Management* 17(1), 99–120.

Borison, Adam. 2003. "Real Options Analysis: Where Are the Emperor's Clothes?" presentation to Real Options Conference, Washington DC, July. http://www.realoptions.org/abstracts/abstracts03.html.

Brandenberger, Adam and Barry Nalebuff. 1995. "The Right Game: Using Game Theory to Shape Strategy." *Harvard Business Review* 73(July–August), 57–71.

Brandenberger, Adam and Barry Nalebuff. 1997. *Co-Opetition*. New York, Doubleday.

Buono, Anthony and James Bowditch. 1989. *The Human Side of Mergers and Acquisitions: Managing Collisions Between People and Organizations*. San Francisco, Jossey-Bass.

Burt, Ronald. 2000. "The Network Structure of Social Capital." *Research in Organizational Behavior* 22, 345–423.

Camerer, Colin. 1985. "Thinking Economically About Strategy." In J. Pennings and Associates (editors), *Organizational Strategy and Change*. San Francisco, Jossey Bass. Ch 2.

Campbell, Andrew, Michael Goold, and Marcus Alexander, 1995. "Corporate Strategy: The Quest for Parenting Advantage." *Harvard Business Review* 73(March–April), 120–132.

Chandler, Alfred. 1962. *Strategy and Structure: Chapters in the History of the American Industrial Enterprise*. Cambridge, MIT Press.

Chatterjee, Sayan, Michael Lubatkin, and Yaakov Weber. 1992. "Cultural Differences and Shareholder Value in Related Mergers: Linking Equity and Human Capital." *Strategic Management Journal* 13(5), 319–334.

Chi, Tailan. 1994. "Trading in Strategic Resources: Necessary Conditions, Transaction Cost Problems, and Choice of Exchange Structure." *Strategic Management Journal* 15(4), 271–290.

Collis, David and Cynthia Montgomery. 1995. "Competing on Resources: Strategy in the 1990s." *Harvard Business Review* 73(July–August), 118–128.

Collis, David and Cynthia Montgomery. 2005. *Corporate Strategy: A Resource-Based Approach*, 2nd edition. New York, McGraw-Hill.

Connor, Kathleen. 1994. "A Historical Comparison of Resource-Based Theory and Five Schools of Thought Within Industrial Organization Economics: Do We Have a New Theory of the Firm?" *Journal of Management* 17(1), 121–154.

Copeland, Thomas and Vladmir Antikarov. 2001. *Real Options: A Practitioners Guide*. New York, Texere.

Cording, Margaret, Petra Christmann, and L.J. Bourgeois. 2002. "A Focus on Resources in M&A Success: A Literature Review and Research Agenda to Resolve Two Paradoxes." *Academy of Management Meetings*, Denver, August.

Crook, T. Russell, David Ketchen Jr., James Combs, and Samuel Todd. 2008. "Strategic Resources and Performance: A Meta-Analysis." *Strategic Management Journal* 29(11), 1141–1154.

D'Aveni, Richard. 1994. *Hypercompetition*. New York, Free Press.

Davis-Floyd, Robbie. 1998. "Storying Corporate Futures: The Shell Scenarios." In G. Marcus (editor), *Corporate Futures: The Diffusion of the Culturally Sensitive Corporate Form*. Chicago, University of Chicago Press. pp. 141–176.

Dierckx, Ingemar and Karel Cool. 1989. "Asset Stock Accumulation and Sustainability of Competitive Advantage." *Management Science* 35(12), 1504–1511.

Eisenhardt, Kathleen and Jeffrey Martin. 2000. "Dynamic Capabilities: What Are They?" *Strategic Management Journal* 21(10/11), 1105–1121.

Fink, Ronald. 2001. "Reality Check for Real Options." *CFO Magazine*, 13 September. http://www.cfo.com/article.cfm/3000665/1/c_3046509.

Fowell, Walter. 1990. "Neither Market Nor Hierarchy: Network Forms of Organization." In B. Staw and L. Cummings (editors), *Research in Organizational Behavior*, vol. 12. Greenwich, JAI Press. pp. 295–336.

Gartner Group. 2011. *Market Share Analysis: Business Intelligence, Analytics, and Performance Management Software, Worldwide, 2010.* http://www.gartner.com/DisplayDocument?ref=clientFriendlyUrl&id=1639015.

Gartner Group. 2012. *Market Share: All Software Markets, Worldwide 2011.* http://www.gartner.com/id=1969315.

Ghemawat, Pankaj. 1991. *Commitment: The Dynamic of Strategy.* New York, Free Press.

Godfrey, Paul and Charles Hill. 1995. "The Problem of Unobservables in Strategic Management Research." *Strategic Management Journal* 16, 519–533.

Goldman Sachs. 2005. *US Technology: Software Investment Perspective.* 17 February.

Ghoshal, Sumantra and Peter Moran. 1996. "Bad for Practice: A Critique of the Transaction Cost Theory." *Academy of Management Review* 21(1), 13–47.

Grantham, Charles, James Ware, and Cory Williamson. 2007. *Corporate Agility: A Revolutionary New Model for Competing in a Flat World.* New York, AMACOM.

Hagel, John. 2010. "Running Faster, Falling Behind: John Hagel III on How American Business Can Catch Up." *Knowledge@Wharton*, 23 June. http://knowledge.wharton.upenn.edu/article.cfm?articleid=2523.

Haleblian, Jerayr and Sydney Finkelstein. 1999. "The Influence of Organizational Acquisition Experience on Acquisition Performance: A Behavioral Learning Perspective." *Administrative Science Quarterly* 44(1), 19–56.

Hall, Richard. 1993. "A Framework Linking Intangible Resources and Capabilities to Sustainable Competitive Advantage." *Strategic Management Journal* 14(8), 607–618.

Hamel, Gary. 1991. "Competition for Competence and Inter-Partner Learning Within International Strategic Alliances." *Strategic Management Journal* 12(Summer), 83–103.

Hamel, Gary. 1996. "Strategy as Revolution." *Harvard Business Review* 74(July–August), 69–82.

Hamel, Gary and C. K. Prahalad. 1989. "Strategic Intent." *Harvard Business Review* 67(May–June), 63–76.

Hamel, Gary and C. K. Prahalad. 1994. *Competing for the Future.* Cambridge, Harvard Business Review Press.

Haspeslaugh, Philippe and David Jemison. 1991. *Managing Acquisitions: Creating Value Through Corporate Renewal.* New York, Free Press.

Hayward, Matthew and Donald Hambrick. 1997. "Explaining the Premium Paid for Large Acquisitions: Evidence of CEO Hubris." *Administrative Science Quarterly* 42(1), 103–127.

Henderson, Bruce. 1968. *Perspectives on Experience.* Boston, Boston Consulting Group.

Henderson, Bruce. 1970. "The Product Portfolio." In C. Stern and M. Deimler (editors), *The Boston Consulting Group on Strategy*, 2nd edition [2006]. New York, Wiley. pp. 35-38.

Huang, Christine and Brian Kleiner. 2004. "New Developments Concerning Managing Mergers and Acquisitions." *Management Research News* 27, 54–62.

Isaacson, Walter. 2011. *Steve Jobs.* New York, Simon & Schuster.

Jemison, David and Sim Sitkin. 1986. "Corporate Acquisitions: A Process Perspective." *Academy of Management Review* 11(1), 145–163.

Jensen, Michael and William Meckling. 1976. "Theory of the Firm: Managerial Behavior, Agency Costs and Ownership Structure." *Journal of Financial Economics* 3(4), 303–360.

Johnson, Gerry and Kevan Scholes. 2006. *Exploring Corporate Strategy: Text and Cases*, 7th edition. London, Financial Times.

Kaplan, Steven. 2009. "How to Fix Business Schools." *Harvard Business Review blog* [blog debate], 9 April. http://blogs.hbr.org/how-to-fix-business-schools/?page=2 (accessed 6 June 2012).

King, David, Dan Dalton, Catherine Daily, and Jeffrey Covin. 2004. "Meta-analyses of Post-Acquisition Performance: Indications of Unidentified Moderators." *Strategic Management Journal* 25(2), 187–200.

Kesner, Idalene, Debra Shapiro, and Anurag Sharma. 1994. "Brokering Mergers: An Agency Theory Perspective on the Role of Representatives." *Academy of Management Journal* 37(3), 703–721.

KPMG. 1999. "Mergers and Acquisitions: A Global Research Report." http://www.imaa-institute.org/docs/m&a/kpmg_01_Unlocking%20 Shareholder%20Value%20-%20The%20Keys%20to%20Success.pdf

Krishnan, Hema, Alex Miller, and William Judge. 1997. "Diversification and Top Management Team Complementarity: Is Performance Improved by Merging Similar or Dissimilar Teams?" *Strategic Management Journal* 18(5), 361–374.

Kroll, Mark, Peter Wright, Lesley Toombs, and Hadley Leavell. 1997. "Form of Control: A Critical Determinant of Acquisition Performance and CEO Rewards." *Strategic Management Journal* 18(2), 85–96.

Krug, Jeffrey and Ruth Aguilera. 2005. "Top Management Team Turnover in Mergers & Acquisitions." In S. Finkelstein and C. Cooper (editors), *Advances in Mergers & Acquisitions*, vol. 4. London, Emerald Group. pp. 123–151.

Lado, Augustine and Mary Wilson. 1995. "Human Resource Systems and Sustained Competitive Advantage: A Competency-Based Perspective." *Academy of Management Review* 19(4), 699–727.

Learned, Edmund, Carl Christensen, Kenneth Andrews, and William Guth. 1969. *Business Policy: Text and Cases*. New York, Richard D. Irwin Publisher.

Luehrman, Timothy. 1998. "Strategy as a Portfolio of Real Options." *Harvard Business Review* 76(September–October), 89–99.

Luehrman, Timothy. 1998. "Investment Opportunities as Real Options: Getting Started on the Numbers." *Harvard Business Review* 76(July–August), 51–67.

Marks, Mitchell. 1997. "Consulting in Mergers and Acquisitions: Interventions Spawned by Recent Trends." *Journal of Organizational Change Management* 10(3), 267–279.

McArthur, John and Bruce Scott. 1969. *Industrial Planning in France*. Boston, Harvard Press.

Mintzberg, Henry, Richard Pascale, Michael Goold, and Richard Rumelt. 1996. "The Honda Effect Revisited." *California Management Review* 38(4), 78–117.

Moran, Peter and Sumantra Ghoshal. 1996. "Theories of Economic Organization: The Case for Realism and Balance." *Academy of Management Review* 21(1), 58–72.

Myers, Stewart C. 1977. "Determinants of Corporate Borrowing." *Journal of Financial Economics* 5(2), 147–175.

Nahapiet, Janine and Sumantra Ghoshal. 1998. "Social Capital, Intellectual Capital, and the Organizational Advantage." *Academy of Management Review* 23(2), 242–266.

Neilson, Gary, Karla Martin, and Elizabeth Powers. 2008. "The Secrets to Successful Strategy Execution." *Harvard Business Review* 86(May–June), 61–70.

Oracle. 2009. *Oracle Buys Sun* [press release], 20 April. http://www.oracle.com/us/corporate/press/018363.

Osterwalder, Alexander and Yves Pigneur. 2010. *Business Model Generation: A Handbook for Visionaries, Game Changers, and Challengers.* Hoboken, Wiley.

Page, Larry. 2009. Commencement address at University of Michigan. Transcript retrieved from http://www.google.com/intl/en/press/annc/20090502-page-commencement.html.

Patnaik, Dev. 2009. "How to Fix Business Schools." *Harvard Business Review blog* [blog debate], 9 April. http://blogs.hbr.org/how-to-fix-business-schools/?page=2 (accessed 6 June 2012).

Penrose, Edith. 1959. *The Theory of Growth of the Firm.* London, Basil Blackwell.

Pepall, Lynn, Dan Richards, and George Norman, 2008. *Industrial Organization: Contemporary Theory and Empirical Applications*, 4th edition. New York, Wiley-Blackwell.

Perrow, Charles. 1981. "Markets, Hierarchies, and Hegemony." In A. H. Van de Ven and W. F. Joyce (editors), *Perspectives on Organizational Design and Behavior.* New York, Wiley. pp. 371–386.

Peteraf, Margaret. 1993. "The Cornerstones of Competitive Advantage: A Resource-Based View." *Strategic Management Journal* 14(3), 179–191.

Pfeffer, Jeffrey. 1981. *Power in Organizations.* New York, HarperCollins.

Pfeffer, Jeffrey. 1993. *Managing with Power: Politics and Influence in Organizations.* Cambridge, Harvard Business Review Press.

Porter, Michael. 1980. *Competitive Strategy.* New York, Free Press.

Porter, Michael. 1985. *Competitive Advantage.* New York, Free Press.

Porter, Michael. 1987. "From Competitive Advantage to Corporate Strategy." *Harvard Business Review* 65(May–June), 43–59.

Porter, Michael. 1990. *The Competitive Advantage of Nations.* New York, Free Press.

Porter, Michael. 1996. "What Is Strategy?" *Harvard Business Review* 74(November–December), 61–78.

Porter, Michael. 2008. *On Competition.* Cambridge, Harvard Business School Press.

Prahalad, C. K. and Gary Hamel. 1990. "The Core Competence of the Corporation." *Harvard Business Review* 68(May–June), 79–91.

Rogers, Paul and Marcia Blenko, 2006. "Who Has the D? How Clear Decision Roles Enhance Organizational Performance." *Harvard Business Review* 84(January–February), 53–61.

Schoenberg, Richard. 2006. "Measuring the Performance of Corporate Acquisitions: An Empirical Comparison of Alternative Metrics." *British Journal of Management* 17(4), 361–370.

Schmidt, Dennis and Karen Fowler. 1990. "Post-Acquisition Financial Performance and Executive Compensation." *Strategic Management Journal* 11(7), 559–569.

Selznick, Philip. 1957. *Leadership in Administration.* New York, Harper & Row.

Senge, Peter. 2006. *The Fifth Discipline: The Art and Practice of the Learning Organization.* New York, Crown Business.

Shanley, Mark and Mary Correa. 1992. "Agreement Between Top Management Teams and Expectations for Post Acquisition Performance." *Strategic Management Journal* 13(4), 245–266.

Simon, Herbert. 1947. *Administrative Behavior.* New York, Free Press.

Sirower, Mark. 1997. *The Synergy Trap: How Companies Lose the Acquisition Game.* New York, Free Press.

Smith, James and Robert Nau. 1995. "Valuing Risky Projects, Option Pricing Theory and Decision Analysis." *Management Science* 41(5), 795–816.

Teece, David, Gary Pisano, and Amy Shuen. 1997. "Dynamic Capabilities and Strategic Management." *Strategic Management Journal* 18(7), 509–533.

Trigeorgis, Lenos. 1998. *Real Options: Managerial Flexibility and Strategy in Resource Allocation.* Cambridge, MIT Press.

Tversky, Amos and Daniel Kahneman. 1983. "Extensional Versus Intuitive Reasoning: The Conjunction Fallacy in Probability Judgment." *Psychological Review* 90(4), 293–315.

Tzu, S. 2008. *The Art of War.* Translated by Lionel Giles. North Clarendon, Charles E. Tuttle Co.

von Neumann, John and Oskar Morgenstern. 1944. *Theory of Games and Economic Behavior.* Princeton, Princeton University Press.

Wack, Pierre. 1985a. "Scenarios: Uncharted Waters Ahead." *Harvard Business Review* 63(September–October), 73–89.

Wack, Pierre. 1985b. "Scenarios: Shooting the Rapids." *Harvard Business Review* 63(November–December), 2–14.

Walsh, James. 1988. "Top Management Turnover Following Mergers and Acquisitions." *Strategic Management Journal* 9(2), 173–183.

Waterman, Robert, Thomas Peters, and Julien Phillips. 1980. "Structure Is Not Organization." *Business Horizons* (McKinsey quarterly in-house journal). http://www.tompeters.com/docs/Structure_Is_Not_Organization.pdf.

Wernerfelt, Birger. 1984. "The Resource-Based Theory of the Firm." *Strategic Management Journal* 5(2), 171–180.

Williamson, Oliver E. 1975. *Markets and Hierarchies: Analysis and Market Implications.* New York, Free Press.

Williamson, Oliver. 1981. "The Economics of Organization: The Transaction Cost Approach." *American Journal of Sociology* 87(3), 548–577.

Williamson, Oliver. 1996. "Economic Organization: The Case for Candor." *Academy of Management Review* 21(1), 48–57.

Williamson, Oliver and William Ouchi. 1981a. "The Markets and Hierarchies Program of Research: Origins, Implications, and Prospects." In A. H. Van de Ven and W. F. Joyce (editors), *Perspectives on Organizational Design and Behavior.* New York, Wiley. pp. 347–370.

Williamson, Oliver and William Ouchi. 1981b. "A Rejoinder." In A. H. Van de Ven and W. F. Joyce (editors), *Perspectives on Organizational Design and Behavior*. New York, Wiley. pp. 387–390.

Zajac, Edward and Cyrus Olsen. 1993. "From Transaction Cost to Transaction Value Analysis: Implications for the Study of Interorganizational Strategies." *Journal of Management Studies* 30(1), 131–145.

ENTREPRENEURSHIP

This chapter traces the evolution of the field of entrepreneurship and applies its literature to managers. In developing business plans for both domestic and international new businesses, Joe recognized that the general model for such plans is to make "best guess" estimates of costs and revenues, and add (or subtract) a percentage to address risk. But what of uncertainty? Given that all risks cannot be quantified and known beforehand, how can a potential entrepreneur plan with any confidence? Understanding that the "unknown unknowns" may radically affect performance, how can one start a business in an economically volatile domestic environment or in a foreign country with limited knowledge, while constant economic changes increase uncertainty? In Section 1 of this chapter, Frank Knight (1921) and Schumpeter (1934) reflect on this common entrepreneurial challenge with insights that are as relevant today as when they were written.

There are three arguments in favor of formally studying entrepreneurship (Shane and Venkatraman 2000).

- Much technical information is embodied in products and services (Arrow 1962; see Chapter 6), and entrepreneurship is a mechanism by which society converts technical information into these products and services.
- Entrepreneurship is a mechanism through which inefficiencies in time and space within an economy are discovered and mitigated, as described by Kirzner (1997; see Section 2).
- Entrepreneurially driven innovation in products and processes is the crucial engine driving the change process in a capitalist society (Schumpeter 1934).

Entrepreneurs are often struck by the thought, "Why didn't someone else already do this?"—why do some people, and not others, discover and exploit opportunities? As discussed in Section 2, Ardichvili, Cardozo, and Ray (2003) infer that opportunities are made, not found, suggesting that the "entrepreneur–opportunity nexus" is at the heart of opportunity exploitation. Joe's prior market and technology knowledge helped him read and interpret trends, enabling the emergence of new ventures, in a manner consistent with the work of Shane and Venkatraman (2000; see Section 2).

We begin in Section 1 with selected articles that define entrepreneurship, identify and describe the main theories in the field, and explain the major theoretical tensions and areas for the development in the field. Section 2 introduces articles that describe opportunities—the heart of entrepreneurship. In Section 3, we introduce other literature describing entrepreneurs: who are they and where do they come from? Section 4 summarizes selected articles that discuss the impact of entrepreneurship on individuals and economies. Section 5 concludes the chapter with a summary of articles that speak to new venture internationalization: why, how, and with what outcome do new ventures move beyond their domestic environment?

1. Entrepreneurship and Why We Should Study It

The articles summarized in this section provide a historical context for entrepreneurship as well as insight into the field's economic and behavioral roots. We begin with an article by Aitken (1963) that frames some of the entrepreneurial thought in the first half of the 20th century. In particular, two writers in the early 20th century laid a foundation for much of the research in entrepreneurship. The first, Frank Knight, published a key work in 1921, while the second, Joseph Schumpeter, wrote a number of books from 1911 to 1942. Both outstanding educators were economists, at the University of Chicago and Harvard respectively. Finally, Joseph Schumpeter (1934) was a major developer of the economic base for entrepreneurship, and his term "creative destruction" has found its way into standard business jargon.

HUGH AITKEN
"The Future of Entrepreneurial Research" (1963), *Explorations in Entrepreneurial History.*

Thesis: *Entrepreneurship* refers to firms based on social relationships, and is studied at the level of the enterprise.

Despite its forward-looking title, Aitken's article presents a brief history of entrepreneurship as a field of study. Entrepreneurship was established to revitalize the whole field of economic history post-World War II, and was one of only four fields of inquiry that economic scholars selected as deserving support in the postwar years (along with the economic role of government, the development of the corporation, and the history of U.S. banking). There was a great diversity of views on the definition of entrepreneurship, and when agreement did occur, it was agreement on a rather fundamental level that took the form of implicit acceptance of a few rather simple propositions.

These propositions suggested that entrepreneurship refers to a kind of behavior characteristic of certain organized associations of individuals (e.g., firms)—it is the association, not the individual, that exhibits entrepreneurship. Therefore, the search for individual entrepreneurs rests on fallacious logic. Additionally, explanations of why one particular association (organization or firm) exhibits more entrepreneurship than another must be sought in the relationships among individuals in the association, and in the relationships between the association and the society (including the economy) of which it was part.

By this logic, the analysis of aspects such as the personalities, social origins, and education of particular individuals alleged to be entrepreneurs is relevant only to the extent that it throws light on the behavior of the associations to which those individuals belong. The concept of social role serves as a key to the analysis both of the intra-firm determinants of entrepreneurship and of the determinants located "outside" the business unit.

Entrepreneurship is characteristic of all organized human activity; it is not a matter of "all or nothing," but a matter of "more or less." The study of entrepreneurship is part of the study of organization, particularly of business organization. Organization is a quality, not a thing, and is an ongoing process, not a fixed state. Future work in the tradition of entrepreneurial history, Aitken concluded, will be concerned largely with studies of economic organizations at the level of the individual enterprise and of the economy as a whole.

FRANK KNIGHT
Risk, Uncertainty and Profit (1921), Chapter 9.

Thesis: As the distribution of known possible outcomes, "risk" is distinct from "uncertainty," which describes that the set of possible outcomes is not known. Firms profit only by bearing uncertainty.

Frank Knight was one of the founders of the "Chicago school" (an economic theory highlighting the benefits of free-market economics and critical of Keynesian government intervention) and counted four Nobel laureates among his students (Paul Samuelson, Milton Friedman, George Stigler, and James Buchanan). In this book, he introduced what has been termed "Knightian uncertainty." Knight examined neoclassical economics, a branch of economic literature which assumes that markets are perfect, questioning its assumptions. Motivated by the seeming paradox that with perfect markets there should be no possibility of earning rents in the long run (except for monopolies), Knight asked, "Why should firms exist?" and "What determines profitability?".

Knight makes a distinction between *risk*, as the known distribution of the outcome in a group of instances, and *uncertainty*, in which "it is impossible to form a group of instances, because the situation dealt with is in a high degree unique" (p. 233). This is a crucial idea, as some sources of change and the associated risk are not quantifiable. A situation is "risky" if you can identify possible outcomes and assign probabilities to their occurrence (e.g., if you engage in a coin toss, you do not know whether you will get heads or tails but know that there is a 50% chance of each). A situation is uncertain if you cannot identify the possible outcomes.

In terms of uncertainty and profit, firms can only profit if they take on uncertainty. In these situations, private information may forestall entry: those with information may not enter, whereas those without information may (i.e., information asymmetry leads to uncertainty). Producers are able to charge a premium for products and for bearing uncertainty for others. Entrepreneurs are individuals with unusually low levels of uncertainty aversion.

Regarding the role of entrepreneurs, their business judgment is not based on true knowledge per se, but is rather more intuitive in nature. "The opinions...which govern the decisions of responsible business managers for the most part have little similarity with conclusions reached by exhaustive analysis and accurate measurement" (p. 230). A crucial source of uncertainty relates to the ability to formulate probabilistic predictions and its likely association with the ability to group events. Knight asks,

> What things are we dealing with, and what are the circumstances which condition their action? From knowledge of these two sets of facts it must be possible to say what behavior is to be expected. (p. 204)

Entrepreneurial success (which entrepreneurs may variously define as length of survival or ability to control events) is determined by four factors:

- the extent of one's ability to address uncertainty,
- confidence in the chosen approach,
- luck in one's predictions, and
- the presence or absence of these qualities in others.

Even in the presence of these factors, it may be difficult to sustain entrepreneurship, as these entrepreneurial advantages are not likely to last forever. Risk may become uncertainty and uncertainty may become risk. Successful entrepreneurs will be able to adjust their focus.

JOSEPH SCHUMPETER
The Theory of Economic Development (1934).

Thesis: *Enterprise* is the carrying out of new combinations, and *entrepreneurs* are the individuals who do so. Economic development emerges when new combinations appear discontinuously in a process of creative destruction.

Joseph Schumpeter was an Austrian economist whose major works span the years 1911 to 1950, though he may be most known for the ideas published in this book. His *Theory of Economic Development* stated that entrepreneurially driven innovation in products and processes is the crucial engine driving the change process in a capitalist society. There is no distinction between the entrepreneur and the firm. Schumpeter stresses four main concepts:

- the circular flow of economic life,
- the fundamental concept of economic development,
- credit and capital, and
- entrepreneurial profits.

The Circular Flow of Economic Life

The mechanism of exchange-economy operations works with great precision because the circular flow of economic periods goes relatively fast and essentially the same thing occurs in every economic period. To properly analyze economic causal relationships, exploratory efforts must continue until the phenomenon that plays the "causal" role is non-economic. This circular flow is closed since all businessmen are both buyers and sellers, and all goods find a market.

The economic system will not change capriciously on its own initiative, but will be connected to a previous state of affairs and, while economic activity may have any motive, its meaning is always the satisfaction of wants. The value system (once established) and the combinations (once given) are always the starting point for every new economic period and have a presumption in their favor. The assumption is that in every period, only products produced in the previous period are consumed (i.e., no inventory), partially by workers and landlords whose services were required for the production of new consumption goods for the following period; therefore, workers and landlords always exchange their productive services for present consumption goods only. Thus, there is no need for them to exchange their services of labor and land for future goods, promises of future consumption goods, or any "advance" of present consumption goods.

In other words, there is no "credit"—rather, a stream of goods is being continually renewed. The system thus tends toward an equilibrium position, as economic life runs on in the same channels, year after year.

The Fundamental Phenomenon of Economic Development
Economic life does experience changes, and it is not possible to explain that change by previous economic conditions alone—one needs to consider the preceding total situation. The ideal state of equilibrium, never attained but continually striven after, changes because the data changes. Mere growth of the economy is not a process of development, as it calls forth no qualitatively new phenomena, being only a process of adaptation.

Spontaneous and discontinuous changes and disturbances of the center of equilibrium appear in industrial and commercial life. Such changes constitute *development*—the carrying out of new combinations—that encompass five cases:

- the introduction of a new good or of a new quality of good;
- the introduction of a new method of production;
- the opening of a new market;
- the conquest of a new source of supply of raw materials or half-manufactured goods; and
- the carrying out of the new organization of any industry, like the creation or dissolution of a monopoly position.

New combinations are, as a rule, embodied in new firms that generally do not arise out of old ones but start producing beside them (e.g., the owner of stage-coaches does not build railroads). New combinations must draw the necessary means of production from some old combinations, thus requiring a business to resort to credit in order to carry out new combinations; unlike an established business, a new business cannot be financed by returns from previous production. Credit is the solution to the problem of detaching productive means (employed elsewhere) from the circular flow and allotting them to new combinations.

Credit and Capital
In the circular flow, since goods are consumed in the period in which they are produced, there are no idle stocks upon which entrepreneurs can draw. Circulating media (e.g., currency) cannot all be redeemed at once, and exist solely for the purpose of granting credit. Capital is embodied in the goods; entrepreneurs cannot draw out their capital from their "investment," because it is already spent. In return for their capital, they have acquired goods that they will not employ as capital (i.e., as a fund in paying for other goods) but rather in technical production.

Entrepreneurial Profits

In the circular flow, total receipts are just big enough to cover outlays, so there is no profit. Since new combinations via "development" are more advantageous, total receipts are greater than total costs, which must yield a profit. Thus, new businesses arise under the impulse of alluring profit, and a new equilibrium position results. However, the entrepreneur is never the risk-bearer. The one who gives credit bears the risk (this may be the same person, but not in the same role as entrepreneur).

Discussion and Implications

Aitken proposed that practitioners will typically be concerned with the ways in which organizational behavior and attitudes are molded by social structure and cultural configurations, and will have a continuing concern with productivity and economic development. While Aitken's focus is on the organizational aspects of entrepreneurship, his conclusion indicates that the economic aspects are central. Indeed, the history of entrepreneurship stems from economics, dating back to the 18th and 19th centuries in the works of Cantillon (1755) and Say (1845), in which entrepreneurs assume certain roles relative to risk, capital, and resources. Aitken's work was in response to literature on entrepreneurial traits suggesting that entrepreneurs possess certain characteristics, such as a need for achievement (McClelland 1961), that others do not possess.

In essence, his work starts to suggest that entrepreneurs are not born, but they can be made. This argument has significant implications for managers, educators, policymakers, and those of us who aspire to be entrepreneurs ourselves. Thus, it is now common for managers to develop entrepreneurial thinking and spirit, entrepreneurship majors to exist at numerous universities, government leaders to develop programs to promote entrepreneurship, and for many of us to take the leap into starting new ventures.

Frank Knight and Schumpeter suggest that managers and entrepreneurs must face a significant amount of uncertainty. All risks cannot be quantified and known *a priori* (beforehand). The presence of the "perennial gale of creative destruction" (Schumpeter 1942, p. 83) identified by Schumpeter means that entrepreneurs and managers must continually seek to improve their capabilities and offerings, as new technologies and innovations from unknown and uncertain sources will eliminate the need for today's products and services.

Frank Knight's argument that information cannot be known ahead of time stands in contrast to later work in economics and strategy theory, which uses models in which markets can infer private information, and to incomplete contracting models in which parties are purportedly fully informed at the time of agreement. Of relevance to entrepreneurs, however, is Knight's notion that risk, which can be quantified probabilistically, is fundamentally different from uncertainty, which may be due to "unknown unknowns" (we do not know what we do not know). It may be the case that entrepreneurs deal better with uncertainty that do managers, allowing them flexibility in strategies.

Further reading in this stream includes articles that seek to define entrepreneurship and entrepreneurs. Hayek (1945) bashes Schumpeter's approach, which he feels disregards the unavoidable imperfection of man's knowledge and the consequent need for a process by which knowledge is constantly communicated and acquired. Leibenstein (1968) developed a view of "x-efficiency," which posited that neither individuals nor groups work as hard or as effectively, or search for new information and techniques as diligently as they could; this lack produces persistent slack that implies the existence of entrepreneurial opportunities. McClelland (1961) proposed that entrepreneurs have particular traits, such as a need for achievement (nAch) that drove them to form new ventures. Additional writings in this area include the following, presented in chronological order.

- **Schumpeter (1942).** An *entrepreneur* is a leader and a contributor to the process of creative destruction, and is the person who carries out new combinations, causing discontinuities. Creative destruction is at the heart of capitalism, as general economic "recipes" do not work. Modern business entails constantly evolving oligopolies based not on price competition, but rather involving technological and organizational battles. In this article, Schumpeter provides an alternative view of monopolies, one that suggests that they are not unhealthy, as was the prevailing view. The profits of large firms stem not from monopolies, but from innovations; that is, firms are not successful because they are monopolies, but because they innovate. Entrepreneurship has been the domain of bold individuals—in a world with limited information, intuitive, extra-rational activity is critical. However, as knowledge is increasingly systemized, it becomes possible to manage innovation in a planned economy, and entrepreneurship loses importance even if the economic process of which entrepreneurship was the prime mover continues unabated.

- **Kets de Vries (1977).** While prior research identifies entrepreneurial roles as innovator, manager, or risk-taker, there is more complexity to the roles entrepreneurs play and the personal attributes that lead to these roles. Family dynamics and early childhood can affect the propensity to engage in entrepreneurial acts and exert control.

- **Drucker (1985).** Three main entrepreneurial strategies are critical for competition: (1) being "Fustest with the Mostest," (2) "Hitting them where they ain't," and (3) finding and occupying a specialized "ecological niche." These strategies result in changing the economic characteristics of a product, a market, or an industry. These entrepreneurial strategies have their prerequisites, as each fits certain kinds of innovation and not others, each requires specific behavior on the part of the entrepreneur, and each has its own limitations and risks.

2. OPPORTUNITIES AND OPPORTUNITY RECOGNITION

A significant portion of the body of entrepreneurship literature focuses on opportunities and whether they exist independent of individuals or if entrepreneurs have specialized traits or abilities to identify or develop opportunities. This section begins with Kirzner (1997), who emphasizes the role of entrepreneurship in identifying opportunities and in driving markets to equilibrium. Full information is not available to all participants, and it is entrepreneurs who gain partial monopolies from new information and drive markets to equilibrium by identifying disparities in prices and qualities. Kirzner examines not just equilibrium but the path taken to get there. Mistakes by one entrepreneur can provide opportunities for another, due to differing abilities to perceive and obtain information. The entrepreneurial process facilitates the identification of such information due to incentives and rivalry.

Kirzner's work informs and influences other studies in this area, two of which are presented in more detail in this section. Shane and Venkataraman (2000) embed the study of entrepreneurial opportunities in a broader integrating framework that invokes Section 1's examination of why entrepreneurship research is of interest and Section 3's focus on why some people discover opportunities and become entrepreneurs. Ardichvili, Cardozo, and Ray (2003) extend these earlier works using a theory-based approach to suggest that opportunities result from being alert, having prior knowledge, being creative, and being optimistic.

ISRAEL KIRZNER
"Entrepreneurial Discovery and the Competitive Market Process: An Austrian Approach" (1997), *Journal of Economic Literature*.

Thesis: Entrepreneurship is a mechanism through which temporal and spatial inefficiencies in an economy are discovered and mitigated.

Kirzner comes from the Austrian approach to economics which, while microeconomics-based, he claims is not ordinarily well-represented in textbooks or journals. In his work, he seeks to represent the Austrian perspective, which he believes is critical for understanding entrepreneurship, and add it to the literature. In earlier work, Kirzner (1985) recognized the central role that entrepreneurial alertness plays in the discovery of previously-overlooked possibilities, through the "speculative ability to see into the future" (Bull and Willard 1993, p. 190). This alertness suggests an arbitrage situation, in which the entrepreneur anticipates market imperfections and imbalances, and seeks to profit from their occurrence.

In this article, Kirzner focuses on specific positive elements of the approach to entrepreneurial discovery that stamp the approach as Austrian. These positive elements focus on the role of knowledge and discovery in the market equilibration process, in which market participants acquire more accurate and complete mutual knowledge of potential supply and demand. Imperfect knowledge involves elements of "sheer" (i.e., unknown) ignorance, which may be related to Knightian uncertainty (F. Knight 1921), and is accompanied by the element of surprise as one realizes one's ignorance. Entrepreneurial discovery gradually pushes back the boundaries of sheer ignorance, increasing mutual awareness among market participants, thereby driving prices, inputs and output quantities, and qualities toward equilibrium values.

Three interrelated concepts comprise the heart of the modern Austrian entrepreneurial discovery theory of the market process: the entrepreneurial role, the role of discovery, and rivalrous competition.

The entrepreneurial role does not exist in neoclassical equilibrium theory—where there is not scope for pure profit, there is nothing for the entrepreneur to do. Kirzner refers to Mises (1949) in defining the *entrepreneur* as one acting in regard to changes in the data of the market. Each market is characterized in opportunities for pure entrepreneurial profit, which are created by earlier entrepreneurial errors resulting in shortages, surplus, or misallocated resources. The alert entrepreneur discovers these errors and buys where prices are "too low" and sells where prices are "too high." Price discrepancies are thus narrowed in the equilibrium direction.

The role of discovery is that profit opportunities have to be discovered and grasped by routine-resisting participants in the entrepreneurial market. An opportunity for pure profit cannot be the subject of systematic search. An overlooked profit opportunity, by its very nature, has been utterly overlooked in that one is not aware at all of missing out on any profit. This opportunity discovery involves surprise, which accompanies a realization that one has overlooked something readily available, as well as discovery. The notion of *discovery* is thus midway between the concept of deliberately-produced information in standard search theory and that of the gain generated by pure chance.

Entrepreneurial boldness and imagination drive the market process, which embodies the series of discoveries that boldness and alertness generate. Through rivalrous competition, entrepreneurs enter the market, compete with others, and outdo rivals with better offerings or prices. That competition results in the revelation of information not known to be lacking. Rivalrous competition depends on the profit incentive to mitigate the occurrence of entrepreneurial error. As a result, the Austrian approach stresses the discovery potential in rivalrous competition and its entrepreneurial character.

SCOTT SHANE and SANKARAN VENKATARAMAN
"The Promise of Entrepreneurship as a Field of Research"
(2000), *Academy of Management Review.*

Thesis: Entrepreneurship involves the study of sources of opportunities to sell goods or services at greater than their cost of production. To sell in this fashion requires different beliefs about the value of resources.

In this article, Shane and Venkataraman define the domain of the field of entrepreneurship, explain why researchers should study it, describe why entrepreneurial opportunities exist, and discuss why some people (and not others) discover and exploit those opportunities. The authors then consider the different modes of exploitation of entrepreneurial opportunities, concluding with a brief reflection on the potential value of their conceptual framework for studying entrepreneurship.

The foundation for this study is the assertion that entrepreneurship is concerned with the discovery and exploitation of profitable opportunities, in contrast to prior research defining the field solely in terms of entrepreneurs and what they do. The prior-research definition is limited because entrepreneurship involves the nexus of two phenomena: the presence of lucrative opportunities and the presence of enterprising individuals (Venkataraman 1997).

Shane and Venkataraman's definition of *entrepreneurship*, "the scholarly examination of how, by whom, and with what effects opportunities to create future goods and services are discovered, evaluated and exploited" (p. 218) has been the guiding definition over the past decade for entrepreneurship research. The field thus involves the study of the sources of opportunities; the processes of discovery, evaluation, and exploitation of opportunities; and the set of individuals who discover, evaluate, and exploit them. The authors use Casson (1982) to define *entrepreneurial opportunities* as those situations in which new goods, services, raw materials, and organizing methods can be introduced and sold at greater than their cost of production.

Organization scholars are primarily concerned with three sets of research questions about entrepreneurship. They want to know why, when, and how:

- opportunities for the creation of goods and services come into existence,
- some people and not others discover and exploit these opportunities, and

- different modes of action are used to exploit entrepreneurial opportunities.

Opportunities are objective phenomena that are not known to all parties at all times, and that require the discovery of new means–ends relationships. Drucker (1985) described three different categories of opportunities: the creation of new information (e.g., new technology), the exploitation of market inefficiencies resulting from information asymmetries, and the reaction to shifts in relative costs and benefits of alternative uses of resources.

Entrepreneurship requires that people hold different beliefs about the value of resources—if all people possessed the same entrepreneurial conjectures, they would all compete to capture the same profit, dividing it to the point where opportunity was eliminated. *Entrepreneurial discovery* occurs when someone makes the conjecture that a set of resources is not put to its best use.

People vary in their ability to identify and to combine existing concepts and information into new ideas; in addition, entrepreneurial opportunities can become cost-inefficient to pursue due to a dependence on information asymmetries and beliefs. The duration of an opportunity depends on monopoly rights; speed of information diffusion; and (in)ability to imitate, substitute, trade for, or acquire the rare resource required to drive the surplus. All opportunities cannot be obvious to everyone all the time, as they depend on the possession of prior rare or specialized information for their identification. Opportunities require that someone (the entrepreneur) possesses certain cognitive properties to perceive that value, such as the ability to identify new means–ends relationships generated by a given change in order to discover entrepreneurial opportunities.

Discovering entrepreneurial opportunity is necessary to success but is not sufficient unto itself—the decision to exploit the opportunity is a function of the joint characteristics of the opportunity and the nature of the individual. Entrepreneurial opportunities vary on several dimensions, and an entrepreneur must believe that the expected value of profit is large enough to compensate for the opportunity cost of other alternatives, the lack of liquidity of investment time/money, and a premium for bearing uncertainty. Relevant individual differences include wealth effects, strength of social ties to resource providers, prior employment knowledge/information, the transferability of information from prior (entrepreneurial) experience, individual differences in perceptions, and tolerance for ambiguity and optimism.

There are various modes of exploitation of entrepreneurial opportunities, differentially organized in the economy. This differential organization considers the modes of creation of new firms (hierarchies) and the sale of opportunities to existing firms (markets).[1] The entrepreneur's choice of mode depends on how

---

[1] See Williamson (1985) for further discussion of markets and hierarchies.

the industry is organized (e.g., concentrated or fragmented), the opportunity, and the *appropriability regime* (e.g., the ease with which intellectual property can be taken by others).

Industrial Organization (IO) research has shown that entrepreneurship is less likely to take the form of *de novo* (new) startups when capital-market imperfections make it difficult for independent entrepreneurs to secure financing. Entrepreneurship is more likely when

- the pursuit of entrepreneurial opportunity requires the effort of individuals who lack incentives in large organizations;
- scale economies, first-mover advantages, and learning curves do not provide advantages to existing firms; and
- industries have low barriers to entry.

 ALEXANDER ARDICHVILI, RICHARD CARDOZO, and SUARAV RAY
"A Theory of Entrepreneurial Opportunity Identification and Development" (2003), *Journal of Business Venturing.*

Thesis: Entrepreneurial opportunities are made (not found), and require alertness, prior knowledge, creativity, and optimism.

 This article combines several theories including entrepreneurial traits, social network, and prior knowledge as lenses through which to explore opportunity recognition, development, and evaluation. Ardichvili et al.'s assertion that opportunities are created builds on prior work, such as that of Kirzner (1997), which stresses the role of opportunity recognition as a central element of entrepreneurship.

The concepts of opportunity recognition and development have a number of major influencers. In particular, the authors discuss entrepreneurial alertness; information asymmetry and prior knowledge; discovery versus purposeful search; social networks (entrepreneurs who have extended networks identify significantly more opportunities); personality traits that emphasize optimism and creativity; and the type of opportunity, which differentiates between opportunities as being known or unknown and those opportunities being defined as addressable or not.

Ardichvili et al. use Dubin's (1978) methodology for theory-building, identifying three units of the theory of entrepreneurial opportunity identification and development:

1. *Opportunity development* reflects "the chance to meet a market need…through a creative combination of resources to deliver superior value" (p. 108).
2. *Opportunity recognition* suggests that "Opportunities begin as simple concepts that become more elaborate as entrepreneurs develop them….[W]e regard

opportunity development as a continuous, proactive process essential to the formation of a business" (p. 109). This consists of three distinct sub-processes: sensing or perceiving market needs and/or underemployed resources, recognizing or discovering a "fit" between particular market needs and specified resources, and creating a new "fit" between heretofore separate needs and resources in the form of a business concept (pp. 109–110).

3. *Opportunity evaluation* "communicates a judgment, which determines whether a developing opportunity will receive the resources to mature to its next stage" (p. 112). The staged model has gates associated with market needs, under-employed resources, business concepts, business plans, business formation, and enterprise success.

The authors then develop a number of propositions relative to entrepreneurial opportunities as a framework for future empirical studies.

- They suggest that successful opportunity-recognition is associated with a high level of entrepreneurial alertness and with the existence and use of an extended social network that includes weak ties, an *action set* (a group of people forming a temporary working relationship for a limited purpose), partnerships, and an inner circle.

- They assert that a convergence of both special-interest knowledge and industry knowledge is critical to successful opportunity-recognition and that prior knowledge of markets, customer problems, and ways to serve markets increases the likelihood of successful entrepreneurial opportunity recognition.

- Further, high levels of entrepreneurial alertness are related to high levels of entrepreneurial creativity and optimism, and the opportunity identification process results in enriching the entrepreneur's knowledge base and increasing alertness, leading to the identification of future business opportunities.

Discussion and Implications

 It is incumbent on executives to create an environment in which entrepreneurial development can be fostered. If one believes, as we do, that entrepreneurs can be made, then recognizing and exploiting opportunities is the means by which they can be made; that is, educators and managers can seek to develop these skills in students and staff. This belief also suggests that firms, whether young or old, small or large, can develop entrepreneurial skills that can focus on renewal and development of new business opportunities. Managers may thus develop and nurture a culture of entrepreneurship in their organizations. Every organization can renew, from the five-year-old company Synetics that Joe worked for, which reorganized in a manner that permitted him to develop an International Business Unit, to the behemoth Oracle for which Eric works, which reorganizes as it identifies market opportunities that result in acquisitions.

Traditional models of competitive equilibrium do not provide an explanation of how systems move to equilibrium, but Kirzner's entrepreneurial theory of the market process does precisely that. Focusing on the entrepreneur's correction of errors through arbitrage and speculation, Kirzner constructs a theory of how economies move toward equilibrium via the activities of arbitrage and speculation that are actually beneficial to ordinary consumers. By defining the entrepreneur as one who perceives profit opportunities and initiates action to fill currently unsatisfied needs or improve inefficiencies, Kirzner recognizes the central role of *entrepreneurial alertness*—what Bull and Willard called the "speculative ability to see into the future" (1993, p. 190). Through this role of alertness and subsequent action, Kirzner links entrepreneurship to the neoclassical economics that underpin modern economic thought.

The literature in this section begins the identification of the "individual–opportunity nexus" of entrepreneurship, which describes how opportunities may exist independent of individuals, but it is the awareness, via specific abilities to recognize opportunities, that separates entrepreneurs from "ordinary" people. Ardichvili et al.'s suggestion that opportunities are made does not undermine the idea of the "individual–opportunity nexus," which is now a basis for entrepreneurship research and teaching.

These studies describe the context for opportunities, which suggests that what might not be an opportunity here-and-now may be an opportunity later-and-elsewhere. This supposition has significant implications for entrepreneurs and other businesspeople, and raises questions such as the following:

- Where might this be an opportunity in the future?
- What institutional or environmental conditions lead to this being an opportunity here and now?
- Where might these conditions exist now or in the future?

As we have worked in technology industries during the growth of Silicon Valley and Boston's Route 128, the consolidation of the computer industry, and the demise and birth of new industries and companies, we have seen how time and context changes everything. The availability of knowledge, materials, and money varies with economic conditions, education programs at young ages, and government support for science. The environment for entrepreneurship in Europe, where Joe works, is very different than the environment in California where Eric works.

This section also highlights the importance of social networks and the "learning advantage" (Autio, Sapienza, and Almeida 2000) by young firms especially as described in the entrepreneurial literature on new venture internationalization (Section 5).

Additional writings in this area include the following, presented in chronological order.

- **Stevenson and Gumpert (1985).** Resources need to be given and assessed incrementally, which does not always fit into how companies may operate; in-course corrections are necessary and environmental issues may predominate. Gradual resource-commitment permits easier adaptation to the internal and external environments. In entrepreneurial ventures, capital investment systems are geared to one investment decision as opposed to multiple investment decisions as in large firms. Bureaucratic systems can stymie incremental resource requests—new ventures need decisions to be fast-tracked. Large, more mature corporations own instead of "rent" resources; new ventures should use outside specialists and avoid obsolescence by renting, thus gaining more flexibility.

- **Van de Ven (1993).** Industrial infrastructure both constrains and facilitates entrepreneurship, so entrepreneurship is deficient if it focuses exclusively on the characteristics and behaviors of individual entrepreneurs. Firms must make a strategic choice on what to do internally and what external resources are necessary: "Entrepreneurial firms that run in packs will be more successful than those that go it alone to develop their innovations" (p. 223). Cooperative and competitive ties between firms will enhance the stability of inter-firm relationships and add flexibility to the overall system. "Aborted efforts at establishing cooperative relationships turn out to become competitive relationships" (p. 225), when there is a smaller number of organizations in an industry as with an oligopoly.

- **Krueger (2000).** To understand how corporate ventures emerge, it is necessary to understand how opportunities emerge. An "organization must develop a cognitive infrastructure among its members, which increases and broadens what members see as desirable and perceive as feasible" (p. 19). An organization might promote an appropriate cognitive infrastructure by increasing perceptions of feasibility and of desirability. To do so, top managers may provide explicit cues of what is feasible and desirable, develop supportive strategic controls, enhance information flows, implement benchmarking and best practices, enhance mentorship programs, and provide developmental experiences.

- **Shane (2000).** Given an invention (e.g., 3D printers), different innovators identified various opportunities for businesses based on their individual knowledge bases—prior knowledge led to the discovery of opportunities in a non-search fashion. In fact, people were blind to the applications that others saw in the invention, despite the fact that many had technical backgrounds. Entrepreneurs should recognize the non-obvious aspect of these opportunities (meaning that not everyone sees them).

3. Entrepreneurial Entry and Organizational Emergence

Where do entrepreneurs come from and why do they become entrepreneurs? Is the number of entrepreneurs in a context bounded? The articles in this section seek to provide answers to these questions, as a means to understand the motivations and mindset of the individual entrepreneur along with the broader macroeconomic context that may facilitate or impede entrepreneurship.

This section first explores the industry context for entrepreneurial entry. Aldrich (1990) and Aldrich and Fiol (1994), respectively, describe the context in terms of population-ecology (is there a limit to the number of new ventures an environment can support?) and institutions (new ventures and new industries need legitimacy to garner resources necessary for growth and survival). The next three articles (Katz and Gartner 1988; Gartner 1985; Khilstrom and Laffont 1979) address entrepreneurial entry as related to new or emerging organizations. The first two explore, respectively, the specific properties such organizations possess and the phenomenon of the creation of these organizations. The third ties the concept of new-venture creation to the risk aversion of the individual entrepreneur. The final two articles (Reuf, Aldrich, and Carter 2003; Evans and Leighton 1989) address issues faced by founding teams and individuals, and how these issues affect their entrepreneurial entry—their move from being employees to being entrepreneurs.

HOWARD ALDRICH
"Using an Ecological Perspective to Study Organizational Founding Rates" (1990), *Entrepreneurship Theory and Practice.*

Thesis: There appears to be an environmental carrying capacity that can limit the formation of new startups when too many already exist in a bounded competitive environment (which can be geographic, industrial, or market-based).

Aldrich examines *de novo* startups and the conditions in which they form, through a review of important population-ecology concepts as they are applied to firm founding-rates. Three explanations for variations in founding rates are presented: intra-population processes (i.e., within the population); inter-population processes (i.e., across populations, at the community level); and institutional processes.

- *Intra-population processes* focus on the key population-ecology concepts of prior deaths, prior births, and density dependence. The number and nature of prior firm deaths and births in an industry affect resource availability and set (potential) entrepreneurs' perceptions of opportunities. Density dependence refers to the dependence of population processes on the size of the population itself (p. 11). Increasing density (more firms in an ecology) can have both positive (e.g., legitimacy) and negative (increased competition) effects. One finding is that the founding rates of many, if not most, organizations are *not* density dependent, although ecology dynamics do come into play. Aldrich states that "[w]hen a population approaches carrying capacity, several negative effects become apparent, including investors' reluctance to fund new organizations, and a dwindling supply of potential organizers, customers, and suppliers" (p. 13).

- *Inter-population relations* take a variety of forms, from full competition (e.g., competition for land between incompatible uses, such as junkyards and shopping malls), to predatory competition (video stores versus cinemas), to neutrality, to commensalism (fast food outlets near an auto plant), to symbiosis (hardware stores and lumber yards). Capital sources, such as banks and venture capitalists, represent inter-population relationships. Some populations facilitate foundings in other populations, and some (e.g., venture capitalists in Silicon Valley) serve as information channels between populations.

- *Institutional forces* include political factors and state policies, spatial location (e.g., proximity to industry/universities), and culture, "probably hav[ing] their greatest impact when a new form of organization is emerging, constraining and imprinting the new form in distinctive ways (Stinchcombe 1965)" (Aldrich, p. 20). A common finding in empirical ecological studies of foundings is that "intra-population processes have had the most consistently significant effects on foundings of all processes studied" (p. 20).

HOWARD ALDRICH and MARLENE FIOL
"Fools Rush In? The Institutional Context of Industry Creation"
(1994), *Academy of Management Review*.

Thesis: New ventures need and seek legitimacy, which is fostered by symbolic behavior, links to established parties, and collective action.

Aldrich and Fiol extend the examination of firm-founding rates to explore the institutional context and social processes surrounding the emergence of new industries. Their focus is on the development of independent new ventures that are not sheltered by sponsoring organizations, and they identify factors hindering and supporting the progression from the founding of a completely new activity, in an institutional void, through development as a legitimate industry.

Reaching legitimacy is important and the process of legitimation can occur in two ways. *Cognitive legitimation* is the spread of knowledge about a new venture, and this type of legitimacy considers that when an activity becomes taken for granted, time and other organizing resources are conserved. *Sociopolitical legitimation* is the process by which key stakeholders accept a venture as appropriate and right, given existing norms and laws.

Entrepreneurs face significant legitimacy constraints. New industries emerge when entrepreneurs succeed in mobilizing resources in response to perceived opportunities, but entrepreneurs' access to capital, markets, and governmental protection is partially dependent on the level of legitimacy achieved by an emerging industry. The number of organizations (e.g., new firms) is the primary force raising the legitimacy of a population. When the number of organizations in a new industry is small, new organizations are thought to have a lower chance of survival; as an industry grows, the increasing number of organizations raises its legitimacy along the cognitive and sociopolitical dimensions.

Aldrich and Fiol share these main propositions regarding cognitive and sociopolitical legitimacy for entrepreneurs in emerging industries. They propose that cognitive legitimacy is gained more quickly:

- by founders who utilize encompassing symbolic language and behaviors, as compared to founders who do not; and
- for industries in which founders encourage convergence around a dominant product/service design, industries that create linkages with established educational curricula, or those in which founding firms promote their new activity through third-party actors.

Aldrich and Fiol further propose that sociopolitical approval is gained more quickly:

- by founders who communicate internally consistent stories regarding their new activity, as compared to founders who do not; and
- for industries in which founders mobilize to take collective action, industries in which founding firms negotiate and compromise with other industries, or those that organize collective marketing and lobbying efforts.

Social contexts present entrepreneurs with many constraints, but also set conditions that create windows of opportunity. There are four levels of social context as progressively broadened sites within which founding entrepreneurs build trust, reliability, reputation, and institutional legitimacy: organizational, intra-industry, inter-industry, and institutional. These are the primary channels for attaining cooperation based on increasing familiarity and evidence.

Trust is a critical first-level determinant of the success of founding entrepreneurs because there is an absence of information and evidence regarding their new activity. In particular, founders of ventures in new industries—lacking the advantages of a taken-for-granted activity and without widespread sociopolitical approval—must first call upon whatever personal and interpersonal resources they possess.

Further, trust plays a strong role in the development of legitimacy, and the effects of progressive building of trust can rise up the hierarchy, collectively reshaping the inter-industry and institutional environments. Many promising new activities never realize their potential because founders fail to develop trusting relations with stakeholders, are unable to cope with opposing industries, and never win institutional support. From a practical perspective, strategy theorists have prescribed uniqueness and imperfect imitability (i.e., hard to mimic) as means of gaining a substantial competitive advantage. Aldrich and Fiol's framework, however, suggests that a single venture's uniqueness during the initial states of an industry's development must be counterbalanced with the collective efforts of all players in the emerging industry to portray the new activity as familiar and trustworthy, if they are to survive as a group.

 JEROME KATZ and WILLIAM GARTNER
"Properties of Emerging Organizations" (1988), *Academy of Management Review.*

Thesis: Emerging organizations require intentional information-seeking, resources, boundaries, and an exchange of transactions. The goal of the article is to better link research on entrepreneurship to organization theory.

 Katz and Gartner outline a set of four properties for the identification of emerging organizations, and for use in researching venture creation. Previous theories—and therefore methods of sampling—have not adequately captured organizations in the emergent phase, but have captured organizations (retrospectively) later in their creation process. The authors suggest that their approach will allow researchers to examine the "pre-organization" phase, acquire a better understanding of the nature of the concept of emergence as it happens, and thus be able to answer the question about how organizations come into existence.

Existing theories are inadequate, in that traditional organization theory, strategy theory, and even existing entrepreneurship theory use a macro perspective (changes studied over long periods of time), while micro perspectives (changes studied primarily at "gestation") are more useful. This article incorporates four major properties for the identification and recruitment of research samples of emerging organizations:

- *Intentionality* refers to an agent's information-seeking that can be applied toward achieving the goal of a new organization.

- *Resources* are the physical components that combine to form an organization (e.g., human capital, financial capital, property).

- *Boundaries* are the barrier conditions between an organization and its environment that establish physical and legal bases for exchange (e.g., incorporation, tax numbers).

- *Exchange* refers to the cycle of transactions, across borders of subsystems, within organizations and across organization boundaries with individuals.

All four properties are necessary for emerging organizations but do not become visible simultaneously. The opportunity to "find" organizations in emergence (especially those that die during the creation process) is affected by these four variables. Using these four properties, researchers can build a framework for analyzing potential sources of new organizations in a way that permits identification of organizations early in the creation process. This identification will allow more adequate analysis of the diversity of new organizations.

Katz and Gartner believe that population ecology has failed to recognize the diversity of new organizations because studies have used samples that are too old. They argue that the diversity of organizations is likely greatest when organizations are being born, which underscores the importance of separating new organizations and small businesses in research.

WILLIAM GARTNER
"A Conceptual Framework for Describing the Phenomenon of New Venture Creation" (1985), *Academy of Management Review.*

Thesis: Differences between entrepreneurial firms themselves may be greater than those between entrepreneurial firms and established firms. This complexity is driven by the interaction of four dimensions in the creation process: individuals, organization, environment, and process.

In this article, Gartner offers a conceptual framework for describing the creation of new entrepreneurial ventures; with this framework, he attempts to organize many variables used in past research to describe entrepreneurs and their ventures. The goal is to challenge past assumptions that entrepreneurs and the ventures they create are "much the same." Previous research has focused on showing the differences between entrepreneurs and non-entrepreneurs, or between entrepreneurial firms and non-entrepreneurial firms. Gartner's approach is not "reductive," but rather shows that entrepreneurship is a complex and multidimensional phenomenon. He seeks to demonstrate that differences between entrepreneurial firms may be much greater than differences between entrepreneurial firms and non-entrepreneurial firms.

Gartner presents a four-dimensional conceptual framework in contrast to the one-dimensional approach used by much prior research (e.g., the work of Pennings (1980, 1982) on environments that support new venture creation, and that of Van de Ven (1980) on the process of venture creation). Gartner's framework addresses the levels of the individual, the organization, the environment, and the process.

This model demonstrates the potential complexity of the interaction of the four dimensions in the organization-creation process and allows meaningful contrasts and comparisons between the different sorts of organizations created. Careful and detailed observation is important, in that key variables distinguishing types of ventures created can, in turn, support the identification of subsets of similar ventures. Homogenous groups, once located, can then lead to the identification of theories or general rules as well as the possibility of describing subsets in the unwieldy set of "all entrepreneurs."

This new framework helps to identify the aspects neglected by previous research and supports the creation of new research that would avoid similar mistakes. Gartner's work also provides a focus with which to compare the actual samples of previous entrepreneurship research. Since this article was published in 1985, researchers still acknowledge the need to examine entrepreneurial issues at the individual, firm, industry, and macro (e.g., country) level. However, there has been a shift from traits-based thinking to an understanding of multiple aspects, such as knowledge (at the individual and firm level) and its effect on entrepreneurial intentions and geographic expansion, as well as institutions and how they similarly affect entrepreneurial entry and expansion.

 RICHARD KHILSTROM AND JEAN-JACQUES LAFFONT
"A General Equilibrium Entrepreneurial Theory of Firm
Formation Based on Risk Aversion" (1979), *Journal of Political Economy*.

Thesis: Individuals who are more risk-averse are less likely to choose to transition from employee to entrepreneur at any given wage, and are less likely to remain an employee at a lower wage.

Starting from the premise that some people choose to remain employed by others while others decide to take risks and leave their jobs to become entrepreneurs, this article seeks to answer a number of questions.

- Why do entrepreneurs and employees coexist?
- What are the dynamics of entrepreneurial entry and exit?
- How are firm sizes distributed?
- What is the relative income of entrepreneurs and employees?

Khilstrom and Laffont develop economic models of choice for individuals to become entrepreneurs or remain employees, based on (a) respective profits and wages, and (b) limited access to labor and existing wealth (i.e., bankruptcy is not possible in their model) for the entrepreneur.

A key result is that if uncertainty is multiplicative, more risk-averse entrepreneurs run smaller firms. If all entrepreneurs are identical, then an increase in risk aversion leads to higher wages: fewer workers are hired by risk-averse entrepreneurs, leading to upward pressure on wages. The dynamics of the adjustment process, assuming that wages can move only a little in each period, indicate that shifts in an individual's "quality" will trigger entry to or exit from entrepreneurship. Wages will then converge to a new equilibrium.

The authors' models indicate that people who are more risk-averse will become employees at lower wages, and that an equilibrium exists for entrepreneurial entry. The implications for social welfare are that if all people's "quality" is the same, each firm should produce the same amount. An efficient outcome would be one in which all entrepreneurs are risk-averse, but in reality, the distribution of firms is uneven, leading to inefficiencies.

MARTIN REUF, HOWARD ALDRICH, and NANCY CARTER
"The Structure of Founding Teams: Homophily, Strong Ties, and Isolation Among U.S. Entrepreneurs" (2003), *American Sociological Review*.

Thesis: Teams compose themselves based on ascriptive characteristics such as gender or ethnicity. Teams with founders from diverse backgrounds are less common, and individuals from minority groups are more likely to be isolated.

In this article, Reuf et al. consider how achieved characteristics— as well as those characteristics often ascribed to entrepreneurs— affect the composition of teams. They also consider how these characteristics are mediated or conveyed by the social context of the entrepreneurial effort.

Sociological literature on group formations identified five general mechanisms that can influence team membership:

1. **Homophily.** Other team members are selected on the basis of similar ascriptive characteristics (e.g., gender, ethnicity, nationality, appearance).
2. **Functionality.** This mechanism describes the extent to which team members possess valuable and complementary competencies that help ensure the success of a collective in the long run.
3. **Status expectations.** High-status individuals (with respect to ascribed or achieved characteristics) have a greater capacity to attract other team members compared to low status individuals.
4. **Network constraints.** Team formation occurs within a pre-existing network of strong and weak ties that constrains the founding team's choice of members.
5. **Ecological constraints.** Spatial proximity and the environmental distribution of potential group members are very important.

Reuf et al. used data from a panel study of entrepreneurial dynamics based on random-digit dialing of 64,622 individuals in the United States (with a final reduced sample of 816 nascent entrepreneurs). They found that all-male and all-female organizational founding teams are not more common than mixed-gender teams, but that controlling for married partners results in significant positive homophily (i.e., results in teams of similar individuals). Additionally, teams with founders from diverse occupational backgrounds will be less common than teams lacking such functional diversity. Individuals who represent the numerical minority along any sociodemographic dimension are more likely to be isolated than those in the numerical majority (e.g., women and minorities are less connected).

DAVID EVANS and LINDA LEIGHTON
"Some Empirical Aspects of Entrepreneurship" (1989), *American Economic Review.*

Thesis: Individuals should be more likely to become entrepreneurs to the extent they have previously been self-employed, are self-directed, and have a high net worth. Therefore, income and job tenure will be negatively correlated with the probability of becoming an entrepreneur.

Evans and Leighton addressed a gap in the empirical evidence of entrepreneurship by using panel (longitudinal) data to test theories from economics, sociology, and psychology. Using the National Longitudinal Survey, they surveyed 4,000 white males age 14 to 24 in 1966 a total of 12 times until 1981. The data included demographic information (e.g., age, marital status, education), assets, and background—including prior self-employment. This data was supplemented by the Current Population Survey of 150,000 white males (U.S. Department of Commerce 1981).

Their analyses show a basic pattern of increasing rates of entrepreneurial entry, followed by a plateau, with decreasing rates of exit. They found that the probability of entrepreneurial transition should increase with previous self-employment, a greater "internal locus of control," and net worth. It should decrease with income and job tenure. Self-employment has positive returns (i.e., is overall positive financially), but wage experience matters more for employees. Finally, the returns from education are even higher in self-employment than the returns from employment, meaning that more education is related to higher entrepreneurial returns than to greater employment wages.

Discussion and Implications

 Aldrich (1990) suggests that entrepreneurs need to consider the population and environment for establishing a venture, including access to capital, labor, and the like; thus, an identified opportunity must be evaluated in the context in which it is to be exploited. Are there sufficient capital and other resources in the environment to support such an initiative? Are there too many entrepreneurs in the environment, causing a rise in the cost of capital or labor? When and where are the best times/places for starting a venture?

The answers to such questions are not clear-cut. For example, consider Silicon Valley with its great number of entrepreneurs, high knowledge spillovers, and aggressive competition for capital. These elements still support entrepreneurial entry in Silicon Valley despite the potential for resource costs (e.g., labor) to increase. In other entrepreneurial environments such as Chicago, many of these factors may exist but labor costs increase due to greater limits on labor mobility, dampening entrepreneurial activity (see Chapter 6 for further discussion of entrepreneurial ecosystems).

The institutional environment plays a key role in these decisions. In describing differences in the evolution of the computer industries of Silicon Valley and Route 128, Saxenian (1994) describes how the firm Fairchild in Silicon Valley incubated many ventures while a similar firm outside Boston, Digital Equipment Corporation (DEC), spawned few. Joe worked in the Route 128 environment at Wang Laboratories, a competitor of DEC, and saw a larger number of ex-DEC managers move to Wang than leave to start their own companies.

It is difficult to identify new industry emergence early in its life. When the first personal digital assistants (e.g., the Palm) and the first cell phones came out, it was not obvious that a new industry was emerging from the convergence of computers and telephony. Aldrich and Fiol suggest a number of interesting perspectives based on industry evolution. A new industry's boundaries are determined by the balance it achieves between competition and cooperation vis-à-vis other groups of firms. Within new industries, key events affecting emergence as stable entities involve the formation of other types of organizations (councils, trade associations, etc.), but investigating those organizations requires anthropologists, political scientists, and others outside the business field. In other words, managers must be prepared to solicit and examine the perspectives of others outside the business field to recognize and react to the emergence of new industries and to understand the manner in which this emergence can be facilitated and bolstered.

There have been many theoretical articles regarding entrepreneurial labor markets, for example on who becomes an entrepreneur and who stays as an employee (e.g., Khilstrom and Laffont), or on why some projects are backed by venture capital and others performed by corporations (e.g., Gromb and Scharfstein 2002). However, empirical work to observe how entrepreneurs actually behave has been limited[2] and has faced the challenges of data availability and issues with definitions. The definition problem is evidenced by the fact that theory describes entrepreneurs as individuals who identify market opportunities, create new firms, and/or hire others, but public data in the United States often identify successful entrepreneurs like Bill Gates and Michael Dell as employees. Thus, many studies focus on self-employment, such as sole proprietors and partners. Even when considering firms, studies largely focus on small entities such as restaurants, hairdressers, or franchises, so that distinguishing truly innovative businesses is difficult. In addition, the quality of and access to government data has declined due to privacy issues and budget cuts. This trend is reversing to some degree, as forces such as the internet, transparency advocates, and research groups have opened the door to data for analyses. In addition, the awareness of such research issues is pushing academics (and peer reviewers) to more carefully select research samples and control for variance in industry.

Katz and Gartner's article concerns how new ventures start and what (potential) entrepreneurs can see in their world that can start ventures. Since their work was published, more studies have collected data regarding how people start businesses (e.g., the PSED or Panel Study of Entrepreneurial Dynamics). This data has permitted researchers to better understand factors that enhance or inhibit one's intentions for becoming an entrepreneur, which is the first step in entrepreneurial entry. In addition, the Global Entrepreneurship

---

[2] Much of the basis for this material comes from a doctoral seminar taught from February to April 2004 by Josh Lerner at Harvard Business School.

Monitor (www.gemconsortium.org) compiles data from entrepreneurs and potential entrepreneurs from approximately 40 countries to permit the analysis of venture emergence in various cultural and institutional contexts.

Katz and Gardner identified differing patterns of motivators for entrepreneurial entry, such as need (e.g., putting food on the table) or pursuit of an opportunity (e.g., moving from employee to entrepreneur to pursue an idea). They also identified distributions of entrepreneurial entry by age and gender, and by the focal country's level of economic development. Beyond aiding research, this data can assist entrepreneurs in pursuing opportunities outside their domestic markets (see Section 5, International Entrepreneurship).

A key element of Khilstrom and Laffont's article is its focus on risk aversion. Consistent with Frank Knight (1921), they assume that some subset of the population (i.e., the entrepreneurs) is particularly willing to bear risk. They further assume no difference in individuals' abilities to pursue entrepreneurial or traditional employee activity. One can argue with a number of the assumptions (e.g., is there really no difference in abilities?), but overall the model is instructive. The value of their model is evident in France, where entrepreneurial entry has often lagged behind that of many other economies. With a very supportive social system (e.g., health and unemployment benefits) and an emphasis on retirement, it is not common for someone to leave their company to start a new venture. Over the past few years, tax regulations (e.g., implementation of the auto-entrepreneur scheme) have been implemented in an attempt to reduce the tax effort and burden (and thus risk) of becoming an entrepreneur.

While insightful, the Evans and Leighton (1989) article suffers from at least two methodological issues. First, the self-employment rate is much lower for women and minorities, but their sample excludes women. Second, there are at least two challenges with the measurement of self-employment: income-based measures tend to understate the number of self-employed, and dual jobs are frequent. Despite these limitations, their article provides interesting insights into self-employment while pointing to the need to carefully consider the sample and framing of the analysis to ensure generalizability and analytical rigor. Entrepreneurs should thus be wary of statistical reports in the press which run counter to their experience, and explore the sample and context for the analyses.

As a whole, the articles in this section provide insight into why and how individuals select self-employment. They are also instructive regarding how industries emerge from the actions of individuals: in essence, the Schumpeterian "new combinations" lead not only to new businesses, but also to new industries. The following are related articles in the area of entrepreneurial entry and organizational emergence, briefly described in chronological order.

- **<u>Saxenian</u> (1994).** This study of the factors that led to different evolutions of the computer industry in Silicon Valley and Route 128 around Boston in the 1980s identified a number of geographic, institutional, and cultural dimensions that resulted in very different evolutionary trajectories. Silicon Valley was bounded by mountains and ocean to the east and west respectively; had laws prohibiting restraint of trade (and, thus, no non-compete clauses in employee contracts); government support; outstanding relationships between industry and academia; and a culture, led by Fairchild, that fostered employee mobility, celebrated spinoffs, and facilitated technological spillovers. While similarly rich in universities, the Route 128 area did not establish solid ties between industry and academia; had a Protestant work ethic that led to different celebrations of success than in Silicon Valley; and was anchored by DEC, which branded as pariahs all employees who left to start a new venture. As a result, the information-technology industry grew at a faster rate and achieved more success in California than in Massachusetts in the 1990s.

- **Amit, Muller, and Cockburn (1995).** The authors studied opportunity cost and its effect on entrepreneurial activity. Using a sample of the Canadian labor force and examining the wages of people who were self-employed and those that were employed by others, they found that lower perceived opportunity-cost led to an increased likelihood that one would choose self-employment (i.e., become an entrepreneur).

- **Hamilton (2000).** This comparison of the earnings of self-employed workers (entrepreneurs) to paid employees proposes that if entrepreneurs deal with risk by having variable income, they should make more than wage earners. In a sample of 8,771 working-age U.S. males, self-employed workers earned 35% less than paid employees (p. 606) , with greater variance in the earnings. The conclusion is that entrepreneurs earn less because they have non-pecuniary benefits—money isn't everything.

- **Azoulay and Shane (2001).** Entrepreneurs select governance structures for their ventures based on routines that come from their prior knowledge. Those entrepreneurs that get it wrong fail, and the others survive. The authors come to this finding by examining the knowledge of new franchisees and the survival of ventures that had exclusive territories (which enhance survival). Some entrepreneurs did not choose exclusive territories because they did not know the value of exclusivity. This article underscores the importance of prior knowledge, the ways that knowledge impacts organizational form, and its evolutionary nature.

4. Entrepreneurial Finance, Resources, and Economic Impact

For entrepreneurs, the source of funds is a critical element related to opportunity-enactment, as access to various forms of capital (financial, social, and human) affects entrepreneurs in a number of ways. Resource availability is impacted by the value that entrepreneurship creates. If entrepreneurship leads to economic development, more resources become available (more taxes are paid, more investors exist, and investor willingness to invest increases) and greater economic growth results.

The articles in this section address resources and their impact on ventures and the economy in which they operate. The first two (Evans and Jovanovic 1989; Gompers 1995) respectively focus on the micro (firm) level, and address capital sufficiency in new ventures and the factors that affect the availability of financial capital. The next two articles (Stuart, Hoang, and Hybels 1999; Gulati and Higgins 2003) focus on the interorganizational level by examining the effect that partnerships and their associated endorsements have on new ventures. Finally, Baumol (1968) and Bruno and Tyebjee (1982) explore the relationship between entrepreneurial activity and the economic context in which entrepreneurial ventures operate, in the macroeconomic and local geographic environments, respectively.

DONALD EVANS AND BOYAN JOVANOVIC
"An Estimated Model of Entrepreneurial Choice Under Liquidity Constraints" (1989), *Journal of Political Economy*.

Thesis: The vast majority of startups remain capital-constrained, despite programs that have been enacted to help.

Small firms have insufficient capital, and common financial intermediaries have failed in funding small firms; thus, there is a gap between very small and more substantial financings. Numerous programs have attempted to address this gap, such as the Small Business Innovation Research (SBIR) program, equity investments via the U.S. Small Business Administration, and similar programs worldwide. However, although the smallest firms may have the most critical capital constraints, they are unable to access even these resources.

The key question raised by Evans and Jovanovic is whether capital constraints block entrepreneurship. Historically, there are contrasting views: <u>Frank Knight</u> (1921) notes that bearing risk is a critical part of entrepreneurship, but <u>Schumpeter</u> (1934) distinguishes between the entrepreneur and the capitalist.

To answer their key question, Evans and Jovanovic develop a one-period model in which an individual must choose between employment and entrepreneurship. Using the National Longitudinal Survey of Young Men in 1976, the model considers entrepreneurial earnings, invested capital, and borrowing among two thousand white males aged 24-34. Evans and Jovanivic sought to identify the determinants of entrepreneurial entry for the 1,443 men who were in the sample for both years, and found that only 89 (4.5%) became entrepreneurs by 1978 (p. 817). The key findings are that most entrepreneurs (approximately 98%) are capital-constrained and that entrepreneurial entry would be almost 50% higher (5.1% vs. 3.8%) without those constraints (p. 824; findings predate increased U.S. VC activity post-1978).

PAUL GOMPERS
"Optimal Investment, Monitoring, and the Staging of Venture Capital" (1995), *Journal of Finance.*

Thesis: Venture capital overcomes capital constraints. Staged investments offset agency conflicts to keep incentives better aligned between startup investors and startup managers.

Venture capital is one means that entrepreneurs use to overcome capital constraints. Venture investments are typically made in stages, with the startup receiving additional funding as it passes through developmental milestones. In this article, Gompers sheds light on venture capital as an investment and investigates how the monitoring of an investment via staged offerings addresses the agency problems inherent in the relationship, which arise from the differing incentives of the startup's investor-owners and managers. While this study of 794 public and private companies focuses on one aspect of venture financing from the venture capitalist perspective, it also provides insight into the issues faced by entrepreneurs seeking to ease their capital constraints.

The pattern of staged investments is not unique to venture capital—banks and credit cards similarly increase credit lines, although not as explicitly as in the venture capital setting. All firms, and particularly entrepreneurial firms, are subject to *agency conflicts*: the different objectives that principals (owners) may have relative to the agents (managers) they hire, whose self-interest may result in different behavior than the owner would find optimal. For example, heightened agency issues can arise in technology industries where *information asymmetries*—

differences in the information possessed by managers and owners—are most severe (Amit, Brander, and Zott 1998).

The staging of investments (i.e., dispersal of capital in rounds) is determined by the agency problems inherent in entrepreneurial firms. Entrepreneurs may choose personally rewarding or excessively risky projects and may inefficiently seek to continue failing businesses. Knowing this, investors may provide funding in rounds tied to performance—a prototype of a product, for example—that ties the manager's goal of getting funding to the investor's goal of getting a suitable return. Gompers found that early-stage companies have smaller financing rounds, use cash more slowly, and have longer intervals between rounds. Such longer intervals also exist when the company is older and when the industry in which the company operates is more prone to agency problems. Gompers also examined the total amount of funding raised by a company and the total number of rounds the company receives, and the results also suggest that staging is a result of agency issues. Statistics show that more successful firms receive more financing.

TOBY STUART, HA HOANG, and RALPH HYBELS
"Interorganizational Endorsements and the Performance of
Entrepreneurial Ventures" (1999), *Administrative Science Quarterly*.

Thesis: Associating with prominent partners facilitates access to resources that ventures need, and this access translates to enhanced performance.

This article investigates how the interorganizational networks of young companies affect their ability to acquire the resources necessary for survival and growth, by shaping potential investors' assessments of the quality of such firms. Interorganizational exchange relationships can act as endorsements that influence perceptions of the quality of young organizations when unambiguous measures of quality do not exist or cannot be observed, for example, when entering a foreign country.

Stuart et al.'s argument here suggests that young companies with prominent alliance partners should garner higher attributions of quality than they would otherwise because of the characteristics of their alliance partners; these higher attributions of quality will be reflected in the young companies' performances.

> An equity investor signals to a broader community that another organization is impressed enough with a young company to put of a stake in it. Equity relations are akin to "strong" ties (Granovetter 1973) and may impart an additional level of confidence in the quality of young companies. (p. 320)

They also note that Podolny and Stuart (1995) demonstrated that inventions in uncertain technological areas were more likely to become widely important when they had been previously adopted by high-status organizations. They continue by observing that Baum and Oliver (1991, 1992) demonstrated that organization-to-institution ties signal conformance to institutional prescriptions and thereby facilitate young organizations' attempts to acquire legitimacy and other resources.

Several possible social mechanisms may lead would-be investors, customers, and other potential exchange partners to consider the characteristics of a focal new venture's affiliates as they strive to assess its unobserved and uncertain quality. In particular, relationships with prominent organizations signal a new venture's reliability and thus its high likelihood of survival.

Stuart et al.'s study of 301 dedicated biotech firms concludes that prominence of exchange partners affects the performance of entrepreneurial ventures. Sponsorship has the capacity to substitute for accomplishment and experience as a basis for the success of young companies. Firms with well-known equity partners were more likely to have prominent alliance partners and use prestigious banks. It is important to stress that credentialing is often an ancillary consideration in the decision of young biotech firms to form strategic alliances and to solicit equity investment. The results of this study show that these inter-firm relations carry reputational consequences, and suggest that the impact of interorganizational relations is driven more by the identity of a young company's associations than by the volume of its relations. Such endorsement benefits were stronger for young and small companies.

 RANJAY GULATI and MONICA HIGGINS
"Which Ties Matter When? The Contingent Effects of Interorganizational Partnerships on IPO Success" (2003), *Strategic Management Journal.*

Thesis: Partnerships with organizations such as venture capital firms, investment banks, and strategic alliance partners can provide endorsement effects that may affect IPO performance.

 Gulati and Higgins investigate the contingent value of interorganizational relationships at the time of a venture's IPO. Specifically, they examine whether endorsement relationships (with VCs and investment banks) and strategic alliance partnerships have different signaling value under different market conditions. They execute this examination by asking the question, "Which ties matter when, in the context of young firms undergoing their IPO?"

Endorsement relationships are interorganizational relationships a firm has with another organization that serves as an intermediary between the focal firm and a third party. For example, in the context of IPOs, the venture capitalists and IPO underwriters are intermediaries between the IPO venture and the potential buyers of the new listing. Prior research has demonstrated that VC backing increases the likelihood that a firm will have a successful IPO (e.g., Megginson and Weiss 1991). In addition to VC investment signaling venture quality and affecting performance via greater monitoring, endorsement by a VC signals a firm's future value.

Using a sample of 858 biotech ventures that went public, Gulati and Higgins find that endorsement by a prestigious VC should be particularly beneficial to the success of a young company's IPO, when the equity markets are either hot (active) *or* cold (inactive). However, network ties are not uniform in their effects on firm outcomes, as they vary across different types of endorsement ties. One benefit to young firms in developing partnerships with well-established firms is access to valuable information and capabilities that can enable young firms to overcome the liabilities of newness and smallness (Baum and Silverman 1999). For investors, uncertainty associated with a firm can arise from firm characteristics (e.g., age, size, location) as well as from exogenous sources such as changes in preferences or regulatory changes (e.g., firms operating in multiple countries are open to more and varied regulatory changes).

WILLIAM BAUMOL
"Entrepreneurship in Economic Theory" (1968), *American Economic Review.*

Thesis: Economic theory should examine how to encourage entrepreneurial activity.

This article examines the grounds on which entrepreneurship should concern the general populace and explains why economic theory has failed to develop an illuminating formal analysis of entrepreneurship. Using the neoclassical (perfect market) economic theory of the firm, Baumol defines the *entrepreneur* as someone whose function is to locate new ideas and put them into effect, potentially via leadership and inspiration—an entrepreneur is the Schumpetarian innovator and more.

There is empirical evidence that the entrepreneurial function is vital to economies, as innovation requires entrepreneurial initiative for its introduction. The theoretical firm must choose among alternative values for price, output, and (perhaps) advertising, suggesting that mathematical calculations are made to determine an optimum outcome that is taken to constitute the business decision. In order to analyze the optimal solution to this type of well-defined problem, the presence of the entrepreneur is critical, but formal theory does not appropriately consider the entrepreneur.

Regarding the supply of entrepreneurship, where do inputs to this supply come from? Economic theory commonly talks about inputs, but never discusses where those inputs come from. Theory needs to induce the appearance of entrepreneurial skills, so a policymaker's interest is what determines the supply of entrepreneurs and entrepreneurship as well as the ways that supply can be expanded. A theoretical approach to entrepreneurship should examine what can be done to encourage entrepreneurial activity, which is a key to stimulation of growth.

People—whether employees, entrepreneurs, or sports stars—will choose the occupation that gives the greatest return. Baumol suggests that how entrepreneurs act depends heavily on the rules of the game and the reward structure (i.e., the institutional environment) in the economy. People will become good entrepreneurs when markets are large and they can keep the profits from their efforts. Good entrepreneurship is argued as being good for the economy due to numerous spillovers (e.g., the development of new and efficient technologies, the need for ancillary services and products, and tax generation). These spillovers are more evident from entrepreneurship than from other activities (e.g., clergy and military activity). For example, in eras when rent-seeking (gaining value without contributing) was the dominant behavior, there was a shift of entrepreneurs into less productive activities and thus a transfer of profits away from entrepreneurs; this shift and consequent change in profit production had a profound impact on the rate of economic growth.

ALBERT BRUNO and TYZOON TYEBJEE
"The Environment for Entrepreneurship" (1982), in C. Kent, D. Sexton, and K. Vesper (editors), *The Encyclopedia of Entrepreneurship*.

Thesis: The environment of startups contributes to their geographic clustering, driven by the availability of venture capital, experienced entrepreneurs, suppliers, government policies, and proximity to universities.

This work extends Baumol (1968) by considering the broader environmental context of entrepreneurship beyond just its economic position. Bruno and Tyebjee present a theoretical perspective on the environmental influences of entrepreneurship and the reasons for geographical clusters of entrepreneurial activity, such as the San Francisco Peninsula and Boston's Route 128.

There are a number of environmental factors related to entrepreneurship, including venture capital availability, accessibility of demand and supply, favorable governmental policies, and proximity to universities (see, e.g., Saxenien 1994). Venture capital availability often comes from already successful entrepreneurs; the presence of experienced entrepreneurs provides role models, and spin-off companies can draw from the resultant technically skilled labor force. Incubator organizations support development and sometimes drive entrepreneurial activity. Accessibility to suppliers, customers, or new markets is often cited, but little published research supports this proposition. Favorable governmental policies (e.g., tax structure, legislation) may affect the ability to collect seed money. Proximity to universities may provide educated young people to recruit and some faculty may start their own companies, but the impact is debatable. Other actors exist, such as availability of land or facilities, accessibility of transportation, receptive population, availability of supporting services, and attractive living conditions (as founders tend to start companies in the areas where they already live and work because they can secure resources more easily).

These factors may be classified in a number of ways: enhancing or inhibiting, level of environmental maturity, cause and effect, venture stage, nature of the innovation, or technological content of the undertaking. Entrepreneurial activity may be measured using types of outcome such as the following:

- startup outcomes (number of startups, equity, legal structure, scale),
- performance outcomes (profitability measures, growth, and market share), and
- residual outcomes (e.g., changes in capital structure).

A variety of theoretical perspectives are relevant for an examination of the environmental factors for entrepreneurship. For resources, organizations depend on their external environment (Pfeffer and Salancik 1978), which is characterized in terms of six constructs:

- *Concentration* is the extent to which power and authority are widely spread.
- *Munificence* describes the availability or scarcity of critical resources.
- *Interconnectedness* is the number and pattern of linkages among different organizations.
- *Conflict* refers to disagreement among stakeholders about the goals of the social system.
- *Interdependence* is the degree to which one organization influences another.
- *Uncertainty* describes the degree to which the future can accurately be predicted.

Bruno and Tyebjee also consider the topic from the perspectives of resource-exchange models and population-ecology models. The former view organizations as entering into a transactional relationship with environmental factors because they cannot generate all the necessary resources internally; thus, organizations actively attempt to secure control over external contingencies. The population-ecology model avers that organizations survive if they are isomorphic (synchronized) with the environment; they are doomed unless they meet the environmental test of fitness.

Discussion and Implications

Entrepreneurship has been viewed as the engine of economies, and thus policymakers must identify the factors and conditions that promote or impede new-venture formation. Capital constraints are a major factor for entrepreneurs, which necessitates programs to provide access to capital, whether via debt (e.g., bank loans) or equity (e.g., via angel financing or venture capital from corporations, universities, or independent entities). While the markets for financing are well developed in the United States and other developed countries, emerging economies are limited in their ability to support new venture development, making it difficult to become players on the world stage.

For ventures requiring capital, the institutional environment is itself a major element in the availability of capital for investment and the terms that investors set on the company. As a result of agency issues, information asymmetries, and legal protections for investors, round characteristics (e.g., round size, interval, syndication) may vary by context as a means to mitigate these risks. As Gompers indicates, venture capitalists dispense funding in rounds to help ensure congruence between investor and manager objectives. Yet, despite the availability of venture capital and other sources of financial capital, ventures are still underfunded, and as demonstrated by Evans and Jovanovic, potential entrepreneurs eschew entrepreneurial entry as a result.

Baumol's (1990) basic argument is consistent with that of Murphy, Shleifer, and Vishney (1991), proposing that people will choose the occupation that gives the greatest return. People will become (good) entrepreneurs when markets are large and they can keep the profits. Good entrepreneurship is positive for the economy, not just for job growth and taxes, but also for the numerous spillovers to society, such as enhanced quality-of-life physically (via new diagnostics) and socially (via social networks, as we have recently experienced). Other activities, such as hairdressing and corner stores, provide few such spillovers. The supply of entrepreneurship is constant, as it relates primarily to the allocation of resources, so one implication of Baumol is that tax laws can help push the distribution of entrepreneurs to greater numbers, to the overall economic benefit of society.

Bruno and Tyebjee's article makes a number of excellent points and summarizes the relevant environmental factors well. For entrepreneurs, it underscores that the external environment in which entrepreneurial ventures operate is crucial and that entrepreneurs must consider environment along a number of related dimensions. It is too easy for entrepreneurs to focus on one aspect, such as market size or availability of critical resources, and ignore the linkages among various stakeholder organizations.

Related literature in entrepreneurial finance and economic impact include the following, listed in chronological order.

- **Sapienza (1992).** The venture capital industry is highly cyclical, with more interest in adding "value" when the supply (of capital) outstrips the demand (e.g., during the internet boom). While investors provide more than just financial capital, they tend to focus on the provision of capital in down periods. Differences in the businesses (e.g., strategy, innovation) in this study related to the value of VC involvement: the greater the innovation pursued by the firm, the more frequent the contact between CEO and VC. VCs added greater value when the communication was more frequent, more open, and less contentious between the entrepreneur and the investor VC. The most effective VCs are those who maintain frequent contact but also strive for openness and minimum conflict, so it is important for entrepreneurs to find a good "partner" and keep communication open and frequent.

- **Cable and Shane (1997).** Why is cooperation the best mechanism for managing the relationship between investor and entrepreneur? The Prisoner's Dilemma framework is an effective approach for understanding entrepreneur–venture capitalist relationships as the parties negotiate their ongoing business relationship. Both parties should increase the level and quality of information transfer to maximize mutual cooperation and minimize defection.

- **Baron and Markman (2000).** Social skills are important in new ventures, as the founding team's face-to-face interactions with outsiders may help form business alliances and enhance new venture success. Entrepreneurs with successful companies communicate more with others than entrepreneurs whose companies fail. Socially skilled entrepreneurs may well evoke higher levels of positive affect among those with whom they interact. So, training in social skills can contribute to social capital and help entrepreneurs succeed; such training should be part of all programs in entrepreneurship, and entrepreneurs should be persuaded to seek it.

- **Sorenson and Stuart (2001).** Venture capitalists show a preference for being near the companies in which they invest. This preference results from the desire to establish and maintain relationships with the founders/management team, communicate directly via regular interactions, and monitor the activities of the venture.

- **Brush, Carter, Greene, Hart, and Gatewood (2002).** Women entrepreneurs receive a smaller percentage of funding than male entrepreneurs. A fundamental aspect of the social capital of new ventures resides within the top management team, their social relationships, and the size and diversity of their networks. Women-led investments, despite "experience," are funded less frequently than male-led investments. The number of women in the VC industry remains very small.

- **Kaplan and Strömberg (2003).** Empirical studies of venture capitalists indicate that they attempt to mitigate principal–agent (agency) conflicts in the three ways suggested by theory: via sophisticated contracting, pre-investment screening, and post-investment monitoring and advising. These three means of risk-mitigation are interrelated.

5. International Entrepreneurship

The study of international entrepreneurship began as a trickle with the publication of Oviatt and McDougall's (1994) identification of "international new ventures," but has since increased significantly. This area of inquiry has two main components: the study of differences in entrepreneurship across countries, and the study of ventures that enter foreign markets at an early age. Internationalization was once thought to be the province of large, mature companies, but Oviatt and McDougall's analysis of international new ventures found that "from inception, [an international new venture] seeks to derive significant competitive advantage from the use of resources and the sale of outputs in multiple countries" (1994, p. 49).

The first two articles in this section address country differences that affect entrepreneurship (Busenitz, Gomez, and Spencer 2000) and institutional and legal differences (La Porta, Lopez-de-Silanes, Shleifer, and Vishny 2000). Two articles by Oviatt and McDougall (1994, 2005) discuss the phenomenon of international new ventures and, more broadly, international entrepreneurship. An article by Zahra and Garvis (2000) examines the environmental hostility faced by internationalizing ventures. Two articles by Gary Knight and Cavusgil (1997, 2005) describe more broadly the emergence of *born-global firms*—those that enter foreign markets at or near inception. The section finishes with a perspective from Autio, Sapienza, and Almeida (2000) on firm-specific factors and how they affect international performance.

LOWELL BUSENITZ, CAROLINA GOMEZ, and JENNIFER SPENCER
"Country Institutional Profiles: Unlocking Entrepreneurial Phenomena" (2000), *Academy of Management Journal.*

Thesis: Country variance in rates of entrepreneurship is based in part on differences in regulatory, cognitive, and normative institutional differences. Understanding these differences—and the competitive advantages they offer to entrepreneurs—is critical for managers seeking to operate in foreign countries.

In this article Busenitz et al. address a basic premise of much of the international business literature, namely that firms are embedded in country-specific institutional arrangements that can guide strategic activities and help determine the amount of innovation occurring in a country. Hofstede's (2001; see Chapter 5) measures of culture—alone—do not explain inter-country differences in entrepreneurial activities. Infrastructure that enhances cooperation among entrepreneurs facilitates problem-solving and increases entrepreneurial activities; in particular, there are three dimensions to consider.

A country's institutional profile describing governmental policies (regulatory dimension), shared social knowledge (cognitive dimension), and value systems (normative dimension) is known to affect domestic business activity.

- The *regulatory dimension* consists of laws, regulations, and government policies that provide support for new businesses, reduce entrepreneurs' risks, and aid efforts to acquire entrepreneurial resources. The U.S. government provides advice and assistance for new business starts and offers grants for technology development.
- The *cognitive dimension* consists of the knowledge and skills possessed by the people in a country pertaining to establishing and operating a new business. How to start a new business, for instance, may be known and dispersed in a country.
- The *normative dimension* measures the degree to which a country's residents respect entrepreneurial activities and value creative, innovative thinking.

Busenitz et al. conducted a survey of six countries that analyzed 636 individuals. The results show that institutional differences explain differences in entrepreneurial activity, but also that country differences are not consistent across the three institutional dimensions. The authors present the results more for their future research directions than for their practical implications; however, government policymakers could use the identified factors to assess their own country's scores on each dimension and devise strategies for improving their domestic institutional environments for entrepreneurship.

The institutional profile can help evaluate the source of each country's strengths and weaknesses, and understand why some countries tend to maintain an advantage in new business development within a particular industry or organizational form. Family businesses, for example, may succeed in countries with certain profiles, whereas initial public offerings may succeed in others.

Businetz et al.'s findings may help globally focused entrepreneurs start firms that have international objectives from inception, by identifying obstacles they may need to overcome before they expand into new countries.

RAPHAEL LA PORTA, FLORENCIO LOPEZ-DE-SILANES, ANDREI SHLEIFER, and ROBERT VISHNY
"Investor Protection and Corporate Governance" (2000), *Journal of Financial Economics*.

Thesis: Countries differ with regard to firm ownership concentration and capital access, but one common element to these differences is the degree to which investors are protected by law from expropriation by the firm's managers and controlling shareholders. The legal basis of these differences may both explain and provide insights into strategies of corporate governance reform.

La Porta et al. argue that the protection of shareholders and creditors by the legal system is central to understanding the patterns of corporate finance in different countries. Expropriation by controlling shareholders can take the form of profit-stealing, selling outputs or assets at below-market prices to another firm owned by those shareholders, installing unqualified family members in managerial positions, or overpaying executives.

In the legal approach to corporate governance, the key mechanism for limiting expropriation is the protection of outside investors via laws and their enforcement. Thus, variations in law and enforcement such as the following are central to understanding why firms raise more funds in some countries than in others.

- Cash flow return from projects to investors cannot be taken for granted and financial claims are subject to contracts.
- The rights of investors are protected and sometimes even specified by the legal system.
- When investor rights, such as shareholder voting rights and liquidation rights, are extensive and well-enforced by regulators or courts, investors are willing to finance firms.
- Investor rights include disclosure and accounting rules, which provide investors the information needed to exercise other rights.

- Protected shareholder rights include the ability to receive dividends, vote for directors, participate in shareholder meetings, and the like.
- Laws protecting creditors deal with bankruptcy and reorganization procedures.

In different jurisdictions, the rules protecting investors come from different sources, including corporate law, securities regulations, bankruptcy law, takeover and competition law, exchange regulations, and accounting standards. Entrepreneurs have the incentive to bind themselves through contracts with investors in order to limit expropriation. These contracts must be enforceable (although they are necessarily elaborate), but courts are often unable or unwilling to invest the resources necessary to ascertain the facts associated with complicated contracts.

The commercial legal systems of most countries derive from a few legal "families" dispersed worldwide through colonization, including the English (common law), the French, and the German. Common law countries have the strongest protection for outside investors, whereas French civil law countries have the weakest, while German civil law and Scandinavian countries fall somewhere in between, as illustrated in Figure 2-1. The legal family shapes the country's legal rules, which in turn influences its financial markets. The state has a relatively greater role in regulating business in civil law countries than in common law ones, as common law evolved to protect private property against the crown and the courts extended this protection to investors over time. Civil

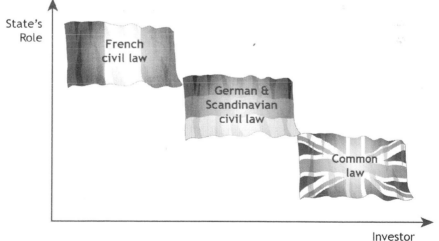

Figure 2-1. "Families" of Law: Investor Protection and the Role of the State.[3]

---

[3] Authors' image; data from La Porta et al. (2000).

law is associated with greater government intervention in economic activity and weaker private property protection than common law.

La Porta et al. conclude that entrepreneurs may wish to keep control of their firms when investor protection is poor; if they disperse control to investors, they give up the "private benefits" premium in a takeover. However, retaining control means limiting the ability to raise external funds from investors. La Porta et al.'s analysis of data on investor rights for 49 countries across various legal families shows that countries with poor investor-protection typically exhibit more concentrated control of firms than do countries with good investor-protection. Countries that protect shareholders have more valuable stock markets and higher IPO rates than unprotected countries.

BENJAMIN OVIATT and PATRICIA MCDOUGALL
"Toward a Theory of International New Ventures" (1994), *Journal of International Business Studies.*

Thesis: New ventures that do business in foreign countries challenge existing international business theory, as they neither possess significant tangible resources nor advantages associated with internationalization.

The domain of academic literature on organizations includes literature on new and established organizations with both domestic and international scope. Of the four possible combinations of these two dimensions, only the combination of international scope and new venture is underrepresented in the literature. This seminal article in the study of new venture internationalization defines and describes international new ventures (INVs) and presents a framework on how INVs fit within the extant theories of multinational enterprises (MNEs).

Resource constraints that new ventures experience require alternate governance structures, locational advantage, and the use of unique resources. Defined as companies "that, from inception, seek to derive significant competitive advantage from the use of resources and sale of outputs in multiple countries" (Oviatt and McDougall 1994, p. 49), INVs represent a phenomenon that is incongruent with traditionally expected characteristics of multinational enterprises. The authors propose a framework to explain the integration of international business, entrepreneurship, and strategic management theories to describe four necessary and sufficient elements for the existence of INVs:

- organizational formation through internalization of some transactions,
- a strong reliance on alternative governance structures to access resources,

- the establishment of foreign location advantages, and
- control over unique resources.

The distinguishing feature of INVs is that their origins are international, as measured by observable and significant commitments of resources in more than one nation. The Stages Theory of MNE internationalization (Johanson and Vahlne 1977; see Chapter 5, Section 1) describes how MNEs develop their international business through incremental, risk-averse, and reluctant adjustments to changes in a firm or its endowments—against the prevailing expectation that firms with large resources take large steps toward internationalization. It is easier to learn about foreign market conditions when they are stable and homogeneous, and experience in similar markets may be generalizable to new target foreign markets. INVs are a unique challenge to this theory.

Large size is often thought to be a requirement for multinationality, but size may be either the cause or the effect of multinational competitive advantage, or may be concomitant of other sources of advantage. The international environment is changing, in that human capital is more internationally mobile, markets now link countries more efficiently than in the past, hierarchies of large, established firms no longer have same competitive advantage that they once had, and firms may skip stages of international development that have been observed in the past.

Four necessary and sufficient elements progressively distinguish subsets of transactions:

- internationalization of some transactions,
- alternate governance structures,
- foreign location advantages, and
- unique resources.

INVs commonly lack sufficient resources to control many assets through ownership, so alternative governance structures, including hybrid structures such as licensing and franchising, are common. Firms are international because they find an advantage (location advantage) in transferring some moveable resources across national borders. Knowledge may be unique, but potentially imitable. Four ways to limit knowledge are to use unique resources such as patents/copyrights, imperfect imitability, licensing, and network governance structures.

The authors also identify four types of INVs based on the number of activities coordinated in the value chain and the number of countries involved.

1. *Export/import startups* coordinate few activities across only a few countries, while
2. *Multinational traders* coordinate few activities across many countries.
3. *Geographically focused startups* coordinate many activities across only a few countries, while
4. *Global startups* coordinate many activities across many countries.

BENJAMIN OVIATT and PATRICIA MCDOUGALL
"Defining International Entrepreneurship and Modeling the
Speed of Internationalization" (2005), *Entrepreneurship Theory and
Practice*.

Thesis: Internationalization speed is influenced by a variety of internal and
external forces.

 This article provides an updated definition of international
entrepreneurship, based on the evolution of the definition of
entrepreneurship and research in the field, specifically related to
opportunity recognition and enactment. Based on the Shane and
Venkataraman (2000) definition of entrepreneurship, but recognizing that
opportunities as objective phenomena must be enacted to be valuable, the
authors define international entrepreneurship as "the discovery, enactment,
evaluation, and exploitation of opportunities—across national borders—to
create future goods and services" (Oviatt and McDougall 2005, p. 540).

The authors model the forces influencing internationalization speed.
Technology is an enabling force, while competition is a motivating force.
Moderating forces include foreign market knowledge and intensity. Network
relationship forces include tie strength, network size, network density. Finally,
entrepreneurial actor perceptions act as a mediating force.

The above forces work on the entrepreneurial opportunity to impact the
speed of internationalization, in terms of the initial entry (age), country scope
(diversity) and commitment (intensity). Noting Coviello and Munro (1995), the
authors aver that foreign market selection and entry stem from network
contacts, rather than strategic decisions. Networks help entrepreneurs identify
international opportunities, establish credibility and often lead to strategic
alliances or other cooperative strategies. The more direct or indirect cross-
border weak ties that an entrepreneurial actor has established, the greater is the
potential country scope of internationalization and the greater possible speed
for increasing that scope.

 SHAKER ZAHRA AND DENNIS GARVIS
"International Corporate Entrepreneurship and Firm
Performance: The Moderating Effect of International
Environmental Hostility" (2000), *Journal of Business Venturing*.

Thesis: Executives' perceptions of the characteristics of the firm's international environment, especially hostility, moderate the relationship between international corporate entrepreneurship and performance.

 Globalization provides an opportunity to study companies' foreign market entrepreneurial activities. This view through the entrepreneurial lens permits the authors to examine questions previously not asked, such as, "Can international corporate entrepreneurship renew a company by improving its ability to compete and take risks by (a) redefining its business concept, (b) reorganizing its operations, and (c) introducing system-wide innovations?"

The authors define international corporate entrepreneurship (ICE) as the sum of a company's efforts aimed at *innovation, proactiveness*, and *risk-taking*.

* **Innovation.** The firm's ability to create new products and successfully introduce them to the market.
* **Proactiveness.** The firm's aggressive pursuit of market opportunities and a strong emphasis on being the very first to undertake innovations in its industry, which has been shown to improve company performance.
* **Risk-taking.** The firm's disposition to support innovative projects (e.g., international ventures), even when the payoff from these activities is uncertain.

International environment hostility is measured by the difficulty in accessing distribution channels, labor, and capital; high rates of bankruptcy among companies in the industry; rapid product obsolescence; and declining demand for industry products.

The study finds that ICE is positively associated with a firm's financial performance, but that this relationship is moderated by the hostility of the international environment. Firms that pursue ICE in environments with higher levels of hostility will have higher profits and higher growth. However, firms that over-pursue ICE in hostile environments will generate diminishing profits and lower growth.

 GARY KNIGHT and S. TAMER CAVUSGIL
"Emerging Organizational Paradigm for International Marketing: The Born Global Firm" (1997), in *Proceedings: 1997 Annual Meeting, Academy of International Business.*

Thesis: Early and successful international market expansion is distinctly different from traditional patterns.

Born global companies are concentrated in high-technology industries with common characteristics:

- their goods can be standardized,
- their goods have broad relatively universal appeal, and
- their intellectual property is well protected.

Facilitating factors and internationalization triggers lead to observed, distinctive features of born globals (BGs). For example, BGs are associated more with radical innovation.

Facilitating factors include the following:

- the globalization of markets for goods and services,
- advances in communication and information technology,
- the inherent advantages of young firms,
- advances in production technology,
- the increasing salience of global market niches, and
- the growing role of global networks.

Internationalization triggers relate to export pull and push, possession of a worldwide monopoly or near-monopoly position, product-market conditions necessitating international involvement, and significant global network relationships.

Global orientation factors relevant to born globals include the following:

- a commitment to international markets,
- international venturesomeness,
- an international market orientation,
- possession of international marketing competence, and
- extensive leveraging of advanced communications technology.

Distinctive marketing strategies that BGs employ are a niche focus, product and product-service quality, product/marketing differentiation, promotion emphasizing personal selling, and foreign distributor effectiveness.

The authors note that there is

> evidence that some young firms are being rapidly moved into the international arena through the intervention of venture capitalist firms, anxious to maximize market potential and receive other benefits from operating abroad...Venture capitalists and other such sponsors can bring specialized knowledge and managerial sophistication to young companies otherwise lacking in these areas. (p. 9)

GARY KNIGHT and S. TAMER CAVUSGIL
"A Taxonomy of Born Global Firms" (2005), *Management
International Review.*

Thesis: "Born global" companies are a distinct type of new venture.

This article reviews literature on born globals and international
new ventures, using cluster analysis on survey results from 365
companies in order to develop typologies of such firms.

The study defines a new construct, *born globalness,* as the
difference between the firm's founding year and the year it first went
international, (e.g., a firm that was international at inception would have a born
globalness value of 0). The authors find that exporting is the initial mode of
foreign market entry for the majority of born global firms.

International performance is the extent to which firm objectives are
attained in foreign markets as a function of specific orientations and strategies.
Generic strategies are reflected by those indicated by Porter (1980):

- **Differentiation.** BGs interviewed emphasized the importance of having
  relatively unique products or differentiated offerings.
- **Focus.** BGs emphasized the role of strong focus on foreign customers.
- **Cost leadership.** Few BGs interviewed identified low cost as their main
  strategy.

In "traditional" international firms, the relevant resources for
internationalization tend to be highly tangible (e.g., plant, property, equipment),
or are largely comprised of financial and human resources. By contrast, the case
studies here suggest that BGs tend to focus on intangible resources, primarily
special knowledge about specific strategies and approaches for international
business.

The study identified four main types of international entrepreneurs:
entrepreneurial strategy and technology leaders, high-tech focusers,
entrepreneurs emphasizing cost leadership, and poor performers "stuck-in-the-
middle." The results indicate that the earlier a firm internationalizes, the better
its ultimate performance in foreign markets. Compared to relatively less BGs,
born-global firms that internationalize the earliest tend to emphasize
international operations and obtain more of their total sales from international
sources.

ERKKO AUTIO, HARRY SAPIENZA, and JAMES
ALMEIDA
"Effects of Age at Entry, Knowledge Intensity and Imitability on
International Growth" (2000), *Academy of Management Journal.*

Thesis: Internationalization early in a company's life is associated with faster
international growth and the knowledge intensity of the venture. Early
international activities induce greater entrepreneurial behavior and confer a
growth advantage.

Research has not sufficiently distinguished between the age at
first international operations and the speed of international
growth, each of which may affect, and be affected by, learning
and knowledge internalization. The process theory of
internationalization (Johanson and Vahlne 1977; see Chapter 5, Section 1)
describes an incremental process of acquiring and internalizing knowledge as
companies move to more geographically and psychically distant countries. The
international new ventures theory (Oviatt and McDougall 1994) suggests that
some entrepreneurs possess skills and knowledge that permit them to see and
exploit opportunities, which they do in foreign environments.

A premise of the study is that knowledge about international markets and
operations is an important determinant of international sales growth for
entrepreneurial firms. Based on data from 59 entrepreneurial ventures over five
years, the authors develop and test a knowledge- and learning-based framework
of Finnish venture internationalization. Organizational learning starts at the
individual level, and a firm's absorptive capacity (Cohen and Levinthal 1990)
depends on its prior, related knowledge that evolved in a path-dependent
fashion. A self-reinforcing pattern occurs whereby exploitation occurs in areas
nearest existing knowledge. Organizational knowledge is reinforced in a firm's
activities and becomes calcified, rendering learning as partly the unlearning of
the old. Internationalization requires acquiring completely new experiential
knowledge and foreign business practices. Thus, *when* a firm internationalizes
impacts how quickly it learns in the international market and how great the
subsequent learning will affect growth.

Early internationalization may occur before a firm gets "locked out" of
certain types of knowledge or develops "competency traps" that limit pursuit of
opportunities suited to existing competencies. Additionally, the earlier a firm
internationalizes, the less well established its political and relational allegiances,
and the more likely to develop foreign alliances alongside domestic ones.

Knowledge intensity, the extent to which a firm depends on the knowledge
inherent in its activities and outputs as a source of competitive advantage, may
relate to international growth. Knowledge-intensive firms may be more able to

deal with knowledge obsolescence than firms with less-developed knowledge-regenerating capabilities. As a result, knowledge-intensive firms may grow faster in foreign environments.

The analyses show that age at international entry is negatively related to international growth (i.e., early internationalization is associated to greater growth), and that knowledge-intensive firms grow faster in foreign environments. Young firms apparently have a "learning advantage of newness" that allows them to adapt to and compete in new, dynamic environments.

New venture managers may thus consider that they can successfully expand internationally, and do so more rapidly than previously thought. Efforts to intensify its knowledge-related abilities may enhance both the firm's output and its capacity to recognize opportunities and assimilate new knowledge.

Discussion and Implications

 The first two articles spark the discussion on country differences in entrepreneurship. The Global Entrepreneurship Monitor (GEM) studies, which survey entrepreneurs in over 40 countries annually, provide insights into where new ventures may expand internationally, the nature of differences one can expect, and why certain types of ventures do not appear in certain contexts. They also explain the emergence of different types of entrepreneurship in different contexts based on the economic conditions and employment options available to the population. For example, some people are forced into becoming entrepreneurs because of need—they have no option but to create a business to feed themselves and their families. Other entrepreneurs may be more driven more by opportunities than by need, in that they may be well fed, but see voids in the market that they can exploit. Regulations can, however, affect the entrepreneur's ability to exploit opportunities. A study by LiPuma, Newbert, and Doh (in press) shows that the regulatory dimension affects small and new firms' export intensity. Armed with this knowledge, entrepreneurs can make better-informed decisions as to the best geographic range for their marketing and sales efforts.

The next set of articles touch on new venture internationalization: the antecedents, processes, and outcomes associated with young companies doing international business. This phenomenon was identified by Oviatt and McDougall (1994) as a contradiction to international business theory. They, along with Gary Knight and Cavusgil (1997, 2005) seek to understand the why, how, and to what ends international new ventures, or born globals, internationalize.

These authors' choice of sample underscore the nascence of the research area of international entrepreneurship, in that Knight and Cavusgil use a figure of 10 years old (to first international experience) as a cutoff for BGs, whereas Oviatt and McDougall use a figure of six years, consistent with statistics in the

U.S. regarding new venture mortality. Additionally, the former use a target figure of 25% FSTS (ratio of foreign sales to total sales), whereas others suggest a less intensive figure of 10% as a cutoff for inclusion as an INV. Clearly differences in national markets, foreign market integration (e.g., NAFTA, the European Union), and regional differences play into the analysis as to why lower levels of international activity for new ventures in one context may be considered strategic whereas higher levels in another context may not be considered such.

In reading these articles, one must also consider that many of these studies focus on manufacturing. As services increasingly account for higher portions of international trade, this begs the question of whether the studies' conclusions hold in other industries, such as services (e.g., consulting, custom software).

Another point of interest relates to resources. The literature as a whole paints a picture of resource constrained entrepreneurs seeking to internationalize, which requires more (and potentially different) resources than solely domestic operations. As the new ventures that internationalize are, coincidentally, young and technology-focused as are recipients of venture capital, how does the receipt of VC, which eases resource constraints, related to new venture internationalization? Venture capitalists invest in industries with high ambiguity, information asymmetries, and with highly specific assets. Research by Fernhaber and McDougall-Covin (2009) and Fernhaber, McDougall, and Shepherd (2009) seeks to understand the relationships between venture capital provision and the internationalization of new ventures. It may be that the presence of venture capitalists influences the aggressive strategies taken by international new ventures as compared to solely domestic new ventures (McDougall, Oviatt, and Shrader 2003).

For new ventures, the resources used for internationalization are more intangible than those used by more mature ventures. Such intangible resources include prior experience of the entrepreneurs, the background of associated third parties (e.g., venture capitalists), and more aggressive strategies. Survival may decrease, but those that survive have greater growth.

Even for corporations that internationalize, the results compellingly suggest that there are upper limits to the potential gains a firm can achieve from aggressive pursuit of international corporate entrepreneurship, when the international environment in which it competes is hostile. We should note, however, that these results may be due to the fact that many of the measures used are not *direct measures*—instead they use measures of CEO/VP *perceptions*. That is, studies may measure an executive's perceptions of environmental hostility, which may be affected by the executive's prior experience, location of education, or country of origin.

Finally, an important element to new venture internationalization is that of knowledge. Autio et al. and subsequent work of Zahra, Ireland, and Hitt (2000) point to the fact that, consistent with "traditional" international business theories, knowledge is the key determinant to venture internationalization (see Chapter 5). New ventures may have a "learning advantage of newness" that lets them more easily take on behaviors and routines for internationalization (and reject routines that do not support internationalization), as well as overcome their liabilities of newness and of foreignness as they enter and expand their international business.

Additional literature in the international entrepreneurship stream, presented in chronological order, includes the following:

- **Coviello and Munro (1995).** The authors build on earlier work showing that entrepreneurial high-technology firms develop multiple relationships for internationalization and use them in parallel across numerous markets. The internationalization process for these firms was compressed, and they did not follow the traditional stepwise approach to internationalization (see Chapter 5). This study focuses on the market development aspect—use of network relationships—to pursue foreign-market activities and conduct international marketing activities. The authors conclude that foreign market selection and entry initiatives emanate from opportunities created via network contacts, rather than solely from strategic decisions by managers in the firm.

- **Bell, McNaughton, and Young (2001).** The authors propose an integrative model that recognizes the existence of different internationalization pathways for "traditional," "born global," and "born-again global" firms. There are distinct differences in internationalization behavior among these three types of firms, along seven dimensions: motivation, objectives, expansion patterns, pace, method of distribution/entry modes, international strategies, and financing. Entrepreneurs interested in entering foreign markets should consider all seven dimensions in their analyses, as the trajectories and outcomes for different patterns may have significant cost and performance implications.

- **Sapienza, Autio, George, and Zahra (2006).** This conceptual article suggests that ventures entering foreign markets at an early age are more subject to issues of survival. However, those international new ventures that do survive perform better than ventures that do not seek to enter foreign markets.

FURTHER READING

If you're interested in reading more on the topics discussed in this chapter, here are some sources to get you started. We do not offer this as a comprehensive or exhaustive list, but rather have selected well-regarded or significant works that space did not permit us to include in the main discussion.

1. WHAT IS ENTREPRENEURSHIP AND WHY SHOULD WE STUDY IT?

Hebert, Robert and Albert Link. 1982. *The Entrepreneur: Mainstream Views and Radical Critiques*. New York, Praeger Press.

Kirzner, Israel. 1973. *Competition and Entrepreneurship*. Chicago, University of Chicago Press.

2. OPPORTUNITIES AND OPPORTUNITY RECOGNITION

Ahuja, Gautam. 2000. "Collaboration Networks, Structural Holes, and Innovation: A Longitudinal Study." *Administrative Science Quarterly* 45(3), 425–455.

Delmar, Frédéric and Scott Shane. 2003. "Does Business Planning Facilitate the Development of New Ventures?" *Strategic Management Journal* 24(12), 1165–1185.

Eckhardt, Jonathan T. and Scott Shane. 2003. "Opportunities and Entrepreneurship." *Journal of Management* 29(3), 333–349.

Sarasvathy, Saras. 2001. "Causation and Effectuation: Toward a Theoretical Shift from Economic Inevitability to Entrepreneurial Contingency." *Academy of Management Review* 26(2), 243–263.

3. ENTREPRENEURIAL ENTRY AND ORGANIZATIONAL EMERGENCE

Bruno, Albert and Tyzoon Tyebjee. 1982. "The Environment for Entrepreneurship." In C. Kent, D. Sexton, and K. Vesper (editors), *The Encyclopedia of Entrepreneurship*. Englewood Cliffs, Prentice Hall. pp. 288–315.

Carroll, Glenn R. and Elaine Mosakowski. 1987. "The Career Dynamics of Self-Employment." *Administrative Science Quarterly* 32(4), 570–589.

Fairlie, Robert W. 2002. "Drug Dealing and Legitimate Self-Employment." *Journal of Labor Economics* 20(3), 538–566.

Low, Murray and Eric Abrahamson. 1997. "Movements, Bandwagons and Clones: Industry Evolution and the Entrepreneurial Process." *Journal of Business Venturing* 12(6), 435–458.

Zucker, Lynne G., Michael R. Darby, and Marilynn B. Brewer. 1998. "Intellectual Human Capital and the Birth of U.S. Biotechnology Enterprises." *American Economic Review* 88(1), 290–306.

4. ENTREPRENEURIAL FINANCE AND ECONOMIC IMPACT

Acs, Zoltan and David Audretsch. 1993. "Innovation and Technological Change: The New Learning." In G. Libecap (editor), *Advances in the Study of Entrepreneurship, Innovation and Economic Growth*, vol. 6. Greenwich, JAI Press. pp. 109–140.

Amit, Raphael, Lawrence Glosten, and Eitan Muller. 1990. "Entrepreneurial Ability, Venture Investments, and Risk Sharing." *Management Science* 36(10), 1232–1245.

Black, Bernard S. and Ronald J. Gilson. 1998. "Venture Capital and the Structure of Capital Markets: Banks Versus Stock Markets." *Journal of Financial Economics* 47(3), 243–277.

Bygrave, William. 1987. "Syndicated Investments by Venture Capital Firms: A Networking Perspective." *Journal of Business Venturing* 2(2), 139–154.

Chen, Hsuan-Chi and Jay Ritter. 2000. "The Seven Percent Solution." *Journal of Finance* 55(3), 1105–1131.

Fluck, Zsuzsanna, Douglas Holtz-Eakin, and Harvey S. Rosen. 1998. "Where Does the Money Come From? The Financing of Small Entrepreneurial Enterprises." Center for Policy Research, Syracuse University Working Paper no. 191.

Gompers, Paul A. and Josh Lerner. 1999. *The Venture Capital Cycle*. Cambridge, MIT Press.

Ofek, Eli, and Matthew Richardson. 2003. "Dotcom Mania: The Rise and Fall of Internet Stock Prices." *Journal of Finance* 58(3), 1113–1137.

Ritter, Jay R. and Ivo Welch. 2002. "A Review of IPO Activity, Pricing, and Allocations." *Journal of Finance* 57(4), 1795–1828.

Shane, Scott and Daniel Cable. 2002. "Network Ties, Reputation, and the Financing of New Ventures." *Management Science* 48(3), 364–381.

Starr, Jeniffer A. and Ian C. MacMillan. 1990. "Resource Cooptation via Social Contracting: Resource Acquisition Strategies for New Ventures." *Strategic Management Journal* 11(Summer), 79–92.

Winborg, Joakim and Hans Landstrom. 2000. "Financial Bootstrapping in Small Businesses: Examining Small Business Managers' Resource Acquisition Behaviors." *Journal of Business Venturing* 16(3), 235–254.

Zacharakis, Andrew and Dean Shepherd. 2001. "The Nature of Information and Overconfidence on Venture Capitalists' Decision-Making." *Journal of Business Venturing* 16(4), 311–332.

5. INTERNATIONAL ENTREPRENEURSHIP

De Clercq, Dirk, Harry J. Sapienza, and Hans Crijns. 2005. "The Internationalization of Small and Medium-Sized Firms: The Role of Organizational Learning Effort and Entrepreneurial Orientation." *Small Business Economics* 24(4), 409–419.

McDougall, Patricia P., Benjamin M. Oviatt, and Rodney Shrader. 2003. "A Comparison of International and Domestic New Ventures." *Journal of International Entrepreneurship* 1(1), 59–82.

Oviatt, Benjamin M. and Patricia P. McDougall. 2005. "Defining International Entrepreneurship and Modeling the Speed of Internationalization." *Entrepreneurship Theory & Practice* 29(5), 537–553.

Westhead, Paul, Mike Wright, and Deniz Ucbasaran. 2001. "The Internationalization of New and Small Firms: A Resource-Based View." *Journal of Business Venturing* 16(4), 333–358.

WORKS CITED

Aitken, Hugh. 1963. "The Future of Entrepreneurship Research." *Explorations in Entrepreneurial History* 1(1), 3–9.

Aldrich, Howard E. 1990. "Using an Ecological Perspective to Study Organizational Founding Rates." *Entrepreneurship Theory and Practice* 14(3), 7–24.

Aldrich, Howard E. 2000. *Organizations Evolving.* London, Sage.

Aldrich, Howard and C. Marlene Fiol. 1994. "Fools Rush In? The Institutional Context of Industry Creation." *Academy of Management Review* 19(4), 645–670.

Amit, Raphael, James Brander, and Christoph Zott. 1998. "Why Do Venture Capital Firms Exist? Theory and Canadian Evidence. " *Journal of Business Venturing* 13(6), 441–466.

Amit, Raphael, Eitan Muller, and Iain Cockburn. 1995. "Opportunity Costs and Entrepreneurial Activity." *Journal of Business Venturing* 10(2), 95–106.

Ardichvili, Alexander, Richard Cardozo, and Suarav Ray. 2003. "A Theory of Entrepreneurial Opportunity Identification and Development." *Journal of Business Venturing* 18(1), 105–124.

Arrow, Kenneth. 1962. "Economic Welfare and the Allocation of Resources for Invention." In *The Rate and Direction of Inventive Activity: Economic and Social Factors*, National Bureau of Economic Research. Princeton, Princeton University Press. pp. 609–626.

Autio, Erkko, Harry J. Sapienza, and James Almeida. 2000, "Effects of Age at Entry, Knowledge Intensity and Imitability on International Growth." *Academy of Management Journal* 43(5), 909–924.

Azoulay, Pierre and Scott Shane. 2001. "Entrepreneurs, Contracts and the Failure of Young Firms." *Management Science* 47(3), 337–358.

Baron, Robert and Gideon Markman. 2000. "Beyond Social Capital: How Social Skills can Enhance Entrepreneurs' Success." *Academy of Management Executive* 14(1), 106–116.

Baum, Joel A.C. and Christine Oliver. 1991. "Institutional Linkages and Organizational Mortality." *Administrative Science Quarterly* 36(2), 187–218.

Baum, Joel A.C. and Christine Oliver. 1992. "Institutional Embeddedness and the Dynamics of Organizational Populations." *American Sociological Review* 57(4), 540–559.

Baum, Joel A.C. and Brian S. Silverman. 1999. *Alliance-Based Competitive Dynamics in the Canadian Biotechnology Industry*. Boston, Harvard Business School Press.

Baumol, William J. 1968 "Entrepreneurship in Economic Theory." *American Economic Review* 58(2), 64–71.

Baumol, William J. 1990. "Entrepreneurship: Productive, Unproductive, and Destructive." *Journal of Political Economy* 98(5, Part 1), 893–921.

Bell, James, Rod McNaughton, and Stephen Young. 2001. "'Born-Again Global' Firms: An Extension to the 'Born Global' Phenomenon." *Journal of International Management* 7(3), 173–189.

Brockhaus, Robert H. 1980. "Risk-Taking Propensity of Entrepreneurs." *Academy of Management Journal* 23(3), 509–520.

Brush, Candida G., Nancy M. Carter, Patricia G. Greene, Myra M. Hart, and Elizabeth J. Gatewood. 2002. "The Role of Social Capital and Gender in Linking Financial Suppliers and Entrepreneurial Firms: A Framework for Future Research." *Venture Capital International Journal* 4(4), 305–323.

Bull, Ivan and Gary E. Willard. 1993. "Towards a Theory of Entrepreneurship." *Journal of Business Venturing* 8(3), 183-196.

Busenitz, Lowell, Carolina Gomez, and Jennifer Spencer. 2000. "Country Institutional Profiles: Unlocking Entrepreneurial Phenomena." *Academy of Management Journal*, 43(5), 994–1003.

Cable, Daniel and Scott Shane. 1997. "A Prisoner's Dilemma Approach to Entrepreneur–Venture Capital Relationships." *Academy of Management Review* 22(1), 142–176.

Cantillon, Richard. 1755. An Essay on Economic Theory. Auburn, Alabama: Ludwig von Mises Institute, 2010. http://library.mises.org/books/Richard%20Cantillon/An%20Essay%20on%20Economic%20Theory.pdf

Carroll, Glenn R. and T. Michael Hannan. 2000. *The Demography of Corporations and Industries*. Princeton, Princeton University Press.

Casson, Mark. 1982. *The Entrepreneur*. Totowa, NJ, Barnes and Noble Books.

Cohen, Wesley and Daniel Levinthal. 1990. "Absorptive Capacity: A New Perspective on Learning and Innovation." *Administrative Science Quarterly* 35(1), 128–152.

Coviello, Nicole E. and Hugh J. Munro. 1995. "Growing the Entrepreneurial Firm: Networking for International Market Development." *European Journal of Marketing* 29(7), 49–61.

Drucker, Peter. 1985. *Innovation and Entrepreneurship*. New York, Harper and Row.

Dubin, Robert. 1978. *Theory Development*. New York, Free Press.

Evans, David S. and Boyan Jovanovic. 1989. "An Estimated Model of Entrepreneurial Choice under Liquidity Constraints." *Journal of Political Economy* 97(4), 808–827.

Evans, David and Linda S. Leighton. 1989. "Some Empirical Aspects of Entrepreneurship." *American Economic Review* 79(3), 519–535.

Fernhaber, Stephanie A. and Patricia P. McDougall-Covin. 2009. "Venture Capitalists as Catalysts to New Venture Internationalization: The Impact of Their Knowledge and Reputation Resources." *Entrepreneurship Theory and Practice* 33(1), 277–295.

Fernhaber, Stephanie A., Patricia P. McDougall-Covin and Dean A. Shepherd. 2009. "International Entrepreneurship: Leveraging Internal and External Knowledge." *Strategic Entrepreneurship Journal* 3, 297–320.

Gartner, William. 1985. "A Conceptual Framework for Describing the Phenomenon of New Venture Creation." *Academy of Management Review* 10(4), 696–706.

Gompers, Paul. 1995. "Optimal Investment, Monitoring, and the Staging of Venture Capital." *Journal of Finance* 50(5), 1461–1490.

Granovetter, Mark. 1973. "Strength of Weak Ties." *American Journal of Sociology* 78(6), 1360–1380.

Gromb, David and Denis Scharfstein. 2002. "Entrepreneurship in Equilibrium." National Bureau of Economic Research Working Paper no. 9001.

Gulati, Ranjay and Monica Higgins. 2003. "Which Ties Matter When? The Contingent Effects of Interorganizational Partnerships on IPO Success." *Strategic Management Journal* 24(2), 127–144.

Hamilton, Barton H. 2000. "Does Entrepreneurship Pay? An Empirical Analysis of the Returns of Self-Employment." *Journal of Political Economy* 108(3), 604–631.

Hayek, Friedrich A. 1945. "The Use of Knowledge in Society." *American Economic Review* 35(4), 519–530.

Hofstede, Geert. 2001. *Culture's Consequences: Comparing Values, Behaviors, Institutions, and Organizations Across Nations*. Thousand Oaks, Sage.

Johanson, Jan and Jan-Erik Vahlne. 1977. "The Internationalization Process of the Firm: A Model of Knowledge Development and Increasing Foreign Commitments." *Journal of International Business Studies* 8(1), 23–32.

Kaplan, Steven N. and Per Strömberg. 2003. "Financial Contracting Theory Meets the Real World: An Empirical Analysis of Venture Capital Contracts." *Review of Economic Studies* 70(2), 281–315.

Katz, Jerome and William Gartner. 1988. "Properties of Emerging Organizations." *Academy of Management Review* 13(3), 429–441.

Kets de Vries, Manfried. 1977. "The Entrepreneurial Personality: A Person at the Crossroads." *Journal of Management Studies* 14(1), 34–57.

Khilstrom, Richard E. and Jean-Jacques Laffont. 1979. "A General Equilibrium Entrepreneurial Theory of Firm Formation Based on Risk Aversion." *Journal of Political Economy* 87, 719–748.

Kirzner, Israel M. 1985. *Discovery and the Capitalist Process*. Chicago, University of Chicago Press.

Kirzner, Israel M. 1997. "Entrepreneurial Discovery and the Competitive Market Process: An Austrian Approach." *Journal of Economic Literature* 35(1), 60–85.

Knight, Frank. 1921. *Risk, Uncertainty and Profit*. Boston, Houghton-Mifflin.

Knight, Gary A. and S. Tamer Cavusgil. 1997. "Emerging Organizational Paradigm for International Marketing: The Born Global Firm." in *Proceedings: 1997 Annual Meeting, Academy of International Business*, Honolulu.

Knight, Gary A. and S. Tamer Cavusgil. 2005. "A Taxonomy of Born Global Firms." *Management International Review* 45(3), 15–35.

Krueger, Norris. 2000. "Cognitive Infrastructure of Opportunity Emergence." *Entrepreneurship Theory and Practice* 24(3), 5–24.

La Porta, Raphael, Florencio Lopez-de-Silanes, Andrei Shleifer, and Robert Vishny. 2000. "Investor Protection and Corporate Governance." *Journal of Financial Economics* 58(1–2), 3–27.

Liebenstein, Harvey. 1968. "Entrepreneurship and Development." *American Economic Review*, 58(2), 72–83.

LiPuma, Joseph A., Scott L. Newbert, and Jonathan P. Doh. (in press) "The Effect Of Institutional Quality on Firm Export Performance in Emerging Economies: A Contingency Model of Firm Age and Size." *Small Business Economics*. doi: 10.1007/s11187-011-9395-7.

McClelland, David C. 1961. *The Achieving Society*. New York, Free Press.

McDougall, Patricia P., Benjamin Oviatt, and Rodney C. Shrader. 2003. "A Comparison of International and Domestic New Ventures." *Journal of International Entrepreneurship* 1(1), 59–82.

Megginson, William L. and Kathleen A. Weiss. 1991. "Venture Capitalist Certification in Initial Public Offerings." *Journal of Finance* 46(3), 879–903.

Murphy, Kevin M., Andrei Shleifer, and Robert W. Vishny. 1991. "The Allocation of Talent: Implications for Growth." *Quarterly Journal of Economics* 106(2), 503–530.

Oviatt, Benjamin M. and Patricia P. McDougall. 1994. "Toward a Theory of International New Ventures." *Journal of International Business Studies* 25(1), 45–64.

Oviatt, Benjamin M. and Patricia P. McDougall. 2005. "Defining International Entrepreneurship and Modeling the Speed of Internationalization." *Entrepreneurship Theory and Practice* 29(5), 537–554.

Pennings, Johannes M. 1980. "Environmental Influences on the Creation Process." In J. R. Kimberly and R. Miles (editors), *The Organization Life Cycle*. San Francisco, Jossey Bass. pp. 135–160.

Pennings, Johannes M. 1982. "Organizational Birth Frequencies: An Empirical Investigation." *Administrative Science Quarterly* 27(1), 120–144.

Pfeffer, Jeffrey and Gerald R. Salancik. 1978. *The External Control of Organizations: A Resource Dependence Perspective*. New York, Harper & Row.

Podolny, Joel M. and Toby E. Stuart. 1995. "A Role-Based Ecology of Technological Change." *American Journal of Sociology* 100(5), 1224–1270.

Porter, Michael. 1980. *Competitive Strategy*. New York, Free Press.

Reuf, Martin, Howard Aldrich, and Nancy Carter. 2003. "The Structure of Founding Teams: Homophily, Strong Ties, and Isolation Among U.S. Entrepreneurs." *American Sociological Review* 68(2), 195–222.

Sapienza, Harry J. 1992. "When do Venture Capitalists Add Value?" *Journal of Business Venturing* 7(1), 9–27.

Sapienza, Harry J., Erkko Autio, Gerald George, and Shaker A. Zahra. 2006. "A Capabilities Perspective on the Effects of Early Internationalization on Firm Survival and Growth." *Academy of Management Review* 31(4), 914–933.

Saxenian, Annalee. 1994. *Regional Advantage: Culture and Competition in Silicon Valley and Route 128*. Cambridge, Harvard University Press.

Say, Jean-Baptiste. 1845. *A Treatise on Political Economy*, 4th edition. Translated by C. R. Prinsep. Philadelphia, Grigg & Elliot.

Schumpeter, Joseph. 1934. *The Theory of Economic Development*. Cambridge, Harvard University Press.

Schumpeter, Joseph. 1942. *Capitalism, Socialism and Democracy*. New York, Harper and Brothers.

Shane, Scott. 2000. "Prior Knowledge and the Discovery of Entrepreneurial Opportunities." *Organization Science* 11(4), 448–469.

Shane, Scott and Sankaran Venkataraman. 2000. "The Promise of Entrepreneurship as a Field of Research." *Academy of Management Review* 25(1), 217–227.

Sorenson, Olav and Toby Stuart. 2001. "Syndication Networks and the Spatial Distribution of Venture Capital Investments." *American Journal of Sociology* 106(6), 1546–1588.

Stevenson, Howard H. and David E. Gumpert. 1985. "The Heart of Entrepreneurship." *Harvard Business Review* 63(March), 85–94.

Stinchcombe, Arthur L. 1965. "Social Structure and Organizations." In J. G. March (editor), *Handbook of Organizations*. Chicago, Rand-McNally. pp. 142–193.

Stuart, Toby, Ha Hoang, and Ralph Hybels. 1999. "Interorganizational Endorsements and the Performance of Entrepreneurial Ventures." *Administrative Science Quarterly* 44(2), 315–349.

U.S. Department of Commerce, Bureau of the Census *Current Population Survey: Annual Demographic File, 1966-1981*, 2nd ICPSR ed. Ann Arbor, Inter-university Consortium for Political and Social Research.

Van de Ven, Andrew H. 1980. "Early Planning, Implementation and Performance of New Organizations." In J. R. Kimberly and R. Miles (editors), *The Organization Life Cycle*. San Francisco, Jossey Bass. pp. 83–134.

Van de Ven, Andrew. 1993. "The Development of an Infrastructure for Entrepreneurship." *Journal of Business Venturing* 8(3), 211–230.

Venkataraman, Sankaran. 1997. "The Distinctive Domain of Entrepreneurship Research: An Editor's Perspective." In J. Katz and R. Brockhaus (editors), *Advances in Entrepreneurship, Firm Emergence, and Growth*. Greenwich, JAI Press. pp. 119–138.

Williamson, Oliver. E. 1985. *The Economic Institutions of Capitalism*. New York, Free Press.

Zahra, Shaker A. and Dennis M. Garvis. 2000. "International Corporate Entrepreneurship and Firm Performance: The Moderating Effect of International Environmental Hostility." *Journal of Business Venturing* 15(5-6), 469–492.

Zahra, Shaker A., R. Duane Ireland, and Michael A. Hitt. 2000. "International Expansion by New Venture Firms: International Diversity, Mode of Market Entry, Technological Learning, and Performance." *Academy of Management Journal* 43(5), 925–950.

LEADERSHIP

Northouse (2012) defines *leadership* as a process whereby an individual influences a group to achieve a common goal. Leadership was practiced, examined, and written about long before other management fields were even defined. In this introduction to leadership, we offer a brief history of the study of leadership practice to provide context for the sources discussed in the chapter.

Niccolo Machiavelli (1513) provided a clear description of how leaders achieve their own ends by manipulating followers; his observations serve as an education for followers regarding how this manipulation occurs, that they might better resist (Section 1). Chester Barnard (1938), a senior executive at New Jersey Bell, started a more modern examination of leadership, exhorting that the primary responsibility of any executive is to define the organization's purpose and instill loyalty so that managers cooperate for the good of the organization. To achieve such loyalty, he suggested, executives should work to satisfy their employees rather than viewing them simply as production inputs (Section 1).

Several researchers have started by observing leaders in practice before offering prescriptions. Henry Mintzberg (1975) observed how leaders spend their time, and found that they do not typically engage in systematic planning. Actual leaders are interrupted constantly, reacting far more than they plan, which leads to incremental decisions made abruptly (Section 2). Along the same lines, Warren Bennis (1989) categorized the contradicting and tangential demands obstructing leaders from actually achieving meaningful goals. Specifically, routine work tends to drive out strategic or creative work, such that leaders must work hard to carve out time for the larger picture and force subordinates to manage the daily operations of the enterprise (Section 2).

Some researchers emphasize the distinction between managing and leading. John Kotter (1990) offered that management is about coping with complexity while leadership is about coping with change; therefore, most companies need more managers than leaders (Section 2). Several authors including Kets de Vries (1989) have demonstrated some of the destructive potential of leadership:

leadership can be isolating, can involve unrealistic expectations, and can lead to self-destruction from guilt or fear (Section 4).

Organizations reflect the personality and style of their leaders. Edgar Schein (2010) examined the critical role of leadership in establishing and maintaining the organizational culture that is the very identity of the group and that represents the deeper level of shared assumptions critical to the organization's success (Section 3). Jean Lipman-Blumen (1996) classified leadership styles and prescribed that leaders must adopt a broader set of styles to achieve the agility required for the shorter timeframes of the modern organization. She also showed distinct differences between men and women, and upper- versus lower-level managers, in how individuals actually lead (Section 4).

Jay Conger and Ronald Riggio hosted a workshop in California in 2006, gathering scholars in particular areas of leadership, and asked them to extract from a large body of research and identify insights that could inform the actual practice of leadership. Riggio and Conger (2006) published the results in a book, in which for the last chapter they summarize the work presented by these other scholars. The prescriptions are varied but contain some common themes: leaders must engage, they must monitor and adapt, they need to model behavior, they have to be proactive, and they should recognize that there are no shortcuts or formulas (Section 5).

1. Leadership Classics

This section presents two early but still relevant classic sources on leadership. Niccolo Machiavelli (1513) offers an unapologetic description of how leaders manipulate their followers to accomplish their aims. He encourages readers not to romanticize leadership but rather to fully expect leaders to engage in the brutish pursuit of power. Chester Barnard (1938) was an executive who was disappointed to find no explanation of his own business experience in organization or economic theory, and set out to fill the gap in instructing others on how to be an effective executive, in as scientific a manner as he could manage. Leadership is not a new endeavor; the passage of time has not diminished the relevance of the insights of either of these authors.

NICCOLO MACHIAVELLI
The Prince (1513). Translated by Robert Adams.

Thesis: Machiavelli provides an objective description of how leaders can and do achieve their own ends by manipulating their followers.

Machiavelli starts by identifying different kinds of nations, including republics and "princely states" (which may be hereditary, newly created, or newly acquired). In hereditary principalities, those who are used to their ruler are less troublesome than new subjects. If a prince is not too ambitious, he[1] will have fewer reasons to offend his subjects. Some states are mixed principalities. When acquiring (i.e., conquering) a new state similar to the leader's own, the most successful path is to extinguish the ruling line to avoid a leadership challenge but maintain the culture the people are used to. If the new state is a different type, the leader should move in and live among the new subjects. "Men ought either to be caressed or destroyed, since they will seek revenge for minor hurts but will not be able to revenge major ones" (p. 7).

In discussing centralized versus decentralized control, Machiavelli suggests that a leader should adjust to his circumstances. For example, a centrally controlling monarchy like Turkey had is difficult to acquire (because the monarchy must be smashed) but easy to hold once acquired. For a country with decentralized control like France, control would fragment upon invasion, making France easy to acquire but difficult to control.

To rule subjects who are used to living under their own laws, there are three possible approaches: you can destroy the subjects, live in their realm, or set up an oligarchy. The problem is that "any man who becomes master of such a city accustomed to freedom, and does not destroy it, may expect to be destroyed by it" (p. 15). On the other hand, principalities that are used to taking orders from others are slower to take up a defense.

For subjects used to living under a king, conquering and holding a new kingdom requires talent, skill, and luck. Princes of great character find power difficult to gain but easy to hold. For those states acquired by other people's might, or by luck, princes who rise through good fortune gain power easily but have difficulty maintaining it.

For those who become rulers by crime, cruelty can be used successfully or unsuccessfully in securing a new province. Cruelty is well used when it is implemented all at once. It is used poorly when it is performed infrequently at first but increasing over time. A prince should live on such terms that no accident can force him to change his conduct.

Both nobles and common people attempt to elevate one of their own to power. A noble's prince experiences conflict with his peers and has difficulty retaining power. A people's prince has independence and more power to lead as he sees fit. The bottom line is that "the prince must have the people well

---

[1] In this book, we are writing for leaders of all genders as our language reflects, but authors in the 16th century did not always appear to appreciate that leadership lessons apply equally to kings and queens.

disposed toward him; otherwise in times of adversity there is no hope" (p. 29). A prince should not trust what he observes in quiet times; in adversity, a prince never experiences a crisis a second time.

To measure the strength of a state, the golden rule is that princes who can stand alone are the strongest. States are founded upon good laws and good arms. Mercenaries are viewed as useless: disunited, ambitious, undisciplined, and untrustworthy. Having one's own troops is key—auxiliary troops are a drain on success. "Unless it has its own armies, no state is really secure; in that case, it depends entirely upon fortune" (p. 40). The principal occupation of a prince should be war. Even in peace, a prince must make the military capital that will position him to resist adversity.

In the real world it is sometimes necessary to do things not perceived as virtues. Often, virtues like mercy lead to ruin and apparent vices result in greater security. A financially liberal reputation requires resources and therefore heavy taxation, causing subjects to eventually hate the taxing prince. A prince should not object to being considered miserly; a prince should incur the charge of cruelty in order to keep subjects united and loyal. "If you have to make a choice, to be feared is much safer than to be loved" (p. 46).

One can fight by law or force, but force must be used when the law is not sufficient. A prince must not keep good faith when it is against his interests (i.e., he should break his word), but he must always appear to have mercy, faith, and integrity. This discussion carries Machiavelli's most known message, that the end justifies the means.

A prince should contrive for his actions to show grandeur. He should fear both his subjects and foreign powers. The remedy for conspiracy is to not be hated by the masses. A prince should delegate the carrying out of unpopular duties. One should always arm rather than disarm one's subjects. Their arms become the prince's own, and those once suspected become faithful. A prince should endeavor to obtain fame for being excellent. A prince should never make common cause with one more powerful than himself, for if the ally wins then the prince rests in that ally's power.

The first impression of a ruler and his wisdom is gained from seeing those around him. A minister who thinks more of himself than of the prince will never be a good advisor. A prince must let those around him speak the truth, but if everyone is allowed to be candid he may lose their respect. A prince must choose specific councillors to give full liberty to speak the truth on those matters he asks about.

Princes who have lost their empires (e.g., Italy) have done so because of common defects in their weapons, the people's hostility to them, and their inability to protect themselves against the nobles. The key is to prepare in good times for times of adversity. The actions of those who seek power must be consistent with the situation. Fortune appears to favor the impetuous rather than the cautious. Italy is ready for a new leader (as of 1513) to restore her to glory.

CHESTER BARNARD, *The Functions of the Executive* (1938), Chapters 15–18.

Thesis: The primary responsibility of an executive is to define the organization's purpose. The executive must demonstrate and instill loyalty so that managers put aside their personal interests and cooperate for the benefit of the larger organization. This in turn requires executives to satisfy their employees rather than view them as production inputs.

Regarding the executive functions of the leader, Barnard first addresses how to maintain organizational communication. The company establishes the means of communication by selecting people for executive functions. The first executive function is to create positions and establish a system of communication. Executives define positions in an organizational scheme, and then they manage the personnel. Managers should foster loyalty by bestowing prestige and other non-material incentives, more than by compensation; promotion, demotion, and dismissal drive control, but such control depends on cooperation. Informal organization is also essential and is achieved by selecting executives compatible with the company and personnel. The second executive function is to secure personal services by recruiting people and ensuring their continuing contribution after they are hired. The third function is to formulate and define the purposes, objectives, and ends of the organization—in this work, it is critical to assign responsibility by delegating objective authority.

Regarding the executive process, Barnard delineates what executives do that is distinct from the work required of other members of the organization. The functions defined in above were defined independently, but they must be carried out simultaneously by an executive process encompassing all of the organization's activities. This complex and ambiguous undertaking relies on intuition and aesthetics—the process is nonlinear, nonrational, and synthetic rather than purely analytical.

Success is pursued in two dimensions: effectiveness and efficiency.

- *Effectiveness* relates to the appropriateness of the means selected to accomplish the objective. These tools are all of the activity patterns of the business, and the executive is concerned with creating a balanced set of processes. Effectiveness is threatened when the organization's focus—as evidenced by the subjects chosen for its control systems—is too narrowly defined. Attention must be paid in a balanced way to all core factors in order to avoid crisis. The executive must prevent crisis by "sensing the whole." In Barnard's view, only an executive elite has the capability to perform this task.

- *Efficiency* means that the contributions received by the organization exceed those inducements it provides. This definition is grounded in Barnard's conception of the organization as a system of cooperative activities geared to producing value.

He describes four types of economies in which an organization trades. In each economy, the organization offers utility valuable to the recipient (money, satisfaction, affiliation, etc.) in exchange for utility valuable to the organization.

- A *material economy* includes the exchange and transformation of useful physical things.
- A *social economy* governs exchange with individuals and other organizations.
- An *individual economy* covers the balance of inducements to and contributions from individuals within the organization.
- An *organizational economy* is the aggregate of these other three economies.

If it were possible to assign value through a common metric, the executive's task would be easier; however, since different forms of utility have different measurement, the best indicator of organizational success is simply survival. Efficient organizations survive, and inefficient ones do not.

Regarding the nature of executive responsibility, Barnard states that cooperation requires leadership. Action in formal organizations depends upon people and their motivation. *Leadership* is the word expressing the moral attributes of chief importance in cooperation—it is the power of individuals to inspire cooperative personal decisions by creating faith in common beliefs, in the probability of success, and in a common purpose. Leadership is the catalyst for combining human efforts and has two aspects: a technical aspect of superiority or competence, and a responsibility aspect yielding persistence, endurance, and courage (what Barnard deems *quality* in a broad moral sense).

Barnard's conception of responsibility is drawn from a broad conception of morality where *morals* refers to private codes that inhibit impulses running counter to the individual's interests and enhance those consistent with them. Such codes may arise from education or training, but also may simply be absorbed from the environment. Executives have a multiplicity of private moral codes, and executives that are responsible with respect to one code are likely to be responsible with respect to others; however, different codes have differing power to inspire responsible behavior, so we can infer some kind of responsibility ranking (valence).

When codes come into conflict, there are three possible results:

- paralysis of action (destructive outcome),
- the violation of one code with accompanying guilt (destructive outcome), or
- the creation of an alternative course of action that satisfies both codes (constructive outcome that strengthens the codes).

Responsibility is distinct from the possession of multiple codes and converts the mere possession of such codes into action. A talented and responsible executive will be predictable and reliable due to both a commitment to codes and a talent at harmonizing them. Compliance based on incentives is to be distinguished from compliance to responsibility based on an intrinsic desire to comply.

Organizations impose a complex set of codes that can conflict with personal codes; participation in multiple organizations also generates inter-code conflict. Complexity can result in general deterioration of moral codes and reduction of sense of responsibility, or it can strengthen the ability of the individual to harmonize the codes or develop alternative solutions to conflicts. Code complexity is magnified by the need to inspire codes that are consistent across subordinates.

The term *responsibility* is a measure of an executive's ability to handle code complexity, which is achieved by analyzing the purpose of codes to resolve inconsistencies among them. The ability to handle lower-level positions in the organization is an indicator of the ability to move up to higher levels with more complex codes. An executive must be able to inspire or create moral codes for others, as this is the highest work of the executive; "the creative function as a whole is the essence of leadership" (p. 281) and requires honesty, sincerity, and conviction. Technologies, systems, and resources are not sufficient—without executive responsibility, results will be diminished. Responsibility allows executives to "bind the wills of men to the accomplishment of purposes beyond their immediate ends, beyond their times" (p. 283).

Barnard's general conclusions include the following:

- **Cooperation.** Cooperation is the synthesis of social factors with physical and biological factors. Cooperative systems have been disturbed by "false ideologies" reinforcing personal biases. More cooperation implies increased moral complexity.
- **Structure.** The structure of the organization matters. All capital is part of the physical environment. All formal organization consists of units, and the properties of unit organizations are determined by social, physical, and biological factors. Organizations themselves form the structure of society. Informal organizations are essential to the vitality of formal organizations; they are mutually dependent.
- **Executive errors.** There are four principal errors: oversimplifying the economy of organization life, disregarding informal organization,

inappropriate focusing on objective over subjective aspects of authority, and confusing morality with responsibility.

- **Decision-making.** Decision is the essential process of adaption. Decision error can be large due to imprecise perception. Cooperative systems contain physical, personal, and social factors; differing versions of how these factors are related to each other (what Barnard refers to as "economies") are intuitively utilized by executives as they make decisions in different specific situations.

- **Strategy.** The strategic factor in cooperation is leadership. The strategic factor in leadership is more creativeness (which depends on technical ability). The strategic factor in social integration is the development and selection of leaders.

Barnard ends by describing the struggle he sees between the political views of extreme individualism (which he sees as a narcissistic barrier to necessary cooperation) and those of extreme cooperation (with its stifling dogmatism). "This study had at its heart this deep paradox and conflict of feelings in the lives of men. Free and unfree, controlling and controlled" (p. 296).

Discussion and Implications

 Many people recoil from Machiavelli's blunt descriptions of how leaders can get things done, with no regard to the morality of the means (e.g., discussing when cruelty is most useful in achieving an objective). A literal reading of his work is indeed offensive, but a more generous interpretation is that Machiavelli was a realist writing a treatise on the psychology of followers. By describing, in pragmatic and candid terms, exactly how leaders seek to manipulate followers to achieve their own ends, he instructs those followers on how to resist the fear that makes them easier to control. His work also encourages people not to be surprised when their leaders' primary goal appears to be the accumulation of power.

Much of Machiavelli's description of human nature has direct analogies to the corporate world, which is why he is still read by both academics and businesspeople. With very little translation, we have transferred the above discussion into advice for corporate leaders shown in Table 3-1.

Table 3-1: Machiavelli's Advice for Readers in the 21st Century

Machiavelli's language	Advice for corporate leaders
Those used to their rule are less troublesome subjects.	The increased mobility of modern workers creates less tenure of the workforce, and makes leading more of a challenge for today's executives.

Machiavelli's language	Advice for corporate leaders
On acquiring a new state, maintain the culture and live among the subjects.	When acquiring a company, maintain those elements of culture that provide identity to the target employees, and immerse yourself in their culture and business as much as possible to create a sense of shared community.
The circumstances of the state dictate the ease of control.	Contingency theory emphasizes the importance of adapting your leadership style to your current context.
Those accustomed to freedom expect it.	Empowered employees will seek to remain empowered.
Cruelty is well-used when performed all at once rather than increased over time.	If layoffs are necessary, it is better to have one significant round early on and then move on, rather than introduce successive iterations of layoffs.
A prince should always arm rather than disarm his subjects.	Empower employees and drive decision-making down to the field manager with the most data in a given situation.
Princes should court goodwill in good times.	Senior management that treats its employees well in profitable periods can ask for more during downturns.
Do not make common cause with one more powerful than yourself.	Be wary of joint ventures with larger companies— once the joint battle is won, will your larger partner then turn against you?
One's subordinates create the initial impression of the leader.	Nothing communicates your values to your employees more clearly than the choice of who you hire, promote, and fire.
It is important to allow some trusted individuals full liberty to speak the truth, but only when asked.	You must have selected people who will challenge your views and keep you from becoming unaligned with reality. However, you must choose when and from whom to get your reality checks.
Spend good times preparing for inevitable adversity.	Be aware of threats to your competitive position. Build relationships with employees and partners when you have the time to invest in those relationships, and it will pay off when the inevitable crisis comes.
Fortune favors the impetuous more than it does the cautious.	Action, even if not consistently optimal, tends to be a more profitable approach than caution.

Note. Authors' table.

Finally, Machiavelli's emphasis on attracting loyalty suggests he might even favor the liberal use of spreading the wealth, perhaps in the form of stock options.

Eric's experience in Silicon Valley corroborates the value of several of these prescriptions. For example, mobile employees who have choices regarding where they work can be more challenging to lead and retain. We have found that employees at technology firms in the western United States are noticeably more willing to challenge directives from their bosses than are those on the east coast, and we also observe shorter average tenures within a given company. In addition, many tech firms drive more decisions down to the employee level (following the maxim of telling employees what needs to happen rather than how to go about it). Layoffs tend to be done in single rounds, and employee loyalty is courted with stock options.

Chester Barnard was not an academic, and generated his theories based on years of personal experience in managing organizations. He wrote this original work in 1938, and thirty years later Kenneth Andrews described the book in its preface as "the most thought-provoking book on organization and management ever written by a practicing executive" (p. xxi). In the forty years since Andrews's statement, Barnard's influence has waned. As one observer put it, "Barnard partly owes this undeserved obscurity to his labored and lugubrious style: he is extremely difficult to read" (Chandran 1998, p. 2).

Despite his less accessible writing style, Barnard's ideas are still relevant to today's corporate leaders. Barnard was one of the first to articulate the concept of organizational purpose, and he assigned defining the purpose of the organization as an executive's foremost responsibility. Unlike Machiavelli, Barnard repeatedly stressed the moral aspects of leadership. For example, he emphasized that the primary contribution required of an executive is loyalty— only by embodying loyalty can the executive convince employees to subordinate their own narrow interests to that of the larger organization. This principled approach necessitates treating employees as subjects to be satisfied rather than simply manipulated.

It is an understatement to say that Barnard's exhortation for employee empowerment was ahead of its time. He also is unique in his argument that a key to rising through the executive ranks is the ability to reconcile competing "codes." For example, when profit clashes with another objective (e.g., treating employees or suppliers fairly), the executive must determine which principle will dominate, or better still, determine how to meet both sets of objectives simultaneously.

2. What Leaders Actually Do

Several academic authors perform the useful service of observing leaders and describing how they actually behave. Mintzberg (1997), Bennis (1989), and Kotter (1990) offer such empirical analysis of leader behavior, rather than developing theories about how leaders should behave (or even trusting that leaders will always accurately remember and report how they spend their time).

HENRY MINTZBERG
"The Manager's Job: Folklore and Fact" (1975), in R. Vecchio (editor), *On Leadership* (2007).

Thesis: Managers do not engage in systematically planning or organizing their activities. In fact, they tend to take on too many projects, encourage interruption and abrupt changes in activity, and respond quickly to any stimulus. They also seek the tangible while avoiding abstract thinking, and make decisions gradually in small increments.

Mintzberg assumes the role of empiricist in analyzing leadership. He observed leaders (5 executives, 56 foremen, and 160 managers) throughout typical days and recorded what he saw. With his analysis, he punctures much of the myth—and academic literature—around leadership. First, he identifies several myths about managerial work (Table 3-2).

Mintzberg then returns to a basic description of how a manager works. The position and its status represent formal authority and lead to interpersonal relations, which then leads to access to information. CEOs hold a number of roles in this chain:

- **Figurehead.** In terms of interpersonal roles, CEOs spend significant time in their role as figurehead: they spend 12% of their time on ceremonial tasks, and 17% of their mail is related to status.
- **Leader and liaison.** They also spend time in their traditional role as leader and their role as liaison in making contacts outside the vertical chain of command.
- **Communication center.** As part of their informational role, a CEO emerges as the nerve center of the organization by virtue of interpersonal contacts. They spend 40% of contact time on information transmission, and 70% of their incoming mail is purely informational.

It appears that communication is the primary element of their work.

Table 3-2: Mintzberg's Folklore Versus Fact for Managers

Folklore	Fact
The manager is a reflective, systematic planner.	Managers work at an unrelenting pace. Their actions are brief, varied, and discontinuous. Of the observed executive activities, 50% lasted less than nine minutes, fewer than 10% exceeded an hour. Managers worked for a half-hour without interruption once every two days.
The effective manager does not have regular duties.	Managerial work involves many regular duties, including participating in ritual and ceremony, negotiating, and processing soft information about the environment.
The senior manager solicits aggregated information via formal systems.	Managers strongly prefer verbal media (e.g., phone calls, meetings) over documents and reports. The observed executives spent 78% of their time in verbal communication.
Management is a science or profession.	The manager's program—to schedule time, process information, make decisions—remains locked deep inside her brain. Observers use words like *judgment* or *intuition* to hide ignorance.

Note. Authors' table; data from Mintzberg (1975).

The CEO also serves several decisional roles that are not easily separable. The CEO is an *entrepreneur* who adapts the unit to changing environmental conditions, a *disturbance handler* who spends time involuntarily responding to pressures, a *resource-allocator* deciding who will receive specific resources, and a *negotiator*.

Managers tend to spend more time in the roles they are most comfortable with. Unfortunately, the difficulty in fully sharing information between individuals makes it very difficult to share a managerial position among more than one person.

This description of how managers allocate their work time should be more useful than any prescription derived from it, because managers' effectiveness is impacted by their insight into their own work. Each manager is challenged to find systematic ways to share privileged information, and

> to deal consciously with the pressures of superficiality by giving serious attention to the issues that require it, by stepping back in order to see a broad picture, and by making use of analytical inputs....The manager is challenged to gain control of his or her own time by turning obligations into advantages and by turning those things he or she wishes to do into obligations. (pp. 50–51)

Management schools need to "get serious" by placing as much importance on skill training as on cognitive learning. Skill training requires practice and feedback, like swimming or any other pursuit. For researchers, Mitzberg advises, it is time to strip away the folklore about managerial work and study it realistically so that we can begin the difficult task of making significant improvements in its performance. (p. 52)

WARREN BENNIS,
Why Leaders Can't Lead (1989).

Thesis: Routine work will drive out all time for strategic thinking, unless leaders engage in a conscious and disciplined effort to (a) empower employees to make decisions, and (b) create time for the leader to attend to the big picture.

Bennis describes a single year in a leadership job, summarizing the acting presidency of Dr. Charles Johnson at University of Oregon. In one year, Dr. Johnson faced several tangential issues that consumed him, including an outcry about the use of obscenities in the student newspaper, a confrontation between two African-American basketball players who refused to cut their Afros and their first-year coach who had ordered it, and a dispute about the use of California grapes in the dining hall.

Using this business case as a touchstone, Bennis identifies two basic truisms about leadership:

- **Routine work drives out nonroutine work and smothers all creative planning.** In Dr. Johnson's case, there were letters in his in-basket demanding responses to the trivial. His staff did not want to take responsibility, so they pushed every decision to the top. Finally, 20% of the year was absorbed by a single issue at the university hospital (Pentagon funding of a study measuring the impact of radiation on cancer patients).

- **Regardless what plans are made, the unexpected or trivial will disturb and disrupt them.** The media make a university into a goldfish bowl, focusing on the lurid or superficial. Media attention on Pentagon funding drew disproportionate interest in a single academic study. A dean who wanted to make a point about equality for women started bringing in his 10-week-old son each day, prompting a flood of letters demanding his dismissal for child abuse.

Given these truisms, Bennis advises the following:

- It is necessary to lead, not manage. Managers do things right, but leaders are people who do the right thing. Don't seek to excel at routine tasks; rather, question whether the routine should be done at all.
- Create time to think about strategy—a president should be a conceptualist.
- Create clear-cut and measurable goals.

He contends that U.S. organizations are both underled and overmanaged.

Bennis studied 60 corporate leaders, most of whom were white males and all of whom remained married to their first spouse. He found four competencies in every member of his group:

- **Management of attention.** One is effective when one knows what one wants.
- **Management of meaning.** Leaders must communicate their vision.
- **Management of trust.** The main determinant of trust is constancy.
- **Management of self.** Know your skills and deploy them effectively.

Bennis concludes that effective leadership is reflected in empowerment. Empowering employees creates an environment in which people feel significant, learning and competence matter, people are part of a community, and work is exciting.

JOHN KOTTER
"What Leaders Really Do" (1990), in R. Vecchio (editor), *On Leadership* (2007).

Thesis: Leadership and management are two distinctive and complementary systems of action. Management is about coping with complexity, while leadership is about coping with change.

The difference between management and leadership is that *management* is about coping with complexity. Management develops the capacity to achieve its plan by controlling and problem solving, including establishing a formal organizational structure and staffing the organization. Planning and budgeting are tools to address complexity.

Leadership is about coping with change: setting a direction to lead the organization to constructive change, and developing a vision of the future along with strategies. Leaders align people by communicating the new direction to those who can create the needed coalitions of employees who understand the vision and are committed to achieving it. Such achievement requires motivation and inspiration. The key to setting such direction is to maintain strong networks of informal relationships. Kotter echoes Bennis' contention that "most U.S. corporations today are over-managed and under-led" (p. 23).

Setting a direction is an activity distinct from planning or budgeting. Planning is a management process, but setting a direction is more inductive. It is crucial to determine how a vision serves important constituencies and how readily it can be translated into a realistic competitive strategy. A frequent mistake is to embrace long-term planning as some kind of panacea for lack of direction and inability to adapt—this can never work. In addition, "in a company without direction, even short-term planning can become a black hole. A competent planning process serves as a useful reality check on direction-setting activities" (p. 28).

Similarly, *aligning people* is a different activity than simply staffing. Interdependence is a central feature of modern organizations, and linkages pose a challenge when an organization attempts to change. Rather than organizing people, executives need to align them. Alignment is more of a communication challenge than it is a design problem. Executives need to empower people with a clear sense of direction that keeps everyone aiming at the same target.

Managers may exert control over people in order to solve problems. The purpose of systems and structure that managers create is to help normal people complete routine jobs successfully day after day.

Leaders, on the other hand, motivate people. Motivation and inspiration energize people by satisfying the human needs for achievement, a sense of belonging, recognition, self-esteem, a feeling of control over one's life, and the ability to live up to one's ideals. Leaders articulate vision in a manner that stresses the audience's values, and involve people in deciding how to achieve the vision. As achieving a vision requires a burst of energy, leaders provide coaching and help employees grow. They recognize and reward success. Through this process, work becomes intrinsically motivating.

In order to create a culture of leadership, it is necessary to recruit people with leadership potential. As part of managing the career patterns of potential leaders, executives should try to lead, take risk, and learn from both triumphs and failures. They should also teach people about both the difficulty of leadership and its potential for producing change, and create challenging opportunities for young employees. Decentralization is often key to making this happen. Strong networks of informal relationships help coordinate leadership activity in the same way that formal structure coordinates management activity. Finally, it is critical to recognize and reward people who successfully develop leaders.

Discussion and Implications

 Many executives may relate to Mintzberg's descriptions of managers who are interrupted constantly and spend the bulk of their time simply passing information back and forth. This feels particularly accurate now that email has amplified the amount of information flowing to and from each manager (especially executive layers of management).

There are several reasons why, as Mitzberg found, executives simply do not take the time to engage in abstract thinking. First, executive schedules do not readily permit the uninterrupted flow of time required for conceptual thinking, and it takes a committed effort to arrange a schedule differently. Second, handling urgent crises is actually easier than engaging in long-term planning around important issues. Crisis management brings people together and tends to be both seductive and energizing.

However, executives can impose control over these dynamics. The first step to avoiding these traps is to recognize them and know that many others are falling into the same trap. As a leader, you must allocate your time consciously and limit the percentage of time spent reacting to unplanned events.

Mintzberg has been criticized for making stereotypes based on a small, homogenous sample of executives, but we give him credit for basing his findings on observed day-to-day behavior rather than on a larger-than-life abstraction of what leaders must be doing. More recently, a team of scholars analyzed the daily schedules of CEOs in another executive time-use project (Bandiera, Prat, Sadun, and Wulf 2012). The authors found that executives averaged 55-hour workweeks, with 18 hours in meetings, 3 spent on calls, and 5 in business meals. The number of direct reports correlated with more and longer internal meetings, and those CEOs with more direct reports had less unplanned time. However, CEOs with CFOs or COOs spent 5.5 hours *less* in meetings than those without those specific subordinates. The researchers found that CEOs' assessment of how they spend their time differs significantly from their actual records.

Bennis describes how single issues can consume a disproportionate share of an executive's time and energy. What prepared an academic, who had moved up from professor to department chair to Dean and then President, to face a campus outraged over whether African-American basketball players should be expected to follow the hair-length rules established by their new white coach?

A more recent example is the Hewlett-Packard pretexting scandal, in which the chairwoman of the board directed the general counsel to determine the source of an information leak from the board regarding the company's long-term strategy. Media reports (beginning with an article by David Kaplan in *Newsweek* on September 5, 2006) revealed that the internal lawyer hired security experts who then recruited private investigators to obtain board directors' telephone records under false pretenses. The resulting furor sparked a media circus, multiple resignations (of a board member, the general counsel, and the chairwoman of the board), congressional hearings, and HP's hiring of a public relations firm.

In both of these examples, one discrete action by a few people consumed the leadership of an organization. The rub for leaders is that, even if they navigate such crises successfully, the time it requires to do so comes at the expense of their ability to get other necessary work done. One of Bennis's key points is that crises like this may be inevitable in a large organization, and that they will crowd out long-term planning. Another of his points is that too many issues are pushed to the most senior person to decide, so that leaders can become hostage to their subordinates' failure to make decisions.

In this context, it becomes challenging but vital for leaders to carve out time to think about strategy so that they can lead, instead of managing each day's small and large unanticipated developments. With this time, they can create measurable goals for each part of the organization (which can be worked on when other parts are distracted). Bennis's study reveals that leaders who are able to create the time to think about long-term issues have in common the ability to manage their attention, communicate their vision, engender trust by exhibiting constancy, and empower their employees.

Within this discussion, Kotter makes an important distinction between executive activities. When a corporate controller implements the systems and hires the accountants needed to provide detailed financial reporting to the public and the SEC, she is managing a complicated undertaking—this is management in the sense of coping with complexity. When the CEO of the same organization identifies that the competitive landscape has shifted, and that the company should pursue a different set of target markets than before, this is leadership in the sense of coping with change.

Management is a necessary skill for organizational success. One of Kotter's main points, however, is that most organizations have a sufficient number of employees skilled at management, and fewer who are able to learn from their wins and losses as well as align employees so they are aiming at a common target.

There are evident similarities between Kotter and Barnard highlighting the importance of leaders in motivating and inspiring their employees to achieve a vision, and recognizing the importance of informal networks in getting that work done. Kotter also offers a useful working definition of management and leadership. In modern organizations, executives must actively address both complexity and change.

It is atypical for a single person to excel at coping with both complexity and change; Kotterman (2006) notes that a frequent tendency is to set aside leadership skills in favor of managing the workplace—after all, a firm has to get through this week before it identifies its vision. Kotter's work is important, though it does not yet provide operational detail such as the best ratio of leaders and managers. Kotterman notes that senior managers often believe they are leading when they are managing, and adds that

> since management and leadership are so misunderstood, most companies believe they need many leaders when in fact what they really need is a few great leaders and many first-class managers. (p. 15)

When companies do not allow newly trained leaders to lead, rather than manage, the would-be leaders often end up frustrated, apathetic, and unhappy. We see this is as a very real downside for companies that pride themselves on hiring "bench strength." If you insist on hiring leaders but only have management work for them to do, you may be setting up conditions for discontent. This is a cautionary note for companies or academic institutions that take advantage of their prestige to hire people in at a lower level than they could obtain elsewhere (e.g., Cisco in 1999, Google in 2005, Facebook in 2012, Harvard in all periods).

While some other authors assert that management and leadership are not mutually exclusive (e.g., Yukl 1989 uses the term *managerial leadership*), Abraham Zaleznik (1992) agrees with Kotter that the two are distinct but complementary. Zaleznik's thesis is that leadership is a creative endeavor that has more in common with artistry than management. He contrasts the two functions in a number of dimensions: personality (rational control versus creativity), attitudes toward goals (impersonal or passive versus active), conceptions of work (as an enabling and mediating process versus a higher-risk pursuit), relations with others (working with others versus working with ideas, meaning, and emotion), senses of self (once-born versus continuous struggle to attain sense of order), developing others, and comfort with having one's ideas challenged.

Although Zaleznik supports his ideas more with anecdotes than data, his approach is similar in spirit to Kotter's. He concludes that talented leaders grasp the significance of anomalies. Further, managers and leaders have an important difference in their conception of chaos and order.

> Leaders tolerate chaos and lack of structure and are thus prepared to keep answers in suspense, avoiding premature closure on important issues. Managers seek order and control and are almost compulsively addicted to disposing of problems even before they understand their potential significance. In my experience, seldom do the uncertainties of potential chaos cause problems. Instead, it is the instinctive move to impose order on potential chaos that makes trouble for organizations. (p. 131)

Finally, creativity and imagination are key. Business schools would be better served to conduct experiments in creativity and imagination than to pursue the logics of strategy.

This segment of the literature raises the question: do managers in many organizations un-train people with leadership qualities by punishing them for taking risks? We think they do.

3. LEADERSHIP AND ORGANIZATIONAL CULTURE

In this section, we examine the critical intersection between leadership and corporate culture. This area was developed in large part by Edgar Schein, who earned his doctorate in psychology at Harvard in 1952 and spent much of his career at the MIT Sloan School of Management.

EDGAR SCHEIN
Organizational Culture and Leadership (2010), Chapters 12–21.

Thesis: The first task of a leader is to create and sustain the organization's culture. *Culture* is the deeper level of assumptions shared by members of the organization, and is critical to its success.

Schein begins the later chapters of his book by discussing how culture emerges in new groups. Norms of behavior evolve through what members do (or do not do) when critical incidents occur. Key assumptions for the purposes of culture include those that evolve about authority (i.e., who influences group behavior) and intimacy (e.g., permission level to attack opposing ideas, level of boundaries around personal issues). Norms that work for the organization then become cultural assumptions.

He then discusses how leaders create organizational cultures, identifying three sources:

- the beliefs, values, and assumptions of the founders of the organization;
- the learning experiences of the group's members as the organization evolves; and
- new beliefs, values, and assumptions brought into the organization by incoming members and leaders.

Founders have the most important impact on the cultural beginnings because they choose the initial mission and environmental context as well as the group members. Founders typically have a major impact on how the group defines itself, and they also do not mind imposing their views on employees and partners.

As the company progresses, a common history evolves among its members. A culture may not survive if the main culture-carriers depart and if the remaining members are in conflict. If the original founders do not have solutions to the problems critical to the group's success, other strong members will emerge as leaders within the organization.

Next, Schein addresses how leaders transmit culture. After founders begin the formation of culture by imposing their own assumptions on a new group, new members learn this culture through socialization. Founders communicate assumptions and values in both deliberate and unintended ways; in some cases, founders may send contradictory messages. Often the conflicting messaging is tolerated because of the founders' power, though in some cases the "idiosyncratic" founder is ousted from the organization (e.g., Steve Jobs at Apple in 1985).

Cultural-embedding mechanisms can be broken into primary and secondary mechanisms. Primary mechanisms create culture, while secondary mechanisms reinforce culture. Primary mechanisms include the following:

- **The focus of leader attention, measurement, and control.** What leaders ask questions about sends a clear message about their priorities. Emotional reactions from the leader are a good indicator that an important assumption is being violated. What a leader does not react to sends an equally clear message (e.g., if cost overruns are ignored in favor of product quality). What leaders consistently pay attention to communicates most clearly their own assumptions and priorities.

- **Leader-reactions to critical incidents and crises.** The way a leader deals with crisis reveals underlying assumptions and creates new norms. Heightened emotional involvement during crisis is a powerful motivator of new learning to reduce anxiety.

- **Observed criteria used by leaders to allocate resources.** How budgets are created sends messages to the team regarding what is valued.

- **Deliberate role modeling.** The leaders' visible behavior best communicates values. Informal messages (e.g., modeling) are more powerful than formal messages because day-to-day actions best reveal one's true assumptions.

- **Observed criteria for allocating rewards.** Constituents learn what the leader values through their experience with promotions and appraisals.

- **Observed criteria for recruitment, promotion, and excommunication.** Nothing speaks louder than who is hired, promoted, and fired. Leaders often choose members who resemble themselves, and are often unconscious of their selection criteria.

Secondary mechanisms are cultural reinforcers rather than creators, particularly in younger organizations, and they only work if they are consistent with the primary mechanisms already in effect. In more mature groups, these can become primary mechanisms that constrain future leaders. Secondary mechanisms include the following:

- **Organizational design and structure.** The organization's primary task is to determine how to structure itself in order to survive the external environment. Organizational design is often initially more a function of the founder's background than any analysis.

- **Organizational systems and procedures.** Daily-to-annual cycles of routines, procedures, and reports are a visible part of organizational life. Though some label these routines as bureaucracy, they provide predictability and reinforce the message of what the leader cares about.

- **Rites and rituals of the organization.** Ritualizing certain behaviors becomes a powerful reinforcer of those behaviors.

- **Design of physical space, facades, and buildings.** Visible features convey a great deal; for example, open-office layouts can convey the value of open communication.

- **Stories about important events and people.** Stories are an unreliable source of values because the message becomes distilled and sometimes ambiguous over time.

- **Formal statements of organizational philosophy, creeds, and charters.** Formal statements also emphasize special things meriting attention within the organization.

Regarding these means of culture-reinforcement, Schein concludes: "When a manager decides to change the assumptions of a work group by using all of these mechanisms, that manager is becoming a leader" (p. 258).

In an organization's early stages, its distinctive competencies tend to be biased toward business functions that reflect the background of the founders. As an organization progresses toward mid-life, the founder becomes less dominant. During this transition, conflicts over culture become surrogates for disagreements about the founder's personality. Change in attitudes and culture comes as subgroups develop their own specific subcultures, and managers are promoted from some of these selected subcultures whose members have assumptions that are better adapted to new external realities. Incremental changes happen through general evolution (i.e., differentiation) and through specific evolution whereby particular parts of the organization adapt to their specific environments. Leadership can influence the nature of this differentiation, which can include: functional or occupational differentiation, geographical differentiation, differentiation by product or market or technology, divisionalization, or differentiation by hierarchical level.

The evolution of culture can be assisted by planned change, or by challenging existing attitudes and using technology (e.g., automation, a total quality program) to develop new attitudes. Some companies use an education intervention (like Peter Senge's 1990 learning organization model) to deliberately build a new set of shared assumptions. Shared assumptions can be changed by changing the composition of dominant groups, as when the board brings in a new CEO from outside the company. This change in leadership may trigger a conflict between the old and new assumptions. If the new leader fails (i.e., improvement does not occur, or the leader does not get credit for improvements that occur, or the new assumptions threaten too much of the core culture), they will be forced out. If the new assumptions result in renewed profitability, however, the new leader is likely to survive.

As the organization becomes fully mature, continued success builds a strong culture, though organizations may also develop espoused values out of sync from the actual assumptions by which they operate. At the same time, growth typically slows as products become obsolete and markets saturated. Assumptions may be unfrozen by scandal and other evidence that operating assumptions are now out of sync with the environment. Change can be implemented through turnarounds, coercive persuasion, or by destruction (merger or bankruptcy) and rebirth.

In his next chapter, Schein discusses how to change culture when the normal evolutionary processes are not working or are too slow, and provides a general model of managed change. He identifies three stages of change.

Unfreezing the Current Set of Assumptions, Creating the Motivation to Change
Disequilibrium is required in this stage where disconforming data causes discomfort. Survival anxiety or guilt is created (e.g., without change, something bad will happen). Finally, psychological safety is created to overcome learning anxiety.

- Learners may recognize the need to learn new ways of thinking, but this creates stress for a variety of valid reasons (e.g., loss of power, fear of incompetence, loss of personal identity, loss of group membership). These fears produce resistance to change, and it is important to recognize that this resistance is not irrational.
- Learners need to find safety in seeing the solution without loss of identity. Visionary leaders tell the group it is okay to change.
- To make this stage work, it is key that survival anxiety must exceed learning anxiety, and that learning anxiety must be reduced. That is, learners need to be more nervous about survival than about change, but not too nervous to function.
- To reduce learning anxiety, the leader must offer a compelling positive vision, formal training, involvement of the learner, informal team training, practice fields, positive role models, support groups, and structures consistent with the new way of thinking.

*Cognitive Restructuring, the Learning of New Concepts, New Meanings for Old
Concepts, and New Standards for Judgment*
This stage involves new learning through trial and error or through the
adaptation of role models. The work of this stage requires the redefinition of
assumptions.

*Refreezing Assumptions and Internalizing New Concepts, Meanings, and
Standards*
In this stage, new behavior and a new set of cognitions should be reinforced.
Data must be confirmed by external stakeholders and internal sources; as
confirming data is received and digested, assumptions are stabilized.

Schein advises those implementing deliberate culture change to follow these
additional general principles:
- Identify the change goal in terms of the problem being fixed, not as "culture
  change."
- Old cultural elements can be destroyed by eliminating the carriers, but new
  elements can only be learned if the new behavior leads to success.
- Culture change is always transformative, requiring a period of unlearning
  that is psychologically painful.

He then describes a ten-step group interview process to give leaders a rapid
way of deciphering the elements of existing culture so they can assess its
relevance to their change program. In the following chapter, he provides
illustrations of the role of culture in organizational change processes.

The next chapter expands on the learning of culture, and the contradiction
of stability and change. The only thing one can know about the future is that it
will be different—leaders must become perpetual learners. Schein identifies the
following core characteristics of a learning culture:
- **Proactivity.** Active problem-solving leads to learning.
- **Commitment to learning to learn.** This characteristic requires getting
  feedback and taking the time to analyze its implications.
- **Positive assumptions about human nature (Theory Y[2]).** Assumptions
  about people become self-fulfilling. Leaders should have faith in people, and
  assume them to be basically good.
- **Belief that the environment can be managed.** Problems are manageable
  and leaders have control.

---

[2] Douglas MacGregor (1960) introduced the term *Theory X* to refer to traditional theories
that assume employees tend to work as little as possible, and so they must be supervised. He
proposed Theory Y as an alternative theory assuming that employees possess ambition, self-
motivation, and self-control.

- **Commitment to truth through pragmatism and inquiry.** Learning cultures have a positive orientation toward the future.
- **Commitment to full and open task-relevant communication.** Learning requires feedback regarding what is and is not working.
- **Commitment to cultural diversity.** The more turbulent the environment, the more likely that an organization with diverse cultural resources will cope with unpredicted events.
- **Commitment to systemic thinking.** Complexity and interdependent connections increase the value of thinking systemically. Most events have multiple causes.
- Belief that cultural analysis is a valid set of lenses for understanding and improving the world.

Leaders should remember that the right culture is contextual: different stages of organizational development require different kinds of culture management, and different strategic issues require focus on different dimensions of the group's culture. When creating culture in a new organization, leaders must have self-insight and recognize their own role in embedding both conscious assumptions and their own inner conflicts into the culture. In organizations or groups at the midlife stage, subgroups develop with their own subcultures, creating the need for integration. Leaders must deal with succession issues, both in terms of the person and in terms of the organizational direction. In mature organizations, the leader must determine how to change the culture when it is no longer adaptive.

Understanding culture is particularly essential in specific strategic situations. When evaluating and integrating mergers and acquisitions, leaders must understand both cultures and convince all involved to take cultural issues seriously. A leader must be able to step back and rise above their own culture. In joint ventures, leaders must surmount their own organizational culture, and typically also their own ethnic and national culture.

There are several implications for the selection and development of leaders. In particular, Schein identifies the following elements that will stimulate cultural learning:

- **Perception and insight.** The learning leader must be able to perceive the problem as well as have insight into the culture and its dysfunctional elements. This element requires leaders to acknowledge their own limitations and seek help.
- **Motivation.** Learning leaders require the motivation and skill to intervene in their own cultural process. They must be willing to disconfirm and unfreeze their own organization.

- **Emotional strength.** Unfreezing an organization requires a leader to create psychological safety, requiring that leader to absorb much of the associated anxiety.

- **Ability to change the cultural assumptions.** Leaders need the ability to induce cognitive redefinition by articulating and selling new values and concepts.

- **Ability to create involvement and participation.** The leader must be able not only to lead but also to listen and involve the group in finding its own insights into cultural dilemmas. The leader needs to manage relationships across both macrocultural boundaries and hierarchical and occupational boundaries.

Schein's final chapter explores how cultural insight can be achieved in today's multicultural settings that cross national and occupational macrocultures. Multicultural projects have been framed as collaborations in recent literature, as they require the group to discover the norms and underlying assumptions dealing with authority and intimacy among the participants involved, usually when the social order makes open discussion of these norms taboo. However, it is usually too time-consuming to try to educate participants about the norms of each culture involved.

A better approach is to focus on cultural capacities and learning skills, which are described by the term *cultural intelligence*. Trying to learn about each macroculture is less adaptive than developing the skills to quickly acquire whatever knowledge is needed in a particular situation. Cultural intelligence requires actual knowledge of some of the essentials of the other cultures, sensitivity or mindfulness about culture, motivation to learn about cultures, and the behavioral skills and flexibility to learn new ways of doing things.

Schein proposes a process to assist in a mutual search for common ground. Groups may develop a "cultural island," which is a situation in which the rules of having to maintain face are temporarily suspended to allow exploration of self-concepts, particularly around authority and intimacy. Focused dialogue can identify points of disagreement that reveal differences in cultural assumptions. Process breakdowns have often been linked to differences in how cultures communicate problems upward to supervisors; one prominent example is how culture influences the willingness of a co-pilot to tell his pilot that the planned course of action may be unsafe.

Discussion and Implications

 Edgar Schein's work on culture is not simply a single piece of research but rather a career, captured in this book. The earlier part of his book defines culture, shows its importance, and specifically describes how to identify a culture. A working definition of *culture* is "what goes without saying" in an organization—this is the corporation's personality.

Culture is very different across companies and can be difficult for even a long-time employee to verbalize, but when evaluating a company it is critical to ask, "What are the unspoken assumptions here?" We would venture that identifying the unspoken assumptions which constitute culture is the single most imperative task a prospective acquirer undertakes in evaluating a target company, and also the most important task an individual has when interviewing with a prospective employer.

The focus in this section has been on the second half of Schein's book, describing the role of leaders in creating organizational culture. It is nearly impossible to doubt that the unique cultures at well-known companies were established by their founders. Taking just the tech sector as an example, consider Steve Jobs at Apple, Bill Gates at Microsoft, Larry Ellison at Oracle, Larry Page and Sergey Brin at Google, and Mark Zuckerberg at Facebook. When Steve Jobs famously asked job candidates from IBM and other leading companies to describe how they lost their virginity, or if they had tried LSD, he was making a clear statement about what kind of culture he did not want to establish.

Leaders communicate which employees are valued by how they spend their time. Many technology companies are engineering-centric, consumer goods companies are often marketing-centric, and other companies (e.g., GM in the 1980s and 1990s) are considered finance-centric. This choice of focus influences the assumptions behind employee interactions and how decisions are made.

Schein's description of building a learning culture borrows from Peter Senge's own work on the same topic (see Senge 1990, 2006); both focus on the role of the leader as designer of the organizational personality. Senge decries social institutions that are designed more toward controlling than toward learning. Through their focus on performing for someone else's approval in the context of an annual performance review, he notes, corporations create the very conditions that guarantee mediocre performance. Senge exhorts organizations to move past adaptive learning geared toward coping, in favor of generative learning oriented toward creating. He echoes Schein's emphasis on systems thinking and agrees that superior performance ultimately requires superior generative learning. A leader in a learning organization promotes such learning as designer, teacher, and steward.

4. CONSTRUCTIVE AND DESTRUCTIVE LEADERSHIP

In this section, we turn to constructive and destructive elements of how leaders utilize their teams to reach their intended goals. Kets de Vries (1989) investigates the dark side of leadership, and Lipman-Blumen (1996) breaks effective leadership into different styles that may be suited toward various leadership situations.

MANFRED KETS DE VRIES
"Leaders Who Self-Destruct: The Causes and Cures" (1989), in R. Vecchio (editor), *Leadership* (2007).

Thesis: Leadership in an organization is isolating, employees tend to have overly high expectations of their leaders, and some leaders create their own failure from guilt or fear.

In this article, Kets de Vries discusses the factors behind destructive leaders. He discusses how leaders are typically isolated from reality, giving truth to the term *loneliness of command*. Leaders have the same normal dependency needs as anyone else (e.g., for contact, support, and reassurance), but fewer avenues to meet those needs. Leaders have less support because CEOs have to avoid the appearance of having favorites, and subordinates have to avoid the appearance of "kissing up." In addition, employees often look to the leader to be infallible, even on a day-to-day level.

Leaders may even become the embodiment of their employees' ideals; psychologists call this *distortion transference*. All interpersonal exchanges involve both realistic and transference reactions, and leaders are particularly susceptible to this kind of confusion. Transference can take several forms:

- Employees may see the CEO as an authority figure, and raise feelings associated with some other past authority figure. Workers may view their leaders as having a parental type of omniscience (which in turn can inflate the leaders' own self-esteem).

- During times of change people are even more prone to look to leaders for guidance, and may go out of their way to please the leader. This makes it hard for a CEO to avoid "yes" people, and further separates even a diligent leader from reality. It also enables the leader to deny culpability for problems since their sounding board is telling them everything is okay.

Some leaders exhibit a fear of success. Upon reaching the pinnacle position they have worked to achieve, they question whether their climb was truly deserved. Then they question their abilities to lead, which can trigger a downward spiral.

Kets de Vries advises leaders to be aware of these psychological forces and work to identify early signs of trouble through a regular process of critical self-evaluation. Leaders should encourage candid feedback from outsiders and

board members with a different frame of reference, and participate in training
programs that bring them together with their peers.

JEAN LIPMAN-BLUMEN
The Connective Edge (1996).

Thesis: Organizations today have shorter timeframes for decision-making and
tighter connections, and such organizations require more speed and agility.
Therefore, leaders must adopt a broader set of implementation strategies than
was required in the past. Empirical work on leadership styles can show
individuals how to employ a style appropriate to a particular context; this
research also reveals differences between upper- and mid-level managers, and
between men and women, in terms of how they lead.

In the first part of her book, Lipman-Blumen discusses the
changing dynamics of leadership. There have been three stages in
the evolution of leadership: the physical era, the geopolitical era,
and now the connective era. Everyone today is connected, and
these tighter connections are reinforced by existing technology.

Lipman-Blumen argues that the conditions of leadership have changed: Old
methods no longer function, and now people look more to individual leaders
than to ideologies. There are multiple sources of change: science and
technology, increasing internationalism, diversity, lost faith in ideologies and
institutions, changes in organizational structure, and new social ills (e.g., AIDS,
drugs, crime, urban decay). Leaders today have shorter timeframes, requiring
more speed and agility with fewer second chances.

The desire for leadership comes from the needs of the followers for (a)
effective group action and (b) protection against uncertainty. Workers live with
two contradictions: Most people preach teamwork but idolize individualism,
and one's individual ego is not always compatible with human institutions. The
legacy of these contradictions is an increased ambivalence toward leadership.

In the second part of the book, Lipman-Blumen takes an empirical look at
how leaders actually behave. She has developed a conceptual tool that can
identify different achieving styles, and analyze how individuals use combinations
of these implementation strategies to accomplish their goals.

Most people utilize a narrow range of achieving styles, habitually drawing
on behaviors that have worked before. These styles are learned and reinforced,
which allows leaders to deliberately learn new styles and gain experience at
matching an achieving style to the specific leadership context. Lipman-Blumen's

connective leadership model breaks out into three sets of three achieving styles, as follows.

Direct achieving styles are centered on mastering one's own tasks; these styles focus on the activities that individuals set for themselves. They reflect independence and the ways in which an individual confronts a task directly.

- **Intrinsic.** In this style it is the content or intrinsic nature of the task that excites the individual. It may be the challenge or importance of the goal that motivates the person; Lipman-Blumen gives examples of climbing Mount Everest or starting one's own company. Intrinsic style is employed by those who are guided by a strict internal standard of excellence.
- **Competitive.** This style reflects the competitive individual's desire to outdo others. Proving that one is the best is what matters.
- **Power.** Those who favor this style are motivated by taking charge and coordinating the actions of others.

Relational achieving styles involve accomplishing goals by contributing to the tasks of others. People who prefer relational achieving easily collaborate in group tasks or contribute to other people's goals, relinquishing control over both the means and the ends of accomplishment.

- **Collaborative.** Those using the collaborative style enjoy working with others, sharing in the work and responsibility as well as the glory. They value the bonds of friendship and camaraderie that accompany a shared project.
- **Contributory.** These individuals derive their satisfaction from helping other people complete their own chosen tasks. They contribute to others' accomplishments.
- **Vicarious.** Those implementing this style do not actively participate in the activities of others, but rather encourage or facilitate other peoples' accomplishments. They may be mentors, or cheerleaders. Many parents are familiar with this mindset.

Instrumental achieving styles are geared toward maximizing interactions between participants. People who prefer instrumental achieving treat every situation as an opportunity to further their goals. In organizations, these are people who navigate informal relationships to get things done.

- **Personal.** This style entails using one's self; it can involve calling on one's own intelligence, charm, and attractiveness to attract supporters. Users of this style are often skilled with dramatic gestures and counterintuitive symbols. They are comfortable using negotiation and persuasion to develop a common point of view.
- **Social.** This style focuses less on using one's own charisma and more on using relationships to get things done. The phrase "it's not what you know but who you know" describes this approach well. Social achievers build and

maintain a network of associates who can be called on to address any particular challenge or problem.

- **Entrusting.** People who use this style expect everyone they know to help them achieve what they consider to be their shared goals. Often this expectation is self-fulfilling, as trust can be motivating and confidence-building for the other people expected to pitch in. Lipman-Blumen argues that when others are entrusted with a leader's vision, they become indebted and repay that obligation by fulfilling the leader's expectations.

With today's tighter connections and faster decision times, leaders must adopt a broader set of implementation strategies than was required in the past. Such modern *connective leaders* draw on multiple styles, selecting the appropriate style for a given challenge or context. They also use instrumental styles ethically (what the author terms "denatured Machiavellianism"). Key elements to this ethical approach are maintaining authenticity and harnessing the leader's ego (i.e., the leader understanding herself as a means to a larger end).

In the third part of her book, Lipman-Blumen describes the results of administering her tool to multiple upper- and mid-level male and female managers. She found that upper-level managers tend to use most of the styles; they are high in the intrinsic and direct categories and only slightly lower in the relational category. Mid-level managers have a similar profile, though they are— perhaps surprisingly—less competitive than their upper-level counterparts.

Lipman-Blumen pays special attention to issues of gender in leadership. U.S. leadership images tend to draw on the direct achieving styles, stressing power, self-reliance, competition, and a belief in one's own abilities. These traditional characteristics of leadership also happen to mirror the traditional U.S. notion of masculinity.

She asserts that a more interdependent and diverse world may play well to strengths developed by women in traditional roles within families, and breaks apart her data for specific gender differences, as follows. The *direct achieving styles* reflect self-reliance, competition, and power:

- **Women surpass men in task orientation.** Both male and female managers favor the intrinsic style, but women do so more. It ranks first for both genders.
- **Women on average are less competitive than are men.** Women are less driven by competition than men, ranking this style ninth out of nine (compared to sixth to eighth place for men).
- **The power style works for both genders.** Both genders use the power style with equal frequency, ranking second.

With regard to *relational achieving styles*, males invade traditionally female territory:

- **Men gain the collaborative advantage, using status as a shield.** The collaborating style ranks fourth for both genders. Upper level managers use the collaborative style more than do mid-level managers. It may be that their higher formal status allows collaboration without a perception of weakness.

- **Contributory action for the highest levels.** Both genders use this style third, and upper management uses this more than mid-level management. As with collaboration, executives' formal power may allow them to employ this style without being perceived as weak (in fact, they may get credit for not relying on their formal power).

- **The vicarious style is overrun by males.** Males use this style more, particularly those in upper-management. Lipman-Blumen perceives that women work to avoid being perceived as traditional females, whereas men may find it less threatening to support the achievements of others. Male upper managers appear to be integrating the intrinsic and power styles with all three relational styles, but remain wary of personal and social styles.

Instrumental achieving styles are still the road less traveled:

- **Avoiding the personal.** The personal style is the mark of charismatic leaders. Both genders appear to be avoiding this style in the workplace, though, using it seventh of nine styles.

- **Social surprises.** Female managers reject social strategies, ranking it eighth. Lipman-Blumen speculates that perhaps women are again not wanting to act "traditionally female."

- **Women entrust more than men, but reluctantly.** Women do use the entrusting style significantly more than men, but still only sixth out of nine. This could reflect a lack of mentors and the need to make it up the corporate ladder on their own.

She ends with the observation that people's fears set them on a search for leaders. Connective leaders can help people integrate multiple visions, accept ambiguity, assemble coalitions, convey complex meanings, and "move beyond individualism to a politics of commonalities and take on serious societal problems" (p. 344). Employees and constituents should therefore beware of self-serving leaders and instead seek more reluctant leaders in the vein of Mahatma Gandhi or Martin Luther King, neither of whom held an official leadership position but who unambiguously led.

Discussion and Implications

 Kets de Vries recommends many questions for leaders to ask themselves, but also acknowledges that most people have the potential for irrational behavior. For some, the power of leadership may cause even those attempting to be self-critical to fall into the trap of changing fantasy into perceived reality.

We see value in maintaining strong relationships with people outside the organization. Family members (especially spouses) and old friends who have known us since our lowest-status days can be excellent sources of reality check whenever we start believing our own hype. After you accept the promotion and acclaim, it is useful to be reminded that you still need to take the trash to the curb before you get to go to bed. As Montaigne (1580) once said, "no man is a hero to his own valet" (p. 574).

In an earlier article, Kets de Vries and Miller (1985) show that leadership effectiveness and organizational dysfunction can often be explained in terms of the narcissistic disposition of the leader. Self-centered and self-confident people often seek leadership positions and sometimes succeed in getting such roles, and the authors detail three types of narcissistic leader (the reactive, the self-deceptive, and the constructive). They then give suggestions to organizations for dealing with the two negative types (reactive and self-deceptive): distribute power through cross-functional teams or committees, encourage 360-degree performance appraisals, and select strong employees who can cope with such managers.

In a similar vein, Jay Conger (1990) examines strategic visionaries and warns about unsuccessful strategic visions that are inconsistent with constituent needs. Misalignment in vision can take several forms: focusing on the internal needs of the leader rather than the market, misallocating resources, having an unrealistic perception of market or constituent needs, or failing to recognize environmental changes.[3] Many leaders deny flaws in their visions, and sometimes constituents are dependent enough on the leader not to raise questions, particularly if the leader is fulfilling a charismatic stereotype.

Lipman-Blumen provides a rare service in the leadership literature by developing a tool that can be used to identify one's own leadership style, and specifically to show how one could develop and use alternative implementation strategies to become a more effective leader. This is actionable research, making this book unique and well worth exploring.

Eric took the survey early in his career and identified a tendency to underuse instrumental styles, so he undertook to broaden his approach to getting things done through other people as opposed to simply doing tasks himself. You arguably do not need to take the survey to think about your own leadership style and evaluate if there are approaches to leadership that you are over- or under-emphasizing.

Do you tend to get things done by direct action, by contributing to other people's ability to accomplish the task, or by maximizing interactions between

---

[3] An excellent example of a leader who forgets the primary goal of his team is found in the portrayal by Sir Alec Guinness of the British Colonel Nicholson in the movie *Bridge On the River Kwai* (1957). The colonel initially protects the soldiers under his command in a prisoner-of-war camp, but becomes obsessed with building a perfect bridge for his captors, forgetting that the goal was to escape from the Japanese rather than to demonstrate impressive British workmanship.

participants? If when given an assignment, you pull several all-nighters and do it yourself, you are engaging in a direct method. If you coach a member of your team to reach the objective, you are exercising relational leadership. If you pull out your rolodex and introduce three people with relevant information to each other, you are implementing instrumental leadership. We agree with Lipman-Blumen that the most effective leaders harness whichever approach works best for the particular task at hand.

That said, Lipman-Blumen's book also showcases some of the challenges involved in attempting to study leadership. Half of the book relies on case studies and anecdotes about individual leaders, an approach that allows the author to find an example of almost any phenomenon (and it seems likely that one could find a counterexample with another leader). The author has developed a leadership-style assessment tool and given this tool to thousands of managers, which allows her to examine differences between subgroups: upper-versus middle-management, male versus female managers. But we do not think she is clear about how the nine achieving styles were arrived at in the first place, or whether the assessment tool validly measures each of the style constructs in a way that allows us to confidently know what it means that we score a six on one style and a five on another. Finally, when differences are found between the scores and ranking of usage of the styles among different subgroups, the author posits potential explanations but cannot yet provide an empirical basis for choosing among them. For instance, when it is found that women do not differ from men in employing a social style (using one's contacts to accomplish a task), does this mean—as the author posits—that female managers are "perhaps trying to put the lie to the stereotype that women get ahead through relationships" (p. 320)? In other words, does using a social style mean that female managers are deliberately compensating, or does it instead just mean that the stereotype does not apply?

Despite these potential shortcomings, Lipman-Blumen's book stimulates each reader to think about how to broaden their leadership approach and tailor it more to the situation at hand, and it does illuminate (even if it cannot always explain) surprising differences and surprising non-differences in self-reported leadership styles between senior and middle management, and between men and women. Her work represents a genuine contribution to a genre overrun with analysis-by-anecdote.

5. LEADERSHIP RESEARCH FINDINGS

Jay Conger and Ron Riggio hosted an academic conference on leadership in 2006 in Claremont, California with the goal of informing practicing leaders about what has been shown to work (and not to work) in organizations. They turned the conference papers into chapters of a book, and wrote the final chapter summarizing the findings of the prior chapters.

RONALD RIGGIO and JAY CONGER
"Getting It Right: The Practice of Leadership," in J. Conger and R. Riggio (editors), *The Practice of Leadership* (2006).

Thesis: Leaders need to engage their followers. They need to monitor, measure, and adapt. Leaders need to model the way forward, and proactively address challenges before they become crises. Effective leadership is a long-term developmental process.

Conger and Riggio first share two broad conclusions before summarizing each of the four parts of the book.

- **More is known about bad leadership than effective leadership.** In particular, research shows that the frequently used method of unstructured interviews is less effective at selecting leaders than other methods. Handwriting analysis has also been demonstrated to be ineffective in assessing leadership ability, but even today some firms believe it matters.
- **Good leadership is tied to the particular circumstances.** Therefore, formulaic approaches to leadership are likely to have mixed results, which is why academics no longer study airline crews or basketball teams to extrapolate lessons for business managers.

The first part of the book concerns leader selection and development. Research has made the most progress in assessing and selecting leaders, and the least progress in developing them. The authors summarize research conducted by the various participants in their conference and book.

Ann Howard reviews various tools for interviewing candidates for leadership positions (e.g., screening tests, biodata, interviews, assessment centers). She concludes that more sophisticated tools (e.g., assessment centers that simulate multiple leader functions) are superior to relying on inferences gained from interviews and a review of a candidate's resume. For those seeking to hire leaders, she recommends the following:

- Use tools that simulate leader behaviors.
- Use multiple selection methods and do not weight any one of them too heavily.
- Tailor your methods to your own needs.

- Ensure that the selection system becomes embedded in the organization and aligned with other systems and values within the organization.

London, Smither, and Diamante emphasize evaluating leader performance for development purposes, and evaluating impact on team performance. They conclude the following:

- Assessing performance and providing feedback must be continuous rather than periodic.
- Assessment needs to attend to the outcomes of a leader's efforts and assist in understanding the process by which leaders do their jobs.
- The organization should use a balanced scorecard of measures, aligning organizational, team, and individual goals with performance indicators to assess high-level leader performance.
- The organization should ensure that assessment methods are appropriate for the specific needs of each of these levels (organization, team, individual leader).

O'Connor and Day argue that individual-focused leaders cannot be expected to deal with the multiple challenges of today's complex environment; rather, collective forms of leadership must be developed that involve people sharing in the creation of a unified leadership. To encourage collective leadership, they recommend the following:

- Build collective identities such that individuals see themselves as part of the shared leadership effort.
- Look for projects that require shared leadership, with managers that are open to an action-learning approach[4] and would benefit from it.
- Invest resources so that action learning becomes integrated into the organization.
- Realize that action learning must be compatible with the organization's current needs and structure.

McCall and Hollenbeck critique existing leadership development programs, which fail because they try to develop a general laundry-list of competencies. Instead, a more customized definition of performance is needed. They echo some of the best practices already described above and recommend the following:

- View development as an ongoing, on-the-job process of providing challenging learning experiences for leaders.

---

[4] *Action learning* refers to instruction that focuses the responsibility of learning on learners. Typically, such learning adheres to the principle of providing early guidance followed by practice in the context of real (not simulated) work, and reflection on how to improve.

- Concentrate development efforts on those identified as high-potential leaders.
- Rely on the leader's own supervisor to tease out important lessons from key experiences.
- Use executive coaches to help leaders develop from their experiences.

The second part of the book focuses on critical tasks performed by leaders, such as using influence to help team members achieve goals, leading for creativity as well as for productivity, and leading in a manner that avoids ethical violations. Yukl advises that to wield such tactics, a leader must consider the situation—including the characteristics of followers, the leader's personal history with them, and other factors. His takeaway messages for leaders includes the following:

- Elicit follower commitment by using effective influence tactics (e.g., rational persuasion, inspirational appeals, consultation, collaboration).
- Link inspirational appeals to an attractive vision and ensure these appeals are consistent with the followers' values.
- Increase involvement and commitment by using consultation and collaboration.
- Use logical combinations of tactics rather than one type of influence alone.

Mumford, Eubanks, and Murphy discuss leading for innovation and argue against the belief that creative groups of knowledge workers tend to be self-led teams incorporating shared leadership. Instead, they argue that leaders of creative teams do perform important functions, in particular, providing a collaborative environment that promotes idea-generation and risk-taking. The leader needs to manage people as well as managing ideas. For leaders, they recommend the following:

- Stay actively involved in developing ideas and bringing them to fruition.
- Use a sense of common purpose to encourage innovation and commitment.
- Lead creative groups by having high levels of relevant expertise as well as the ability to lead the process.
- Promote sophisticated creativity training for leaders of such groups.

Craig Johnson asserts that leaders have an obligation to shoulder the ethical burdens of leading, including a focus on ethics as a key part of conducting business. Ethical leaders must proactively take steps to avoid a climate that condones unethical behavior, and serve as continuing role models. He makes specific recommendations for ethical leaders:

- Stay aware of and avoid unhealthy motivations (insecurity, greed, ego).
- Develop methods to critically evaluate situations from an ethical perspective.

- Work to develop one's own virtues and patterns, and encourage this in others.

Stagl, Salas, and Burke also argue that team leaders remain vital, despite the fact that many professional workers manage themselves and share leadership. They name the following best practices for team leaders:

- Define team-member roles and foster successful interdependence (rather than letting this evolve on its own).
- Clearly define responsibilities, outcomes, and goals for individuals and the team.
- Provide motivation via a compelling vision.
- Use experts to coach team members on how to better coordinate activities and facilitate team performance.

The third part of the book explores leadership at the organizational level. Specific topics include the leader's role in organizational transitions, effective leadership at the strategic level, and the role of boards.

Regarding organizational transitions (mergers, downsizing, etc.), Marks demonstrates that leading during a transition is best approached step-by-step, with distinct phases for the leader. He recommends these best practices for leaders managing organizational transitions:

- Recognize natural reactions to stress (fear, anger, resentment, resistance to change) and take steps to acknowledge these while helping individuals resolve them.
- Get people involved by providing honest information and empowering them to participate in the positive transition from the old to the new state.
- Demonstrate commitment to the transition through a compelling vision of what the future will look like, and by providing the necessary resources to get there.
- Attend to aligning the vision, enforcing appropriate job behaviors, and tracking the new structure and culture.

Waldman addresses the practice of leadership at strategic levels, providing evidence that socially responsible firms outperform other firms over time and avoid the scandals that have brought down once-great organizations (e.g., Adelphia, Enron, WorldCom). Socially responsible leaders have a broad view of the organization's impact, covering relationships with multiple stakeholders (customers, stockholders, employees, community). He suggests the following best practices for responsible leaders:

- Articulate a shared vision that energizes followers and appeals to multiple stakeholders.
- Promote shared leadership that involves followers in the strategic process.

- Foster an environment in which members engage and live their moral values at work.
- Demonstrate integrity and act transparently by sharing information that has an impact on the organization's stakeholders.

Conger begins with the premise that leadership by corporate boards is often lacking, and highlights high-profile disasters that might have been averted with appropriate board oversight. He specifically argues against allowing a CEO to chair the board, given that splitting these two critical functions brings in at least one more view at the top; one alternative can be strong committee leadership, although this structure provides no centralized board authority. He recommends the following practices for improved board leadership:

- Board members should view their role as leaders and not as advisors.
- Independent directors should constitute a majority, and should chair key board committees.
- The board should conduct independent analyses of issues without receiving their information solely from the CEO.
- The board should conduct serious and regular evaluations of CEO performance, as well as engaging in proactive succession planning.

Part Four addresses leading in the complex world of 2011 and forward. Mitroff examines leadership in times of crisis, emphasizing the need for proactive thinking and planning. He suggests that the very *form* of successful leadership will differ from that in normal periods, and recommends that leaders prepare during normal periods:

- Explore worst-case scenarios in advance, and question your own and others' assumptions about what is normal.
- Prepare emotionally and spiritually for the shock and loss a crisis will eventually cause you.
- Create a mechanism to deal with crisis, train key individuals, and run practice scenarios.
- Learn the leadership requirements needed for uncertain circumstances.

Offermann and Matos explore the challenge of leading increasingly diverse organizations, as well as its benefits (multiple viewpoints and problem-solving perspectives, increased ability to retain employees) and costs (increased divisiveness and dissatisfaction). To maximize these advantages and minimize the complications, the authors suggest the following for those running organizations:

- Think broadly about diversity, seeing beyond simple gender and racial elements to consider culture and subcultural differences. Provide a unifying vision and culture committed to common goals.

- Be sensitive to differences, and aware of how a person's own culture can impact others.
- Be flexible, adaptable, insightful, and inclusive. Communicate challenging goals and positive expectations for all members.
- Use mentoring programs to manage work groups and help mentor-leaders better understand their diverse teams.

Teagarden addresses cross-cultural leadership. She names the following qualities needed for effective global leadership:

- Become culturally intelligent, so that you can cross contexts and function effectively.
- Develop competency step-by-step by building a knowledge base for dealing with complexity, acting inquisitively, and adapting to different environments.
- Require executives to gain experience living and working in international assignments.
- Develop leaders by integrating the selection of best prospects, cross-cultural training, international assignments, and ongoing performance feedback.

Riggio and Conger close their summary of the contributions to their book by identifying common themes in this array of topics in modern leadership:

- Leaders need to engage and involve followers.
- Effective leaders monitor, measure, and adapt.
- Leaders need to model the way.
- Leaders need to be proactive.
- There are no shortcuts; effective leadership is a long-term, developmental process.

Discussion and Implications

 The chief value of the conference that resulted in this book was its explicit theme of informing leaders about what does and does not work. Practice lags behind research findings, as demonstrated by the multitude of companies that still rely primarily on unstructured interviews for hiring (not to mention those that still hang on to handwriting analysis), or that over-extrapolate results from studying sports teams to the entirely different context of business leadership.

We find that the research conclusions make broad sense. For example, tools that simulate leader situations and behaviors have been found to produce superior hiring results than interviews alone. Indeed, we have been surprised by the number of hiring managers willing to base such an important decision on a

30-minute interview.[5] For leader selection and development, we also agree that assessment of leaders with a balanced scorecard creates better performance (we believe in the adage "what gets measured gets managed"), and that leadership development is more effective when programs are customized.

For tasks performed by leaders, our experience is consistent with the findings that leaders are more effective when they tailor their approach to the particular situation, when they provide a collaborative environment to their creative teams, when they focus on ethics deliberately on an ongoing basis, and when they explicitly define team member roles.

Our own board experience in the United States and elsewhere reinforces that boards are more effective when members view themselves as independent leaders rather than simply advisors. Lastly, in a more complex era, organizations must place a higher emphasis on executives who can lead in crisis, manage increasingly diverse teams, and lead across cultures with different values and symbols.

This conference and book represent practitioner-oriented research that deserves an audience among executives rather than in academic settings.

FURTHER READING

If you're interested in reading more on the topics discussed in this chapter, here are some sources to get you started. We do not offer this as a comprehensive or exhaustive list, but rather have selected well-regarded or significant works that space did not permit us to include in the main discussion.

1. LEADERSHIP CLASSICS

Burns, James MacGregor. 1978. *Leadership*. New York, Harper Collins.

Drucker, Peter. 1993. *Management: Tasks, Responsibilities, Practices*. New York, HarperBusiness.

Lewin, Kurt, Ronald Lipitt, and Ralph White. 1939. "Patterns of Aggressive Behavior in Experimentally Created 'Social Climates.'" *Journal of Social Psychology* 10(2), 271–299.

Wren, Thomas. 1995. *The Leader's Companion*. New York, Free Press.

---

[5] Eric has discovered that surprisingly few of his colleagues over the years actually check a candidate's multiple references. In his own reference checking, several former supervisors have told Eric that they would not rehire the individual. What is more surprising than the fact that candidates list such references is that they often get hired anyway, possibly because many hiring managers "trust their gut" rather than doing such investigation.

2. What Leaders Actually Do

Bass, Bernard and Ruth Bass. 2008. *Bass's Handbook of Leadership*, 4th edition. New York, Free Press.

Zaccaro, Stephen. 2007. "Trait-Based Perspectives of Leadership." *American Psychologist* 62(1), 6–16.

3. Leadership and Organizational Culture

Able, Richard. 2007. "The Importance of Leadership and Culture to M&A Success." Paper, Human Capital Institute, Towers Perrin HR Services.

Northouse, Peter. 2012. "Culture and Leadership." In *Leadership: Science and Practice*, 6th edition. Los Angeles, Sage. Ch. 15.

4. Constructive and Destructive Leadership

Lipman-Blumen, Jean. 2005. *The Allure of Toxic Leaders*. New York, Oxford University Press.

Maccoby, Michael. 2000. "Narcissistic Leaders: The Incredible Pros, the Inevitable Cons." *Harvard Business Review* 78(January–February), 69–77.

5. Leadership Research Findings

Avolio, Bruce. 2010. *Full Range Leadership Development*, 2nd edition. Los Angeles, Sage.

Day, David and John Antonakis. 2011. *The Nature of Leadership*, 2nd edition. Los Angeles, Sage.

Kaiser, Robert, Robert Hogan, and Bartholomew Craig. 2008. "Leadership and the Fate of Organizations." *American Psychologist* 63(2), 96–110.

Works Cited

Bandiera, Oriana, Andrea Prat, Raffaella Sadun, and Julie Wulf. 2012. "Span of Control and Span of Activity." Harvard Business School Working Paper. http://www.hbs.edu/research/pdf/12-053.pdf.

Barnard, Chester. 1938. *The Functions of the Executive*. Cambridge, Harvard University Press.

Bennis, Warren. 1989. *Why Leaders Can't Lead*. New York, Jossey-Bass.

Bridge on the River Kwai. 1957. [Film] Directed by David Lean. USA, Columbia Pictures.

Chandran, Jay. 1998. "The Relevance of Chester Barnard for Today's Manager." Unpublished paper, Devos Graduate School of Management, Northwood University.

Conger, Jay. 1990. "The Dark Side of Leadership." In R. Vecchio (editor), *Leadership*, 2nd edition [2007]. Notre Dame, University of Notre Dame Press. pp. 199–215.

Conger, Jay. 2006. "Best Practices in Corporate Boardroom Leadership." In J. Conger and R. Riggio (editors), *The Practice of Leadership*. San Francisco, Jossey-Bass. pp. 244–260.

de Montaigne, Michel. 1580. *Essays of Michel de Montaigne*. Translated by Charles Cotton [2009]. Sioux Falls, NuVision.

Kets de Vries, Manfred. 1989. "Leaders Who Self-Destruct: The Causes and Cures." In R. Vecchio (editor), *Leadership*, 2nd edition, 2007. Notre Dame, University of Notre Dame Press. pp. 216–227.

Kets de Vries, Manfred and Danny Miller. 1985. "Narcissism and Leadership: An Object Relations Perspective." In R. Vecchio (editor), *Leadership*, [1997]. Notre Dame, University of Notre Dame Press. pp. 194–214.

Kotter, John. 1990. "What Leaders Really Do." In R. Vecchio (editor), *Leadership*, 2nd edition, [2007]. Notre Dame, University of Notre Dame Press. pp. 23–32.

Kotterman, James. 2006. "Leadership vs. Management: What's the Difference?" *Journal for Quality and Participation* 29(2), 13–17.

Lipman-Blumen, Jean. 1996. *The Connective Edge*. New York, Oxford University Press.

Machiavelli, Niccolo. 1513. *The Prince*. Translated by Robert Adams [1992]. New York, Norton.

Mintzberg, Henry. 1975. "The Manager's Job: Folklore and Fact." In R. Vecchio (editor), *Leadership*, 2nd edition [2007]. Notre Dame, University of Notre Dame Press. pp. 33–50.

Northouse, Peter G. 2012. *Leadership: Theory and Practice*, 6th edition. New York, Sage.

Riggio, Ronald and Jay Conger. 2006. "Getting It Right: The Practice of Leadership." In J. Conger and R. Riggio (editors), *The Practice of Leadership*. San Francisco, Jossey-Bass. pp. 331–344.

Schein, Edgar. 2010. *Organizational Culture and Leadership*, 4th edition. San Francisco, Jossey-Bass.

Senge, Peter. 1990. "The Leader's New Work: Building Learning Organizations." *Sloan Management Review* 32(1), 7–23.

Senge, Peter. 2006. *The Fifth Discipline: The Art and Practice of the Learning Organization*. New York, Crown Business.

Stagl, Kevin, Eduardo Salas, and C. Shawn Burke. 2006. "Best Practices in Team Leadership: What Team Leaders Do to Facilitate Team Effectiveness." In J. Conger and R. Riggio (editors), *The Practice of Leadership*. San Francisco, Jossey-Bass. pp. 172–198.

Teagarden, Mary. 2006. "Best Practices in Cross-Cultural Leadership." In J. Conger and R. Riggio (editors), *The Practice of Leadership*. San Francisco, Jossey-Bass. pp. 300–330.

Waldman, David. 2006. "Best Practices in Leading at Strategic Levels: A Social Responsibility Perspective." In J. Conger and R. Riggio (editors), *The Practice of Leadership*. San Francisco, Jossey-Bass. pp. 224–243.

Yukl, Gary. 1989. "Managerial Leadership: A Review of Theory and Research." *Journal of Management* 15(2), 251–289.

Zaleznik, Abraham. 1992. "Managers and Leaders: Are They Different?" *Harvard Business Review* 70(March–April), 126–35 [1977].

ORGANIZATION & PROCESS

Amy Kates and Jay Galbraith (2007) define organizational design as the alignment of structure, process, rewards, metrics, and talent with the strategy of the business. There has been a wealth of research about organizational design and effectiveness over the past forty years. Much of it has been conducted outside of business schools by organizational psychologists, and so may be less familiar to management faculty as well as to managers in organizations. Any survey will necessarily only scratch the surface, but this chapter presents several contributions we find particularly useful to practicing executives.

One of the primary roles of leaders in any organization is to establish and sustain the group's unique culture. Over a long career, Edgar Schein (e.g., 2010) has helped frame culture and used that lens to better understand the behavior seen in organizations. He and others (including Trice and Beyer 1993) have explored the barriers and benefits of changing an organization's culture (Section 1 below). Philip Zimbardo (1972) conducted a famous experiment showing that situations can be a stronger determinant of individuals' behavior than the actual personality or values of the individuals involved, meaning that organizational structure may predetermine constructive or destructive outcomes (Section 2). Sim Sitkin (1992) demonstrated the value of cultures that allow and encourage intelligent failures, based on the organizational resiliency fostered by such failures (Section 3).

Organizations create incentives that drive the behavior of their members. As Steven Kerr (1995) demonstrated, organizations of all kinds consistently reward behaviors that are in conflict with the desired behavior; these counterproductive incentives can be confronted and reversed, but it takes work. Henry Parsons (1975) found that attention itself (in the form of research or simply of management communication) can alter the behavior of those being studied, by giving workers more feedback on their performance than they may have had previously (sometimes coupled with financial incentives; see Section 4).

A tremendous amount of research over the past fifty years has explored what motivates workers. We review two articles that surveyed this field (Locke and Henne 1986; Latham and Pinder 2005). The research demonstrated some surprising conclusions, such as that the level of compensation by itself is only weakly motivating, and that there is little link between job satisfaction and productivity. Other conclusions are perhaps less surprising: setting specific and difficult goals enhances performance, and employees are motivated by being part of a larger cause (Section 5).

We also examine the role of power in organizational settings. Salancik and Pfeffer (1977) found that power accrues, at least initially, to those members of an organization who cope with its problems, and therefore power represents the underappreciated foundation of success. Kanter (1979) cataloged sources of power and positions of powerlessness. Both sources we review agree that power can be challenging to openly analyze, but that those who ignore its impact on decision-making will find themselves repeatedly surprised (Section 6).

We end by exploring the economic value of information technology. Research in this area reaches sometimes-conflicting conclusions, but several articles conducted at the level of the firm (e.g., Kohli and Devaraj 2003) indicated a significant positive relationship between the use of IT and organizational productivity (Section 7).

1. ORGANIZATIONAL CULTURE

In this section, we explore the power of shared assumptions within any group, starting with Edgar Schein's description of culture and how to understand it. We also review Trice and Beyer's work showing how organizations can deliberately alter their personality.

EDGAR SCHEIN
"The Concept of Organizational Culture: Why Bother?" and
"The Three Levels of Culture" (2010), *Organizational Culture and Leadership*.

Thesis: Identifying the pattern of shared basic assumptions within a group is a powerful tool to understand organizational behavior.

We covered Schein's work on the role of leaders in creating culture in our separate chapter on leadership (Chapter 3). In this chapter, we focus on his discussion of the concept and role of culture overall.

Schein opens his book with the observation that cultural forces are powerful because people are often unaware of them. The concept of culture may illuminate much of the apparently irrational behavior observed in organizations, and the primary important task of leaders may be to create and manage culture. "If leaders do not become conscious of the cultures in which they are embedded, those cultures will manage them" (p. 22).

Culture is a deep and complex phenomenon, but a powerful tool to understand behavior. As culture is an abstract concept, observable elements are needed to make it useful. An anthropological model identifies observable events and underlying forces, including observed behavioral regularities when people interact, group norms, espoused values, formal philosophies, rules of the game, climate, embedded skills, habits of thinking, shared meanings, root metaphors, and formal rituals.

The concept of culture implies structural stability, depth, breadth, and patterning or integration. Schein offers the following formal definition of *organizational culture*:

> A pattern of shared basic assumptions learned by a group as it solved its problems of external adaptation and internal integration, which [pattern] has worked well enough to be considered valid, and therefore, to be taught to new members as the correct way to perceive, think, and feel in relation to those problems. (p. 18)

These "shared basic assumptions" are learned responses that come to be taken for granted. Culture cannot be inferred from regular behaviors because those behaviors may be environmentally rather than culturally caused.

In the second chapter of his book, Schein shows that culture can be analyzed at several levels (i.e., degress of visibility to the observer). He defines three major levels of cultural analysis: artifacts, espoused beliefs and values, and basic underlying assumptions.

Artifacts are the most visible, surface level of the culture, including what can be seen and heard directly as part of the constructed physical and social environment. While easy to observe, these artifacts may be hard to decipher (e.g., how status is demonstrated by members). It can therefore be dangerous to try to infer deeper assumptions based only on artifacts without imposing one's own assumptions on the culture being observed.

Espoused beliefs and values encompass ideals, goals, values, aspirations, ideologies, and rationalizations (which may or may not be congruent with behavior and other artifacts). Values represent a sense of what "ought to be" rather than what is. If a value can be validated to work reliably in solving problems then that value can go through a process of cognitive transformation, becoming a belief and ultimately an assumption. As values begin to be taken for granted, they drop out of consciousness; however, some values remain conscious because they serve a function in guiding members in how to deal with certain situations. Be aware of "espoused values," which may be stated but not operative (e.g., "we value people"). When espoused values are congruent with assumptions, they can serve as a source of identity and mission. Values only provide a partial understanding of a culture (i.e., they may be incomplete, internally inconsistent, or incongruent with observed behavior).

Basic underlying assumptions are unconscious, taken-for-granted beliefs and values that determine behavior, perception, thought, and feeling. When a solution works repeatedly, it becomes taken for granted, such that one finds little variation within a social unit. Members may then find behavior based on any other premise inconceivable. Like "theories-in-use" (Argyris and Schon 1996) these assumptions are nonconfrontable. Such assumptions can drive how a person frames the world (i.e., is a colleague shirking or thinking when she stares at the wall?), and can provide a basic sense of identity.

In an organization, if a leader's approach continues to work, the leader's assumptions gradually come to be shared assumptions. In this way, a founder defines the character and identity of a group. Schein makes the additional point that those who study culture, whether leaders or members of an organization or even researchers, must actively participate with the members to understand the culture; they cannot just observe.

Unconscious assumptions can lead to "Catch-22" situations. For example, for a U.S. boss whose highest priority is solving a problem, and an Asian subordinate whose highest priority is not contradicting or embarrassing the boss, successful outcomes are difficult and frustration often ensues.

HARRISON TRICE and JANICE BEYER
"Changing Organizational Cultures" (1993), in J. M. Shafritz, J. S. Ott, and Y. S. Jang (editors), *Classics of Organization Theory* (2005).

Thesis: With cultural change, losses are more certain than gains; therefore, managing change entails convincing people that the likely gains outweigh the losses.

Trice and Beyer define *cultural change* as change that is planned, more encompassing, and more substantial than changes that arise spontaneously or are part of efforts to keep culture vital. A relatively slow and drawn-out process, cultural change does not represent simply the introduction of new practices. Culture change involves an underlying duality of destruction of one culture and creation of another, which takes different forms including the following:

- **Revolutionary and comprehensive culture change.** An example of this is the U.S. postal service in the 1970s, which completely overhauled its culture across the organization.
- **Efforts confined largely to specific subcultures or units.** An example is the L-1011 plant at Lockheed, which had a set of challenges specific to that location which were addressed by the corporation.
- **Efforts which are gradual and incremental but accumulate into a large reshaping.** An example is the Cadbury confectionary company which evolved into a wholly different culture over a thirty-year period.

To assess the amount of change, Trice and Beyer suggest evaluating the change over four dimensions:

- *Pervasiveness* refers to the proportion of organizational activities affected.
- *Magnitude* describes the distance of new values from old ones.
- *Innovativeness* is the degree to which ideas/behaviors are unprecedented versus borrowed.
- *Duration* refers to the length of time a change effort is likely to take.

They then define three categories of change, mapped against those four dimensions, as follows. *Revolutionary change* occurs when pervasiveness is high, magnitude is high, and innovativeness and duration are variable. *Subunit change* occurs when pervasiveness is low, magnitude is moderate to high, and innovativeness and duration are variable. Finally *cumulative change* occurs when pervasiveness is high, magnitude is moderate, innovation is moderate, and duration is high.

Trice and Beyer give eight specific, action-oriented recommendations to managers and leaders for the difficult task of changing organizational cultures.

1. **Capitalize on propitious moments.** Obvious problems are changes in circumstances that provide the opportunity to implement changes in culture. Those affected must be persuaded that change is justified, and one can blame problems on the environment. Trice and Beyer suggest taking advantage of inflection points when people are more receptive to change.
2. **Combine caution with optimism.** An optimistic outlook is essential, and visible doubts are toxic. Change is inevitable, so leaders may as well channel and initiate it. Leaders can help people envision the change as achievable.
3. **Understand resistance to culture change.** People tend to resist change, and managers should understand common sources of resistance. At the individual level, people resist change based on fear of the unknown, self-interest, selective attention and retention, habit, dependence, and the need for security. At the group level, resistance is often based on threats to influence, lack of trust, differing goals, and resource limitations.
4. **Maintain some continuity.** It is important to remind people of the sustaining principles that will not change, even as some practices do. For

example, HP underwent change in their processes and structures continuously over decades, but retained the notion of "the HP way," which asserted that employees' brainpower was the company's single most important resource, and that a relatively decentralized structure with employee-friendly perquisites was the best way to maintain that asset.

5. **Recognize the importance of implementation.** Ninety percent of strategy changes fail in execution. The institutionalization of change depends on well-managed, persistent, and pervasive implementation efforts at all levels of management.

6. **Select, modify, and create appropriate cultural forms.** Culture is defined in symbols, rituals, language, stories, and role models—manipulate symbols. Employees listen to those leaders who "walk the talk." Managers must be seen to spend time on that which they define as important. Metaphors also matter (e.g., when AT&T replaced its image of "Ma Bell" with that of a connected globe). Developing new metaphors, myths, and role models can be useful.

7. **Modify socialization tactics.** Rites of passage (or even of degradation) can show people the positive (and negative) consequences of adapting to the new environment.

8. **Find and cultivate innovative leadership.** Senior management should reward leaders who have self-confidence, convictions, and the ability to preach the new vision. Executives should remove existing leaders who embody the old culture, if and only if they are unwilling to change. The most concrete signal senior management can send is what kind of person and behavior gets promoted.

Discussion and Implications

When a senior executive leaves a company, it is not usually due to lack of technical competence but rather to a lack of fit with the organizational culture. Similarly, the failed merger of two organizations also often reflects a problem with meshing the two distinct corporate cultures.

These observations have been made in the literature. For example, Adolph, Elrod, and Neely (2006) observed that "bringing disparate groups of people together as one company takes real work and represents an effort that is often largely overlooked. Culture change management is not indulgent; it is a critical aspect of any transaction" (p. 1).

Time Warner's acquisition of AOL in 2001 provides a concrete example. This $350 billion deal was the biggest merger ever; ten years later, the combined entities were worth less than one-seventh of their merger values. The acquisition is considered by many to be the worst in history. In an interview, the former co-COO of the merged company agrees with those who say that cultural misalignment was the primary reason for its failure: "The thing that makes a merger work is culture. These were two mergers of equals. And now you're trying to put two together and if the cultures aren't somewhat aligned, you're going to have problems. And we had big problems" (Arango 2010, p. 1).

Our experience is consistent with these conclusions. We believe that cultural fit may be the single biggest determinant of whether a merger will succeed, or whether an executive will succeed in a company. When being interviewed, we recommend testing your cultural fit by always asking, "What are the unique assumptions that 'go without saying' in this organization?" Given that employees are not always explicitly conscious of the organization's assumptions, this question may also serve as a test of the level of self-awareness of the interviewer. We also recommend assessing whether your organization's espoused values are congruent with the actions you observe. Where there is a disconnect, we recommend tagging the observed behaviors as reflective of the actual operating values.

It is hard to overstate the importance of culture. When two people from different countries are not communicating, as in Schein's example of a U.S. supervisor (whose priority may be solving a problem) and an Asian subordinate (whose priority may be to avoid contradicting the boss), it pays to examine the unconscious assumptions that may be in play. Although these differences may be more obvious when the players are from different national cultures, the dynamics play out equally when the players are merely from different industries or companies. We have experienced as much culture shock going from east-coast U.S. companies to Silicon Valley as we have moving from one country to another. In fact, domestic corporate culture shock can have a bigger impact— because it is not telegraphed by differences in language or appearance, it can more easily catch people by surprise.

We agree with Trice and Beyer that changing culture is hard. It is far easier to establish a culture at the beginning of an organization, and worth taking the time to do so deliberately rather than by default. However, even a culture that is initially aligned to its environment can become misaligned as the competitive environment changes, and as new leadership takes over. This misalignment can necessitate a need to alter the organization's personality.

We also agree with Trice and Beyer's specific recommendations for how to go about culture change. In particular, our experience points to the importance of understanding resistance and to the use of symbols. We have seen organizations invert organization charts, change logos, create new heroes and villains, and visibly show the CEO allocating his or her time in a very different way.

It appears that companies want to manage change but do not know how. In one survey, 90% of companies stated they were unable to implement changes in corporate strategy (Kiechel 1979, p. 110). In another survey, 62% of corporate presidents stated they were trying to create a mindset of change (Cotter 1995, p. 56). Cotter recommends a push/pull strategy to fight barriers to change. *Pull initiatives* include reaching consensus about change, developing the capability to change by engaging those who have done it before, and introducing new skills with training. *Push initiatives* often emerge spontaneously, and include taking advantage of new investment opportunities, starting new business units, and creating a crisis intentionally.

Markus (1998) points out that major organizational change projects can fail in at least three ways: *technical failure* (project does not work), *social failure* (project succeeds technically but people do not use the new system), or *bad-idea failure* (project does not produce the desired results). Faithfully following a particular methodology does not prevent social or bad-idea failures.[1]

Senior management cannot make every decision in a business of any size. By establishing the culture, management makes it clear to those making the decisions in the field what principles would guide their leaders if the leaders were in fact making those decisions, and so culture is a critical tool to ensure that businesses act in a consistent and aligned fashion. President Reagan was reputed to have told his cabinet secretaries to think of his principles and make decisions consistent with them, without necessarily meeting with him first (Mitchell 2005).

Our experience matches the literature discussed above on cultural change. When old assumptions are no longer effective, particularly if the business is not as successful or the environment has changed, it becomes especially critical for the new leadership to identify and communicate what the new shared operating norms are. Members of the organization present during an earlier, more successful period may be reluctant to alter what has always worked in the past. This resistance must be acknowledged and discussion facilitated, and the people doing the work of the organization must be persuaded that the change is necessary. Getting people aligned is crucial for success, so the leaders must make their argument and then remove those who cannot be persuaded.

In this discussion of corporate culture and how to change it, the question arises as to whether the cultural norms of Silicon Valley provide a model for adaptability. Delbecq and Weiss (1988) argue that the rapid pace of Silicon Valley is facilitated by its culture: decision-making is more intuitive and less formal, and communication structures are eclectic and decentralized. There are fewer formal controls over business units, but more intense informal

---

[1] Markus (1998) also warns against goal displacement in specific initiatives. A manager implementing a new performance-measurement system may be evaluated on the cost and schedule performance of their project rather than on whether anyone is using the new system, and so the manager may avoid focusing on how the system is being adopted. The goal "implementing a new measurement system" can thus replace "improving the organization's performance against its strategy."

communication between units and the executives at headquarters. Labor is mobile, and reward structures are geared toward equity rather than the security of pensions. They conclude that a loosely coupled, fluid organization is a prerequisite for innovation. We agree, and would go further by saying that the relatively rapid rate of changeover in the Silicon Valley workforce makes it easier to change the culture (whether senior management wants to change or not—it takes energy to sustain a stable culture through multiple generations of employees).

Hwang and Horowitt (2012) argue convincingly that no city or country can recreate the success of Silicon Valley by simply marrying a research university to a supply of venture capital, but rather that success requires importing the distinct cultural norms of behavior that apply among the startup companies, the venture capitalists, and the established technology companies. We agree, and in particular would point to the value of failure. Nowhere else in the world is failure looked upon as positively as in the Valley. Pouring venture capital into a nation with a culture that is judgmental about those involved in any failed business venture is not likely to succeed.

2. THE IMPACT OF STRUCTURE AND SITUATION

In this section we describe an experiment conducted by a Stanford psychologist that has become possibly the most (in)famous academic experiment ever conducted. Philip Zimbardo's prison experiment has significant implications for those who are establishing organizational structure and culture.

PHILIP ZIMBARDO
"Pathology of Imprisonment" (1972), Society.

Thesis: In determining the behavior of individuals in groups, situations can have a larger impact than the inherent personalities involved. Poor organizational structure can predetermine destructive outcomes.

In this rather modest article, Zimbardo (who had recently become a tenured psychologist at Stanford) describes a simple experiment he conducted in August 1971. The setup involved the selection of 24 undergraduates from 75 applicants to play the roles of guards and prisoners in a mock prison over a two-week period. Those students who were selected had been classified as emotionally stable. The student volunteers were offered $15 a day to participate, and roles were assigned at random. "Prisoners" were arrested at their homes by cooperating Palo Alto police, charged with armed robbery, and processed with fingerprinting and mug shots before being taken to a mock prison in the basement of Stanford's Psychology Department in Jordan Hall.

The mock prison was maintained for only six days, with three main results:

- **Participants adapted to their roles startlingly far beyond expectations.**
- **Guards quickly began displaying authoritarian and even cruel measures.** Examples included identifying prisoners solely by number, forcing them to count off (with punishment for errors), refusing to allow prisoners to relieve themselves, removing mattresses to force prisoners to sleep on the concrete floor, forcing some prisoners to go naked, and spraying them with fire extinguishers. Experimenters concluded that one-third of the guards engaged in genuinely sadistic behaviors.
- **Prisoners accepted humiliating treatment from the guards.** Prisoners experienced high levels of stress and evolved from rebellion to inhibition within a few days. One prisoner broke into a screaming rage within 36 hours and was released, along with two others in the first four days. No other prisoners quit the experiment, though some offered to forfeit their pay to gain parole. When told that their parole applications were denied within the context of the experiment, none quit the experiment. That is, they accepted the ruling of the "parole board," despite giving up their participant pay, and did not assert their right to simply walk away. Though none left the formal experiment, by the fourth day several prisoners spoke of escape. Zimbardo himself asked to move the prisoners to the actual Palo Alto police station when Stanford officials said they could no longer participate in the exercise.

When Zimbardo's girlfriend (herself a psychologist) visited the experiment five days in, she strenuously objected to the appalling conditions and convinced Zimbardo to terminate the experiment on the sixth day. Of the 50 people involved in the experiment (including friends and family members allowed to visit the prisoners), she was the first to question its morality.

> At the end of only six days we had to close down our mock prison because what we saw was frightening. It was no longer apparent to most of the subjects (or to us) where reality ended and their roles began. The majority had indeed become prisoners or guards, no longer able to clearly differentiate between role playing and self. There were dramatic changes in virtually every aspect of their behavior, thinking and feeling. In less than a week, the experience of imprisonment undid (temporarily) a lifetime of learning; human values were suspended, self-concepts were challenged and the ugliest, most base, pathological side of human nature

surfaced. We were horrified because we saw some boys (guards) treat others as if they were despicable animals, taking pleasure in cruelty, while other boys (prisoners) became servile, dehumanized robots who thought only of escape, of their own individual survival and of their mounting hatred for the guards. (p. 5)

Zimbardo concluded that the acceptance by the prisoners of the continuing authority of the experimenters to keep them confined was evidence that they had internalized their roles thoroughly, accepting their powerlessness and fully assuming the role of prisoners. He views the results as inconsistent with the idea that personality drives behavior (dispositional attribution), and more consistent with the hypothesis that situation drives behavior (situational attribution).

In a later piece, Zimbardo, Maslach, and Haney (1999) summarized the lessons from the study as follows:

- When trying to understand behavior or motivation, start with a situational analysis and only use a personality-driven explanation as a fallback.
- Situational power is most salient in new settings with few precedents for the individuals involved.
- Situational power often comes with an ideological cover story to inhibit ordinary norms from governing behavior.
- Role-playing, even when understood to be pretend, can exert a profound impact on how people act. Values are modified to conform to the role-playing actions as individuals minimize any cognitive dissonance.
- Good people can be induced into evil behavior by immersion in total situations.
- Human nature can be transformed in social settings.
- Results of experimental research are generalizable to how people behave everywhere.
- Selection procedures for some jobs might benefit from role-playing as a supplement to the more commonly used personality testing.

Discussion and Implications

 This experiment was severely criticized from within and outside of the academy. Zimbardo concluded that he himself had become too absorbed in his role as prison superintendent and was too slow to terminate the study. Many made comparisons to the 1961 Milgram experiment at Yale in which students willingly complied with faculty instructions to provide electric shock to other students (as described in Milgram 2009). Neither of these experiments would pass the current ethical standards of the American Psychological Association.

The experiment was criticized on methodological as well as ethical grounds.

- The number of participants was small, and the observations anecdotal.

- Were participants merely role-playing? We think not, as Zimbardo convincingly shows that participants internalized the roles as the study progressed.
- Given that the guards were instructed to behave oppressively, some take this more as a study of tyrannical leadership (Zimbardo's) than of situational-driven behavior.

This profound academic experiment covers a lot of ground, and has significant implications for understanding human behavior in organizations. It demonstrates the power of role-playing in any context, from explaining dynamics in supervisor–subordinate relationships to understanding why so many people enjoy dressing up for Halloween (or other, more private, occasions). Zimbardo's study also demonstrates how quickly people can feel powerless and become paralyzed when they feel they have little control over their situation.

Regardless of whether the guards' poor behavior was driven by an overdeveloped willingness to accept direction (to treat prisoners poorly), or by the structure of the situation itself (people become their roles), there are clear and powerful implications for all who have the authority to give instructions and to create organizational structure. Executives can and must clearly ask:

- Who am I promoting into positions of power over other employees?
- What assumptions (explicit or implicit) are embedded in the actual organization chart?
- If team members are behaving in unexpected ways, what is it about the situation that is creating or contributing to that behavior?
- What are the intended and unintended consequences of a strong organizational culture? To what extent do we want our organizational mindset to replace behavioral norms from outside the organization?

Creating a strong culture can foster a sense of team and loyalty, and spur employees to work hard to advance the company. This cultural strength can result in an inspired and motivated workforce, distinct and separate from that of other companies. Creating a strong culture can also have side effects: the local corporate culture can replace other values from outside. Many of these consequences can be beneficial, but they should be deliberate. For example, if you have a culture that promotes vigorous competition and debate among peers, you should understand the impact this could have on team collaboration, rather than assuming that somehow outside norms about cooperation will override the competitive race you have established.

We would emphasize Zimbardo's finding that new settings especially foster the power of the situation to drive behavior, over the power of personality or norms from the outside world. We would also hypothesize that age may play a role; with less exposure to competing workplace cultural norms, young employees may be more prone to internalize a unique corporate culture (for better and for worse). Consider the work environment of a typical startup, with young employees working with a passionate commitment to change the world and a healthy disdain for how larger and slower companies operate. Long hours and sleep deprivation can isolate the team from the outside world, and success in the market reinforces the culture. Such an environment may unintentionally replicate that of a cult: in both situations a strong culture is developed by replacing the values the participants had going in.

In fact, academic research has matched the culture of specific well-known companies to the conditions of a cult. For example, Tourish and Vatcha (2005) draw on academic studies of cults and show how the culture at Enron matched those conditions. We find this danger more pronounced in a corporate context, because if the company is prestigious the employees (and those who form their support system) will have a tougher time recognizing and breaking out of the situation.[2]

Establishing a unique set of norms can lead to great accomplishments, and in fact there are often large benefits to deliberately doing so (the military has long understood this and is very deliberate about establishing new norms in training). However, leaders need to think consciously about what values are being created or replaced, and not be surprised if some values (good and bad) that many people take for granted may become weaker drivers of behavior.

3. Organizational Learning

In Section 1, we described the importance of corporate culture and suggested that Silicon Valley's unique culture may be particularly suited toward fostering success. In this section, we examine the nature of this connection by looking at conditions that facilitate organizational learning.

 SIM SITKIN
"Learning through Failure: The Strategy of Small Losses" (1992), in B. Staw and L. Cummings (editors), *Research in Organizational Behavior.*

---

[2] This research resonates with us. Eric joined Cisco Systems in 1999 when it was one of the three most valuable companies in the world and a sought-after workplace. Few of Eric's friends understood why anyone would seriously consider resigning a position from such a successful and trendy company.

Thesis: Failure is an essential prerequisite for learning. Organizations must allow people to fail in order to grow. Success fosters reliability, while failure fosters resilience.

 Learning requires failure, as failure stimulates necessary experimentation. Sitkin describes an experiment in which six bees and six flies are placed in a bottle, which is placed on its side with the bottom facing a light and the top open. The bees will kill themselves trying to get out of the bottom, since they "know" that the exit is toward the light. The flies will fly wildly and randomly about until they all escape the bottle. Which behavior is more adaptive?

Success has benefits: it tends to maintain the status quo, and reliability can be efficient. Sitkin generates nine hypotheses and justifies why he expects these to hold. He theorizes that the following benefits are linked to a high degree of or consistency with prior success:

1. goals and values shared by employees to a high degree,
2. greater efficiency achieved through focused search and proven procedural routines,
3. increased operational stability and subunit coordination across the organization, and
4. greater motivation and confidence to persist in face of minor obstacles.

Success also carries liabilities: complacency, restricted search and low levels of attention, and homogeneity. Regarding these liabilities, Sitin hypothesizes that the following are also linked to higher degree of or consistency with prior success:

5. less expansive search activities,
6. less attention paid to discrepant information,
7. greater complacency about experimenting with new procedures,
8. greater levels of risk aversion, and
9. higher proclivity to homogenize subcultures and procedures.

Strategic failure, characterized by learning by experimentation, represents an alternative to success. There are distinct benefits to failing:

*   **Attention to and the processing of potential problems.** Failure stimulates search.
*   **Ease of recognition and interpretation.** Failing provides a clear signal of what does not work.
*   **Stimulation of search processes.** Small failures are survivable and better.
*   **Motivation to adapt.** People will see a need for correction.
*   **Requisite variety.** As in the process of evolution, variety is good, providing diversity in determining what does and does not work, and helping to better identify the common denominators.

- **Practice.** Practice is helpful in mastering any new skill.

In Sitkin's next group of hypotheses, greater incidence of small prior failure is linked to the following:

- increased attention and deeper processing of information,
- more potential problems being recognized and interpreted,
- a greater level of search,
- increased flexibility and openness to change for the group and its members,
- a greater level of risk tolerance,
- more variety in personnel and procedures used, and
- more experience and relevant practice for the organization.

Success and failure both impact organizational learning. Organizational reliability is promoted by success, while organizational adaptability is promoted by failures and experimentation. Not all failures result in learning, however.

Five key characteristics contribute to the intelligence of failures: (1) They result from thoughtfully planned actions that (2) have uncertain outcomes, (3) are of modest scale, (4) are executed and responded to with alacrity, and (5) take place in domains familiar enough to permit effective learning. Intelligent failure can be facilitated by the following sets of organizational conditions.

1. **Focus on process over outcome.** Challenge aspiration levels by creating meaningful goals for attention and learning. Scale reductions increase the number of actions possible (i.e., more experiments are possible if they are smaller). Practice fast feedback and slow learning: do not revise plans until you observe a sufficient number of outcomes.
2. **Legitimize intelligent failure.** Visibly recognize intelligent failure at all levels of leadership. Intelligent failures should not lead to career setbacks or affect career mobility. Publicize, legitimize, and reward intelligent failures.
3. **Establish a learning culture and design.** Train for surprise and novelty: people cope with surprise better when they are used to it. Commit resources to failure and to the monitoring of failure. Develop an "intelligent failure ideology."
4. **Establish failure management systems.** Include compensatory programs that foster "play" by drawing attention to, legitimating, and rewarding intelligent failure to fill out the distribution of observed outcomes.

In terms of research implications, management researchers should work to address the following: the conditions under which failure is more acceptable than other outcomes, the effect of outcome history on new risk perception, the question of whether learned helplessness can be avoided and self-efficacy promoted by understanding responses to changes in scale, the effect of human resource policies on experimentation, and the extent to which legitimacy is affected by failure.

Sitkin applies his hypotheses to organizational phenomena. Intelligent failure can assist in fostering innovation and in managing hazards in organizations. Failure can also improve acquisition decision-making and integration, since bad acquisitions can be part of a longer-term learning plan. Overall, failures are valuable.

Discussion and Implications

 Context is critical to an organization's attitude toward risk. An environment that prizes reliability (e.g., a power plant or mobile phone network) may want to stick solely to proven procedures with demonstrated effectiveness. In this context, the organization should prize processes and people that have a steady track record of success. An environment that values resilience will find value in failures, and in those who have failed; many startup companies fall into this category. Larger companies should decide what combination of reliability and innovation to promote.

We find personal resonance in this message for individuals in their careers as well as for the organizations that employ them. We know more than one venture capitalist who prefers to fund entrepreneurs who have failed (intelligently) and taken appropriate lessons from the experience. In our own careers, we have found (more than once) that failure has laid the groundwork for later success. One of our favorite interview questions remains "tell me about a time when you failed"—the response can reveal a lot about the perspective and self-awareness of the applicant.

Sitkin's analysis is consistent with other academic work. For example, Sheryl Axline (2001) emphasizes the role of proactive adaptation in team learning, whereby teams revisit earlier decisions (and failure would be more likely to trigger such revisiting). She finds that team learning processes are determined largely at the outset by team features.[3] More recently, complex-systems theorist Scott Page (2008) extended Sitkin's point about flies versus bees, by demonstrating how organizations can thrive through assembling individuals from different backgrounds. To build an effective team, the single biggest factor may be compiling those with different backgrounds and perspectives who will approach a problem or challenge differently. Complex problems may be solved by diversity in approach more than by attacking the problem with more individuals with the same perspective. We agree, having seen that organizations and bosses looking to hire people who complement their own skills succeed more than those who hire people just like themselves.

---

[3] This finding also supports, at the level of teams, Zimbardo, Maslach, and Haney's (1999) contention about individuals—namely that structure plays a key role in determining behavior.

4. ALIGNING ORGANIZATIONAL INCENTIVES

Capitalistic societies tend to have economies based on an understanding that individual incentives matter. However, in this section, we find evidence in various organizational contexts that are rewarding individual behavior wholly inconsistent with the behaviors desired.

STEVEN KERR
"On the Folly of Rewarding A While Hoping for B" (1995),
Academy of Management Executive [1975].

Thesis: Organizations repeatedly reward behaviors inconsistent with behavior that is desired. This misalignment of incentives can be confronted and reversed.

Kerr first establishes the universality of the pattern of "rewarding antiproductive behavior" across a spectrum of contemporary organizational life:

- **Politics.** Politicians who declare operative goals with specifics (e.g., about what sacrifices are required and by whom, what programs will cost, and which other objectives will be given lower priority) are not elected by voters. Voters therefore reward the antiproductive behavior of having intentionally vague official goals.

- **War.** In World War II, soldiers went home only when the war was over. In Vietnam, U.S. soldiers went home when their tour of duty was over regardless of the status of the war. Kerr asks if this difference in incentives could have impacted the effectiveness of the U.S. war effort.[4]

- **Medicine.** Doctors can make two types of errors: (1) declare a healthy patient sick, or (2) diagnose a sick patient as healthy. Doctors in the United States are incented to make the first type of error (thus creating income with little likelihood of patient death) and to avoid making the second type (thus creating the risk of expensive liability lawsuits). Doctors thus are financially rewarded for unproductive, higher-cost behavior, while patients

---

[4] We do not think that Kerr intends to malign the efforts of those who fought in the Vietnam War. He cites unnamed research indicating that the average level of acceptance of superior officers' authority was lower in Vietnam than in World War II. It is sufficient for his argument if the different incentives, at the margin, could have impacted the actions of a significant enough subset of soldiers to make a difference.

merely hope that doctors will not engage in unnecessary and expensive testing and procedures.

- **Rehabilitation centers and orphanages.** Federal and local U.S. governments support orphanages with the goal of providing homes for parentless children, but also impose regulations and adoption criteria on social service agencies that can inhibit adoptions. With this sort of *goal displacement*, the means (i.e., criteria and conditions for adoption) become ends in themselves that displace the original goal (adoption). Other rewards can reinforce this displacement, including the allocation of budget and hiring based on the number of unplaced children.

- **Universities.** Teaching awards are limited in number and bestow little to no money or prestige; in contrast, faculty can receive significant rewards for research, and punishment (i.e., no tenure) if they are minimally published. Similarly, it is not knowledge but grades and test scores that drive graduate school prospects, employment, parental appreciation, and so on. Grades become an anti-productive end to themselves, and students direct their behavior toward efficiency in producing grades and scores rather than on obtaining useful knowledge.

- **Ecology.** Kerr presents the hypothetical example of a corporation making a decision to invest in anti-pollution equipment or risk a 10% chance of being caught in non-compliance of environmental regulations, with a fine equal to 10% of the cost of the investment. In this scenario, the threat of regulatory punishment creates no financial incentive to influence behavior, so the desired outcome occurs only if management feels a stronger responsibility to social concerns than to shareholders.

Kerr finds similar dynamics in the evaluation of training programs, in team sports, and in management by objectives (MBO) systems. In each context, the most common reward systems incent behaviors that are directly opposite to the desired outcome.

Three business examples are particularly relevant. First, examining dollar-approval levels at a typical manufacturing firm, the author finds that risk overavoidance is rewarded at lower levels of management, even while the reward system was properly aligned at higher levels. Second, an insurance company attempted to measure and reward accuracy in paying claims quickly by tracking returned checks and customer complaints. This approach ended up encouraging less-stringent claims review and subsequent overpayment: the adjusters found that following up on claims made it impossible to process the claims within two days, so they tended to approve immediately. Lastly, many companies have evaluation systems in which merit increases differ very little between "outstanding" (top 5%) and "average" (near the 50th percentile) employees.

Kerr then identifies four factors explaining why reward systems achieve unintended effects:

- Companies strive for simple measures without realizing that objective measures often conceal predetermined and subjective elements.
- Some behaviors are more easily observed than others; important elements like creativity and teamwork are hard to measure and so are not easily rewarded.
- The behavior incented may be what is actually desired—even if it is not acknowledged as desired. For example, it is the norm in many jurisdictions that judges' campaigns may receive contributions from defense attorneys but not from prosecutors, with the predictable impact on judges' ability to be "tough on crime."
- Factors other than the organizational compensation systems may prevent the establishment of a system that rewards the behaviors desired by senior management. Loyalty, morality, or a sense of fairness may play a larger part than tangible rewards in creating the behavior. U.S. voters who feel obligated to vote in an election may end up voting for politicians who refuse to specifically discuss substantive issues, as those candidates may seem like the least difficult choice to support.

In both the third and fourth factors above, the system is actually generating the behavior desired by the rewarder (even if the rewarder claims to want a different behavior).

Kerr identifies two strategies that have limited utility in achieving improved behavioral influence:

1. **Selection.** Assume that the company can employ only those whose goals coincide with management's (unsurprisingly, Kerr sees limited potential here).
2. **Training.** Assume that a company can educate individuals to align their goals with management; however, history shows that people respond to their individual incentives.

A third strategy, altering reward systems, has better potential:

- Start with identifying which behaviors are currently being rewarded.
- Ensure that rewards reinforce desired behaviors without adding obstacles.

Changing the formal reward system is the only way to escape the necessity of selecting only desirable people (i.e., those who will do the right thing even if it is not in their specific interest), or of altering the behavior of undesirable people.

In his 1995 postscript to the article, Kerr concludes that these ideas are based on common sense:

> I believe that most readers already knew, and act on in their non-work lives, the principles that underlie this article. For example, when we tell our daughter (who is about to cut her birthday cake) that her brother will

select the first piece, or inform our friends before a meal that separate checks will be brought at the end, or tell the neighbor's boy that he will be paid five dollars for cutting the lawn after we inspect the lawn, we are making use of prospective rewards and punishments to cause other people to care about our own objectives. Organizational life may seem to be more complex, but the principles are the same. (pp. 13–14)

HENRY PARSONS
"What Happened at Hawthorne?" (1975), *Science.*

Thesis: *Any* change that involves giving employees feedback with financial incentives will improve productivity—what gets measured gets managed.

From 1924–1932, Western Electric executives commissioned researchers to conduct studies of productivity at their Hawthorne Works factory outside Chicago. Workrooms were given higher and lower levels of light, but researchers found higher productivity during the study period regardless of whether the light was increased or decreased. They similarly found that any type of change (cleaner work stations, clearing floors of obstacles, relocating work stations) resulted in higher productivity. In these studies, operators were told what their output rates were, and those with higher rates received more pay. Since productivity increased under most of the changes made, this created the myth that group dynamics caused faster work under *any* change.

Parsons considers two theories of consequences:

1. **Instrumentality theory.** This theory emphasizes the contingency relationship between performance and wages in terms of (a) the valence of wages (i.e., the value the employee places on the wages), (b) worker perceptions of that relationship, and (c) worker intentions. None of this relationship depends on workers knowing their own productivity results.[5]

2. **Operant conditioning.** This theory (constructed primarily by Skinner 1953) holds that productivity increases as a result of the systematic application of contingent reinforcement, that is, the coupling of a behavior with triggered consequences to influence the likelihood of that specific behavior. More simply, being able to observe one's own production rate,

---

[5] Although Parsons uses the term *instrumentality theory*, we believe the intended term was *expectancy theory* (also called valence-instrumentality-expectancy or VIE theory). Expectancy theory was framed initially by Victor Vroom (1964), and is addressed in Section 5.

and being rewarded for a higher rate, causes workers to determine what actions work best.

Parsons considers various explanations and concludes that operant conditioning is the simplest explanation consistent with the Hawthorne findings.

Change itself is not good for productivity—rather, the Hawthorne experiments themselves introduced information feedback with financial reward. Workers simply learned how to be more productive, and exhibited progressive increases in response rate (typical of operant conditioning).

Discussion and Implications

 We find it very easy to generate examples of unintended-yet-predictable consequences from incentive systems, which demonstrates the ongoing relevance of Kerr's simple but deep article. If you reward your accounts payable and accounts receivable clerks based on the number of transactions they process, you should not be surprised when errors go up along with processing speed. If an employee who is rated as "meets expectations" gets a 3% raise and an employee who is rated as "far exceeds expectations" receives a 5% raise, your organization is not incenting employees to put in the extra 10-20 hours a week it takes to excel. If you are the CEO of Enron and pay your employees based on the return on their investment projects, should you be surprised to find your finance and trading departments taking an unusual amount of risk?

Kerr's article remains a staple of graduate management class syllabi, and played a role in his landing stints at GE and Goldman Sachs in addition to a presidency of the Academy of Management (AOM). Amusingly, the article was initially rejected by the Eastern Academy of Management and recommended for rejection by one of the two initial reviewers at *Academy of Management Journal* (the reviewers thought the tone inappropriate for an academic audience, which the author met by creating more "data" in the form of a table).[6]

Some may find Kerr's conclusion about changing formal rewards somewhat simplistic for the complexity and changeability of modern organizational life. In a 1995 AOM survey, however, 90% of respondents indicated that Kerr's folly was still prevalent in U.S. corporate culture twenty years after his initial article. It is easy to become discouraged by the number of examples of misaligned reward systems compared to the paucity of specific examples of organizations that have realigned their reward systems for improved productivity. On the other hand,

---

[6] This judgment may be evidence that the decision process at academic journals represents an example of the phenomenon Kerr studied. Is the goal of such journals to highlight original articles that help us understand how to manage more effectively, or have the means (tone, data, rigorous number-crunching) become goals in themselves regardless of the value of the content?

we see definite examples where reward systems have been overhauled: the changes made to welfare programs by the U.S. government in the early 1990s, or the success of sports teams using statistical regression to identify previously-unmeasured individual player characteristics that correlate most highly with team success.[7]

One does not need a graduate degree to see situations where outcomes can be improved by letting one child cut the cake and another child select the first piece. The key is organizational self-awareness—what incentives are you creating in your own organization in terms of how you evaluate, pay, and promote your employees?

Parsons's discussion is an excellent reminder of how observing a phenomenon can change that same phenomenon. Research involves measurement of inputs and outcomes, and that very measurement is used by people to work more effectively. Elton Mayo (1945) introduces an additional potential explanation, which is that the attention paid to the workers caused them to feel better (due to the interest of the observers), and that this attention was itself motivating. Under either explanation, these findings offer support for the adage that "what gets measured gets managed."

One corollary of this dynamic is that organizations often find it easier to manage aspects of the business that are easily quantifiable. Paying a bonus to a division manager based on that division's profit is straightforward; making the bonus depend in part on how that division manager contributed to the profit of other divisions may be harder. Introducing other desired criteria (how well does the manager train junior employees, how is she viewed by suppliers, is she a team player, etc.) can be more challenging still.

If a company wants to incent behaviors that lack easy and objective measures, it is a very good investment in time to develop better measures (e.g., what percentage of subordinates moves on to higher responsibility, and how do suppliers and peers rank her on a scale of 1-10). More nuanced measures can then ensure that desired behaviors are managed and rewarded.

5. MOTIVATION

In this section, we describe two articles that are themselves surveys of research over several decades into what motivates employees. Locke and Henne survey

---

[7] See, for example, the book *Moneyball* by Michael Lewis (2004; also a movie in 2011), which describes how the Oakland As identified superior baseball players overlooked by other teams relying on traditional measures, or *Basketball on Paper* by Dean Oliver (2004), which provides a similar statistical re-examination of which basketball player skills correlate most with team success.

the research up to 1986, and Latham and Pinder review evidence from 1986 through 2005.

EDWIN LOCKE and DOUGLAS HENNE
"Work Motivation Theories" (1986), in C. L. Cooper and I. T. Robertson (editors), *International Review of Industrial and Organizational Psychology*.

Thesis: Job satisfaction does not actually drive job performance. Setting goals—particularly, specific and challenging goals—does lead to higher job performance.

This article presents a model of motivation and reviews major theories (up to 1986) in terms of this model. Locke and Henne discuss need theories, value theories, equity theories, goal theories, and self-efficacy theory, along with job satisfaction and turnover.

Need Theories

Need theories include all of the following elements.

- *Needs* are the requirements for an organism's survival and well-being.
- *Cognition* is a factor behind individual differences; establishes identity including one's own abilities and competencies.
- *Values* describe what an individual considers good (perhaps subconsciously), ranked in a hierarchy.
- *Goals* are more specific than values—closer to action.
- *Emotions* refer to the result of value or goal appraisal. Where feedback determines whether the value was achieved or not, emotions result.

Locke and Henne perceive the class of need theories as too limited. Maslow (1970) is well known for presenting a hierarchy of needs whereby people must first meet their physiological needs (air, food, etc.), and then safety, love, esteem, and self-actualization. Once each set of needs is met, a person can pursue the next higher-level set. However, this hierarchy is very difficult to operationalize in terms of explaining work motivation. Herzberg (1968) presents a two-factor theory of (1) motivators that arise from intrinsic conditions of the job itself, and that do or do not provide satisfaction; and (2) hygiene factors, like status and salary, which do not provide satisfaction when present but do create dissatisfaction when absent. Locke and Henne's view is that this two-factor theory has never been adequately tested and it is not valid.

Value Theories

Next, they review two separate value theories, finding them intriguing but concluding that value theories need more conceptual development and experimental work. The first value theory is the Hackman-Oldham (1980) job characteristics theory, which states that task characteristics that satisfy growth needs will lead to satisfaction and internalized work motivation, thereby affecting work performance. There are five core task characteristics: variety, task identity, task significance, autonomy, and feedback. Those individuals with higher growth needs will also have higher levels of three psychological states (experienced meaningfulness, experienced responsibility, and knowledge of results). When these three states are present, the worker will get satisfaction and motivation for high quality work.

Locke and Henne's analysis of this theory is that the job satisfaction criterion appears valid, the growth need has inconsistent results, and the link of characteristics to performance is weak and inconsistent. The main problem is that the job characteristics theory is unclear regarding how one gets from core characteristics to high performance, or how desire for enriched work leads to performance standards or goals.

The second value theory, Deci's (1980) intrinsic motivation theory, states that an employee's desire for competence and self-determination (i.e., intrinsic motivation) should be measured by observing the time spent on a task during a free-choice period. This motivation can be facilitated by enhancing the employee's sense of self-determination by giving her choices or enhancing her sense of competence through positive feedback. Unfortunately, Locke and Henne conclude, no study provides direct evidence in support of all or substantial parts of this model.

Equity Theories

Equity theory is focused on the value of equity/inequity, where equity is the ratio of outputs to inputs. Employees may compare the ratio of their outputs-to-inputs to the same ratio for other people. Locke and Henne find some empirical support for this theory of motivation, but it is stronger for the subset of people who feel undercompensated. The authors view this theory as too flexible: it can explain any behavior but cannot explain why something is an input rather than an outcome without reference to other motivational concepts. They conclude that equity is just one of many values.

McClelland's (1961; see also Miner 1980) achievement and power-motivation theories hold that people who are high in achievement motivation will value tasks where (a) performance is related to their efforts; (b) there is concrete, immediate feedback regarding performance; (c) employees have a moderate future orientation; and (c) novel solutions are allowed or encouraged. The thematic apperception test can be used to measure the subconscious motivation of entrepreneurs. However, as Locke and Henne discuss, this test has been shown to have low internal consistency (except with large numbers) and low re-test reliability, and is not considered valid for women. Furthermore, the tests covered only entrepreneurial environments (i.e., a limited subset of employees).

Miner's (1978, 1985) role-motivation theory presents a specific motivational system or values set associated with success in bureaucratic organizations. Success is measured on six dimensions: authority, competition, assertiveness, the imposition of wishes on others, independence (standing out), and routine administration. Locke and Henne find that tests of these values show consistent validity, and do correlate significantly with managerial success in organizations that are hierarchical and structured (e.g., the military).

Expectancy theory (also known as valence-instrumentality-expectancy theory) describes the process of selecting one alternative among many possible actions (Vroom 1964). A person's motivation should depend on the following: valences (values), instrumentality (perceived probability of possible outcome), and expectancy (successful performance of act). Locke and Henne find some positive empirical support for this theory, though the theory is often criticized. They conclude that it may be more appropriate for explaining job choices than in explaining work motivations.

Goal Theories

Finally, Locke and Henne discuss goal theories (Locke's own specialty). The large majority (90%) of studies examined show that setting goals enhances performance. Goal theory, as espoused by Locke (1984) and by others (including Locke, Shaw, Saari, and Latham 1981), also asserts the following:

- **Specific and difficult goals lead to higher performance.** Having no goals or only vague goals is associated with lower performance.
- **Goals affect task performance.** Performance is enhanced by direct attention or action, mobilizing effort, increased persistence, and a motivated search for strategies.
- **Goal commitment is necessary for goals to affect performance.** Goal commitment is unaffected by participation in goal setting, but is affected by expectancy of goal success and valence of (value placed on) success.
- **Money may interact with goal-setting.**
- **Demographic and individual differences are not related to effectiveness.**

This theory represents a breakthrough, as it resolves the apparent conflict between *expectancy theory* (which holds that expectancy is positively related to performance) and *goal theory* (which holds that hard goals with low expectations correlate with performance). Goal theory applies between groups and expectancy theory applies within groups.

Self-Efficacy Theory

Having covered the major categories of motivation theories (need theories, value theories, and goal theory), Locke and Henne then address Bandura's (1982) self-efficacy theory as a theory of cognition whose effects are primarily motivational. *Self-efficacy* is a judgment of how well one can execute the actions required to deal with prospective situations, and it includes one's convictions about one's total capacity to perform a task (ability, adaptability, ingenuity, and capacity to perform under stress). There is a strong relationship between self-efficacy and performance, in domains ranging from clinical settings to workplace: believing you are competent noticeably helps your performance.

Job Satisfaction

The authors look at both the causes (inputs) for job satisfaction as well as its consequences for motivation (outputs). A number of variables have been shown to be associated with job satisfaction: race, sex, rural/urban, alienation and job quality, union status, volunteer versus paid status, self-esteem and job attributes, autonomy, role ambiguity, role conflict and organizational level, tension, self rated performance versus pay, realistic expectations, value importance, and flexible hours. In terms of performance, early theorists believed that satisfied workers were more productive. However, despite repeated examination, researchers have not been able to document job satisfaction as a significant driver of job performance.

Employee Turnover

It has been hypothesized that more dissatisfied workers are most likely to leave. This hypothesis has been generally supported by the data, but the magnitude of the correlation is not large. Researchers should look for ways to improve prediction of turnover. Other data validates the expected negative correlation of absenteeism and lateness with job satisfaction.

Locke and Henne conclude by rating each group of theories on a scale of 1 to 5 in terms of validity (Table 4-1). The ratings are higher as the theories get closer to describing action.

Table 4-1: Locke and Henne's Motivation Theory Ratings

Theory Type	Validity Rating
Need theories	1.25
Value theories	2.75
Role motivation theories	4.00
Expectancy theories	3.50
Goal theories	4.67

Note. Authors' table; data from Locke and Henne (1986, p. 26).

GARY LATHAM and CRAIG PINDER
"Work Motivation Theory and Research at the Dawn of the
Twenty-First Century" (2005), *Annual Review of Psychology.*

Thesis: Context is the key to job motivation, particularly that provided by
culture, job characteristics, and job fit. Also, workers are motivated by
subconscious as well as conscious sources.

This article is a more recent literature survey examining both
theoretical and empirical progress made in work-motivation
theory. Latham and Pinder emphasize the importance of context
(established by recent research) as key to understanding
organizational behavior. They focus in particular on three contextual variables:
job design characteristics (common in studying motivation), and the two newer
elements of national culture and person-environment fit.

Latham and Pinder's framework for reviewing literature is consistent with
Locke and Henne's. They categorize the research into seven core areas: needs,
traits, values, context, fit, cognition, and emotion.

Needs

Maslow's (1954) hierarchical needs theory has received more testing since 1986.
For example, Haslam, Powell, and Turner (2000) find that when personal
identity is dominant, the need to self-actualize and enhance self-esteem through
personal advancement becomes dominant. On the other hand, when social
identity is emphasized, the need to enhance group esteem and relatedness takes
center stage. When supervisor and employee have different identities, behavior
is more externally controlled (this theory of external control is commonly
referred to as *Theory X*). When the two have similar identities, self-direction is
more common (self-direction is referred to as *Theory Y*). Overall, however,
Latham and Pinder caution that while needs-based theories explain why a
person acts, they do not predict specific actions nor account for individual
differences.

Traits

Research on personality has been a growing part of the motivation literature.
Research shows that personality traits (including extroversion,
conscientiousness, self-regulation and monitoring, tenacity, and goal-
orientation) predict or influence choice of job as well as job performance and
satisfaction.

Values

Values influence behavior because they are standards used to choose among alternative courses of action. Values are similar to goals, though less specific; goals are the mechanism by which values lead to action. In one study, Malka and Chatman (2003) find that business school graduates with an external work orientation (i.e., motivated by external measures of success like money or grades) are more satisfied with their work than those who focus on intrinsic aspects of work.

Context

One aspect of context is national culture, which plays a role in determining key components of motivation, including people's self-concept, norms about work ethic and achievement, and environmental factors (education, prosperity, political systems). Steers and Sanchez-Runde (2002) conclude that these factors influence self-efficacy beliefs, motivation levels, and goals. Several other researchers show that projecting values from one culture to another, when those two cultures differ on collectivism-versus-individualism and on power distance, can seriously impact employee motivation and performance (see Earley 2002).

Another element of context is job design characteristics and their fit with a person's values. Characteristics such as job autonomy, learning, performance, organizational citizenship behavior, and satisfaction have all been demonstrated to impact motivation.

Person-Context Fit

Cable and DeRue (2002) find that employees differentiate among person-environment fit, needs-supplies fit, and the fit between job demands and employee abilities. An attraction-selection-attrition model states that people gravitate to jobs congruent with their values (Schneider, Smith, and Paul 2001).

Cognition

Cognition is itself broken down by Latham and Pinder into seven subcategories.

- **Goal-setting theory.** This idea remains the single most dominant theory in the field of motivation. A significant body of research validates that performance is enhanced by goals that are specific, challenging, and committed to by the employee. In addition, high goals can lead to performance and rewards, leading to higher self-efficicacy, in a virtuous cycle (Latham, Locke, and Fassina 2002).
- **Contextual conditions.** Goal-setting can be complicated in certain situations. Self-enhancing personal goals can reduce group performance when the individual and group goals differ (Seijts and Latham 2000). For complex tasks, urging employees to do their best yields better performance than a specific high goal, but a high learning goal in terms of discovering a

specific number of ways to solve a complex task does even better (Winters and Latham 1996).

- **Implementation of intentions and auto-motive goals.** Goal intentions accompanied by implementation intentions on complex tasks lead to higher goal attainment than do goal intentions only (Golliwitzer 1999). Implementation intentions link situations to responses (i.e., "whenever situation x arises, the individual will initiate the goal-directed response y). Nonconscious goals produce the same favorable outcomes as conscious ones (Bargh and Ferguson 2000).

- **Feedback.** Active feedback-seeking by new employees correlates with performance (Ashford and Black 1996). However, feedback is more helpful for people with high self-esteem; those with low esteem may lack the resilience to seek feedback or to keep it from affecting their self-appraisal.

- **Self-regulation.** Setting goals and seeking feedback are the core of self-regulation. Employees can be trained to engage in self-enabling rather than self-debilitating self-talk when confronted by setbacks.

- **Expectancy theory.** Naylor, Pritchard, and Ilgen's (1980) expectancy theory[8] holds that motivation is a process of allocating time and energy to a variety of tasks, where the relationship between energy and resulting need satisfaction determines how much energy is devoted to any particular action. Updating the motivational component of Naylor et al.'s work, Pritchard and Payne (2003) developed a "ProMes" productivity measurement system that identifies objectives, measures the extent to which they are met, and provides feedback regarding performance. This system has been found to lead to productivity improvements in European countries regardless of culture.

- **Social cognitive theory.** Research shows that the effect of environmental antecedents and consequences is mediated by cognitive variables. People are motivated by the foresight of goals, not just the hindsight of shortfalls. There is some debate about whether high self-efficacy leads to new and higher goals, or whether at times it may lead to complacency or inappropriate task persistence. This theory downplays the importance of personality traits.

Affect/Emotion

People with higher positive affect (i.e., those who appear or act happier) tend to be more persistent and motivated on tasks (Erez and Isen 2002). Negative mood may correlate with creativity, however, because the bad mood signals dissatisfaction with the status quo (George and Zhou 2002). Another driver of

---

[8] Although similarly named, this is a different theory than the expectancy theory (valence-instrumentality-expectancy) coined by Vroom (1964) that was discussed earlier in the section.

motivation, consistent with equity theory described earlier by Locke and Henne, appears to be the individual's view of organizational justice. Individuals develop beliefs about the work inputs they provide and the outcomes they receive, and compare the ratio for themselves to that of others. Fair procedures enhance acceptance of organizational outcomes. When employees feel unfairly treated, they commit less and leave more often.

Latham and Pinder reach ten conclusions from this broad overview of motivation research.

1. Three theories have dominated the motivation literature: goal-setting, social cognitive theory, and organizational justice.
2. Research no longer predominantly focuses on cognition as it did from 1950–1975; recognition is also given to the importance of affect and behavior.
3. The ability to understand motivation has broadened in scope to include needs, values, cognition, affect, and behavior.
4. Today's research seeks to explain more variables (ranging from citizenship to counterproductive behavior) than earlier measures of job performance and satisfaction.
5. Experimental and correlational psychology have combined forces to explore how particular mechanisms (like personality traits) mediate between causes and impacts in motivation.
6. The importance of context to motivation is now much better recognized, in lieu of one-size-fits-all conclusions. Culture, job characteristics, and job fit all matter.
7. Motivation now acknowledges not only conscious sources of motivation but also pre- or sub-conscious sources.
8. Theorists are spending less time destroying other theories and more time constructing developments from what is already known.
9. The understanding of motivation is broader than before, but knowledge is not growing at a rate commensurate with the energy invested over the past thirty years.
10. There have been few fundamentally new models with the same impact as Maslow's need theory, Vroom's expectancy theory, or Locke and Latham's goal-setting theory.

Discussion and Implications

Most of the academic theories on motivation included in Locke and Henne's 1986 review have received significant press despite a dearth of any evidence that they actually describe what motivates workers. For example, contrary to the belief of many human resource practitioners, the evidence does not indicate that job satisfaction correlates with performance. However, the literature has shown a few approaches that do work.

- Setting goals enhances performance.
- The more specific and ambitious the goals, the higher the increase in performance.
- Humility is a limited virtue.
- Believing you are good at your job helps you perform better at it, which might help explain the large egos in many who hold positions of power.

In other work, Locke (1996, 2000) describes goal-setting in more detail, and provides explicit guidance to executives. Specifically, one can expect higher performance with the following:

- more difficult goals,
- more specific goals,
- goals employees believe are important,
- goals that employees believe they are capable of making progress toward, and
- goals that allow for feedback on progress made.

Surprisingly, it makes little difference whether the employees identify the goals themselves or are given those goals by their managers.

Tying compensation to goals creates some real tension, which creates the unhelpful incentive of employees trying as hard as possible to make sure that their goals are easy to achieve. Locke (2000) quotes an executive who describes management-by-objectives as "the procedure by which smart managers tried to convince their bosses that their easy goals were actually hard" (p. 52). One alternative is to motivate by goals but reward by performance, so that an employee who sets challenging goals which are not met can be paid more than one who fully meets easier goals (Locke 1996, 2000).

We agree; based on our experience, for a company to move toward setting real stretch goals to stimulate performance, this approach will only work if the company simultaneously ensures that employees are rewarded based on their actual achievement rather than on the percent-of-goals-achieved. Otherwise, employees are likely to feel exploited—after working on challenging goals and not getting paid for the extra effort—and will redouble their efforts to ensure that future goals are set lower.

If management-by-objective results in goals that are too easy, critics have also taken aim at the related ritual of annual performance reviews. Culbert (2008) makes a persuasive case for abolishing such reviews, in large part because of the very different agendas of the two participants. "The boss wants to discuss where performance needs to be improved, while the subordinate is focused on such small issues as compensation, job progression and career advancement" (p. 1). Again we agree; we think it is vital to assess performance and also to discuss the employee's individual goals, but that it is unproductive to have these two separate discussions as part of the same conversation.

In Latham and Pinder's review of what motivates employees, as with Locke and Henne's, many theories have not been borne out by the evidence; nonetheless, research has uncovered salient tools for managers to utilize in motivating employees. Too few executives appear to know that the absolute level of compensation alone has not been found to be tremendously motivating. However, employees appear highly motivated by *relative compensation*, that is, how they are paid relative to other people in the same organization (or relative to those in other organizations with the same role).[9] This focus on local ranking is probably due to the importance to employees of organizational justice. We think that many managers intuitively understand the importance of relative pay, which is why most companies work very hard to prevent individual employees from knowing the compensation offered to their peers within the company.

Firms may be able to get away with underpaying everyone better than they can get away with being seen to pay some workers more, when those workers are not viewed by their peers as deserving. Firms benefit by tying compensation to performance in ways that are perceived as objective and consistent, and leaders need to think carefully through what incentives are created (e.g., the previously-discussed incentive to have overly easy goals within a management-by-objectives framework).

Context has also been demonstrated to play a large role in motivation. Individuals from different cultures are motivated differently (e.g., the role of the group versus individual in the culture, and norms regarding the acceptable range of power between the least and most powerful members).

It is easy to forget that employees are motivated by recognition: simple praise and acknowledgement can go a long way. The book *1501 Ways to Reward Employees* (Nelson 2012) gives a concrete list to managers looking for inexpensive ways to recognize performance and maintain motivation.

Employees are also motivated by being part of a larger cause. It is no coincidence that Google's period as a highly desirable employer came at the same time as their founders' exhortation "Don't be evil." Cisco does not sell internet plumbing, but rather "transforms how people connect, communicate, and collaborate." Eric's experience at Cisco (when it had one of the highest market capitalizations in the world) bears out that employees work harder when

---

[9] Some understand this instinctively. In his informative and entertaining 1989 book *Liar's Poker*, Michael Lewis tells the story of receiving his first bonus at Salomon Brothers. His initial joy at receiving a six-figure bonus check quickly turned to anger when he found that some of his coworkers received higher amounts.

they believe they are changing the world. Facebook connects people to their friends. These larger causes are effective in recruitment and retention.

6. POWER

In this section, we review research on power in organizations. *Power* is the ability to get things done, and is not always aligned with position in a hierarchy. Salancik and Pfeffer examine who obtains power in an organization, and Kanter shows how a number of positions actually lack power.

RICHARD SALANCIK and JEFFREY PFEFFER
"Who Gets Power and How They Hold on to It: A Strategic Contingency Model of Power" (1977), *Organizational Dynamics.*

Thesis: Power accrues to those who cope with the organization's problems. Power is therefore the secret of success.

Political power is one of the few mechanisms available for aligning an organization with its own reality. However, institutional power tends to buffer the organization from reality; it is hard to define power, but easy to recognize its consequences.
Power is the ability to get things done the way one wants them to be done. Salancik and Pfeffer studied more than twenty organizations, with two interesting findings: an unusual level of agreement amongst respondents when asked who is influential in the group, and very few questions regarding what was meant by influential.

Power Facilitates the Organization's Adaptation to Its Environment
Those subunits most able to deal with the organization's critical problems acquire power. When an organization faces a number of life-threatening lawsuits, the legal department gains influence. If a person or unit is critical to other units, they will have power, regardless of whether that is recognized by more senior levels of management. The basis for power in an organization derives from the ability of a person or unit to take (or not take) actions desired by others.

Power Is Shared Because No One Can Control All the Scarce, Critical Resources
Because power derives from activities rather than individuals, that power is never absolute and derives ultimately from the context of the situation. One's

own power always depends on other people, partly because of their ability to substitute for one's unique contribution.

Power rarely organizes around abundant resources, but rather around activities that are both scarce and important; one way to remove power is to deemphasize the importance of the controlled activity.

Power Accrues from Aligning an Organization with Its Environment
The environmental context determines what resources are needed, and therefore, the problems to be dealt with. Subunits contributing to critical resources will gain influence, which may sound obvious, but many managers appear to assume that all departments in the same tier on an organizational chart actually hold the same status.

Salancik and Pfeffer tested the above three hypotheses (representing a model of power) by analyzing 29 departments in a university over 18 months, and conclude that those departments bringing more critical resources to the university were more powerful. They found that three factors accounted for 70% of the variance in perceived power: the relative contribution of each department in outside grants received, the number of courses taught, and national departmental rankings.

Power Impacts Decision-Making
However, since power is used sparingly by those who have it, decisions will not always be made by those with the most power. A rational model of budgeting university departments might be to make budgets proportional to student demand for courses, or based on each department's research reputation. A power-based model would predict that budgets will depend on grant funds obtained. If there are several possible alternatives for a rational basis, then there will be differences of opinion about how to weight them, and decisions will become more likely to reflect the goals of those who prevail in political contests.

The authors propose three conditions that are likely to affect the use of power:

- **Scarcity.** Subunits will exert influence when resources are scarce (if resources are abundant, the unit can get what it wants without exerting new effort).
- **Criticality.** A subunit will attempt to influence decisions to obtain resources that are necessary to its own activities (and will not fight over trivial decisions).
- **Uncertainty.** When individuals do not agree about what the organization should do or how to go about it, power will affect decisions. If there are no clear-cut criteria for resolving conflicts, then resolution will follow a social process. If there is no real consensus, the powerful manager can usually make the most persuasive case.

The university evidence shows that department power is the single biggest predictor of the percentage of the university budget achieved by each department. When the total budget is cut back, budget allocations mirror power even more closely. A department's need for resources (i.e., student demand for that department's courses) is a very weak predictor.

Power Influences the Selection of Key Leadership Positions

The choice of leaders further aligns the organization to its environment. Chief administrators in hospitals were found to have backgrounds in whatever form that dollar-inflows occurred: for business hospitals, administrators were experienced in patient billing; and for social service hospitals, they were experienced at obtaining government funding. In addition, rural hospitals with fewer problems tended to have longer-serving administrators, and hospitals facing more challenges tended to have more turnover. Troublesome conditions in individual organizations tend to be misattributed to the executives themselves. Tenure is affected by the status of a hospital's budget—not so much by level of the surplus or deficit, but rather by the relationship with those providing the funding.

When Critical Contingencies Change, Power Changes in Turn

This effect holds true for both individuals and the organization. The dominant coalition will tend to be the group that can best contend with the biggest current challenge. For example, until the 1950s, corporations tended to be led by former production-line managers. As this function became mechanized, marketers were more likely to become the leaders. Marketing benefited from size, and the finance executives who could facilitate mergers and investments became heavily represented in the 1960s.

Adaptation Can Have Nonadaptive Consequences

Those with the ability to get the job done are given the job to do, but in addition, the definition of the job will expand and become less clear. Power is a capacity for influence that extends beyond the original bases that created it; power also tends to take on institutionalized forms that enable it to endure long beyond its usefulness. Those in power will not easily give it up and will pursue policies that facilitate their continued domination. According to Salancik and Pfeffer, "change and stability operate through the same mechanism, and, as a result, the organization will never be completely in phase with its environment or its needs" (p. 17). Hospital administrators with a longer tenure tend to be found in private hospitals with diffuse ownership as opposed to those depending on one or two external organizations. Similarly, corporations with diffuse ownership appear to have poorer earnings and longer-tenured executives than those in which there is a dominant shareholder.

It Is Often Easy to Mistake Critical Contingencies
More powerful units may extend their power by arguing for resource allocation criteria that favor them, even if these are not the most rational criteria. Since the appropriate criteria are often not obvious, those with prior credibility may be listened to.

Those in Power Can Create Structures to Institutionalize Themselves
For example, they can name their functions as critical, structure the organization in a way that favors themselves, structure information systems to ensure their access to critical data, and distribute rewards and resources. A consumer company might enhance the power of marketing by establishing a coordinator role between production and marketing, and by appointing a marketing manager to that role. Interestingly, turnover among executives who have had the ability to structure the organization is rare; if opposition is designed out, leadership may remain constant until a crisis develops that is so severe that the failure of leadership to stay aligned with challenges becomes obvious. This ability to structure the organization can be another source of misalignment between organizations and their environments.

There are some clear implications for how to manage power in organizations. One should start outside the organization to understand power within it, by identifying groups that mediate the organization's outcomes but are not within its direct control. Construct an accurate model of the environment to ensure that those with the relevant expertise are incorporated into the decision-making process.

ROSABETH MOSS KANTER
"Power Failures in Management Circuits" (1979), *Harvard Business Review*.

Thesis: Powerlessness (not power) breeds bossiness. Power can mean efficacy and capacity. To expand power, share it.

It is easier to talk about money and sex than about power. Effectiveness from power evolves from access to resources, and from the ability to get cooperation in doing what is necessary. Organizational sources of power derive from connections and consist of three lines: lines of supply, lines of information, and lines of support. Such systemic aspects of power derive from two sources:

- **Job activities.** Power accumulates in jobs that allow discretion.

- **Political alliances.** Power comes when one has close contact with sponsors or peers.

Many positions are in fact positions of powerlessness. First-line supervisors are evaluated by certain rules while limited by others; they cannot control events but must react. Staff professionals tend to get stuck in specialized roles, lack growth prospects, and become turf-minded, resisting change. Even top executives can lack supplies, information, and support. Finally, female managers experience special power failures. Women are often overprotected, bypassed, lacking in informal networks, and viewed as recipients of sponsorship rather than sponsors themselves.

To expand power, share it. All the groups named above can experience powerlessness and often react by exercising dictatorial, rules-minded management styles. Many modern bureaucracies minimize dependence on individual intelligence and so are surprised that people in routine jobs can in fact make sophisticated decisions.

Discussion and Implications

A central conclusion by Salancik and Pfeffer is that those elements of an organization that are most able to deal with the larger organization's critical problems acquire power. We see this at both macro and micro levels. Fifty years ago, manufacturing departments tended to dominate. As more corporations pursued economies of scale to become conglomerates, finance became more important. As companies battle increasingly in court (over patents) or in congress (over legislation), legal and government affairs get more influence. We have personally seen that, in most technology companies, the engineers rule.

In any industry, we find it informative to look at the distribution of CEOs' professional backgrounds. Are they coming from marketing, engineering, finance, supply chain management, or elsewhere? The predominant CEO background says a lot about which functions have the power in that industry.

There are several models of power that have some overlap with Salancik and Pfeffer. Astley and Sachdeva (1984) develop a model of organizational power as the joint product of three sources: hierarchical authority, resource control, and network centrality. They view power as linked to the reach of important organizational goals, but they do not determine how such goals are developed. Shafritz, Ott, and Jang (2010) define *power* as the ability to get things done, stemming from resources, information, and access. Pfeffer (1981) clarifies that power is separate from authority, and represents a store of potential influence; politics then involves activities to develop and use this power.

Organizational leaders must see the world as it is, not as they wish it to be. Some find it distasteful to spend time thinking through ways to get more power;

they are likely to end up with less of it as a result, and to be more often surprised by the decisions that get made on other-than-rational criteria. Humans are hierarchical. Decisions are not always made by the most powerful voice, but overall we agree with Jeffrey Pfeffer's (1981) observation that if a political/power model of making decisions is the natural inclination of most people, it will require constant energy to apply any different model within a particular organization.

Kanter concisely describes how various categories of people end up low in power. A common thread is that those who have less access to real information will have less real power to influence outcomes. The less-informed can be lower-level employees, who may be thought of as "not needing to know" the larger context in order to focus on efficiency in their own small part of the company (e.g., a salesperson who knows the product line but not the company's overall competition strategy). Higher-level employees may not know what is really happening in the field. Women may be excluded from the informal networks that supplement the flow of information from official channels with useful gossip and background. Our own (admittedly anecdotal) belief is that senior executives in many companies restrict information flow, with the stated justification of protecting proprietary information about company strategy—but in reality, keeping their staff less knowledgeable and therefore less powerful.[10]

In an organizational setting, much depends on the level of centralization or decentralization an organization has in decision-making. We suggest that what is important as a leader is to consciously direct the level of autonomy you want in your team. Do you want the first-line supervisors in the field where they have access to some of the most relevant information, making decisions? Or do you want the executives in headquarters, with more decision-making experience and possessing "the big picture," to be driving those decisions?[11] Either is defensible, with implications for the type of employees you should be recruiting at all levels. The ability to make decisions is a skill that increases with practice and rusts with disuse, so your choice may also drive whether your next senior-level leaders will be found internally or externally. Sharing power can make you more efficacious and thereby increase your own power.

---

[10] It would be interesting to run an experiment whereby senior management shares meaningful short-term strategic information with middle and lower management, to see if the resulting increase in the team's ability to assist in achieving the desired outcomes might outweigh the loss of some competitive intelligence to the outside world. However, we do not know many senior teams that want to run such an experiment.

[11] It is interesting to observe how different presidencies approach this dilemma. George W. Bush is said to have preferred to manage crises from the White House with his core team, and so he was not as concerned about who he appointed to cabinet and other posts. Similarly, Johnson was known for micromanaging the generals in Vietnam. Other presidents, like Kennedy (who recruited "the best and brightest") and Reagan, gave more power to their subordinates.

7. Information Technology and Productivity

In this section, we review process-improvement approaches that have been in and out of fashion since 1990, and focus on how these approaches involve the use of information technology (IT). Then we examine the assumption that information technology creates more value-added in productivity than the technology itself costs. We review a survey article that dissects multiple studies about the relationship between IT and productivity, and finds common denominators among those studies that do find a positive correlation.

MICHAEL HAMMER
"Reengineering Work: Don't Automate, Obliterate" (1990),
Harvard Business Review.

Thesis: Modern information technology can enable organizations to eliminate non-value-added activities instead of merely automating them to make them more efficient.

U.S. companies have spent years restructuring and downsizing by rationalizing and automating processes, but have obtained only a fraction of the necessary or possible improvements. Hammer argues that this gap largely results from leaving existing processes intact and merely using computers to incrementally speed up those processes. Many processes were built on a model of decentralization and labor specialization, but involving multiple people tends to blur accountability.

Instead of "paving the cow paths," as they have been doing, companies can use IT to fundamentally redesign processes from the ground up. Such reengineering breaks ingrained patterns of thinking about one's business—an all-or-nothing proposition with an uncertain result but tremendous promise.

In the early 1980s, Ford looked for ways to make its accounts payable (a department of over 500 employees) function more efficiently. The existing process went as follows:

1. The purchasing department wrote an order and sent a copy to accounts payable (AP).
2. The materials department received the goods, and sent a list of those goods to AP.
3. AP compared the two documents, and if they matched, issued a payment.

Predictably, the department spent most of its time investigating differences between the two documents. Rather than use technology to make this investigation more efficient, Ford instituted invoiceless processing.

1. Purchasing enters an order into a database.
2. When the goods arrive at the receiving dock, the receiving clerk checks the database for a match with a purchase order.
3. If there is a match, the clerk accepts the shipment and enters into the system for AP to pay. If there is not a match, the shipment is rejected.

This new system allowed Ford to reduce payables staff by over 75%.

Mutual Benefit Life achieved similar savings when it reengineered how it processes insurance applications. The old process involved several steps performed by different people in assembly-line style (checking credit, quoting, rating, underwriting). The new process put each application under a single case manager, which allowed the department to significantly reduce staffing and double the volume of applications processed at the same time.

Hammer suggests seven principles to guide cross-functional teams in achieving better outcomes.

1. **Organize around outcomes, not tasks.** Have one person perform all the steps in a process, designing their job around an entire objective rather than a single task within an objective.

2. **Have those who use the output of the process perform that process.** Co-locating the "doers" with the users of a process eliminates the overhead associated with managing the actual work of the process. If accounting needs pencils, accounting can order pencils directly rather than going through purchasing.

3. **Subsume information-processing work into the real work that produces the information.** Rather than having receiving send information into accounts payable, receiving can process the received goods itself.

4. **Treat geographically dispersed resources as though they are centralized.** Companies can use telecommunications and computing networks to achieve the benefits of scale and coordination (that previously required centralization) while maintaining the benefits of flexibility and service that come with decentralization.

5. **Link parallel activities instead of integrating their results.** Forge links between parallel functions while the activities are taking place, rather than waiting for them all to finish and then redesigning the parts to fit. For example, different units within a bank should not have to wait to know if another department has extended credit to a customer.

6. **Put the decision point where the work is performed, and build control into the process.** Organizations no longer need to distinguish between those who do the work and those who monitor the work. Processes can

have built-in controls, enabling the flattening of management layers within an organization.

7. **Capture information once and at the source.** This principle is essential to avoid repetitive and conflicting data.

Hammer emphasizes the importance of creative thinking to obtain all the value that information technology can offer an organization.

> We have the tools to do what we need to do. Information technology offers many options for reorganizing work. But our imaginations must guide our decisions about technology—not the other way around. We must have the boldness to imagine taking 78 days out of an 80-day turnaround time, cutting 75% of overhead, and eliminating 80% of errors. These are not unrealistic goals. If managers have the vision, reengineering will provide a way. (p. 112)

 RAJIV KOHLI and SARV DEVARAJ
"Measuring Information Technology Payoff: A Meta-Analysis of Structural Variables in Firm-Level Empirical Research" (2003), *Information Systems Research.*

Thesis: Studies employing better methodologies tend to find a positive connection between IT and organizational productivity.

 Business managers consider IT to be an enabler for improved organizational efficiency. Despite the fact that some recent studies have put to rest the "productivity paradox" (i.e., the observation that continuing improvements in computing power do not seem to yield similar improvements in productivity), not all studies have demonstrated a clear payoff from IT investment. Kohli and Devaraj undertake a systematic analysis to understand the structural differences between studies that find a positive payoff and those that do not. They catalog the literature and examine variables influencing different findings.

In reviewing the literature, Kohli and Devaraj begin with a review of IT-payoff research. Past studies at the firm level have explored what element of productivity is measured, how it is measured, and where it is measured. In studies gauging the correlation of IT investments with measures of productivity, the source of data and the analysis approach both matter. Study characteristics (e.g., duration of data collection and process of IT investment) describe how the data is measured. Even when IT spending is shown to improve intermediate variables like communication, that result does not necessarily lead to improvements in productivity. In addition, IT payoff appears harder to measure in some industries than others. Prior studies have differed in terms of contexts, characteristics, data sources, and variables employed in firm-level studies.

Based on the literature, Kohli and Devaraj catalog the structural variables that have been explored in 66 empirical firm-level studies conducted from 1990-2000 that measured the impact of IT on company performance. They develop and test propositions to examine the influence of various variables on the payoff from IT. From each specific prior study, they identify the dependent variable, sample size, data source, IT impact examination, IT asset identification, and industry. They also employ a variable that measures continuous IT payoff. They label each study as either showing a positive or nonpositive impact of IT on the payoff measure. In their results, Kohli and Devaraj find support for most of their propositions.

The authors summarize the results of other studies and identify common factors that find a positive impact of IT on performance:

- IT had a higher positive impact for some industry sectors (e.g, manufacturing and service businesses) than others (e.g., nonprofits and governments).
- A positive impact of IT correlated with larger sample sizes.
- Data collected from the firms themselves showed a higher positive impact of IT.
- Studies that measured productivity rather than simply profitability (as dependent variables) tended to show a higher positive impact of IT.
- There was higher positive impact of IT in studies that identified an intermediate process-variable related to the IT asset (though not to the impact of IT).

Some of Kohli and Devaraj's predictions related to the data analysis were not supported:

- Studies applying regression or economic models do not show a higher IT payoff than those applying simpler correlation-based analyses.
- Studies with a longitudinal design (looking at individual firms over time) do not show a greater IT payoff than those with cross-sectional designs (looking at different firms at a single point in time).
- Higher IT payoff in studies capturing IT assets and IT impacts (a process orientation) is not demonstrated compared to those studies lacking this more detailed process orientation.

Kohli and Devaraj acknowledge the limitation that the studies they utilized came primarily from the information systems discipline, and that the source studies themselves may not always have measured variables accurately. They find that how studies of IT payoff are conducted makes a meaningful difference to the conclusions reached.

Discussion and Implications

 The Hammer article, the subsequent book by Hammer and Champy (1993), and a similar article by Davenport and Short (1990)[12] sparked something of a revolution in companies in the 1990s in implementing business process reengineering (BPR).

BPR became trendy.[13] Consulting firms (including Andersen Consulting, Bain, Boston Consulting Group, McKinsey, and others) embraced and evangelized the BPR message, and information technology (IT) was central to that message.

Hammer and Champy (1993) identify disruptive technologies that challenge the conventional wisdom on how processes should be managed: shared databases, expert systems, telecommunications networks, decision-support tools, wireless communication, automated identification and tracking, and high-performance computing. Enterprise Resource Planning (ERP) vendors (including SAP, Oracle, JD Edwards, and PeopleSoft) demonstrated how ERP serves as a natural tool for process redesign. In fact, given the amount of money that companies were spending on consultants for both IT implementation and process redesign, Oracle and other software vendors have been successful at convincing customers that it is less expensive and more efficient to adapt their firms' processes to the software applications (which are themselves developed specifically for each industry) rather than attempting to customize software applications to their existing business processes.

Of course, IT itself does not guarantee successful reengineering. Markus and Benjamin (1997) explore why many IT change management projects result in failure, and conclude that too often managers see IT as a "magic bullet," forgetting that each project must have an assigned change agent to ensure that the tools are utilized as intended. Focusing on IT rather than the need for change can cause managers to avoid resolving the real issues involved with changing process. Other elements driving success and failure of BPR projects (including the importance of an adequate IT infrastructure) are found in Covert (1997) and Al-Mashari and Zairi (1999). Critics of reengineering focus on the fact that companies have downsized in the name of reengineering (Davenport 1995).

At about the same time as BPR's emergence, W. Edwards Deming (2000a, 2000b) and others developed Total Quality Management (TQM) which

---

[12] Davenport and Short (1990) state that "business process design and information technology are natural partners, yet industrial engineers have never fully exploited their relationship. The authors [Davenport and Short] argue, in fact, that it has barely been exploited at all. But the organizations that *have* used IT to redesign boundary-crossing, customer-driven processes have benefited enormously" (p. 11).

[13] In 1993, 60% of Fortune 500 claimed in their annual reports to have initiated reengineering or to have plans to do so (Hamscher 1994, p. 71).

emphasizes long-term success through customer satisfaction. In these last two books, Deming repeated his philosophy that organizations can increase quality and simultaneously reduce costs (by reducing waste, rework, staff attrition, and litigation while increasing customer loyalty). The key to this improvement in both quality and cost is to practice continual improvement and think of manufacturing as a system. Deming also emphasized that a focus on cost alone is likely to increase cost rather than decrease it, and he stressed the use of statistical methods in improving quality.

Over time, TQM gave way to Six Sigma,[14] which was developed by Motorola in 1986 and implemented by Jack Welch at General Electric in 1995. Six Sigma seeks to improve process quality by identifying and removing the causes of defects and minimizing variability in manufacturing and business processes (Antony 2008). A core of this approach is that improvements in quality and cost are not inversely related but rather tend to go together.[15] As with other quality improvement approaches, software and other forms of IT can play a key role.

Increasingly, businesses use technology tools (either buying the computing power or leasing it from cloud providers) to search through very large, imprecisely contained data sets ("big data") to find exploitable patterns in customer behavior. Therefore, we expect IT use to continue to grow.

Kohli and Devaraj review a number of separate academic studies which examine the payoff of investments in IT, broadly defined. They find a greater payoff for IT investment in studies utilizing better inputs (larger sample sizes and data from the companies themselves) and better outputs (productivity instead of profitability). Some managers may be surprised by the lack of consensus among studies of the payoff from investing in IT, but the literature is full of studies reaching opposing conclusions. Kohli and Devaraj make a real contribution by demonstrating that those studies employing methodologies generally considered to be better are more likely to find a positive connection between investment in IT and organizational productivity. Of course, this is a general conclusion; their study does not make even basic distinctions between types of IT investment (e.g., hardware versus software), and there definitely is more work to be done.

Melville, Kraemer, and Gurbaxani (2004) also review the literature on the payoff to investment in IT. In addition to highlighting Kohli and Devaraj's

---

[14] The term originated from statistical modeling, in which a six-sigma process is one in which 99.99966% of product outputs are expected to be error-free, or 3.4 defects per million (Motorola University n.d., under "Six Sigma as a Metric").

[15] 3M was a big user of Six Sigma through 2006, but in 2007 (after the arrival of a new CEO, George Buckley) the company dialed back its commitment out of concern that the focus on this approach resulted in incremental improvements in manufacturing quality at the expense of larger creative efforts (Hindo 2007).

analysis about IT contributing to economically valuable performance improvement, they make other observations about prior empirical work:

- **IT's value depends on context.** Specific variables include type of IT, management practices, organizational structure, and the macro environment.

- **Software usage is associated with firm performance.** In particular, enterprise resource planning systems are associated with higher financial market valuation in the long-term (short-term, there may be a dampening of an organization's effectiveness during and immediately after implementation; Hitt, Wu, and Zhou 2002).

- **Return on IT spending exceeds that on non-IT capital spending.** The gross marginal product for computer capital is 81% (Brynjolfsson and Hitt 1996).

- **Managerial IT skills confer a sustainable competitive advantage.** Technical IT skills do not give the same sustainable advantage (Mata, Fuerst, and Barney 1995).

- **The impact of IT on productivity differs by employee category.** Firms with high levels of information technology that have also reduced their clerical and professional ranks have higher productivity (Francalanci and Galal 1998).

A variety of "how-to" guides for managers cover the deployment of tech tools that are now available. For example, a 2010 book by Davenport, Harris, and Morrison offers practical advice on how to utilize information analytics to access data and drive better decision-making. Davenport et al. describe five elements (spelling "DELTA") of successful analytics adoption:

- **Data.** Analytics data should be high quality and accessible.

- **Enterprise.** A whole-business orientation to analytics is key.

- **Leadership.** Company leaders should use and support an analytical approach.

- **Targets.** The development of strategic capabilities is important to successful analytics.

- **Analysts.** The importance of managing analysts as a strategic resource should not be understated.

Davenport et al. believe that embedding analytics in business processes will yield better decisions throughout the enterprise.

We may be biased (Eric works at an IT-firm whose whole business model is predicated on the value-added of investment in hardware and software), but we firmly believe that IT investment on average adds value, and the non-academic evidence we have seen in our work environments bears out this conclusion. Our own expectation is that, as computing becomes ever cheaper and more powerful, the economics around investing in IT will most probably improve—

so long as managers recognize that IT must be complemented by the understanding that technology is a tool toward the end of efficient processes, and not an end in itself. We agree with Melville et al. that companies would benefit from focusing as much on managerial IT skills as on technical expertise.

FURTHER READING

If you're interested in reading more on the topics discussed in this chapter, here are some sources to get you started. We do not offer this as a comprehensive or exhaustive list, but rather have selected well-regarded or significant works that space did not permit us to include in the main discussion.

1. ORGANIZATIONAL CULTURE

Kotter, John and James Heskett. 2011. *Corporate Culture and Performance*. New York, Free Press.

Kreps, David. 1990. "Corporate Culture and Economic Theory." In J. E. Alt and K. A. Shepsle (editors), *Perspectives on Positive Political Economy*. New York, Cambridge University Press. pp. 90–143.

O'Reilly, Charles. 1989. "Corporations, Culture, and Commitment: Motivation and Social Control in Organizations." *California Management Review* 31(4), 9–25.

2. THE IMPACT OF STRUCTURE AND SITUATION

Arnott, David. 1999. *Corporate Cults: The Insidious Lure of the All-Consuming Organization*. New York, AMACOM.

Katz, Daniel and Robert Kahn. 1978. *The Social Psychology of Organizations*, 2nd edition. New York, Wiley.

Morgan, Gareth. 2006. *Images of Organization*. New York, Sage.

Perrow, Charles. 1988. *Complex Organizations: A Critical Essay*, 3rd edition. New York, Random House.

Zimbardo, Philip. 2008. *The Lucifer Effect: Understanding How Good People Turn Evil*. New York, Random House.

3. ORGANIZATIONAL LEARNING

Argyris, Chris. 1999. *On Organizational Learning*, 2nd edition. New York, Wiley-Blackwell.

4. ALIGNING ORGANIZATIONAL INCENTIVES

Ventrice, Cindy. 2009. *Make Their Day! Employee Recognition that Works*, 2nd edition. San Francisco, Berret-Koehler.

5. MOTIVATION

Latham, Gary. 2011. *Work Motivation: History, Theory, Research, and Practice*, 2nd edition. New York, Sage.

Pink, Daniel. 2011. *Drive: The Surprising Truth About What Motivates Us.* New York, Riverhead Trade.

6. POWER

Kellerman, Barbara. 2010. *Leadership: Essential Selections on Power, Authority, and Influence.* New York, McGraw-Hill.

Montana, Patrick and Bruce Charnov. 2008. "Leadership: Theory and Practice." In *Management*, 4th edition. New York, Barron's Educational Series. Ch. 14.

Pfeffer, Jeffrey. 1993. *Managing with Power.* Cambridge, Harvard Business School Press.

7. INFORMATION TECHNOLOGY AND PRODUCTIVITY

Ahire, Sanjay. 1997. "Management Science—Total Quality Management Interfaces: An Integrative Framework." *Interfaces* 27(6), 91–105.

Drnevich, Paul. 2006. "Overview of the Business Value of IT Literature." In Resources, Capabilities, and Performance Heterogeneity. Dissertation, Purdue Krannert School of Management. http://www.krannert.purdue.edu/academics/mis/workshop/PD0_032406.pdf.

Franz, Peter and Mathias Kirchmer. 2012. *Value-Drive Business Process Management: The Value-Switch for Lasting Competitive Advantage.* New York, McGraw-Hill.

George, Michael, John Maxey, David Rowlands, and Mark Price. 2004. *The Lean Six Sigma Pocket Toolbook: A Quick Reference Guide to 100 Tools for Improving Quality and Speed.* New York, McGraw-Hill.

Harris, Michael, David Herron, and Stasi Iwanicki. 2008. *The Business Value of IT: Managing Risk, Optimizing Performance, and Measuring Results.* New York, Auerbach Publications.

Jacowski, Tony. 2007. "Six Sigma vs. Total Quality Management." *The Project Management Hut*, 28 May. http://www.pmhut.com/six-sigma-vs-total-quality-management.

Malhotra, Yogesh. 1998. "Business Process Redesign: An Overview." *IEEE Engineering Management Review* 26(3), 27–31.

McDonald, Mark. 2010. *Improving Business Processes.* Cambridge, Harvard Business Review Press.

Pande, Peter, Robert Neuman, and Roland Cavanaugh. 2000. *The Six Sigma Way: How GE, Motorola, and Other Top Companies Are Honing Their Performance.* New York, McGraw-Hill.

Pyzdek, Thomas and Paul Keller. 2009. *The Six Sigma Handbook*, 3rd edition. New York, McGraw-Hill Professional.

WORKS CITED

Adolph, Gerald, Karla Elrod, and J. Neely. 2006. "Nine Steps to Prevent Merger Failure." *Harvard Business School Working Knowledge for Business Leaders*, 27 March. http://hbswk.hbs.edu/archive/5271.html.

Al-Mashari, Majed and Mohamed Zairi. 1999. "BPR Implementation Process: An Analysis of Key Success and Failure Factors." *Business Process Management Journal* 5(1), 87–112.

Antony, Jiju. 2008. "Pros and Cons of Six Sigma: An Academic Perspective." *Improvement and Innovation.com*, 7 January. http://www.improvementandinnovation. com/features/article/pros-and-cons-six-sigma-academic-perspective/.

Arango, Tim. 2010. "How the AOL-Time Warner Merger Went Wrong." *New York Times*, 10 January. p. 1, Media & Advertising section.

Argyris, Chris and Donald Schon. 1996. *Organizational Learning II*. Reading, MA, Addison-Wesley.

Astley, W. Graham and Paramjit Sachdeva. 1984. "Structural Sources of Intraorganizational Power: A Theoretical Synthesis." *Academy of Management Review* 9(1), 104–113.

Axline, Sheryl. 2001. "Proactive Adaptation in ERP Teams: Mechanisms of Team Learning." Unpublished doctoral dissertation, Claremont Graduate University.

Brynjolfsson, Erik and Lorin Hitt. 1996. "Paradox Lost? Firm-level Evidence on the Returns to Information Systems Spending." *Management Science* 42(4), 541–558.

Cotter, John. 1995. *The 20% Solution: Using Rapid Redesign to Create Tomorrow's Organization Today*. New York, Wiley.

Covert, Michael. 1997. *Successfully Performing BPR*. Visible Systems Corporation. http://www.ies.aust.com/papers/BPR.html.

Culbert, Samuel. 2008. "Get Rid of the Performance Review." *Wall Street Journal*, 20 October. http://online.wsj.com/article/SB122426318874844933.html.

Davenport, Thomas. 1995. "Reengineering: The Fad that Forgot People." *Fast Company* November. http://www.rotman.utoronto.ca/~evans/teach363/fastco/reengin.htm.

Davenport, Thomas, Jeanne Harris, and Robert Morrison. 2010. *Analytics at Work: Smarter Decisions, Better Results*. Cambridge, Harvard Business Press.

Davenport, Thomas and James Short. 1990. "The New Industrial Engineering: Information Technology and Business Process Redesign." *Sloan Management Review* 31(Summer), 11–27.

Delbecq, Andre and Joseph Weiss. 1988. "The Business Culture of Silicon Valley: Is It a Model for the Future?" In J. Weiss (editor), *Regional Cultures, Managerial Behavior and Entrepreneurship*. New York, Quorum Books. pp. 123–141.

Deming, W. Edwards. 2000a. *Out of the Crisis*, 2nd edition. Cambridge, MIT Press.

Deming, W. Edwards. 2000b. *The New Economics for Industry, Government, Education*, 2nd edition. Cambridge, MIT Press.

Earley, Chris. 2002. "Redefining Interactions Across Cultures and Organizations: Moving Forward with Cultural Intelligence." In B. M. Staw and R. M. Kramer (editors), *Research in Organizational Behavior: An Annual Series of Analytical Essays and Critical Reviews*. Kidlington, UK, Elsevier. pp. 271–299.

Francalanci, Chiara and Hossam Galal. 1998. "Information Technology and Worker Composition: Determinants of Productivity in the Life Insurance Industry." *MIS Quarterly* 22(2), 227–241.

Hammer, Michael. 1990. "Reengineering Work: Don't Automate, Obliterate." *Harvard Business Review* 68(July–August), 104–112.

Hammer, Michael and James Champy. 1993. *Reengineering the Corporation: A Manifesto for Business Revolution.* New York, Harper Business Books.

Hamscher, Walter. 1994. "AI in Business-Process Reengineering." *AI Magazine* 15 (4), 71–72.

Hindo, Brian. 2007. "At 3M, a Struggle Between Efficiency and Creativity." *Business Week*, 10 June, 81N–141N.

Hitt, Lorin, D. J. Wu, and Xiaoge Zhou. 2002. "Investment in Enterprise Resource Planning: Business Impact and Productivity Measures." *Journal of Management Information Systems* 19(1), 71–98.

Hwang, Victor and Greg Horowitt. 2012. *The Rain Forest: The Secret to Building the Next Silicon Valley.* Los Altos Hills, Regenwald.

Kanter, Rosabeth Moss. 1979. "Power Failures in Management Circuits." *Harvard Business Review* 57(July–August), 65–75.

Kates, Amy and Jay Galbraith. 2007. *Designing Your Organization: Using the Star Model to Solve Five Critical Design Challenges.* San Francisco, Jossey-Bass.

Keichel, Walter. 1979. "Playing the Rules of the Corporate Strategy Game." *Fortune* 25 September, 110–115.

Kerr, Steven. 1995. "On the Folly of Rewarding A While Hoping for B." *Academy of Management Executive* 9(1), 7–14 [1975].

Kohli, Rajiv and Sarv Devaraj. 2003. "Measuring Information Technology Payoff: A Meta-Analysis of Structural Variables in Firm-Level Empirical Research." *Information Systems Research* 14(2), 127–145.

Latham, Gary and Craig Pinder. 2005. "Work Motivation Theory and Research at the Dawn of the Twenty-First Century." *Annual Review of Psychology* 56, 485–516.

Lewis, Michael. 1989. *Liar's Poker.* New York, Norton.

Lewis, Michael. 2004. *Moneyball.* New York, Norton.

Locke, Edwin. 1996. "Motivation through Conscious Goal Setting." *Applied & Preventive Psychology* 5(2), 117–124.

Locke, Edwin. 2000. "Motivation by Goal Setting." In R. Golembiewski (editor), *Handbook of Organizational Behavior.* New York, Marcel Dekker. pp. 43–56.

Locke, Edwin and Douglas Henne. 1986. "Work Motivation Theories." In C. L. Cooper and I. T. Robertson (editors), *International Review of Industrial and Organizational Psychology*, vol. 1. New York, Wiley. pp. 1–35.

Markus, M. Lynne. 1998. "Lessons from the Field of Organizational Change." *Journal of Strategic Performance Measurement* 2(2), 36–45.

Markus, M. Lynne and Robert Benjamin. 1997. "The Magic Bullet Theory in IT-Enabled Transformation." *Sloan Management Review* 38(2), 55–68.

Mata, Francisco, William Fuerst, and Jay Barney. 1995. "Information Technology and Sustained Competitive Advantage: A Resource-Based Analysis." *MIS Quarterly* 19(4), 487–505.

Mayo, Elton. 1945. *The Social Problems of an Industrial Civilization*. London, Routledge [2007].

Melville, Nigel, Kenneth Kraemer, and Vijay Gurbaxani. 2004. "Information Technology and Organizational Performance: An Integrative Model of IT Business Value." *MIS Quarterly* 28(2), 283–322.

Milgram, Stanley. 2009. *Obedience to Authority: An Experimental View*. New York, Harper Perennial.

Mitchell, David. 2005. *Making Foreign Policy: Presidential Management of the Decision-Making Process*. Burlington, Ashgate Publishing.

Motorola University. n.d. *What is Six Sigma?* http://www.motorola.com/web/Business/_Moto_University/_Documents/_Static_Files/What_is_SixSigma.pdf (accessed 20 August 2012).

Nelson, Bob. 2012. *1501 Ways to Reward Employees*. New York, Workman.

Oliver, Dean. 2004. *Basketball on Paper: Rules and Tools for Performance Analysis*. Dulles, Potomac Books.

Page, Scott., 2008. *The Difference: How the Power of Diversity Creates Better Groups, Firms, Schools, and Societies*. Princeton, Princeton University Press.

Parsons, Henry. 1975. "What Happened at Hawthorne?" *Science* 183(4128), 922–932.

Pfeffer, Jeffrey. 1981. "Understanding the Role of Power in Decision Making." In J. M. Shafritz, J. S. Ott, and Y. S. Jang (editors), *Classics of Organization Theory*, 7th edition [2010]. Belmont, Wadsworth. pp. 277–290.

Salancik, Richard and Jeffrey Pfeffer. 1977. "Who Gets Power and How They Hold on to It: A Strategic Contingency Model of Power." *Organizational Dynamics* 5(3), 3–21.

Schein, Edgar. 2010. *Organizational Culture and Leadership*. San Francisco, Jossey-Bass.

Shafritz, Jay, Steven Ott, and Yong Suk Jang. 2010. *Classics of Organizational Theory*, 7th edition. Belmont, Wadsworth.

Sitkin, Sim. 1992. "Learning through Failure: The Strategy of Small Losses." In B. Staw and L. Cummings (editors), *Research in Organizational Behavior*. New York, Elsevier Science. pp. 231–266.

Skinner, Burrhus Frederic. 1953. *Science and Human Behavior*. Oxford, Macmillan.

Tourish, Dennis and Naheed Vatcha. 2005. "Charismatic Leadership and Corporate Cultism at Enron." *Leadership* 1(4), 455–480.

Trice, Harrison and Janice Beyer. 1993. "Changing Organizational Cultures." In J. M. Shafritz, J. S. Ott, and Y. S. Jang (editors), *Classics of Organization Theory*, 6th edition [2005]. Belmont, Wadsworth. pp. 383–392.

Vroom, Victor. 1964. *Work and Motivation*. New York, Wiley.

Zimbardo, Philip. 1972, "Pathology of Imprisonment." *Society* 9(6), 4–8.

Zimbardo, Philip, Christina Maslach, and Craig Haney. 1999. "Reflections on the Stanford Prison Experiment: Genesis, Transformations, Consequences." In T. Blass (editor), *Obedience to Authority: Current Perspectives on the Milgram Paradigm*. Mahwah, Erlbaum. pp. 193–237.

INTERNATIONAL BUSINESS

Business is such that companies—even new companies in new industries—must consider the global environment in which they operate. This chapter summarizes some of the key international business literature in an array of dimensions: theories of multinational enterprises, international political economy, multinational management, and culture. Exploration of these dimensions provides managers with many of the tools and concepts necessary for establishing, developing, and managing multinational companies.

Section 1 introduces the main theories for international business and multinational enterprises (MNEs). Section 2 presents articles describing some of the approaches firms take and advantages they derive from internationalization. The articles in Section 3 discuss international political economy, which describes the interaction between multinationals and the economic and political environments in which they operate. Section 4 articles address the means, methods, and issues of managing multinational enterprises. Finally, the articles in Section 5 describe culture: what it is and how it affects internationalization and multinational management.

1. THEORIES OF THE MULTINATIONAL ENTERPRISE (MNE)

While international trade has occurred for centuries, only in the past 35 years has understanding of the reasons, processes, and outcomes associated with multinational business been subjected to deep academic scrutiny. This section presents some of the major theories of the multinational enterprise and provides a foundation for later sections. Presented in chronological order, the articles begin with Hymer's (1960) doctoral dissertation on international operations and the control-based forms of multinationals. Vernon (1971) describes a theory based on product lifecycles, followed by Johanson and Vahlne's (1977) introduction of the stages theory: the incremental development of international business into psychically more distant environments. Dunning's

(1988) article presents his view that internationalization is based on three sets of advantages (ownership, location, and internalization). Finally, Hennart (2001) puts the various theories in context and relates them to theories in strategy.

STEPHEN HYMER
The International Operations of National Firms: A Study of Direct Foreign Investment (1960).

Thesis: Foreign investment is driven not by differing interest rates, but by the desire to achieve control of a foreign subsidiary and to increase profits. Foreign investment appears to be particular to certain industries and firms.

Published posthumously, Hymer's book describes foreign investment and explains why companies enter foreign markets. A portfolio investment explanation, in which investors try to maximize profits by investing where returns are highest, does not explain why certain industries historically garner more foreign investment than others. Hymer develops a theory for one type of direct investment—international operations—in which companies own and control an entity in a foreign market.

Direct investment has behaved differently from portfolio investment over various time periods, economic climates (e.g., depression, war), and countries. In the *blind eye portfolio* approach, the investor determines foreign market entry based solely on the highest interest (return) rate. This approach is complicated by risk (all things being equal, one would go for the lower risk opportunity), uncertainty (i.e., currency rate fluctuations), and barriers to the movement of investments. The distribution of direct investment, both in terms of industry and country, further undermines interest-rate theory as the basis for direct investment (if interest rate is the main driver, one should see investment in all industries in a country, rather than the "lumpiness" evidenced in the data).

The relationship between a headquarters operation and that of a foreign subsidiary has two dimensions:

- the amount of control headquarters has over the foreign subsidiary, and
- the legal ownership (i.e., the percent of equity in the subsidiary owned by headquarters).

Equity ownership via direct investment is but one way of achieving control (a board of directors seat is another).

A firm may have a number of reasons for wanting to control an enterprise in another country:

- **To protect investments.** First, companies may earn more profit by controlling enterprises in more than one country as a means to remove competition between them or to substitute centralized decision-making for decentralized decision-making.

- **To appropriate the returns on certain skills or abilities.** Companies may find it profitable to exploit advantages in a particular activity by establishing foreign operations.
- **To diversify.** This more minor reason may be more economics-based. Diversifying can be an attempt to control profits long-term as economic conditions change due to success in one industry.

A variety of forms of international operations exist, with varying degrees of investment, control, and risk. From lowest cost/commitment/control to highest, these include licensing arrangement, minority interest, joint venture, branch plant, majority-owned subsidiary, and wholly owned subsidiary. The form depends in part on the type of control desired. If the motivation is to separate markets and prevent competition between units, control of price decisions and output decisions must be complete. Control increases as the product structures of the parent and the subsidiary are more similar; the greater the need for local adaptation, the less control the parent has.

There are four pure cases of international operations, as follows.

- **Market impurity.** International operations occur in those industries in which enterprises of different countries sell in the same market or sell to each other under conditions of imperfect competition.
- **Unequal ability.** International operations occur in industries where some firms have advantages over other firms (patents, strong discrimination against foreigners via tariffs protecting domestic companies, etc.).
- **Interdependence.** Interdependent enterprises in different countries may exist for other reasons, such as profits in one country increasing while decreasing in another (e.g., due to currency rates), leading to diversification by having operations in more than one country.
- **No international operations.** This case probably represents the majority of production in countries (i.e., percentage of the value of goods produced).

While licensing is one way of utilizing a firm's advantages, a firm must also decide whether (and when) to use the advantage itself instead of licensing it. Licensing can mean selling the advantage to one power in a firm's market, creating difficulty controlling price and outputs. Profits may not be maximized, and there is an inherent danger of losing the advantage due to substitutions or reverse engineering. When there are few firms, licensing problems arise, in which case the firm may be best served by establishing foreign operations and pursuing the advantage itself.

The theory of international operations implies that the relevant units of study are industries and firms, rather than aggregates of international operations. A survey of available data suggests that U.S. foreign operations are concentrated in a few industries and by a small number of firms, and that in these industries, U.S. firms account for a large (or major) share of output in foreign countries. In a country where U.S. firms have a large share of output, a firm from that country often also operates in the United States, so that international operations are in place in both directions.

RAYMOND VERNON
Sovereignty at Bay: The Multinational Spread of U.S. Enterprises (1971), Chapters 2–3.

Thesis: U.S. firms gather raw materials or manufacture goods overseas to achieve lower-cost production. Key elements are time, oligopoly, production factors, innovation, demand, price, risk, market change, and the cost of technology transfer.

Chapters 2 and 3 of Vernon's book provide essential insights into why U.S. firms decide to extract/refine raw materials or manufacture goods in foreign countries. Innovation and export induce a process that includes U.S. enterprises seeking lower-cost production sites, leading the firms to produce abroad and serve their markets from a foreign location.

This decision to engage in multinational activities may be understood using the *product cycle model*:

$$Initiation \Rightarrow Exponential\ Growth \Rightarrow Slowdown \Rightarrow Decline$$

The key elements that Vernon explores regarding their relationship to the international product cycle are as follows:

- time,
- oligopoly,
- production factors (resources, capital, labor, R&D),
- innovation,
- demand (internal, external),
- price,
- uncertainty/risk,
- market change, and
- cost of technology transfer.

Each of these elements is deemed to be necessary but not sufficient in explaining the international product cycle. Vernon elaborates on the insights introduced above by examining two archetypes of ventures: those that extract and process raw materials, and those that manufacture goods.

The Raw Material Ventures

The power of foreign-owned raw material enterprises has traditionally been considered a function of the following:

- the scale of undertaking required for effective performance,
- the complexity of technology associated with the activity, and
- the importance of captive overseas markets as an outlet for the raw material.

The characteristics or superior capabilities allowing initial advantage can erode over time and, as technology grows more complex, restoring the initial advantage also becomes more complicated.

Vernon uses the oil industry to illustrate insights into why and how this strength and strategic response shift over time. By the 1960s, oil companies were in an oligopolistic market and firms had achieved a high level of concentration and scale, with a large percentage of output to foreign markets. The growth of investment did not occur until the industry had became more concentrated, as the initial strategy was to buy the distribution network, meaning that entry into the marketing end of the business was much too easy. A shift to vertical integration strategies led to a willingness to assume the costs and risks of oil production in foreign countries. As one company adopted the vertical strategy, others followed in due course and copied the strategy to remain competitive. Once a vertical strategy was selected, multi-nationalizing minimized the threat that competitors might find a cheaper source of raw materials, ultimately stabilizing prices in the market. Competing companies were often operating in the same geographic locations, which also helped to stabilize the market. Committing to a vertical integration strategy also helped to diversify sources of raw materials.

Multinational enterprises leave some foreign markets because governments increase their share of profits and control over time, via the introduction of state-owned firms. When a raw material is first discovered, the host country often lacks production, marketing, or finance capability. The government therefore enters into self-denying commitments (e.g., tax breaks) to lure in foreign investment for exploration, exploitation, and infrastructure development—all of which the host country receives for the relatively low cost of the tax it foregoes. If the project succeeds, the level of risk drops and the host country re-assesses the foreign company returns as too high for the adjusted level of risk. At the same time, the foreign enclave produces its own infrastructure and the surrounding economy acts eagerly to provide what foreigners need. Foreign production fails to shift to local sources of supply, and politicians reopen agreements to gain power by showing independence from foreign investors. As foreign investor operations become more integrated in the host country's economic life, however, the economy is perceived as more dependent on the foreign investor. The government reacts by introducing state-owned enterprises into the industry. While state-owned firms may not displace foreign companies, they have been successful in obtaining a voice in the management decisions of the foreign companies.

There are some consistent lessons in history regarding raw materials ventures.

- Foreign enterprises whose successful establishment had rested on some superior capability or knowledge have lost security-of-position as time eroded their initial advantage.
- Enterprises have sometimes had their initial advantages restored as the technology of the industry grew more complex.

The oil industry at end of 1969 exhibited the characteristics of the oligopolistic strategy shift described earlier. In the case of the oil industry, U.S. oil companies worried that competitors might have access to cheaper sources of oil, threatening world oil prices. This threat led to a policy of participating in joint exploration of new areas.

The Manufacturing Industries

In manufacturing industries, there was a gradual fanning out of skill oriented products from areas of the world that are geographically and culturally familiar to those that are remote. Innovation and export induce a process in which U.S. enterprises seek lower-cost production sites, leading them to produce abroad and serve their domestic markets from a foreign location.

The product cycle model is based on the relative availability of production factors:

- **Resources.** Production is affected by access to and the relative cheapness of, for example, power, forest products, and arable land.
- **Labor.** The existence of scarce artisan labor that innovates is crucial for processing these resources.

The resulting reduced cost of capital or labor forms the basis for the export of goods and high per-capita income. Firms introduce new products/processes abroad through exports under the following conditions:

- no initial incentive for a producer to look outside the home country for lower production or labor costs,
- large internal markets (including military purchases),
- demand that is less sensitive to price for new innovation, and
- high need for effective communication inside enterprises.

With international markets, flexibility and response become more important in location selection than capital and labor cost. When the export position is threatened, companies establish foreign subsidiaries to exploit what remains of their advantage. Export can be threatened by the following developments:

- Technology moves to a point where it is transferable at reasonable cost (thus, production can happen elsewhere).

- Domestic demand significantly increases, making the average delivered cost for overseas production comparable to domestic production.
- The cost of production becomes dominated by cost of capital and cost of labor.
- Threats such as political instability and tariffs vary, thereby changing the calculus for subsidiary versus export decisions.
- Decreasing margins induce U.S. producers to place production closer to foreign markets to reduce cost.

All oligopolistic advantage based on the original lead eventually erodes completely, so there is no longer any cost advantage over competitors both foreign and domestic, even for foreign subsidiaries operating in the same economic environment as their competitors.

JAN JOHANSON and JAN-ERIK VALHNE
"The Internationalization Process of the Firm: A Model of Knowledge Development and Increasing Foreign Commitments" (1977), *Journal of International Business Studies.*

Thesis: Knowledge is the most important scarce resource to be maximized; internationalization facilitates the acquisition and use of knowledge. Companies geographically diversify as they incrementally internalize knowledge from ever more psychically-distant countries.

Based on data from Scandinavian firms, Johanson and Vahlne develop and present a theory emphasizing the evolutionary process of internationalization that is characteristic of firms in the United States and elsewhere. While they do not claim that this process is universal, the impression given is that the model both describes what companies do and prescribes the best way to do it.

The basic assumptions of the so-called Uppsala model are that a lack of knowledge about foreign markets and operations is an obstacle in the development of international operations, and that the necessary knowledge can be acquired through operations abroad. These assumptions hold for both increasing involvement of the firm in an individual foreign country and then establishing operations in other countries.

The major contribution of this theory is the importance and emphasis given to knowledge as the focus of analysis—knowledge is seen as the most important scarce resource to be maximized. The incremental process of internationalization is directly related to the gradual acquisition, integration/internalization, and use of knowledge. Knowledge is what is ultimately being transferred: knowledge of the host market as well as knowledge

of the production of a good or service. The internationalization process is one
of incremental learning and adjustment to changing conditions between the firm
and the social environment. Although not explicitly highlighted, we can
conclude that the ability to learn and adapt is part of the knowledge of the firm.

Lack of market knowledge (i.e., information about markets and operations
in those markets) due to differences such as language and culture is an obstacle
in the decision-making connected with the development of international
operations. Data on Swedish companies suggested a pattern of
internationalization that did not appear to be the result of a strategy for
optimum allocation of resources, but rather a process of incremental
adjustments to the firm's changing conditions and environment. Lacking
routines for the solution of such sporadic problems, management "searches in
the area of the problem" (Cyert and March 1963, p. 46). A constraint on solving
the problem is the lack of, and difficulty in obtaining, market knowledge in
international operations. The incremental approach to internationalization is
due to lack of market information and the uncertainty created by that lack.

The time sequence of internationalization is related to *psychic distance*: the
psychological or cultural factors that prevent the flow, understanding, and
codification of information to and from the foreign market. Regarding psychic
distance, Johanson and Vahlne's theory proposes four main constructs grouped
into the categories of state and change.

State Aspects

Market commitment is composed of the amount of resources committed (size of
investment, including marketing and personnel) and the degree of commitment
(integration and specialization of resources for market entry).

Market knowledge considers the knowledge of opportunities and evaluation
of alternatives. Knowledge can be acquired through objective means (i.e., can be
taught) or experiential means (i.e., can only be learned); experiential knowledge
is increasingly important as the activities and required knowledge area are less
structured and defined. Market knowledge can also be applied more generally or
for a specific market.

- *General knowledge* concerns marketing methods and the common
  characteristics of certain types of customers.
- *Market-specific knowledge* includes the characteristics of the specific national
  market, its business climate, its cultural patterns, the structure of the market
  system, and the characteristics of individual customer firms.

Market knowledge relates to market commitment: The better the
knowledge, the more valuable are the knowledge resources, and the stronger the
commitment to the market. This relationship is especially true of experiential
knowledge, which is usually associated with particular conditions of the market.

Change Aspects

Current activities consider how the time lag between activities and their consequences determines the level of commitment and the source of experience. Both firm experience and market experience are essential in order to perform marketing activities. Individuals on the boundary between the firm and the market must interpret information. If the activities are production-oriented, companies may find it easier to substitute hired personnel or advice for current activities, as the activities are neither knowledge-intensive nor dependent on firm-specific knowledge.

Commitment decisions are made in relation to alternatives in response to problems or opportunities. There is an opportunity horizon, in which activities are likely to be suggested by those responsible for operations, such that we have scale-increasing decisions if the risk is below the maximum tolerable risk level, whereas we have uncertainty-reducing decisions if the risk exceeds the maximum tolerable level for the firm. Additional commitments will be made in small steps unless the firm has large resources or market conditions are stable or the firm has experience in other similar markets.

JOHN DUNNING
"The Eclectic Paradigm of International Production: A Restatement and Some Possible Extensions" (1988), *Journal of International Business Studies.*

Thesis: The determinants of foreign direct investment (FDI) can be classified into three categories based on the ownership, location, and internalization (OLI) advantages available to multinational corporations (MNCs).[1]

Dunning first presented the concept of the eclectic paradigm of international production in 1977, as a holistic framework for identifying and evaluating factors influencing the initiation and growth of foreign production. Dunning used the word *eclectic* to convey the idea that it is necessary to draw on various economic theories to explain MNCs' international activities.

The eclectic paradigm states that the extent, form, and pattern of international production are determined by the configuration of ownership, location, and internalization (OLI) advantages available to MNCs.

- *Ownership factors* encompass organizational-level factors that are unique to the organization including management expertise, trade secrets, and the potential for uniform governance across one firm.

---

[1] The terms multinational enterprise (MNE) and multinational corporation (MNC) refer interchangeably to the same type of business organization operating in multiple countries.

- *Location advantages* are associated with where the production takes place. Foreign production makes sense when it can be combined with some home country assets, or when trade barriers or transport costs prompt greater regional specialization.
- *Internalization advantages* exist when it is in the best interest of the MNC to transfer ownership advantages across national borders within their own organizations. This may be the case due to risk and uncertainty, exploitation of economies of scale, or costs or benefits external to the transaction (Dunning 1976).

The eclectic paradigm relates the OLI configuration facing MNCs to structural or contextual variables, such as country or industry. In some industries, there are as many differences between MNE characteristics in the same sector as there are between companies in different sectors. Each firm faces different strategic options and their evaluation of these options and associated risks vary, even if the conditions they face are identical (Dunning 1976).

In this paper published 12 years later, Dunning responds to commentators by proposing an investment-development path. He suggests that a country's propensity to engage in foreign direct investment, either inward or outward, will vary according to the following factors:

- the country's stage of economic development,
- its factor endowments and markets,
- its political and economic systems, and
- the nature and extent of market failure in the transaction of intermediate products across its borders (e.g., high tariffs for import of component products).

As a country passes through economic development stages, so will its international investment position.

JEAN-FRANCIS HENNART
"Theories of the Multinational Enterprise" (2001), in A. Rugman and T. Brewer (editors), *The Oxford Handbook of International Business*.

Thesis: Theories of multinationalization focus on the firm rather than on the nation. Explanations for multinationalization include product market competition and transaction cost economics.

In his chapter, Hennart provides a critical survey of some of the theories that have sought to explain why multinational enterprises (MNEs) exist. He defines the MNE as a private institution devised to organize (through employment contracts) interdependencies between individuals located in more than one country. In tracing the evolution of the theory of the multinational enterprise, Hennart analyzes trade theories, industrial organization theories, and transaction cost/internationalization theories.

Trade Theories

In trade theories, Hennart explains, foreign direct investment (FDI) measures the export of capital from one country to the rest of the world. While academics make heavy use of FDI in research, it is an imperfect measure because a firm establishing a presence in a foreign country can expand without capital exported from the home country by borrowing locally or by reinvesting profit. From 1966 to 1972, only a modest percentage of the funds invested abroad by a sample of U.S. MNEs came from the United States. Observed investment does not match portfolio diversification patterns, given that most foreign affiliates are in the same industry as their parents (Levy and Sarnat 1970).

Industrial Organization Theories

Hennart locates the roots of industrial organization theories related to internationalization in Hymer, who brought the focus from the nation to the firm. The crux of Hymer's argument was that MNEs were instruments by which competitors reduced competition in industries where large barriers to entry had created and were sustaining local monopolies. Hymer's thesis was that MNEs were internalizing externalities[2] due to competition on markets for final products. As firms compete, they lower the price they can charge consumers and give up monopoly profits, through which consumers gain what the MNE loses.

Transaction Cost/Internationalization Theories

Applying these theories, when natural market imperfections are high, the expansion of firms across national boundaries may be a more efficient way to internalize these externalities. Transaction cost theorists like Oliver Williamson (see Chapter 7) seek to explain why MNEs organize international interdependencies that could also be handled by markets. Transaction cost economics argues that firms arise when they are the most efficient institution to organize these interdependencies. MNEs thrive when they are more efficient than markets and contracts in organizing interdependencies among agents in different countries. Economic agents have cognitive limitations (boundedly

---

[2] An externality exists whenever one firm's actions affect the well-being of another firm—for better or for worse—in ways that need not be paid for according to the existing definition of property rights. For example, polluting firms negatively affect the environment, raising costs for other firms dependent on forests (for example). Contracts or laws act to internalize externalities by, for example, requiring polluters to remedy the damage caused by their pollution.

rational) and some are opportunistic, thus organizing this cooperation among agents will incur transaction costs for information, bargaining, and enforcement. Firms use two basic methods to organize transactions:

- **Hierarchy.** This method replaces markets' output constraints with behavior constraints. In the price system (whereby the price of goods coordinates the decisions of consumers, producers, and resource owners), the focus is on outputs: Prices for outputs convey to all agents the value of goods and services, and reward agents in proportion to their measured output. However, if output is hard to measure, then agents can be rewarded on their behavior instead (i.e., obeying the boss). This relationship is an employment contract, but decoupling reward from output may decrease the incentive to work hard.

- **The market.** Since markets are not perfect, (a) prices may not convey an accurate estimate of the value of goods and services due to an inability to define and measure property rights; (b) agents will find it difficult to measure output, so money will have to be spent to enforce trades or there will be cheating; and (c) agents engage in bargaining when there is an insufficient number of buyers and sellers.

The price system is heavily dependent on the definition and measurement of outputs. A hierarchy may be better when measurement and enforcement costs are high and the small number of buyers and sellers renders prices endogenous.

In applying transaction cost theory to the multinational firm, Hennart notes that the MNE expands abroad when it can organize interdependencies more efficiently. This decision to expand implies the following:

- Interdependent agents are in different countries.
- An MNE must be the most efficient way to organize interdependencies.
- The costs to do so must be lower than the benefits.

When such conditions are likely to be met depends on four factors: know-how, reputation, raw materials and components, and distribution and marketing.

- **Know-how.** Markets for know-how suffer from information asymmetries, as buyers do not generally know the exact characteristics of the know-how they are purchasing, and sellers cannot provide that information without giving it away for free (Arrow 1962). The patent system helps to solve this paradox, but is limited due to the difficulty of writing tacit knowledge into patents and to imperfect enforcement of patents. Knowledge transfer within a firm can be more efficient, as both buyer and seller are rewarded for effective transfer—internalization of the markets for know-how provides the advantages for MNEs.

- **Reputation.** Franchising contracts typically stipulate that agents pay a royalty on sales for use of trademarks and agree to franchiser's behavior constraints. International interdependencies of goodwill (e.g., brand value, reputation) will be organized through international franchising contracts if it is relatively easy to write contracts that specify quality and whose violation is easy to detect and prove (e.g., fast food, hotel), and if it would be costly to control shirking employees (e.g., management consultants). *Free-riding* (maximizing income by decreasing quality) is a problem with franchising if free-riding is easy to detect by consumers (who will then avoid other franchise holders) or there is the potential for repeat customers. When managers have difficulty defining quality, employment contracts may be better than having franchise agents.

- **Raw material and components.** Interdependencies arise when different stages of the value chain are optimally handled by different agents in different countries. Parties with transaction-specific investments can protect themselves by writing a long-term contract that specifies *ex ante* the terms and conditions of the exchange and the penalties in case of breach. The alternative to the contract is to have buyers and sellers become employees of the same firm.

- **Distribution and marketing.** Selling internationally requires physical and intellectual investments. As for raw materials and components, the market for distribution services will be inefficient if it is narrow. If it is difficult to separate the performance of manufacturers from that of distributors, it is better to integrate manufacturing and distribution within a firm. Manufacturers may integrate with a foreign distribution firm when the quality of their products could be affected by improper handling and service. Inversely, distributors have backward-integrated into foreign production when the quality of products they were buying was difficult to assess (e.g., bananas).

Discussion and Implications

 International business theories vary. This section discusses theories based on finance and strategy (Hymer), product lifecycle (Vernon), and stages of development (the Uppsala model of Johanson and Vahlne). We also present the eclectic OLI theory (Dunning), which is based on sources of competitive advantage and also considers aspects of various economic theories.

Hymer's analysis of international operations, the highest control form of foreign market entry, provided the impetus for much of the following research into foreign market entry modes and the nature of internationalization. The concept that companies' control of their foreign presence had a number of forms and dimensions, each with varying levels of cost and commitment, has contributed to managers' understanding of the range of options open to them as they enter foreign markets. Joe dealt directly with this range of options at

Synetics, where the company entered England as a greenfield subsidiary (see Harzing 2002 in Section 2), and as an international joint venture in Saudi Arabia (which required majority ownership by a Saudi citizen). As Joe's executive experience preceded his academic training, retrospective examination of his experience through the academic lens reveals how a better informed approach to the issues of various foreign market entry modes would have enhanced the experience (and performance) of his subsidiaries.

Vernon's product lifecycle model addresses how the outcomes of multinational enterprises (MNEs) develop over time, and assumes that MNEs and sovereign nations are formally structured.[3] Further, MNEs are assumed to be able to choose behaviors, their choices are based on a consistent set of preferences (economically or politically driven), their choices occur prior to the action taken, and the action is goal-directed. These assumptions invite overgeneralization; for example, is it really likely that any one multinational can, or should, co-determine its behaviors with any one government? Therefore, Vernon's argument may be more appealing and generally useful for the evaluation of the overall process for the international spread of business enterprises. The dynamic process described may not hold for all organizations—service and information-based industries (e.g., law), for example, may not follow the same cycle.

The Uppsala model of Johanson and Vahlne suggests that the higher the knowledge, the higher the commitment to a particular market, but in fact we can imagine a situation in which more knowledge of a market may indicate the need to exit from it, since risk management is one of the most important aspects of the evolutionary process of internationalization. Market commitment emphasizes the degree of commitment of an asset (e.g., specialized equipment needed for production to conform to a foreign regulation) in terms of its integration with the business, which can be seen as a factor related to exit barriers. However, exit barriers should be analyzed differently depending on the type of business: manufacturing and service businesses differ considerably in this regard. Johanson and Vahlne's theory should also consider that integration occurs not only in the context of the business being developed in the focal (local) market, but also in other markets operated by the same firm. Therefore, it is possible that a firm such as PepsiCo or Carrefour has a strategy that involves different markets at the same time, in combination, and thus the management of markets does not occur in isolation. Although the model they

---

[3] Of course, all sovereign nations are formally structured and so are companies. However, unless one is discussing a command economy (e.g., China in the 1970s), the formal structure of a nation cannot contain the operations of all parts to the degree that an MNE could (and even that is limited).

propose is quite practical and objective, it seems simplistic in explaining all the complexities of real-life strategies.

Johanson and Vahlne's "stage model" describes incremental foreign expansion as based on the internalization of knowledge regarding more psychically-distant countries. Their work suggests the knowledge gained by the firm in its internationalization is most relevant for foreign market expansion. In contrast, however, there are international new ventures (INVs) or born-globals (BGs), which enter foreign countries at or near inception for access to resources or markets; for these ventures, it is generally the prior experience or knowledge of the founders or top management team that drives international growth. Early researchers in this area are Oviatt and McDougall (1994) and Knight and Cavusgil (1997), and their work is presented in Chapter 2, Section 5. Both of these models are relevant and appropriate, and as more research is applied to younger, smaller companies, we may see a blending of these theories describing how young ventures incrementally gain knowledge but in a more rapid fashion, permitting them to go through internationalization phases more quickly.

Additional significant readings on theories of the MNE, presented in chronological order, are:

- **Caves (1996).** Firms internationalize when they possess monopolistic advantages. Transaction cost economics can explain a combination of macroeconomic issues (e.g., capital flows, income distribution, employment, wages, taxation, economic welfare, technology and productivity, and less developed countries), microeconomic issues (e.g., organization, growth, investment behavior, market competition), and public policy issues. Chapter 6 of this book is particularly relevant to the question of capitalization and investment in internationalization.

- **Buckley and Casson (1998).** The international business agenda focuses on a variety of issues, including uncertainty and market volatility, flexibility and the value of real options, cooperation through joint ventures and business networks, entrepreneurship, managerial competence and corporate change, and organizational change. Flexibility is related to the size and scope of the firm; network firms and virtual firms have "fuzzy" boundaries. The search for flexibility has implications for the firm's external environment, boundaries, and internal organization.

- **Caves (1998).** Using Gilbrat's Law, which states that the growth rate of a firm is independent of size, Caves suggests that barriers to entry do not affect market entry—but do affect survival. Industry concentration decreases firm entry and exit.

2. Internationalization Advantages and Approaches

Internationalization is intended to provide companies with competitive advantages, and this section describes the various approaches companies take to their foreign market entry and expansion. In the first article, Dunning (2001) provides an overview of the literature on internationalization from 1960–2000, summarizing the main themes and academic perspectives on internationalization in the context of broader economic, political, and business activities. Dunning's article sets the stage for the subsequent papers in this section, which are presented in chronological order. Kogut and Zander (1993) describe the role of knowledge acquisition and internalization as the key to multinational corporate evolution. Chung (2001) focuses on one type of knowledge—technology—and how it relates to firm internationalization and to the environments into which firms enter. Harzing (2002) examines two high control, high commitment foreign-market entry modes: the acquisition of other ventures, and greenfield (new venture) investments. Finally, Vermeulen and Barkema (2002) discuss the pace, rhythm, and scope of foreign expansion.

JOHN DUNNING
"The Key Literature on IB Activities: 1960–2000" (2001), in A. Rugman and T. Brewer (editors), *The Oxford Handbook of International Business.*

Thesis: The literature on internationalization over the past forty years has emphasized the determinants of ownership and examined the impact of changes in the external environment on research itself.

Dunning traces the main thrust and content of two interrelated, influential strands of internationalization literature:

1. **Determinants of key MNE strategies.** These sources discuss the determinants of the ownership, industry sectors, and geographic scope of multinational enterprise (MNE) activity.
2. **External conditions influencing MNE activity.** This literature examines the main changes in the external technological, economic, and political environment that have helped fashion these explanations.

Both strands are examined across three time domains: mid-1960s to mid-1970s, mid-1970s to late 1980s, and late 1980s to 2000.

Determinants of key MNE strategies

During the mid-1960s to mid-1970s, Hymer (1960), <u>Vernon</u> (1971), and Bain (1956) sought to examine ownership and internalization. While Hymer paid no attention to strategic or managerial issues, Bain explained ownership and the competitive structure of various U.S. industrial sectors according to entry or exit barriers that provide advantages (e.g., ownership of proprietary rights, absolute cost and scale economies, privileged access to product or factor markets). Vernon emphasized country-specific factors influencing both the competitive advantages of firms and the location of value-added activities arising from those firms. Exploited initially in domestic markets and then shifted abroad, these advantages enabled U.S. firms to penetrate the markets of foreign rivals and created barriers to potential competitors.

After Hymer and Vernon, research on the theory of international production followed four main paths.

- The first path focuses on those advantages enabling firms to penetrate foreign markets in the first place.
- The second path extends Vernon's work to other national contexts and confirms the importance of the location-bound characteristics of home countries. Those characteristics influence the industry sector distribution of outbound foreign direct investment (FDI) and inbound geographic profile (i.e., geographic source of inbound FDI).
- Along the third path, scholars in the early 1970s started to pay more attention to the strategic behavior of firms.
- Finally, the fourth path addressed the interests of international finance scholars, perceiving FDI as the means by which firms could spread exchange rate and other risks and internalize imperfect foreign exchange and capital markets.

During the 1970s to late 1980s, research shifted away from the act of FDI per se (which was the focus of research in the 1960s to mid-1970s) in favor of the institution making the investment and its reasons for extending value-added activities outside its home country. One literature stream was primarily concerned with explaining the sequential or incremental process by which firms internationalize their activities, postulating that firms first enter markets about which they are most familiar and then move to less familiar territories. The second stream addressed the questions, "What is distinctive about MNEs?" and "Why do firms headquartered in one country prefer to own value-adding activities in another country rather than engage in arm's-length or contractual transactions with foreign firms?".

Economists of this era argued that the foreign production of firms as market-replacing activities would occur whenever and wherever firms perceived that the net benefits of using cross-border markets to organize the transactions were less than those of hierarchical control. The real question became, "Why do firms (rather than markets) internalize cross-border transactions?" The market failure that might inspire a firm to choose internationalization over cross-border partnership was identified in the following:

- the costs of opportunism, bounded rationality, information asymmetry, moral hazard, adverse selection, reputation protection, agency misrepresentation, and uncertainty;
- the inability of the market for any good, asset, or service to capture economies external to the transaction involved; and
- the market's failure to permit firms to engage in price discrimination.

This market failure analysis became the leading explanation for the existence and growth of the MNE.

By the early 1980s, the MNE was perceived as an institution that coordinates the use of intermediate assets generated in one country with value-added activities arising from these assets in another country. During this period, Dunning's OLI paradigm emerged (described in Section 1).

The late 1980s to 2000 period produced insights about the determinants of FDI and foreign activities of MNEs as being either country- (region-), industry-, or firm-specific. There were three major intellectual thrusts during this time.

- Awareness grew that firms go abroad to augment their competitive advantages or seek new advantages as well as exploit them. The term *metanational* emerged—an MNE that harnesses resources and intellectual capabilities from throughout the world and integrates these to best advance its long-term strategic objectives.
- International business scholars observed and attempted to explain the increasing diversity of forms of foreign investment (foreign portfolio investment, M&As, strategic alliances, and network relationships).
- Attention increased around embracing the growing variety of cross-border, non-equity cooperative associations within a general theory of international economic involvement.

External Conditions Influencing MNE Activity

In mid-1960s, MNEs were predominately active in manufacturing (and related services), and their manufacturing efforts were designed to produce products for host country markets and determined by production and spatially related cost advantages. Natural resource-based activity was intended to supply agricultural products and minerals for the home market. Attention was focused on the act of FDI per se, rather than on the institution making the investment.

During this time, research was interested in understanding the conditions under which FDI would replace trade, the determinants of the sectoral composition of such investment, and the identity of countries in which such investment was most likely to occur. Early studies were oriented toward trade-type explanations, but later the focus shifted to industrial organization (IO) models. In the 1960s, the likely impact of outward FDI on investing countries' balance of payments was an important policy issue. Studies showed that inbound FDI generally benefited the recipient economies via transfer of technology, management and marketing skills, organizational competences, and new forms of entrepreneurship.

In the 1970s and late 1980s, there was a redirection of academic interest toward the international firm (MNE) as the owner of resources and controller of the way in which those resources are deployed. Jean Jacques Servan-Schreiber's book *The American Challenge* (1967), which proposed actions Europe could take in its silent economic war with the United States, helped to prompt the shift, as did the U.N.'s ECOSOC examination of the impact of MNEs on economic development. The U.N. researchers sought to identify the economic and social impact of MNE strategies on the people of the countries where affiliates operate. They pinpointed several reasons for the emergence of the global enterprise:

- an increase in multinational activities by leading foreign investors,
- the growth of non-U.S. multinational firms in Europe and then Japan,
- the slower rate of technological innovation in the 1970s,
- an increase in the size and product diversification of leading MNEs, and
- increasing interdependence among the market economies of the world (e.g., governments accepting the need to harmonize monetary and exchange rate policies).

At this time, two main schools of thought emerged. The first viewed the international firm as an exploiter and creator of monopolistic advantages that it used to reduce competition. The second saw the MNE as a compensating instrument for intrinsic cross-border market failures and a more efficient allocator of scarce resources. The emergence of Third World MNEs (Brazil, Korea, Taiwan, Hong Kong, Singapore, and India) raised the question of whether there are differences in the determinants and structure of this group versus the First World group studied previously. Some academics also considered country-specific differences (United States vs. Japan) as the explanation for most differences in the level and structure of foreign investments.

From the 1980s to 2000, academic discourse on internationalization focused on three great trading blocs (North America, Western Europe, and Japan) and the rapid growth of FDI in Europe. The role of domestic or foreign-based MNEs increased, with privatization and deregulation opening up opportunities for FDI.

BRUCE KOGUT and UDO ZANDER
"Knowledge of the Firm and the Evolutionary Theory of the
Multinational Corporation" (1993), *Journal of International Business
Studies.*

Thesis: Firms exist because they are repositories of social knowledge that
structure cooperative action. Knowledge includes information (e.g., a
description of how to ride a bicycle) and know-how (e.g., knowing how to ride a
bike).

Kogut and Zander's theory shares many similarities with
Johanson and Valhne (1977, discussed in Section 1), but comes to
a different conclusion. Kogut and Zander concur with the
emphasis on the evolutionary stages of internationalization and
the identification of knowledge as the main scarce resource being transferred, as
well as recognize similarities with transaction cost economics (TCE) in regard to
the challenge of explaining why firms exist. However, for them, firms exist
because they are repositories of social knowledge that structure cooperative
action.

Thus, their theory explains the firm in a positive way, rather than just as a
condition to safeguard the investment from market hazards. The firm justifies
itself by having differentiated capabilities, distinct from its competitors. The
knowledge created by a firm constitutes an ownership advantage, and attributes
of this knowledge determine the mode by which technology is transferred.

Kogut and Zander developed empirical research in the Swedish market,
contrasting two groups: licensing/joint-venture and subsidiary. Their research
objective was to test the effectiveness of innovation transferred across borders
by measuring the underlying dimensions of knowledge (i.e., codifiability,
complexity, and teachability). The results support the notion that internalization
occurs not because knowledge is a public good, but because knowledge is a
complex good with a high level of tacitness. Thus, firms exist to create and
transfer knowledge that is difficult to encode for the purpose of external
dissemination; in this case it is better to transfer knowledge through a subsidiary
than through a third party.

One important contribution of this theory is the formal distinction between
two types of knowledge: information and know-how. Although this objective
versus experiential distinction was already highlighted by others (e.g., Polanyi
1966 and Johanson and Valhne 1977), Kogut and Zander further develop the
distinction via the example that *information* is related to, for example, the
instruction on how to ride a bike (an intellectual process), while *know-how*
involves the actual process of riding the bike (learning from experience).

WILBUR CHUNG
"Identifying Technology Transfer in Foreign Direct Investment:
Influence of Industry Conditions and Investing Firm Motives"
(2001), *Journal of International Business Studies.*

Thesis: Multinationals transfer some capabilities to unaffiliated firms, such that
the host country's industry gains from the presence of the MNE's subsidiaries.

To obtain the greatest returns, MNEs transfer capabilities across
national boundaries to their foreign subsidiaries. This article asks
whether some of these capabilities are also transferred to
unaffiliated firms, and therefore the host industry overall gains
from the presence of an MNE's subsidiaries. Research conducted on Australia,
Canada, and Mexico suggests that knowledge leakage does occur, but the
motives of existing firms (e.g., exploiting advantages, searching for skills) mask
effective analysis of technology transfer. Findings also show that foreign MNEs
establish R&D in the United States to obtain access to science and technology;
therefore, differences in R&D intensity between the home and host country
may indicate the motive of augmenting or exploiting skills.

Using manufacturing (4-digit SIC) data from 11,000 firm-year observations
from Compustat for 1987–1991, the study tests two hypotheses:
H1. Inward FDI will increase host industry productivity when prevailing
     industry competition is low, while controlling for changes in competition.
H2. The higher the prevailing level of industry competition, the less inward
     FDI will increase host industry productivity.

Chung presents three main findings.
- An increased foreign presence of U.S. manufacturing significantly affects
  change in productivity when there are multiple investment motives (i.e.,
  both augmenting and exploiting skills).
- In industries where one entry motive (i.e., augmenting or exploiting skills) is
  more likely than another, increased foreign presence in relatively
  uncompetitive industries is subsequently associated with productivity
  increases.
- Increased foreign presence in relatively competitive industries is
  subsequently associated with productivity stagnation.

The results indicate that when competition is low, technology transfer
occurs. At a point of increasing competition (as measured by product markup),
technology transfer positively impacts productivity. When competition is higher,
productivity gains shrink as foreign entrants both exploit existing capabilities
and source new capabilities.

ANN-WIL HARZING
"Acquisitions Versus Greenfield Investments: International
Strategy and Management of Entry Modes" (2002), *Strategic
Management Journal.*

Thesis: A multinational's strategy links the choice of entry mode to the type of
subsequent management. Overseas acquisitions are initially less controlled by
headquarters and more responsive to local conditions than are greenfield
overseas-startup subsidiaries.

Expansion requires decision on two issues. The company must
choose between non-equity modes (e.g., exporting through
agents, licensing) and equity-based modes (e.g., foreign direct
investment) of foreign market entry. If an equity mode is chosen,
the second decision concerns whether to acquire an existing firm or set up a
new plant (greenfield).

Harzing's study introduces a key explanatory variable: the MNC's
international corporate strategy, that is, the way in which the organization
positions itself with respect to the global business environment and creates or
sustains competitive advantage across national boundaries. Based on a survey of
122 MNEs and the managing directors of 1,650 subsidiaries in 22 countries,
Harzing identifies the MNC strategy as the link between the choice for *entry
mode* and subsequent *management type*, and analyzes whether greenfields and
acquisitions are managed the same way.

The article explores how international corporate strategy influences MNC
marketing service strategy, focusing on the distinction between global and
multidomestic strategies (see <u>Bartlett and Ghoshal</u> 1998, in Section 4).

- **Global firms.** Characterized by a high level of globalization of competition,
  global firms have interconnected national product markets and focus on
  capturing economies of scope and scale. The dominant strategic
  requirement is efficiency, leading to standardized products.
- **Multidomestic/multinational firms.** Characterized as a decentralized
  network with relatively autonomous subsidiaries, multinational firms
  experience a lower level of global competition and compete mainly on a
  domestic level, adapting products and policies to various markets.
- **Transnational firms.** Hybrids of the above, transnational firms participate
  in the global market while also competing on a domestic level. They seek to
  couple the efficiencies of global firms with the local responsiveness of
  multidomestic/multinational firms.

Two theoretical perspectives come into play. The first suggests that
different firm-specific advantages are associated with the two strategies (global

or multidomestic/multinational). The second suggests that different levels of internal versus external similarities in structure (isomorphism) are portrayed by subsidiaries using the two strategies. FDI as the entry mode implies that internalization advantages exist.

Global and multidomestic strategies are associated with different types of firm-specific advantages (FSAs). *Location-bound* FSAs depend on being used in a set of locations (sourced from home and host country), while *non-location bound* advantages can be used on a global basis (i.e., are location independent). Linking these two concepts, global companies tend to focus on exploiting non-location-bound, home-based advantages (e.g., proprietary technology) while also exploiting location advantages in host countries. Multidomestic companies exploit location-bound advantages using host-country-specific advantages, thus requiring product and policy customization (and implying that they will thus choose acquisition strategies for their FDI).

The process of *homogenization* is defined as isomorphism. A subsidiary's external environment includes its parent, the host government, and local interest groups. MNC subsidiaries are pressured to become isomorphic to the parent's organizational norms and external norms. This integration/responsiveness framework suggests that global strategies focus on internal isomorphism and go greenfield, whereas multidomestic strategies focus on external isomorphism and prefer acquisition.

The choice of entry mode influences the headquarters–subsidiary relationship. The headquarters (HQ) does not have the knowledge or resources to make subsidiary decisions, but cannot leave all decisions to the subsidiary, as their interests may differ. One would expect that adopting a global strategy will cause HQ to exercise high control over greenfield subsidiaries (and assign more expatriates in management), while utilizing a multidomestic strategy will result in less control, instead employing local management and tapping into local knowledge.

From substantial data, Harzing shows that acquisitions are more likely for multidomestic firms, and that greenfields are more likely for global companies. Her findings thus support the main hypotheses that acquisitions experience a lower level of control from headquarters, employ fewer expatriates, and demonstrate a significantly higher level of local responsiveness. Overall, acquisitions as subsidiaries have stronger external links with the local environment than internal links with headquarters, and the reverse is true for greenfields. However, over time, greenfields will see reductions in expatriate presence, and acquisitions will cede some of their control and local responsiveness, becoming more integrated in corporate networks and more similar to greenfields.

FREEK VERMEULEN and HARRY BARKEMA
"Pace, Rhythm and Scope: Process Dependence in Building a
Profitable Multinational Corporation" (2002), *Strategic Management Journal.*

Thesis: The characteristics of a firm's international expansion impact its
profitability. It takes time to accumulate resources, and there is a limit to each
company's capacity to absorb new experience.

 Some firms increase profits as a result of international expansion
while others do not. Vermeulen and Barkema investigate how the
relationship between foreign subsidiaries and firm profitability is
moderated by various characteristics in the international
expansion process.

The article utilizes an organizational behavior perspective (consistent with
the evolutionary theory of the firm), conceptualizing firm expansion as a dynamic
process in which history and time matter and where the path taken determines
the reward. This perspective outlines both sides of foreign expansion:

- **Benefits.** Foreign expansion allows the firm to learn from foreign
  subsidiaries, transfer intangible assets overseas, and improve its
  innovativeness.
- **Complexities.** Learning how to operate in different institutional and
  cultural contexts and adapting systems, processes, and organizational
  structures to the international setting adds complexity to the firm and its
  operations.

The extent to which the firm is able to exploit these benefits is constrained by
the capacity of the firm to absorb the complexity of the international process.

Vermeulen and Barkema's theoretical argument is built on two concepts.

1. **Time compression diseconomies.** There is a mechanism of diminishing
   returns when the pace of processes increases. In other words, to speed up a
   process, you must add additional resources that end up providing less value
   per unit (Dierickx and Cool 1989; see Chapter 1, Section 3).
2. **Absorptive capacity.** The firm has a finite capacity to absorb new
   knowledge and put it to commercial use. Given the bounded rationality of
   individuals, limits in their cognitive scope, and organizational inertia, the
   absorptive capacity of the firm is constrained in time (Cohen and Levinthal
   1990).

Overloading the firm's absorptive capacity through an intensive foreign
expansion could lead to diseconomies of time compression and could negatively
impact the performance benefits arising from the foreign subsidiaries.

To measure the "intensity" of the international process, the authors choose four characteristics—pace, rhythm, product scope, and geographical scope—and develop four hypotheses. Each of these four characteristics can negate some of the benefits arising from the corporation's foreign subsidiaries.

H1. **Pace.** The pace of internationalization is the amount of foreign expansion a firm undertakes in a certain period of time. The greater the pace, the greater likelihood that management devotes suboptimal time or attention building greenfields, evaluating and implementing acquisitions, integrating new units into the corporate organization, evaluating foreign experience, assimilating it, and applying it to commercial ends. This lack of management attention prevents the firm from realizing full profit potential from its foreign subsidiaries.

H2. **Rhythm.** The rhythm of foreign expansion measures the regularity of the international process. Large peaks of rapid expansion and long periods of inactivity could lead to a reduction of absorptive capacity and to time compression diseconomies. During peaks, managers do not have enough time to completely absorb expansions; during long periods of inactivity, organizations forget what they have learned and become more rigid in terms of structures, systems, cultures, and mental models.

H3. **Product scope.** The product scope measures the dispersion of foreign subsidiaries in different product markets. A high product scope could lead to time compression diseconomies because new business in new countries requires new knowledge, different routines and business practices, and a different corporate culture. A foreign expansion with high product scope takes significant management time and attention, and the likelihood that the firm makes suboptimal choices will increase.

H4. **Geographical scope.** The geographical scope is the number of countries involved in the international process. Individual countries have different (a) cultural and institutional characteristics, (b) local networks of suppliers and customers, and (c) educational systems and so forth, requiring different organizational systems and processes.

The authors summarize the above concepts to generate two overarching hypotheses. First, a faster or irregular pace moderates the impact of a firm's foreign subsidiaries on its profitability. Second, a higher product or geographic scope also negates some of the benefits of a firm's foreign subsidiaries on its profitability.

They tested these two hypotheses over a longitudinal database of 22 multinational Dutch firms that, during a period of 26 years, performed 67% of their foreign expansion in the EU. The analysis supports the hypotheses and highlights the tradeoffs between the positive effects of having foreign subsidiaries and the moderating effects of speed, geographical scope, product scope, and irregularity.

Discussion and Implications:

 The knowledge-based aspects of the Uppsala model and evolutionary theory (Kogut and Zander) play into the manner of internationalization via entry mode pace, rhythm, and scope. Kogut and Zander identify knowledge as a key competitive advantage of the firm; as an asset it is difficult to replicate due to its sometimes tacit nature, and temporal and contextual aspects make it relevant in certain times and under certain conditions (i.e., knowledge of an industry in a country at a certain time may not be relevant in other markets at other times). A firm's competitive advantage is based on its ability to create and transfer specialized knowledge, and it is the attribute of knowledge that draws the boundaries of the firm. The authors apply their theory to predict that in more advanced stages of internationalization, subsidiaries will have a more active role as knowledge creators, developing the notion of a network of subsidiaries characterized by the cross-border transfer of learning. Eric's experience with the importance of knowledge acquisition relates to the learning-versus-planning debate in the discussion of strategy of Chapter 1; learning allows the serendipitous generation of know-how which can drive strategic decisions.

In establishing a subsidiary in the United Kingdom, Joe sought to facilitate knowledge sharing between the U.S. headquarters and the subsidiary by assigning U.S. staff to work on one-year assignments. A greenfield approach was used instead of an acquisition, as the company's specialization in systems integration was partially based on the company's Boston-based relationship with Lotus Corporation. To augment local knowledge, Joe hired an experienced executive from Lotus U.K. to head the subsidiary. This approach worked well in the United Kingdom; however, in the more psychically-distant environment of Saudi Arabia, an international joint venture was necessary, as companies in that country must be majority owned by Saudis. This arrangement was less conducive to knowledge transfer and internalization for the subsidiary, as fewer U.S. staff were willing to move to Saudi Arabia, and the firm was unable to sustain any competitive advantage in that country.

Dunning's approach considers the inherent dynamics of the environment in which the MNC's subsidiaries operate. The differentiation between the MNC's organizational level and the host country's location-specific determinants (e.g., labor or raw material endowment) sets the stage for the parent–host duality that affects each specific subsidiary's behavior. Initially, there may be a dominant influence on the subsidiary from either direction (i.e., corporate headquarters or host country government) depending upon the factors used to drive the FDI decision, although the objective of any subsidiary would be to add value to the MNC as opposed to the host country. The result is that each foreign subsidiary of the MNC is confronted with two distinct sets of pressures and a need to maintain legitimacy within both the host nation and the MNC, underscoring the importance of selecting country subsidiary managers who can balance these pressures.

Chung's article complements prior research and demonstrates FDI's complex influence on host markets, with three outcomes:

1. Foreign firms enter the market and technology transfer is possible, but incumbents are unable to absorb new technology.
2. Foreign firms enter, technology transfer occurs, and overall production rises.
3. Foreign firms enter by sourcing new capabilities, but those entrants are relatively less productive and the overall productivity of the host market stagnates.

As we have seen since the year 2000, emerging economies have benefited from the FDI experience of multinationals from developed economies and, in many cases, the second of Chung's three outcomes has resulted. In our consideration of the case of China, the findings that host countries gain capabilities from MNE subsidiaries may be a motivation for China's encouraging the development of local contract manufacturing sites. China has been better at fast-copying innovation (and making it more efficient)—generating spillovers—than in generating creative new ideas, but that could change.

Vermulen and Barkema offer two general results regarding firm growth and management decisions. The theory of the growth of the firm (Penrose 1959) suggests that to fully understand the organization's expansion, one may have to consider how the organization arrived there; this path-dependence suggests that the path an organization takes influences both its profitability and its future growth. In terms of management, firms need to follow a path of balanced growth, making clear strategic choices about which of the different dimensions they privilege. For example, increasing the pace of internationalization means that a firm will likely need to restrict the product or the geographic scope of the process. This consideration of strategic choice relates to Harzing's article on the internationalization choices that companies face when acquiring a local firm or starting anew in a foreign market. These choices relate to many environmental factors, including culture, as discussed in Section 5 of this chapter. The observation that overseas acquisitions are less controlled by HQ than are greenfields could be part of why such a small percentage of acquisitions are overseas. At the MNEs where Eric has worked, acquisitions have been overwhelmingly (more than 90%) domestic (U.S.).

Additional readings in this area include, in chronological order, the following.

- **Luo and Park (2004).** In international equity joint ventures, there is a strong positive impact of cooperation between partners on performance, as perceived both by the partners and the venture management team.

- **Vachani (1991).** It is important to distinguish between related and unrelated international global diversification when measuring the impact on an MNE's profit and stability.

3. International Political Economy

The environment in which MNEs operate affects—and is affected by—the MNEs. As economic actors, MNEs affect other companies, the labor force, technological growth, and overall economic growth in the countries in which they operate. As political actors, MNEs may influence the political environment in these countries in ways that are inconsistent with the political aims of the corporate headquarters. Globalization of MNEs emphasizes their roles as actors at the level of countries and supra-national organizations.

This section begins with Kobrin's (2001) description of how an MNE interacts with the objectives and actions of the sovereign nation in which it operates. Gilpin (2001) extends the focus on country and MNE economics to examine the distribution of gains from market activities. Murtha and Lenway (1994) describe how multinational and country strategies interact to provide a competitive advantage for firms. Following this idea, Blumentritt and Nigh (2002) discuss the connection between strategic and political activities via the actions of the MNE's subsidiaries. Finally, Stiglitz (2002) returns the discussion to a broader level, examining the effects of globalization and the involvement of institutions such as the World Bank and the International Monetary Fund.

STEPHEN KOBRIN
"Sovereignty@Bay: Globalization, Multinational Enterprise, and the International Political System" (2001), in A. Rugman and T. Brewer (editors), *The Oxford Handbook of International Business*.

Thesis: International business research has touched on the relationship between multinationals and governments but has not (a) predicted the end of the nation-state, (b) shown that sovereignty is fatally compromised, nor (c) defined terms like *sovereignty*, *autonomy*, and *control*. The MNE and nation-states are inextricably linked.

Political and other non-economic issues were not addressed in international business research until the second half of the 20th century. Penrose (1959) first introduced the theory of the growth of the firm, Lilienthal (1960) "defined" the MNC, Vernon (1971) examined the threat MNEs pose to national sovereignty, and Dunning (1988)

described the OLI (eclectic) paradigm. In this article, Kobrin focuses on the MNE's impact on a country's sovereignty, autonomy, and control.

Kobrin defines *multinational enterprises* as international or cross-border entities that are *of* the existing interstate system, firmly rooted in national territorial jurisdiction. His view of the traditional MNE–state relationship focuses on three central issues: jurisdictional asymmetry, jurisdictional overlap, and control. Kobrin believes that the hierarchical structure of traditional MNEs originally reinforced the core values of the international political system, rather than threatening state sovereignty. In the current MNE world, however, this has changed: globalization now compromises territorial sovereignty due to the limited nature of economic and political governance (traditionally enforced within a specific geographic jurisdiction). Several factors have contributed to this change, including advances in technology, strategic alliances, global electronic networks, the importance of transnational actors, and the importance of international civil society.

The political authority of states (i.e., countries) was originally based upon and defined by geographic parameters: everything within its borders was under its jurisdiction. There are three basic elements to this traditional sovereignty:

1. **Formal sovereignty.** A state is legally recognized as independent of outside authorities in the exercise of its authority.
2. **Internal sovereignty.** A monopoly of force is assumed within the nation's territory (i.e., there is only one ruler).
3. **External sovereignty.** There is both mutually exclusive territoriality (no disputed border areas) and mutual recognition by like units.

Autonomy is a central issue when examining issues surrounding a state's control, policymaking, and policy implementation. However there is no clear line between autonomy and internal sovereignty.

Overall, Kobrin sees the activities of the traditional MNE as constraints on the implementation of sovereignty while at the same time reinforcements for external sovereignty. Literature reveals four sets of problems that MNEs pose for states and the state system:

- appropriate distribution of the costs and benefits associated with MNEs, both within and across states;
- jurisdictional asymmetry between the state's control over geographic jurisdiction and the international network of the MNE and its affiliates;
- jurisdictional conflict and overlap as well as "underlap," including the problem of extraterritoriality; and
- a weakening of national control over the economy and economic actors.

In practice, these problems are interrelated. The distribution issue is generally state-related, as the MNE is responsive to all of the states in which it operates but is not controlled by any one. There is a duality for the MNE subsidiary, which is subject to both the laws of the host nation and the overarching strategy of the MNE. Taxation is a major issue resulting in underlap—corporate taxes may be uncollected by any state. Antitrust laws put subsidiaries in potentially difficult situations. Countries often attempt to extend their jurisdiction through the MNE (e.g., trying to tax foreign income), making it difficult to draw the line when determining the "nationality" of a subsidiary. MNEs organize international economic transactions through internalization, becoming a vehicle for moving management, labor, and technology across borders.

Considering the modern state system and the MNE, internal sovereignty is absolute in theory, but not in practice. The linkage between trade and FDI reduces state control of the economy, and states require the assistance of MNEs to satisfy certain economic objectives; however, the two have different overall objectives that do not always substantially overlap. External sovereignty is more of an absolute construct, as compromising external sovereignty will compromise the state and the system. Traditional MNEs do not compromise external sovereignty because they are incorporated (i.e., registered as legal entities) in each country. Therefore the MNE is a collection of national corporations and exists because the state provides for their creation.

Globalization applies to social, cultural, and political processes and economic organization, and implies a connection between a number of organizations that are not under the jurisdiction of one state. Kobrin argues that MNEs impact the interstate system and sovereignty via deep integration, technology, networks and alliances, transnational actors, and cyberspace. Internationalization of production implies that MNEs coordinate international economic flows. States find control a difficult issue because the transactions are so complex, forcing the state to focus on regulation instead of direct control. Firms need to internationalize in order to amortize the costs of R&D expenses, and thus states become dependent upon MNEs for advances in technology and competitiveness.

Transnationals are autonomous actors in world politics that command significant resources, extending across national borders and influencing politics without state mechanisms. MNEs serve as a source of private authority in world politics through their governance of international economic transactions. The movement of markets and MNEs to cyberspace will further impact sovereignty, as cyberspace destroys the significance of the physical location. MNE networks may thus become nearly impossible to map, undermining the relevancy of territorial jurisdiction given the nature of electronic commerce.

ROBERT GILPIN
Global Political Economy: Understanding the International Economic Order
(2001).

Thesis: International political economy extends the focus of economics to examine (a) the *distribution* of gains from market activities and (b) the impact of the world economy on nations' power, values, and political autonomy. The three archetypes of national economies are the U.S., Japanese, and German models.

Neoclassical economics (NCE) primarily concerns itself with efficiency and the mutual benefits of economic exchange, and regards markets as self-regulating mechanisms isolated from political affairs. Neoclassical economics is generally indifferent to the role of institutions in economic affairs. NCE and International Political Economy (IPE) ask different questions.

International political economy (IPE) is also interested in the distribution of gains from market activities. While over the long term every society gains, those gains are seldom distributed equally among all economic actors, and states are concerned with their relative gain. IPE is interested in the impact of the global economy on nations' power, values, and autonomy. States have the incentive to enact policy to manipulate market forces to safeguard their own values and interests; states attempt to influence the design and functioning of institutions in order to advance their own political, economic, and other interests.

Gilpin begins by defining key terms.

*   *Industrial policy* represents the deliberate efforts by a government to determine the structure of the economy through such devices as financial subsidies, trade protection, or government procurement.
*   The *regime* is a set of conditions, most often of a political nature.
*   An *international regime* comprises a set of implicit or explicit principles, norms, rules, and decision-making procedures around which actors' (e.g., countries') expectations converge in a given area of international relations. This term encompasses rules and organizations such as the IMF and GATT (now the WTO).

Economics, in general, emphasizes the efficient allocation of scarce resources and absolute gains to everyone, and purports that exchange takes place because of mutual gain (positive sum vs. zero sum). IPE offers a state-centric interpretation, emphasizing the distributive consequences of economic activities, and argues that relative (vs. absolute) gain is important. States are interested in the distribution of gains affecting, for example, domestic welfare, national wealth, and military power, with military power being the most important consideration: states are reluctant to trade military security for economic gain.

The Politics of International Regimes

A liberal international economy needs rules to deal with cheating and free-riding, and institutions such as the World Bank, IMF, and WTO exist for this purpose. The theory of hegemonic stability states that a liberal international economy requires a *hegemon* (a leading or paramount state powerful enough to influence events throughout the world) committed to liberal economic principles. A hegemon is a necessary but not sufficient condition for establishment of a liberal international economy, for without a hegemon, international cooperation in trade, finance, and most other matters becomes difficult, if not impossible, to achieve. Stability of the international monetary system is dependent on a dominant power.

Arising in response to the theory of hegemonic stability, *regime theory* suggests that international regimes are a necessary feature of the world economy, as they reduce uncertainty, minimize transaction costs, prevent market failures, and preserve and stabilize the international economy. Regime theory arose in the 1970s in response to a perceived decline of U.S. power, as a means to reassure those inside and outside the United States that a liberal international order would survive a U.S. economic decline. The precise rules and decision-making techniques embodied in international regimes are determined by technologic, economic, and political factors. Regimes rest on international cooperation and are instituted to achieve interstate cooperation, promote information sharing, and solve common problems.

Regime theory frequently sidesteps the problem of national autonomy and interests. For example, every nation joining an international regime reserves the right to withdraw if its interests change. Even in NATO, each member reserves the right not to come to the aid of another member. International regimes invariably affect the economic welfare, national security, and political autonomy of individual states, who thus try to manipulate regimes for their own economic and political advantage. For an international regime to be effective and its rules enforced, it must also rest on a strong political base.

Governance of the Global Economy

International regimes require international leadership and a governance structure, which they cannot directly provide because they lack the power to enforce compliance. The regime leader may be the most powerful state in the group. In normal times, the leader must maintain the flow of capital to poor countries, provide some order in foreign exchange rates (at least for key currencies), and arrange for moderate coordination of macroeconomic policies among leading economies. In times of crisis, the leader must provide open markets for distressed goods during times of economic depression, be a source of extra supply when goods are tight (e.g., during oil crises), and be the lender of last resort in the event of a serious international financial crisis. The leader must encourage other states to obey the international regime and its rules and must promote—but not necessarily pay for—"public goods" such as lighthouses (which protect all vessels, foreign and domestic), open trading systems, and a stable international monetary system.

National Systems of Political Economy

The primary purpose of economic activity varies by society, from promoting consumer welfare to pursuing national power. In liberal societies, which emphasize consumer welfare and market autonomy, the role of the state tends to be minimal. In societies where communal or collective purposes prevail, the role of the state is more intrusive and interventionist.

There are three archetypes of national economies: the U.S., Japanese, and German systems (see Table 5-1). The differences between these three were most apparent in the late 1960s and 1970s as a consequence of the increasing interdependence of national economies. The U.S. system incorporates neoclassical precepts regarding the organization and function of an economy and is intended to maximize consumer satisfaction and facilitate adjustment to change. The Japanese system places a high priority on social harmony and national power, but critics describe it as inflexible, mercantilist, and unresponsive to concerns of other societies. The German emphasis on the social market shares both virtues and vices of the other two systems.

The idea that nations qua nations are in a zero-sum game for market share and economic superiority is anathema to every mainstream economist—international competition takes place between individual firms and not between national economies. Although nations may not compete with one another in a narrow economic sense, nations can be said to compete in their ability to manage their economic affairs effectively. Several solutions to international competition exist:

- **Convergence.** In economic performance or in economic institutions and business practices, convergence—nations evolving toward the same practices or level of performance—requires patience.
- **Harmonization.** Based on international negotiations and reciprocity, harmonization leads to the elimination of national differences: the eradication of national differences should be an explicit goal of international negotiations.
- **Mutual recognition.** Nations agree to honor one another's economic and business practices, suggesting an acceptance of the legitimacy of the rules by which other nations manage their economies. This approach may be more possible for the "Western world."

Table 5-1: Characteristics of Three National Economy Archetypes

Characteristic	U.S.	Japanese	German
Economic type	Market-oriented capitalism	Development capitalism	Social market capitalism
National policy character	Neoclassical: competitive market economy	Neo-mercantilism	Welfare state capitalism or corporatist
Primary purpose	Benefit consumers, maximize wealth creation	Pursue sociopolitical objectives	Balance social concerns and market efficiency
Emphasis	Consumption	Exports and savings	Savings and investment
Outside investment availability	Open to outside world, unless specifically closed (embargoes; import restrictions)	Open, but *keiretsu* limits foreign firms' access	Open and codified to ensure fair treatment of foreign business
Principal driving force	Maximize profits	Maximize sales, market share, and corporate growth	Long-term growth and stability
Markets	Competitive; competition prompted if insufficient	Oligopolistic and Schumpeterian	Oligopolistic; dominated by bank-corporate alliances
Role of state	Laissez-faire	Central	Indirect
Government industrial policy	Limited role to correct market failure	Major role via subsidies, finance, and administrative guidance	Modest role; not activist, but heavy spending on R&D
Control of financial system	Treasury, Federal Reserve, and other legislative and judicial actions	Ministry of Finance has virtual monopoly power	Bundesbank
Regulation	Legal (quasi-autonomous public agencies) and uniform	Self-regulated and policed; potential for inequities	Legal

Characteristic	U.S.	Japanese	German
Industry voice	Fragmented (e.g., Chambers of Commerce)	Focused: *keidanren*	Federated German Industries
Voice of labor	Fragmented with many voices from separate unions	Fragmented into company unions with little influence	Single representative for auto, metal workers, and others
Corporate governance	Stockholders	Banks	Banks, labor, and larger society
Source of capital	Stock market	Retained earnings and affiliated bank	Bank loans
Control of business	Largest stockholders usually own < 5%, often < 2%	70% or more of stock held in *keiretsu*	Banks own large portions of companies
Corporate responsibility	To shareholders	To stakeholders	To stakeholders
Social responsibility	Limited	Committed	Accepting of welfare state
Business practices	Large firms invest and produce abroad	Investment and production at home	Corporate takeovers considered destructive to business relationships

Note. Authors' table; data from Gilpin (2001, Chapter 7).

THOMAS MURTHA AND STEFANIE LENWAY
"Country Capabilities and the Strategic State: How National Political Institutions Affect Multinational Corporations' Strategies" (1994), *Strategic Management Journal.*

Thesis: Multinational strategies interact with state strategies. National institutions contribute to state capabilities, forming a basis for competitive advantage.

This article discusses the implementation of industrial strategy. Successful implementation relies on collaborative interaction between business and governments (Lodge 1990). Formal economic models of effective industrial-strategy implementation rely on the assumption that government policies represent credible commitments (Spencer and Brander 1983; Brander and Spencer 1985) and that governments entering credible commitments (Williamson 1996) therefore bind themselves to nonreversible courses of action (Schelling 1960).

Industrial strategies are government plans to allocate resources to meet long-term national economic objectives, including growth and international competitiveness. *Target specificity* is the degree to which a state can disaggregate and isolate component activities of the national economy as objects of policy intervention. This disaggregation and isolation ranges from macroeconomic tools (e.g., monetary and fiscal policy) to microeconomic tools (e.g., loans, subsidiaries). As a state's target specificity increases, so does its government's ability to single out industries and firms for benefits.

The authors' theoretical argument is influenced by strategic trade theory, which combines game theory with the theory of public externalities. In this context, one fundamental function of government is to influence MNC behavior in an effort to ensure that externalities (public goods) associated with the foreign MNC's strategies do not undermine proper functioning of the market. Crucial questions become, "How can government influence MNC strategy?" and "What is the basis of this capacity?". *Strategic capabilities* (formulating and implementing national industrial strategies that in turn affect MNCs' strategies) are seen as functions of national institutional arrangements. The strategic capabilities of a country are measured by the allocation of property rights between the public and the private sectors and by the degree to which the system relies on markets versus public planning to govern the transactions among existing organizations. Different strategic capabilities lead to different feasible sets of effective industrial strategies, and are the basis of the country's competitive advantage in the global economy.

Murtha and Lenway propose a taxonomy of national systems of interest intermediation, differentiated by their mix of institutional arrangements (proportion of real assets allocated to private vs. state ownership, and proportion of inter-organizational transactions governed by the price vs. plan mechanisms):

- *Transitional* systems are governed by the market, with property rights allocation skewed toward the public.

- *Command* systems have authoritative coordination, with property rights allocation skewed toward the public.

- *Pluralist* systems are governed by the market, with property rights allocation skewed toward the private ownership.

- *Corporatist* systems have authoritative coordination, with property rights allocation skewed toward the private ownership.

In terms of strategy *formulation*, their differences rest on how a policy network institutionalizes and formalizes interest reconciliation among the public and private property-rights holders that collaborate with the government in setting industrial strategies; in other words, different processes for formulating an industrial strategy. In pluralist economies, for example, state institutions tend to be decentralized, weak, and composed of fragmented interest groups that are not institutionalized, while in corporatist economies there is formal recognition of a few interest groups (labor and business). From a strategy *implementation* perspective, policy specificity increases the country's capacity to discriminate between domestic and foreign companies as well as among local firms. Policy credibility is a necessary condition to cause a real change in MNC strategy—if the country is not credible in implementing a certain industrial strategy, a firm adapts to that national strategy only when it is coherent with the firm's own, preexisting strategy.

Murtha and Lenway propose a framework that identifies the impact of the different state models on the strategy choices of home firms and incoming MNCs. Furthermore, their model seems to suggest the "optimal" strategy that the country should follow in different situations. We synthesize these implications in Table 5-2.

The authors' framework suggests that governments and MNCs can achieve more by understanding and acting upon each others' unique capabilities than they can by simply replicating the strategies of other countries. In both corporatist and pluralist economies, for example, private property rights systems foster the development of firm-specific advantages, driving firms to compete in international markets by investing abroad. For both transitional and capitalist states, policy credibility plays a critical role in determining whether the home or host government's strategies actually influence MNC strategy or only appear to do so. Governments can pursue credible strategies provided they formulate them to fit within their states' capabilities.

Table 5-2: State Economic Models and Their Impact on Home Firm and Incoming MNE Strategy

Dimension	Command and transitional models	Corporatist model	Pluralist model
Home firm form of internationalization	Export	FDI with limits: the system imposes pressure for global strategies (see Porter 1986)	FDI with greater strategic discretion: sources of pressure are diffuse and non-binding; pressure of host countries for responsiveness leads to multifocal strategies
Incoming MNC strategies	Flexible; strategy not dependent on government inducements for commercial success (due to the country's low policy-credibility) or affected by host-country industrial strategies	Strategy affected by host-country industrial strategies	Strategy affected by host-country industrial strategies
Host country strategies	Increase credibility by (a) transitioning toward market, (b) not using the most specific policy instruments, and (c) running disciplined macroeconomic planning	Support industries and exclude foreign firms; can reduce the international competitiveness of home firms and industries	Support sectors (no possibility of excluding foreign firms)

Note. MNE = multinational enterprise; FDI = foreign direct investment; MNC = multinational corporation. Authors' table; data from Murtha and Lenway (1994, pp. 123–126).

TIMOTHY P. BLUMENTRITT AND DOUGLAS NIGH
"The Integration of Subsidiary Political Activities in Multinational
Corporations" (2002), *Journal of International Business Studies*.

Thesis: Strategic and political activities are connected: the more a corporate
subsidiary is integrated with its affiliates strategically, the more it is integrated
with other subsidiaries politically.

Blumentritt and Nigh use resource dependence theory (Pfeffer
and Salancik 1978) as a foundation to combine literature on
MNCs and international business–government interactions. They
were interested in whether an MNC's political activities, as well as
the competitive activities of its subsidiaries, might exhibit differentiation as well
as integration. Two streams of existing literature—international business-
government interactions and international strategic management of political
activities—conflicted around certain questions:

- How does a firm manage an imperative found in one country that may
  affect the activities of a subsidiary in a different country?
- What is the significance of the location of decision-making authority (HQ
  or locally-based) over political acts?

Since governmental structures and procedures differ and issues vary across
regions, MNC subsidiaries are likely to differ with respect to their available
resources and strategic roles. Consequently, the political activities that MNCs
and subsidiaries employ are likely to differ: MNCs might take a global strategic
position in their interactions with governments, while host-country contexts
might demand specified activities by the subsidiaries (Hillman and Keim 1995;
Hillman and Hitt 1999). Firm-specific advantages, managerial positions, and
host-government characteristics influence an MNC's adoption of integrated or
locally responsive interactions with governments (Rugman and Verbeke 1998).

Blumentritt and Nigh's examination of extant literature led to the question,
"How do MNCs and their subsidiaries coordinate or differentiate their political
activities given diverse material and geographic environments?" To answer this
question, the authors examined the influence of external factors on an
organization's practices and success. Using a sample of 88 subsidiaries of 22
MNCs in 37 countries, the authors find that MNC interactions with host
governments are characterized by degrees of both *localization*, based on the
characteristics of each subsidiary and its host country, and *coordination*, based on
the overall objectives of the MNC and possible knowledge-sharing within the
firm. Subsidiaries integrate their political activities with affiliates based on the

influence of both inter-subsidiary strategic factors and host country environments.

These findings lead to an enhanced view of foreign subsidiaries, as one cannot assume that the positions taken and methods used by an MNC in its home country are equally prudent in other countries. The more integrated a subsidiary is with affiliates in a strategic sense, the greater its integration with other subsidiaries in a political sense.

This article demonstrates a connection between strategic and political activities. MNC political activities occur not only within the countries in which MNCs operate and have subsidiaries, but between those subsidiaries as well. There is "something special" about MNCs and their political activities in that, as cross-national interdependence of economic activities within MNCs increase and while external political and economic actors become more interdependent, the MNC is driven to develop a more integrated political strategy to achieve its objectives.

JOSEPH STIGLITZ
Globalization and Its Discontents (2002).

Thesis: Globalization has brought both gains (e.g., faster growth, better technology, improved literacy) and losses; institutions like the World Bank and the International Monetary Fund have a mixed record. The IMF should adopt non-economic objectives, become more transparent, customize its approach more to each country, and engage in a staged process rather than all-at-once interventions.

Whether there has been a net gain or loss due to globalization depends on one's point of view. Many countries have grown faster than they would have otherwise, foreign aid has brought benefits to millions, technology has spread, and literacy has improved. There have also been many protests that, in some cases, have resulted in policy changes like the international land mine treaty, debt forgiveness for some of the poorest countries, and a reduction in drug prices for HIV/AIDS.

Several international organizations have charters that attempt to deal with various problems in the world (e.g., finance, health, or labor issues). On financial issues, both national governments and private institutions play a role in international affairs.

- **International Monetary Fund.** The IMF reports to finance ministers and central banks to provide global macroeconomic stability.
- **World Bank.** The bank addresses structural issues and lending for projects such as roads and dams, with the slogan "Our Dream Is a World Without Poverty."[4]
- **World Trade Organization.** The WTO addresses international trade relations via Trade Ministers, and differs from the IMF and World Bank in that it does not set rules, but rather provides a forum for trade negotiations.

Other players include the United Nations (UN), World Health Organization (WHO), International Labor Organization (ILO), various nongovernmental organizations (NGOs), industrialized countries, regional banks, and treasuries.

These international organizations have leaders, philosophies, and policies that affect individual countries as well as global economics. Prior to 1980, for example, the World Bank viewed the economy as consisting of market failures and therefore perceived a higher need for government intervention. In 1980, the World Bank underwent a change in administration, resulting in a new school known as the "Washington Consensus" that is more market-based with a reduced role for government.

The IMF's original charter was concerned with economic stability, so that in times of crisis it would intervene at the macroeconomic level; however, for countries in a seemingly constant state of crisis, the IMF became a fixture in the country's policy-making. The economic school of thought within the IMF viewed "liberal financial markets" solely from an economic perspective and was thus less likely to understand the "bigger system" including social forces.

The IMF has several procedures to keep countries honest with respect to loans, and the institutionalization of these procedures raises certain organizational issues, including a lack of transparency and the IMF's tendency to get involved politically. These issues help to explain some of conflict between the IMF and developing countries: While participating countries have voting rights, large developed countries dominate. Overall, one picture of the IMF that develops is that of a powerful, politically motivated, and Western-driven bureaucracy.

Stiglitz is critical of the IMF's procedure of demanding market reforms, suggesting that the IMF confuses the ends with the means and that the "means" should involve sequencing and pacing, rather than moving directly to the end "solution" of free markets. He makes specific recommendations as follows:

- **Organization.** Sitglitz advocates for more transparency, especially since the IMF is a public institution.

---

[4] This was the slogan of the World Bank at the time Stiglitz wrote his book. Their slogan is variously reported, and as of this writing their website uses "Working for a World Free of Poverty."

- **Policy.** He recommends that the IMF broaden its perspective to understand that there are other aspects to problems (e.g., social), in addition to the economic viewpoint.
- **Procedures.** Stiglitz would like to see more "customization" with respect to how a development plan is created for a particular country, and recommends that the IMF view development as a process that needs to be done in stages, rather than as a "shock" treatment.

Discussion and Implications

 Whereas countries are sovereign entities with geographic and legal boundaries, Kobrin explains that MNEs operate in multiple countries via subsidiaries that are recognized legal entities in each country. The internalization of transactions within MNEs, which is necessary to decrease transaction costs and consistent with transaction cost economics (TCE), can undermine country sovereignty. The emergence and ubiquity of the internet has, as Kobrin predicted in 2001, heightened these issues—note the 2011 Kim Dotcom[5] case of file sharing via websites. Managers must recognize the role of sovereign states in the world order, and realize that the number of countries in the world has increased significantly since the 1960s, and is expected to continue increasing.

Nations take different approaches to their political economy, and international political economy (IPE) studies delineate attempts by governments to influence the structure of the economy, both internally and externally. Political economic theory focuses on relational gain (am I doing better than my neighbor) versus the absolute (zero-sum) gain of neoclassical economics. This focus relates to the relationship between MNC strategy and the local government's industrial strategy. The articles on IPE and MNCs suggest a number of relevant questions for managers:

- Is there a "one best way" based on the trade-offs between the private and public sector, as proposed by Murtha and Lenway?
- Is their proposed approach too deterministic?

These questions underscore the symbiotic relationship between corporations and governments, and relate to the international political economics view that the economy is not zero-sum.

The interaction of MNEs with the political environments in which they operate is affected by and through the MNE's subsidiaries. The sources

---

[5] The Kim Dotcom/Megaupload case is an example of 21st century technology dissolving national borders. Mr. Dotcom (neé Schmitz) was arrested in a commando-style raid at his New Zealand home at the behest of U.S. FBI concerning his Hong Kong-based file sharing site, Megaupload, alleging copyright infringement. See Hutchison (2012) and Taylor (2012) for background and details.

discussed in this section, in general, point to how MNC managers must recognize the role that subsidiaries play in the countries where they operate and in the parent company. Stiglitz, however, does not say much about MNCs. While he does state that FDI has played an important role in MNCs and the macroeconomic environment, he focuses primarily on the banking industry. His opinion is that large MNC banks have hurt smaller domestic banks, and furthermore, have played a role in assisting MNCs to internationalize.

While the IMF is often criticized for its failures, the institution has had some successes. For example, Stiglitz mentions that Latin America has seen successful IMF reforms. Many of the problems in the late 1990s in South America seem connected to IMF policies but suggest that *sustained* stability may not have occurred because of insufficient development of "infrastructure." Stiglitz seems to conclude that in the distant past the IMF was successful, though in some cases economic stability was not sustained due to a multitude of factors.

Additional writings in this area include the following, presented in chronological order.

- **Rugman and Verbeke (1998).** Firm-specific advantages and managerial positions, as well as host-government characteristics, influence MNCs' decisions regarding integrated or locally responsive interactions with governments.
- **Hillman and Hitt (1999).** An MNC might take a global strategic position with respect to interacting with governments, while host-country contexts might demand specified activities by the MNC's subsidiaries.
- **Furman, Porter, and Stern (2002).** National innovative capacity may explain differences in innovation intensity across advanced economies. The variation of R&D inputs is a critical determinant of the level of innovation intensity—national innovative capacity influences downstream commercialization.

4. MULTINATIONAL MANAGEMENT

Section 3 addresses how MNEs, as headquarters and subsidiary units, affect the environment in which they operate, both politically and economically. How, then, should MNE managers structure activities between headquarters and subsidiary? How should the structure map to the firm's strategy, learning, and the market needs of the industry globally and locally? The sources in this section address the evolution of MNE organization, and its fit and strategy relative to the needs of the industry.

This section begins with a focus on the structural evolution of the firm (Stopford and Wells 1972), and then examines such structures from the subsidiary perspective (Birkinshaw 2001), as subsidiaries are increasingly concerned with resource development (rather than market positioning). Bartlett and Ghoshal (1998) speak to the need for the organizational forms discussed in the first two articles (i.e., firm and subsidiary), to match competitive demands in a global environment. Rugman and Verbeke (2001) further analyze firm-specific and subsidiary-specific advantages based on competencies that are unique to the company and to the location of each subsidiary. Finally, Inkpen (2001) presents relationships between the firm and outside entities as cooperative arrangements that utilize resources from autonomous organizations in different countries to create value that would be unachievable by either parent acting alone.

JOHN STOPFORD AND LOUIS WELLS JR.
Managing the Multinational Enterprise (1972).

Thesis: A firm's structure evolves as its international activities increase. If the mismatch between a firm's structure and strategy is severe, it may incur higher costs or miss opportunities.

In their book, Stopford and Wells identify the structural stages that companies go through as they evolve from simple, unitary, domestic firms to growth-oriented firms to multi-divisional enterprises. The structures to address international and global business develop in concert with this evolution. The *structure of an organization* represents the design through which the enterprise is administered, and that design has three major aspects:

- the authority and responsibility of each executive,
- the kinds of information that flow along communication lines, and
- the procedures established for channeling and processing information.

Companies often pass through three stages of structural evolution.

1. A simple firm normally begins with a functional structure administered by a single person, such as the owner or founder.
2. Functional departments are created that are capable of accommodating considerable growth, and a hierarchy develops in which these departments report to the office of the president. Creating functional departments achieves certain advantages, but each department develops its own language/code that enhances intra-department communication at the expense of inter-department communication.
3. A balance is struck between central coordination and independence for each subsystem, as each division resembles the functional hierarchy of Stage

2. Finance is now controlled by the central office, and each division is a profit center. Divisional subsystems and the central office are linked by a control function (e.g., performance monitoring, correction action signaling, fund allocation) and a planning process. The president's role now concerns determining strategy and divisional balance, rather than the daily coordination of functional departments.

International growth is seen first as being small and entrepreneurial, but when the international group becomes large relative to corporate headquarters, an international division is formed with a general manager reporting into executive management. This division coordinates the activities of foreign subsidiaries, adjusts transfer prices, and raises capital for overseas subsidiaries, but does not have the same autonomy as domestic product divisions. The international division is the locus of all international expertise, and serves as training ground for more managers. However, in this structure there may be a communication gap between the domestic and international product groups.

A global structure develops when top managers realize that strategic planning and major policy decisions must be made centrally to maintain a worldwide perspective on the interests of the firm. This structure can have different forms, including area divisions, worldwide product divisions, or a mixture of the two. A major issue with this structure is a shortage of adequate managers.

Product diversification develops to capitalize on superior marketing skills or as a response to the threat of falling profit margins or lower growth rates. Levels of diversity are defined by the number of industries in which the product lines operate. Product diversification is related to the third stage structure, as firms can transfer the manufacture of an added product line to foreign locations, developing global structures using worldwide product divisions.

If structure does not match strategy, a firm may incur higher costs or miss opportunities. This mismatch may result from a lag in reorganization, which can occur when managers do not immediately recognize the need for a change, so that their biases and preferences for the future organizational structure delay negotiation. Whether product- or area-designed, global structures have inherent inefficiencies due to the prioritization of one concern over another (e.g., product over area). Organization components (e.g., committees, teams, the grid system, matrix systems) are designed to improve information flow, but may have drawbacks (e.g., potential conflict due to dual supervisors or slow decision-making by committees and teams).

Interestingly, significant effects on performance are only seen in the case of extreme mismatches between strategy and structure. This difference may be due to the complexity of factors that affect performance.

JULIAN BIRKINSHAW
"Strategy and Management in MNE Subsidiaries" (2001), in A.
Rugman and T. Brewer (editors), *The Oxford Handbook of
International Business*.

Thesis: Subsidiaries are increasingly concerned with resource development over
market positioning, and subsidiaries have some freedom to shape their own
strategy separate from headquarters. Companies need to install structures that
allow the local managers sufficient autonomy.

Birkinshaw holds that MNE subsidiaries face a dilemma. On the
one hand, subsidiaries are at the heart of MNE action, which
means they are expected to act more independently concerning
their own local market while staying under the MNE
headquarters' strategic control. On the other hand, as the MNE becomes more
globally integrated and globally oriented, the subsidiaries' powers and
responsibilities become diluted.

The author reviews the literature on MNE subsidiaries and offers some
perspectives on how the literature may evolve. The focus is on the wholly-
owned subsidiary company as the primary unit of analysis. Birkinshaw first
describes four literature streams during the 1970s-1980s.

1. **The Strategy-Structure stream.** This literature focused on the strategies
    and structures of MNEs from a classical hierarchical perspective (e.g.,
    Stopford and Wells 1972) and gave little explicit attention to subsidiaries.
2. **The HQ–Subsidiary Relationship stream.** This research focused on how
    the center could control its subsidiaries, and on the centralization and
    formalization of decision-making, coordination, and integration (e.g.,
    Brandt and Hulbert 1977; Gates and Egelhoff 1986).
3. **The MNE Process stream.** Process stream literature focused on issues
    such as strategic MNE decision-making and organizational change, and
    demonstrated the complexity of the relationship—in which structure is less
    important than management systems or culture as a way to control
    subsidiary managers (e.g., Prahalad and Doz 1981).
4. **The Subsidiary Role stream.** These studies moved the level of analysis
    down to the subsidiary and showed that the subsidiary is not just an
    instrument of the parent, but has some freedom in shaping its destiny (e.g.,
    Poynter and Rugman 1983).

While instructive, these categorizations are limited as they give little regard
to theoretical issues; in addition, additional streams of literature are evident
since the 1990s. The first considers the increasingly specialized roles taken
within MNEs, such as the emergence of centers of excellence, different roles of

R&D units in subsidiaries, emergence of regional HQs in subsidiaries, and the role of divisional HQs. The second stream examines the evolution of subsidiary roles over time and the ways that the process of sequential investment affects a subsidiary. In this view, subsidiary evolution can be driven from within (through the initiative of subsidiary managers) or from without (through parent investment or external forces). The third stream examines the flows of information between the subsidiary and its network (which can be internal or external to the MNE), and the patterns of information flow between the subsidiary and the MNE headquarters. This literature considers the transfer of best practices between units and the linkages between the subsidiary and the local business environment (e.g., how the subsidiary draws from and contributes to the local knowledge pool, the extent to which subsidiaries are embedded in the local environment). The final literature stream examines the HQ–subsidiary relationship using concepts such as procedural justice; feedback-seeking behavior in subsidiary managers; and perception gaps between HQ and subsidiary managers, and their consequences. Foundational to this work is the idea that the subsidiary is not just an instrument of the parent company, but has degrees of freedom in shaping its own destiny.

The theories used in MNE research are problematic: they are eclectic and often incommensurable, and the relevant level of analysis for most theory is the MNE as a whole, not the subsidiary.

- *Transaction cost-based theory of international production* is widely used and seeks to explain the existence of MNEs in terms of ownership-specific advantages vis-à-vis incumbent domestic competitors, location-specific advantages, and intermediate market failure that favors internalization. This application of the theory assumes that ownership advantages originate in the MNE's home country, whereas in reality they sometimes arise in subsidiaries.
- The *resource-based view of the firm* is a dominant conceptual paradigm in strategic management, but there is not much attention to this view in MNE literature. The resource-based view implicitly assumes that resources and capabilities are developed and held in a monolithic firm, whereas in an MNE some may be in the HQ while others are in a subsidiary.

Institutional theory, however, provides a way of understanding why competing firms are often similar.

Birkinshaw hypothesizes that subsidiary strategy is increasingly concerned with resource development rather than with market positioning, and considers that while the subsidiary's role is assigned to it by the parent, the concept of "subsidiary strategy" suggests some level of choice or self-determination. For example, in market positioning there are many types of subsidiaries with varying mandates in many types of markets, which suggests that most subsidiaries have less control over market positioning than the traditional approach suggests.

There are trends underway that serve to limit subsidiaries' degrees of freedom in shaping market positioning:

- the emergence of global customers who demand consistent products and services on a worldwide basis,
- global integration of supply chains (to mirror the emergence of global customers),
- pressure on R&D organizations to deliver more efficient outputs, and
- global market transparency due to e-commerce.

Competition is increasingly global, requiring the coordinated management of a portfolio of subsidiaries and decreasing degrees of freedom for individual subsidiary managers. Most tangible resources are held primarily at the subsidiary, whereas most intangible resources (e.g., reputation) are held at the firm level.

 CHRISTOPHER BARTLETT and SUMANTRA GHOSHAL
Managing Across Borders (1998).

Thesis: Organizational forms must match competitive demands. To compete globally, a transnational company must develop global competitiveness, multinational flexibility, and worldwide learning capability simultaneously.

 Bartlett and Ghoshal's book is based on a five-year study of nine large corporations, and provides practicing managers with guidance and recommendations for managing across borders. Their objective was to understand the organizational and administrative tasks facing managers in companies with worldwide operations in a time of major environmental change, and to identify and conceptualize the forces of change and strategic challenges.

Their study examined companies in the areas of branded packaged goods (Procter & Gamble, Unilever, Kao), consumer electronics (General Electric, Philips, Matsushita), and telecommunications (ITT, Ericsson, NEC). Bartlett and Ghoshal identify various strategic demands faced in these industries.

- **The force for global integration is driven by a need for efficiency (e.g., GE).** Major technological innovation forces a fundamental realignment of industry economics: consumer tastes and preferences begin homogenizing, major external discontinuities (e.g., oil shocks) facilitate change, and MNEs enter a game of "global chess."
- **The force for local differentiation centers on a need for responsiveness (e.g., Kao).** While there is movement toward

homogeneity of tastes and preferences, we are not there yet. International travel and communication have reduced differences, while barriers and countertrends force continued sensitivity to national differences and local interests. There are differences in national market structures and impediments to the globalizing forces of scale economics: the benefits of scale economies are offset by the additional costs of central supply (freight and administrative costs), the realities of flexible manufacturing, and the reactions of national governments that see their markets flooded by MNC products.

- **The force for worldwide innovation is based on a need for learning (e.g., ITT).** The ability to link and leverage knowledge is a key factor that differentiates winners from survivors and losers. There is a trend to seek global volume in order to amortize R&D costs or to transfer new technologies voluntarily via licensing, joint development, and/or strategic alliances.

Company performance in the five-year study was based primarily on the fit between the dominant strategic requirements of the business and the firm's dominant strategic capability.

The authors first define three types of cross-border organizational forms:

- *Multinational companies* manage a portfolio of national entities.
- Driven by a need for global efficiency, *global companies* centralize strategic and operational decisions.
- *International companies'* strategy is based primarily on transferring and adapting the parent company's knowledge or expertise to foreign markets.

Bartlett and Ghoshal believe in a new approach to managing a company's worldwide operations, which will be particularly effective in highly competitive, volatile, and changing business environments. At a fundamental level, each business is characterized by one of the above dominant strategic demands, and a firm can compete effectively as long as its capabilities fit the strategic demand.

A *multinational industry structure* (multiple structures loosely connected across national boundaries) was most relevant when technology adoption, distribution, legal and regulatory conditions, and production conditions are tantamount. These conditions create a need for local differentiation in products and strategic approaches, and the underlying economics allow achievement of minimum-scale efficiencies.

The *multinational decentralized federation* was adopted by companies expanding in the prewar period and is characterized by distributed resources and delegated responsibilities. A global industry structure (basic characteristics defined by need for global scale, relatively unimpeded by national differences) is relevant in consumer electronics, where the trend through the 1970s was an increase in the benefits of world-scale economies driven by technological changes and reinforced by homogenization of customer tastes and the decline of trade barriers.

The *global centralized hub* consolidates assets, resources, and responsibilities, and views the world as a single economic entity. This international industry structure (developing products and processes centrally, and moving overseas by transferring technologies and marketing expertise) is relevant when the development of products is prohibitively expensive, when significant scale economies exist in production, and when the key to success lies in the ability to transfer knowledge and manage the product life cycle efficiently and flexibly.

A key task of the *international coordinated federation* is the transfer of knowledge and expertise to overseas environments. In this model, management takes a somewhat superior and parochial attitude toward international operations.

These organization models have different strategic capabilities. Multinational models allow sensitivity and responsiveness to local differences and demands, international models provide an effective means for companies to transfer knowledge and skills, and global organizations facilitate the development of coordinated strategies to capture global-scale efficiencies. The environment–strategy–structure linkage suggests that superior performance comes from a good fit between strategy and environmental demands, as well as between organization structure and strategy.

Each of these three organizational models (multinational, global, international) has built-in efficiencies for appropriate learning and information exchange, but each also has inherent inefficiencies related to resources.

- Global companies may achieve efficiency by exploiting scale economies, and centralizing knowledge to efficiently manage innovation. However, national subsidiaries are managed without any slack resources, limiting their ability to respond to local market needs, while a central "innovation" group lacks understanding of market needs and production realities outside the home market. Thus, learning opportunities overseas are lost due to limited national resources and a narrow national role.
- MNCs' dispersed resources permit responsiveness to local needs, but fragmentation of activities carries efficiency penalties, learning suffers, and local innovations represent efforts to protect turf and autonomy.
- International companies are able to leverage knowledge and the capabilities of the MNE's parent, but resource configurations and operating systems negatively impact efficiency.

Bartlett and Ghoshal propose a fourth organizational type, the *transnational company*, which seeks efficiency as a means to achieve global competitiveness and also acknowledges the importance of local responsiveness as a tool for achieving flexibility in international operations. Innovation is regarded as the outcome of a larger process of organizational learning, resulting in selective decisions regarding the centralization and decentralization of resources. The outcome is a complex configuration of assets and capabilities that are distributed yet specialized, requiring strong interdependencies that may be reciprocal or sequential.

Transnationals develop responsiveness by building multinational flexibility: designing slack into production facilities, adopting flexible automation, creating products with modular structures, and building the systematic differentiation of roles and responsibilities into different parts of the organization. In determining subsidiary roles, transnationals consider customer tastes, government regulations, the availability of leading-edge technologies, and the position of global competitors. Transnationals recognize that innovations are created by subsidiaries in addition to central R&D, so they pool resources to develop worldwide solutions.

The transnational must develop a multidimensional organization that maintains the viability and effectiveness of each organizational group, requiring highly flexible coordination processes to cope with both short-term shifts in specific role assignments and long-term realignments of basic responsibilities and reporting relationships. The company has to coordinate and mange three crucial flows:

- the flow of parts, components, and finished goods;
- the flow of funds, skills, and other scarce resources among units; and
- the flow of intelligence, ideas, and knowledge that are central to innovation and learning.

Transnationals must build coordinating processes of centralization (substantive decision-making by senior management), formalization (institutionalization of systems and procedures), and socialization (building a context of common purpose, values, and perspectives among managers to influence their judgments).

A summary of the key elements of each of the organizational forms discussed by Bartlett and Ghoshal is provided in Table 5-3. The transnational model can be seen both as a hybrid or a distinct model. As a hybrid, it selects and incorporates the perceived best features of the three basic models. As a distinct model, it brings in a new dimension not covered by the previous models—emphasizing aspects such as interdependence, integration, and sharing.

Bartlett and Ghoshal close by identifying four types of subsidiaries.

1. *Strategic leaders* are located in countries or regions critical to an MNE's competitiveness, and act as both recipient and source of the MNE's most advanced non-location-bound knowledge bundles.
2. *Contributors* derive their role from internal knowledge-development capabilities, not from the external country-specific advantages of their location.

Table 5-3: Key Elements of Organizational Forms for Businesses That Grow Beyond Their Home Market

Organizational features	Multinational	Global	International	Transnational
Key capability	National responsiveness	Global-scale efficiency	Worldwide transfer of home country innovation	All three: national responsiveness, global-scale efficiency, and worldwide transfer of home country innovation
Configuration of assets, decisions, and responsibility	Decentralized, self-sufficient subsidiaries	Concentrated, centralized	Key competences centralized; other resources distributed	Distributed, interdependent, specialized
Role of foreign subsidiaries	Sensing and exploiting local opportunities	Implementing parent company strategies	Exploitation and adaptation of parent company's competences	Differentiated contributions to worldwide integrated operations
Development and diffusion of knowledge	Knowledge is developed and kept by subsidiaries	Knowledge is developed and kept by the headquarters	Knowledge is developed at the headquarters and transferred to subsidiaries	Joint development and sharing on a worldwide scale
Preferred control mechanism	Socialization	Centralization	Formalization	All three: socialization, centralization, and formalization

Note. Authors' table; adapted from Christopher Bartlett and Sumantra Ghoshal, *Managing Across Borders* (1998).

3. *Implementers* may be important for an MNE's overall cash flow, but location is not considered critical to the MNE's sustained competitiveness, nor are implementers expected to develop new non-location-bound knowledge themselves.
4. *Black holes* have non-location-bound information that was transferred in from other parts of the firm, but this transferred knowledge does not represent a real firm-specific advantage in the subsidiary's market.

ALAN RUGMAN AND ALAIN VERBEKE
"Subsidiary-Specific Advantages in Multinational Enterprises"
(2001), *Strategic Management Journal.*

Thesis: Multinationals develop firm-specific and subsidiary-specific advantages based on competencies that are unique to the MNC and to the location of each subsidiary.

This article discusses internal patterns of MNE competence-building, with a focus on the creation of foreign subsidiary capabilities. Rugman and Verbeke analyze the development and diffusion processes of firm-specific advantages (FSAs), and distinguish between FSAs (advantages regarding the MNE as a whole) and subsidiary-specific advantages (SSAs). MNEs are differentiated networks of dispersed operations (as well as resources and capabilities); subsidiaries perform specific value-creating activities embedded in the host countries' knowledge development system.

Prior analytic approaches to MNE/subsidiary research focused on the subsidiary manager as the unit of analysis, and examined the process by which these managers make strategic decisions and undertake "subsidiary initiatives." The eclectic paradigm (Dunning 1988, 1993) dominating the mainstream international business approach was based on three assumptions:

1. It is possible to evaluate subsidiary roles and capabilities solely from a corporate "portfolio analysis" perspective.
2. HQ employs a "simple allocation" of roles and capabilities to subsidiaries.
3. HQ coordinates and controls activities through the design of an appropriate "structural context."

Rugman and Verbeke investigate the functioning of a subsidiary within an MNE through the theoretical lens of development and diffusion within the MNE network. Specifically, they track FSAs (which can be functional), production-related proprietary assets (know-how), and organizational capabilities to efficiently coordinate and control the MNE's asset base. Also important to the framework are country-specific advantages (CSAs) from which firms obtain a competitive advantage in the international marketplace.

An MNE is able to achieve a superior performance if it develops some type of FSA. There are two main characteristics of FSAs:

- **Location of internal development in the home country, in the host country, or through a joint action of various units in the MNE network.** This characteristic is related to CSAs: individual countries are path-dependent in their knowledge development trajectories, making the knowledge difficult to replicate. Therefore only firms with foreign affiliates located within the national borders will benefit from the country-specific, technological, and organizational capabilities.

- **The distinction between location-bound and non-location-bound advantage.** By definition, location-bound FSAs cannot be easily transferred across borders, as they require significant adaptation for use in other locations. Non-location-bound FSAs (e.g., functional assets, production-related proprietary assets, organizational capabilities) can easily be transferred across borders and lead to benefits of scale, scope, or exploitation of national differences.

Firms differ in their ability to accumulate competencies and capabilities that are rare, valuable, non-substitutable, and difficult to imitate.

Rugman and Verbeke identify ten potential patterns of FSA development and diffusion characterized by different mixes of these two characteristics and different evolution trajectories in the development and diffusion process, as seen in Table 4. They find that several of these capability-development processes are associated with SSAs; thus, the configuration of dispersed operations cannot be entirely controlled through decisions about FDI taken by headquarters.

Patterns 5, 6, and 7 are associated with idiosyncratic resources and capabilities of foreign subsidiaries that cannot be diffused throughout the MNE. These patterns agree with empirical observation: an increasing number of MNEs have regional organizational units and powerful affiliates that build upon both the national knowledge-development system and the global profit opportunities provided by the host country.

There are three interaction drivers of subsidiary evolution and capability creation: head office assignment, subsidiary choice of action, and local environment determinism. SSAs reflect the competencies and capabilities that can be exploited globally without the internal diffusion of the bundle of knowledge itself. The development process of these SSAs is contingent upon the subsidiary's ability to incorporate knowledge that is tacit and fundamentally context-specific, as well as its ability to reflect the existence of a capability gap with other MNE affiliates. The SSAs can only be sustained— and will only be supported by HQ—if they do not negatively impact other MNE operations.

Synergies must exist between the rent creation potential of MNE-level, non-location-bound FSAs, and SSAs at the affiliate level; that is, the SSA should be synergistic with other non-location-bound FSAs so that the MNE, and not just the subsidiary, can extract value from the SSA.

Table 5-4: Patterns of Development and Diffusion for Firm-Specific Advantages (FSAs)

Pattern	Location bound?	Location developed	Subsequent action taken with FSA
1	No	Home base	Diffused across borders
2	Yes	Home base	Transformed into non-location-bound and diffused
3	No	Home base	Diffused to create location-bound FSAs in host countries
4	Yes	Host country	Used in host country
5	No	Host country	Diffused
6	No	Host country	Linked to home guidelines and diffused
7	Yes	Foreign subsidiaries	Transformed by subsidiaries into non-location-bound and diffused
8	No	Jointly by subsidiaries	Diffused throughout network
9	No	Jointly by subsidiaries	Associated with some location-bound activities
10	Yes	Network of subsidiaries	Transformed into non-location-bound and diffused

Note: Authors' table; data from Rugman and Verbeke (2001, pp. 237–250).

A single subsidiary may be associated with several "generic" FSA development and diffusion processes in its value-creating activities. This association implies that attempts to classify subsidiaries according to their specific "role" in the MNE have become less relevant.

ANDREW INKPEN
"Strategic Alliances" (2001), in A. Rugman and T. Brewer (editors), *The Oxford Handbook of International Business*.

Thesis: Strategic alliances are enduring inter-firm cooperative arrangements that employ resources from autonomous organizations in different countries to create value unachievable by either parent organization acting alone.

 Strategic alliances were traditionally considered collaborative organizational arrangements that use resources or governance structures from more than one existing organization. Inkpen incorporates cross-border flows and linkages to produce a new definition of *international strategic alliances* as (relatively) enduring inter-firm cooperative arrangements using resources from autonomous organizations based in two or more countries. This definition suggests that pooling resources creates value in a way that each of the parent organizations could not achieve by acting alone.

This pooling of resources relates to four strategic objectives: gain economies of scale, reduce risk and promote stability, gain legitimacy (capitalize on another's reputation), and gain access to another's knowledge or ability.

The reasons firms choose to enter into an alliance have been examined from several perspectives.

- **Transaction cost.** Firms may enter an alliance due to an inefficient market for intermediate goods (i.e., a high degree of asset specificity). In inefficient or imperfect markets, arm's-length contracts may not be ideal. Alliances may eliminate uncertainty, provide a rapid means of establishing a competitive position (especially when acquiring businesses foreign to one's own), and offer low risk (as there is no transfer of ownership, the deal can be broken).

- **Organizational learning.** Alliances provide a platform for organizational learning: each partner can access the other's knowledge, take advantage of mutual interdependence and problem-solving, and observe alliance activities and outcomes. This platform reduces the risk that the knowledge will be lost quickly.

While practitioners often write about alliance failures, academics have noted the difficulty in measuring alliance performance. Not only is alliance stability used as an indicator of performance, but there are also issues of instability and competing definitions of alliance stability (e.g., changes in percent holdings, shifts in alliance control, unplanned equity changes). Cultural issues are also important, as compatibility and congruency are critical to alliance success.

Control issues between alliance partners are at the heart of management conflicts, as the presence of more than one "parent" leads to problems in exercising control.

Trust also plays a crucial role in alliance formations and should be regarded as an evolving concept, as relationship and dependence evolve. Despite the necessity for growth and evolution, limited attention has been given to the midlife or the developmental dynamics of alliances. Most work has been done on the attachment process, that is, why entities form alliances with specific entities.

Discussion and Implications

 Stopford and Wells observe that organizational structures for managing international business develop and evolve over time. The conditions under which the stages of development occur are not deterministic, and vary with industry, country, and managers' capabilities. It is clear, however, that a unitary form with one manager leading everything, as is common in small young companies, will not work for a business crossing country borders with an array of offerings. The best structure is dictated by the appropriate industry strategy and the availability of competent managers. Subsidiaries may be a source of headquarters managers, but only if appropriate knowledge flows up and down the hierarchy. The roles and responsibilities accorded to subsidiaries provide the means for developing appropriate international managerial talent.

At Synetics Corporation, Joe assumed the role of Vice President–International as the company was evolving from Stopford and Wells's Stage 3 structure to one addressing international business. A variety of engagements with the Agency for International Development and the U.S. Trade and Development Agency, along with an interest in establishing a foreign subsidiary, were being loosely managed in various departments. Coalescing these initiatives into one internationally-focused division facilitated the development of policies and procedures for their management, allowed for a united international strategy, and increased efficiency of operations. These actions led to the successful acquisition of portions of Synetics (including the international business unit).

There is not a "one size fits all" approach for subsidiary roles and MNE organizations, as Bartlett and Ghoshal note. The balance between local responsiveness and global effectiveness is greatly influenced by the industry and its specific characteristics. Kogut and Zander discuss the need for learning by both headquarters and subsidiaries, as well as the role of knowledge and knowledge-sharing within the organization. Internationalization requires absorbing knowledge, and a multinational—via its network of subsidiaries—provides a broader platform for knowledge integration. Knowledge is most useful when it is easily transmitted around the MNE.

The scope of subsidiary autonomy as noted in Bartlett and Ghoshal is also important; local responsiveness can best happen when subsidiaries have the authority to address local needs. The degree to which this responsiveness is allowed (and from which the MNE derives value) requires monitoring by headquarters, including the heads of the international, product, and market groups. Cultural aspects also come into play, as presented in Section 5. When

Eric was at Flextronics, the CEO (Michael Marks) said that he wasn't sure if centralization or decentralization was better, since each has advantages and disadvantages, but he was pretty sure that whichever way you had been doing it, it would probably be a good idea to switch periodically to keep the disadvantages from becoming too ingrained.

As subsidiaries act in accordance with local market needs, they may develop subsidiary- specific advantages (SSAs). Rugman and Verbeke note that the distinction between FSAs and SSAs raises interesting questions for management:

- Should parent companies incentivize the creation of SSAs, or should they reduce the local embeddedness of the knowledge creation process (i.e., focus solely on organizational routines)?
- Should subsidiary managers be rewarded or sanctioned for creating specialized knowledge bases?
- What are the implications for MNE strategies of SSAs and similar knowledge that present high mobility barriers?

As these questions reflect, it is important for managers to understand both industry and global dynamics, as Birkenshaw recommends. Bringing these two dynamics together requires

- systems to ensure that subsidiary managers are involved in market-facing decisions,
- a shift in subsidiary roles toward greater depth and less breadth, and
- internal-market structures and systems for sharing knowledge.

The common theme in these three points is that systems and structures must be established to ensure that the subsidiary manager is her own boss while also being integral to the corporate network.

Moving beyond subsidiaries, Inkpen addresses the use of alliances—organizational forms frequently employed by MNEs. Companies may posess technological knowledge, but lack the market knowledge of local (foreign) partners. As a result, an alliance with a local partner may provide access to necessary market information more readily than the development of a subsidiary. While alliances have less direct cost than subsidiary development, they may also introduce issues of risk to intellectual property or goal mis-alignment. In addition, while the lack of equity participation between alliance partners serves to speed development, it can also hinder control between the headquarters unit and the local alliance partner.

Additional readings in this area include the following, presented in chronological order.

- **Martinez and Jarillo (1989).** This article moved the MNE research focus from "what to do" to "how to do it." Formal mechanisms of internationalization include departmentalization, centralization, formalization and standardization, planning, and output and behavior control. Informal mechanisms include lateral or cross-department relations, informal communications, and socialization. These lists progress from broadest and easiest to implement to narrowest and harder to implement. Complex strategies in MNEs need to add (not substitute) mechanisms further down the list, as far as necessary to implement a strategy.

- **Harzing (2000).** The author identified variables that underpin the global, multidomestic, and transnational strategies defined by Bartlett and Ghoshal. These variables are environment/individual, corporate-level strategy, corporate-level organizational design, subsidiary strategy and role, subsidiary structure, control mechanisms, and international human resource practices.

5. CULTURE

In Chapter 4 we explore the importance of corporate culture to any organization, drawing on the work of Schein (2010) and others to map the role of unspoken assumptions in making each organization unique. In the international context, which is the focus of this chapter, corporate culture mixes with national culture and becomes even more central to organizational performance.

This section presents two papers from 2001, beginning with Hofstede's follow up to his 1980 study of culture via the analysis of IBM managers. Manev and Stevenson then focus on cultural aspects related to the nature of relationships among multinational managers.

GEERT HOFSTEDE
Culture's Consequences: Comparing Values, Behaviors, Institutions, and Organizations Across Nations (2001).

Thesis: National culture has five dimensions: power distance, uncertainty avoidance, individualism/collectivism, masculinity/femininity, and long-term/short-term orientation. The basic values of a multinational are determined by the nationality and personality of its founders and leaders; cultural profiles have distinctly different sets of competitive advantages and disadvantages.

This book follows up on Hofstede's (1980) work that explored the construct of culture, which had been seen as a critical component of international business but had yet to be treated in an academic fashion. In response to the question, "Why is national culture relevant?", Hofstede notes that culture has a number of implications for business strategy, management, marketing and advertising, business etiquette, and intercultural negotiations. As a founder of the science of culture, Hofstede worked for IBM as a psychologist from 1967 to 1973.

The concept of "culture" originated in discussions of national character, which were expanded in the 20th century by studies of organizational climate (e.g., Blake and Mouton 1964), organizational culture (e.g., Pettigrew 1979), and corporate culture (e.g., Silverzweig and Allen 1976). *In Search of Excellence* (Peters and Waterman 1982) described how culture supports excellence. Schein (1985) added elements of leadership to that of organizational culture. *Culture* was later defined as "a shared system of meanings…[that] dictates what we pay attention to and how we act" (Trompenaars 1993, p. 13).

Hofstede (2001, p. 9) defines *national culture* as "the collective programming of the mind that distinguishes the members of one group or category of people from another." The key constructs in Hofstede's book are values, mental programs, and culture. *Mental programs* are "software of the mind" that can be found at the individual, collective, or universal levels. In general, behavior is the enactment of mental programs, which are best examined via *values*: broad tendencies to prefer certain states of affairs over others. Mental programs thus relate to a conception of the desirable that influences the selection of available means and ends for actions. To say that a person holds a value is to say that she has an enduring belief, that a specific mode of conduct or end state of existence is personally and socially preferable to other alternatives. With this background, Hofstede focuses on culture in his book.

Cultural Dimensions
Hofstede finds that culture is comprised of five dimensions as described in Table 5-5: power distance (PDI), uncertainty avoidance (UAI), individualism/collectivism (IDV), masculinity/femininity (MAS), and long-term orientation (LTO). In situations where cultures meet, communication, cooperation, and the acculturative stress that such processes generate work together to create barriers that often result in culture shock. This shock can lead to failure or ineffectiveness of expatriates. While training may raise awareness of one's own cultural "baggage" and provide awareness of other cultures, it cannot develop intercultural skills—those result solely from experience.

Table 5-5: Hofstede's Five Dimensions of Culture and Relationship to
International Negotiations

Dimension	Definition	Effect on international negotiations
Power distance (PDI)	The extent to which the less-powerful members of organizations and institutions accept and expect that power is distributed unequally.	Affects the degree of centralization of the control and decision-making structures, and the importance of the status of the negotiators.
Uncertainty avoidance (UAI)	Society's tolerance for uncertainty and ambiguity.	Affects the (in)tolerance of ambiguity and (dis)trust in opponents who show unfamiliar behaviors and the need for structure and ritual in the negotiation procedures.
Individualism/ collectivism (IDV)	The degree to which individuals are integrated into groups.	Affects the need for stable relationships between (opposing) negotiators. In a collectivist culture, replacement of a person means that a new relationship will have to be built, which takes more time than in an individualist culture. Mediators (go-betweens) have an important role in maintaining a viable pattern of relationships that allows negotiators to discuss problem content.
Masculinity/ femininity (MAS)	The distribution of emotional roles between the genders.	Affects the need for ego-boosting behavior and the sympathy for the strong on the part of negotiators and their superiors, and the tendency to resolve conflicts by a show of force. Femininity-oriented cultures are generally more likely to resolve conflicts through compromise and to strive for consensus.
Long term orientation (LTO)	The time horizon of a society	Affects the perseverance with which desired ends are pursued, even at the cost of sacrifices.

Note: Authors' table; data from Geert Hofstede, *Culture's Consequences: Comparing Values, Behaviors, Institutions, and Organizations Across Nations* (2001).

Intercultural Contact and Expatriates

As the general principles of communication and cooperation have shown, intercultural contact is not the same as mutual understanding. Stereotypes of others can help to get communication started, but can also affect an individual's perception of events. Exposure to a foreign culture can generate a high level of stress, which manifests itself as "acculturative" stress for a local culture subject to modernization, and "culture shock" for expatriates.

The intercultural contact process comprises four phases: euphoria, culture shock, acculturation, and a stable state that helps to explain culture shock and expatriate failure. Culture shocks are environment-specific, so moving to another country with a new culture produces a new shock. Previous successful expatriation is the only valid predictor of future manager success, but a low rate of expatriate failure may still include damage from expatriate insensitivity in the host country. The primary reason for the early return of expatriates working abroad is their spouse's culture shock. Hofstede also notes that expatriates' reintegration into their home culture can be problematic, as a degree of adaptation to the foreign culture has occurred.

International Negotiations

While negotiators share some universal characteristics (e.g., a common need for agreement due to expected gain), models of negotiation are based on assumptions about the negotiators' values. In intercultural negotiations, cultural differences affect negotiators goals and tactics (see Table 5, column 3), but do not necessarily affect outcomes. Effective intercultural negotiations demand language and communication skills, organization skills, and insight into the range of cultural values to be expected among partners.

Subsidiaries and MNE Management

Managing an MNE requires balancing culture, strategy, structure, and control. Strategy is deeply affected by the strategist's cultural values, and structure and control systems determine how the strategy is elaborated. No single structural principle is likely to fit an entire corporation, as optimal solutions change over time and external variety requires flexibility. Control systems are influenced by the culture of the MNE's home country and are related to cultural distance between the MNE and its subsidiary.

Internally, foreign subsidiaries function more according to the host culture's value systems and beliefs, even if they formally adopt home-culture ideas and policies. Biculturalism is required for task-related issues, while other aspects of business may be guided by home country values only; individualist cultures tend to see culture as relevant more at the MNE level. Having a dominant national culture is an asset rather than a liability for the functioning of an organization, and such a culture should be fostered carefully; a dominant culture can mitigate the emergence of culture-based issues. However, subsidiaries with high cultural distance from headquarters are less likely to follow home country practices; this effect can be countered by increasing the number of expatriate employees and focusing on communication.

As MNEs mature and tariff and technological advantages wear off, competition shifts toward cultural advantages and disadvantages.

- Small power distance means more acceptance of responsibility.
- When uncertainty avoidance is weak, basic innovation can result; when it is strong, precision may be the focus.
- Collectivism may lead to employee commitment, whereas individualism may permit more management mobility.
- Cultures high in femininity may deliver more personal service with more custom-made products, whereas masculine cultures may excel in mass production and efficiency.
- While short-term oriented societies may adapt quickly, long-term oriented societies may be better in development of new markets.

These culture-based competitive advantages suggest that companies locate activities in countries, regions, and organizational units that possess the cultural characteristics necessary for competing in these activities.

Hofstede makes a number of observations and suggestions regarding MNE operations within these cultural dimensions. While values and talents vary widely within cultures, and different national cultures overlap in many respects, the author notes the following.

- Differences in power distance are a likely source of trouble in hierarchical arrangements.
- Differences in power distance and individualism/collectivism are especially problematic for interaction among colleagues.
- Ambiguous group tasks should be chaired by a person from a low-uncertainty-avoidance culture, who is likely to have better performance on such tasks.
- For clearly defined and urgent tasks, people from high-uncertainty-avoidance cultures will likely perform better.
- In general, people from low-uncertainty-avoidance cultures can more easily acquire cross-cultural sensitivity than those from high-uncertainty-avoidance cultures.

Culture also relates to international marketing, advertising, and consumer behavior. Consumption decisions can be driven by function or social needs that are culture-bound; thus, uniform international advertising campaigns can have unpredicted local impacts. The ways in which a sales force is managed and compensated should reflect cultural values in addition to the industry's characteristics.

Foreign Market Entry

International acquisitions, mergers, and joint ventures are highly subject to cultural considerations, which vary by mode of entry into foreign countries as seen in Table 5-6. Cultural issues affect both the choice of entry mode and the rate of success.

Table 5-6: Foreign Market Entry Modes and Cultural Fit

Mode	Speed	Risk	Cultural fit
Greenfield	Slow	*Limited*	*Good*: Founder selects employees who fit corporate culture
Foreign acquisition	Fast	*Considerable*: Executives are eager to extend their power; financial experts don't look beyond purchase price	*Poor*: As an arm's length transaction, clashes are resolved through brute power with potential for destruction of human capital
International merger	Moderate	*High*: Executives are eager to extend their power; financial experts don't look beyond purchase price	*Bad*: Conflicts cannot be resolved through a one-sided show of power
Foreign joint venture	Slow	*Low*: One partner may supply all management	*Good*: Local partner may transfer culture to foreign partner
Strategic alliance	Slow	*Most prudent*: Alliance may be broken without endangering either partner's survival	*Varies*: Fit may be tested on a temporary basis

Note. Authors' table; data from Geert Hofstede, *Culture's Consequences: Comparing Values, Behaviors, Institutions, and Organizations Across Nations* (2001).

Looking Ahead

Culture also relates to international marketing, advertising, and consumer behavior. Consumption decisions can be driven by function or social needs, which are culture-bound; thus, uniform international advertising campaigns can have unpredicted local impacts. The ways that a sales force is managed and compensated should be based on both cultural values and the industry's characteristics.

Culture also dominates technology, since people select information to be consumed based on their values and on what reinforces their preferred points of view. New technologies alone will not reduce the need for intercultural understanding, but they may be useful tools for intercultural learning.

Successful intercultural encounters presuppose that the partners believe in their own values—one does not need to think, feel, and act like someone else in order to agree with that person on practical issues and to cooperate. People from some cultures (generally those with lower power distance and lower uncertainty-avoidance) will cooperate more easily with foreigners than others. There is no evidence of international convergence of cultural values over time, except toward increased individualism for countries that have become richer.

Everyone looks at the world from the biased position of their own culture: there is no "normal" position in cultural matters. Culture is relative, and only those with different mental programs can help us find the limitations of our own.

 IVAN MANEV AND WILLIAM STEVENSON
"Nationality, Cultural Distance, and Expatriate Status: Effects on the Managerial Network in a Multinational Enterprise" (2001), *Journal of International Business Studies.*

Thesis: The characteristics of multinational managers influence how those managers exchange knowledge and adopt practices. Informal expressive ties tend to be stronger than formal instrumental ties, and such expressive ties are strengthened by having managers from the same nations and by having managers with smaller cultural distance and from similar status levels.

 Manev and Stevenson discuss how the characteristics of an MNE's managers influence its managerial network, suggesting a number of implications for MNE management. An *MNE managerial network* is the set of relatively stable interactions among managers (e.g., knowledge exchange between subsidiaries as well as the fast and successful adoption of organizational practices across subsidiaries, carried out through interpersonal interactions). Managerial networks are important forces for coordination and integration in the MNE, functioning as conduits for information exchange and as the glue of that holds these organizations together.

The key properties of managerial networks are strength, emotional intensity, intimacy and reciprocal service, and *multiplexity*, which is the coexistence of expressive ties and instrumental ties.

- *Instrumental ties* are more formal relationships between MNE managers that usually relate to their job by facilitating the transfer of physical, informational, or financial resources. Although similar to the traditional view of a formal structure defined by how it facilitates work, instrumental ties can bypass the hierarchy and occur directly via a managerial network.

- *Expressive ties* are more personally passionate, usually dealing with providing friendship and social support.

Interactions within the same or different informal groups constitute a solid foundation for the formation of a managerial network—not as an extension to the traditional formal structure, but as a new and extensively interrelated pattern among and across the boundary of each individual subsidiary.

Three manager characteristics are relevant to these networks:

- **Nationality.** Much like gender and age, a common nationality can generate shared perspectives, leading to more interactions and hence stronger ties among managers. Similarly, there are more friendly and intimate interactions among compatriots within the same MNE.

- **Cultural distance.** When managers are from different nations, cultural distance exists between them. People may prefer to interact more with others with whom they have small cultural distance, reducing misunderstanding and obstacles for communication.

- **Expatriate status.** Because of differences in culture, power position in the hierarchy, and language, expatriate managers in an MNE often have a different status than local managers.

Integrating these three into one differentiated category suggests that managers of the same nationality/with smaller cultural distance/from one and the same status group are more likely to develop stronger ties.

Manev and Stevenson tested these hypotheses using a sample from a UK-based nongovernmental, nonprofit MNE that operates in more than 30 countries and whose managerial network is not inordinately large. They conclude that managers' international background characteristics have a measurable impact on MNE network, in that managers from the same nations, those with smaller cultural distance, and those from the same organizational status (e.g., first-level managers) tend to have stronger expressive ties than instrumental ties. Conversely, managers from different nations, with larger cultural distance, or from different organizational status tend to have strong instrumental ties instead of expressive ties.

From a practical perspective, these findings provide some guidance for MNE management. For example, larger cultural distance can be beneficial as long as the benefit brought forth by the enhanced instrumental ties exceeds the potential cost of the weak expressive ties or the misunderstandings and difficulty in communication. Since strong expressive ties may result in ethnocentrism or even factionalism in an MNE, management should promote communication across diverse groups of managers by arranging forums, encouraging teamwork across subsidiaries, and using the social capital of centrally located managers in the network to balance the overwhelming power of expressive ties.

Discussion and Implications

 This section provides an overview of some of the contextual cultural issues that multinational enterprises face—and of which managers must be aware. The political and economic landscape sets the stage for market entry, expansion, and growth, and indicates that managers are affected by, and can affect these landscapes in host countries. Effective and value-producing MNE management depends on having the right structure for the industry's drivers, and on managing relationships between headquarters and subsidiary. Culture plays a big role in this management, and should be assessed in all areas of internationalization from market entry to the selection of country managers and the staff with whom they work.

Hofstede's original research was criticized for its limited data: its examination of managers of one company, and its sole emphasis on managers. However, Hofstede's groundbreaking work continues to be used by multinational companies and is instructive for understanding issues related to foreign-market entry mode, international negotiations, expatriate success/failure, joint venture performance, and a variety of other cross-border situations. Certainly Hofstede's descriptions of culture are very general, and many individuals may not fit the cultural norms he identified. The mobility of managers, many of whom are educated in more economically developed countries, may erode their initial cultural traits.

Joe sees this erosion in the MBA students he encounters. With an average of seven years of professional experience, many MBA students from more economically developed countries have had the opportunity to work in various countries, and hence have experienced intercultural issues in their jobs. Students from emerging economies (or even those from developed but more ethnically isolated countries) can experience some challenges working with culturally diverse project teams. It seems to be as much an issue of erosion of cultural traits (which implies something is lost) as it is an enhancement of cultural traits in assuming more and more varied experience (implying that something is gained). In teaching management, we hope to imbue students with that sense of gain.

In management practice, we have witnessed how ongoing management localization can solve the high cost and difficulty of management communication in MNE subsidiaries. It is an open question how management localization can be successfully carried out in MNEs, but training, meeting, and other kinds of cross-subsidiary activities may achieve the optimal practice.

On the topic of culture literature as applied to international business, one additional reading is of particular interest.

- **Schwartz (1999).** Groupings of culturally related nations are identified on the basis of the dimensions of conservatism versus intellectual/affective autonomy, hierarchy versus egalitarianism, and mastery versus harmony. The emphasis on cultural value may be compatible or conflicting for various dimensions of work, such as work centrality, social norms about working, and work values. For example, the pursuit of power values is likely to be more acceptable in cultures where hierarchy and mastery values are emphasized, such as in the United States.

FURTHER READING

If you're interested in reading more on the topics discussed in this chapter, additional sources follow. This is not a comprehensive or exhaustive list, but rather we have selected well-regarded or significant works that space did not permit us to include in the main discussion.

1. THEORIES OF THE MULTINATIONAL ENTERPRISE

Aharoni, Yair. 1966. *The Foreign Investment Decision Process.* Cambridge, Division of Research, Harvard Business School.

Buckley, Peter J. and Mark Casson. 1985. *The Economic Theory of the Multinational Enterprise.* London, St. Martin's Press.

2. INTERNATIONALIZATION ADVANTAGES AND APPROACHES

Aharoni, Yair. 1966. *The Foreign Investment Decision Process.* Cambridge, Division of Research, Harvard Business School.

Barkema, Harry G. and Freek Vermeulen. 1998. "International Expansion Through Start-Up or Through Acquisition: An Organizational Learning Perspective." *Academy of Management Journal* 41(1), 7–26.

Buckley, Peter J. and Mark Casson. 1985. *The Economic Theory of the Multinational Enterprise.* London, St. Martin's Press.

Casson, Mark. 1982. "Transaction Costs and the Theory of the Multinational Enterprise." In A. Rugman (editor), *New Theories of the Multinational Enterprise.* New York, St. Martin's Press. pp. 24–43.

Caves, Richard E. 1996. *Multinational Enterprises and Economic Analysis*, 2nd edition. New York, Cambridge University Press.

Caves, Richard E. 1998. "Research on International Business: Problems and Prospects." *Journal of International Business Studies* 29(1), 5–20.

Leonidou, Leonidas C. and Constantine S. Katsikeas. 1996. "The Export Development Process: An Integrative Review of Empirical Models." *Journal of International Business Studies* 27(3), 517–551.

Lu, Jane W. and Paul W. Beamish. 2006. "Partnering Strategies and Performance of SMEs' International Joint Ventures." *Journal of Business Venturing* 21(4), 461–486.

Rugman, Alan and Alain Verbeke. 2001. "Subsidiary-Specific Advantages in Multinational Enterprises." *Strategic Management Journal* 22(3), 237–250.

3. INTERNATIONAL POLITICAL ECONOMY

Boddewyn, Jean J. and Thomas L. Brewer. 1994. "International-Business Political Behavior: New Theoretical Directions." *Academy of Management Review* 19(1), 119–143.

Brown, L. David, Sanjeev Khagram, Mark H. Moore, and Peter Frumkin. 2000. "Globalization NGOs and Multisectoral Relations." In J. S. Nye and J. D. Donahue (editors), *Governance in a Globalizing World*. Washington, Brookings Institution. pp. 271–296.

Encarnation, Dennis and Sushil Vachani. 1985. "Foreign Ownership: When Hosts Change the Rules." *Harvard Business Review* 63(September–October), 152–160.

Eden, Lorraine. 1993. "Bringing the Firm Back In: Multinationals in International Political Economy." In L. Eden and E. H. Potter (editors), *Multinationals in the Global Political Economy*. New York, St. Martin's Press. pp. 25–58.

Krugman, Paul 1999. *The Return of Depression Economics*. New York, Norton.

Porter, Michael E. 1998. "Clusters and the New Economics of Competition." *Harvard Business Review*, 76(November–December), 77–90.

Pralahad, C. K. and Yves Doz and C. K. Prahalad. 1987. *Multinational Mission*. New York, Free Press.

Rugman, Alan M. 2001. *The End of Globalization: Why Global Strategy is a Myth & How to Profit from the Realities of Regional Markets*. New York, AMACOM.

Stopford, John M. and Susan Strange. 1991. *Rival States, Rival Firms: Competition for World Market Shares*. Cambridge, Cambridge University Press.

Strange, Susan. 1988. *States and Markets*. London, Pinter Publishers.

Vernon, Raymond. 1977. *Storm Over the Multinationals*. Cambridge, Harvard University Press.

Vernon, Raymond. 1998. *In the Hurricane's Eye: The Troubled Prospects of Multinational Enterprises*. Cambridge, Harvard University Press.

4. MULTINATIONAL MANAGEMENT

Birkinshaw, Julien, Neil Hood, and Stefan Jonsson. 1998. "Building Firm-Specific Advantages in Multinational Corporations: The Role of Subsidiary Initiative." *Strategic Management Journal* 19(3), 221–241.

Egelhoff, William G. 1982. "Strategy and Structure in Multinational Corporations: An Information Processing Approach." *Administrative Science Quarterly* 27(3), 435–458.

Etemad, Hamid and Louis Seguin Dulude. 1986. *Managing the Multinational Subsidiary.* London, Croom Helm.

Otterbeck, Lars (editor). 1981. *The Management of Headquarters-Subsidiary Relations in Multinational Corporations.* Hampshire, Gower Publishing.

Tallman, Stephen, & Li, Jiatao. 1996. "Effects of International Diversity and Product Diversity on the Performance of Multinational Firms." *Academy of Management Journal* 39(1), 179–196.

Wolf, Joachim and William G. Egelhoff. 2002. "A Reexamination and Extension of International Strategy-Structure Theory." *Strategic Management Journal* 23(2), 181–189.

5. CULTURE

Berger, Peter L. 2002. "Introduction: The Cultural Dynamics of Globalization." In P. Berger and S. Huntington (editors), *Many Globalizations: Cultural Diversity in the Contemporary World.* New York, Oxford University Press. pp. 1–16.

Chen, Chao C., Xiao-Ping Chen, and James R. Meindl. 1998. "How Can Cooperation be Fostered? The Cultural Effects of Individualism-Collectivism." *Academy of Management Journal* 23(2), 285–304.

Gomez-Mejia, Luis R. and Leslie E. Palich. 1997. "Cultural Diversity and the Performance of Multinational Firms." *Journal of International Business Studies* 28(2), 309–335.

Rao, Asha and Keiji Hashimoto. 1996. "Intercultural Influence: A Study of Japanese Expatriate Managers in Canada," *Journal of International Business Studies* 27(3), 443–466.

Schuler, Randall S. and Nikolai Rogovsky. 1998. "Understanding Compensation Practice Variations Across Firms: The Impact of National Culture." *Journal of International Business Studies* 29(1), 159–177.

Schwartz, Shalom H. 1994. "Beyond Individualism/Collectivism: New Cultural Dimensions of Values." In U. Kim, H. Triandis, C. Kâğitçibaşi, S. Choi, and G. Yoon (editors), *Individualism and Collectivism: Theory, Method, and Applications.* Cross-Cultural Research and Methodology Series, vol. 18. Thousand Oaks, Sage. pp. 85–119.

WORKS CITED

Arrow, Kenneth. 1962. "Economic Welfare and the Allocation of Resources for Invention." In *The Rate and Direction of Inventive Activity: Economic and Social Factors.* National Bureau of Economic Research. Princeton, Princeton University Press.

Bain, Joe S. 1956. *Barriers to New Competition.* Cambridge, Harvard University Press.

Bartlett, Christopher A. and Sumantra Ghoshal. 1998. *Managing Across Borders*. Cambridge, Harvard Business School Press.

Birkinshaw, Julien. 2001. "Strategy and Management in MNE Subsidiaries." In A. Rugman and T. Brewer (editors), *The Oxford Handbook of International Business*. New York, Oxford University Press. Ch. 14.

Blake, Robert and Jane Mouton. 1964. *The Managerial Grid: The Key to Leadership Excellence*. Houston, Gulf Publishing.

Blumentritt, Timothy P. and Douglas Nigh. 2002. "The Integration of Subsidiary Political Activities in Multinational Corporations." *Journal of International Business Studies* 33(1), 57–77.

Brander, James A. and Barbara Spencer. 1985. "Export Subsidies and International Market Share Rivalry." *Journal of International Economics* 18(1–2), 83–100.

Brandt, William K. and James M. Hulbert. 1977. "Headquarters Guidance in Marketing Strategy in the Multinational Subsidiary." *Columbia Journal of World Business* 12(Winter), 7–14.

Buckley, Peter J. and Mark Casson. 1998. "Models of Multinational Enterprise." *Journal of International Business Studies* 29(1), 21–44.

Caves, Richard E. 1996. *Multinational Enterprise and Economic Analysis*. Cambridge, Cambridge University Press.

Caves, Richard E. 1998. "Industrial Organization and New Findings on the Turnover and Mobility of Firms." *Journal of Economic Literature* 36, 1947–1982.

Chung, Wilbur. 2001. "Identifying Technology Transfer in Foreign Direct Investment: Influence of Industry Conditions and Investing Firm Motives." *Journal of International Business Studies* 32(2), 211–229.

Cohen, Wesley M. and Daniel A. Levinthal. 1990. "Absorptive Capacity: A New Perspective on Learning and Innovation." *Administrative Science Quarterly* 35(1), 128–152.

Cyert, Richard M. and James G. March. 1963. *A Behavioral Theory of the Firm*. Engelwoods Cliffs, Prentice Hall.

Dierickx, Ingemar and Karel Cool. 1989. "Asset Stock Accumulation and Sustainability of Competitive Advantage." *Management Science* 35(12), 1504–1511.

Dunning, John H. 1977. "Trade, Location of Economic Activity and the MNE: A Search for an Eclectic Approach." In B. Ohllin, P. O. Hesselborn, & P. M. Wijkman (editors), *The International Allocation of Economic Activity*. London, Macmillan. pp. 395–418.

Dunning, John H. 1988. "The Eclectic Paradigm of International Production: A Restatement and Some Possible Extensions." *Journal of International Business Studies* 19(1), 1–30.

Dunning, John H. 1993. "Internationalizing Porter's Diamond." *MIR: Management International Review* 33 (Extensions of the Porter Diamond Framework), 7–15.

Dunning, John H. 2001. "The Key Literature on IB Activities: 1960–2000." In A. Rugman and T. Brewer (editors), *The Oxford Handbook of International Business*. New York, Oxford University Press. Ch. 2.

Furman, Jeffrey L., Michael Porter, and Scott Stern. 2002. "The Determinants of National Innovative Capacity." *Research Policy* 31, 899–933.

Gates, Stephen R. and William G. Egelhoff. 1986. "Centralization in Headquarters-Subsidiary Relationships." *Journal of International Business Studies* 17(2), 71–92.

Gilpin, Robert. 2001. *Global Political Economy: Understanding the International Economic Order.* Princeton, Princeton University Press.

Harzing, Anne-Wils. 2000. "An Empirical Test and Extension of the Bartlett and Ghoshal Typology of Multinational Companies." *Journal of International Business Studies* 31(1), 101–120.

Harzing, Anne-Wils. 2002. "Acquisitions versus Greenfield Investments: International Strategy and Management of Entry Modes." *Strategic Management Journal* 23(3), 211–227.

Hennart, Jean-Francis. 2001. "Theories of the Multinational Enterprise." In A. Rugman and T. Brewer (editors), *The Oxford Handbook of International Business.* New York, Oxford University Press. Ch. 5.

Hillman, Amy J. and Michael Hitt. 1999. "Corporate Political Strategy Formulation: A Model of Approach, Participation, and Strategy Decisions." *Academy of Management Review* 24(4), 825–842.

Hillman, Amy J. and Gerald Keim. 1995. "International Variation in the Business-Government Interface: Institutional and Organizational Considerations." *Academy of Management Review* 20(1), 193–214.

Hofstede, Geert. 1980. *Culture's Consequences: International Differences in Work-Related Values.* Newbury Park, Sage.

Hofstede, Geert. 2001. *Culture's Consequences: Comparing Values, Behaviors, Institutions, and Organizations Across Nations.* Thousand Oaks, Sage.

Hutchison, Jonathan. 2012. "Megaupload Founder Goes From Arrest to Cult Hero." *The New York Times,* 3 July. http://www.nytimes.com/2012/07/04/technology/megaupload-founder-goes-from-arrest-to-cult-hero.html?pagewanted=all.

Hymer, Stephen H. 1960. *The International Operations of National Firms: A Study of Direct Foreign Investment.* Cambridge, MIT Press, 1976.

Inkpen, Andew. 2001. "Strategic Alliances." In A. Rugman and T. Brewer (editors), *The Oxford Handbook of International Business.* New York, Oxford University Press. Ch. 15.

Johanson, Jan and Jan-Erik Valhne. 1977. "The Internationalization Process of the Firm: A Model of Knowledge Development and Increasing Foreign Commitments." *Journal of International Business Studies* 8(1), 23–32.

Knight, Gary A. and S. Tamer Cavusgil, 1997. "Early Internationalization and the Born-Global Firm: Emergent Paradigm for International Marketing." Michigan State University Working Paper CIBER.

Kobrin, Stephen J. 2001. "Sovereignty@Bay: Globalization, Multinational Enterprise, and the International Political System." In A. Rugman and T. Brewer (editors), *The Oxford Handbook of International Business.* New York, Oxford University Press. Ch. 7.

Kogut, Bruce and Udo Zander. 1993. "Knowledge of the Firm and the Evolutionary Theory of the Multinational Corporation." *Journal of International Business Studies* 24(4), 625–645.

Levy, Haim and Marshall Sarnat. 1970. "International Diversification of Investment Portfolios." *American Economic Review* 60(4), 668–675.

Lilienthal, David. 1960. "The Multinational Corporation." In M. Ashen and G. L. Bach (editors), *Management and Corporations, 1985*. New York, McGraw-Hill. pp. 119–159.

Lodge, George. 1990. *Perestroika for America*. Boston, Harvard Business School Press.

Luo, Yadong and Seung Ho Park. 2004. "Multiparty Cooperation and Performance in International Equity Joint Ventures." Journal of International Business Studies 35(2), 142–160.

Martinez, Jon I. and J. Carlos Jarillo. 1989. "The Evolution of Research on Coordination Mechanisms in Multinational Corporations." *Journal of International Business Studies* 20(3), 489–514.

Manev, Ivan M. and William B. Stevenson. 2001. "Nationality, Cultural Distance, and Expatriate Status: Effects on the Managerial Network in a Multinational Enterprise." *Journal of International Business Studies* 32(2), 285–303.

Murtha, Thomas and Stephanie Lenway. 1994. "Country Capabilities and the Strategic State: How National Political Institutions Affect Multinational Corporations' Strategies." *Strategic Management Journal* 15(S2), 113–129.

Oviatt, Benjamin and Patricia P. McDougall. 1994. "Toward a Theory of International New Ventures." *Journal of International Business Studies* 25(1), 45–63.

Penrose, Edith. 1959. *Theory of the Growth of the Firm*. New York, Oxford University Press.

Pettigrew, Andrew. 1979. "On Studying Organizational Cultures." *Administrative Science Quarterly* 24(4), 570–581.

Peters, Thomas J. and Robert H. Waterman. 1982. *In Search of Excellence*. New York, Harper & Row.

Pfeffer, Jeffrey and Gerald R. Salancik. 1978. *The External Control of Organizations: A Resource Dependence Perspective*. New York, Harper & Row.

Polanyi, Michael. 1966. *The Tacit Dimension*. Garden City, Doubleday.

Poynter, Thomas A. and Alan M. Rugman. 1983. "World Product Mandates: How Will Multinationals Respond?" *Business Quarterly* 47(3), 54–61.

Prahalad, C. K. and Yves L. Doz. 1981. "An Approach to Strategic Control in MNCs." *Sloan Management Review* 22(4), 5–13.

Rugman, Alan M. and Alain Verbeke. 1998. "Multinational Enterprises and Public Policy." *Journal of International Business Studies* 29(1), 115–136.

Rugman, Alan M. and Alain Verbeke. 2001. "Subsidiary-Specific Advantages in Multinational Enterprises." *Strategic Management Journal* 22(3), 237–250.

Schein, Edgar. 1985. *Organizational Culture and Leadership*. San Franciso, Jossey-Bass.

Schein, Edgar. 2010. *Organizational Culture and Leadership*, 4th edition. San Francisco, Jossey-Bass.

Schelling, Thomas. 1960. *Micromotives and Macrobehavior*. New York, Norton.

Schwartz, Shalom H. 1999. "A Theory of Cultural Values and Some Implications for Work." *Applied Psychology: An International Review* 48(1), 23–47.

Sevran-Schreiber, Jean-Jacques. 1968. *The American Challenge*. Translated by Ronald Steel with a foreword by Arthur Schlesinger Jr. London, Hamish Hamilton.

Silverzweig, S. and R. F. Allen. 1976. "Changing the Corporate Culture." *Sloan Management Review* 17(3), 33–49.

Spencer, Barbara and James A. Brander. 1983. "International R&D Rivalry and Industrial Strategy." *Review of Economic Studies* 50(4), 707–722.

Stiglitz, Joseph E. 2002. *Globalization and its Discontents*. New York, Norton.

Stopford , John M. and Louis T. Wells Jr. 1972. *Managing the Multinational Enterprise*. New York, Basic Books.

Taylor, Jerome. 2012. "It's Game Over for Kim Dotcom, the Mr. Big of File Sharing." *The Independent*, 21 January. http://www.independent.co.uk/news/world/americas/its-game-over-for-kim-dotcom-the-mr-big-of-filesharing-6292290.html.

Trompenaars, Fons. 1993. *Riding the Waves of Culture*. London, Nicholas Brealey.

Vachani, Sushil. 1991. "Distinguishing Between Related and Unrelated International Geographic Diversification: A Comprehensive Measure of Global Diversification." *Journal of International Business Studies* 22(2), 307–322.

Vermeulen, Freek and Harry Barkema. 2002. "Pace, Rhythm and Scope: Process Dependence in Building a Profitable Multinational Corporation." *Strategic Management Journal* 23(7), 637–653.

Vernon, Raymond. 1971. *Sovereignty at Bay: The Multinational Spread of U.S. Enterprises*. New York, Basic Books.

Williamson, Oliver. 1996. "Economic Organization: The Case for Candor." *Academy of Management Review* 21(1), 13–47.

INNOVATION

The essence of this chapter is not "how to innovate" but rather "how to understand the environment for innovation." This chapter addresses literature in four areas: an overview of some key issues in technology and innovation strategy (Section 1); patterns of technological innovation, industry emergence, and technology trajectories (Section 2); technology competition (Section 3); and macro issues such as science, government technology policy, and economic growth.

Contexts for innovation exist on three levels:

- **Location.** Why are some cities more innovative and entrepreneurial than others?
- **Industry.** What industry characteristics (e.g., knowledge intensity and lifecycle stage) foster more innovative activity?
- **Country.** What demographic and institutional factors drive innovation and subsequent economic growth?

In this chapter we examine how innovation diffuses or spreads, and how current technology such as the web and social media might affect the adoption of innovative outputs. In creating and managing innovation strategies, it is essential that managers understand the contexts for innovation at the firm, industry, and country levels. We also discuss how to even measure innovation in order to determine its presence and effect—are the measures of innovation suitable for managerial decision-making?

1. Issues in Technology and Strategy

Ideas, information, invention, and innovation are related and require investment in order for those who create them to extract returns. The economics associated with perfect markets and the market for information may result in underinvestment in innovative activities, thwarting invention and subsequent economic growth. Managers must therefore develop strategies and policies to promote innovative cultures and practices within companies, and identify means for measuring innovative output. Managers and governments often use patents as economic indicators to develop scientific and strategic policies, but economic incentives associated with these policies may have differential impacts on innovation.

To illustrate the interrelations among ideas, information, invention, and innovation, we begin this section with an article (Arrow 1962) that discusses how resources and information affect invention. Next, Solow (1957) and Griliches (1990) address the measurement of technology change, while Griliches (1998) and Nelson (1962) address the role of research and development (R&D) and invention. The last three articles (Pavitt 1990; Van de Ven 1986; Stern 2004) consider more firm-level issues in innovation.

KENNETH ARROW
"Economic Welfare and the Allocation of Resources for Invention" (1962), in *The Rate and Direction of Inventive Activity: Economic and Social Factors*.

Thesis: Perfect competition results in a non-optimal allocation of resources and leads to underinvestment in invention due to underproduction of the information needed to pursue new invention. The "Arrow paradox" describes how owners of information cannot convince potential buyers of its value without disclosing the information.

Invention is the production of knowledge, and Arrow avers that optimal resource-allocation for invention depends on the technological characteristics of the invention process and the nature of the market for knowledge. *Welfare economics* asks the question, "To what extent does perfect competition lead to an optimal allocation of resources?" Three of the classical reasons for the failure of perfect competition to achieve optimal resource allocation are indivisibilities, inappropriability, and uncertainty.

When producing a given commodity under uncertainty, if a market exists for all commodity-options, the firm knows its output (e.g., crop production) under each state of nature (e.g., amounts of sunshine) and sells a corresponding quantity of commodity-options. The firm's revenue is thus completely determined, and it may choose its inputs to maximize its profits. On the other side of the firm–consumer equation, consumers maximize their expected utility by selling labor given their income constraint. *Pareto optimal equilibrium*, the point at which no one can be made better off without making at least one individual worse off, is reached on all commodity-option markets just as it would be in competitive equilibrium under certainty—markets serve the function of achieving an optimal allocation of risk-bearing among members of the economy (including producers and consumers).

However, real economic systems do not possess markets for all commodity-options, and at the other extreme there is no provision for reallocating risk-bearing; firms determine inputs, produce outputs due to states of nature, and set prices to clear markets. The inability of individuals to buy protection against uncertainty gives rise to a loss of welfare. If insurance were available against any conceivable event (e.g., cloudy days), optimal allocation would be achieved. However, shifting of risks in the real world is incomplete. Moral hazard exists: the difficulty in distinguishing between a state of nature (e.g., cloudy day) and a decision by the insured (e.g., to not apply fertilizer) means that insurance policies can have the effect of dulling incentives.

Steps that improve efficiency in the economy with respect to risk-bearing may therefore also decrease its technical efficiency. As far as inventions are concerned, success in such activities depends on a tangle of objective uncertainties and decisions of entrepreneurs; therefore, invention success is uninsurable. Nonetheless, such activities should be undertaken if the expected return exceeds the market rate of return. Inventors can sell stock to decrease their risk, but this also decreases their incentive to invent due to a decrease in their reward.

Uncertainty creates more subtle problems in resource allocation, in that information becomes a commodity. Information has economic value: anyone possessing it can make greater profits than would otherwise be the case. Frequently, the cost of transmitting information is very low, and a given piece of information is an indivisible commodity. In the absence of special legal protection, the owner of information cannot simply sell it in the open market, as anyone who purchases the information can destroy the monopoly (i.e., reproduce and distribute it at almost no cost). The only effective monopoly is the use of the information by the original possessor, who may or may not be able to exploit it as effectively as others.

Information is also imperfectly appropriable.[1] If information could be legally protected, appropriating it would be a useful strategy, but using the information inevitably reveals at least part of it. The demand for information has uncomfortable properties: its use is subject to indivisibilities, its value for purchasers is not known until they have the information, and its potential for non-optimal purchase and allocation is high. These properties lead to difficulty in creating a market for information (if one should be desired), and the costs of transmitting information create allocative difficulties. There is therefore a case for centralized decision-making because within a centralized structure such as a

---

[1] That is, one that can be appropriated—or taken for one's own use—usually without the owner's permission.

firm, leaders can help ensure that information is freely available for decision-making.

Invention and research are devoted to the production of information. Thus, invention is risky, in that the output cannot be predicted perfectly from the inputs. Insurance against failure would weaken the incentives to succeed, so the only way to minimize the risks is to "self-insure" by conducting research in large institutions with many projects. However, there are deeper problems of misallocation due to the nature of the product—any information obtained should, from a welfare perspective, be available free of charge, which ensures optimal utilization of the information but leaves no incentive for investment in research.

The profitability of invention therefore requires a non-optimal allocation of resources: whatever the price, the demand for information is less than optimal. Patent laws restrict the range of appropriable information, reducing incentives to engage in inventive and research activities. Information is not only the product of inventive activity; with the inventor's talent, it is also a major input. Basic research—the output of which is only used as an information input to other inventive activities—is especially unlikely to be rewarded. Arrow expects free enterprise economies to under-invest in invention and research due to its inherent risk.

Incentives to invent can exist even under perfect competition in the product markets though not in the "market" for information contained in the invention. For a new product invention, the inventor can receive a return equal to the monopoly profits by charging a suitable royalty to a competitive industry. The incentive to invent is less under monopolistic than competitive conditions, but even in the latter case it will be less than is socially desirable.

If the government and other nonprofit institutions are to compensate for the under-allocation of resources to invention by private enterprise, two problems arise:

- how to determine the amount of resources to devote to invention, and
- how to encourage efficiency in their use.

Cost plus fixed-fee contract awards depend, in part, on past performance and thus still create some incentives for efficiency. Payment by results would involve great risks for the inventor, and risks against which he could hedge only in part.

ROBERT M. SOLOW
"Technical Change and the Aggregate Production Function"
(1957), *Review of Economics and Statistics.*

Thesis: Technical change is a critical element in modeling production.

Solow's contribution is a move toward measuring technical change, since a macroeconomic model based solely on capital and labor cannot explain everything. Solow's model is based on the *aggregate production function* and examines the effect of changes in capital, labor, and technology on production growth. The model allows the segregation of variations in production based on technical change due to changes in capital or labor.

The success of the model is demonstrated by its ability to explain the impact of technology on growth in U.S. markets from 1909 to 1949. Solow makes several assumptions:

- The general form of the aggregate production function states that production is a function of capital, labor, and technical change.
- Assuming neutral technical change (here defined to mean that the shifts in the aggregate production function were purely due to growth, e.g., the scaling up of the productive economy), changes in technology do not affect the marginal rates of capital or labor.
- The only inputs to production are capital and labor.

Using this model to analyze the real, private, U.S. non-farm GDP per person-hour shows a strong upward trend, with a higher slope in the second half of the period. There is a sharp dip after World War I, a leveling off at the end of the 1920s, a sustained rise beginning in the 1930s, and another sharp dip after World War II. The gross output per person-hour doubled over the interval, with 87.5% of the increase attributable to technical change and 12.5% due to the increased use of capital (p. 320). These findings suggest that technical change within the period had little effect on marginal rates of capital or labor.

Solow concludes that under certain assumptions and conditions, the aggregate production function model allows segregation of the impact of technical change. U.S. non-farm data for 1909–1949 shows a good fit to the model.

ZVI GRILICHES
"Patent Statistics as Economic Indicators: A Survey" (1990), *Journal of Economic Literature.*

Thesis: Patent statistics are useful economic indicators, and can be a good measure of differences in inventive activity across different large firms.

Griliches describes how patent statistics have been and can be used as economic indicators of various interesting and important phenomena. He summarizes some results of empirical work in this area, addresses issues with respect to data and indicates ways to resolve them, and raises new and interesting research problems for which patent statistics may provide evidence.

The goal of patents is to encourage invention and technical progress by both providing a temporary monopoly and forcing early disclosure of the details of the innovation. A patent granted by a government gives the patent-holder the right to exclude others from producing or using a new device, apparatus, or process for a set number of years. The device, apparatus, or process must meet standards of novelty and utility, and the right is enforced by (threats of) lawsuits only. Patents may be assigned to other owners, sold, and licensed. Patent documents contain data about the inventor, application date, the patented item itself, citations of prior work, patent classes (technology categories), the owner (usually a firm), and applicant location.

Researchers look for correlations between patent counts and other variables, such as R&D expenditures, productivity growth, profitability, and stock market value. Correlations are weak at best, but show that patents are good indicators of inputs into inventive activity. Researchers would like patents to measure both inputs and outputs of the innovation process: what is happening and why. There are a variety of problems, however, in that not all inventions are patentable, not all are patented, and there are quality and value issues associated with patents. In addition, the differences between small and large firms, for example, limit extrapolation from broad patent studies.

Key problems in using patents for economic analysis relate to classification and relation of patent activity to R&D activity:

- Should one assign a patent to the industry of origin, production, or use?
- Are patents good indicators or indices of inventive activity?
- Is R&D productivity declining?
- How does one measure patent "quality" and R&D "quality"?
- How do patent statistics illustrate the process of innovation and technical change across firms, across industries, and over time?

Results of Griliches's analyses suggest that patents are good indicators of differences in inventive activity across different firms, especially firms over a minimum size: in the absence of detailed R&D data, patent data can be used as an indicator of inventive input and output. However, care must be taken in interpreting across time, as the high variance and skewness in the distribution of patent values makes it hard to use patent counts as indicators of short-run changes in R&D. For example, the appearance of an absolute decline in inventive activity (in the 1970s) was largely a statistical mirage due to U.S. Patent

Office budget inadequacies and a reduced number of patent examiners. Finally, R&D expenses per patent are rising, but this may be due to a "shrinking yardstick" (resulting from inflation) or a rise in patent quality. In addition, expenses may be mostly on the development side, which does not do much patenting as compared to the research side.

ZVI GRILICHES
"Issues in Assessing the Contribution of R&D to Productivity Growth" (1998), in E. Wolff (editor), *The Economics of Productivity*, volume 1.

Thesis: It is possible to quantitatively measure some effects of R&D investment, but real returns on R&D cannot be predicted using such measures.

In this article, Griliches asks what innovation is, whether we can measure its output, and what are its implications—in essence, he inquires as to the real return on R&D investment. He offers a critical discussion of the methodological possibilities and operational difficulties in such an inquiry. His emphasis here is on econometric estimates through the production function approach, focusing on the measurement of output in R&D and the stock of knowledge capital.

In general, R&D output is poorly measured or not measured at all, and does not reflect quality improvements. There are also issues in the measurement and definition of R&D knowledge, including:

- the need to aggregate knowledge that is expressed in various forms (e.g., patents, books, people, and oral traditions);
- the lag structure effect, such as that between invention and production, or between invention and acceptance;
- the depreciation effect; and
- the spillover effect (e.g., among firms and industries).

Production function approaches consider total output as a function of past investment. In this study, Griliches proposes a model employing a national income accounting framework (aggregate productivity measures). His conclusion is that effects can be measured based on some assumptions, but predictability is not possible. There are many issues still to be solved, such as a lack of relevant data, limitation of measures employed, and poor overall conceptual adequacy as relates to the lag structure, technological distance, externalities and spillovers, the role of basic research, and cyclical factors.

RICHARD R. NELSON
"The Link Between Science and Invention: The Case of the
Transistor" (1962), in *The Rate and Direction of Inventive Activity:
Economic and Social Factors*, National Bureau of Economics
Research.

Thesis: Bell Labs succeeded by letting scientists pursue pure science research of
their own choosing. Learning and advancing knowledge led to serendipitous
discovery.

In this article, Nelson focuses on factors affecting the allocation
of research resources in science-oriented industrial research
laboratories. He uses the case of basic research in industry that
led to the invention of the transistor and the case of the
organization responsible for the research—the Bell Telephone Lab (Bell
Labs)—as the means to examine these factors.

The research at Bell Labs leading to the discovery of the transistor effect
was conducted by men who observed something they were neither looking for
nor expecting—a natural phenomenon in research activity. Because of great
uncertainty, much research effort is directed toward learning rather than toward
the achievement of a specific and well-defined result. While the group of people
at Bell Labs possessed a variety of skill sets, the nature of their interaction could
not have been predicted or planned in advance; the goal was first to advance
knowledge and then to invent devices with possible payoffs.

While the bulk of research has been conducted outside the industrial system
(i.e., in universities, for the government, and by private individuals), Nelson
examines the research process within a large corporation (Bell Labs). The
overarching criterion for research management at Bell Labs was that the area of
research should be one related to the applications of the company's technology.
This policy assumed that scientific worth is highly correlated with potential
technical value. The resulting decentralized decision-making freed the individual
scientists to choose the projects they considered of greatest interest, permitting
the allocation of resources by free choice.

KEITH PAVITT
"What We Know about the Strategic Management of
Technology" (1990), *California Management Review*.

Thesis: Successful firms recognize that their company structure and
competitive strategy impact their technology strategy. These firms develop

routines to align their technology strategy, use trial and error, learn from experience, and train their employees well.

 Innovation is not just about new products and processes but also involves new forms of organization, markets, and sources of raw materials. Schumpeter (1942) stressed the central importance of innovation in firm competition and the evolution of industrial structures and processes on economic development. Pavitt notes, however, that Schumpeter says little regarding the theory of the innovating firm, sources of innovation, the importance of continuous incremental improvements, or the organizational characteristics of the major sources of technical change in established firms.

The accepted characteristics of technological innovation activities are those that utilize continuous collaboration across specialized groups, but that are also uncertain, cumulative, and differentiated (requiring specific, specialized technical skills that are not easily transferable). This restriction has a number of implications for theory and action, related to the following:

1. **Content of technological strategy.** Conventional resource allocation choices do not take into account the variety in sources of technological opportunities and in the rate and direction of their development. Innovative opportunities depend on an organization's size and its core business. In the technology race, it is not often clear where the start and finish lines are or what the race is about. Because innovation is cumulative, an uncritical application of conventional project-appraisal techniques will result in myopic technology strategies.

2. **Implementation of technology strategy.** Company structure and overall strategy play major roles in technology strategy formation. Factors associated with successful innovations include the quality of the technical work, a strong horizontal linkage among functional departments, and strong links with customers and outside sources of relevant technical expertise.

3. **Creation of institutional continuity in the face of technological discontinuity.** Successful firms develop routines reflecting the content and process of strategy implementation, use trial and error, learn from experience, and have good employee training. They engage in frequent communication among specialists and functions, especially through personal contact at a physical location. They work toward both technological discontinuities and institutional continuities, which can coexist because large firms have R&D labs, experience integrating technologies, and experience hiring and integrating professionals from new areas. Large firms have oligopolistic power, along with resources and the time to link technological discontinuities to their core competencies through learning.

An important conclusion for management is to beware the conventional wisdom. It is not useful to ask if the firm should be a leader or a follower, broad or narrow, or pursue product or process—these strategies follow from firm size and the nature of accumulated technological competence. Similarly, conventional project appraisal methods may be inappropriate.

Implementation matters as much as definition, and there is an additional need for learning capacity. It is important to orchestrate and integrate functional and specialist groups to implement innovation; to continuously question the appropriateness of existing markets, missions, and skills; and to take the long view.

ANDREW VAN DE VEN
"Central Problems in the Management of Innovation" (1986),
Management Science.

Thesis: Companies must create a culture of innovation by maintaining a balance between dividing work into reasonable tasks (differentiation) and coordinating activities into a meaningful whole (integration).

Van de Ven offers a general management perspective in this article on how to create and maintain a culture of innovation. He presents critical success factors for launching new organizations, joint ventures, and innovative projects by maintaining a balance between differentiation and integration (Pfeffer and Salancik 1978).

Innovation is defined as the development and implementation of new ideas by people who, over time, engage in transactions with others within an institutional context. Technical and administrative innovations are often interdependent, as changes in technology require changes in institutional and organizational arrangements. It is often impossible to look at a new idea and determine if it is an innovation or a mistake.

Innovation frameworks address factors such as new ideas, people, transactions, and institutional context. The new idea is central, and once taken up by people in positions of power, a web of transactions is created as the idea becomes an institutionalized innovation. For its part, the institution can work either to thwart or enable the innovation. There are a number of related problems, however, including the management of attention, the management of process, the relationship between the part and the whole, and institutional leadership.

While individuals have ideas, innovations require social networks that must be managed and maintained. The management of ideas requires the recognition that innovation is inevitably a disruption or threat to the existing order and that the problems encountered are interdependent. There often exist insufficient ideas to solve problems, and there are physiological limits to handling complexity that are associated with a preference for stability and for conforming to group norms.

Attention must also be managed to facilitate innovation: individuals have short attention spans and groups can develop "group think," which decreases the diversity of individual thought. Structure and system can displace thought, requiring consideration of the organization. Managers may often need to confront the problem of constrained thinking face-to-face, which causes stress. The development of double-loop learning (in which one evaluates the evaluation criteria) versus single-loop learning (in which one uses the existing criteria) can enhance innovation.

Emergent organizational networks can make innovation impossible, in which case it becomes incumbent on the leader to establish a more favorable culture. Innovation requires network adoption, in which the team manages the innovation process via self-organizing units, redundant functions, requisite variety (mimicking the complexity and breadth of the environment), and temporal linkage (linking the innovation to past, present, and future transactions). Leaders set the culture, and they must distinguish between institutional and technical processes. Technology reduces uncertainty, but the institution must maintain a certain level of uncertainty, as innovation processes require discontinuities.

SCOTT STERN
"Do Scientists Pay to Be Scientists?" (2004), *Management Science.*

Thesis: More scientifically-oriented researchers tend to be paid less; in other words, scientists pay to be scientists.

Stern's article evaluates the relationship between wages and the scientific orientation of R&D organizations. Using a survey of scientists at the time of their first post-postdoc job offer, he seeks to understand whether researchers have intrinsic preferences for interaction with discipline-specific scientific communities (the *preference effect*) or if their participation in science may be motivated by the benefits to private firms themselves (the *productivity effect*). In the design of the study, Stern makes several assumptions:

- There are no *wealth effects* (which may include having more publications, a better network, or more money at the time of analysis).

- Scientists of higher ability place a higher value on science-oriented research environments.
- Differences in firms' perceptions of candidates are uncorrelated with their scientific orientation.

The results show a strong negative relationship between wages and level of scientific orientation; in addition, the adoption of science orientation is more likely as firms expect to have access to higher-ability researchers. Stern concludes that, conditional on scientific ability, scientists do indeed pay to be scientists.

From a public policy perspective, these results suggest that while there is broad agreement for government subsidies of basic research, the exact form of that subsidy is contentious. A professional ethic—participation in the public scientific community—has effects on an economic observable (wage) and may have effects on observed productivity. From the perspective of managing technology, the economics of staffing need to be reexamined: a science-oriented firm will pay 20% less (on average) for scientists, meaning that they can employ 15% more scientists (p. 846). Finally, the professional ethic, shown here to have an effect on wages (and maybe on productivity), may also exist in other professions such as law and medicine.

Discussion and Implications:

 This section highlights a number of issues in innovation that are relevant for managers. Griliches asks, "What is innovation?" and "How can we measure its output?", while Solow explores "What is technical change and how do we measure it?" In essence, one must look both inside and outside the company to measure and understand whether the activities being performed are (or are not) productive in terms of innovation. It was one thing for a research-oriented entity such as Bell Labs (now Avaya) to do basic science and innovate, as the production of ideas is a key strategic competence in such an environment. It is quite another thing for a company focused on making products to engage only in innovative activities that have a measurable output.

Griliches offers a good overview of what can and cannot be measured, but leaves open questions such as whether patents can be used to infer a firm's position in "technological space" or to illuminate the results of R&D spillovers and strategic rivalries. Patents in and of themselves may not have economic value, and an important question is ignored: Does the patent holder make money with the patent?

Once a measure exists, it can be used as a basis to question

- how to apply resources to facilitate innovation,
- what level of resources is available, and

- how to structure the organization to manage innovation.

When Joe worked in R&D at Wang Laboratories in the mid-1980s, his focus in one of his positions was to examine all R&D projects to identify the "Nifty 50" that were most likely to provide productive output.[2]

Information flows are necessary for innovation, so it is important to understand the factors that impede or facilitate these flows. Given the indeterminate nature of the value of information (as Arrow discussed), a hierarchy may or may not be the most efficient way to manage innovation. Entrepreneurs are sometimes skittish about starting their ideas for fear of appropriation (theft). While this may be less of an issue if the information sharing is done within a company rather than between individuals or companies, the richness of information to aid innovators may be less as compared to the information available in the market. Even though some information is easily codified and flows well, we still see certain industries evolving near universities where the information was developed. Why was (and is) Stanford so important to Silicon Valley if information can be easily packaged and instantaneously sent around the world?

While Nelson's case studies of innovation at Bell Labs may be hard to generalize, they are instructive regarding the management of basic research. It is important to note that AT&T (the owner of Bell Labs for many years) was a monopoly at the time of the study. Monopolies can most efficiently do basic research, as there is no one to take spillovers and derive value (potentially at the expense of the monopolist). But a number of questions remain:

- Do monopolistic firms innovate, or do new firms rise and embody innovation (as suggested by Van de Ven)?
- What is the track record for a single firm innovating (e.g., a pharmaceutical giant or a company like 3M)?
- How and why do certain innovative ideas get implemented while others do not? Is it the entrepreneur's ability to disclose yet protect his knowledge and use his network?
- How and why do people only pay attention to certain ideas and ignore the rest?
- What is more important: the idea or power (e.g., the power of a large company to keep innovators out of the market)?
- Is there an optimal position within a social network for ideas to originate?
- In what way does the shape of a social network matter (and how do social network tools such as Facebook affect innovation)?

---

[2] Unfortunately, while the Nifty 50 list was intended to focus resource allocation on the top 50 projects, the final list actually contained 52 projects, underscoring the issue of focus that many R&D organizations experience.

- Can the adoption of an idea within a network be measured? In fact, how can one measure invention?

Although Nelson considers teamwork in his research, the structure of appropriate teams is not emphasized, nor is the relationship between free choice and teams. If everybody starts doing the same thing, the earnings the firm expects will deteriorate due to too much supply. In another article, Milgrom and Roberts (1990; discussed below) consider the relationship between the individual and the organization in terms of rent-seeking, and investigate how the assignment of resources (e.g., team members) depends on knowing the value of projects before assigning the team resources who are better equipped to estimate that value.

Stern notes that firms adopting a science orientation may gain earlier and more-detailed access to new scientific discoveries. In this way, they may be purchasing a "ticket of admission" that pays off in terms of higher R&D productivity and a higher rate of technological innovation. Stern's article relates to the discussion in Chapter 4, Section 5 regarding compensation as a motivator; scientists may not mind being paid less than non-scientists, but each one wants to make more than the other scientists in her organization.

Additional writings in this area include the following, presented in chronological order.

- **Milgrom and Roberts (1990).** This article focuses on the management of technological resources. The term *rent-seeking* implies the extraction of uncompensated value from others without making any productive contribution. There is a relationship between information availability and openness, and the potential for redistribution of rents. How can equitable arrangements be made so that both the individual (e.g., engineer or scientist) and the organization are not rent-seeking? For example, how can compensation schemes ensure that engineers do not work at companies for private benefit (e.g., develop a product unbeknownst to management) and that managers reward engineers appropriately for their contribution?
- **Jaffe, Trajtenberg, and Henderson (1993).** This analysis of patent citations suggests that knowledge spillovers are geographically localized at various levels—country, state, and local (e.g., Metropolitan Statistical Area).
- **Florida (2002).** The presence of "bohemians" (e.g., artists and free-thinkers) is positively related to high human capital in an economic area, indicating a greater level of openness and thus low perceived industry entry barriers. There is also a positive relationship between having bohemians in an area and a high concentration of high technology.

2. PATTERNS OF TECHNOLOGICAL INNOVATION, TECHNOLOGY TRAJECTORIES, AND INDUSTRY LIFECYCLES

Traditional economic theory may not be the best for explaining the birth, growth, and death of firms; this section presents the perspective of evolutionary theory on the life cycle of firms. First, Nelson and Winter (1982), David (1985), and Mokyr (1990) discuss how innovation associated with venture emergence and growth is path-dependent: the history of the entrepreneur and the heritage of the company matter. Invention and innovation are complements, and some societies have more creative individuals and more economic growth than others.

Next, Abernathy and Utterback (1978), Foster (1986), and Utterback (1994) discuss how firms at different stages of development approach innovation differently. As industries and firms evolve, they establish dominant product designs as outputs and move from radical or evolutionary product innovation to process innovation. All innovations follow an S-curve relating effort to performance: the impact of effort on performance varies over time from low to high to low. Technology cycles in an industry from one set of innovations to another through the emergence of dominant designs.

Finally, Tushman and Rosenkopf (1992) and Klepper (1996) describe how technological progress is associated with community norms. Larger firms are better able to appropriate the returns from R&D, spurring innovation, and firms with different expertise will pursue different types of production innovations. Economic factors, social factors, and information availability affect innovation; these ideas are addresses by Griliches (1957), Ryan and Gross (1943), and Gort and Klepper (1982), respectively.

RICHARD NELSON and SIDNEY WINTER
An Evolutionary Theory of Economic Change (1982), Parts I and II.

Thesis: Evolutionary theory does a better job than traditional economic theory at explaining the birth, growth, and death of firms.

In the first parts of their book, Nelson and Winter make several arguments regarding firms and the life cycle of firms:

- Firms grow and die though natural selection.
- Firms are relatively rigid and operate in both blind and deliberate processes.

- Firms have routines and *stochastic* (undetermined) elements.
- Firms co-evolve with industries.

The authors assert that orthodox economic theory is based upon static models with unrealistic assumptions that ignore real-world phenomena. They contend that evolutionary theory is dynamic, process-based, and better explains the industrial, real world in terms of knowledge, innovation, firm differences, and adjustment processes.

The behavior of more "traditional" types of firms ("large firms in technological change," p. 39) may be characterized by their business routines, which represent the genes for organizational evolution, and that evolution is itself dependent on *organizational memory*. Memory goes beyond formally recorded activities, and organizational memory is embedded within repetitive routine activities. This concept of memory suggests a continuous mechanism of "knowing": members "own" routine repertoires (combinations of routines), the performance of which may involve communicating with other members or the environment via an exchange of messages (verbal, written, or behavioral) and the interpretation of the information embedded within those messages.

Organizational memory thus lies within the continuous and cyclic interaction between the "know-how" possessed by individual members and the application of that know-how within the organizational context. *Organizational knowledge* involves the following:

- *Ingredients* include skills, plant, equipment, technologies, production capabilities, and so on.
- *Recipes* describe the knowledge or instruction of how to use the ingredients.
- *Coordination* refers to routines for applying the right recipes and using the right ingredients, which are developed based on the exchange and interpretation of messages.

Because routines lie within networks rather than within the elements (nodes) of those networks, they are harder to replicate and imitate. Routines play a role in organizational culture by helping to resolve conflicts and creating organizational truce. There is a tension between "routine-preserving" and "routine-changing/creating" forces, which management may address with a variety of tactics, including the following:

- *Selection* is the tactic of acquiring resources that fit well with routines.
- *Modification* refers to accustoming the resources to the routine.
- *Monitoring* includes detecting and preventing deviations.
- *Adaptation* is changing the routine to be more flexible to heterogeneity.

The first three tactics above are more often used for routine-preserving.

While a feasible pattern of productive activity can be replicated, perfect routine replication is not likely due to the heterogeneity of resources and external conditions. The imitation of another firm's successful routines may be even more challenging. Routines and innovation contradict—yet feed—each other, and the tension between them is an engine of the evolution process.

PAUL DAVID
"Clio and the Economics of QWERTY" (1985), *American Economic Review*.

Thesis: Innovation is path-dependent and history matters in the adoption of innovation; the "best" innovation may not ultimately be the winner.

In this article, David demonstrates how much history matters, in the sequencing of events, toward establishing path dependency and a standard. This theoretical paper is "a piece of narrative economic history in which 'one damn thing follows another'" (p. 332), showing that in order to figure out the logic (or illogic) of the world around us, it is sometimes necessary to understand its dynamics. The key research question is why the arrangement of the keys in the topmost row of a keyboard is QWERTYUIOP, better known as QWERTY, rather than one of the more efficient sequences like DSK (the Dvorak Simplified Keyboard, developed in 1932).

Different typewriters with different improvements were developed between 1867 and the early 1880s. Sholes-Glidden-Soule patented the first in 1867, with a keyboard in alphabetical order but that suffered from clashes between the mechanisms that imprinted on the page. Six years of improvements followed. The alphabetical order changed to a four-row model approaching the QWERTY standard. Densmore and Remington & Sons succeeded Sholes-Glidden-Soule in 1873 with limited modifications and in which the first row contained the letters to write the brand (TYPE WRITER). The Hammond and Blickensderfer model (1892) had a keyboard arrangement that is more sensible than QWERTY, namely DHIATENSOR.

However, from the beginning of the typewriter boom (1880s), QWERTY became "the Universal." From that point, progress focused upon typewriter engineering, and any rationale for QWERTY's continued use was removed by its market dominance. How did usability come to be sacrificed as a design consideration?

The typewriter is an element of a more complex system of production. The "touch" typing method gave rise to three features of that evolving production system.

- **Technical interrelatedness.** The keyboard does not have value per se, but its value depends on the software—or in other words, on the availability of typists who know that particular arrangement of the keys. Since the learning effects of a particular system are appropriable only by the individual, firms did not have incentives in shaping that choice of system. However, the learning effects also produce positive "network externalities" in that if the number of people who know that system increases, the benefits go to people who have already learned it. In other words, one's choice influences and at the same time is influenced by the choice of the other people.

- **Economies of scale.** Technical interrelatedness implies decreasing overall user costs in adopting a particular system (termed *system scale economies*), leading to a de facto standard. The choice of standard depends on the choices made by producers and users at or near to the beginning of the process (path-dependence), such as the QWERTY arrangement.

- **Quasi-irreversibility of investment.** There is a high cost for a typist to convert to another system. Once typists know QWERTY, conversion to a different keyboard becomes costly to them—and, more particularly, to their employer.

JOEL MOKYR
The Lever of Riches: Technological Creativity and Economic Progress
(1990), Chapters 1, 2, and 11.

Thesis: Invention and innovation are complements. The existence of knowledge is necessary, but not sufficient—it must also be disseminated and stored. Societies and their knowledge of innovation evolve via "technological DNA."

In his book on technological creativity, Mokyr examines "how the world works" (*propositional*) knowledge and "how to manipulate the world" (*prescriptive*) knowledge. Regardless of its veracity, if prescriptive knowledge results in positive impacts, it is "useful knowledge." Mokyr states that "new knowledge that is not applied makes no difference to economic welfare" (p. 10), noting that technology change is primarily the study of outward shifts of the *production possibility frontier*: a curve showing the combinations of two or more goods and services that can be produced while using all of the available factor resources efficiently.

In these chapters, Mokyr focuses on aspects of economic growth that result in shifts of the production frontier, that is, the aspects that allow producers to produce more goods with the same resources. He identifies four categories of economic growth:

- investment,
- commercial expansion,

- scale or size effects, and
- increases in the stock of human knowledge.

He defines *technological progress* as "any change in the application of information to the production process in such a way as to increase efficiency, resulting either in the production of a given output with fewer resources, or the production of better or new products" (p. 6).

On an aggregate level, Mokyr explores why there were (and are) some societies that have more creative individuals than others, and why economic growth occurs in some societies and not others. On an individual level, he examines how technological change involves an attack by an individual on a constraint that everyone else takes as a given.

Mokyr believes invention depends on factors that determine individual behavior, and differentiates between *micro-inventions*, or "small, incremental steps that improve, adapt and streamline existing techniques already in use" (p. 13), and *macro-inventions*, "in which a radical new idea, without clear precedent, emerges" (p. 13). The essential feature of technological progress is that macro- and micro-inventions are not substitutes but complements—innovation requires interaction with other individuals and depends on institutions and markets, and thus is largely social and economic in nature. There are two basic components:

- **Mind over matter.** Technical problems involve control of the physical environment.
- **Social interaction.** The innovator has to interact with a human environment comprised of competitors, customers, suppliers, and the like.

Classical economies, such as the Romans and Greeks, employed organization, trade, order, and the use of law and money. It is difficult to judge whether these cultures were technologically successful; we know that science was applied to some things and that in areas that mattered to them (literature, science, mathematics, medicine, and political organizations), the Greeks and Romans achieved huge success and made technological advances in both public works and war. However, positive externalities were also missed; these societies mastered the use of gears and applied geometry but did not find an economic purpose for them. At the time, iron-making was slow and produced a poor product, and many inventions that could have led to major economic changes were underdeveloped, forgotten, or lost.

If traditional economic tools are not suitable to create value from such technological advances, what is the alternative? A *steady-state economy*—a form of growth that is itself constant and predictable (e.g., "technological drift" or "evolutionary progress")—is a possibility, but the fundamental problem is that evolution has two meanings: "gradual or continuous change" or "mutations and selection." Mokyr prefers a biological analogy that "the knowledge of how to produce a good or service in a specific way...[has] an evolutionary character"

(p. 275). He concludes that there is an intergenerational transmission of "technological DNA" (p. 277) that occurs through the training of apprentices by people possessing the technological information.

Biological theories of innovation have changed over time, from Neo-Darwinism (slow change), to natural selection, to Goldschmidt's (1940) micro- and macro-mutations, to *punctuated equilibria* (long periods of small change interrupted by major changes). In technology innovation, there are only a few macro-inventions that represent a clear break from previous techniques. Macro-inventions need to be both technically and economically feasible in the social environment of the time. Many major technical breakthroughs have also occurred through micro-inventions: small conceptual changes or simple ideas that led to drastic differences in production methods.

The distinctions between macro- and micro-inventions matter because they each appear to be governed by different laws. Micro-inventing suggests an intentional search for improvements, whereas macro-inventing employs individuals and "luck"; the two appear to occur in clusters, as they influence each other.

WILLIAM ABERNATHY and JAMES M. UTTERBACK
"Patterns of Industrial Innovation" (1978), *Technology Review.*

Thesis: Firms at different stages of development approach innovation differently. As firms grow, they establish a dominant product design and move from radical to evolutionary product innovation.

In this article, Abernathy and Utterback create a model relating patterns of innovation within a unit to that unit's competitive strategy, production capabilities, and organizational characteristics. Their model describes the shift from radical to evolutionary product innovation due to the development of a dominant product design. They conclude that a unit's capacity for and methods of innovation depend critically on its stage of evolution, from small technology-based enterprise to major high-volume producer. Changes in innovative pattern, production process, and scale and type of production capacity all occur together in a consistent, predictable way. As a result, process and incremental innovation may have equal or greater commercial importance than product innovation.

This understanding has implications for technology management: as a unit moves from radical innovation toward large-scale production, goals evolve from ill-defined and uncertain targets to well-articulated design objectives. Innovation moves from the province of users to that of manufacturers.

Firms decrease their need for R&D as they mature. The nature of R&D evolves from high target uncertainty and technical uncertainty, toward informal R&D, so there is little incentive for formal R&D through the middle of this evolution. Firms with the largest investment in R&D (i.e., science-based firms) operate in the middle between new uncertain technologies and very specific improvements. *Units* (i.e., smaller companies or business units in corporations) are often large and integrated with large market share, and have little need for R&D at maturity. Equipment moves from being general purpose to specific and integrated. Coordination and control evolve by reducing the need for information processing, moving from oriented toward high capacity information processing, to dealing with high uncertainty, to dealing with complexity. The organization structure becomes more formal, with more levels of authority.

Abernathy and Utterback's models predict that units in different stages will respond to differing stimuli and undertake different types of innovation. Their model helps to identify the full range of issues with which the firm is confronted at different stages in the innovation cycle. Failure of the company is due to the "consistency" of management action—since there are stages of firm development, management action also needs to evolve to match the needs of the firm. Therefore, the model suggests the following:

- A firm cannot simultaneously increase the variety and diversity of product lines and maximize efficiency.
- A firm cannot simultaneously reduce costs through backward integration and have a high rate of product innovation.
- Government policy to maintain diversified markets is not consistent with a firm policy seeking high rates of effective product innovation.
- A firm cannot give employees more challenging/less repetitive tasks and at the same time mechanize to reduce labor needs.
- Government cannot stimulate productivity by forcing product standardization before there is a dominant design.

RICHARD FOSTER
"The S-curve: A New Forecasting Tool" (1986), in *Innovation, The Attacker's Advantage*, Chapter 4.

Thesis: Innovations follow an S-curve: The impact of effort on performance varies over time from low to high to low.

Foster was the head of innovation consulting at McKinsey, and his article provides qualitative advice for managers: in a nutshell, managers need to manage discontinuities, which sometimes means abandoning the old and going for the new. His premise is that innovations follow an S-curve relating effort to performance. The dependent variable is a performance measure such as "survival time in weeks" for an artificial heart or "chip density" in the semiconductor industry; the independent variable is effort (which is not necessarily time). For the artificial heart case study, effort was "cumulative laboratory work" and for semiconductors effort was "dollars per year."

Foster focuses on understanding the relationship between effort put in and results achieved, and the way this relationship changes over time in a consistent manner. He outlines three phases of innovation in an S-curve over time, as illustrated in Figure 6-1.

1. **Trial and error.** The beginning of innovation has a low slope, as there is much effort required to improve a technology only a small amount. Innovation is a "trial and error" process—after one problem is solved, another comes up. In the development of the artificial heart, for example, several technical issues kept many hearts non-feasible.

2. **Growth.** Once the learning of phase one is done, significant progress is made during the growth phase for relatively little expenditure of effort. The slope of the innovation curve is high, as performance increases greatly relative to effort.

3. **Diminishing Returns.** In the third phase, each new step makes less progress, illustrating a low slope. In the development of the pocket watch, for example, as thinness reached its limits, other performances parameters such as area, reliability, ease-of-use, and cost gained in importance.

Using this analysis, Foster develops a forecasting tool. His view is that the S-curve might be useful to examine the extent to which current products can be improved and identify the amount of effort it will take to get them to higher performance levels. Other applications of this concept might include forecasting how products will fare in the future, or even predicting what new products might be worth developing.

Foster notes that the strategic management of discontinuity is important. There is discontinuity between S-curves when one technology replaces another, and these transitions can be quite chaotic. Most companies are operating in a "Third Era"[3] focused on the strategic management of technology, in which they

---

[3] The "First Era" was the period after World War II when research activity received little corporate guidance, and the "Second Era" was the age of marketing's dominance that put R&D into a reactive mode.

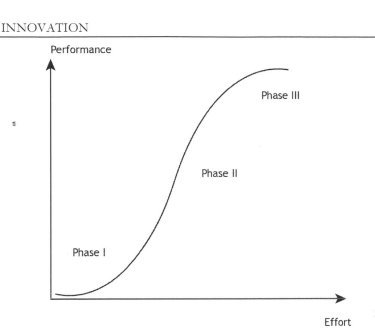

Figure 6-1. Foster's S-Curve.[4]

invest in research to know where they are on relevant S-curves. Firms become sophisticated at massaging the shape of the curve by developing new products and processes faster; however, this approach focuses on efficiency rather than effectiveness. A company may underestimate the rapid advent of a new technology and face a dilemma as to when to abandon an old technology and reallocate resources to developing something new (i.e., selecting a new S-curve on which to operate). The key for companies will be to enter a "Fourth Era" that entails the management of discontinuities.

JAMES UTTERBACK
Mastering the Dynamics of Innovation (1994), Chapter 2.

Thesis: Technology cycles through the emergence of dominant designs from product innovation by many firms, after which the few surviving firms focus on process innovations to improve efficiency.

The theoretical argument in Utterback's study of five industries is based on a view that new products lead to new markets. During a period of new products, there is no preferred product design or manufacturing process and no dominant firm. Innovation is

---

[4] Authors' image.

directed at the product. When a dominant design emerges, the industry changes from one with many firms and many designs to one with few firms and few designs. Once the design is dominant, innovation is directed at process—making the product cheaper and faster. At that point, the firms that cannot sufficiently innovate to drive down costs and drive up efficiencies must exit the industry. This situation results in an industry with little product innovation and a few large, stable firms.

Dominant design is the result of new products using a synthesis of old features from prior products and innovations. The resulting design is good in many markets, but great in none. Without an array of other options, users are *satisfied* (i.e., resigned to use of the dominant design), but while the design may basically satisfy many, it optimizes for none. Features become implicit in the design. The emergence of the dominant design may be due to a chance event, something in the technology, or the result of social or organizational features. The dominant design cannot be predicted until it emerges.

Performance measurement is established when a dominant design emerges; prior to this state, there is no agreed-upon metric by which products are evaluated. The shift toward process innovation in manufacturing permits a shift away from a skilled labor force with general-purpose equipment to less-skilled labor with specialized equipment. Concurrently, the organization shifts from entrepreneurs to efficiency managers, and from organic to mechanistic growth. Process improvements are less easily copied than product innovations, making it easier to defend the market position after the dominant design emerges.

MICHAEL L. TUSHMAN and LORI ROSENKOPF
"Organizational Determinants of Technological Change:
Towards a Sociology of Technological Evolution" (1992), in B.
M. Staw and L. L. Cummings (editors), *Research in Organizational Behavior*.

Thesis: Technological progress is not rational but rather infused with value beyond the technical requirements of the current need. The community of practitioners defines the norms that drive science.

Organization theory considers technological change to be an influential determinant of organizational phenomena, but studies have neglected the impacts of organizations on the technological progress. Little is known about the determinants of technology, which is usually seen as a "black box." Tushman and Rosenkopf's objective was to analyze the non-technological determinants of technological change by adopting a system perspective to understand its evolution. In this article, they build a model of technological progress and generate typologies through lessons taken from historical case studies.

Rather than viewing technology as an autonomous force acting on organizations or as a predictable outcome of an elite set of experts, Tushman and Rosenkopf argue that technology evolves through a combination of random chance events, the actions of organizations, and competition between interested players. Technological progress is under-determined by factors internal to the technology; rather, the interaction of the technological options generated by organizational and inter-organizational dynamics shapes the path of progress. Evolution is driven by a combination of technical, economic, social, political, and organizational processes.

The authors' main conclusion is that technological progress is not coldly rational, but is infused with value, evolving "through the combination of random and chance events...organizations shaping industry standards, and the invisible hand of...a technological community" (p. 337). Science is driven by core norms and values that are carried, interpreted, and defined by the community of practitioners. The social dynamics among these practitioners are accentuated in the realm of technological change because of the underlying nature of technology. Unlike science, technological evolution involves more uncertainty and "dis-sensus" (as opposed to consensus). Uncertainties associated with technological progress can only be adjudicated by the evolving community, and such progress can be seen as driven by social dynamics—an example of the intrusion of non-technical factors into technological change.

Technology can be seen as an outcome of community dynamics, and technology change can be characterized by sociocultural evolutionary processes:

- **Variation.** Stochastic (undetermined) technological breakthroughs, in which discontinuities initiate rivalry between alternative technology regimes, drive the development of multiple technical options.
- **Selection.** Technological rivalry is not settled by technology logic, but by socio-organizational dynamics that lead to the selection of a dominant design.
- **Retention.** The selected variants evolve through retention periods marked by incremental changes and increased interdependence within a community of practitioners.

For complex products, the emergence of dominant designs is not a function of the economics of technological determinism; rather, dominant designs evolve from a negotiated logic made active by agents with interests in competing technological regimes. There is more than one "best" way to implement a product or process. Whereas technological discontinuities may be driven by random events and strokes of genius, dominant designs are driven by the visible hands of organizations interacting with other organizations. Dominant designs are also driven by practitioners committed to shaping the dimensions of merit and industry standards in order to maximize local needs. As an example of local drivers,[5] threatened technological communities resist technological change by increasing the persistence of the prior regime and political actions; therefore, significant discontinuities tend to be generated from outside the established communities of practice.

Understanding products as technological *systems* permits a greater understanding of the conditions under which sociopolitical processes affect technological progress. Non-assembled and simple, assembled products require sequentially interlinked steps or subprocesses; when there is clarity regarding the dimensions of merit and relative ease of measurement, sociopolitical dynamics are minimal in shaping technology progress for these products.

Assembled systems (complex products) are made up of distinct subsystems that interact with each other, linked together via interface and linkage technologies. They are heavily driven by sociopolitical processes constrained by technological boundaries and incompatible dimensions of merit.

- *Closed systems* are hierarchically ordered and sociopolitically-bounded, such that core subsystems affect complementary change in the interdependent subsystems.
- *Open systems* are sets of closed systems linked together through interfaces but without boundaries. They are inherently complex and require the evolution of multiple organizations, demanding political processes between players that represent complex interests.

The more complex a product is, the greater the number of interfaces among components, and the greater its technological and contextual uncertainty. Increasing levels of uncertainty are expressed by an increasing level of sociopolitical intrusion into technology evolution.

STEVEN KLEPPER
"Entry, Exit, Growth, and Innovation Over the Product Life Cycle" (1996), *American Economic Review*.

Thesis: A simple model can explain all the features of the product life cycle theory of industry evolution. The model suggests that larger firms are better able to appropriate returns from R&D, and that firms with different expertise will pursue different types of production innovations.

---

[5] The geography defined by "local" can vary widely: think Route 128 versus Silicon Valley in the 1980s and 1990s, or United States versus Europe as related to FCC technological standards.

In this article, Klepper develops a model based on the process/product dichotomy and industry evolution in previous papers (e.g., Nelson and Winter 1982; Jovanovic 1982) in order to shore up the logical foundations of the industry evolutionary pattern known as the product life cycle (PLC). His goal is to show how a simple model can explain all of the PLC's central features. The model makes two assumptions:

- The demand for a firm's product affects its incentive to innovate.
- Firms are randomly endowed with distinctive capabilities that influence the kinds of innovations they develop (Porter 1980).

Klepper's formal model builds on theories of industry evolution (Nelson and Winter 1982; Jovanovic 1982) and efforts to model the link between market structure and R&D (e.g., Nelson and Winter 1978).

The number of entrants (or producers) may rise over time from the industry's inception, or it may attain a peak at the start of the industry and then decline over time despite continued growth in industry output; in both cases, the number of entrants eventually becomes small. Eventually, the rate of change for the largest firms' market share declines and industry leadership stabilizes. The diversity of competing versions of the product and the number of major product innovations also tend to reach a peak as the number of producers grows, and then fall.

When the number of producers is growing, the most recent entrants account for a disproportionate share of product innovations, while over time producers devote increasing effort to process innovation. Product innovation is principally designed to attract new buyers, and differences in capabilities manifest themselves in product innovations by specialization. Process innovation, on the other hand, is principally designed to lower a firm's average cost of production. The incentive for process innovation is dependent on the total quantity demanded of the firm's product; it is incremental and based on information that firms commonly generate through production.

Subject to a number of assumptions regarding innovative expertise, distribution of opportunities, and supply and demand drivers, Klepper proposes the following sequence:

1. Initially, the number of entrants who gain a foothold via distinctive product variants may rise or decline, but eventually it will decline to zero. Incumbent costs are lower due to their having more process R&D. Price decreases over time increase the incumbent advantage and reduce the number of new entrants.

2. Initially, the number of firms may rise but eventually will decline steadily. Over time, price falls, the more-innovative incumbents expand, and the less-innovative ones exit and are replaced by more innovative, smaller

entrants. Incumbent growth leads to insurmountable advantages, and entry ceases while exit continues as firms less able to innovate leave.

3. As each firm grows, the rate of change in its market share will decline over time. Standard product profit margins determine the rate of incumbent expansion. An inevitable decline in margins induces firms to expand their market share. Larger firms will be the first to see their growth slow, and they perform the most process R&D.

4. After entry ceases, the expected number of industry product innovations declines over time.

5. For each firm remaining in the market in a given period, the ratio of spending on process-to-product R&D will be higher than in the previous period.

6. In all periods, new entrants will be more innovative (on average) than incumbents in order to survive the disadvantage of smaller size and lower profits.

7. For each period, the larger the firm's output at the start of the period, the greater its total spending on R&D and the greater the fraction of its total R&D is devoted to process innovation.

8. For each period, the average output of process R&D versus product R&D varies inversely with the size of the firm.

9. In each period, firm average cost varies inversely with firm size.

10. The largest and most profitable firms will come from the first cohort of entrants. These firms will increase their market shares over time and consistently earn supernormal profits.

Klepper's proposed model grounds the PLC with two simple forces:

- The ability to appropriate the returns to process R&D depends critically on the size of the firm.

- Firms possess different types of expertise, which lead them to pursue different types of product innovations.

ZVI GRILICHES
"Hybrid Corn: An Exploration in the Economics of Technological Change" (1957), *Econometrica*.

Thesis: Innovation consists of the availability and acceptance of a new product, and can be studied using economic analysis.[6] As an example, economic analysis

---

[6] Griliches considered that the lag in the entry of seed producers and the long-run use of hybrids can be explained by economic considerations such as profitability. Additionally, the allocation of both private and pubic funds was economically efficient in that sector.

shows that the hybrid seed industry expanded rationally by allocating its resources first to the areas of highest returns.

 In this article, Griliches shows that innovation can be studied through economic analysis (which Griliches chooses to use broadly) and identifies two parts to an innovation: its *availability* (date or origin) and its *acceptance* (rate of growth). His study examines the diffusion of hybrid corn in the United States from the 1930s to 1950s, data that appears to follow an S-form. To statistically analyze the diffusion of hybrid corn, Griliches used a logistic model in which the dependent variable is the percentage of hybrid corn, influenced by the equilibrium value of the long-run percentage of corn and the rate of growth.[7]

Descriptive statistics indicate that U.S. states varied in their adoption of hybrid corn, with the Corn Belt starting first and having the fastest rate of growth. In Corn Belt states, 100% of the corn area was quickly converted to hybrid. In other states, adoption was later, growth was slower, and less land was converted.

To answer the question of why the diffusion process differed among states, Griliches identifies a number of factors. An economic interpretation[8] suggested examining acceptance versus availability. Was it a matter of farmers accepting the new seed or was it a matter of the seed's levels of availability?

Variation in the date of origin was identified with supply factors created when seed producers ranked different areas according to the expected profitability of entry and marketing there. This ranking depended on market size (measured as market density), marketing cost (based on average sale size), and cost for innovating.

Variation in growth rate was associated with demand factors, and the rate itself is assumed to be largely a demand or "acceptance" variable. Demand, in the form of acceptance by farmers, is based on two factors:

- **Time.** It takes time for customers (farmers) to realize things have changed.
- **Differences in profitability.** The increase in yield per acre and the average pre-hybrid yield determine differences in probability.

Variation in the equilibrium value was also associated with demand factors, and was a function of the average profitability and the distribution of this profitability. This finding indicates that the same technical superiority may mean different things in different parts of the country.

---

[7] $P = K / (1 + e^{-(a + bt)})$ where the dependent variable P is the percentage planted with hybrid corn. The independent variables were K (ceiling or equilibrium value), a (constant of integration which positions the curve on the time scale), and b (rate of growth).

[8] Here, Griliches contrasts "economic" with "financial," "sociological," "agricultural," and so on.

Griliches concludes that given a limited set of resources, the hybrid seed industry expanded according to a pattern that made sense, allocating its resources first to the areas of highest returns. The process of innovation is therefore amenable to economic analysis.

BRYCE RYAN and NEAL C. GROSS
"The Diffusion of Hybrid Seed Corn in Two Iowa Communities" (1943), *Rural Sociology*.

Thesis: Social factors impact the diffusion of innovation. Knowledge and adoption of an innovation by others have differential influence over time.

In contrast to Griliches, Ryan and Gross's study of hybrid seed corn diffusion in two different Iowa communities attempts to show that social factors matter in the diffusion of innovation. Their analysis showed that the rate of adoption is not explained through the superiority of the new breed, as few farmers took over hybrid seed for their entire acreage the first year. There are two time-lagged steps in the diffusion of new input: knowledge and adoption. In each step, different actors play different roles: the commercial channel (salespeople) is involved in the diffusion of knowledge, while neighbors influence the adoption of the new seed. The commercial channel loses its importance (as a source of knowledge) as the number of operators using the new product increases. Thus, the most important source of the original knowledge was not the most influential one: salesmen were the most important source of knowledge for early adopters, while later adopters valued their neighbors' knowledge.

MICHAEL GORT and STEVEN KLEPPER
"Time Paths in the Diffusion of Product Innovations" (1982), *Economic Journal*.

Thesis: The probability of a new product entry depends on the returns that can be maximized based on information regarding its technology. Innovation plays a critical role in entry rates and in the number of firms in an industry.

In this article, Gort and Klepper seek to measure and analyze the diffusion of product innovation, where *diffusion* is defined as the spread in the number of producers engaged in manufacturing a new product (i.e., the industry's net entry rate). The theoretical basis is evolutionary theory, constructed and contrasted with alternate theories of entry such as scale economics, technical change and shifts in optimum firm size, dynamic adjustment costs, and entry and technological change.

The central question concerns what determines the probability of entry at a particular time. The general hypothesis is that entry probability depends on which returns can be maximized based on available information on the new product technology. Information is the key point. In this study, information comes either from outside the industry for new products, or from inside the industry as "learning by doing," and is a determinant of market entry.

Applying the evolutionary theory of diffusion of innovations, product innovation has two steps: technical development and the introduction of new products. The latter is hypothesized to have five stages, described in Table 6-1.

Information on new product technology arises from two sources:

- **I_1, or new information emanating from experience in production by existing firms.** Transferable components of I_1 information cannot be appropriated and are available for adoption by other firms. Non-transferable components of information accumulate over time as "learning by doing," and operate as a barrier to entry.

- **I_2, or technological information emanating from sources outside current producers.** I_2 has a positive effect on entry and reduces the value of experience accumulated through past production.

I_2 is dominant in Stages I and II, during which time the number of producers increases greatly. I_1 is dominant in Stages III through V, with the number of new producers reaching its maximum in Stage III. The growth rate in the number of producers declines sharply, and the total number of producers declines in Stage IV, before leveling off in Stage V.

The transition from I_2 to I_1 innovations corresponds to a retardation in the rate of technological advance. In contrast with other theories, the equilibrium number of firms is path-dependent. Innovation plays a critical role in determining entry and exit rates, and the resulting number of firms. The number of potential entrants in technologically adjacent industries also influences entry rates.

Gort and Klepper also examine alternative theories of entry. Findings indicate that major early-stage innovations are of greater importance than those occurring later, and that the exit of less-efficient producers in Stage IV is associated with intensified technology competition from sources internal to the industry.

In summary, most new products appear to pass through at least five distinguishable stages. New industries pass through a stage in which the number of producers declines significantly. Rises and declines in innovation rates are associated with the rate of entry, and the character, importance, and sources of

Table 6-1: Stages of Technical Development and New Product Introduction

Stage	Characteristics	Observations
I	Commercial introduction of new product by first producer; stage ends with sharp increase in rate of entry of new competition	Length of stage is related to the ease of imitation, the size of market, and the number of potential entrants.
II	Period of sharp increase in the number of producers	Entry rate increases due to technological information emanating from sources outside current producers (I_2) and profit. As technology matures, the rate of important innovations decreases, leading to a decrease in entry rate.
III	Number of entrants balanced by the number of exiters	Structural change in the industry is reflected in the balance of entrants and exiters
IV	Net entry is negative; end of structural industry changes	The decrease in the rate of major innovations moves profits and prices to competitive levels, leading to a pressure to increase innovation rate (I_1), reinforcing barriers and forcing less efficient firms from the market.
V	Second period of near-zero net entry, continues until the eventual shrinkage of the market	The increase in the rate of patenting over time, particularly in this stage, is associated with intensified technological competition from sources internal to the industry.

Note: I_1 = new information emanating from experience of existing firms. I_2 = information emanating from sources outside current producers. Authors' table; data from Gort and Klepper (1982, p. 650).

innovations appear to change over the product lifecycle. In general, the results support the conclusion that the structure of markets is shaped, in part, by technological change and the flow of information among existing and potential producers.

Discussion and Implications:

 Innovation in companies and industries follows patterns. In companies, patterns are based on routines that develop over time and become embedded in the network of employees and managers (e.g., many people in a company will know who knows or does certain things). As Nelson and Winter describe, such routines can facilitate information exchange and in turn enhance innovation, but can also impose rigidity and inertia that can impede innovation. Utterback shows how in industries, the emergence of dominant designs—a generally accepted way of doing or making something—facilitates innovation. Once a dominant design exists, suppliers can innovate to develop better components with a positive effect on the overall product. As an example, in the early history of airplanes there were many designs with different wing configurations (and numbers) and different fuselage styles. Once a dominant design arose, engine suppliers could focus on producing better, lighter, stronger engines consistent with the overall architecture at lower costs.

The path leading to a standard is based on the interrelatedness of technology, economies of scale, and the quasi-irreversibility of investment, as illustrated by David. One of David's key takeaways is that technology adoption is not necessarily efficient, as network externalities determine whether there will be convergence on a standard. If there are high switching costs, there could be convergence to the wrong standard. Managers may thus consider buying the installed base (e.g., pricing at low profit for maximum market share as early as possible) in order to obtain the network externalities (e.g., maximizing the number of typists using QWERTY). We can relate this to our discussion on complex systems (Chapter 8, Section 4), which shows that most models for management are built for simple linear processes, and that managers have less experience modeling the path-dependent processes exhibited by technology adoption.

Resources are allocated to those areas from which the returns are highest, suggesting a dynamic process associated with innovation—this observation was a key improvement of the evolutionary model of technological advances (see Nelson and Winters). The stochastic (undetermined) evolutionary process incorporates key components of reality otherwise overlooked, such as the role of routines in companies and the sticky nature of knowledge embodied in routines. How do managers take advantage of this stickiness and how do they eliminate it if it impedes innovation? When General Motors decided to start the Saturn division, it created a new facility away from headquarters and built a new organization without GM's usual set of embedded routines. Even small companies experience the impact of routines. A "skunk works" was instituted at the 100-person company, Tessera, where Joe worked in the mid-1990s, to more efficiently develop a product within this IT service-based company.

Mokyr focuses on what drives economic growth and concludes that it is the production of knowledge, specifically useful knowledge. Changes in access costs (caused by institutions, such as governments) determine the use and value of knowledge; managers must know what information is where in organizations, as well as how to tap into that knowledge efficiently. In high-technology firms, it is common to have "brown-bag lunches" during which engineers share their knowledge broadly; Joe observed, however, that they were as much about sharing information as feeding egos and letting others know where information (and power) resides in the organization.

An interesting follow-up to Foster's article on the S-curve and managing discontinuities is *The Innovators Dilemma* by Clayton Christensen (1997), in which he analyzes the computer disk drive industry. Christensen finds that innovators created disruptions in technology, pushing leading incumbents out of business again and again, and demonstrating performance S-curves that are associated with industry evolution and disruptive innovation.

Some patterns of industry growth and decay suggested by Utterback's model may be context-dependent, and so may not apply in international contexts or with certain types of products. Certainly, the globalization and market integration fostered by the internet erode some contextual differences. It is not always easy to observe where you are in an industry evolution, and products with less focus on design may not have the same dependence on, or pattern of, dominant design emergence.

A nice example of the concepts illustrated in Tushman and Rosenkopf is the case of the video cassette recorder (Rosenbloom and Cusumano 1987); the study describes how rival companies worked together to establish VHS as the standard over the more technologically advanced Betamax. Many factors involving learning and leadership resulted in greater development of the "software" (the movies), permitting household penetration of the specific hardware (the VHS video recorder/player) on which the movies could run. This relationship underscores the impact of complementary products.

Klepper ties together the product/process dichotomy by focusing on product (vs. service) industries. The analogy of "service as a product" may carry one a little ways down the path of applying Klepper's model to service industries, but specialization of knowledge in some industries (e.g., law) may not result in predicted price declines. Since much of Klepper's model depends on such price declines, it may not apply to services—especially in high-end, knowledge-intensive services where there are fewer economies of scale.

We are left with the question, "So what?" Does Klepper's model provide an opportunity to develop metrics for industries to see where they are on the lifecycle, permitting managers to make strategic decisions? Certainly metrics can be developed, and most are easily created and employed in more static or geographically-bounded industries. As we have seen in recent years, however, industry lines blur (note the convergence of communications and computers) and industry evolution varies by geographic context.

If smaller firms are more innovative but larger firms are more able to appropriate returns from R&D, do we have a natural explanation for the level of acquisitions in innovative industries like technology? Oracle has emphasized economies of scale (spreading out R&D over a larger revenue base), thereby making M&A a logical choice. It is intuitive that companies like Oracle and other technology acquirers may be better positioned to extract returns from the R&D of the target companies, because they are already in most customers' buying patterns and they have more experience protecting the acquirer's intellectual property.

Industry evolution is dependent on the diffusion of information about the product, and of the product itself. While individual consumers are adopters of innovations, firms are important innovation adaptors and not all new products are innovations. We are left with pertinent managerial questions such as the following:

- Why do some good innovations fail to diffuse?
- Which types of innovation are more likely to diffuse?
- How do installed bases, switching costs, and social influences affect diffusion?

If diffusion is a matter of availability, as suggested by Griliches, then communication technology (e.g., internet) and transportation can immensely affect innovation diffusion. We can see this effect in the rapidity with which products have penetrated the market over the past hundred years: To reach 150 million users in the United States, the telephone needed almost 90 years, the television nearly 40 years, mobile phones 14 years, and Facebook only 5 years.

In many of the studies presented in this section, industry variation is an important component, as suggested by Gort and Klepper. Promotional activities may play a role in influencing the behaviors of early entrants (marketing implications for sellers) and the size of the early movers (large firms could exercise a higher influence upon the later entrants).

Additional literature in the realm of technological innovation and trajectories, presented in chronological order, includes the following:

- **Tushman and Anderson (1986).** Innovations can be competence-enhancing or competence-destroying, and competition is based on who can develop the standards and "rules of the game" by which firms in the industry are forced to play. This article suggests that these types of innovation-motivations supercede economic incentives to invest. Competence-enhancing innovation is primarily done by incumbents in an industry, whereas competence-destroying innovation is done mainly by entrants.

- **Klepper and Graddy (1990).** These authors decompose industries into three evolutionary stages and compute the average growth rate in the population of firms in each stage, finding a large decline in the second stage. Entrants may bring additional skills into the industry, to which incumbents may not respond effectively. Output growth is driven by entry and capacity. With certain assumptions, they find a pattern of falling prices and rising output, of growth rates in the number of firms, and inter-industry differences.

- **Jovanovic and MacDonald (1994).** Motivated by the observed prevalence of periods of rapid growth and shake-out in industries, this study accounts for technological innovation. Examining the value maximization decision for high-, low-, and no-technology firms, the authors find equilibrium where increasing the fraction of high-technology firms leads to more output and lower prices. This equilibrium depends on the distribution and advantage of high- and low-technology firms.

- **McGahan (2004).** There are four distinct trajectories of industy evolution: progressive, creative, intermediation, and radical. These trajectories differ in the degree to which core assets are threatened (foundational change) or core activities are threatened (architectural change). CEOs must specifically understand and identify which industry they are in, and determine the trajectory of their industry, as strategies consistent with these trajectories are essential for survival and growth. If the firm operates in different industries, managers must consider the industry and trajectory relevant for each business unit.

3. Technology Competition

The articles in this section describe how innovation and innovative competition may vary based on the size and position of the firm and the nature of the industry in terms of R&D intensity and market structure. After describing various types of innovation, Henderson and Clark (1990) focus on *architectural innovation*, which uses a firm's competencies to change the way product components are linked together without changing the core design concept. Other sources discuss how innovation may be driven by incumbents (firms already in the industry), new entrants, or users (von Hippel 1988).

Protecting proprietary information is key for innovators. Patent laws exist for this reason but are only one mechanism preventing general access to new innovation. *Appropriability*, or who gets the value from innovation, is the topic of the next set of authors. Teece (1987) examines the determinants of the share of profit of innovation, while Levin, Klevorick, Nelson, and Winter (1987) provide findings on the various means of protecting intellectual property and the ways these means vary by industry. Gans and Stern (2003) suggest that there is value in ideas, and that the market for ideas affects innovation competition.

Firm resources also play into technology competition. Henderson and Cockburn (1994) analyze firm competence and its relationship with research productivity—information and the ability to recognize the value of new information, accumulate it, assimilate it, and exploit it are based on related prior knowledge. The *absorptive capacity* of a firm (Cohen and Levinthal 1990) is the firm's ability to assimilate and transfer information. These abilities are better within firms than in the market (Kogut and Zander 1992). Beyond knowledge, the firm's or industry's prior offerings provide a basis for technological competition, as first-mover advantage may be lost when the market develops slowly or the speed of imitation increases (McGahan, Vadasz, and Yoffie 1996).

Innovators do not always outperform followers; the innovator's share of profits is determined by the appropriability regime, the dominant design paradigm, and complementary assets. The presence of resources such as a star scientist dramatically affects technological competition (Zucker, Darby, and Brewer 1998).

The final three articles in this section address geographic and network aspects of competition. Saxenian (1994) compares the geographic (and institutional) characteristics of the computer industry's evolution in Silicon Valley and Boston's Route 128. The nature of network collaboration (Ahuja 2000) and syndication (Sorenson and Stuart 2001) provides insights to managers, entrepreneurs, and investors.

REBECCA M. HENDERSON and KENNETH CLARK "Architectural Innovation: The Reconfiguration of Existing Product Technologies and the Failure of Established Firms" (1990), *Administrative Science Quarterly*.

Thesis: Innovation can be incremental, radical, or architectural. Architectural innovation changes the way product components are linked together without changing the core design concept.

Henderson and Clark's article describes differences between incremental innovation and radical innovation. In particular, each type of innovation generates different consequences that lead to the requirement of different organizational capabilities, which are difficult to create and costly to adjust.

- *Incremental innovation* entails refining and improving the current concept by introducing minor changes to the existing product, facilitating the exploitation of the established design's potential and reinforcing the dominance of established firms. Incremental innovation tends to reinforce existing capabilities.

- *Radical innovation* introduces a new concept based on a different set of principles, opening up new markets and new potential applications, creating great difficulties for established firms, and providing the basis for the successful entry of new firms. Radical innovation forces a new set of challenges (e.g., new questions, new skills, and new problem-solving approaches) that undermine existing capabilities.

However, these two types of innovation are insufficient to explain all the different technological innovations in the real world. Some innovations involve apparently modest changes to the existing technology but have quite dramatic competitive consequences. Why do certain seemingly incremental innovations have radical consequences?

Henderson and Clark propose a new kind of innovation, *architectural innovation*, which changes the way the components of a product are linked together while leaving the core design concept untouched. This type of innovation destroys the usefulness of a firm's architectural knowledge but preserves the usefulness of its knowledge about the product's components.

The authors apply design theory, which relates to the distinction between the product as a whole and the product in its parts (system vs. components). This distinction underscores the idea that successful product development requires two types of knowledge:

- *Component knowledge* is an understanding of each of the core design concepts and the way in which they are implemented in a particular component.
- *Architectural knowledge* concerns the ways in which the components are integrated and linked together into a coherent whole.

This understanding is a source of insight into both the ways that innovations differ from each other and their effect on organizations.

Traditional views of innovation and organization suggest that different kinds of innovation have different competitive effects, that product evolution is characterized by periods of great experimentation followed by the acceptance of a dominant design, and that organizations build knowledge and capabilities around the recurring tasks they perform. When viewing architectural innovation's impact on the organization, Henderson and Clark note the following mechanisms created by the firm to cope with complexity:

- **Communication channels.** Developing around critical interactions to conduct the task, the use of communication channels leads to relationships around which the organization builds architectural knowledge.
- **Information filters.** Filters allow the firm to quickly identify what is most crucial in its information stream, permitting it to achieve greater focus and efficiency of information.
- **Problem-solving strategies.** Using the firm's stores of knowledge about solutions already tested, problem-solving strategies lead to solutions to routine problems.

These mechanisms are efficient precisely because they do not have to be actively created or executed each time they are needed; they have become implicit and embedded. This embeddedness may, however, be a source of problems in situations of architectural innovation exactly because the embedded knowledge is a source of inertia and is difficult to change.

ERIC VON HIPPEL
The Sources of Innovation (1988), Chapters 1–4.

Thesis: Sources of innovation vary, and include manufacturers, suppliers, and users, based on expectations of appropriation of profits. *Lead users*—users at the front of a trend—are those who innovate in the application of new products and services in an attempt to gain innovation profits. Product innovation occurs more in industries in which such users expect to realize these *rents* (i.e., returns in excess of the resource owner's opportunity cost).

 In the first chapters of his book, von Hippel presents a series of cases providing evidence that the sources of innovation vary greatly according to the type of innovation. He explores why this variation occurs and how it might be predicted in order to better manage the innovation process. The studies he includes consider the functional source of innovation by categorizing firms and individuals in terms of the functional relationship through which they derive benefit from a given product, process, or service innovation.

Von Hippel tries to predict the functional sources of innovation by analyzing the temporary profits expected by potential innovators in disparate industries. His work discredits the long-held assumption that manufacturers were the principal source of innovation. Innovations in scientific instruments, semiconductors, and printed circuit board assembly processes prove the central role of users in the invention, information diffusion, pre-commercial replication, and use phases of innovation.

The central role of users or other potential innovators is connected to their expectations of economic rents. Expectations of profits are formed and distributed across users, manufacturers, suppliers, or other sources according to underlying strategies and rules determined by the informal exchange of know-how. This process consists of an exchange of valuable information between traders that is kept secret from non-traders. The informal information-exchange process occurs almost exclusively when proprietary know-how offers little competitive advantage; informal exchange is preferred for its lower transaction costs, as more formal agreements usually generate higher costs.

Von Hippel finds that variations in the sources of innovation are caused by variations in potential innovators' expectations of profits; to predict the likely source of innovation, it is necessary to understand how those profits are distributed. By changing the distribution of profit expectations, it is possible to shift the likely source of innovation.

Although the role of market research seems crucial to predict the source of innovation, market research is actually constrained by user experience and overly connected to the individual analyst's ability. Users "at the front of the trend" (Urban and von Hippel 1988, p. 570) who expect high rents from a potential solution are *lead users* who can induce user innovation, becoming one of the most important sources of innovation. The high level of product innovation found among lead users of computer-aided design software, for example, can only be expected in product areas where the potential rents are sufficient to induce user innovation.

 DAVID TEECE
"Profiting from Technological Innovation: Implications for Integration, Collaboration, Licensing and Public Policy" (1987), in *The Competitive Challenge: Strategies for Industrial Innovation and Renewal.*

Thesis: Innovators do not always outperform followers. The innovator's share of profits is determined by the appropriability regime, the dominant design paradigm, and complementary assets.

 In this article, Teece explains why a fast runner-up or even a slow third entrant might outperform the innovator. He investigates the question, "What determines the share of profits captured by the innovator?" (as opposed to the profits of followers, suppliers, complementors, customers, etc.). The framework he develops also explains inter-firm activities such as joint ventures, co-production agreements, cross-distribution arrangements, and technology licensing.

Teece builds his framework on the following concepts:

- **Appropriability regime.** This concept includes the nature of technology and the efficacy of legal mechanisms of protection (e.g., patents do not protect process innovations, trade secrets, or tacit knowledge). The appropriability regime can be tight (like the recipe for Coca-Cola), or loose (like the Simplex algorithm used for linear programs).

- **Dominant design paradigm.** Discussed in more detail under Abernathy and Utterback (1978) above, the dominant design paradigm is more suited to mass markets with homogenous consumer tastes, rather than niche markets using generalized equipment. When (a) imitation is possible, (b) occurs, and (c) is coupled with design modification before the emergence of a dominant design, followers have a good chance of becoming the industry standard.

- **Complementary assets.** Successful commercialization of an innovation almost always requires know-how to be combined with other capabilities or assets (e.g., marketing, after-sales support, or competitive manufacturing). Some complementary assets are *specialized*, meaning they involve a unilateral dependence (e.g., the production of a product needs a specialized machine), and may be a key requirement for least-cost production. *Co-specialized* assets involve a bilateral dependence (e.g., the specialized machine can only be used for that product).

The boundaries of the firm may thus be an important strategic variable, as the ownership of complementary assets helps determine who wins and who loses—not only who profits most, but ultimately who survives. Teece notes that the distribution of profits among innovators and followers is determined by the structure of firms (rather than markets), particularly the scope of their boundaries coupled with national policies regarding the development of complementary assets.

This framework has a number of implications for strategic management, public policy, and international trade and investment.

- **For the firm.** Since one cannot always win, managers need an R&D portfolio and a focus on innovations in a tight appropriability regime or for a regime where the company already owns specialized assets. Therefore, a firm's history and asset stock should condition its R&D investment decisions. Large firms can more easily "win" because they have the assets. As industries mature, new entrants need to form coalitions and other relationships to succeed.

- **For public policy.** In weak appropriability regimes, issues around imitation, contracting between markets (e.g., having one nation design and another manufacture), transfer of know-how, and intangible asset pricing are all difficult to gauge *ex ante* (beforehand). Innovating nations also need to have complementary assets, and should enhance the protection their laws and policies afford worldwide to intellectual property. Governments can block investment into and ownership of complementary assets by foreign firms, but this move can backfire if these assets are not unique or critical, as restrictive practices only redistribute profit with respect to domestic sales.

Channel strategy issues exist regarding how best to control the complementary assets that Teece shows are often critical to successful innovation:

- **Using a mixed mode to control the asset.** In the real world, mixed modes are most common and may be transitional or be used in an attempt to reduce risk. In other words, it may be best to contract for the use of a complementary asset while one ensures there is sufficient market for a product, after which it may be prudent to obtain the asset.

- **Contracting for control of the asset.** Various contracting modes (licensing, buy/sell agreements, etc.) or types of strategic partnerships exist, but each has differing profiles of risk that may require more capital commitments. For example, strategic partnerships are open to opportunism.
- **Integrating the asset.** Integration modes involve ownership, which facilitates incentive alignment and control.

RICHARD LEVIN, ALVIN KLEVORICK, RICHARD NELSON, and SIDNEY WINTER
"Appropriating the Returns from Industrial Research and Development" (1987), Brookings Papers on Economic Activity.

Thesis: Patents are only one mechanism preventing general access to new innovation. Appropriability is imperfect; imitation is costly and takes time.

This paper examines industry patent policy and other factors that affect firm innovation. It is commonly known that appropriability is not perfect: on the one hand patents provide little protection, and on the other hand public disclosure through the patent system does not result in diffusion. Levin and his coauthors surveyed high-level R&D managers of large, public manufacturing companies, but were concerned with measurement error, especially since "subjective, semantic scales" were used. They also note that some potential competitors are not represented in their sample because the firms failed.

Whereas prior researchers wanted to know whether there are systematic relations between the degree of appropriation and other observable economic variables, Levin et al. seek to understand the relationship between patents and other factors for either protecting or acquiring competitive advantage. The dependent variables used were the protection of innovation, the acquisition of a competitor's knowledge, and the cost and time to imitate rivals. Independent variables fell into two categories:

- **For the protection of innovation.** Independent variables included patents, secrecy, lead time, learning curve, and sales or service efforts.
- **For the acquisition of a competitor's knowledge.** Independent variables included licensing, patent disclosure, publications or technical meetings, conversations, the "poaching" of R&D staff, reverse-engineering, independent R&D, and the cost of duplication.

The results vary both inter- and intra-industry.

- **Innovation protection.** Patents are not always a main factor in protecting competitive advantage. Some companies use patents to evaluate scientific contributors or for entry into international markets. Variables such as lead time and learning curve are important in process innovations, whereas sales and service are more important in product innovations.

- **Acquisition of a competitor's knowledge.** Independent R&D had the highest rating for acquisition of competitor's knowledge, followed by licensing technology. Reverse engineering was more of a factor for products than for process, and conversations with employees of competing firms were the least important factor. Regarding the cost and time required for imitation, major innovations take longer to copy—and those that are patented take longer and cost more than the unpatented.

The results of Levin et al.'s study have a number of policy implications, given that patents are not the only—nor necessarily the primary—barriers preventing general access to what would otherwise be public goods. In examining a proposed adjustment of the patent system or related institutions, it is important for policymakers to recognize that the incremental effect of the policy change depends on the protection provided by other mechanisms. Also, policy changes should be assessed at the industry level, as industries vary in their means of protecting intellectual property.

IAIN COCKBURN and ZVI GRILICHES
"Industry Effects and Appropriability Measures in the Stock Market's Valuation of R&D and Patents" (1988), *American Economic Review*.

Thesis: Appropriability may be higher in some industries than in others. Patents are more highly valued in industries with stronger patent protection.

Recognizing that the effectiveness of patents as a mechanism for appropriating the returns on R&D is not constant for all industries, Cockburn and Griliches's main objective in this article is to examine R&D and patenting while attempting to control for inter-firm variability. The concern here is the market value of the firm, and the study uses the market's relative valuation of the capital invested as the dependent variable. Since value is the result of an activity derived from assets, valuation is a function of both tangible and intangible assets.

First, the authors constructed appropriability measures to compare the equality of industries. Non-patent measures showed no significant difference between industries, whereas patent measures did show significant differences. In fact, a single variable, "patents provide protection" (PPP), successfully accomplished the same as 10 dummy variables representing industries. For industries where patent protection is more effective, the authors make two observations:

- The models indicate a higher valuation of patents.
- The market values "news" on R&D as more relevant than past industry investment.

Cockburn and Griliches conclude that it is useful to question the effectiveness of patents as a mechanism for protecting the return from innovation. Their study provides evidence of the existence and significance of the interaction between industry-level measures of patent effectiveness and the market valuation of a firm's past R&D and patenting performance. Patent counts should be taken cautiously, as R&D expenditures are a stronger measure of input to the innovative process than patents are of its "output."

JOSHUA GANS and SCOTT STERN
"The Product Market and the Market for Ideas: Commercialization Strategies for Technology Entrepreneurs" (2003), *Research Policy*.

Thesis: A firm's commercialization strategy should reflect its environment. The value earned on ideas is greater than that from access to specialized assets. Returns depend on the timing of collaboration and the pacing of competition. Investments in innovation should align with the highest-return option (e.g., selling products vs. ideas).[9]

Gans and Stern provide a framework synthesizing the drivers of startup commercialization strategy and the implications of these drivers on industrial dynamics. They define the *commercialization environment* as the microeconomic and strategic conditions facing a firm that is translating an idea into a value proposition for customers. The authors examine the cooperation/competition decision of innovators in the context of access to complementary assets and imitability. They apply a variety of theoretical lenses to the analysis, including the boundaries of the firm, elements of transaction cost economics (imperfect contracts and asset specificity), and the resource-based view (Chapter 1, Section 3).

The main problem faced by small firms is not invention but commercialization, the effective strategies for which vary across industries. Two

---

[9] Although this last sentence may seem obvious, most innovators ignore this recommendation and try to produce a product rather than license the idea—even if they have no idea how to produce it. Calculating the return is, unfortunately, often based on hubris and optimism.

elements of the commercialization environment determine the share of the innovation's value received by the firm:

- **The nature of the appropriability environment.** What works best to protect the innovation's value to the innovator (e.g., patents or secrecy)?

- **The distribution of ownership and control of specialized complementary assets.** Such assets may include, for example, distribution and manufacturing capabilities or brand-name reputation. Firms that control key complementary assets are the most likely and most effective product market imitators.

Pursuing cooperation with firms controlling key complementary assets can be hazardous if they are also product market players with incentives to expropriate the innovator's technology and commercialize it themselves. The choice between cooperation and competition requires a fine-grained *ex ante* analysis of the costs and benefits of each option, as there are costs and constraints on switching later.

To profit from innovation through the product market, an innovator must aggressively invest, manage uncertainty, focus scarce resources on establishing market presence, persuade customers of the value proposition, and avoid "detection" and aggressive responses by established players. Profiting through cooperation requires agreements with firms who serve as conduits for the commercialization of technology. The value of cooperation is positively related to the threat posed. Cooperation can take a number of forms:

- licensing, in which parties maintain organizational independence;
- acquisition of the innovator by an established firm; and
- intermediate contracting relationships such as joint ventures.

Cooperation is a two-sided coin, with positive and negative facets.

- **Benefits of cooperation.** It reinforces established market power and softens market competition. Cooperation also allows startups to avoid investments in complementary assets, and provides incentives to innovate on current technology. In addition, established firms avoid investments in imitative research programs.

- **Detriments of cooperation.** It limits the investment in downstream commercialization, as it is difficult to both cooperate and compete. Additional drawbacks include the costs of identifying and accessing appropriate partners, and the paradox of disclosure (Arrow 1962): to gauge value, you have to know information, but once you know it, you do not need to pay for it to exploit it.

The authors identify two drivers of startup commercialization strategy:

- **Excludability environment.** This strategy driver describes to what extent successful technological innovation by the startup can preclude effective development by an incumbent with knowledge of the innovation. Not all appropriability mechanisms are created equal (e.g., trade secrecy may work for competitors but not for partners, while patents may permit disclosure while preserving bargaining power).

- **Complementary asset environment.** This driver defines the extent to which the incumbent's complementary assets contribute to the value proposition of the new technology. Substantial product market-entry startup costs reduce the returns to competition and weaken the startup's relative bargaining position. An increase in the importance of complementary assets encourages collaboration over competition.

An effective commercialization strategy results from the interaction between excludability and complementary asset environments, resulting in four distinct scenarios, described in Table 6-2.

Gans and Stern conclude that competitive interaction between startup innovators and established firms depends on the presence or absence of a "market for ideas." They offer some new insights into effective commercialization strategies:

- Appropriability, reputation, and economic institutions play a role in shaping strategic choice.
- Commercialization strategy has an impact on competitive dynamics.

A key driver of effective commercialization strategies should be the type of appropriability. Reputation and economic institutions (e.g., banks and investors) play a role for ideas in trading in "mixed" environments, as intermediaries such as venture capitalists facilitate the market for ideas via their knowledge of a startup innovator's reputation.

These insights have a number of implications for technology entrepreneurs:

- The commercialization strategy should reflect the firm's commercialization environment.
- The value earned in the market for ideas extends beyond the value of access to specialized complementary assets.
- The returns on cooperation depend on the timing of collaboration; the returns on product market entry depend on the pacing of competition.
- Investments in innovation should be sensitive to the most attractive commercialization environment.

Table 6-2: Commercialization Strategy Environment Scenarios

Scenario	Startup behavior	Incumbent behavior	Expected competitive dynamics
"Attacker's advantage": Innovation overturns an incumbent's asset value	Performance depends on stealth product-market entry	Strategy should be based on its competitive advantage in products and on tight integration of its value chain	Dynamics based on market leadership determined by technological leadership, and on startup investments in complementary assets
"Greenfield competition": Incumbent's complementary assets unimportant, and innovators preclude effective imitation	Performance depends on the strength of technological competition	Competitive advantage is based on products, requiring the development of a strong innovative performance	Focus on technology leadership, competition for technological priority, and investment in new platforms and complementary assets
"Reputation-based ideas trading": Innovation reinforces the incumbent's complementary assets	Performance depends on the existence of incumbent's commitment to trading	Strategies include focused R&D and a competitive advantage based on both competencies and products	Established firms face few competitive threats from startups
"Idea factories": Technology leaders focus on research and commercialization via partnerships	Performance depends on securing bargaining power	Need to find a balance between internal and external innovation	Technological leadership may frequently change, startups compete with each other for negotiation priority with incumbents, and startup innovations will reinforce existing platforms

Note. Authors' table; data from Gans and Stern (2003, p. 341).

WILLIAM COHEN and DAVID LEVINTHAL
"Absorptive Capacity: A New Perspective on Learning and
Innovation" (1990), *Administrative Science Quarterly*.

Thesis: The ability to recognize the value of new information—as well as
accumulate it, assimilate it, and exploit it—is based on related prior knowledge.

Cohen and Levinthal's article empirically evaluates the
importance of absorptive capacity for innovation by modeling
firm investments in R&D and relating that model to the
knowledge that underlies technical change within an industry.
The authors define *absorptive capacity* as the ability to recognize the value of new
information, assimilate it, and apply it to commercial ends. Absorptive capacity
is conferred by prior related knowledge, which permits the assimilation and
exploitation of new knowledge. Some portion of that prior knowledge should
be very closely related to the new knowledge to facilitate assimilation, and some
fraction of that prior knowledge must be fairly diverse, although still related, in
order to permit effective, creative utilization of the new knowledge.

A company's accumulation of absorptive capacity in one period will permit
its more efficient accumulation in the next period. In an uncertain environment,
absorptive capacity affects the formation of expectations, permitting the firm to
more accurately predict the nature and commercial potential of technological
advances. If absorptive capacity is important and R&D contributes to it, then
whatever affects the firm's incentives to learn should also influence R&D.

To understand the impact of the characteristics of the learning environment
on R&D spending, Cohen and Levinthal examine three variables that determine
R&D intensity: demand, appropriability, and technological opportunity. Their
results indicate the following.

- When the quality of the targeted knowledge is less (i.e., when learning is
  more difficult), an increase in the relevance of knowledge has a stronger
  positive effect on R&D intensity.
- The ease of learning may enhance the effects of knowledge spillovers.
- The positive absorption incentive associated with knowledge spillovers is
  likely greater in industries in which the difficulty of learning is greater.
- The positive effect of spillovers will increase in industries in which firms are
  less interdependent.

These findings have a number of implications for innovative activity.

- Since R&D creates a capacity to assimilate new knowledge, firms may invest
  in basic research even when the preponderance of findings spill over to the
  public domain.

- The ease of learning, and thus technology adoption, is affected by the degree to which an innovation is related to the pre-existing knowledge base of prospective users.
- Cooperative research ventures are found more typically in industries that employ more mature technologies, rather than in industries in which technology is moving ahead quickly.

Cooperative ventures that have been initiated to pursue basic research (as well as more applied research objectives) have been subjected over the years to increasing pressure to focus on more short-term research objectives. An explanation for that phenomenon is connected to the costs of assimilating and exploiting knowledge from such ventures.

 BRUCE KOGUT and UDO ZANDER
"Knowledge of the Firm, Combinative Capabilities, and the Replication of Technology" (1992), *Organization Science*.

Thesis: Firms are better than markets at creating, sharing, and transferring knowledge through a dynamic process of learning new skills by recombining current capabilities.

 Why do firms exist? The prevailing view is that firms exist in order to suppress the transaction costs that arise from the self-interested motivation of individuals. Kogut and Zander's view is that firms are better than markets at creating, sharing, and transferring knowledge (both information and know-how). An analysis of what firms can do must therefore understand knowledge as embedded in the organizing principles by which people cooperate within an organization. Paradoxically, the efforts of a firm to grow by replication of its technology may enhance the potential for imitation. Codification and simplification of knowledge induce the likelihood of imitation, which is a principal constraint to firm growth.

By considering how firms can deter imitation via innovation, Kogut and Zander develop a more dynamic view of how firms create new knowledge. They build this dynamic perspective by suggesting that firms learn new skills by recombining current capabilities. Because new ways of cooperating cannot be easily acquired, growth occurs by building on the social relationships that currently exist in a firm. What a firm has done before tends to predict what it can do in the future. In this sense, a firm's cumulative knowledge provides options to expand in new but uncertain markets in the future.

Kogut and Zander categorize knowledge into information (declarative) and know-how (procedural). They examine personal expertise and social knowledge to argue that firm capabilities in general rest in the organizing principles of relationships as structures: relationships among individuals, within and between groups, and among organizations. They introduce the concept of a firm's combinative capability for synthesizing and applying current knowledge, and presume that knowledge of the firm is socially constructed (i.e., resting in the organizing of human resources). Firms differ in their information and know-how, and these differences affect performance due to codifiability and complexity that make information and know-how difficult to transfer and imitate.

They apply their observations to make-or-buy decisions and firm capabilities. Conventional wisdom asserts that markets for technology transfer fail due to high transaction costs. As it is often cheaper to produce in-house than outside, the technology says inside because, argue the authors, the innovator has already developed the right capabilities. The decision to make or buy depends on three things:

- how good the firm currently is at doing something,
- how good the firm is at learning specific capabilities, and
- what the value is of these capabilities as platforms into new markets (i.e., the economic gain).

This theory of knowledge ignores the issue of individual motivation by focusing on organizing principles as the unit of analysis to understand variations in firm performance. These principles represent procedures by which social relations are recreated and coordinated. Firms are repositories of capabilities determined by the social knowledge that is embedded in enduring individual relationships, structured by organizing principles. Switching to new capabilities is difficult, and the stability of these relationships generates observed inertia in a firm's capabilities.

 ANITA MCGAHAN, LESLIE L. VADASZ, and DAVID YOFFIE
"Creating Value and Setting Standards: The Lessons of Consumer Electronics for Personal Digital Assistants" (1996), in D. Yoffie (editor), *Competing in the Age of Digital Convergence*.

Thesis: First-mover advantage is powerful but may be lost when the market develops slowly or the speed of imitation increases. Network externalities drive toward separate hardware and software industries to generate buyer value. Products need backward compatibility to utilize previous standard technology.

McGahan et al.'s management policy-oriented study of product innovations in the personal digital assistant (PDA) industry is of particular interest to managers, providing three general lessons.

1. First mover advantage (FMA) is powerful, but when the market develops slowly or the speed of imitation increases, this advantage may be lost. FMA is powerful because there is no installed base from which to switch users to a new technology. For the second mover, incumbents may try to prevent new product innovation.

2. Network externalities are critical, requiring that separate and independent hardware and software industries must develop to generate buyer value.

3. Backward compatibility, in that new offerings must be able to utilize previous standard technology, facilitates and hastens market acceptance.

The authors examine these lessons in the context of seven different product introductions, as follows.

- Apple's Newton was a pen-based computing device, initially with no keyboard or hard disk.

- AT&T's EO was an early tablet computer with (poor) handwriting recognition.

- FM radio was proposed by an RCA employee to the firm, but denied in order to protect RCA's share of AM radio.

- Color television required an ultra-high frequency transmission system.

- The audio cassette was introduced by Lear Jet, who contracted with RCA's music library and Ford.

- The VHS format for video cassette recorders was first introduced for commercial use; when the cheaper Betamax format came on the market, the two systems vied for market dominance.

- The Palm Pilot was a Personal Digital Assistant (PDA) introduced after Palm's first PDA, Zoomer, failed.

Table 6-3 summarizes McGahan et al.'s analysis of these products vis-à-vis the three general lessons of first mover advantage, network externalities, and backwards compatibility.

The paths of these various technologies illustrate and underscore the elements of first mover advantage, network externalities, and backward compatibilities necessary for the successful introduction of a new technological innovation. In 1996, McGahan et al. proposed that incentives for investment in PDAs and software would be driven by the presence of complementary systems such as wireless communications.

Table 6-3: Summary of Product Introduction Analysis

Technology	Year introduced	First mover?	Network externalities	Backwards compatible?	Outcome
Apple's Newton	1993	Yes	Apple loyalists	No interface with previous Apple technology	Repositioned successfully but discontinued in 1995
AT&T EO	1993	Yes	None	No	Discontinued in 1994
FM radio	1933 (AM 1919)	No	Little: few FM stations	No	Widespread use delayed for 30 years
Color television	1940s (B&W 1939)	No	None	Not until 1950s	Market penetration delayed for 20 years
Audio cassette	1966	No	Negative: 8-track owner resistance	No	LP price increases in 1970s drove consumers to cassettes
Video cassette recorder	1956	Yes	None until 2-hour tape became standard	N/A	Took 20 years to be commercially viable; had good run until DVD
Palm Pilot	1996	No (device) Yes (firm)	Not initially	Link to Win95	Fastest-selling computer through 1998

Note. Authors' table; data from McGahan et al. (1996, pp. 227–264).

LYNNE G. ZUCKER, MICHAEL R. DARBY, and
MARILYNN B. BREWER
"Intellectual Human Capital and the Birth of U.S. Biotechnology
Enterprises" (1998), *American Economic Review*.

Thesis: Basic scientific research by "star" scientists is central to the formation
of new high-technology industries and is a powerful predictor of firms'
geographic distribution.

In their research, Zucker, Darby, and Brewer were in pursuit of
several goals:

1. to empirically demonstrate that the commercialization of biotech is
   intrinsically related with the development of scientific knowledge and
   its localized effects;
2. to examine the relationship between the intellectual capital of scientists
   making frontier discoveries, the presence of great university bioscience
   programs, the presence of venture capital firms, and federal research
   support; and
3. to quantify the separable effect of each of these main variables in order
   to encourage local economic development through geographically
   localized knowledge spillovers.

Some innovations specifically related to methods of inventing are better
characterized as creating "rivalrous" human capital, which has natural
excludability due to the complexity or tacitness of the information required to
practice innovation. In other words, not everyone has access to the human
capital (e.g., one person's knowledge), as such complex capital transcends a
simple set of instructions for combining inputs and outputs. Biotech
innovations should be seen as naturally excludable knowledge held by a small
initial group of discoverers, in which "genius" and "vision" play an important
role in knowledge applications (by defining the exact research focus and
promising areas). In a second phase of industry growth, strategic knowledge
spreads sufficiently widely to become part of routine science, easily diffused by
learning institutions.

Zucker et al. collected data for 14 years in 183 regions, including 751 firms,
327 "star" scientists, and more than 4,000 published articles (pp. 291–292).
They found that the number of active star scientists is a powerful predictor of
the geographic distribution of biotech enterprises, as are the presence of top
quality universities and federal research grants. The quality of the labor force is
more relevant that its size, and the number of venture capital firms is significant
and negatively associated with the geographic concentration of firms.

Further, intellectual human capital plays a strong role in determining where biotech firms are located. Star scientists play a crucial role in the process of spillovers and geographic agglomeration: The location of biotech enterprises relates to the areas in which star scientists become active. However, the scientist's value decreases with knowledge diffusion, so universities play a more important role in attracting new ventures to an area. The overall results provide strong evidence on the relevance of basic scientific research as central to the formation of new high-technology industries spawned by scientific breakthroughs.

ANNALEE SAXENIAN
Regional Advantage: Culture and Competition in Silicon Valley and Route 128 (1994).

Thesis: A set of geographic, sociological, and regulatory differences led Silicon Valley and Route 128 to develop different cultures, which led to differences in economic performance. The more flexible form generated more innovation.

 The Silicon Valley and Route 128 regions were extremely important to the development of the computer and information technology industries. Different cultures emerged after the initial industrial shock, and these different cultures led to differences in performance. Saxenian's book examines these cultural factors in an attempt to describe how a more flexible form led to more innovation and greater success.

Silicon Valley

Silicon Valley was characterized by competition and community. In the early 1980s, chipmakers relinquished the market for semiconductors to the Japanese. In the mid-1980s, a new generation of semiconductor and computer startups (e.g., Sun) grew alongside established companies (e.g., HP, Intel). With limited prior industrial experience, these new startups had a sense of being pioneers and outsiders to the industrial traditions of the East, which led to experimentation with organizational forms. The close proximity of suppliers, producers, and financiers (due to being bounded by the Pacific Ocean to the west and mountains to the east) forced interaction and occupational mobility. Many workers found that job hopping was less disruptive to life than relocating to another region.

Silicon Valley developed a primarily individualistic society with a culture of greater loyalty to one's craft than to one's company, resulting in less trade secrecy and a localized accumulation of technological knowledge that enhanced the viability of startups. Leading firms such as Fairchild enhanced collegiality and openness to risk-taking: Fairchild celebrated managers leaving to start spinoff ventures. The interconnectedness of managers and technologists due to job-hopping was an accepted (and almost encouraged) feature of the resource pool. There was extensive information sharing in both formal (e.g., industrial associations) and informal (e.g., the Wagon Wheel bar) settings. Status was defined by entrepreneurship and by one's technical capabilities. Failure was socially acceptable. Venture capitalists here had entrepreneurial or technical backgrounds, and thus understood the issues faced by technology entrepreneurs. Managers had limited experience with and within hierarchical structures, and so created more decentralized organizational structures and delegated more readily. There was extensive use of equity compensation: having a piece of the pie was critical, and stock was the "mother's milk" of Silicon Valley.

The industry structure was fragmented, leading to a diverse and adaptable industrial ecology. Redundancy was a means to reliability, as there were 3,000 electronics firms (p. 43), 85% with fewer than 100 employees (p. 44), with significant cooperation via cross-licensing and second-sourcing. The ecosystem was further characterized by a localized, relatively tight integration and involvement of service providers (e.g., lawyers and market research firms), universities (e.g., Stanford), and government. Organizations such as business associations facilitated connections with government and provided services to assist the management of small firms, and similar organizations helped develop standards that prevented duplication and waste.

Route 128
In contrast, the Route 128 area around Boston in the early 1980s consisted of minicomputer companies that watched customers shift to workstations and PCs. Route 128 inherited *autarkic* (i.e., self-sufficient and not relying on others) practices and structures (e.g., secrecy and territoriality) that kept enterprises stuck as autonomous entities, with few interdependencies. These practices and structures provided advantages of scale and stability at the expense of adaptability and responsiveness. The environment was replete with Puritan traditions, a strong work ethic, a high value on privacy, ties to families, and communities—with a strict separation between work and social life. Technology leaders did not develop public profiles or a sense of community, and did not encourage entrepreneurs: those who started firms had little previous work experience. The main career path was to move up the corporate ladder. Two of the key CEOs, Ken Olsen (DEC) and Edson DeCastro (ex-DEC, Data General founder), demanded loyalty to the company, resulting in low staff turnover. This was a collectivist society, with the collective being the firm.

Northeast venture capitalists were bankers and financiers first and foremost; it was rare for one to have operating experience in the technology industry. The widespread involvement of companies in military procurement contracts enhanced autarky, separation, and insularity, and led to vertical integration versus supplier relationships. The matrix structure instituted in many Route 128 firms masked a centralization of decision-making and control. There were significant status differences and a strong hierarchy inherent in these companies, with equity and perks (such as covered parking spaces) reserved for top executives.

Implications

Comparing track records, Route 128 had over 2.5 times the electronics and semiconductor employment of Silicon Valley in 1959. By 1970, Silicon Valley had 1.5 times the employment of Route 128, and by 1980, Silicon Valley had 3.5 times the employment (p. 79). Saxenian suggests that the identified factors were main contributors to this difference in growth, with the implication that more detailed analysis of geographical context can lead to an understanding of the complex web that affects innovation environments.

GAUTAM AHUJA
"Collaboration Networks, Structural Holes, and Innovation: A Longitudinal Study" (2000), *Administrative Sciences Quarterly*.

Thesis: Structural holes, direct ties, and indirect ties can each affect a firm's innovative output, but the context determines the nature of the effect.

The goal of Ahuja's empirical longitudinal study is to assess the effects of a firm's network of relations (structure) on innovation output. The focus is not on the network, per se, but on the "ego nodes" and on an ego network analysis of the effect of direct ties, indirect ties, and structural holes on innovative output. Using patents in the international chemical industry as a measurement, Ahuja focuses on the horizontal technical linkages among firms in this industry.

Network relationships can be seen as network resources. Densely embedded (closed) networks can help the focal actor; while open networks provide brokerage opportunities to help (Burt 2000). The value derived by the actor depends on specific benefits provided by direct versus indirect ties in terms of magnitude and content; the type of tie may matter. Examination of the relationships between network positions and innovation output can elucidate the role of different elements of network structure and indicate the effectiveness of knowledge flows. This approach is different from that of studies of innovation adoption or diffusion.

Ahuja hypothesizes that direct and indirect ties both have a positive impact on innovation, but that the impact of indirect ties is moderated by the number of direct ties. Structural holes (gaps in networks) may have both positive and negative influences on innovation.

The number of direct ties can affect a firm's innovation output positively due to knowledge sharing, complementarity, and scale. Ties lead to knowledge spillovers through inter-firm exchange processes, which can be significant due to the information gathering and screening aspects of the network. For firms with many direct ties, the information also reaches competitors via partners. Structural holes permit brokerage (a form of power) and maximize information availability, but a dense network is better for sharing resources, curbing opportunism, and developing efficient and effective knowledge-sharing routines.

A firm must consider three factors when evaluating its balance of indirect and direct ties.

- Direct and indirect ties are not substitutes for each other.
- The magnitude of indirect-tie benefits may be much smaller. Both types of ties are resources for getting information, but many indirect ties are also competitors for using the information via the common partner.
- The interaction of direct and indirect ties is negative.

Whether direct or indirect ties are better depends on the context, nature and content, type of outcome, and broader network structure. When increasing trust and reducing opportunism matter more than diverse information (e.g., in joint research), structural holes may not be helpful. Unfortunately, Ahuja concludes, there is no simple answer.

OLAV SORENSON and TOBY STUART
"Syndication Networks and the Spatial Distribution of Venture Capital Investments" (2001), *American Journal of Sociology*.

Thesis: The likelihood of a venture capitalist's investment in a new venture declines sharply with the physical and industry distance between the investor and the target.

Sorenson and Stuart's article is an empirical study of how inter-firm networks in the U.S. venture capital (VC) market affect spatial patterns of exchange. Their central argument is that the distance from the investment target matters in VC investing: relationships with other VCs and VC-specific factors influence the effect of distance in their investments. The authors demonstrate the prevalence of localized exchange by showing that the likelihood of a venture capitalist's investment in a new venture declines sharply with the physical and industry distance between the VC and the target. Social networks in the VC community, built through the industry's extensive use of syndicated investing, diffuse information across borders and therefore expand the spatial radius of exchange.

The probability of forming a relationship declines with physical and social distance, as distance decreases the chances of random interactions. The VC community aligns with the movement of capital for at least two reasons.

- Investors must be aware of investment opportunities before they capitalize on them. Many young, private ventures lack public exposure, and personal and professional relationships provide one of the primary vehicles for information dissemination.

- Investors carefully investigate the quality of opportunities before they determine whether to support them or not.

Both information and trust require social interaction. The relatively more modest flow of information across geographic and industrial spaces deters distant investments. Yet, inter-firm relationships in the VC community effectively reduce the spatial limitations on the flow of information.

Discussion and Implications:

The articles summarized in this section demonstrate (a) the need for greater interaction between theoretical and empirical literature, and (b) the need for managers to understand the nature of analyses related to inter-firm differences (vs. industry differences) in innovative activity and performance. The nature of network relationships in access to knowledge, as discussed in Ahuja, ties into Cohen and Levinthal's analysis of R&D which suggests that firms are sensitive to the characteristics of the learning environment in which they operate.

Absorptive capacity based on prior knowledge appears to be part of a firm's decision calculus in allocating resources or innovating activity. It is easier to invest resources in innovative projects related to things one knows about (based on one's past) than in projects that are unrelated to experience. Knowledge is sticky, and the concept of intellectual capital is based on the idea that the costs of mastering specialized bodies of knowledge play a central role in delimiting the boundary of the firm, as there are certain things that people will only do within the boundaries of a company.

A person possesses intellectual capital if she holds a specialized body of knowledge that enables her to earn extraordinary returns on the cost of obtaining knowledge (as related to Zucker, Darby, and Brewer). Scientific discoveries vary in the degree to which others can be excluded from making use of them, so that every discovery has a degree of "natural excludability." To really understand the diffusion and commercialization of a scientific breakthrough, it is essential to focus on the scientific elite and the forces shaping their behavior. The method of protecting intellectual property (as described in Levin, Klevorick, Nelson, and Winter) must be consistent with the industry and the ability for patents, secrecy, and other means to protect it.

The discussion in Teece and in Gans and Stern regarding the ownership of complementary assets is nicely reflected in the various books about who really invented television. The story is that Philo T. Farnsworth invented television, but RCA owned the complementary asset: the transmission towers necessary for signal transmission, which RCA owned for radio. As a result, RCA kept Mr. Farnsworth from commercializing his invention by controlling the asset he needed, while simultaneously attempting to develop the television for itself.

Saxenian's book underscores the role that context and culture play in the development of industries and agglomeration zones. Although social and cultural issues certainly led to the success of Silicon Valley versus Route 128, the difference in roles taken by universities was underplayed in the book but was nonetheless important. Additionally, policy issues (e.g., California's law restricting restraint of trade) had an effect on spillovers—maybe more so than the "cultural" issues.

Sorenson and Stuart also address the issue of location. In national investment, location matters as proximity permits communication and the development of trust. Both Eric and Joe have seen this significance directly: Eric via his involvement with the venture capital industry in Silicon Valley, and Joe through his work with VC-backed ventures in the Route 128 area. Surprisingly, by the mid-1990s, Silicon Valley Bank was a major investor in Route 128-based ventures, one of which was Tessera Enterprise Systems (at which Joe was an executive). But how does one explain cross-border investment, which is increasingly common? Do networks of venture capitalists that cross borders exhibit similar needs for communication and trust, or does technology mitigate that need?

Other research in this area includes, in chronological order:

- **Gilbert and Newbery (1982).** If dominant firms emerge in an industry, they are likely to last forever. R&D is likely to be increasingly performed by the monopolist, subsequently with a limited role for entrepreneurs or new entrants.

- **Reinganum (1983).** In this economic model, an incumbent firm and an entrant engage in a game of innovation under stochastic (non-determined) conditions. Entrants stimulate progress both through their own innovative behavior and through their provocation of incumbent firms. In equilibrium, they contribute a disproportionate share of important innovations. Reinganum's model suggests that, under uncertainty, a new entrant will invest more in new technology than will an incumbent. Incumbents will invest more under deterministic conditions. Reinganum concludes that the degree of cost reduction and the degree of uncertainty are related; more-drastic innovations tend to be more uncertain. Certainty models are more appropriate for incremental innovations. However, there are cases when the innovation is not drastic, but the incumbent will still invest less than the challenger.

- **Acs and Audretsch (1988).** The authors examine the conditions (industry differences) under which small and large firms are more innovative (i.e., produce new products). Innovations are negatively related to industry concentration and unionization, and positively related with R&D, skilled labor, and the degree to which large firms comprise the markets.

- **Acs and Audretsch (1993).** Small entrepreneurial firms play a key role in generating innovations. These findings are not constant across industries, but depend upon market-structure characteristics (e.g., scale economies), concentration, and firm size distribution.

- **Henderson and Cockburn (1994).** Both the ability of firms to integrate knowledge and the allocation of research resources in a collaborative manner have positive impacts on research productivity. Moving beyond the broad "firm fixed effect" (i.e., idiosyncratic firm factors) as the source of variance in pharmaceutical research productivity across firms, the authors analyzed research competence as a source of competitive advantage. They distinguished component capability and architectural capability as two broad classes, finding that architectural competence (the ability to integrate knowledge) and the allocation of key research resources through collaborative (rather than dictatorial) processes positively relate to research productivity.

- **Audretsch and Feldman (1996).** Even after controlling for the degree of geographic concentration in production, innovative activities cluster more in industries where knowledge spillovers play a decisive role (e.g., industries with higher R&D intensity). Resource-dependent industries also tend to be more geographically concentrated.

4. INSTITUTIONS AND INNOVATION: THE ROLE OF THE GOVERNMENT IN INNOVATION AND UNIVERSITY–INDUSTRY INTERACTIONS

What role does—or should—government play in developing an environment for innovation? Is it possible to develop, from scratch, an innovation-oriented culture? Consider that Jamaica and Singapore became independent countries in 1962 and 1965 respectively. In 1965, the GDP per capita of the two countries were very similar (Jamaica at $2,850 and Singapore at $2,650). Forty years later, in 2006, their respective GDPs per capita were $4,800 and $31,400 (Lerner 2009, p. 18). How was this possible?

Governments can help to create an environment conducive to innovation, entrepreneurship, and economic growth. In Singapore, the government offered support for entrepreneurship through the provision of public funds for venture investors seeking to locate in the city-state, subsidies for firms in targeted technologies, the encouragement of potential entrepreneurs and mentoring for fledgling ventures, subsidies for leading biotech researchers to move their labs to Singapore, and awards for failed entrepreneurs (with the hope of encouraging risk-taking). Conversely, the Jamaican government is essentially unsupportive: the World Bank's Ease of Doing Business survey of 178 countries studied ranked Jamaica 170th in burden of complying with tax regulations (Singapore was 2nd) and 108th in cost of registering property (13.5% vs. 0.5% in the United States; Lerner 2009, p. 19). Jamaican entrepreneurs may not be able to grow their ventures.

This final section presents four works that examine the role of macro-level institutions in innovative activities. Nelson (1993) presents a cross-country study of similarities and differences in innovation systems. Furman, Porter, and Stern (2002) delve into the specific nature of national innovative capacity and the ways that countries profit from innovation. Finkelstein (2003) analyzes how specific economic incentives influence technological progress in a particular industry. The final reading, a recent book by Hwang and Horowitt (2012), presents a view of innovation as a complex, interrelated system with limited geographic boundaries.

RICHARD R. NELSON
National Innovation Systems (1993).

Thesis: Countries have significant similarities and differences in their systems of innovation, with implications for national policy.

Nelson's book describes, compares, and illuminates similarities and differences across countries in innovation systems. His objectives are twofold:

- to broaden the debate from single-country analyses or dual-country comparisons into an exploration of high-technology industries in terms of national policy and relevance, and
- to explore whether it is still appropriate to analyze innovation policy at the country level, or better to analyze at the policy level.

The book is framed by Nelson's definition of *innovation* as
the processes by which firms master and get into practice product designs and manufacturing processes that are new to them, if not to the universe or even to the nation. (p. 4)

A *system* is the

> set of institutions whose interactions determine the innovative
> performance…of national firms…[T]he 'system' concept is that of a set
> of institutional actors that, together, plays the major role in influencing
> innovative performance. (p. 4)

Science and technology are intertwined. R&D facilities are the principal vehicles through which technological advance proceeds, regardless of how strongly various fields of science support the advance. A simplified view is that science leads to technology, although there is much evidence that in fact technology leads to science: the steam engine led to the science of thermodynamics, the chemical industry led to the advance of chemical engineering, and the need to scale production led to "process science."

Thus, the intertwining of science and technology is a principal reason why universities and corporate laboratories are essential to innovation systems. True invention is rare, and much innovation is incremental improvements via experimentation and trial and error.

Various institutions are involved in the research and technology development arena. The major institutional actors in many countries are industrial research laboratories (IRLs), which represent the dominant locus of R&D and spawn innovation for many fields, due to the IRL's closeness to the value chain and profit. These are followed by research universities, which are a source of trained scientists and engineers, research findings, and experimental techniques. Reliance on universities, IRLs, and government laboratories varies by country, as does the use of public monies to help the development of industrial technologies (this is the "public interest" argument, whereby tax revenues are invested in research for the public good). Other significant entities are schools and training institutes, labor and management institutions, financial institutions, and firm governance regulators. In addition, component producers take active roles, including component innovations and process equipment innovations; these roles vary by industry.

The key interactions and networks are not the same in all industries or technologies; however, technological advance in all fields proceeds via the work of a community of actors. To what extent are there "national" communities, and how do they differ? While the "U.S. model" was dominant post-WWII, it was different in the United States (vs. the rest of the world) due to firm size differences, the relative strength of the university system, domestic ownership, and market factors. The European Union and Japan represent emerging models, with the former being less "national," and the latter exemplifying the value of an explicit national technology program (at the time of publication in 1993). In recent years, technological communities have become transnational due, in part, to the convergence of education and living standards. The internationalization of business and technology erodes the extent to which national borders define boundaries that are meaningful in analyzing technological capabilities and technical advance.

Nelson grouped countries by income for a first-cut analysis: large high-income countries (U.S., Japan, Germany, Britain, France, Italy), smaller high-income countries (Denmark, Sweden, Canada, Australia), and lower-income countries (Korea, Taiwan, Brazil, Argentina, Israel). Analyses showed strong intra-group similarities and inter-group differences. In all countries, the bulk of education is conducted in public institutions, and the government is presumed to have the majority of the responsibility for funding basic research.

Underlying country differences in innovation systems include differences in economic and political circumstances and priorities.

- Size and affluence matter, and affect comparative advantage at a basic level.
- The abundance of natural resources shapes innovation systems, as without resources there is a focus on imports, which forces economies toward export-oriented manufacturing and an innovation system that supports it.
- National security concerns also shape innovation systems, such that in high-income countries, defense R&D accounts for the majority of the difference among countries in government funding of industrial R&D. Industries from which the military procures are R&D intensive.

In all countries in the sample, firms are expected to fend for themselves in competitive markets, but beliefs regarding the role of government in shaping industrial policy differ by country. The institutionalization implied by these beliefs suggests continuity in a nation's innovation system.

Nelson also articulates a set of common characteristics for effective innovation performance. "Innovation" in this study basically stands for what is required of firms if they are to stay competitive in industries where technological advance is important.

- Firms in the industry were highly competent in what mattered to be competitive in that line of business, suggesting that the bulk of the effort in innovation needs to be done by the firms themselves.
- Being strong did not mean that firms were large, nor did it imply that firms were not benefitting from publicly funded R&D or favored procurement status. Becoming strong involved actually being exposed to strong competition and being forced to compete and address the needs of a demanding home market.
- Firms in industries where a country is strong have strong interactive linkages with suppliers.
- Strong firms arise "spontaneously" and arise as a result of education and training systems (industry requires literate, numerate people, not just scientists and engineers), strong research at university or public laboratories (the value of which varies by field), and a package of fiscal, monetary, and trade policies. The policies targeting technological advance do not lend

themselves to strong generalizations, as illustrated by the value of "infant industry" protection policies that varies greatly (there is an interesting little debate about this on p. 515).

Finally, a focus on technology as the means to enhance advantage to national economies is not strongly supported empirically.

 JEFFREY FURMAN, MICHAEL PORTER, and SCOTT STERN
"The Determinants of National Innovative Capacity" (2002), *Research Policy.*

Thesis: *National innovative capacity* is the ability of a country to make and profit from a flow of new technology over the long term. R&D inputs have a significant impact on the level of this capacity for each country.

 Furman, Porter, and Stern introduce the concept of national innovative capacity to integrate previous perspectives on the country-specific sources of differences of the intensity of innovation and R&D productivity. In this article, the empirical model used to examine these differences is derived from a relationship between the production of international patents and observable contributors to national innovative capacity. The study employs a novel dataset of patenting activity and its determinants in a sample of 17 Organization for Economic Cooperation and Development (OECD) countries from 1973 to 1996.

National innovative capacity is the ability of a country to produce and commercialize a flow of innovative technology over the long term. The national innovative capacity framework seeks to integrate three perspectives regarding the sources of innovations:

- idea-driven growth theory,
- microeconomics-based models of national competitive advantage and industrial clusters, and
- research on national innovation systems.

Whereas idea-driven growth and cluster theory focus on the economic impact of the geography, the national innovation systems literature focuses more on the political implications of geography.

In their analysis of the determinants of national innovative capacity, Furman et al. begin by categorizing them into three classes:

- the common pool of institutions, resource commitments, and policies that support innovation across the economy;

- the particular innovation environment in the nation's industrial clusters; and
- the linkages between them.

The results suggest that the level of R&D inputs is a critical determinant of the variation across countries in the level of innovation intensity. Factors associated with differences in R&D productivity (e.g., policy choice) also played an extremely important role. Further, national innovative capacity influences downstream commercialization (i.e., high market share of high-tech export markets).

AMY FINKELSTEIN
"Health Policy and Technological Change: Evidence from the Vaccine Industry" (2003), NBER Working Paper.

Thesis: Economic incentives influence technological progress. Supply-side oriented policies to increase the return on investing in vaccine development do, in fact, increase that activity. Demand-side policies have a lesser impact.

Finkelstein's article provides empirical evidence of the consequence of policy on the development of technology relevant to the fields of health economics and the economics of technological change. The author examines the investment response to policies that increase the demand-side incentive by focusing on the vaccine subsector of the pharmaceutical industry, to investigate the theory that if technological progress is influenced by economic incentives, then society can affect change through targeted policy. The focus on the role of demand-side factors reflects the fact that demand-side incentives induce innovations more so than do traditional supply-side subsidies.

Finkelstein identified policy changes in the vaccine sector and set selection criteria to isolate the changes from trends affecting R&D, such as the state of science., She then identified policies related to enlarging the market or reducing product liability expenses, examined variables that reflect expenditure decisions (pre-clinical trial, clinical trial, patent application, and patent approval).

The study examines whether medical investment responds to demand-side incentives in health policy and, if so, which margins of the process of R&D appear responsive to the incentives and what is the magnitude of their response. The results show that investment in vaccine development responds to policies that increase the return on such investment: the number of new clinical trials per year increases, as does the number of newly approved vaccines. However, there is no effect on new pre-clinical trial and new patent filings which represent novel development efforts, as opposed to research already in the pipeline.

These results point to limits in the ability of demand-side incentives to induce technology change. Induced investment seems to affect the commercialization of existing technologies but not the creation of new technologies. Fundamental development efforts (as measured by new pre-clinical trials and the filing of successful patent applications) are not directly influenced by demand-side incentives.

 VICTOR W. HWANG and GREG HOROWITT
The Rainforest: The Secret to Building the Next Silicon Valley (2012).

Thesis: Innovation requires a complex system of individuals, social behaviors, capital, and policies.

 Hwang and Horowitt's book is about the nature of innovation, or more precisely, the nature of complex systems of innovation and how they can be built. The approach is a foil to neoclassical economics, as the authors note that the ingredients of economic production are less important than the recipe for their integration.

While people are designed to trust those closer to them, more economic value is created via transactions between people most different. While such transactions have higher cost, social behaviors in Silicon Valley, for example, overcome these transaction costs, facilitating the free flow of talent, ideas, and capital. Key elements are diversity of talent, trust across social barriers, motivations that rise above short-term rationality, and social norms to promote rapid "promiscuous" collaboration and experimentation. Schumpeterian creative destruction is not sufficient; creative reassembly is far more important.

Hwang and Horowitt begin by comparing San Diego and Chicago: both large, vibrant cities with universities, similar legal and regulatory environments, infrastructure, expertise, and capital. The former became a successful center of innovation, whereas the latter did not. The explanation lies in the manner in which these ingredients were put together. The authors define a *Rainforest* as "a human ecosystem in which human creativity, business acumen, scientific discovery, investment capital, and other elements come together in a special recipe that matures budding ideas so they can grow into flourishing and sustainable enterprises" (p. 22).

People are key in the Rainforest, but the development of people via education and science does not directly lead to business starts and development: regions are not necessarily getting back what they are putting in. Hwang and

Horowitt note the inadequacy of cluster theory (Porter 1998) to improve the situation, suggesting that defining a cluster is a description of a phenomenon, not a prescription for policy. Therefore, the development of clusters and agglomeration zones may not have the intended effect on growth, requiring a deeper look at the drivers of innovation and growth in the context of 21st century communication technology.

What economic activity is *not* happening because of geographic and cultural distance and lack of trust, and how can social institutions help people overcome these barriers? Much of the authors' discussion is based on the nature of the critical agents in a Rainforest, specifically *keystone people* who are integrative, influential, and impactful. Rainforests also need entrepreneurs who are not risk-taking (but rather opportunity seeking, considering the odds of success), information integrators and non-linear thinkers, and students of real-life who can learn from a variety of non-academic situations. The science of innovation is undergoing a development that can help better understand the antecedents of innovation as prescriptions, rather than descriptions that may only apply in certain contexts.

Hwang and Horowitt propose a series of axioms for Rainforests (p. 103):

1. While plants are harvested most efficiently on farms, weeds sprout best in Rainforests.
2. Rainforests are built from the bottom up, where irrational economic behavior reigns.
3. What people typically think of as free markets are actually not that free.
4. Social barriers—caused by geography, networks, culture, language, and distrust—create transaction costs that stifle valuable relationships before they can be born.
5. The vibrancy of a Rainforest correlates to the number of people in a network and their ability to connect with one another.
6. High social barriers outside of close circles of family and friends are normal in the world.
7. Rainforests depend on people who actively bridge social distances and connect disparate parties together.
8. People in Rainforests are motivated for reasons that defy traditional economic notions of "rational" behavior.
9. Innovation and human emotions are intertwined.
10. The greater the diversity in human speculation, the greater the potential value of exchange in a system.
11. The instincts that once helped human ancestors survive are hurting people's ability to maximize innovation today.
12. Rainforests have replaced tribalism with a culture of informal rules that allow strangers to work together efficiently on temporary projects.
13. The informal rules that govern Rainforests cause people to constrain their short-term self-interest for long-term mutual gain.

14. Rainforests function when the combined value of social norms and extra-rational motivations outweigh the human instincts to fear.

Rainforests thrive because of normative culture that accelerates the evolution of human organizations into ever-increasing patterns of efficiency.

Discussion and Implications:

 Nelson's landmark study of innovation systems broadly examines country innovation systems while observing that the country level may not be the best setting for such an examination. The role of science is key, but much scientific discovery requires long-term investments that are traditionally the province of governments. With the growth of multinationals with sufficient resources for R&D activities, there is a shift from government to internationally-based industrial research laboratories. We believe that this shift, coupled with the greater globalization of business evidenced by organizations such as the WTO, may erode the extent to which national borders define meaningful boundaries associated with innovation.

We wonder, however, what conclusions might have been drawn if a different set of 15 countries was selected. China was not in the study, but has seen tremendous growth in scientific publications. We also note that Japan was in its ascendance at the time—would the study have the same conclusions now? What is the shelf-life of this type of study? The emergence of China as an economic force, along with the increasing strength of other emerging economies, reminds us that innovation is not solely the province of developed economies with strong academic institutions. Repatriated, U.S.-educated engineers and scientists are promoting significant scientific and technological advancement in Asia, Africa, and South America. Along with the development of global managers that Joe observes at a French business school, the prospects for scientific discovery worldwide are growing.

Furman, Porter, and Stern focus on the innovative capacity of nations as measured by the ability to produce and commercialize a flow of innovative technology over the long term. There is convergence among OECD countries[10] in terms of their estimated level of innovative capacity. Yet we wonder whether this convergence results in a group of "haves" (the OECD countries) and the "have-nots" (e.g., emerging economies)? Does this convergence of capacity lead to less geographical concentration of the commercial exploitation of

---

[10] Countries belonging to the Organization for Economic Cooperation and Development as of this writing: Australia, Austria, Belgium, Canada, Chile, Czech Republic, Denmark, Estonia, Finland, France, Germany, Greece, Hungary, Iceland, Ireland, Israel, Italy, Japan, Korea, Luxembourg, Mexico, Netherlands, New Zealand, Norway, Poland, Portugal, Slovak Republic, Slovenia, Spain, Sweden, Switzerland, Turkey, United Kingdom, and the United States.

technological opportunities, in that more geographically-dispersed countries have the capacity to innovate? We also note that absent from this discussion is the question of whether emerging economies can build such capacity. The example of Singapore at the beginning of the chapter suggests that such innovative systems can be built—successfully!

Finally, the Rainforest book by Hwang and Horowitt provides an interesting and current counterpoint to the prior two readings. Nelson's idea that countries may not be the most relevant unit of analysis for innovation systems is supported in this book, which suggests that innovative Rainforest ecosystems can transcend localization. However, the idea that a viable startup company today is a multinational corporation from the day of its founding (see the discussion of international new ventures in Chapter 2, Section 5), drawing upon the right people with the right ideas, talent, and capital wherever they happen to be located, may be true in some industries for some types of companies, but this is a small subset of innovators. Innovation happens in many industries, technologies, and commodities, both emerging and mature. Disruptive innovations may be more global in nature; incremental innovations in cottage industries may not be global. The geographic unboundedness suggested by the Rainforest model has implications for government sovereignty, international taxation and regulatory organizations, and multinationals. The Rainforest model uses different mechanisms (i.e., rather than spillovers) for distribution of knowledge, market, and adoption of technology. While some research indicates that trust and proximity are what drive innovation (note Saxenian's 1994 book), there is a lot about routines that can enhance or inhibit the flow of new ideas.

The importance of location and country culture was underscored to Eric while listening to a panel of venture investors and entrepreneurs discuss building innovation hubs outside of Silicon Valley in Shanghai. One panelist noted the critical importance of national culture. In Finland, he said, if you start a company and build something and fail, you are branded a failure and likely to lose your status and friends. If you start a company and build something and succeed, you are branded as pretentious and likely to lose your friends.[11] Putting a university next to sources of venture capital in such an environment is unlikely to result in innovation until that element of national culture is modified.

Other useful sources in this discussion of institutions and innovation include the following.

- **Cohen and Noll (1991).** The authors investigate the factors leading to a successful commercial R&D program, concluding that long-term, risky government investments are inherently problematic. This conclusion argues for favoring generic research activities rather than large-scale

---

[11] Affinity Conference, Kauffman Fellows Program, 26 October 2011, Shanghai, China.

commercialization programs. A government's focus of responsibility can enhance the success of both types of activities.

- **Owen-Smith, Riccaboni, Pammolli, and Powell (2002).** The authors study cross-national differences in the organization of innovative labor in the life sciences, examining the structure and evolution of networks involving public research organizations, science-based biotechnology firms, and multinational pharmaceutical corporations. They find that innovative research in biomedicine has its origins in regional clusters in the United States and in European nations, but that the composition of these regions varies in consequential ways.

FURTHER READING

If you're interested in reading more on the topics discussed in this chapter, here are some sources to get you started. We do not offer this as a comprehensive or exhaustive list, but rather have selected well-regarded or significant works that space did not permit us to include in the main discussion.

1. ISSUES IN TECHNOLOGY AND STRATEGY

Barley, Stephen R. and Beth A. Bechky. 1994. "In the Backrooms of Science: The Work of Technicians in Science Labs." *Work and Occupations* 21(1), 85–126.

Bechky, Beth A. 2003. "Sharing Meaning Across Occupational Communities: The Transformation of Knowledge on a Production Floor." *Organization Science* 14(3), 312–330.

Jaffe, Adam B. 1986 "Technological Opportunity and Spillovers of R&D: Evidence from Firms' Patents, Profits, and Market Value." *American Economic Review* 76(5), 984–1001.

Kline, Stephen J. and Nathan Rosenberg. 2000. "An Overview of Innovation." In C. Edquist and M. McKelvey (editors), *Systems of Innovation: Growth, Competitiveness and Employment*, vol. 2. Cheltenham, UK, Edward Elgar Publishers. pp. 1–33.

Scherer, F. M. 1965. "Firm Size, Market Structure, Opportunity, and the Output of Patented Inventions." *American Economic Review* 55(5), 1097–1125.

Schmookler, Jacob. 1966. *Invention and Economic Growth*. Cambridge, Harvard University Press.

Watson, James, D. 1968. *The Double Helix*. New York, Atheneum.

2. Patterns of Technological Innovation, Technology Trajectories and Industry Lifecycles

Abernathy, William J. and Kim Clark. 1985. "Innovation: Mapping the Winds of Creative Destruction." *Research Policy* 14(1), 3–22.

Mansfield, Edwin. 1968. *Industrial Research and Technological Innovation.* New York, Norton.

Mokyr, Joel. 2002. *The Gifts of Athena.* Princeton, Princeton University Press.

Nelson, Richard R. 1995. "Recent Evolutionary Theorizing about Economic Change." *Journal of Economic Literature* 33(1), 48–90.

Rogers, Everett. 1995. *Diffusion of Innovations,* 5th edition. New York, Free Press.

3. Technology Competition

Allen, Thomas J. 1977. *Managing the Flow of Technology.* Cambridge, MIT Press.

Argyres, Nicolas. 1995. "Technology Strategy, Governance Structure and Interdivisional Coordination." *Journal of Economic Behavior and Organization* 28(3), 337–358.

Burgelman, Robert A. 1994. "Fading Memories: A Process Theory of Strategic Business Exit in Dynamic Environments." *Administrative Science Quarterly* 39(1), 24–56.

Cohen, Wesley M. and Daniel A. Levinthal. 1989. "Innovation and Learning: The Two Faces of R&D." *Economic Journal* 99(3), 569–596.

Freeman, Christopher. 1991. "Networks of Innovators: A Synthesis of Research Issues." *Research Policy* 20(5), 499–514.

Griliches, Zvi. 1992. "The Search for R&D Spillovers." *The Scandinavian Journal of Economics* 94(Supplement), 29–47.

Hsu, David, Joshua Gans, and Scott Stern. 2002. "When Does Start-Up Innovation Spur the Gale of Creative Destruction?" *RAND Journal of Economics* 33(4), 571–586.

Jaffe, Adam B. 1989. "Real Effects of Academic Research." *American Economic Review* 79(5), 957–970.

Katz, Michael. 1987. "R&D Rivalry with Licensing or Imitation." *American Economic Review* 77(3), 402–420.

Klevorick, Alvin K., Richard C. Levin, Richard R. Nelson, and Sidney G. Winter. 1995. "On the Sources and Significance of Interindustry Differences in Technological Opportunities." *Research Policy* 24(2), 185–205.

Levin, Richard C., Wesley M. Cohen, and David C. Mowery. 1985. "R&D Appropriability, Opportunity, and Market Structure: New Evidence on Some Schumpeterian Hypotheses." *American Economic Review* 75(2), 20–24.

Mowery, David C. and Nathan Rosenberg. 1979. "The Influence of Market Demand Upon Innovation: A Critical Review of Some Empirical Studies." *Research Policy* 8(2), 102–153.

4. INSTITUTIONS AND INNOVATION: THE ROLE OF THE GOVERNMENT IN INNOVATION AND UNIVERSITY/INDUSTRY INTERACTIONS

Furman, Jeffrey L. and Scott Stern. 2011. "Climbing Atop the Shoulders of Giants: The Impact of Institutions on Cumulative Research." *American Economic Review* 101(5), 1933–1963.

Henderson, Rebecca M., Adam B. Jaffe, and Manuel Trajtenberg. 1998. "Universities as a Source of Commercial Technology: A Detailed Analysis of University Patenting 1965–1988." *Review of Economics and Statistics* 80(1), 119–127.

Jaffe, Adam B. 2000. "The U.S. Patent System in Transition: Policy Innovation and the Innovation Process." *Research Policy* 29(2), 531–537.

Mowery, David, Richard R. Nelson, Bhaven Sampat, and Arvids Ziedonis. 2001. "The Growth of Patenting and Licensing by U.S. Universities: An Assessment of the Effects of the Bayh-Dole Act of 1980." *Research Policy* 30(1), 99–119.

Mowery, David C. and Nathan Rosenberg. 1979. "The Influence of Market Demand Upon Innovation: A Critical Review of Some Empirical Studies." *Research Policy* 8(2), 102–153.

Rosenberg, Nathan and Richard R. Nelson. 1994. "American Universities and Technical Advance in Industry." *Research Policy* 23(3), 323–348.

WORKS CITED

Abernathy, William J. and James M. Utterback. 1978. "Patterns of Industrial Innovation." *Technology Review* 80(7), 40–47.

Acs, Zoltan J. and David B. Audretsch. 1988. "Innovation in Large and Small Firms: An Empirical Analysis." *American Economic Review* 78(4), 678–690.

Acs, Zoltan J. and David B. Audretsch. 1993. "Innovation and Technological Change: The New Learning." In G. Libecap (editor), *Advances in the Study of Entrepreneurship, Innovation and Economic Growth*. Greenwich, CT, JAI Press. pp. 109–140.

Ahuja, Gautam. 2000. "Collaboration Networks, Structural Holes, and Innovation: A Longitudinal Study." *Administrative Science Quarterly* 45(3), 425–455.

Arrow, Kenneth. 1962. "Economic Welfare and the Allocation of Resources for Invention." In *The Rate and Direction of Inventive Activity: Economic and Social Factors*, National Bureau of Economic Research. Princeton, Princeton University Press. pp. 609–626.

Audretsch, David B. and Maryann P. Feldman. 1996. "R&D Spillovers and the Geography of Innovation and Production." *American Economic Review* 86(3), 630–640.

Burt, R. (2000). "The network structure of social capital." *Research in Organizational Behavior* 22, 345-423.

Christensen, Clayton. 1997. *The Innovator's Dilemma*. Cambridge, Harvard Business School Press.

Cockburn, Iain and Zvi Griliches. 1988. "Industry Effects and Appropriability Measures in the Stock Market's Valuation of R&D and Patents." *American Economic Review* 78(2), 419–423.

Cohen, Wesley M. and Daniel A. Levinthal. 1990. "Absorptive Capacity: A New Perspective on Learning and Innovation." *Administrative Science Quarterly* 35(1), 128–152.

Cohen, Linda R. and Roger G. Noll. 1991. Introduction and Conclusion. *The Technology Pork Barrel*. Washington, The Brookings Institution. pp. 1–16, 363–390.

David, Paul. 1985. "Clio and the Economics of QWERTY." *American Economic Review* 75(2), 332–337.

Finkelstein, Amy. 2003. "Health Policy and Technological Change: Evidence from the Vaccine Industry." NBER Working Paper 9460.

Florida, Richard. 2002. "Bohemia & Economic Geography." *Journal of Economic Geography* 2(1), 55–71.

Foster, Richard. 1986. "The S-curve: A New Forecasting Tool." In R. Foster, *Innovation: The Attacker's Advantage*. New York, Summit Books. Ch. 4.

Furman, Jeffrey L., Michael E. Porter, and Scott Stern. 2002. "The Determinants of National Innovative Capacity." *Research Policy* 31(6), 899–933.

Gans, Joshua and Scott Stern. 2003. "The Product Market and the Market for Ideas: Commercialization Strategies for Technology Entrepreneurs." *Research Policy* 32(2), 333–350.

Gilbert, Richard and David M. Newbery. 1982. "Preemptive Patenting and the Persistence of Monopoly." *American Economic Review* 72(3), 514–526.

Goldschmitdt, Richard. 1940. *The Material Basis of Evolution*. New Haven, Yale University Press.

Gort, Michael and Steven Klepper. 1982. "Time Paths in the Diffusion of Product Innovations." *Economic Journal* 92(367), 630–653.

Griliches, Zvi. 1957. "Hybrid Corn: An Exploration in the Economics of Technological Change." *Econometrica* 25(4), 501–522.

Griliches, Zvi. 1990 "Patent Statistics as Economic Indicators: A Survey." *Journal of Economic Literature* 28(4), 1661–1707.

Griliches, Zvi. 1998. "Issues in Assessing the Contribution of R&D to Productivity Growth." In E. Wolff (editor), *The Economics of Productivity*, vol. 1. Cheltenham, UK, Edward Elgar. pp. 256–280.

Henderson, Rebecca M. and Kim B. Clark. 1990. "Architectural Innovation: The Reconfiguration of Existing Product Technologies and the Failure of Established Firms." *Administrative Science Quarterly* 35(1), 9–30.

Henderson, Rebecca M. and Ian Cockburn. 1994. "Measuring Competence? Exploring Firm Effects in Pharmaceutical Research." *Strategic Management Journal* 15(Special Issue: Competitive Organizational Behavior), 63–84.

Hwang, Victor W. and Greg Horowitt. 2012. *The Rainforest: The Secret to Building the Next Silicon Valley*. Los Altos Hills, Regenwald.

Jaffe, Adam B., Manuel Trajtenberg, and Rebecca Henderson. 1993. "Geographic Localization of Knowledge Spillovers as Evidenced by Patent Citations." *Quarterly Journal of Economics* 108(3), 577–598.

Jovanovic, Boyan. 1982. "Selection and the Evolution of Industry." *Econometrica* 50(3), 649–670.

Jovanovic, Boyan and Glenn MacDonald. 1994. "Competitive Diffusion." *Journal of Political Economy* 102(1), 24–52.

Klepper, Steven. 1996. "Entry, Exit, Growth, and Innovation Over the Product Life Cycle." *American Economic Review* 86(3), 562–583.

Klepper, Steven and Elizabeth Graddy. 1990. "The Evolution of New Industries and the Determinants of Market Structure." *The RAND Journal of Economics* 21(1), 27–44.

Kogut, Bruce and Udo Zander. 1992. "Knowledge of the Firm, Combinative Capabilities, and the Replication of Technology." *Organization Science* 3(3), 383–397.

Lerner, Josh. 2009. *Boulevard of Broken Dreams: Why Public Efforts to Boost Entrepreneurship and Venture Capital Have Failed—and What to Do About It*. Princeton, Princeton University Press.

Levin, Richard C., Alvin K. Klevorick, Richard R. Nelson, and Sidney G. Winter. 1987. "Appropriating the Returns From Industrial Research and Development." *Brookings Papers on Economic Activity* 3(3), 783–831.

McGahan, Anita M. 2004. *How Industries Evolve*. Boston, Harvard Business School Press.

McGahan, Anita M., Leslie L. Vadasz, and David Yoffie. 1996. "Creating Value and Setting Standards: The Lessons of Consumer Electronics for Personal Digital Assistants." In D. Yoffie (editor), *Competing in the Age of Digital Convergence*. Boston, Harvard Business Review Press. pp. 227–264.

Milgrom, Paul and John Roberts. 1990. "The Efficiency of Equity in Organizational Decision Processes." *American Economic Review* 80(2), 154–159.

Mokyr, Joel. 1990. *The Lever of Riches: Technological Creativity and Economic Progress*. New York, Oxford University Press.

Nelson, Richard R. 1962. "The Link Between Science and Invention: The Case of the Transistor." In *The Rate and Direction of Inventive Activity: Economic and Social Factors*, National Bureau of Economic Research. Princeton, Princeton University Press. pp. 549–586.

Nelson, Richard R. 1993. *National Innovation Systems*. Oxford, Oxford University Press.

Nelson, Richard and Sidney Winter. 1978. "Forces Generating and Limiting Concentration under Schumpeterian Competition." *Bell Journal of Economics* 9(2), 524–548.

Nelson, Richard and Sidney Winter. 1982. *An Evolutionary Theory of Economic Change*. Cambridge, Harvard University Press.

Owen-Smith, Jason, Massimo Riccaboni, Fabio Pammolli, and Walter W. Powell. 2002. "A Comparison of U.S. and European University–Industry Relations in the Life Sciences." *Management Science* 1(48), 24–43.

Pavitt, Keith. 1990. "What We Know about the Strategic Management of Technology." *California Management Review* 32(3), 17–26.

Pfeffer, Jeffrey and Gerald R. Salancik. 1978. *The External Control of Organizations: A Resource Dependence Perspective*. New York, Harper & Row.

Porter, Michael E. 1980. *Competitive Strategy*. New York, Free Press.

Reinganum, Jeniffer F. 1983. "Uncertain Innovation and the Persistence of Monopoly." *American Economic Review* 73(4), 741–748.

Rosenbloom, Richard S. and Michael A. Cusumano. 1987. "Technological Pioneering and Competitive Advantage: The Birth of the VCR Industry." *California Management Review* 29(4), 51–76.

Ryan, Bryce and Neal C. Gross. 1943. "The Diffusion of Hybrid Seed Corn in Two Iowa Communities." *Rural Sociology* 8, 15–24.

Saxenian, AnnaLee. 1994. *Regional Advantage: Culture and Competition in Silicon Valley and Route 128*. Cambridge, Harvard University Press.

Schumpeter, Joseph. 1942. *Capitalism, Socialism and Democracy*, 2nd edition. London, George Allen & Unwin.

Solow, Robert M. 1957. "Technical Change and the Aggregate Production Function." *Review of Economics and Statistics* 39(3), 312–320.

Sorenson, Olav and Toby Stuart. 2001. "Syndication Networks and the Spatial Distribution of Venture Capital Investments." *American Journal of Sociology* 106(6), 1546–1588.

Stern, Scott. 2004. "Do Scientists Pay to Be Scientists?" *Management Science*, 50(6), 835–853.

Teece, David J. 1987. "Profiting From Technological Innovation: Implications for Integration, Collaboration, Licensing and Public Policy." In D. J. Teece (editor), *The Competitive Challenge: Strategies for Industrial Innovation and Renewal*. Cambridge, Ballinger. pp. 185–219.

Tushman, Michael L. and Philip Anderson. 1986. "Technological Discontinuities and Organizational Environments." *Administrative Science Quarterly* 31(3), 439–465.

Tushman, Michael L. and Lori Rosenkopf. 1992. "Organizational Determinants of Technological Change: Towards a Sociology of Technological Evolution." In B. M. Staw and L. L. Cummings (editors), *Research in Organizational Behavior*. Greenwich, JAI Press. pp. 311–347.

Urban, Glen L. and Eric von Hippel. 1988. "Lead User Analyses for the Development of New Industrial Products." *Management Science* 34(5), 569–582.

Utterback, James M. 1994. *Mastering the Dynamics of Innovation*. Boston, Harvard University Press.

Van de Ven, Andrew. 1986. "Central Problems in the Management of Innovation." *Management Science* 32(5), 590–607.

Von Hippel, Eric. 1988. *The Sources of Innovation*. New York, Oxford University Press.

Zucker, Lynne G., Michael R. Darby, and Marilynn B. Brewer. 1998. "Intellectual Human Capital and the Birth of U.S. Biotechnology Enterprises." *American Economic Review* 88(1), 290–306.

FINANCE

Finance is the study of how investors allocate assets over time under conditions of certainty and uncertainty, and typically examines the relationship between money, time, and risk. Only recently has finance been considered a field separate from economics. In this introduction, we outline the evolution of finance theory and literature from the inception of the field in the 1950s to the late 2000s, to provide context for and outline the literature reviewed in the chapter.

In the 1950s, Franco Modigliani and Merton Miller developed a pathbreaking series of four articles. The Modigliani and Miller theorem they established (Section 1) expresses that the value of a company is unaffected by how it is financed (if we assume that stock prices go up or down randomly, and that there are no taxes or bankruptcy costs).

Also in the 1950s, Harry Markowitz was one of the first to investigate the behavior of stock prices, and introduced the hypothesis that investors seek to maximize return while minimizing the risk of that return as measured by its variance. The capital asset pricing model (CAPM) was introduced in the mid-1960s by at least four separate authors, including Jack Treynor, William Sharpe, John Lintner, and Jan Mossin. The CAPM provides a price for any security or portfolio based solely on the riskless rate of interest, the expected return for the market, and a measure called *beta* calibrating how that security moves with the overall market. This model is part of the foundation of modern finance, though it depends on several assumptions whose validity was called into question over the following decades. The arbitrage pricing theory (APT) holds that returns and prices for an asset may depend on several factors, rather than just a single equity beta, and it arose as a competing theory; however, the APT is more complex to use and has been subjected to some of the same criticisms (Section 2).

By 1970, Eugene Fama had developed an integrated theory of market efficiency, defining a market as efficient if prices reflect available information

(Section 3). Much research followed, with results consistent with the semi-strong form of market efficiency whereby prices reflect all publicly available information. However, some research in the 1970s and 1980s identified recurring exceptions to semi-strong efficiency in the form of abnormal returns to low price-to-earnings stocks, small-firm stocks, and stocks held in the month of January. This research generated a lasting debate on whether these discrepancies reflect a problem with market efficiency or a problem with the asset pricing model used to estimate what a "normal" risk-adjusted return should be.

At roughly the same time, researchers made progress in the theory of the firm. Jensen and Meckling developed a model in which corporations are not single agents, but rather exist as a nexus of contracts between individuals with different levels of risk aversion and sometimes conflicting incentives (Section 4). In Section 5, we discuss work by other researchers exploring the implications of agents having different information sets. Leland and Pyle explored what credible signals corporate insiders can use to convey that they have high-quality investment prospects when they are seeking outside investment capital. Myers and Majluf demonstrated how asymmetric information can cause managers to pass up attractive investments, and can also create significant value for using cash or debt instead of equity to finance new investment opportunities.

Practical finance research examined how to get past the deficiencies of traditional accounting metrics in giving managers the data needed to make appropriate investment decisions. Two of the resulting systems, which generated a lot of popular attention in the 1990s, were the balanced scorecard (Kaplan and Norton, 1996) and economic value added (Stern, Stewart, and Chew, 1995), which are described in Section 6.

In the 1970s, psychologists Daniel Kahneman and Amos Tversky conducted a series of groundbreaking experiments demonstrating that people as economic agents are not only irrational, but also that many biases are consistent and so do not even cancel out in groups. In the 1980s their insights started to be applied to the finance arena (Section 7), creating an explosive growth in the field of behavioral finance and sparking an ongoing debate between those who believe in rational agents and market efficiency versus those who believe that people make investment (and other) decisions subject to cognitive biases and limited rationality. The rise and fall of the tech bubble in the late 1990s and the financial crisis in 2008 both provided a popular backlash against market efficiency.

Due to space constraints, this chapter's summary of finance by necessity omits several key elements of a literature that now has multiple subfields and strands, but we have included the elements we view as central to management practitioners. Many finance scholars use mathematical models and statistical regressions to develop their arguments; for readers who are not statistically fluent, focus on the thesis and discussion for these articles, and be assured that most of the contributions arrive at conclusions that all of us managers can appreciate.

1. Capital Structure

In the 1950s, Franco Modigliani and Merton Miller were faculty at the business school of Carnegie Mellon University, assigned to teach corporate finance for business students despite a lack of experience in the field. When they read the existing material, they found it so deficient that they were forced to develop consistent principles essentially from scratch. The article summarized here was part of the result.

FRANCO MODIGLIANI and MERTON MILLER
"The Cost of Capital, Corporate Finance and the Theory of Investment" (1958), *American Economic Review*.

Thesis: The value of a company is unaffected by how that firm is financed (in an efficient market absent taxes or bankruptcy costs).

The Modigliani-Miller *irrelevance theorem* states that the value of a company is unaffected by how that firm is financed, under the following assumptions:

- a random walk statistical process for stock market prices;
- no taxes, bankruptcy costs, agency costs, or asymmetric information; and
- an efficient market (i.e., a market in which one cannot earn consistent above-average returns based on available information).

That is, valuation is not impacted by the firm's choice to use debt or equity to raise capital, nor by the firm's dividend policy.

Consider two firms that are identical except for financial structures. Firm U is *unlevered* (i.e., financed solely by equity). Firm L is *levered* (i.e., financed in part by debt). The authors introduce two key propositions:

1. The value of the two firms will be the same; otherwise, an investor could purchase shares of the unlevered firm, borrow the same amount of money as the levered firm would borrow, and make a different return. This will force the returns and prices of the two firms to become equal, so long as (a) the investor has the same borrowing rate as the levered firm, (b) there are

no taxes, and (c) there are no transaction costs. This proposition is expressed as $V_U = V_L$.

2. The cost of (i.e., required rate of return on) equity equals the unlevered cost of equity, plus the debt-to-equity ratio times the difference between the cost of equity and the cost of debt. A higher debt-to-equity ratio must lead to a higher required return on equity, because of the higher risk involved for equity holders in a company with more senior debt holders. The formula $k_e = k_0 + (D/E)(k_0 - k_d)$ simply expresses the weighted average cost of capital.

V_U = value of unlevered firm
V_L = value of levered firm
D/E = debt-to-equity ratio
k_0 = unlevered cost of equity
k_d = cost of debt
k_e = cost of equity

Discussion and Implications

Modigliani and Miller's work says that, subject to some assumptions, when a company needs to raise money to pay for a project, it does not affect the value of the firm whether the money is raised by borrowing versus through issuing new shares of stock. If a firm is worth $100 and needs to raise $10 to pay for a more modern plant, it is the value of the project that should drive the company's worth. That is, investors should focus on how the new plant will change future profitability—not on whether the company borrows $10 or issues new shares of stock to raise $10.

Later, these authors and others adapted the propositions to account for taxes (see Modigliani and Miller 1963). Using debt to pay for projects enables tax-deductible interest payments to replace non-deductible dividend payments. The tax deductible interest payments will increase the value of the company by lowering taxes; this deductibility will cause companies to develop a preference for 100% debt.[1] Taken at first glance, this work can be used to justify essentially unlimited financial leverage, unless one introduces the offsetting consideration of the increased risk of financial distress. Later papers (e.g., Kraus and Litzenberger 1973) introduced the notion of bankruptcy costs that would lead a company to less than 100% debt, consistent with observed debt ratios which are neither zero nor 100%.

Other modifications of Modigliani and Miller's work include the following:

---

[1] Technically, when adding taxes to the framework, Modigliani and Miller are saying that $V_L = V_U + T_C D$ where $T_C D$ is the tax rate times the value of debt. The required rate of return on levered equity will equal the return on unlevered equity plus a financing premium: $r_e = r_0 + (D/E)(r_0 - r_d)(1 - T_C)$.

- **Miller (1977).** With a constant corporate tax rate, a quantity of debt is obtained that is optimal for the economy as a whole but not for any one specific firm.

- **DeAngelo and Masulis (1980).** The corporate tax rate is not constant. Firms that have fewer substitutes for debt will hold more debt.

- **Jensen and Meckling (1976).** Expect more debt for firms that are less susceptible (often because of debt covenants restricting their behavior) to ways in which stockholders can take advantage of bondholders *ex post*. An example would be for a company to issue newer debt to finance a large dividend; this represents a wealth transfer from debtholders directly to stockholders, which can be prevented with stringent covenants limiting how debt proceeds can be spent.

The irrelevance theorem itself is unarguably true based on the assumptions made, so its chief value is to force anyone who concludes that capital structure does impact valuation to explore how relaxing those assumptions leads to a different result. As corporate finance managers, we have received frequent sales pitches from investment banks telling us that changing the company's debt–equity structure will increase the value of our company. The Modigliani-Miller model has encouraged us to be skeptical, to start with an assumption that valuation is unlikely to be easily affected by financial engineering, and to probe what element of taxes and costs of financial distress or other factors might justify such a recommendation. The model does allow for capital structure to impact value, but only through a narrow set of factors, and we think that those should be a focus of such a discussion.

2. CAPITAL ASSET PRICING

Harry Markowitz (1952) introduced the hypothesis that investors seek to maximize return while minimizing risk. Sharpe (1964) was one of several authors to build on this idea to develop a formal model of how capital assets (usually stocks) are priced in the market. Later work (mentioned in this section but not summarized) offers alternative theories of asset pricing.

HARRY MARKOWITZ
"Portfolio Selection" (1952), *Journal of Finance.*

Thesis: Investor diversification can eliminate stock-specific risk so that only non-diversifiable market risk remains. Investment choice then becomes a matter of adding (a) a single riskless asset and (b) one combination of risky assets.

In this article, Markowitz investigates the behavior of stock prices. He rejects the idea that investors seek solely to maximize the presented, discounted value of returns—if this were true, everyone would hold the single stock with the highest expected return and diversified portfolios would not exist.

Rather, he introduces the hypothesis that investors seek to maximize return while minimizing the risk of that return as measured by its variance. Under this rule, investors diversify funds among all securities with maximum expected return. If this results in a portfolio of a sufficient number of independent securities, then the actual yield would be close to the expected yield, such that the variance would be close to zero; however, the correlation among securities means that diversification cannot eliminate all variance. This creates a tradeoff between maximizing expected return and minimizing variance.

If there are a large number of possible portfolios, investors will prefer the lowest variance for a fixed level of expected return, and will prefer the highest expected return for a fixed level of variance. This set of preferences reduces the investable set of all possible choices to a smaller set of *efficient* portfolios. How investors choose among this efficient set depends on their own risk–reward preference.

This model does reasonably well in predicting that investors will diversify in a manner similar to that actually observed. "Not only does the E-V [expected returns–variance of returns] hypothesis imply diversification, it implies the 'right kind' of diversification for the 'right reason'" (p. 89). Diversification across dissimilar industries will be preferred to simply buying an equal number of stocks in related industries. This model can be used both to predict investor behavior and to actually select portfolios.

WILLIAM F. SHARPE
"Capital Asset Prices: A Theory of Market Equilibrium Under Conditions of Risk" (1964), *Journal of Finance.*

Thesis: Given a riskless rate and the expected return for the market, the capital asset pricing model (CAPM) provides a price for any security, based solely on how sensitive that security's return is to the market return.

The market presents an investor with the price of time (interest rate) and price of risk (additional expected return per unit of risk borne). Some risk can certainly be avoided through diversification; Sharpe's article isolates the particular non-diversifiable component of risk that remains relevant. This model represents a market equilibrium theory of asset prices in the presence of risk.

Sharpe first derives the optimal investment policy for an individual, based on that investor's preference function, the investment–opportunity curve, and the pure rate of interest. An individual investor assesses possible investment results in terms of a probability distribution.

- **Preference.** The investor cares about two parameters: the expected value of the investment, and the standard deviation measuring the range of possible outcomes around that expected value. Investors prefer the highest expected value for a given standard deviation, and lowest deviation for any given level of expected value.

- **Investment opportunity.** From a set of opportunities, the investor chooses the one maximizing utility. A plan is *efficient* if (a) no alternative has the same expected return and lower deviation, and (b) no alternative has the same deviation and higher expected return. That is, from among the smaller set of efficient portfolios, the investor chooses the one maximizing utility based on her own tradeoff between risk and return.

- **Pure rate of interest.** The rate for a riskless asset (e.g., treasury bills) is considered the *pure interest rate*. All combinations of a risky set of assets plus the riskless asset form a plan (in Sharpe's mathematical representation, a line). The ability to lend or borrow at the pure rate allows the investor to choose any point on the line connecting (a) the combination of expected return (and a standard deviation of zero) for the riskless asset with (b) the combination for any risky set of assets.

Sharpe then turns to equilibrium in the capital market. Assuming that investors can borrow or lend at the riskless rate, and that all investors have the same expectations regarding the expected values and risk of potential investments, equilibrium can be derived. This equilibrium will cause prices to adjust until every asset is part of a combination on the capital market line. There will still be multiple alternative efficient combinations of risky assets.

Finally, having established a simple linear relationship between expected return and the standard deviation of that return for efficient asset combinations, the CAPM model can determine the prices of individual capital assets. Undiversified holdings can be improved upon to achieve lower risk for the same expected return. The type of risk that matters for prices is *systematic risk*: the component of risk that cannot be diversified away. The expected return of an asset, and therefore its price, will be directly related to the level of this systematic (undiversifiable) risk. "[O]nly the responsiveness of an asset's rate of return to the level of economic activity is relevant in assessing its risk. Prices will adjust until there is a linear relationship between the magnitude of such responsiveness and expected return" (pp. 441–442).

Discussion and Implications

 Diversifying across assets can lower the risk of an investment portfolio. That is, if you own a mix of 100 stocks, you are likely to experience lower percentage ups and downs than if you hold a single stock. Markowitz was the first to explicitly add risk to return as an investment consideration and his work made a lasting contribution. He developed this approach further in his follow-up 1959 book on portfolio selection. Markowitz's model implies that investment choices can be broken down into (a) determining the unique optimal combination of risky assets and (b) allocating funds between a single riskless asset and this particular combination of risky assets. His work also provided the foundation for the development of the capital asset pricing model (CAPM) in the 1960s. Below we discuss the evolution of the CAPM, its potential flaws, and some alternative theories of asset pricing that have been offered.

The CAPM was introduced independently by at least four authors, including Jack Treynor (1961, 1962), William Sharpe (1964), John Lintner (1965a, 1965b), and Jan Mossin (1966). Under certain assumptions, the CAPM provides a price for any security or portfolio based solely on the riskless rate, the expected return for the market, and the *beta*, which is a sensitivity measure capturing the percentage that the expected return varies for a 1% change in the return of the overall market portfolio.

As an example, if Apple stock on average moves four-fifths as much as the market moves, then the beta for Apple is 0.8. If the risk-free rate is 3%, and the expected return for a market portfolio is 6%, then the expected return for Apple is as follows:

$E(R_A)$ = expected return of security
R_f = risk-free rate of return
β_A = security's beta
$E(R_m)$ = expected market return

$$E(R_A) = R_f + \beta_A [E(R_m) - R_f]$$
$$= 3\% + 0.8 [6\% - 3\%] = 5.4\%$$

This formula states: the expected return for Apple is equal to the risk-free rate, plus the beta for Apple times the risk premium (which is itself the difference between the expected return for the market and the risk-free rate). If Apple is currently priced at $700 per share and pays no dividend, this model implies that investors expect the stock price to be $737.80 in one year.

The CAPM suggests that an asset is correctly priced when its estimated price is the same as the present value of future cash flows of the asset, discounted at the rate provided by the model. This model was a breakthrough, both in terms of explaining observed investor behavior (e.g., the tendency of investors to accept lower returns from assets which are relatively unresponsive to changes in the economy than from assets which move with the economy) as well as in providing a foundation to guide investor behavior. The model suggests that investors should diversify investments to reduce risk, and price an additional investment based on how its value moves with the value of the overall portfolio.

The model also allows easy estimation of a company's cost of equity, which can be combined with the known cost of debt to arrive at the firm's weighted average cost of capital. Corporate practitioners have thus been able to generate "hurdle rates" that their investments must out-earn in order to assure the firm provides a higher return to investors than they would expect in alternative uses of their capital. In the example above, Apple would not invest in new projects unless the annual return to those projects exceeded 5.4% (assuming the projects have the same level of systematic risk as the rest of the company).

The model also has provided the foundation for much of the following three decades of finance literature by providing the underpinning for the development of the efficient markets hypothesis. Markowitz and Sharpe shared the Nobel Prize in Economics with Merton Miller in 1990.

Despite the model's innovation and usefulness, the math depends on a number of assumptions whose validity was called into question over the following decades:

- Asset returns are assumed to have statistically normal distribution, but larger swings from the mean have been observed in financial markets than would be consistent with a normal distribution.

- Variance is assumed to be an appropriate risk measure, but other measures might better reflect what investors are concerned about, particularly if return distributions are not in fact normal. Some suggest that probability of loss is a better indication of financial risk, as it is asymmetric (having a higher-than-expected gain may not be a problem, but having a higher-than-expected loss is an issue).

- Investors' probability assessments are assumed to match the true distribution. If investor expectations are biased (as argued in later decades by behavioral economists), this assumption becomes invalid.

- The model assumes no taxes or transaction costs, though it can be modified to accommodate these real-world complications.

In addition to the limitations of these assumptions, scholars have pointed out other shortcomings.

- The observed variation in stock returns is not explained. For example, low-beta models appear to offer higher returns than the model would suggest (as initially pointed out by Black, Jensen, and Scholes in 1969).

- A true "market portfolio" should include all types of assets. Tests using CAPM typically use a stock index as the market portfolio, but any stock index is not the same as "all assets." This distinction may make the CAPM empirically untestable. Richard Roll (1977) contends that the CAPM is not really a valid theory since it cannot be refuted.

Stephen Ross (1976) attacked the simplicity of the CAPM, arguing that asset pricing has more than one dimension. Ross (1976) and Ross and Roll (1980) developed an alternative pricing model—arbitrage pricing theory (APT)—which models the expected return of an asset as a linear function of various macroeconomic factors, not just the equity beta (which shows how sensitive that stock's return is to market movements). In the APT, the sensitivity of the expected return to each factor is represented by a factor-specific beta coefficient.

As with the CAPM, this multi-factor model assumes that any divergent price will be brought back into line by arbitrage, but the APT is less restrictive in its assumptions. For example, it allows each investor to hold a unique portfolio rather than having all investors hold one market portfolio. The APT can be viewed as a supply-side model, since shocks to the macro factors will change expected returns on assets. The CAPM is more demand-side, focusing on the maximization of each investor's utility function and the resulting equilibrium in the market. Unlike the CAPM, the APT does not require the identification of the priced macro factors; these will simply be identified by examining the data to see which factors appear important, though they should still represent undiversifiable influences.

Chen, Roll, and Ross (1986) determined several factors within an APT model that appear to help explain security returns:

- surprises in inflation,
- unexpected GNP,
- surprises in investor confidence (from changes in the default premium in corporate bonds), and
- surprise shifts in the yield curve.

Many find the empirical tests of the APT to be inconclusive in the sense that agreement has not been reached on the value of the coefficients Chen et al. (1986) identified or of other potential explanatory variables. Tests also tend to show that various independent variables are correlated, and modeling to generate non-correlated factors typically has resulted in a single dominant factor. Finally, Jay Shanken (1982) argues that the APT suffers from the same basic challenge in testability/refutability as does the CAPM; the market portfolio must still be well-enough diversified with respect to a given set of factors. Dybvig and Ross (1985) argue that the challenge is not as large as for the CAPM, and that if the portfolios are large enough then the APT can be tested (but it appears that consensus has not arrived at what defines "large enough").

A weakness of the APT models above is that the theory does not tell us what the factors should be. Fama and French (1993) generate a three-factor model that does in fact identify the factors—market premium, size premium, and book-to-market premium—and generates estimates of the size of these three premiums. Fama and French's model appears to explain a higher percentage (than the CAPM) of the returns for diversified portfolios, and is consistent with the evidence that small-cap and value portfolios experience higher expected returns. This model does not appear to have gained the traction among practitioners of the easily used CAPM, however.

In the corporations where we have worked, when finance managers are tasked with determining the cost of capital to be used as a hurdle rate that company projects must earn as return, we have used the CAPM, and most of the other practitioners we know have also used this simpler model. The one complication we have seen is to identify different betas for different projects, recognizing that not every project has the same risk level as the average level of risk embedded in the company's equity beta.[2]

3. MARKET EFFICIENCY

In this section, we trace the foundation and evolution of one of the great debates in modern finance over the past 50 years: how much publicly available information is (or is not) embedded, on average, in the prices of tradable assets.

EUGENE FAMA
"Efficient Capital Markets: A Review of Theory and Empirical Work" (1970), *Journal of Finance*.

Thesis: Asset prices reflect all information contained in the history of past prices, and also reflect all publicly available information. Prices may even reflect much non-public information (except the detailed information held by stock exchange specialists and corporate insiders).

---

[2] Too frequently, we see companies employ a single hurdle rate, failing to acknowledge that some projects and business units are riskier than the average for the company and others are less risky. It is more appropriate to use different hurdle rates (i.e., to calculate different costs of capital based on project-specific equity betas). This approach is considered sophisticated by corporate standards, but still represents a simple variation of the CAPM as opposed to utilizing an alternative pricing model.

In this article, Fama summarizes the efficient market theory he developed in his doctoral dissertation at University of Chicago in the early 1960s, which he also presented in a 1965 *Journal of Business* article. He posits that a market is efficient if prices fully reflect available information, and the set of available information is typically broken down into three possible categories:

- **Weak form efficiency.** Prices reflect all information contained in past prices.

- **Semi-strong form efficiency.** Prices reflect all publicly available information. This includes any information about the company in the public domain, including information contained in earnings announcements, press releases, announcements of dividends or stock splits, and so on.

- **Strong form efficiency.** Prices reflect all information both public and private.

In reviewing the theory of efficient markets, Fama examines several types of models used by researchers to translate a hypothesis about prices fully reflecting information into testable implications.[3] The market may be efficient so long as traders take account of available information, transactions costs are not large enough to prevent prices from reflecting information, and investors (on average) understand the implications of information for pricing.

Fama then turns to the evidence on market efficiency. Several studies have confirmed the weak-form efficiency hypothesis; all information contained in security price history seems to be reflected in current prices. Empirical articles in the random walk literature test whether past prices help predict future prices. This is a test of "serial correlation," and such correlation would imply the existence of trading rules with expected profits. An example of a trading rule is that if a stock price moves up by y%, buy and hold until it goes down y% from a subsequent high price. Some researchers (including Fama and Blume 1966)

---

[3] Specifically, he describes three models:
1. **Expected return or "fair game" models.** If equilibrium prices are generated in a two-parameter model, the expected value of the price of a security in the next period, based on a set of information, is equal to 1 plus the expected one-period percentage return, divided by the current period price of that security. This setup means that any test of the theory is simultaneously a test about expected value as well as a test of the efficiency of the market.
2. **The submartingale model.** In this model, the expected value of next period's price (based on current information) is equal to or greater than the current price.
3. **The random walk model.** Successive price changes or one-period returns are independent and identically distributed, so knowing the last price move does not help predict the next price move.

find that for very small filters (values of y between 0.5-1.5%), this approach can outperform buy-and-hold, but only when ignoring any associated trading costs.

Looking at distributional evidence, Fama finds

> at this date the weight of the empirical evidence is such that economists would generally agree that whatever dependence exists in series of historical returns cannot be used to make profitable predictions of the future. (p. 399)

Fama acknowledges evidence that stock returns do not actually follow a normal statistical distribution, meaning that unusually high and low returns occur more than a normal distribution would predict. He also reviews his own test of a multiple security expected return model; Fama, Fisher, Jensen, and Roll (1969) find that the observed properties of the market model are consistent with the expected return efficient markets model.

Research then turned to semi-strong tests concerned with the speed of price adjustment to new public information (announcements of stock splits, annual reports, equity issuance, etc.). Each test examines whether market prices reflect one particular type of information, with the idea that accumulating such results may generalize to establish the validity of the model. Fama et al. (1969) focus on the information contained in stock splits. A two-for-one stock split doubles the number of shares. Since this does not increase the claims to real assets, by itself this does not represent new information. They find that, on average, stock price tends to increase prior to a stock split, which indicates that a company's good financial performance appears to trigger the split. After a stock split, on average the stock price does not move by more or less than the market.

Separating the group of firms who follow their stock split with a dividend increase from those with a dividend decrease, it turns out that increasers experience higher stock returns post-split than do decreasers. This difference indicates that when a split is declared, investors perceive a signal that earnings are higher to support the dividend on an increased number of shares, so the stock price goes up. However, if no such dividend increase is forthcoming, the stock price moves back down to its average level five months prior to the split, wiping out the apparent impact of the split. The market appears to make unbiased forecasts of the implications of a split for future dividends, and this is fully incorporated into the price of the stock in the month of the split announcement. This behavior is all consistent with an efficient market. Several studies use similar techniques to examine the impact of other types of public announcements, all with similar conclusions: Ball and Brown (1968) look at annual earnings announcements, Waud (1970) at Federal Reserve discount rate changes, and Scholes (1969) at secondary offerings of common stock.

Finally, Fama reviews strong form tests of efficiency. The notion that insiders have information that is relevant to prices but is not incorporated in prices goes back a long way, and there are clear examples contradicting the strong-form hypothesis that prices reflect all public and private information. Niederhoffer and Osborne (1966) find that NYSE specialists make monopoly profits based on having access to unfilled limit orders, and Scholes (1969) finds that corporate officers have monopolistic access to information about their own firms. The logical question is whether it pays a particular investor to expend resources searching out nonpublic information, and who in the investment community has access to special information. Jensen (1968) studies managers of open-ended mutual funds. Jensen estimates the appropriate, risk-adjusted, expected returns earned by mutual fund managers, and then examines whether these managers can utilize information to earn returns significantly higher than expected; in this sense, he is testing both a pricing model and market efficiency. Jensen finds that despite managers' access to information, in the aggregate they appear unable to earn returns sufficiently above the norm to cover the fees they charge their investors. In his sample of 115 mutual fund managers, he cannot even identify individual managers earning a return above or even at the market norm.

Fama concludes that the results are strongly in support of weak-form market efficiency, as knowing past prices does not help predict future prices. The results also favor semi-strong market efficiency: the examination of various discrete information announcements does not reveal that these predict prices. Researchers have found that corporate insiders and stock exchange specialists gain returns from monopolistic access to information, but surprisingly these are the only two deviations found (up to Fama's point of publication) even for strong-form market efficiency.

Discussion and Implications

Saying that markets are efficient does not mean that stocks are accurately valued. However, it does mean that prices on average reflect existing information, so that an investor cannot use existing information to do a better job than other investors of predicting that stock's future price. In an efficient market, knowing Apple stock is $700 a share does not mean that $700 is the "right" price; it simply means you can expect equal odds that the price is too high as that it is too low.

If stock prices follow a random walk statistically, then each change in price is independent of the prior movements, and knowing what the history is does not help one predict the future prices or returns. If you are flipping a fair coin, it does not matter what the past ten results were—the probability of heads or tails remains 50-50.

Despite decades of research consistent with at least weak-form efficiency, there remain a surprisingly large group of investors who pursue the technical analysis of stocks, in which patterns of price history are identified and analyzed to generate "resistance prices" or other indicators of what the price is about to do. Enough research has been done on weak-form efficiency to convince us that such efforts are a misguided waste of time.

If you want to pick stock winners, our conclusion is that it is better to look for underappreciated information than to study the past year of company stock prices and look for a "head and shoulders" or other pattern in the graph of the historical stock price over time. Be very skeptical of marketing targeted to quantitative-minded investors who think that "charting" recent stock prices can help their investment performance (these are increasingly common in the United States and Asia).

Since the initial work of Fama and the authors he cites in the 1960s, there have been countless empirical studies testing market efficiency. Several possible exceptions to semi-strong market efficiency have been identified, as follows.

- **Value effect.** *Stocks with low price-to-earnings (P/E) ratio outperform other stocks.* In an efficient market, the P/E ratio is public information; any information it contains should be reflected in the price, such that knowing the P/E does not provide an advantage in predicting future returns. However, Basu (1977, 1983) finds that low-P/E stocks perform better than the capital asset pricing model (CAPM) would predict, and higher-P/E stocks perform worse. Basu concludes that investors understate growth expectations for lower P-E stocks, leading to overpessimism (and conversely they overstate growth expectations for high P-E stocks). This "value effect" is also observed in several other studies (e.g., Reinganum 1981). Other studies similarly found that stocks with low price to cash flow ratios and low price to book value ratios have also outperformed predicted returns. Stattman (1980) and Rosenberg, Reid, and Lanstein (1985) find the ratio of a firm's book value of equity to its market value positively related to stock returns.

- **Size effect.** *Small firm stock returns outperform those of other stocks.* Looking at data from 1936–1977, Banz (1981) showed that firms with a low market capitalization generate higher returns than those predicted by the CAPM. This is referred to as the "size effect."

- **January effect.** Keim (1983) shows that stock prices tend to increase in the month of January, creating an opportunity for investors to buy stock before January and sell afterwards, in a way not predicted by asset pricing models. This January outperformance is actually observed more for smaller stocks, and so is often considered a part of the size effect. One potential explanation is that tax-sensitive individual investors holding smaller stocks sell stocks for tax reasons at year-end in order to capture a capital loss, and reinvest after the first of the year.

- **Momentum effect.** Jegadeesh and Titman (1993) show that buying past winners and selling past losers does generate higher returns over the following year than what would be predicted by a pricing model. This finding is particularly challenging to market efficiency, since it challenges not just the semi-strong form but even the weak form, by using only past prices to pick outperforming stocks. The authors conclude that this momentum effect arises because investors underreact to specific new information, so that good news and bad news both persist in their impact on stock price.

One challenge with any study that identifies an exception to market efficiency is that each test is simultaneously a test of the asset pricing model and of efficiency. That is, the test has to first determine the *expected* return on each stock in the dataset, and then use that to determine if the realized return was unusually high or low. So, an abnormal average return can result from either an inefficient market or from a mis-specified model for determining the expected return. This ambiguity creates a fair amount of debate among researchers about the implications for whether markets are efficient, as Bill Schwert (1983) describes in the context of the size anomaly:

> The search for an explanation of this anomaly has been unsuccessful. Almost all authors of papers on the "size effect" agree that it is evidence of misspecification of the capital asset pricing model, rather than evidence of inefficient capital markets. On the other hand, none of the attempts to modify the CAPM to account for taxation, transaction costs, skewness preference, and so forth have been successful at discovering the "missing factor" for which size is a proxy. (p. 9)

Fama weighs back in to this debate (Fama and French 1992) by providing evidence that the measure of risk serving as the foundation for the CAPM, beta, does not in fact adequately capture risk. Market betas measure the volatility of individual stocks relative to that of the market as a whole. Fama and French find that that average stock returns are not consistently related to market betas; rather, size and book-to-market equity proxy for dimensions of risk. Fama and French (1993) go further, developing a new asset pricing model which adds two additional risk factors to equity beta: size and book-to-market ratio. Their model explains 90% of portfolio returns compared with 70% using just the beta as in the CAPM. So, they interpret the anomalous evidence above not as implying market inefficiency but rather as showing the shortcomings of the CAPM. Fama and French remain convinced that markets price risk efficiently, investor behavior is rational, and that any challenges are in measuring the elements of risk that are important to investors.

Lakonishok, Schleifer, and Vishny (1994) investigate the performance of value stocks (based on book-to-market, price-to-earnings, and other ratios) relative to growth ("glamour") stocks over a 26-year period through 1990 and find that value stocks outperformed growth stocks by wide margins. They conclude that value investing exploits suboptimal investor behavior and that the relatively better performance of such value investing does not reflect any higher level of risk. A more recent study by the Brandes Institute (2008) replicates their methodology through 2008 (thereby including the 1990s era of growth stock performance) and reaches the same conclusions.

In Section 7 of this chapter, we describe research in behavioral finance, and return to the debate about market efficiency. For now, our own view of the evidence since 1970 is that researchers have identified that significant asset mispricing does occur but a consistent method of profiting from such mispricing has not been identified, so that investors should act as if prices are right on average.

4. AGENCY THEORY

Prior to the 1970s, most research in economics and finance tended to treat companies as single agents, with a unified objective like profit maximization. Jensen and Meckling started from the assumption that a firm is a nexus of contracts between various individuals with differing levels of risk aversion and conflicting incentives, and found that a model built on this assumption leads to predictions consistent with observed behaviors within firms.

MICHAEL JENSEN and WILLIAM MECKLING
"Theory of the Firm: Managerial Behavior, Agency Costs, and Ownership Structure" (1976), *Journal of Financial Economics*.

Thesis: When one group (managers) performs on behalf of another group (owners), the interests of the two groups can diverge. Contracts can minimize the differing incentives, and it can be in the best interest of managers to contractually restrict their own behavior.

This unusually long journal article by Jensen and Meckling draws on the theory of property rights, agency, and finance to develop a theory of ownership structure for the firm. The theory introduces differing incentives and can help explain many phenomena, including how the managers of companies are monitored and compensated by owners.

The specification of individual rights determines how costs and rewards are contractually allocated among the participants in any organization. An *agency relationship* is a contract under which the principals engage an agent to perform service on their behalf involving the delegation of decision-making authority to the agent. In a corporation, the principals are often the shareholders who delegate decisions to management. The agent's own interests may not always coincide with the principal's maximum welfare. *Agency costs* are defined to be the sum of (a) the monitoring expenditures by the principal, (b) the bonding expenditures by the agent, and (c) the residual loss.

Where prior literature focuses on how to structure contracts to align incentives, Jensen and Meckling examine the incentives faced by each party, and the implications and determinants of the equilibrium form of their contractual agreement. Most organizations are legal fictions serving as a nexus for contracting relationships; a corporation is one form additionally characterized by divisible residual claims on assets and cash flows that can be sold without the permission of other counterparties.

The Agency Costs of Outside Equity

The authors investigate the effect of outside equity on agency costs by comparing the behavior of a manager who owns 100% of the firm to a manager who owns only a fraction. Managers who are also owners will maximize their utility: both the monetary return and the non-monetary rewards, such as the attractiveness of his office space and relationships with coworkers. Once the manager owns only part of the company, things change:

- The manager will bear only a fraction of the costs of any non-monetary benefits but will still receive all of the benefit.
- He may become lazy, as he will bear all the burden of working hard to identify new sources of profit but retain only a fraction of those profits.
- She may be incented to overspend on perks, generating agency costs. This overspending can be offset when stockholders monitor the manager (which brings its own set of costs).

The owner bears the wealth effect of these agency costs to the extent that they are expected and understood by anyone who buys or sells ownership shares. Therefore, the wealth costs to the owner of obtaining additional cash in the equity markets will rise as her fractional ownership falls.

Jensen and Meckling develop a theorem to formalize the source of agency costs of equity and identify who bears them. If a manager self-funds new projects, he can reach the value-maximizing point (described as V*) for the company and enjoy a combination of wealth and perks. However, if outside financing is required for the investments and there are costs to monitoring, then the owner will not reach this value-maximizing point.[4] This lack of value

---

[4] Technically, if the owner sells part of the firm and retains a percentage stake α, then the sold ownership portion will be $(1 - \alpha)$. Outsiders will pay only $(1 - \alpha)$ times the value they expect the firm to have, given the induced change in the behavior of the manager. To determine the optimal scale of a firm that is all equity financed, the wealth of the owner is initial wealth $W + V(I) - I$, or the net increment from exploiting new investment opportunities. If the manager covers all investment to reach the value-maximizing point $I*$, he will

maximization reflects agency costs. The manager stops increasing the size of the firm when the gross increment in value is offset by the incremental loss involved in consuming additional fringe benefits due to the manager's smaller fractional interest in the firm.

The manager's behavior can potentially be controlled through monitoring. Outside equity holders will take these monitoring expenses into account in determining the price they will pay for shares. It can therefore become in the manager's interest to restrict his consumption of non-monetary items, to increase the value of the firm and therefore his own share. No matter who makes the monitoring expenditures, the owner-manager bears the full amount of these costs. The value-maximizing size of the firm will involve an optimal level of monitoring costs and bonding expenditures.

There is a difference between the value maximizing point (V*) with no monitoring or bonding costs, and the value with monitoring and bonding expenses. These costs, plus the residual loss from not arriving at V*, are an unavoidable set of agency costs of the relationship between external owners and managers, and are borne by the decision-making manager. A number of factors can affect the size of the agency costs:

- the tastes of the managers,
- the ease with which they can exercise their own preferences,
- the size of monitoring and bonding costs,
- the costs of measuring the managers' performance,
- the cost of devising and applying an index for compensating the managers that correlates with the owner-principal's welfare,
- the cost of devising and enforcing specific behavioral rules, and
- the market for managers (i.e., the cost of replacing managers).

The size of agency costs will also be impacted by the market for the firm itself (i.e., capital markets). However, the owners of firms with monopoly power will have the same incentives to limit agency costs as do the owners of competitive firms.

Why, given positive agency costs, is the corporate form of organization with widely diffuse ownership so prevalent? Limited liability does not eliminate the risk of failure but does shift some of that risk. Jensen and Meckling believe that agency costs provide a way to understand that future cash flows are not in fact independent of ownership structure, contrary to Modigliani and Miller's model.

The Agency Costs of Debt
Having the manager become sole equity holder is one way to avoid agency

---

reach this point of valuation V* and enjoy a mixture of wealth (with value W + V* − I*) and non-pecuniary benefits F*. However, if outside financing is required to cover the necessary investment and monitoring costs are non-zero, then the owner will not reach this value-maximizing point.

costs, so why don't entrepreneurs own all the equity with the rest of the capital borrowed? Some possible reasons are as follows.

- **The incentive effects of debt.** Creditors will not loan to a company where the entrepreneur's equity is low, as this will create a moral hazard problem incenting the owner to take large risks. The owner would get the upside while leaving the downside to the creditors.

- **The monitoring costs created by these incentive effects.** To monitor managers, bondholders could (in principle) introduce covenants to the debt indenture documents limiting bad managerial behavior (limits on using bond proceeds to simply pay dividends to equity holders, limits on future debt issuance, maintenance of working capital, etc.). Complete protection would require incredibly detailed restrictions, however, and it would be almost impossible to think in advance of each way managers could expropriate value.

- **Bankruptcy costs.** The existence of bankruptcy costs also limits the amount of debt a firm will choose to incur.

All these factors discourage the use of corporate debt, but two potential benefits cause debt to be used anyway: the tax benefit of interest expense, and the ability to exploit investment opportunities that are otherwise limited by the resources of the owner.

A Theory of the Corporate Ownership Structure
Jensen and Meckling use this model to determine the ratios of inside equity (held by the manager), outside equity (held by external shareholders), and debt. The optimal proportion of capital to be obtained from outside equity versus debt, for a given level of inside equity, is that which results in minimum total agency costs. Using more outside financing increases total agency costs and increases the optimal fraction of outside funds obtained from equity over debt. The larger the firm becomes, the larger the total agency costs due to higher monitoring costs.

Jensen and Meckling's model implies that managers will first invest all of their wealth in the firm, to minimize agency costs, before seeking any outside funding. However, this is not what is typically observed—most managers have personal wealth outside the company. This diversification can be explained by risk aversion and optimal portfolio selection. The optimal fraction of the firm to be held by outsiders is determined by the best tradeoff between marginal agency costs and the manager's demand for outside financing. This tradeoff also determines the total agency costs borne by the owner. The optimal scale of the firm is determined by the expansion path reaching the highest indifference curve (level of utility), where the managers best balance their interest in owning more of the company with their desire to diversify their own assets.

Qualifications and Extensions of the Analysis

The authors consider several extensions that add realism at the cost of making the model more complicated.

- **Multiperiod aspects.** The ability of managers to develop a reputation over time for not taking non-monetary benefits can reduce, but not eliminate, agency costs.

- **The control problem.** If outside equity holders have voting rights, then the tradeoff will no longer involve purely financial considerations—managers will be concerned about the impact of reducing their fractional ownership below the point where they lose effective control of the corporation.

- **The existence of inside debt and the use of convertible financial instruments.** The analysis has not incorporated debt held by the manager (i.e., inside debt). A manager might be able to reduce agency costs by binding himself to hold a fraction of the total debt equal to the fraction of equity he holds, so that he loses incentive to reallocate wealth from debtholders to stockholders. This is not typically observed in practice. It is possible that the wage contract has some characteristics of debt that accomplish a similar benefit. If this debt feature of wages were strong enough, the manager might even gain incentives to transfer wealth from stockholders to debtholders. Stock options might be a way to offset that risk.

- **Monitoring and the social product of security analysts.** Those who believe that markets are efficient (based on institutional investors who make use of equity analysts not outperforming the market) may conclude that equity research is a social loss (adding no value to the system). But if equity analysts play a useful role in monitoring managerial behavior, they can reduce agency costs—this could explain the presence of equity analysts even in an efficient market.

- **Specialization in the use of debt and equity.** The theory predicts that in industries where it is easy to for managers to expropriate value (e.g., the restaurant industry), there would be less outside equity. Where the incentive effects of debt are large relative to those of equity (e.g., conglomerates that can change acquisition policy), there would be less debt. Bank lending policies might reveal which industries enable managers to change the distribution of outcomes by more or by less.

- **Application to the large, diffuse ownership corporation.** According to Jensen and Meckling, one limitation of the analysis is that it has not yet been worked out for a very large modern corporation whose managers own little or no equity.

- **The supply side of the incomplete markets question.** Prior literature has explored welfare improvements from introducing new contingent claims to incomplete markets, providing an analysis of demand conditions for new markets. However, an analysis of the supply of such claims seems to be lacking. What causes individuals to create and sell contingent claims of various sorts? Jensen and Meckling's model can be considered a first step in addressing this question.

The authors conclude that

> agency costs are as real as any other costs. The level of agency costs depends among other things on statutory and common law and human ingenuity in devising contracts. Both the law and the sophistication of contracts relevant to the modern corporation are the products of a historical process in which there were strong incentives for individuals to minimize agency costs. (p. 72)

Discussion and Implications

 At its core, Jensen and Meckling are examining the incentive to overspend that is created when a manager in a firm is spending other people's (stockholders') money. This phenomenon may be familiar to anyone who is not self-employed and who orders dinner on a reimbursable business trip. The authors cover a lot of ground in this article, and address several different subfields within economics.

A primary contribution is the suggestion to consider the differences in objectives or risk preferences that can arise when a principal (stockholder) delegates decision-making to an agent (manager), and to consider observed norms as tools for minimizing the agency conflict. At its core, this article explores what happens to managers who reap the benefit of spending other people's money.

When considering how to compensate your employees, it is critical to engage in this type of thinking and consider what incentives any compensation structure will create. Offering bonuses based on return-on-investment can result in too-low levels of investment. Offering stock options with an asymmetric payoff (i.e., a large payoff for increased share price, and zero payoff for flat or decreasing share price) can promote risk-taking. Such options can compensate for the risk aversion of managers who want to maximize the odds of keeping their jobs (e.g., by holding more cash than is needed) rather than maximizing stockholder value. Or, it can work too well and create an incentive for taking more risk than is optimal (e.g., if the firm is in trouble, rolling the dice on a bet-the-firm long shot in the hopes of getting a boost to stock price).

One key insight of the analysis is that it can make sense for an agent to restrict his own behavior. If you can credibly commit to shareholders not to act opportunistically (e.g., signing a debt covenant eliminating your ability to use borrowed proceeds to enrich stockholders at bondholders' expense), then you can borrow money more easily, and your firm and yourself can both earn more.

Another contribution of Jensen and Meckling's article is that it breaks away from treating a corporation as a single monolithic agent (like a person). The authors generate fresh insights by considering the differing incentives of the various individuals who make up the corporation.

This literature has also been extended and applied to other contexts. For instance, legislators (principals) delegate decision-making to agents (bureaucrats) with different preferences (e.g., for preserving the scope and tenure of their agencies).[5] Jensen and Meckling's framework is also useful for analyzing the nature of the employment contract. Environments with varying incentives and differing ability to monitor employee performance can give rise to options, profit sharing, and deferred compensation. The framework can explain why salespeople are paid via commission, production workers by hourly wage, office workers monthly, and hospitality employees with tips. In each case, the payment structure is matched to the incentives of that type of worker.

Relevant to this discussion, Milgrom and Roberts (1992) identify four principles of contract design:

- **Informativeness principle.** When information is imperfect, any performance measure that reveals information about the agent's effort level should be part of the compensation contract.

- **Incentive-intensity principle.** The optimal intensity of incentives depends on the incremental profits created by more effort, the precision with which the desired activities are assessed, the agent's risk tolerance, and the agent's responsiveness to incentives.

- **Monitoring intensity principle.** Situations in which the optimal intensity of incentives is high correspond to situations in which the optimal level of monitoring is also high.

- **Equal compensation principle.** Activities that are equally valued by the employer should be equally valuable to the employee. The authors provide many examples of the phenomenon that those activities which are rewarded will get emphasized to the detriment of others (teachers teaching "to the test," software programmers paid by line of code generating overly long programs, etc.).

Another line of research also holds that organizations are susceptible to economic analysis and is termed "the economics of organization" or "transaction cost economics," summarized by Oliver Williamson (1996). This approach views firms and markets as alternative forms of governance, and

---

[5] The agency model can be applied in a government context—not just to legislators-and-bureaucrats, but also to taxpayers-and-government. If a government agency acquires power by spending, this outcome can create an incentive to overspend. The agency model also provides a potential solution: perhaps if an agency can credibly restrict its own future behavior, then taxpayers will be more likely to support that agency's initial creation.

demonstrates how many observed business phenomena (including mergers and unusual contracting processes) arise from the incentive to minimize transaction costs. Williamson provides many examples, including the following:

- A blast furnace and rolling mill both require heat, so they tend to be found next to each other. Although they could in principle be owned by different entities, their common dependence creates contractual hazards that may best be solved by common ownership. Therefore, do not infer monopoly behavior when they are found together.

- Economies of scale often argue for larger companies, but if such economies are all that matter, then there should naturally only be one corporation in the world. Examining at what size an organization minimizes transaction costs helps explain which industries have large versus small participants.

- Countries in which politicians pick winners and losers among companies often have trouble attracting investment even from those dubbed winners, because firms know that even if they are picked as winners now, their political fortunes can change. In order to invest, firms need credible commitments in the form of political structures that limit the degree to which it matters whether they are popular with a given country's ruler (i.e., legal protections against expropriation, targeted costs, or taxation). Such commitments represent a form of minimizing transaction costs.

We think that anyone who has worked in an organization (i.e., a company with more than one employee) has experienced the different incentives and objectives of the different members of the organization. In our experience, the Jensen-Meckling framework offers a disciplined way to think about how differing incentives can be addressed with creative contract terms, particularly with regard to how members are compensated and managed.

5. IMPERFECT INFORMATION

Having addressed the implications of agents having differing incentives, we turn now to the analysis of what happens when agents have different information sets. Leland and Pyle (1977) create a model which shows how corporate managers can signal to the market that they have high-quality projects, and Myers and Majluf (1984) show how information differentials can lead to a failure to finance even high-quality investments.

HAYNE LELAND and DAVID PYLE
"Informational Asymmetries, Financial Structure, and Financial Intermediation" (1977), *Journal of Finance*.

Thesis: When entrepreneurs have inside information about their project quality, the value of the firm will increase with the share held by that entrepreneur. Financing does matter.

 There are numerous markets characterized by informational differences between buyers and sellers, particularly in financial markets. Although entrepreneurs know intimately the quality of their projects, their lenders cannot distinguish the quality of entrepreneurial projects in their potential lending portfolio, causing market value to reflect average project quality. This average quality may be low if there is a large potential supply of poor projects, causing even high-quality projects not to be undertaken due to the resulting high cost of capital. Where informational asymmetry coexists with poor projects, venture capital markets may cease to exist. Credible information about project quality can be transferred, however, by the actions of entrepreneurs. The willingness of the entrepreneur to invest in the project or firm signals true project quality.

Leland and Pyle develop a model of capital structure and financial equilibrium for a situation where entrepreneurs with inside information seek project financing and convey project quality by their own willingness to invest. The resulting equilibrium differs from traditional models in that the value of the firm increases with the share held by the entrepreneur, and capital structure will vary with the project or firm value. Signaling will result in entrepreneurs taking larger equity positions than they would otherwise, but will result in the same set of investment projects as if there were no information asymmetry. This model also predicts financial intermediation, which is difficult to explain in traditional models.

The authors develop a signaling model. Based on her own information and analysis, an entrepreneur assigns a specific value to the expected end-of-period value of a project (μ), but has no credible way to convey this information. Other shareholders will respond to a signal by the entrepreneur regarding his evaluation of μ if they know it is in his self-interest to send true signals. The fraction of equity in the project retained by the entrepreneur, represented by α, will be taken by others as a noiseless signal of the true μ.

This model will lead to specific valuation schedules in equilibrium, theorized as follows.

- **Theorem 1.** The equilibrium valuation function $\mu(\alpha)$ is strictly increasing with α over the relevant domain, if and only if the entrepreneur's demand for equity in his project is normal. *Normal demand* is when more of an asset is demanded as its price falls. This theorem states that higher entrepreneurial ownership signals a more favorable project.

- **Theorem 2.** In equilibrium with signaling by α, entrepreneurs with normal demands will make larger investments in their own projects than they would if they could costlessly communicate their true mean. The cost of signaling the true μ to the market through α is the welfare loss resulting from investing in one's own project beyond the level that would have been optimal with symmetric information.

Leland and Pyle offer three initial propositions.

1. **A project will be undertaken if—and only if—its true market value, given μ, exceeds its cost.** This proposition implies that information transfer via signaling is efficient, in that the set of projects undertaken is the same as if information could be communicated costlessly.

2. **An increase in risk aversion or project risk will reduce the entrepreneur's equity position.** An increase either in the specific risk Z of the project or in the risk aversion b of the entrepreneur will reduce the entrepreneur's equilibrium equity position $\alpha^*(\mu)$. This is true for any value of μ at which the project is undertaken.

3. **An increase in specific risk results in greater expected utility for the entrepreneur.** This is true for any level μ at which the project is undertaken. The expected utility cost of signaling varies with the specific risk Z of the project, meaning that more projects which are more distinct from the market are easier to signal.

The traditional Modigliani-Miller theorem states that there is no systematic relationship between how a firm is financed and the firm's value. However, this theorem does not hold in a world with asymmetric information, which leads to a fourth proposition.

4. **Greater project variance implies lower optimal debt.** Even independent of higher bankruptcy costs, firms with riskier returns will have lower optimal debt levels. This low-debt equilibrium holds for any level of expected project value μ.

The authors finish by discussing how differing levels of information can explain the existence of financial intermediation. In traditional models, lenders can purchase primary securities directly and avoid the costs of intermediaries. Transaction costs could explain intermediation—if they were higher—but asymmetric information can provide a more compelling explanation for intermediation. If non-public information can be obtained with an expenditure of resources, then it is more economical for one intermediary to gather and sell this information than for every potential lender or investor to separately collect it. However, stand-alone sellers of information may have trouble appropriating a return for their product, and it may be challenging for users to distinguish good information from bad. These two obstacles can be overcome if the firm gathering the information becomes an intermediary that buys and holds assets on the basis of its information. The intermediary's information is now embedded in its own portfolio, and its own equity signals the quality of that information. So, the information asymmetry model predicts and explains the existence of intermediaries as a natural response to a world with asymmetric information about portfolio companies.

 STEWART MYERS and NICHOLAS MAJLUF
"Corporate Financing and Investment Decisions When Firms Have Information that Investors Do Not Have" (1984), *Journal of Financial Economics*.

Thesis: Knowing that management has inside information, investors will interpret any issuance of equity as evidence that the company is overvalued. This will cause firms with limited debt capacity to pass up good investments.

 Myers and Majluf also explore the implications of management being better informed than investors. Traditional finance theory advises a firm to accept every project with positive net present value (NPV), regardless of whether the firm has cash or needs to issue equity to pay for it. However, if a firm's managers know more about the value of its assets and opportunities than do outside investors, this can create some interesting incentives. In some cases, the inside information about the firm's value is so favorable that management knows the current stock price is undervalued. Acting in the interest of existing shareholders, management will not want to issue new shares even if it means passing up a profitable investment opportunity. Investors, aware of their ignorance, will reason that a decision not to issue shares is a signal of good news, and will interpret a decision to issue shares as less good news. This negative signal in turn affects the price investors will pay for the new issue, which affects the actual investment decision. This can cause the firm to pass up opportunities in a way that misallocates real investment capital and reduces firm value. If managers try to avoid this phenomenon, the model makes some predictions about financing choices that appear consistent with observed corporate behavior.

The authors establish assumptions, build a model of information asymmetry, and provide an example of what can happen to project financing. *Financial slack* consists of cash, liquid assets, or unutilized borrowing capacity.

- Slack has value because it allows firms to accept an investment opportunity without issuing stock. In this model where investors know that managers have superior information, investors will assume the firm is less likely to issue stock when it is undervalued, so they will take a stock issue as a signal that the stock is more likely to be overvalued.

- Slack would lose its value if the firm could compel existing stockholders to buy and hold any new issue, preventing conflict between old stockholders and new stockholders.

- Slack would lose its value if the firm could costlessly and credibly convey all of its inside knowledge to both existing and potential new stockholders, but educating investors is costly, and any communication may also provide proprietary information to competitors.

Myers and Majluf then develop a general formulation and solution of their model. They assume that management acts in the interest of "old" (existing) stockholders.

- If these stockholders are assumed to be passive, and to not adjust their portfolios in response to the firm's investment decision, then financing will matter (i.e., how a project is financed will drive which projects are undertaken). A firm with cash will take all positive-NPV opportunities. A firm without cash will not want to issue equity at a discount to raise capital, so will not take all positive-NPV projects. In addition, firms will prefer debt to equity when they do need external funds.

- If these existing stockholders are active, and rationally rebalance their portfolios as they learn from the firm's actions, then they will adjust to company developments. They can maintain a constant fractional ownership of the company by participating in new equity issues (rebalancing). In this case financing will not matter (i.e., how a project is financed will not impact which projects are undertaken). However, if stockholders rebalance, this will generate conflicts of interest between old and new shareholders even if the firm has ample slack. In this case, even firms that have plenty of cash will still pass up some positive-NPV investment opportunities. Myers and Majluf do not think this happens, because they do not think existing stockholders rebalance their portfolios based on evolving company developments.

They conclude that the empirical predictions of their passive-stockholder assumption are supported by the observed data. Firms may pass up good opportunities rather than selling stock to raise funds. The decision to issue stock always reduces stock price in this model (unless the issue is known to be unavoidable).

The model can be adapted to include the choice between debt and equity issuance to raise funds for a new project. The ability to issue risky debt alleviates (but does not eliminate) the problem of the firm passing up some positive-value investment opportunities. However, now the firm will not issue equity; if it invests, it will do so with debt proceeds. If we change the assumption that changes in value have a known constant variance rate, to assume that the variance rate is subject to its own information asymmetry, this will allow circumstances where the firm might still issue equity some fraction of the time. However, Myers and Majluf believe that asymmetric information about firm value is a stronger determinant of financing behavior than is asymmetric information about risk.

Concerning the choice between debt and equity in a version of the model with information asymmetry about both firm value and the variance rate in value, the authors find that slack allows the firm to avoid financing, and so has value if management acts in the interest of existing stockholders who are passive. Myers and Majluf explore how rational stockholders react to firm investments, and demonstrate that their reaction does not depend on how the investment is financed. "We think it more likely that managers having superior information act in old stockholders' interest. We also think that existing empirical evidence supports our view" (p. 212). Specifically, stock prices tend to fall when new stock issues are announced.

The fall in stock prices, the building of cash or other forms of slack, and the preference for debt over equity all suggest that stockholders are more passive than active. Existing stockholders do not simply take a proportional share in any new stock issue.

If firms can issue stock before there is any difference in their information set, the problem created by asymmetric information goes away; if the asymmetry is permanent, the problem persists. If financial slack has value, then there is value to increasing slack by merging with another company with surplus liquidity. However, the same information asymmetry can rule out a successful merger proposal of a seller to a buyer. This one-on-one asymmetry can be mitigated if it is easier to convey internal information to a merger partner than to public investors, or if the buyer (rather than seller) takes the initiative.

The authors conclude with a number of suggestions:

- It is generally better to issue safer debt securities than riskier equity securities.
- Firms with investment opportunities and limited debt capacity may pass up good investments.
- Firms can build up slack by restricting dividends in times of modest investment requirements, or by issuing stock when informational asymmetry is lowest.
- Firms should not pay a dividend if they have to recoup the cash by selling stock.
- Stock price will fall upon a new stock issue when managers have superior information.
- A merger of a slack-rich and a slack-poor firm increases combined value, but negotiating will not work unless the slack-poor firm can convey their own inside information to the buyer.

Discussion and Implications

 The intuition of the information asymmetry models is reflected in the fact that the seller of a used car knows more about its prospects than does the potential buyer, which can make the buyer wary of any car that the current owner wants to sell. Based on the simple insight that corporate managers have more information about their company's prospects than do outsiders, Leland and Pyle build an elegant model that predicts real-world phenomena much closer to what executives see in practice. That is, firms appear reluctant to issue equity—even if they are constrained in their ability to borrow to pursue investment opportunities. In their model, firms with low expected returns could pretend to have a higher expected return to increase their valuation (academics refer to this as a "moral hazard problem"). Intermediaries (like banks) can solve this problem by monitoring the actions of firms and coming to their own conclusions (the equivalent of taking the car to an objective mechanic). Firms can use retained equity to more credibly signal their own information about a project, such that (unlike the Modigliani-Miller model) a firm's financial structure is now related to the value of the company.

Leland and Pyle's article stimulated a host of research further exploring the implications of asymmetric information and use of signaling in a variety of situations. To take just one example, Allen and Faulhaber (1989) extend to a signaling model, where in addition to ownership retention rate, a second signal of IPO quality is the deliberate undervaluation by the issuer. The high-value firm signals its type by underpricing, because this will allow the charging of high prices in later offers.[6, 7]

This work in information asymmetry complements agency theory in identifying instances in which the incentives of the various parties differ, and in stimulating thoughts about what contractual or institutional solutions can realign those incentives and raise value. Both the Leland-Pyle and Myers-Majluf models imply that owners should retain a stake after an IPO. Beyond that, these models do not just apply to the example situations provided by the authors, but also teach a way for managers to think through their own incentives in any situation, and suggest how to modify arrangements to ensure that the incentives

---

[6] One academic criticism of Leland and Pyle is that they assume the existence of an incentive signaling equilibrium. Campbell and Kracaw (1980) note that if such an equilibrium existed, then firms would be properly valued even without intermediaries.

[7] We recently attended a venture capital seminar in which an Italian participant complained of the same asymmetric information phenomenon in venture funding. He described how poor-quality entrepreneurial teams in Italy have made it challenging for even high-quality teams to obtain funding from investors who have trouble distinguishing the team quality (Affinity Conference, Kauffman Fellows Program, 11 July 2012, Palo Alto, CA).

of other parties are matched to the same outcomes as one's own. In this sense, these two articles are consistent with applied game theory and strategy.

Myers and Majluf construct another model built on the assumption of information asymmetry. If the buyer of a used car knows that the seller has more information about the car, the buyer may decide that only bad cars will be offered for sale and will adjust any offering price accordingly. This model is also considered an adverse selection model of equity issuance, in which firms issue equity only if they have no choice, knowing that buyers of their equity may assume the firm is likely to be overvalued at its recent price. Myers (1984) builds on this work to characterize the pecking order theory of capital structure, namely that companies prioritize their financing sources according to their level of least resistance: cash, then debt, then equity.

This "pecking order theory" is often contrasted with the *tradeoff theory*, in which a company chooses a debt and equity mix by balancing the costs of the debt with its tax savings (agency costs can be included in the balance as well). A host of studies evaluate the empirical evidence for this theory; Fama and French (2002) find evidence for and against both theories. They find a negative relation between leverage and profitability (contrary to the tradeoff model) and large equity issues for small growth firms (contrary to the pecking order model), but also find predictions common across the two models to be broadly supported. In addition, the pecking order theory may have better support for dividend-paying firms, while the tradeoff theory may be better supported for non-payers. Frank and Goyal (2003) find evidence inconsistent with the pecking order theory, especially for small firms where one should expect amplified information asymmetry compared to larger firms.[8]

In his survey of the field of corporate finance, Jay Ritter (2003a) notes that recent years have seen more empirical work than path-breaking theoretical work, and specifically pinpoints the lack of seminal theoretical articles since Myers and Majluf's contribution. He considers this evolution an unavoidable tendency of a maturing field.

We see information asymmetry in the real world in multiple contexts: between corporations and investors, merger targets and acquirers, entrepreneurs and venture capitalists, and buyers and sellers of goods on eBay. We find the models of this section to be useful for thinking through how to credibly signal knowledge from the better-informed to the less-informed party. For example, eBay set up a system allowing buyers to rate sellers, with the results visible to subsequent buyers. When sellers have a public reputation based on their prior transactions, this reputation alters the incentive a seller might have to exploit

---

[8] We are sympathetic to Miller's (1977) analogy that this balancing of common taxes with rare bankruptcy is akin to the disproportionate balance between one horse and one rabbit in a horse-and-rabbit stew. If this tradeoff drove capital structure, firms should have much higher debt levels than we actually observe.

her superior information about the quality of a product. As this example reflects, the internet provides more opportunities for sharing information. Leland and Pyle's model predicts that increased information flow may lessen the role for intermediaries like credit rating agencies, equity analysts, and other keepers and analyzers of information.[9]

6. BUSINESS MEASUREMENT

Despite the fact that accounting standards evolve constantly, ours is not an accounting book and so we will not cover the evolution of how external financial statements are prepared and reported. However, a major field within finance concerns how managers collect and utilize the information needed internally to make informed decisions, that is, information that supplements the standard financial information that is collected and used to prepare required financial statements. In this section, we describe two efforts to provide managers with such data: the balanced scorecard of Kaplan and Norton (1996) and the measure of economic value added (EVA) developed by Stern, Stewart, and Chew (1995).

ROBERT KAPLAN and DAVID NORTON
The Balanced Scorecard: Translating Strategy into Action (1996).

Thesis: Executives can only manage what is measured. The financial statements prepared for investors are an inadequate source of information for managerial decision-making; companies need to identify which metrics best capture their performance, and build a link from this scorecard to ongoing executive action.

David Norton was the CEO of Nolan Norton, a strategy consulting firm, and Robert Kaplan is an academic consultant at Harvard Business School. They met bimonthly with representatives of a dozen companies (including Apple,

---

[9] We find the crash of the mortgage-backed securities market in 2008–2009 to be an instructive example for agency issues and information asymmetry. The ownership of household mortgage payment cash flows was sliced into multiple pieces, and the originator often retained very little stake. The originators thus lost the incentive to perform even basic due diligence, and investors assumed that such analysis had been done by the better-informed originators. Investors also relied on rating-agency evaluations that did not incorporate the lack of creditworthiness of many borrowers or the stronger-than-expected linkage between the safer and the riskier tranches (portions) of mortgage payment flows.

BellSouth, HP, DuPont, and GE) to discuss how to best measure performance. This work resulted in articles in *Harvard Business Review* in 1992 and 1993, after which they concluded that the balanced scorecard had evolved from an improved measurement system to a core management system so that it was being used "not only to clarify and communicate strategy, but also to manage strategy" (p. ix). Our summary of their 1996 book is longer than some others in the chapter, in order to provide more detail about the specific types of measurement Norton and Kaplan propose.

The Need for a Balanced Scorecard

Kaplan and Norton argue that new measurement is called for in the information age. A manager's operating environment requires cross-functions, links to customers and suppliers, customer segmentation, global scale, innovation, and knowledge workers. They propose that companies develop a scorecard balancing an emphasis on financial objectives with non-financial drivers of such profitability objectives, which can then translate strategy into performance measures. They assert that a balanced scorecard can itself become a strategic framework for action and can assist in clarifying strategy, communicating goals to employees, setting targets, and allowing for learning to adapt the strategy over time.

With regard to financial measures, Kaplan and Norton discuss the inadequacy of existing measures that were created centuries ago to deal with arm's-length transactions between independent entities. These traditional measures cannot adequately value a company's intangible and intellectual assets.

As an alternative, they offer a scorecard that translates the mission and strategy of an organization or unit into four types of objectives and measures:

- *Financial measures* include return on capital and economic value added, among others.
- *Customer measures* refer to satisfaction, retention, acquisition, and so on.
- *Internal business process measures* include the cycle time for processes, such as the average time it takes to convert sales to accounts receivable to cash.
- *Learning and growth measures* include employee satisfaction and retention, among others.

These four types of objectives are aimed at providing a template rather than a straitjacket.

They make a number of recommendations regarding the development of a scorecard.

- Develop objectives and measures that are consistent and mutually reinforcing.
- Establish use-and-effect relationships between outcome and measures, and the performance drivers of those outcomes.

- Use a mix of outcomes (lagging indicators) and performance drivers (leading indicators).
- Provide more information to management about plans, opportunities, risks, and uncertainties.
- Focus more on factors that create longer-term value.
- Better align information reported externally with the information reported internally to senior management.
- Link performance measures across the different types of measures.
- Include only those stakeholders vital for the success of the unit's strategy, not all stakeholders.

The Financial Perspective
Financial objectives and measures must play a dual role: defining the financial performance expected from the strategy, and serving as the ultimate targets for the objectives and measures of the nonfinancial measures. (In other words, a nonfinancial measure like customer satisfaction is expected to eventually impact revenue and profitability.) Kaplan and Norton divide financial measures into several themes (Table 7-1).

Financial metrics can also help executives oversee their risk management objectives: understanding variance in revenues, forecasting better to predict cycles, and reducing deviation between projected versus actual results. In addition, the scorecard should provide incentives to encourage stretch goals.

The Customer Perspective
Firms identify customer and market segments in which to compete (i.e., sources of revenue). This identification allows the alignment of the unit's performance with targeted customers and market segments. Part of the process is identifying the performance drivers (differentiators) of customer outcomes. What must the company deliver to its customers to achieve the desired outcomes? Core measures of the customer perspective are as follows:

- *Market share* reflects the proportion of business in a given market (in terms of number of customers, dollars spent, or unit volume sold) that a business unit sells.
- *Customer acquisition* measures (in absolute or relative terms) the rate at which a business unit attracts or wins new customers or business.
- *Customer retention* tracks (in absolute or relative terms) the rate at which a business unit retains or maintains ongoing relationships with its customers.
- *Customer satisfaction* assesses the satisfaction level of customers along specific performance criteria within the value proposition.

Table 7-1: Potential Financial Measures

Theme and elements	Associated metric
1. Revenue growth and mix	
New products	% revenue from new products
New applications	% revenue from new applications
New customers/markets	Market share
New relationships	% revenue from cooperative relationships
New product/service mix	Revenue from new mix
New pricing strategy	Profitability by product, service, customer
2. Cost reduction / productivity improvement	
Revenue productivity	Revenue per employee (and % increase)
Unit costs	Find and track cost components for each department over time
Channel mix	% business done in each channel
Operating expenses	% revenue as operating expenses
3. Asset utilization / investment strategy	
Working capital management	Cash-to-cash cycle
Asset utilization	Return on capital and economic value added (improve by leveraging infrastructure of physical and intellectual assets)

Note. Author's table; data from Kaplan and Norton (1996, pp. 51–60).

- *Customer profitability* measures the net profit of a customer (or a segment) after allowing for the unique expenses required to support that customer. Firms should retain profitable customers in targeted segments, eliminate unprofitable customers in non-targeted segments, transform unprofitable customers in targeted segments, and monitor profitable customers in non-targeted segments.

By selecting specific objectives and measures across these classes, managers can focus their organization on delivering superior value to their targeted customer segments.

The Internal Process Perspective
In terms of internal process, Kaplan and Norton describe how managers identify processes critical to achieving customer and shareholder objectives, and suggest doing so after financial and customer perspectives described above

(because that sequence helps focus). The authors suggest using a modified Porter value chain to highlight the principle internal processes around innovation, operations, and post-sales activities (Table 7-2).

Managers identify critical processes at which they must excel to meet the objectives of shareholders and targeted customers. The balanced scorecard approach derives demands for internal process performance from the expectations of specific external constituencies.

The Learning/Growth Perspective

The ability to meet ambitious targets and achieve company objectives depends on organizational capabilities for learning and growth, and such capabilities require investments in the people, systems, and processes representing infrastructure. Kaplan and Norton acknowledge that the drivers of organizational learning and growth are less developed than those for other scorecard areas. Some potential core measurements for the learning perspective are described in Table 7-3.

The authors suggesting using a half-life metric for managers' improvement of processes. For instance, to improve on-time shipping, the amount of time to halve the percentage of product that is late-shipped may be ten months.

Linking Scorecard to Strategy

A successful balanced scorecard is one that communicates a strategy through an integrated set of financial and non-financial measurements. It should be possible to "see" the strategy through the scorecard. This measurement creates shared understanding, creates a holistic model of the strategy, and focuses change efforts. There are three principles in building a scorecard to translate a strategy into measurements:

1. A properly constructed scorecard should tell the story of the strategy through a series of cause/effect relationships.
2. A good balanced scorecard should have a mix of outcome measures and performance drivers. *Outcome measures* are generic measures that are lagging indicators, necessary to tell whether actions have been successful. *Performance drivers* are specific measures (unique to particular business unit) that are leading indicators, necessary to know how outcomes are to be achieved.
3. Causal paths from all the measures on the scorecard should be linked to financial objectives.

The scorecard should be viewed as instrumentation for a *single* strategy, and measures can be diagnostic or strategic. The authors recommend that a scorecard should be a mix of 15-25 financial and nonfinancial measures, be grouped into four types or perspectives (financial, customer, internal, and learning), tell the story of a strategy, be transparent, link outcomes and

Table 7-2: Internal Process Measures

Process Type	Description
Innovation	Identify the market by delineating your existing customers, the size of the market, the nature of preferences, and price points for targeted product or service.
	Create a product/service offering: Attract new customers by meeting their emerging needs.
	Use measures for basic and applied research such as the following: • percent of sales from new products, • percent of sales from proprietary products, • new product introduction vs. competitors' products, • rate of actual versus planned new product introduction, • manufacturing process capabilities, and • time to develop the next generation of products.
	Use measures for product development such as the following: • ratio of operating profit to development cost, and • break-even time (pioneered by HP).
Operations	These processes represent value creation, starting with receipt of a customer's order and finishing with the delivery of the product or service to the customer.
	This activity is traditionally assessed with financial measures based on standard costs, budgets, and variances. However, today's business requires augmenting these traditional measures with measurements of quality and cycle time.
	Kaplan and Norton use the term *manufacturing cycle effectiveness* (MCE). Although this description is manufacturing-oriented, MCE can also be applied to service delivery.
	$$\text{MCE} = \frac{\text{processing time}}{\text{throughput time}}$$
	$$\begin{array}{c}\text{throughput} \\ \text{time}\end{array} = \begin{array}{c}\text{processing} \\ \text{time}\end{array} + \begin{array}{c}\text{inspection} \\ \text{time}\end{array} + \begin{array}{c}\text{movement} \\ \text{time}\end{array} + \begin{array}{c}\text{waiting/} \\ \text{storage} \\ \text{time}\end{array}$$
Post-sales service	This is the final stage in the internal value chain: • warranty and repair activities, • treatment of defects and returns, and • payment processing (i.e., credit card administration). One can develop and use metrics to gauge the efficiency of these activities.

Note. Author's table; data from Kaplan and Norton (1996, pp. 92–125).

Table 7-3: Learning and Growth Measures

Category	Potential core measurements
Learning perspective	Employee satisfaction (considered to be the driver of the other outcome measurements)
	Employee retention
	Employee productivity
Company-situation specific	Reskilling the workforce (staff competencies)
	Information systems capabilities (technology infrastructure)
	Motivation/empowerment/alignment (climate for action)
	• Motivation is critical.
	• Even skilled employees with information will not contribute to success if they are not motivated to act in the best interest of organization, or they are not given the freedom to make decisions and take actions.
	Situation-specific drivers (climate for action):
	• measures of suggestions made/implemented,
	• measures of improvement,
	• measures of individual/organizational alignment, and
	• measures of team performance.

Note. Author's table; data from Kaplan and Norton (1996, pp. 126–146).

performance measures together, and measure a series of cause-and-effect relationships.

Strategy and Structure
Kaplan and Norton briefly describe using a scorecard for entities other than a business unit (i.e., corporations, joint ventures, and nonprofits). For corporations with highly autonomous business units, use of the financial perspective only is highly recommended. For corporations with business units that interact or share key functions (e.g., purchasing, finance, information systems), the scorecard could clarify corporate themes (values, beliefs, explicit transactions among business units) that must be shared across units, translated into metrics for each unit. The scorecard should also clarify the corporate role (i.e., the actions mandated at the corporate level, and shared corporate services).

In a joint venture or alliance, the scorecard can be used to define the shared agenda. The prime obstacle for joint ventures is the difficulty of defining the goals of both parties for the venture. The scorecard should be used to measure performance of the unit with which the joint venture operates.

Usage of the scorecard can also prevent shared resources from becoming a corporate disadvantage. Functional departments should be a source of advantage, and the scorecard should transform a functional department to a customer-focused organization. Staff units may benefit from developing and communicating a strategy for delivering focused value propositions to internal customers.

For government and not-for-profits, success should be measured by how effectively the organization meets the needs of its constituencies. Here, the financial perspective forms a constraint rather than an objective, and the scorecard can define and help achieve "tangible objectives." A scorecard can also provide focus in assessing the rationale for existence, and in communicating to external and internal constituents.

Achieving Strategic Alignment
The authors describe four scenarios in which effective strategy implementation is not possible:

- the vision and strategy are not actionable (e.g., the senior team does not communicate an easily-understood strategy),
- strategy is not linked to team and individual goals (e.g., goals with different time frames),
- strategy is not linked to resource allocation (this can happen if there are separate processes for long-term planning and short-term budgeting), and
- feedback is tactical rather than strategic (due to a lack of measurement on how the strategy is being implemented and whether it is working).

Implementing a strategy begins by educating and involving those who must execute it. By communicating and linking the strategy to personal goals, a scorecard creates shared understanding and commitment among all organization participants. A shared framework communicates strategy and allows individuals to see how their particular actions contribute to achieving the business unit's objectives. A feedback process collects performance data and allows the testing of interrelationships among objectives and initiatives. Finally, team problem-solving processes analyze and learn from performance data, and adapt strategy to emerging conditions/issues.

Three means are used to translate strategy into local objectives, to influence personal and team priorities: communication and education programs, goal-setting programs (translate high level objectives into personal objectives), and a reward system linkage. The alignment of the organization toward the strategy must ultimately be motivated through the incentive and reward systems. Kaplan and Norton make two specific recommendations:

- Turn off formula-based incentives so that managers are not asked to attend to a balanced set of objectives while being rewarded only for achieving short-term financial performance.

- Avoid all-or-nothing compensation thresholds. Weight individual objectives with incentive compensation calculated by the percent of achievement on each objective. This approach permits substantial compensation even when performance is unbalanced.

Attempting to gain organizational commitment to balanced performance across a broad set of leading and lagging indicators will be difficult if existing bonus and reward systems remain anchored to short-term financial results.

Resource Allocation and Budgets

To use a scorecard in integrated, long-range strategic planning and the operational budgeting process, managers need the following four-step process.

1. **Set stretch targets.** To achieve change, managers should establish targets for measures 3-5 years out that, if achieved, will transform the company. Performance drivers and lead indicators enable the identification of operational factors. Use a scenario-planning process based on cause-and-effect relationships.

2. **Identify strategic objectives.** When the scorecard is used as management system cornerstone, the various initiatives can be focused on achieving the organizational objectives, measures, and targets. There are three ways a planning process can improve and channel creativity: the "missing measurement" program (if you cannot measure it, you cannot manage it), continuous improvement programs linked to rate-of-change metrics, and strategic initiatives linked to radical improvement in key performance drivers.

3. **Identify critical cross-business and corporate initiatives.** An important element in planning is to identify the linkages of one strategic business unit (SBU) to other SBUs and other functional activities at the corporate level. The scorecard provides a common framework for organizing the planning process of corporate support departments, enabling these departments to understand the strategies of the entire corporation and the individual units so that departments can better service operating units.

4. **Link to annual resource allocation and budgets.** Strategic planning and operational budgeting processes are too important to be treated as independent. Managers need to test both the theory underlying strategy and the way that strategy is being implemented; a necessary condition for such testing is formulation of specific short-term targets for scorecard measures.

Feedback and Strategic Learning

Organizations need the capacity for *double-loop learning*: the learning that occurs when managers question their assumptions and reflect on whether the theory under which they were operating is still consistent with current evidence, observations, and experience.

The authors cite the work of Henry Mintzberg (1987, 1990) and Robert Simons (1995), who identify key aspects of adaptation: strategies are incremental and emerge over time, intended strategies can be superseded, strategy formulation and implementation are intertwined, strategic ideas can arise throughout the organization, and a strategy is a process.

Implementing a Balanced Scorecard Management Program
Measurement is powerful, but a measurement framework should be deployed to develop a management system. This distinction is subtle but crucial: a *measurement system* is a means to achieve an important goal, while a *management system* should help executives implement and gain feedback about their strategy. By identifying and measuring the most important objectives, a scorecard provides a framework for a strategic management system that organizes issues, information, and a variety of vital management processes.

The authors conclude by making implementation suggestions.
1. Pay attention to the dynamics of mobilizing an organization, by phasing in a management system over time with each change linked to a consistent message.
2. Build an integrated management system by tying the scorecard into other management programs (e.g., budgeting, target-setting).

Integrating a management system is not as simple as it seems. There are two primary reasons for failure: structural defects (e.g., using only lagged indicators, incorrectly identifying critical success factors), and organizational defects (e.g., delegating the process to middle management, emulating the measures used by other companies viewed as world-class). In addition, three critical roles must be played in building and embedding a scorecard as a strategic management system: architect, change agent, and communicator.

Companies have a variety of reasons for adopting a scorecard, including the following: clarifying and gaining consensus on strategy, forcing organizational change initiatives, developing leadership capabilities at SBUs, and gaining coordination and economies across multiple business units. A balanced scorecard can be a cornerstone of a company's management system since it aligns and supports key processes.

Kaplan and Norton finish with a brief summary of how to build a balanced scorecard. First, establish objectives for the scorecard program and select the architect. Then begin the process by defining the measurement architecture (i.e., selecting the appropriate organizational unit and identifying business unit linkages), building consensus around objectives, selecting and designing measures (involving subgroup meetings and an executive workshop), and building an implementation plan.

JOEL STERN, BENNETT STEWART, and DON CHEW
"The EVA Financial Management System" (1995), *Journal of Applied Corporate Finance*

Thesis: Companies can better manage for shareholder value if they use an economic measure of value-added rather than an accounting measure that ignores investment. A value-added measure is straightforward to compute and has a higher correlation with changes in market value.

The objective of *economic value added* or EVA is to replace accounting measures like earnings with a measure that can capture economists' concept of *residual income* (the value left over after stockholders and other stakeholders have been compensated). The EVA metric is a refined financial measurement of value that starts with operating income before taxes and net operating profit after taxes, and adjusts to recoup artificially expensed items and reduce the economic cost of capital.

In this article, Stern, Stewart, and Chew discuss how the business environment has been changing, as companies become more decentralized and conglomerates disaggregate. Information technology enables the decentralization of control functions, but is less helpful for motivating a search for opportunities or allocating capital. EVA is intended to provide such motivation; it measures total factor productivity and also provides a common financial management language company-wide.

There are several problems with the measures driven by the generally accepted accounting principles or GAAP (e.g., earnings per share):

- GAAP-driven metrics typically accompany top-down capital allocation.
- When setting goals for these measures, division management often engages in *sandbagging*, or setting low goals that will be easy to meet or surpass, as well as *satisficing*, or working to meet the target goal but not working to hit achievable performance well in excess of that negotiated target level.
- This suboptimizing behavior results in a value for the conglomerate that is often less than the sum of its parts.
- The market response is leverage buyouts (LBOs) and hostile takeovers, to bring in management to tap the unrealized potential of these business units.

EVA can be used to attain the benefits of such LBOs without the risks inherent to them.

The purpose of EVA is to create efficiency in operations. It also motivates investment in opportunities when return on capital exceeds its cost, and reduction in capital allocation when return is less than cost. Finally, EVA allows companies to push capital cost decisions to lower levels of management.

Stern et al. consider EVA to be more than a financial metric—rather, it is the foundation of an integrated system that incents managers to more productive behavior. Elements of this system include EVA measurement, a cash bonus plan, a bonus bank, and leveraged stock options (LSO).

- **EVA measurement.** In order to remove distortions, adjustments need to be made to the operating income before taxes (OIBT) and net operating profit after taxes (NOPAT). Positive adjustments are needed, increasing income by reversing the inappropriate (accounting-driven) expensing of items. A negative adjustment, in the form of reducing income by the cost of capital employed, must also be incorporated. Stern et al. also recommend customized adjustments for certain strategic investments with a long-term payoff (depending on the extent to which they are significant within the particular business using the measure). There are approximately 120 such potential custom adjustments.

- **Cash bonus plan.** In order to incent the pursuit of business actions that maximize the aggregate amount of activities with a return on capital greater than the cost of that capital, the authors suggest tying bonuses to improvements in EVA rather than simply to the level of EVA. Using improvements instead of levels equalizes managers who have inherited a "cash cow" business with those who have been put in charge of "dogs." It also motivates efforts, is inherently self-funding, and automatically adjusts the following year's goals. The payout of these bonuses should be deferred at least one year.

- **Bonus bank.** In order to remove a short-term focus and retain top performers, Stern et al. suggest that both bonuses and penalties be "banked," that is, absorbed over multiple years. For example, bonus payments can be settled with one-third after the first year, and with two-thirds coming in subsequent years. These banked bonuses represent a form of equity and induce high-performers to remain with the company; non-performers acquire penalties and are incented to leave (one need not even fire them, as they will be incented to leave on their own).

- **Leveraged stock options.** Another tool is to allow or require employees to purchase options with an adjusted exercise price. Employees can be encouraged to purchase options from the their bonus bank account. They can also obtain a reduced exercise price with high leverage, with the exercise price adjusted by the cost of undiversified and non-liquid capital.

In summary, Stern et al. recommend that companies measure performance with EVA, tie cash bonuses to improvements in EVA, establish bonus banks to eliminate short-term focus, and provide LSOs with an adjusted exercise price to obtain leverage for shareholder value. They focus on the economic man (consistent with Jensen and Meckling) and warn that the EVA framework is only a financial management system.

Discussion and Implications

 Kaplan and Norton's balanced scorecard moves beyond the traditional financial statements oriented toward the investors in a public company. A disciplined attempt to consider the interests of all stakeholders, the scorecard has become quite popular. Kurtzman (1997) cites work by the Institute of Management Accountants, which finds 64% of U.S. companies using some form of a scorecard (p. 1).

The balanced scorecard has also received criticism.

- Academics point out that it is not driven by theory, or even by previous experience, which is reflected in the fact that the authors do not cite any prior work in their early papers. (Later work by the authors does provide more integration with previous research.)

- Others have criticized the scorecard for simply being a "laundry list" of metrics that does not create a bottom line single score or conclusion. See Michael Jensen's (2001) observation that the "theory is flawed because it presents managers with a scorecard which gives no score—that is, no single-valued measure of how they performed" (p. 298).

- It is hard to link use of the scorecard to better decision-making or larger profits, because each scorecard is different. In analyzing any single company it is challenging to know what the results would have been in the absence of the framework.

That said, there are studies that conclude the scorecard is useful. For instance, Malina and Selto (2001) examine data and interviews from multiple divisions of a large multinational manufacturer to assess the control and communication effectiveness of the scorecard, and find it "an effective device for controlling corporate strategy" (p. 47).

Neither of us has used a formal balanced scorecard ourselves, and we consider that full implementation is a complex exercise requiring a large investment of scarce management time and focus. However, our view is that even if you do not choose to go through the process of developing a scorecard, the Kaplan-Norton framework provides a concrete and useful method of thinking about measurement, the relationship and interconnectedness of different measures, and the incentives created by tying compensation to various measures.

EVA is an important, self-consistent framework that addresses specific inadequacies of accounting-driven metrics. If you invest $100 in a project, which creates $11 in revenues and $10 in expenses in its first year, an accountant will tell you that you had a $1 profit. However, this accounting ignores your investment of capital—your threshold for economic profitability is not zero, but rather the return at which you could have alternatively invested your $100. If you could have invested at 5%, then your threshold for whether this was a good use of capital will be $5, not zero. An EVA measure would tell you that your economic profit is $1, less the required return of $5, for an economic profit of negative $4. EVA is a better indicator of whether you are earning more on your capital than it could earn in an alternate use, and therefore indicates how well your capital is deployed.

EVA also can eliminate other distortions enabled by accounting metrics. For example, a company can lower its apparent capital investment by entering into operating leases for its equipment, despite the fact that the company is still tying up physical capital even if that capital does not reside on its own balance sheet. By adjusting net operating profit by capitalizing leases, EVA reflects this use of equipment regardless of its balance sheet owner. Leasing companies have long targeted operating divisions with limited budgets by giving them a monthly payment instead of a capital investment; this is why leasing remains popular even though most economic lease-versus-buy models indicate that ownership is cheaper over the long term for most assets. EVA is a great tool for eliminating the incentive to over-lease created by standard accounting measures.

Bennett Stewart (1990) argues that because EVA as a measure is closer to an economic measure than an accounting measure, it also correlates more closely with stock price than does earnings-per-share (EPS) or other accounting metrics. Several analyses by Stern and Stewart (including Stern, Stewart, and Chew 1995) repeat this conclusion; however, Dodd and Chen (1996) find EVA does no better than return-on-assets in explaining stock price. If one accepts EVA as "closer" to stock prices, then one advantage is the ability to break down the EVA drivers by business unit and compensate managers based on the levers of EVA they actually control, rather than using traditional stock options in which everyone in the firm is compensated by a single unified stock price (to which each unit only partially contributes).

Having said that, EVA is subject to creating its own set of suboptimal incentives.

- Many authors (e.g., Stangeland 2006) argue that EVA may result in underinvestment and a focus on near-term performance at the expense of long-run maximization. (Stangeland offers his own alternative, cash flow minus amortized capital or CFMAC to address these challenges.)
- Damodaran (2009) points out some measurement issues with EVA, in particular how the amount of capital invested is measured given that book capital reflects its own accounting distortions. If managers can make investments that do not show up as capital, they can make the EVA measure appear higher.

- Damodaran also finds instances where a focus on current-year change-in-EVA can result in a short-run focus. He suggests this can be overcome if the objective is restated as maximizing the present value of EVA over time (rather than maximizing this year's improvement in EVA). However, such an approach removes the simplicity of EVA that is part of its attractiveness, as maximizing current year improvement in EVA is basic enough to be understood by non-financial managers.

- Chermushkin (2008) finds issues in calculating the capital charge as the combination of a cost of capital derived based on market values of debt and equity, applied against an accounting-derived estimate of invested capital. He suggests using an accounting-based cost of capital instead.

In addition to these objections, even if one uses market values of debt and equity, the cost of equity in EVA is often estimated based on the capital asset pricing model or CAPM (for which we have already detailed some deficiencies).

Eric has been part of teams evaluating, devising, and implementing EVA at AT&T and Avery Dennison in the 1990s. AT&T built a comprehensive EVA system and spent a year shadow-testing it by showing what the metrics and compensation would have been, compared to continuing using the old incentive system. Just at the time the new EVA system was scheduled to be implemented, however, AT&T executives scaled it back. We suspect this choice was made because the company generated a significant boost in EVA, and would therefore have generated strong bonuses, and AT&T had some large layoffs that year (it was 1994). Instituting a financial measure that boosts executive compensation in a year where many rank-and-file employees lose their jobs is not likely to be viewed as a positive public relations move. In any event, AT&T stepped back from implementing the system as fully as had been anticipated. Avery Dennison also chose a less-complete implementation of EVA, and several managers dubbed the program "EVA-Lite." Managers at Avery made fewer adjustments to NOPAT (net operating profit after taxes). The resulting measure was not as "pure," but it was very straightforward for managers to understand how their decisions would (or would not) be reflected in the basic measure. We think this made for a better program overall.

Financial metrics appear to come in and out of fashion. EVA was very hot in the 1990s, but appears to be less so now. One potential reason may be the relative growth within the economy of firms stronger in intellectual assets than physical assets. For companies like Oracle, Microsoft, or Google, efficient deployment of physical capital is less crucial to success, and accurately estimating intellectual capital is more challenging than measuring the capital invested in physical assets. We support the EVA framework but acknowledge it is easier and potentially more relevant for companies with a higher percentage of assets that are physical in nature.

7. BEHAVIORAL FINANCE

Behavioral finance is a subset of behavioral economics; much of the work stems from the same core, which demonstrates that individuals are not rational wealth maximizers but rather behave consistently in irrational ways. We devote Chapter 8, Section 2 to behavioral economics and cognitive bias as they apply to general managerial decision-making, but it is also useful to highlight the specific ways in which documented irrational behavior affects finance and investing behavior in particular.

Behavioral finance is a young field, with no single pioneering paper that we can point to as the start. So, we have chosen to include an article that is itself a survey of literature in a field that is growing every year—and faster than most described in this book.

NICHOLAS BARBERIS and RICHARD THALER
"A Survey of Behavioral Finance" (2003), in G. M. Constantinides, M. Harris, and R. Stulz (editors), *The Handbook of the Economics of Finance*.

Thesis: Agents are not rational, and markets are not efficient. People exhibit persistent and significant cognitive biases in how they process information, assess risk, and make investment decisions. These risks are consistent enough across people to be predictable.

The traditional finance paradigm seeks to understand markets using models in which agents are rational, meaning that (a) they update their beliefs correctly upon receiving new information, and (b) based on their beliefs, they make choices that are normatively acceptable (i.e., consistent with maximizing their utility). Barberis and Thaler discuss how it is now clear that the observed cross-section of average returns and individual trading behavior are not explainable in this framework. Behavioral finance argues that some financial phenomena can be better understood using models in which one or both of the two tenets of agent rationality are relaxed.

Limits to Arbitrage

Barberis and Thaler consider a common objection: that even if some agents are not fully rational, through arbitrage rational agents will prevent those nonrational agents from influencing security prices for a long time. Several "limits to arbitrage" papers address this objection and demonstrate that irrationality can have a substantial and persistent impact on prices.

Traditionally, a security's price is considered its fundamental value; that is, the sum of expected future cash flows discounted at an appropriate interest rate based on their risk, where expectations reflect all available information. Markets are efficient if prices reflect fundamental values. In such a market, there is "no free lunch." Friedman (1953) argues that rational traders will quickly undo any dislocations created by irrational traders, by identifying an investment opportunity and then trading on it, thus altering prices back toward their fundamental levels. Behavioral finance disputes this claim that mispricing will necessarily create an actionable investment opportunity—just because there is "no free lunch" does not mean that prices must be correct.

The disconnect between mispricing and investment opportunity arises because real-world arbitrage itself is often costly and risky:

- **Fundamental risk.** Arbitrageurs would want to use a substitute security as part of their trade. If Ford is underpriced, they will want to short GM while buying Ford. The problem is that substitutes tend to be imperfect; shorting GM may protect investors from industry-wide developments, but still leaves them vulnerable to Ford-specific negative developments.

- **Noise trader risk.** DeLong et al. (1990) and Shleifer and Vishny (1997) explore the real risk that the mispricing being exploited by an arbitrageur may worsen in the short run. If Ford is underpriced now, future price movements can increase the divergence of its price from fundamental value. This risk can force arbitrageurs to liquidate their positions early, particularly if they are managing other people's money (i.e., a separation of brains and capital)—investors will see early negative returns and pull their money from the manager. So, arbitrageurs not only have to identify mispricing but need to do so when the time horizon toward repricing is short enough to exploit.

- **Implementation costs.** Transactions costs (e.g., commissions, bid-ask spreads, price impact), short-sale constraints, and search costs can all combine to reduce or even eliminate the returns to exploiting a mispricing. In particular, finding the mispriced assets can be tricky. Shiller (1984) demonstrates the error of the argument that predictable returns should result from speculative traders influencing stock prices, and calls this argument for the thesis that markets are efficient "one of the most remarkable errors in the history of economic thought" (p. 459). Shiller (and also Summers 1986) show that even noise trader demand that creates significant mispricing may not generate predictability in returns, and so may remain very hard to detect.

Turning to the evidence, any example of persistent mispricing would reveal the limits of arbitrage; however, it is rare to establish mispricing beyond any reasonable doubt, because that requires estimating what the price should have been (what Fama called the "joint hypothesis problem"). In spite of this

challenge, researchers have uncovered several phenomena that appear to be
compelling examples of mispricing.

First is the example of twin shares. In 1907, Royal Dutch and Shell
Transport agreed to merge interests on a 60–40 basis while remaining
independent entities. If prices equal fundamental value, then the value of Royal
Dutch equity should always be 1.5 times the value of Shell equity. Froot and
Dabora (1999) show that from 1980–1995, Royal Dutch varied from 35%
underpriced to 15% overpriced relative to this benchmark. In this case there is
little fundamental risk (the stocks are good substitutes), but there is noise trader
risk: anyone trying to trade faced the fact that mispricing at one point in time
often became even more pronounced before it narrowed.

A second area of evidence is the inclusion of stocks in a stock index.
Shleifer (1986) and Harris and Gurel (1986) examine when a company in the
S&P 500 index is removed and replaced with another firm. They document that
when a stock is added, it jumps in price by an average of 3.5%, and most of the
increase is permanent; Yahoo jumped by 24% the day it was added. This
increase happens despite the fact that inclusion in the index does not change the
fundamental value of the stock. In this case, both the lack of substitutes and the
potential persistence of mispricing may play a role.

The third example is found in internet carve-outs. Lamont and Thaler
(2003) examine 3Com's sale of 5% of Palm in a March 2000 IPO with a
commitment to spin off the remainder of Palm within nine months. After the
IPO, Palm traded at $95, which should have implied a value for 3Com of
$142—but 3Com actually traded at only $81, implying that the rest of 3Com
had a negative value of minus $60 per share. This situation persisted for several
weeks. Lamont and Thaler conclude that implementation costs played a role;
investors trying to borrow Palm shares to sell them short were told that no
shares were available or were quoted a high borrowing price.

Psychology

Barberis and Thaler turn to exploring the nature of deviations from
fundamental pricing. When identifying irrational financial behavior, cognitive
psychologists have examined beliefs and preferences.

As a source of irrationality, within the category of beliefs several specific
types have been found.

- **Overconfidence.** There is extensive evidence that people are
  overconfident in their judgments. First, the confidence intervals people
  assign to their estimates of quantities are far too narrow. Alpert and Raiffa
  (1982) show that 98% confidence intervals include the true quantity only
  60% of the time. Second, most people are poorly calibrated at estimating
  probabilities. For example, events that people think are certain to occur end
  up happening only 80% of the time, and events deemed impossible occur
  20% of the time (Fischhoff, Slovic, and Lichtenstein 1977).

- **Optimism and wishful thinking.** Over 90% of people surveyed think they are above average in common domains such as driving ability, ability to get along with others, and sense of humor (Weinstein 1980).[10] People also predict that tasks will be completed much sooner than actually happens (Buehler, Griffin, and Ross 1994).

- **Representativeness.** Kahneman and Tversky (1974) show that people tend to confuse probability with how representative a description sounds. This representativeness heuristic generates several biases, including failure to account for the base rate. When participants were told of a person named Linda who is intelligent and concerned with issues of social justice, and were asked to pick the most probable statement about her, more chose the statement "Linda is a bank teller and is active in the feminist movement" over the statement "Linda is a bank teller" (p. 1064). This is despite the fact that the first statement is a subset of the second, so the second statement must be more likely! Another bias is sample size neglect. Seeing a coin generate 500 heads and 500 tails in 1,000 tosses should cause a person to have more confidence that it is a fair coin than if six tosses resulted in three heads and three tails. However, most people inaccurately find the two sets of tosses equally informative. So, people make inferences about the process based on too few data points (e.g., concluding that a financial analyst is talented after he makes four good stock picks). You can see these same biases in sports (belief in the "hot hand") or in gambling (believing that, after five heads in a row, tails are somehow "due").

- **Conservatism.** While representativeness leads people to underweight base rates, in other contexts people overweight base rates. Edwards (1968) runs an experiment in which people's probability assessments appear biased in the direction of 50–50 even when the evidence indicates other probabilities are in play.

- **Belief perseverance.** Once people form an opinion, they hold it too tightly and for too long in the face of contradicting evidence. People appear to be reluctant to search for evidence that contradicts their beliefs, and when they do encounter such evidence they tend to be excessively skeptical (Lord, Ross, and Lepper 1979).

- **Anchoring.** When forming estimates, people often start with an initial or arbitrary value and adjust away from it. Kahneman and Tversky (1974) asked subjects to estimate the percentage of UN countries from Africa, by asking if their guess would be higher or lower than a randomly generated number between zero and 100. Those asked to compare their estimate to 10% estimated 25%, while those asked to compare their estimate to 60%

---

[10] Weinstein's survey is of over 200 college students, and surveys of other populations about optimism have reached similar results.

estimated 45%. These results occurred even when people knew the anchor was completely unrelated to the topic at hand.

- **Availability biases.** When judging the probability of an event, people overweight more recent or salient events.

An interesting element to these biases is that they persist even when people are told about them. Expertise turns out to be a hindrance; experts like doctors exhibit more overconfidence than laypeople (i.e., with training in a field, confidence increases faster than actual ability!). Camerer and Hogarth (1999) find that while incentives can reduce the magnitude of bias exhibited, no study has made irrational behavior disappear by increasing incentives.

Within the category of preferences as a broad source of irrationality, one way that preferences can play a role is described in prospect theory. There are a multitude of experimental studies showing that investors do not evaluate investments according to the expected utility (EU) framework, particularly when choosing among risky gambles. Prospect theory is an alternative to EU that is more consistent with much of this evidence. Prospect theory is positive (simply describing behavior) rather than normative (describing what behavior should be).

Kahneman and Tversky (1979) find survey respondents to be risk-averse over gains (preferring the sure small gain to the uncertain larger gain with the same expected amount) and to be risk-seeking over losses (preferring the larger uncertain loss to the smaller sure loss). As a result, they find that framing a question as a gain or loss can drive the outcome. For example, how a problem is defined (e.g., being given $1,000 with a chance to double it, versus being given $2,000 with a chance to halve it) leads to different choices—despite ending in the same final wealth position. It turns out that preferences shift dramatically: as much as 30-40% depending on simply the wording of the question. Thaler (2000) uses the term *mental accounting* to describe the process by which people frame questions for themselves.

A second preference-related source of irrationality is ambiguity aversion. Barberis and Thaler describe evidence that suggests people do not like situations where they are uncertain about the probability distribution of a gamble. People prefer a bet where the odds are known over a bet where they do not know the odds (even if the odds may be in their favor).

The Aggregate Stock Market

Barberis and Thaler share three striking facts about the U.S. stock market:

1. **The equity premium.** Stocks return almost 4 percent higher than short-term debt.
2. **Volatility.** Stock returns and price–dividend ratios are highly variable.
3. **Predictability.** Stock returns are forecastable.

All three of these phenomena are puzzles in that they are hard to rationalize in a simple model.

The *equity premium puzzle* concerns how, even though stocks appear to be an attractive asset, with high average returns and low covariance with consumption growth, investors demand a substantial risk premium to hold them. Some studies (e.g., Barberis, Huang, and Santos 2001) show that loss aversion can partially explain the high ratio of reward-to-risk for the aggregate stock market. Thaler, Tversky, Kahneman, and Schwartz (1997) run experiments in which subjects are asked to pick portfolios, and demonstrate that how the allocation decision is framed (e.g., showing return data on a monthly, annual, or five-year horizon basis) has a significant impact on the allocation chosen. Since investors are often uncertain about the distribution of a stock's return, how they respond to ambiguity may also play a role; they may demand a return for ambiguity as much as for risk.

The *volatility puzzle* may be driven by beliefs or preferences, with a number of possible stories providing explanations.

- Investors may believe that mean dividend growth is more variable than it actually is. They perceive a dividend surge as indicating that the overall dividend growth rate has increased, pushing up prices relative to dividends and amplifying the volatility of stock returns.

- An investor who has formed an opinion about cash flow growth based on public information does some private research and becomes overconfident about the accuracy of his own information. If that information is positive, he pushes prices up too high.

- Investors may extrapolate past returns too far into the future.

- Investors may confuse real and nominal quantities when forecasting future cash flows.

All of these stories are belief-based potential explanations for volatility in stock returns and price-dividend ratios.

The volatility puzzle may also be explainable by preferences. Experimental evidence suggests that the degree of loss aversion is not the same in all circumstances, but depends on prior gains and losses. Participants are more likely to take gambles after prior gains, and to refuse gambles after prior losses (the "house money effect"). Barberis et al. (2001) show that a model of this kind can help explain volatility.

The Cross-Section of Average Returns
The behavior of the aggregate stock market has generated both rational and non-rational explanations; however, studies of the behavior of individual stocks have generated facts that are harder to reconcile with rational models. One particular set of facts documents that one group of stocks earns higher average

returns than another group, in a manner inconsistent with the capital asset pricing model (CAPM). This fact set includes the following:

- **The size premium.** Fama and French (1992) document that the average return on the smallest 10% of stocks (in the NYSE, Amex, and Nasdaq exchanges from 1963–1990) is 0.74% per month higher than the average return on the largest stock decile (i.e., the largest 10% of individual stocks).

- **Long-term reversals.** DeBondt and Thaler (1985) demonstrate that a strategy of trading NYSE stocks based on their prior three-year cumulative return (i.e., selling recent winners and buying recent losers) generates a return 8% higher for the portfolio consisting of recent losers.

- **The predictive power of scaled-price ratios.** Book-to-market and earnings-to-price ratios appear to predict stock returns (supported by several studies, including Fama and French 1992).

- **Momentum.** Jegadeesh and Titman (1993) group NYSE stocks into deciles based on their prior six-month return and find that the biggest recent winners outperform the biggest recent losers by 10% annually. Note that results differ depending on the length of time one looks backward in forming portfolios.

Barberis and Thaler also describe various types of event studies examining stock returns that follow important corporate announcements: earnings announcements, dividends, stock buyback, and primary and secondary offerings. They review the challenges in rational-based explanations, including the joint test of market efficiency and asset pricing.

Behavioral researchers have developed belief-based models to explain how groups of stocks outearn other groups. Barberis, Shleifer, and Vishny (1998) develop a model in which investors make systematic errors in using public information to form expectations of future cash flows, based on two biases from updating their beliefs:

- **Conservatism.** Underweighting new information, which means that investors underreact to good earnings.

- **Representativeness.** Using too small or short a sample to make inferences about the population, which means that after a small series of good announcements, investors overreact and push the price up too high.

This model creates several observed phenomena (e.g., post-announcement drift, momentum, long-term reversals, cross-sectional forecasting power for price ratios). Similar studies stress an overconfidence bias in interpreting private information, which can also create predictions consistent with market observations.

Combining belief-based investor irrationality with institutional constraints generates further anomalous cross-sectional evidence. For example, short-sale constraints can explain why stocks with high price-earnings ratios earn lower returns. Miller (1977) shows that if bullish investors can buy, and bearish investors cannot sell short, prices will be too high and subsequent returns lower. Scheinkman and Xiong (2003) argue that investors may buy an overvalued stock in anticipation of it becoming more overvalued later, particularly when other investors cannot close the gap with short sales. Barberis and Thaler describe several papers testing and confirming the model's prediction that stocks with wider disagreement will have higher price-earnings ratios and lower returns.

Preferences may also help explain the cross section of average returns. Barberis and Huang (2001) show that combining loss aversion and narrow framing with assumptions about changing loss aversion over time can explain long-term reversals and price ratios. When investors hold a number of stocks, narrow framing may cause them to derive utility from gains and losses on individual stocks and not just on their portfolio. The pain of loss on one stock depends on that stock's past performance; this causes stocks with a poor return for several periods to be discounted at a higher rate, lowering the stock's price and P-E and leading to higher subsequent returns.

Closed-End Funds and Comovement

Closed-end funds issue a fixed number of shares so that buyers must find a seller. The puzzle is that average fund share prices trade at approximately a 10% discount to net asset value, despite the fact that upon termination the gap must become zero. Lee, Shleifer, and Thaler (1991) argue that some of the investors of these funds are noise traders with irrational swings in their expectations about future fund returns. Changes in their sentiment impact not only fund prices but also the difference between those prices and net asset value. Their own model predicts and confirms that the prices of these funds should move together, and also be correlated with price changes for small stocks.

Another question is whether similar behavioral models can explain other patterns of comovement. Lee, Shleifer, and Thaler (1991) observe that many investors trade only a subset of available securities, altering their exposure to this subset as their sentiment changes, which induces a common factor across this subset. Barberis and Shleifer (2003) argue that many investors first group stocks into asset class categories, and then allocate across them. Noise traders may move funds from one category to another, creating a factor common to the securities within that category, even if their cash flows are basically uncorrelated. Barberis and Shleifer find support for this view by examining otherwise dissimilar stocks added to the S&P 500 index.

Investor Behavior

Behavioral finance also seeks to explain what portfolios investors choose to hold and how they trade over time. As transaction costs fall and defined-contribution plans become a larger element of retirement planning, more individuals are responsible for their own retirement. Several biases for individual investors have been documented, including the following.

- **Insufficient diversification.** Investors diversify their portfolio much less than what is recommended by almost any normative model of portfolio choice. First, investors have a pronounced home bias; French and Poterba (1991) find that investors in the United States, Japan, and the United Kingdom allocate 94%, 98%, and 82% of their equity investments in domestic equities, despite the fact that their human capital is already overly dependent on their home country. Other studies find this local bias extends to overinvestment in an investor's own part of the country. At the extreme, over 30% of defined contribution plan assets in large U.S. companies are invested in the investors' own employer stock (Benartzi 2001). These findings are consistent with the evidence that investors dislike ambiguity and value familiarity.

- **Naïve diversification.** Benartzi and Thaler (2001) find that when people do diversify, they do so in a simplistic fashion. Many allocate $1/x$ of their savings to each of the x available investment options, whether in a lab experiment or in actual defined contribution plans. 401(k) plans that offer more stock funds will end up with investors invested more heavily in stocks.

- **Excessive trading.** Rational models of investing predict very little trading, but the sheer volume of trading on stock exchanges is much higher than this prediction. Studies of individuals and institutional managers suggest that both groups trade more than what can be rationally justified. Barber and Odean (2000) examine trading and find that the average return of investors is much lower than it would be if they simply traded less often. This low return appears to be driven both by transaction costs and by poor security selection. This result is consistent with overconfidence. In fact, those who trade the most (and so may be the most confident) earn the lowest returns. Consistent with studies that show overconfidence is higher for men, men trade more often and earn lower returns on average than women. Interestingly, investors who switch from telephone to online trading, and thereby get better information flow, appear to increase overconfidence, as online traders perform worse than before they make the switch.

- **The selling decision.** Several studies show that investors are reluctant to sell assets at a lower price than their purchase price. A tenet of rational investing models is that the purchase price should not matter, and only the forecast of cash flows from this point forward should drive buy-and-sell decisions. Furthermore, tax considerations actually favor selling assets below their cost. There are at least two behavioral explanations. First, investors may have an irrational belief that stock prices will exhibit mean reversion (i.e., will return to a previous price level after a significant move upward or downward). Second, investors may be subject to prospect theory and narrow framing, whereby not selling a stock that is below its purchase price represents a gamble that the stock will eventually break even and save the investor from a painful loss.

- **The buying decision.** Although sold stocks are likely to be above their purchase price and so are "prior winners," purchased stocks are evenly split between prior winners and losers (Odean 1999). In fact, a disproportionate number of purchased stocks are large prior winners and losers, which is consistent with an attention effect. People buy a stock that has caught their attention, either by going up or down significantly.

Corporate Finance

Do the irrational investors discussed earlier affect the financing and investment decisions of firms? How should a rational manager maximize stock price with such investors? Stein (1996) shows that a manager should issue shares in times of investor exuberance, and buy back shares when the price is low. Baker and Wurgler (2002) show that the share of equity issues among all issues is in fact higher prior to a downturn in the stock market. When CFOs issue stock, Graham and Harvey (2001) report that two-thirds consider the amount by which they assess their stock as undervalued (almost none of the CFOs assess their stock as overvalued). Barberis and Thaler consider some additional initial research exploring whether a market timing framework can serve as the basis for a theory of capital structure.

A second corporate finance application is study of why firms pay dividends at all, given that they have typically been taxed at a higher rate than capital gains. Stock buyback allows a similar result at a lower tax rate. Shefrin and Statman (1984) posit that many people have self-control problems causing them to prefer rigid rules (e.g., consuming only dividends rather than portfolio capital). A second behavioral explanation is based on mental accounting: dividends can make it easier to segregate gains from losses. Third, firms that pay dividends may help investors avoid regret. People regret action that loses money (e.g., selling shares which then rise) more than they regret inaction that loses money (e.g., failing to reinvest the dividend in stock which then rises).

A third corporate finance application is modeling managerial irrationality rather than investor irrationality. If managers think they are maximizing firm value, even if they are not, then no amount of aligning incentives is likely to help. Roll (1986) evaluates the evidence on takeover activity, and concludes that overconfident managers will be too quick to bid when their own valuation exceeds the market price of the target. The predictions of his "hubris hypothesis," that the price of the target will rise by the same amount the price of price of the bidder falls, are consistent with the data. Heaton (2002) predicts that overly optimistic managers will be reluctant to issue equity unless they have exhausted other sources of capital, consistent with the evidence.

Conclusion

In just twenty years, behavioral finance has made progress in explaining various phenomena.

- Researchers have investigated anomalous facts, such as DeBondt and Thaler's (1985) finding that stock prices appear to experience long-term reversals.

- There are limits to the ability of arbitrage to close pricing gaps, such that mispricing can exist in the absence of a profitable investment strategy.

- There is now a long catalog of ways people appear to form expectations and make choices, with some models that incorporate limited rationality.

- Finally, theories of behavioral finance have been developed, including investigation of behavior by individual and corporate investors.

In terms of future research, there is a chance to combine earlier work. Models to date concern isolated elements of investor beliefs or preferences, or the limits to arbitrage, but not all three. If asset pricing anomalies are more pronounced in smaller stocks, this may reflect more significant limits to arbitrage, but such interplay has not yet been meaningfully explored. One potential weakness of the field is the competing explanations: if the long list of biases allows too much freedom in explaining behavior, that is a weakness of the model. Barberis and Thaler argue that rational models involve auxiliary assumptions themselves in order to generate predictions.

Discussion and Implications

 For those with even elementary training in economics, the growing volume of research showing that people are anything but wealth-maximizing, rational agents threatens much of what is in that training. Consider the findings of the research described in the Barberis-Thaler review:

- Individuals mis-estimate probabilities, respond to how an issue is framed as much as to the underlying fact pattern, are not internally consistent in the choices they make, and exhibit marked overconfidence in their own ability to assess probability.

- Furthermore, experts are the most overconfident. The fact that arrogance increases faster than ability has large implications for the level of trust we all place, not just in fund managers as the focus of this finance section, but also in the experts we entrust in various fields: policymakers, doctors, pilots, and CEOs, among others.

- Markets do not close obvious pricing gaps.

- Investors overtrade, do not diversify or diversify across funds rather than assets, sell their winners too soon, and sell their losers too late.
- Firms overpay dividends and overbid for M&A targets.

Barberis and Thaler themselves acknowledge a central weakness to behavioral explanations of financial markets, which is summarized by Ritter (2003b):

> One of the major criticisms of behavioral finance is that by choosing which bias to emphasize, one can predict either underreaction or overreaction. This criticism of behavioral finance might be called "model dredging." In other words, one can find a story to fit the facts to *ex post* explain some puzzling phenomenon. But how does one make *ex ante* predictions about which biases will dominate? (p. 432)

Any model that generates too wide a set of predictions is a weaker model than one that generates narrow and refutable predictions.

Another criticism is that results from lab experiments may not apply to market situations, which have more opportunity for learning and competition, and some question whether models like prospect theory may be more applicable to a one-off decision problem in a lab context. Behavioral researchers argue that neoclassical models may be subject to some of these same criticisms, in terms of failing to predict real-world observed outcomes.

The debate between market efficiency and behavioral finance has developed into a central part of the finance literature over the past several years, and this debate has bubbled over into the popular media. Fama contends that the behavioral literature is essentially a collection of anomalies, and that such anomalies are often priced out of the market over time. He also argues that many of the findings in behavioral literature contradict each other (Fama 1998). In a series of question-and-answer postings to the Fama/French forum, Fama (2009) characterizes the limits of arbitrage as a theory that has not yet generated solid enough empirical support to discredit market efficiency, though French (Fama and French 2010) is more persuaded that the framework assists in understanding asset pricing. French cites Mitchell and Pulvino (2010), who examine periods of stress (crash of 1987, bubble of 1998–2001, and financial crisis of 2007–2008) for evidence on such limits. French concludes that mispricing does not mean easy profits, and that investors should act as if prices are right. Fama's comments about market efficiency in the wake of the 2008 financial crisis are included in an end note to this section.

We fall out roughly with Ken French on this. Eric coauthored a paper (Ball, Chiu, and Smith 2011) which concludes that even sophisticated market participants like venture capitalists cannot predict stock market movements in order to time issuances like IPOs, as suggested by some behavioralists (we found that VCs appear to react to run-ups in the stock market but do not appear able to predict downturns). Assets are often not priced accurately, but the opportunities to earn risk-adjusted abnormal profits are rare, and we think that unless one has very specific information it is best to act as though prices are right. Having said that, we also agree with Jay Ritter's (2003a) conclusion:

> My own summary of the empirical evidence on market efficiency is that the market gets the little things right, but sometimes gets the big things wrong. The stock market bubble of the late 1990s, in my opinion, is the financial economics equivalent of the Great Depression to macroeconomics—an outlier event so huge, and so difficult to explain within the context of the framework that explains investor behavior most of the time, that it will affect future empirical studies dramatically. (p. 2)

We also think it is worthwhile to evaluate in what domains and contexts we should assume that a manager, agent, or consumer is a rational economic person versus a biased decision-maker. People do make tradeoffs and respond to incentives well, both in economic and social arenas.[11] Your managers and customers can be trusted to make tradeoffs in most areas. At the same time, the behavioral literature shows that you should be particularly concerned about decision-making when probabilities play a significant role, given that even experts' probability estimates are consistently erroneous. At a minimum, this would include decisions related to both real and financial investments, safety, and a company's approach to corporate mergers (as discussed in Chapter 1, Section 8, most mergers fail, and we think decision-making biases play a role in these failures).

This discussion is part of a larger dynamic within research in management and the social sciences. By assuming that agents are rational and that they maximize a given utility or wealth function, we generate tractable models that can be developed mathematically. Most of the economics and finance literature over the past century has used mathematical models and tools and the "hard" physical sciences to prove certain outcomes and predictions based on assumptions. The problem with such models is that researchers often end up studying the problems that can be modeled rather than the most important problems (e.g., how do we build a rigorous model of leadership?). Conversely, research that does not limit itself to assumptions allowing for tractability, and thereby gaining more flexibility to tackle important problems, often ends up

---

[11] Gary Becker (1993a) describes his Nobel-prize-winning career focusing on how people make economic tradeoffs in sociological areas, including discrimination, criminal activity, education, and family planning. Becker (1993b) also describes how increased sexual activity may be a result not of changing moral attitudes but simply of the fact that birth control has made the cost of such activity lower. Jensen and Meckling (1994) point out that regulators may face tradeoffs different than what legislators intended: FDA officials are incented to keep potentially unsafe drugs off the market but have less counteracting incentive to expedite the introduction of potentially effective new drugs to the market.

simply telling stories or generating lists of possible explanations without a framework to determine which one should dominate in any particular circumstance. This tension arises across multiple areas in social sciences, but is particularly pronounced in the debate between rationality and market efficiency on the one hand and behavioral finance and cognitive bias on the other hand.

End Note

Eugene Fama (2009) gets to the heart of the debate about whether the 2007–2008 financial crisis killed the theory of market efficiency. A *Fama/French Forum* user posted this question:

> Justin Fox ("The Myth of the Rational Market") and many other financial writers claim that much of the blame for the financial meltdown is attributable to a misguided faith in market efficiency that encouraged market participants to accept security prices as the best estimate of value rather than conduct their own investigation. Is this a fair assessment? If so, how should policymakers respond?

Fama responded at length in a November 4, 1999 posting titled, "Q&A: Is Market Efficiency the Culprit?"

> The premise of the Fox book is that our current economic problems are largely due to blind acceptance of the efficient markets hypothesis (EMH), which posits that market prices reflect all available information. The claim is that the world's investors and their advisors in the financial industry bought into this model. Because they ceased to investigate the true value of assets, we have been hit with "bubbles" in asset prices. The most recent is the rise and sharp decline in real estate prices which froze financial markets and led to the worst recession since the Great Depression of the 1930s.
>
> The book is fun reading, but its main premise is fantasy. Most investing is done by active managers who don't believe markets are efficient. For example, despite my taunts of the last 45 years about the poor performance of active managers, about 80% of mutual fund wealth is actively managed. Hedge funds, private equity, and other alternative asset classes, which have attracted big fund inflows in recent years, are built on the proposition that markets are inefficient. The recent problems of commercial and investment banks trace mostly to their trading desks and their proprietary portfolios, and these are always built on the assumption that markets are inefficient. Indeed, if banks and investment banks took market efficiency more seriously, they might have avoided lots of their recent problems. Finally, MBA students who aspire to high paying positions in the financial industry have a tough time finding a job if they accept the EMH.

I continue to believe the EMH is a solid view of the world for almost all practical purposes. But it's pretty clear I'm in the minority. If the EMH took over the investment world, I missed it.

The Fox book is an example of a general phenomenon. Finance, financial markets, and financial institutions are in disrepute. The popular story is that together, they caused the current recession. I think one can take an entirely different position: financial markets and financial institutions were casualties rather than the cause of the recession.

But suppose we buy into the more common negative current view of finance. There is still a big open question. Beginning in the early 1980s, the developed world and some big players in the developing world experienced a period of extraordinary growth. It's reasonable to argue that in facilitating the flow of world savings to productive uses around the world, financial markets and financial institutions played a big role in this growth. Despite any role of finance in the current recession, are the market naysayers really ready to argue that worldwide wealth would be higher today if financial markets and financial institutions didn't develop as they did?

Toward the end of the book, Fox concludes that passive investing is the right choice for almost all investors. My academic friends in behavioral finance (for example, Richard Thaler) almost always end up with a similar conclusion. In my view, this is an admission that the EMH provides a good view of the world for almost all practical purposes. At which point, I say I won. (para. 1–7)

FURTHER READING

If you're interested in reading more on the topics discussed in this chapter, here are some sources to get you started. We do not offer this as a comprehensive or exhaustive list, but rather have selected well-regarded or significant works that space did not permit us to include in the main discussion.

1. CAPITAL STRUCTURE

Black, Fischer. 1976. "The Dividend Puzzle." *Journal of Portfolio Management* 2(2), 5–8.

Brealey, Richard, Stewart Myers, and Franklin Allen. 2010. *Principles of Corporate Finance*, 10th edition. New York, McGraw-Hill/Irwin.

Hennessy, Christopher and Toni Whited. 2005. "Debt Dynamics." *Journal of Finance* 60(3), 1129–1165.

Jensen, Michael and Clifford Smith. 1984. *The Modern Theory of Corporate Finance*, 2nd edition. New York, McGraw-Hill.

Timmer, Jan. 2012. "Understanding the Fed Model, Capital Struture, and Then Some." Working Paper. http://dx.doi.org/10.2139/ssrn.1322703.

2. CAPITAL ASSET PRICING

Mehrling, Perry. 2005. *Fischer Black and the Revolutionary Idea of Finance*. New York, Wiley.

Rubinstein, Mark. 2006. *A History of the Theory of Investments: My Annotated Bibliography*. New York, Wiley.

3. MARKET EFFICIENCY

Fama, Eugene, Lawrence Fisher, Michael Jensen, and Richard Roll. 1969. "The Adjustment of Stock Prices to New Information." *International Economic Review* 10(1), 1–21.

Malkiel, Burton. 2012. *A Random Walk Down Wall Street*, 10th edition. New York, Norton.

Shiller, Robert. 2006. *Irrational Exuberance*, 2nd edition. New York, Crown Business.

4. AGENCY THEORY

Bolton, Patrick and Mathias Dewatripont. 2005. *Contract Theory*. Cambridge, MIT Press.

Eisenhardt, Kathleen. 1989. "Agency Theory: An Assessment and Review." *Academy of Management Review* 14(1), 57–74

Jensen, Michael and Kevin Murphy. 1990. "Performance Pay and Top Management Incentives." *Journal of Political Economy* 98(2), 225–264.

5. IMPERFECT INFORMATION

Akerlof, George. 1970. "The Market for 'Lemons': Quality Uncertainty and the Market Mechanism." *Quarterly Journal of Economics* 84(3), 488–500.

Copeland, Thomas, Fred Westin, and Kuldeep Shastri. 2004. "Imperfect Information and Agency Theory." *Financial Theory and Corporate Policy*, 4th edition. New York, Addison Wesley. Ch. 12.

6. BUSINESS MEASUREMENT

2GC Limited. 2009. *2GC Balanced Scorecard Usage Survey 2009*. http://www.2gc.co.uk/pdf/2GC-RP-BSCuseSurvey2009-091007.pdf

Hope, Jeremy and Steve Player. 2011. *Beyond Performance Management: Why, When, and How to Use 40 Tools and Best Practices for Superior Business Performance*. Cambridge, Harvard Business Review Press.

Hubbard, Douglas. 2010. *How to Measure Anything: Finding the Value of Intangibles in Business*. New York, Wiley.

Kaplan, Robert and David Norton. 2006. *Alignment: Using the Balanced Scorecard to Create Corporate Synergies*. Cambridge, Harvard Business Review Press.

Voelpel, Sven, Marius Leibold, and Robert Eckhoff. 2006. "The Tyranny of the Balanced Scorecard in the Innovation Economy." *Journal of Intellectual Capital* 7(1), 43–60.

7. Behavioral Finance

Davies, Greg and Arnaud de Servigny. 2012. *Behavioral Investment Management: An Efficient Alternative to Modern Portfolio Theory*. New York, McGraw-Hill.

Shefrin, Hersh and Meir Statman. 2000. "Behavioral Portfolio Theory." *Journal of Financial and Quantitative Analysis* 35(2), 127–151.

Shleifer, Andrei. 2000. *Inefficient Markets: An Introduction to Behavioral Finance*. New York, Oxford University Press USA.

Works Cited

Allen, Franklin and Gerald Faulhaber. 1989. "Signaling by Underpricing in the IPO Market." *Journal of Financial Economics* 23(2), 303–323.

Ball, Eric, Hsin-Hui Chiu, and Richard Smith. 2011. "Can VCs Time the Market? An Analysis of Exit Choice for Venture-Backed Firms." *Review of Financial Studies* 24(9), 3105–3138.

Banz, Rolf. 1981. "The Relationship between Return and Market Value of Common Stocks." *Journal of Financial Economics* 9(1), 3–18.

Barberis, Nicholas and Richard Thaler. 2003. "A Survey of Behavioral Finance." In G. M. Constantinides, M. Harris, and R. Stulz (editors), *The Handbook of the Economics of Finance*. New York, Elsevier Science B.V. pp. 1052–1121.

Basu, Sanjoy. 1977. "Investment Performance of Common Stocks in Relation to Their Price-Earnings Ratios: A Test of the Efficient Markets Hypothesis." *Journal of Finance* 32(3), 663–682.

Basu, Sanjoy. 1983. "The Relationship between Earnings' Yield, Market Value and Return for NYSE Common Stocks: Further Evidence." *Journal of Financial Economics* 12(1), 129–156.

Becker, Gary. 1993a. "The Economic Way of Looking at Behavior" [Nobel address]. *Journal of Political Economy* 101(3), 385–409.

Becker, Gary, 1993b. *A Treatise on the Family*, enlarged edition. Cambridge, Harvard University Press.

The Brandes Institute. 2008. "Value vs. Glamour: A Global Phenomenon." Brandes Institute Research Paper. http://www.brandes.com/Institute/Documents/Value%20vs%20Glamour%20Global%20Phenomenon%200808.pdf

Campbell, Tim and William Kracaw. 1980. "Information Production, Market Signaling, and the Theory of Financial Intermediation." *Journal of Finance* 35(4), 863–882.

Chen, Nai-Fu, Richard Roll, and Stephen Ross. 1986. "Economic Forces and the Stock Market." *Journal of Business* 59(3), 383–403.

Chermushkin, Sergei. 2008. "What's Wrong with the Economic Value Added?" Mordovian State University Working Paper. http://dx.doi.org/10.2139/ssrn.1120917.

Damodaran, Aswath. 2009. "Valuation: Closing Thoughts." Damodaran Online Lectures, New York University. http://people.stern.nyu.edu/adamodar/pdfiles/eqnotes/valcloseFall09.pdf.

Dodd, James and Shimin Chen. 1996. "EVA: A New Panacea?" *Business and Economic Review* 42(July–September), 26–28.

Dybvig, Philip and Stephen Ross. 1985. "Yes, the APT Is Testable." *Journal of Finance* 40(4), 1173–1188.

Fama, Eugene. 1970. "Efficient Capital Markets: A Review of Theory and Empirical Work." *Journal of Finance* 25(2), 383–417.

Fama, Eugene. 1998. "Market Efficiency, Long-Term Returns and Behavioral Finance." *Journal of Financial Economics* 49(3), 283–306.

Fama, Eugene F. 2009. "Q&A: Is Market Efficiency the Culprit?" *Fama/French Forum*, 4 November. http://www.dimensional.com/famafrench/2009/11/qa-is-market-efficiency-the-culprit.html.

Fama, Eugene and Kenneth French. 1993. "Common Risk Factors in the Returns on Stocks and Bonds." *Journal of Financial Economics* 33(1), 3–56.

Fama, Eugene and Kenneth French. 2002. "Testing Tradeoff and Pecking Order: Predictions About Dividends and Debt." *Review of Financial Studies* 15(1), 1–37.

Fama, Eugene F., and Kenneth R. French. 2010. "Q&A: The Limits of Arbitrage." *Fama/French Forum*, 14 July. http://www.dimensional.com/famafrench/2010/07/qa-the-limits-of-arbitrage.html.

Frank, Murray and Vidhan Goyal. 2003. "Testing the Pecking Order Theory of Capital Structure." *Journal of Financial Economics* 67(2), 217–248.

Ch_Layout_7.docxFriedman, Milton. 1953. "The Case for Flexible Exchange Rates." In *Essays in Positive Economics*. Chicago, University of Chicago Press. pp. 157–203.

Jensen, Michael. 2001. "Value Maximisation, Stakeholder Theory, and the Corporate Objective Function." *European Financial Management* 7(2), 97–317.

Jensen, Michael and William Meckling. 1976. "Theory of the Firm: Managerial Behavior, Agency Costs, and Ownership Structure." *Journal of Financial Economics* 3(4), 305–360.

Jensen, Michael and William Meckling. 1994. "The Nature of Man." *Journal of Applied Corporate Finance* 7(2), 4–19.

Kaplan, Robert and David Norton. 1996. *The Balanced Scorecard: Translating Strategy into Action*. Cambridge, Harvard Business Review Press.

Keim, Donald. 1983. "Size-Related Anomalies and Stock Return Seasonality: Further Empirical Evidence." *Journal of Financial Economics* 12(1), 13–32.

Kurtzman Joel. 1997. "Is Your Company Off Course? Now You Can Find Out Why." *Fortune* 17 February, 128–130.

Lakonishok, Josef, Andrei Shleifer, and Robert Vishny. 1994. "Contrarian Investment, Extrapolations, and Risk." *Journal of Finance* 49(5), 1541–1578.

Leland, Hayne and David Pyle. 1977. "Informational Asymmetries, Financial Structure, and Financial Intermediation." *Journal of Finance* 32(2), 371–387.

Malina, Mary and Frank Selto. 2001. "Communicating and Controlling Strategy: An Empirical Study of the Effectiveness of the Balanced Scorecard." *Journal of Management Accounting Research* 13(1), 47-90.

Markowitz, Harry. 1952. "Portfolio Selection." *Journal of Finance* 7(1), 77–91.

Miller, Merton. 1977. "Debt and Taxes." *Journal of Finance* 32(2), 261–275.

Modigliani, Franco and Merton Miller. 1958. "The Cost of Capital, Corporation Finance and the Theory of Investment." *American Economic Review* 48(3), 261–297.

Myers, Stewart. 1984. "The Capital Structure Puzzle." *Journal of Finance* 39(3), 575–592.

Myers, Stewart and Nicholas Majluf. 1984. "Corporate Financing and Investment Decisions When Firms Have Information that Investors Do Not Have." *Journal of Financial Economics* 13(2), 187–221.

Reinganum, Marc. 1981. "Misspecification of Asset Pricing: Empirical Anomalies Based on Earnings Yields and Market Values." *Journal of Financial Economics* 9(1), 19–46.

Ritter, Jay. 2003a. "Introduction." In J. Ritter (editor), *Recent Developments in Corporate Finance*. Northampton, MA, Edward Elgar Publishers. pp. 1–13.

Ritter, Jay. 2003b. "Behavioral Finance." *Pacific-Basin Finance Journal* 11(4), 429–437.

Roll, Richard. 1977. "A Critique of the Asset Pricing Theory's Tests." *Journal of Financial Economics* 4(2), 129–176.

Roll, Richard and Stephen Ross. 1980. "An Empirical Investigation of the Arbitrage Pricing Theory." *Journal of Finance* 35(5), 1073–1104.

Rosenberg, Barr, Kenneth Reid, and Ronald Lanstein, 1985. "Persuasive Evidence of Market Inefficiency." *Journal of Portfolio Management* 11(3), 9–17.

Ross, Stephen. 1976. "The Arbitrage Theory of Capital Asset Pricing." *Journal of Economic Theory* 13(3), 341–360.

Shanken, Jay. 1982. "The Arbitrage Pricing Theory: Is It Testable?" *Journal of Finance* 37(5), 1129–1140.

Sharpe, William. 1964. "Capital Asset Prices: A Theory of Market Equilibrium under Conditions of Risk." *Journal of Finance* 19(3), 425–442.

Stern, Joel, Bennett Stewart, and Don Chew, 1995. "The EVA Financial Management System." *Journal of Applied Corporate Finance* 8(2), 32–46.

Stangeland, David. 2006. "Using the EVA Financial Management System to Make the Wrong Decision." *Journal of Business & Economics Research* 4(11), 43–56.

Stewart, G. Bennett. 1990. *The Quest for Value: The EVA^{TM} Management Guide*. New York, HarperBusiness.

Williamson, Oliver. 1996. "The Economics of Organization: A Primer." *California Management Review* 38(2), 131–146.

EMERGING TOPICS
IN MANAGEMENT

We consider the four topics presented in this chapter to be essential for executives in the 21st century, but not to require an entire chapter for each. Peter Drucker was one of the first academic thinkers to view management as a profession, and his specific management advice for nonprofit managers is also useful in a broader business context (Section 1). Developing since the 1970s, the new field of cognitive bias and decision-making can help executives across all business functions (Section 2). In Section 3, we address the role of marketing in a modern organization. To end the chapter, we turn to the role and promise of the field of complex adaptive systems, which can provide a better understanding of a wide variety of social phenomena (Section 4).

1. MANAGING NONPROFITS (AND BUSINESSES)

In November 2005, one of *Business Week*'s cover stories referred to Peter Drucker as "the man who invented management" (Byrne and Gerdes 2005, cover). He published 39 books from 1939 through 2008, and wrote *The Practice of Management* (1954) to address his frustration that there was no book on how to pursue the profession of management, in contrast to the quantity of literature available for professions like medicine or law. He spent much of his later career focused on the increased role of nonprofit organizations in U.S. society, and on ways to make these organizations more effective at creating changed human beings.

Drucker wrote the first edition of *Managing the Nonprofit Organization* in 1990, and in this section we summarize the business reprint edition (2005). It is worth noting at the outset that almost all of the principles of this book apply to business managers as much as to nonprofit leaders.

PETER DRUCKER
Managing the Nonprofit Organization: Principles and Practices, 7th edition
(2005).

Thesis: Ensure everyone lives the mission. Be action-oriented and driven by
results. Know who your customers are. Define performance concretely and
keep score on yourself. Allocate your own life, make yourself a leader by
focusing on what you want to be remembered for. Develop your strengths, not
your weaknesses.[1]

Half of U.S. adults volunteer, making nonprofits the country's
largest employer and a sector representing 2-3% of the GNP (p.
xiii). Their product is not a material good but rather a changed
human being, but there are few tools or materials designed to
their specific management needs. Nonprofits have unique challenges in
converting donors into contributors, and giving community and common
purpose (replacing the role that used to be played by small towns). Drucker
believes that nonprofits historically were viewed (even by themselves) as
marginal to society, but by 1990 had become "central to American society and
indeed its most distinguishing feature" (p. xiii). In this book, he seeks to meet "a
real need among the nonprofits for materials that are specifically developed out
of their experience" (p. xv).

The Mission Comes First, and the Role of Leader
In making a commitment, it is not charisma but the mission that matters, and
the first job of a leader is to define the institution's mission simply and to set
concrete action goals. The mission of a hospital is not "health care"—the
hospital addresses illness, and each person addresses their own health care. A
hospital mission of "health care" also fails because it does not specify what
action or behavior must follow from the mission. "A mission statement has to
be operational, otherwise it's just good intentions" (p. 4). The task of the
nonprofit manager is to convert the mission into specifics.

A successful mission requires opportunities, competence, and commitment.
The leader should examine the nonprofit's strength and performance and align
the mission with what the organization is good at. Rather than pretending to do
everything, investigate opportunities and needs outside the organization and

---

[1] Drucker tended to write in a more direct style than most academic authors. In particular,
he often used the command voice, exhorting the reader to definitely *do* one set of activities
and to avoid others. As with our other summaries, we attempt to capture the tone of the
author, and so this summary maintains Drucker's somewhat directive voice.

determine where it is possible to make a difference. Finally, consider what the leader, the organization, and the employees and volunteers really believe in.

Leadership is a foul-weather job, and the most important task of a leader is to anticipate crisis, which always comes. Success has ruined more organizations than failure. Nonprofits must make hard choices, and need the discipline of organized abandonment. To do anything well, nonprofit managers have to determine what they are *not* going to do. Start by recognizing that change is not a threat. Look for changes from unexpected success in your own organization (e.g., colleges getting demand from older, already-educated adults), population changes (e.g., demographic shifts), and changes in mindset and mentality in the population at large.

Next, the nonprofit needs a way to bring the new solution to the marketplace, which requires hard work on the part of true believers (who work full-time or not at all). You need to make sure that those doing the planning also understand the details (e.g., if you convert your museum to educational outreach, do you have enough restrooms?).

To pick a leader, first look at the candidates' strengths. Most committees focus on each candidate's deficiencies, but you can only perform with strength. Second, identify the one immediate key challenge and match the leader to it. Third, look for character and integrity—would you want your children to work for this person? Nonprofits need leaders who take their roles seriously but do not take themselves seriously. Anyone who considers themselves "a great man" or "great woman" will kill their own effectiveness and the agency.

Your own personal leadership role has to fit in three dimensions. It must match who you are (e.g., if you are a comic, do not try to play Hamlet), it has to fit the task, and it has to fit expectations. Effective leaders never say (or think) "I", but rather think in terms of the team, accepting responsibility but ensuring that "we" get any credit. Leaders are visible and are constantly on trial; some are more effective in routine, and others in crisis. Most organizations need someone to lead regardless of the circumstances, by working on basic competences: willingness and discipline to listen, willingness to communicate, refusal to alibi yourself, and willingness to recognize your own unimportance compared to the task. Separate yourself from the task, and give not your life but rather your best efforts to leading.

People are not "born leaders." Leadership cannot always be taught but it can be learned—most leaders are not born or made, but are self-made, like Harry Truman. Drucker explores how to set new goals and discusses "what the leader owes" (p. 37).

A leader must balance several dimensions:

- the long- and short-range,
- the concentration of resources on one goal and the diversification of goals,

- caution and rashness ("I've seen more institutions damaged by too much caution than by rashness, though I've seen both" (p. 24)), and
- opportunity and risk.

Reversible decisions can incur more risk, and sometimes there are risks the organization cannot afford not to take.

A leader has "do nots" of leadership as well as "do's":

- Do not believe that the necessity of specific actions is obvious to team members.
- Do not be afraid of strengths in your organization—ambition is better than mediocrity.
- Do not pick a successor who reminds you of your younger self (do not hire a "carbon copy"). Beware also of faithful assistants; people who are able to make decisions rarely stay in the support role for long, and good number 2s often do not make good number 1s. Avoid anointed "crown princes," as often they have avoided responsibility.
- Do not hog the credit.
- Do not publicly criticize your subordinates.
- Do keep your eye on the task and not on yourself—you are a servant of the organization.

Make sure everybody sees, hears, and lives the mission. Periodically evaluate whether the mission needs refocusing due to a change in demographics, efforts not getting results, or the accomplishment of the objective. Look for the opportunity (need). Remain action-oriented in the short-term even when planning for the long-term. Be driven by results. Think through priorities. Set an example, whether you are CEO or a three-hour-per-week volunteer.

Effective Strategies for Marketing, Innovation, and Fund Development
In order for a nonprofit to convert good intentions into results, the end user must in fact be a doer rather than a user. As leader of the nonprofit, you need a plan, marketing, people, and money. Do not put your scarce resources where results will not follow. Know your customers.

Create a fund development strategy, because you raise funds not from the beneficiaries but from those who participate by donating; in fund development, you create a constituency that supports the organization because they view the organization as deserving support. Drucker discusses building the donor constituency, where the first constituency is one's own board, and the ultimate goal of development is contributors who see support as self-fulfillment.

To develop a winning strategy, remember that good intentions do not move mountains—bulldozers do—and strategies are the bulldozers. Strategies are action-focused, describing not what is hoped for but what can be worked for.

- **Improve what the organization already does well.** Strategy is needed for each factor of production. The first factor is people: work smarter and place people where they can produce. The second is money, namely how to get more out of what you already have. The third factor is time—you need ambitious productivity goals. Follow this process: clearly define the goal and convert it into specific results and targets, create a marketing plan for each target group, provide communication and training, handle the logistics (i.e., what resources are required), and define when you have to see results. Do not try to reach different market segments with the same message.

- **Innovate.** Refocus and change the organization when you are successful. An organization that does not improve will go downhill quickly. Look at change as an opportunity rather than a threat. Ask the questions, "How can this give us a chance to contribute?" and "Who in our organization should work on this?".

Drucker provides a list of common mistakes in developing strategy:

- Moving directly from idea to full-scale operation, ignoring the fact that new ideas require testing.
- Basing decisions on common knowledge, instead of examining the actual details of what is happening (Drucker exhorts his readers to look out the window).
- Righteous arrogance—managers must adapt their innovation to reality.
- Failing to adapt, even though everything has a different market than what the innovator expected.
- Patching up the old rather than going all out for the new.
- Overpersistence—if you get no results, try a second time, then move on to something else.

Strategy converts the mission into performance, but too many nonprofit managers convert strategy with a selling effort. Strategy *ends* with a selling effort, but *begins* with knowing who the customers are. It is important to constantly improve strategies and innovate, and critical to develop a strategy to build the donor base. All of these strategies begin with research (starting with researching the people who should be customers) and then training. Abandon what no longer works or is no longer needed. Strategy exploits the right moment, and commits the organization to action.

Managing for Performance: How to Define and Measure Performance
Drucker asks and addresses the question, "What is the bottom line when there is no bottom line?" Many nonprofits de-emphasize performance despite the fact that results are more important for a nonprofit than a for-profit business. Businesses at least provide profitability as a benchmark. The nonprofit manager must first identify the desired results, even before figuring out how to measure

them. It is not enough to serve a need—good nonprofits create a want. Resist the temptation to be reckless; concentrate resources where the results are and do not make promises you cannot meet. Also resist the temptation to go for easy results rather than those that further the mission (e.g., university presidents are often pressured to accept money for department chairs who would detract from the school's mission).

Nonprofits must plan for performance. As they always have multiple constituencies, the toughest task is to get all constituents to agree on long-term goals. It is also common but dangerous to confuse moral and economic causes; such confusion squanders resources. Supporters of moral causes often interpret the absence of results as evidence that efforts must be increased. Put your resources where results are, rather than tilting at windmills (e.g., trying to convince humans not to have sex).

Drucker addresses basic rules for managing for performance:

- Do not become inward-looking or see the institution as an end in itself.
- Do not spend time trying to make workers feel better without addressing the root causes of their dissatisfaction.
- Do not suppress dissent—it is essential, though feuding and bickering must not be tolerated.
- Do not tolerate discourtesy. Immature people resent good manners as dishonesty, viewing them as substance rather than as vital lubricating oil for social friction. Good causes never excuse bad manners, which leave permanent scars.
- Do build the organization around information and communication rather than hierarchy.
- Do delegate, but maintain your own accountability for performance by following up to ensure the task is done, and done right.

Organizations need to control standards. Standards must be set high (slow is different from low), and must be well-defined. High performers should be made visible, and appraisals should always start with what is done well. One can only base performance on strengths. In addition, force people to be outside the organization often enough to know what the organization exists for—inside an institution, there are no results but only costs.

Businesses often define performance too narrowly but at least concretely; for nonprofits, however, it is not enough to say, "We are serving a good cause." Nonprofits use other people's money, making it harder but necessary to quantify results as much as possible, both immediate and long-term. For example, the Salvation Army knows the percentage of alcoholics who stay sober and of criminals who do not get rearrested. Only when key performance areas are defined can goals be set.

Risk and Decision-Making

Effective decision-making is key. Executives spend little time making decisions, despite the fact that this is the one thing they cannot delegate without rendering themselves ineffective. The least effective decision-makers are those who do it constantly, while the most effective make few decisions and concentrate on the important decisions. Many people misapply their time by spending it on easy or irrelevant decisions. Decisions always involve risk-taking, time, and thought. Do not waste time on decisions that lack meaningful consequences.

There are three kinds of risks: those we can afford to take, irreversible decisions, and those where the risk may be high but should not be avoided (sometimes you actually do have to "bet the organization" on a course of action). Too many decisions remain pious intentions. This may arise from selling rather than marketing a decision, going systemwide immediately, not designating who will carry out the decision, or not identifying who needs to do what. Decisions always have to be reevaluated (or as Drucker puts it, "rescued") as circumstances change.

Dissent is essential—if there is consensus on an important matter, you probably have not thought it through well enough. You should not ask who is right or even what is right, but rather assume that each faction is giving the right answer to a different question. Moving from dissent to a common understanding is more critical for nonprofits, which have a higher propensity for internal conflict because everyone is committed to a good cause. Dissent also has the benefit of encouraging the nonconformists upon whom progress depends. Use dissent and disagreement to resolve conflict.

People and Relationships: Staff, Board, Volunteers, and Community

In making people decisions, executives who believe they are good judges of people often end up making the worst decisions because they rely on their "gut" instinct. To be effective, an executive must commit to a diagnostic process. Selection begins with an assignment, and Drucker makes the following recommendations for executives.

- Force yourself to look at more than one candidate.
- Focus on performance and not on personality. Avoid silly questions like "Do you get along with others?" or "Do you have initiative?". Ask what the candidates have accomplished in their last three assignments, and evaluate what they are capable of.
- Check references from people who have known the candidate far longer than you have.

The selection process does not end until 90 days after the person starts, when you evaluate if you have selected the right person.

In developing people, Drucker advises avoiding the following obvious mistakes.

- Do not try to build on their weaknesses; personalities are set by adulthood.
- Do not take a shortsighted view of development—develop workers for a career, not for immediate skills.
- Do not establish "crown princes" (i.e., a fast track for promotion), as there is low correlation between promise at age 23 and performance at age 45.
- If someone tries and fails, give them another chance. If they do not try, ensure that they leave immediately.
- Remember that you can always relax standards but can never raise them.

The best way to develop people is to use them as teachers.

To build a team, start not with the people but the job. There are two keys to personal effectiveness on the job: understanding your own role in detail, and taking responsibility for thinking through what needs to be done. Eighty percent of working effectively is telling people what they do that helps and hinders you, and asking them what you do that helps and hinders them. The executive must encourage everyone to ask what top management really has to know.

The executive must also build reciprocal relationships with the staff, Board, community, donors, volunteers, and alumni. The test of a relationship is not whether it solves problems but whether it functions despite problems. To build community relations, contact those served by the nonprofit (alumni) months later, and let them know you are still concerned with how they are doing.

Unpaid staff are increasingly important to nonprofits, which comes with its own set of challenges. Drucker recommends reframing employees from volunteers to unpaid staff. Sometimes people volunteer because they are lonely, so although the work can meet their desire for interaction, some fraction of volunteers are not skilled at working with others and so must be put into a role that does not depend on such work or be asked to leave. The decision to fire a person is difficult, but allowing non-performers to stay lets down the organization and its cause. One common problem is people who have simply been in the same job for too long; in that case, you can "re-pot" them rather than terminate them. Others must go.

Nonprofit executives deal with a wider variety of stakeholders, so it is more important to manage relationships. Remember that people require clear assignments, the organization must be information-based, nonperformers must be reassigned or told to leave, and the executives have a responsibility to both learn and teach.

Developing Yourself as a Person, as an Executive, and as a Leader
The executive's first priority for development is to strive for excellence. The satisfaction of the team is based on achieving important work essential to a goal that they believe in. A nurse with 32 orthopedic patients should remember that they are her job, and the doctors and the insurance paperwork are impediments.

Drucker advises executives that one can only make *oneself* effective, and that performing is the only thing that will bring trust and support. Review your own performance critically once or twice a year, to identify where you have made a difference and where you have wasted your time. Hold yourself accountable and recognize your responsibility. Reward good performance with a raise. Promote only those people who leave behind a bigger job than they initially took on. The leader sets the standard, and so does every member of an organization. Ask yourself, and others, what do you want to be remembered for? No young person can answer this question, but if you still cannot answer it by your 50s you will have wasted your life. The question pushes you to see yourself as the person you can become rather than who you now are.

Drucker offers the following advice for young people just starting out in their career:

- As you begin the process of self-placement, take your own temperament and personality seriously because they are not too subject to change by training.
- If you have to understand a decision completely before acting, you do not belong on a battlefield, but may excel at another role.
- If you do not feel you belong where you now work, make sure you identify the core reasons why.
- Promotion is not important, but consideration for it is. If you are not being so considered, it is better to leave before you start accepting the organization's second-rate opinion of yourself.
- Sometimes "repotting yourself" is essential to stimulate yourself again, particularly over a longer career.
- Force yourself out of routine—burnout is often just a copout for being bored, and nothing is more fatiguing than going off to work when you don't give a damn. Recognize that most work is repetitive, though, and that the excitement is in the result rather than the work.

Doing the right things well is key. Most of us work at a surprisingly low yield of effectiveness, even when working hard. Effectiveness is a matter of habits and following a few elementary rules.

- Decide what are the right things to do—doing things right (i.e., efficiency) is irrelevant until you are working on the right things.
- Identify strengths by performance. Strengths are not skills, they are capacities. It is vital to know about yourself whether you are a reader or listener (i.e., do you understand concepts better by reading them or hearing them?).
- Listen. Too many think they are good with people because they talk well; being good with people actually means listening well.

- Expect your job to stimulate you only if you work on your own self-renewal and the most effective way to do so is to look for unexpected success and run with it.

In summary, you are responsible for allocating your life—nobody else will do it for you. Self-development means developing both the person's strengths and the skill to contribute. A good boss can also assist with employee development, which does not mean ignoring your weaknesses, but rather overcoming by developing strengths. Work on the tasks to be done and the opportunities to be explored. Proceed in parallel with improvement (do better what you already do well) and change (do something different)—both are essential. Listen for the signal that it is time to change, and do it when you are successful. Ask, "Would I go into this today knowing what I now know?" Keep score on yourself. Development is not a philosophy or set of intentions: it is action. "What will you do tomorrow as a result of reading this book? And what will you stop doing?" (p. 224).

Development begins with striving toward an idea outside of yourself, not with leading. Leaders are self-made, which requires focus. Asking what you want to be remembered for is the beginning of adulthood; the answer changes as the person matures, but the question is required to enable focus and direction.

Discussion and Implications

 By now you probably have recognized that only a portion of Drucker's insights from *Managing the Non-Profit Organization* are specific to the nonprofit community. Drucker explores the essence of management and decision-making in any context. He has been sometimes criticized for his failure to base his conclusions on quantitative research, and he certainly did not gather measurable data from multiple organizations to run regressions. Though he wrote 39 books that sold well, relatively few were considered academically rigorous enough to be read in graduate level courses in management outside his own school.

Our view is that he exemplifies the best of qualitative research, rigorously investigating the behavior of managers and the reasons for the behavior. For example, he wrote about the increasing importance of "knowledge workers" in the 1970s, decades before the term came into constant usage. Drucker consulted for businesses, government leaders and presidents, nonprofits, and academic institutions. We believe that, more than any other person, he successfully straddled the academic and business worlds and showed each what could be learned from the other. In that sense, this book represents our own effort to emulate his approach. We also find his work harder to summarize concisely, precisely because of the density of insight he provides.

Following are some additional observations from another of his books (*Innovation and Entrepreneurship*, 2007) and from his lectures:

- Cultural differences are harder to navigate than language differences (language is obvious, cultural differences create misaligned assumptions).
- One should know accounting as a means of self-defense.
- Drucker's friends were told, accurately, that they were too highly educated to succeed in commerce.
- To manage your boss, first understand how he or she learns (reader vs. listener, morning vs. afternoon, blocks vs. snippets). Tell your subordinates whether you are a reader or listener. Second, knowing when to leave is the single most important thing in managing one's boss.
- We now stay in school too long, and are too disconnected from our physical world.
- Humans require community, and community is defined by who it excludes.
- Government is not competent to tackle substantive community challenges. He recommends less government spending and more tax incentives by offering deductions in excess of donation amounts.
- Free advice is not followed—if you want them to listen then you should charge.
- All industry transitions come from outside.
- The biggest problem in business is bad manners.
- The world is full of bright people who get nothing done because they rely on being smart—it is more important to be conscientious.
- Even if shooting from the hip, you still need to shoot at a target.
- The secret of success is prioritization. What one postpones one abandons. You cannot go back and marry your old sweetheart.
- Social phenomena follow the 80-20 rule, not a bell curve. To raise the average, first raise the peak.
- You owe nothing to a toaster. Do not commit to a product; that is idol worship.
- Systematic innovation requires you not to be too clever. Creative imitators often do better than inventors. First systematize; being clever comes last.
- Don't do what you are only competent at if you are excellent at something else.
- Financial analysts never understand business.
- Workers are assets, not costs.
- There is no business without a customer.
- Ask, if you were not already in your business, would you enter it now?

2. DECISION-MAKING

Bazerman and Moore's book is the seventh edition of a textbook that competently catalogs and summarizes various biases, as well as relating not just to experimental situations but also to the types of decisions made by managers. Theirs is an excellent summary of the relevant experimental results, covering multiple researchers and publications and presenting the results in one place.

 MAX BAZERMAN and DON MOORE
Judgment in Managerial Decision Making (2008).

Thesis: People are bounded in the time they take to make decisions, their rationality, their awareness, and their ethicality. Individuals tend to take cognitive shortcuts, which result in mis-estimating risk and probability and making suboptimal or inconsistent decisions even when the stakes are high. Understanding these tendencies can support better decision-making and better evaluation of others' decisions.

 Judgment refers to the cognitive aspects of decision-making. A rational approach to decision-making would be to define the problem, identify the criteria, weight the criteria, generate alternative courses of action, rate each alternative on each criterion, and calculate the optimal decision. However, most of the time people do not reason in the logical manner just described, which Bazerman and Moore describe as System 2 thinking.

- *System 1 thinking* is intuitive (fast, automatic, implicit, and emotional). People make most decisions using this type of thinking, and yet judgment errors (or biases) are more likely to occur in this type of thinking.
- *System 2 thinking* is slower, conscious, effortful, explicit, and logical. Busier people are more likely to rely on the faster System 1 thinking.

Bazerman and Moore's book studies decision-making descriptively (how decisions are *actually* made) rather than prescriptively (how decisions should be made). People tend to satisfice,[2] rather than optimize, to save time and cost and to utilize their imperfect ability to process information. This book describes how Kahneman and Tversky began a series of experiments in 1974 to catalog

---

[2] Herbert Simon (1956) introduced the term *satisfice* to describe an activity, different from optimization, that satisfies some criteria but sacrifices other criteria in the interest of saving time.

biases influencing judgment, and found that people rely on a number of simplifying rules of thumb (heuristics) when making decisions; these save time but can lead to significant errors. Richard Thaler suggested in 2000 that decision-making is not only bounded in terms of rationality, but also may be bounded regarding willpower (people give too much weight to the present relative to the future), self-interest (people do care about others), awareness, and ethicality.

Common Biases

The authors introduce judgmental heuristics (shortcuts), and catalog common biases that arise from these four shortcuts.

The availability heuristic. People assess the probability or causes of an event by the degree to which occurrences are readily available in memory. The *ease of recall bias* is based on vividness and recency. Which is riskier, driving or flying 400 miles? More people say flying, though driving is riskier. The *retrievability bias* is based on memory structures. Are there more words in the English language starting with an *r* or with *r* as the third letter? Most people say the former when the latter is true.

The representativeness heuristic. When making a judgment about a person or object, people look for traits that correspond with previously formed stereotypes. If someone thinks good salespeople are extroverts, he will favor that type of person for sales jobs. This stereotyping can work on a conscious or subconscious level.

Insensitivity to base rates refers to people's tendency to ignore population proportions. In one example, people were told that 30% of a population are engineers, then were told about one member of that population who enjoys puzzles, is good at math, and is an introvert. Most people concluded this person was an engineer, ignoring the fact that engineers are a minority and therefore unlikely. *Insensitivity to sample size* describes how most people take the result of a small sample as equally valid to that of a large sample.

Misconceptions of chance describes how most people fail to realize that independent events are unrelated. For example, they might think the odds of success are higher after several consecutive failures. *Regression to the mean* refers to people's failure to account for the tendency of many processes to regress to the mean. That is, extreme observations in either direction tend to reverse direction so that subsequent observations are closer to the average.

The *conjunction fallacy* describes how people make associations to create a plausible story, not realizing their story is less likely. When experimenters described a college student interested in women's issues and asked what her career would likely be, most thought it more likely that she would become a "feminist bank teller" than a "bank teller," despite the fact that the first is a subset of the second and by definition less likely.

Positive hypothesis testing. People use data selectively, which can lead to the confirmation bias (people tend to better notice evidence that supports their own hypotheses rather than looking for disconfirming evidence) and to other biases.

The *confirmation trap* refers to people checking for confirming evidence rather than disconfirming evidence of a hypothesis. To determine if a hypothesis is true, finding an example that fits it proves nothing, but finding an example that contradicts it proves it wrong. People should always look for disconfirming examples, but most only look for consistent evidence.

With the *anchoring bias*, when estimating a number or value, people are influenced by any value that they hear at the same time—even if they know it to be irrelevant. In one example, people were asked to estimate the number of countries in Africa by spinning a roulette wheel and saying whether the number of countries was higher or lower than the roulette result. The spin of the wheel had a large impact on the value of the estimate made. In another example, random assignment of students into two groups caused teachers to treat them differently based on an initial description of the group as gifted, average, or below-average. People tend to give too much weight to first impressions even when later evidence indicates that the first impression was wrong or random.

The *conjunctive and disjunctive events bias* describes people's overestimation of the probability of events that must occur in conjunction with each other. If the odds of an event are 90% each time, the odds of five such events in a row are only 59%, but people will see the odds as higher. Similarly, people underestimate the probability of events that occur independently. When multiple events all need to occur, people overestimate the likelihood; when only one event needs to occur, people underestimate the probability. This bias explains many problems with projects that require multistage planning, as well as the fact that large projects seldom finish on time or on budget.

The *overconfidence bias* describes how, if you ask a person to give an estimate for a number that they are 90% confident of, the true number will fall outside that range not 10% of the time but 43% of the time. People believe they can be more precise than they actually can be.

With *hindsight* and the *curse of knowledge*, knowing how a decision turned out makes it "obvious" to people that this was the only possible result. People do not tend to think an incorrect decision might have been justified based on the information available at the time. People tend to overestimate their own foresight and underestimate that of others. In addition, people are unable to ignore knowledge that they have that others do not possess: product designers cannot see how hard their device might be to use for someone seeing it for the first time, and teachers cannot see how hard academic material is to someone being exposed to it for the first time. People are surprised when recipients of ambiguous messages do not understand their meaning (this is particularly true of emails, which lack other cues to meaning); after all, senders know what they meant.

The affect heuristic. Many judgments are evoked by an affective (emotional) evaluation occurring before any reasoning takes place.

Bounded Awareness
In addition to bounded rationality, people also have bounded awareness, which prevents them from noticing or focusing on useful and observable data. People focused on one task fail to notice obvious information (e.g., talking while driving interferes with noticing relevant environmental cues), which is referred to as *inattentional blindness*. People engaged in one task do not notice changes in their environment (*change blindness*). People give probabilities to competing outcomes that sum to well over 100% (*focalism* and the *focusing illusion*). Bounded awareness has specific effects in particular settings:

- **Groups.** The awareness of groups is bounded by the information that becomes part of the discussion. Groups are created to share information, but usually spend their time discussing knowledge that is already commonly understood, and ignoring knowledge that only a subset of the members possess.
- **Strategic settings.** People make consistent errors due to their failure to think rationally about a game, which can also affect assessments of competitors. Entrepreneurs are too eager to enter simple contests (with many other competitors) and too reluctant to enter difficult competitions (with few competitors).
- **Auctions.** The *winner's curse* results from the highest bidder's failure to consider the implications of bidding higher than everyone else who had the same information. Winning bidders in auctions of highly uncertain commodities commonly pay more than the asset is actually worth; whether the asset is a small good sold in an eBay auction or a large company being acquired.

Framing and the Reversal of Preferences
How issues are framed makes a huge difference in how decisions are made. Framing a medical decision in terms of a "90% chance of survival" versus a "10% chance of dying" leads to diametrically different choices, even by experts who should be immune to mere differences in wording. Imagine a disease that is expected to kill 600 people. People are offered a choice between a program that will certainly save 200 people versus an alternative with a one-third chance of saving all 600. They will choose differently if they are offered a program that will lose 400 people versus a two-thirds chance of losing everyone. People are

also more likely to spend payments labeled bonuses than those named rebates. In addition, people can also state a preference for the sum of two undesirable outcomes to the sum of two desirable ones.

Bazerman and Moore suggest that it is usually best to be risk-neutral and to take any bet with a positive expected value, except for very large bets such as taking a job, buying a house, corporate acquisition, and so on.

People tend to value a reduction in the probability of a bad outcome more when the outcome was initially certain (rather than merely probable). Most people will pay more to remove a single bullet from a game of Russian Roulette than they will pay to reduce the number of bullets from two to one, despite the fact that these are identical improvements in one's probability of survival. People favor options that assure certainty rather than those that only reduce uncertainty—referred to as *valuing pseudocertainty*.

Framing is used to oversell insurance. A policy that protects against fire but not against flood will be marketed as "full protection against fire." Most respond differently to the concept of "paying premiums" than to "accepting sure losses." Research shows that the purchase of extended warranties is usually a bad investment (as they have large profit margins for the providers), but these warranties sell well, usually at the time of purchase and usually framed as an insurance provision. As a last example of framing, the way a problem is worded tends to affect how much people value their time; for example, people will drive out of their way to save $40 on a $50 purchase, but will not drive out of their way to save $40 on a $2,000 purchase.

People tend to engage in mental accounting, with separate mental accounts for different financial activities, and then apply very different decision rules to different accounts. People react less to both losses and gains that occur in clusters, so it makes sense to group one's losses and spread out one's gains. Many value transactional utility (i.e., the quality of the deal) instead of simply valuing a good based on what that item is intrinsically worth. People tend to overvalue what they already own, which makes it likely that they will hold on to an asset for too long.

In the short-run, people regret their actions more than their inactions; in the long run, however, people regret more the positive actions that they did not take. People feel worse about bad events caused by action than bad events caused by inaction. Policymakers prefer harms of omission (letting people die) over harms of commission, even when the harms of inaction are much larger (the omission bias). This interest in working harder to avoid harm from overt acts rather than to avoid harm from failure to act is also reflected in an overvaluation of the status quo (when in doubt, people tend to leave things alone).

Finally, Bazerman and Moore describe preference reversals that are joint versus separate. There are many examples in which people place a higher value on one option than another when looking at options individually, but reverse their preferences when looking at two or more options simultaneously. People may go for what they want in separate evaluations, but recognize the more logical decision regarding what they should do in joint evaluations. People also are better able to evaluate differences when thinking about choices at the same time.

People get used to what they have and take it for granted. This allows an already-rich person to value new income, but it also has the result that "we find ourselves on a hedonic treadmill in which we strive for an imagined happiness that forever slips out of our grasp, beckoning us onward" (p. 83). This treadmill is good for work motivation, and bad for happiness.

Motivational and Emotional Influences on Decision Making

Emotion and cognition often collide when decisions must be made and actions taken—Ulysses tied himself to the mast to ensure he would not succumb to the sirens. People have multiple selves, reverse their preferences, and allow value to be impacted by time. We must work to reconcile our internal conflicts: Bazerman and Moore recommend having your "want" self explicitly negotiate with your "should" self.

Perceptions are often biased in a self-serving manner, and people tend to be unaware of their own vulnerability to bias. People tend to view themselves in a more positive light than is objectively accurate, which boosts self-esteem, makes them persist at difficult tasks, and facilitates coping with adverse events. People tend to believe they are worse than others on hard tasks (i.e., riding a unicycle) and better than others on easy tasks (i.e., driving a car), because they have less information about the skills of others than about their own skills.

Emotions influence both memory and decision-making. Some early evidence indicated that good moods increased bias in judgments, but more recent evidence has found exceptions (e.g., sad people are more affected by irrelevant anchoring information and make worse decisions). Specific emotions (happiness, sadness, fear, disgust, and anger) have been found to influence judgments. Emotions from one context do bleed over and affect decision-making in another context. People have mood-congruent recall, that is, they remember more good things when happy and more bad things when upset.

People are motivated to avoid the feeling of regret, separate from the outcome achieved. People are more upset by missing a plane by two minutes than by two hours. Silver medal winners are less happy than bronze winners; the bronze medalist is just happy to be a medalist, while the silver medalist focuses on how narrowly they missed the gold.

The Escalation of Commitment

People escalate commitment to a previously selected course of action beyond that which a rational decision model would prescribe, in what is termed *nonrational escalation.* Economists advise ignoring sunk costs, but people find that impossible and instead allocate resources in a way that justifies previous commitments—whether or not those initial commitments still appear valid. Escalation can be driven by perceptual biases, judgmental biases, impression management, and competitive irrationality.

Escalation can be unilateral, as when NBA teams give higher-drafted (more expensive) players more playing time than lower-drafted players who turn out to be equally talented. Mountain climbers tend to ignore information suggesting they turn around. Some organizations recognize this phenomenon: hedge funds have a different trader make the decision to sell than the one who bought.

Escalation can also be competitive. In many contexts, competition with another party amplifies the motivation to escalate commitment beyond a point that makes rational sense. Bazerman and Moore give several examples of bidding situations (including the merger wave of the 1980s) where both bidders reach a price that is higher than the target is worth to either, stemming from a desire to "win" and not just to acquire a target of value.

Many situations look like opportunities but prove to be traps once the likely reaction of others is considered. People need to be open to dropping an initial commitment as new evidence is collected; however, it is also necessary to recognize that continuing a commitment may provide new options as one moves forward. The key to navigating this tradeoff is to make decisions about the future without regard to sunk costs, focusing solely on the future benefits and costs.

Fairness and Ethics in Decision-Making

Perceptions of fairness and concern for others can also lead to nonrational decisions. The consequences of supply and demand can sometimes seem unfair. People resist unfair allocations even when their allocation is a windfall. Concern about the outcomes for others can also impact decisions. Organizations strive to conceal compensation data to avoid social comparisons and perceptions of unfairness. Research shows that teams perform better with a narrower range between the highest- and lowest-paid members. These norms can be manipulated, as when someone offers to split the difference 50-50 between two numbers but those numbers are themselves arbitrary.

People sometimes exhibit what Bazerman and Moore refer to as *bounded ethicality.* Cognitive biases can lead honorable people to behave unethically without realizing that they are doing so. People violate their own standard of ethics in predictable and systematic ways, often unconsciously. For example, research shows that a friendship between two people makes it impossible for one to objectively assess issues involving the other. Other examples include overclaiming credit, in-group favoritism, discounting the future, implicit attitudes, conflicts of interest, indirectly unethical behavior, and situations in which different positive values point toward different decisions.

Common Investment Mistakes

The S&P index outperforms 75% of actively managed mutual funds, and only 18% of hedge funds outperform their relevant benchmarks after fees—why do investors invest this way? Behavioral finance focuses on how biases can impact individuals and markets and finds the following.

- Overconfidence produces excessive trading.
- People tend to be overly optimistic.
- Investors deny that random events are random.
- Investors tend to naïvely spread their 401(k) allocations across the choices offered.
- Traders fall prey to a status quo bias, keeping investment allocations unchanged over time even as their circumstances change.
- Investors sell stocks above their purchase price too soon, and sell those below their purchase price too late.
- Active trading appears to reinforce biased decision-making; those who trade the most frequently on average perform worse.

Bazerman and Moore's advice is to determine investment goals and avoid the trap of thinking the stock market is predictable.

Making Rational Decisions in Negotiations

Game theory approaches often assume super-rational negotiators, but a decision-analytic approach may be better in that it focuses on how normal people actually behave. Decision analytics outline the following best practices for negotiation:

1. Determine the best alternative to a negotiated agreement.
2. Identify all of the parties' interests. Separate the other party's stated position from its interests.
3. To claim value, usually there is a range over which both parties would be better off, so seek to occupy the optimal point in this range.

To create value in negotiation, there is usually a chance to find tradeoffs across multiple issues that add value. Differences from one another are what creates value; if the other party values something more, let them have it, but get something in return that you value more than they do. It is possible to avoid disagreements about predicted outcomes by developing contracts that are contingent upon the outcome actually realized. Tools for adding value are found in building trust and sharing information, asking questions, strategically disclosing information, negotiating multiple issues simultaneously, making multiple offers simultaneously, and searching for post-settlement settlements.

Negotiator Cognition

Bazerman and Moore explore six common cognitive mistakes made in negotiation and make recommendations for managing each of them.

- **The mythical fixed pie of negotiation.** Do not focus exclusively on allocating the value of the object of negotiation, but rather remember to examine how to increase the value for each side.

- **The framing of negotiator judgment.** Adopt a frame that expresses outcomes in terms of what is gained, rather than what is lost, to maintain a risk-averse rather than risk-seeking posture. Pick anchor points deliberately, for both sides of the negotiation.

- **Escalation of conflict.** Work to avoid the escalation that occurs when each party becomes focused on "beating" the other side. Announcing a position makes it harder to back off of that position. The other side will hold out when they have too much invested in their position to stop.

- **The overestimation of value in negotiation.** Do not forget to eventually say yes. In this context overconfidence has a price.

- **Self-serving biases in negotiation.** Many dilemmas have asymmetry in the parties' contribution to the problem and willingness to cooperate with proposed solutions. This asymmetry is a key driver of self-serving biases; ambiguity enables individuals to justify what they want to do rather than what they should do. People do not usually have a desire to be unfair, but do have difficulty interpreting information in an unbiased manner.

- **Anchoring in negotiations.** Evaluation of value is impacted by the listing price. Making the first offer (anchor) leads to better deals for the offerer, but also increases the likelihood of an impasse. First offers are more effective when high ambiguity exists about the value.

Improving Decision Making
Bazerman and Moore offer concrete suggestions for how individuals can improve the effectiveness of their decisions. In particular, they outline six strategies.

Use Decision Analysis Tools. A linear model is a formula that weights and adds up relevant predictor variables to make a quantitative prediction. These linear models can lead to superior decisions because individuals are better at coding information than in integrating it. Most people resist linear models because such models are viewed as unfair and incomplete, not capturing gut feelings (intuition) that are deemed superior. Linear models have been demonstrated to improve both university admissions decisions and hiring decisions.

Acquire Expertise. Tversky and Kahneman (1986) argue that basic judgmental biases are unlikely to be corrected in the real world, and others reach similar conclusions. However, Neale and Northcraft (1989) propose that biases can be lessened through the development of expertise. Larric and Wu (2007) find that, when estimating the size of the bargaining zone, experience only corrects errors in overestimating its size (resulting in one's offer being rejected), because when the offer is too generous the opponent will not accept immediately. So, experience can actually be a detriment in this particular context. Expertise requires monitoring and awareness of one's own decision-making processes, and conceptualizing decision-making allows skills to be taught.

Debias Your Judgment. Fischoff (1982) proposes four strategies: warn about the possibility of bias, describe the direction of the bias, provide a dose of feedback, and offer extended coaching. Bazerman and Moore suggest unfreezing, changing, and refreezing judgmental practices.

Unfreezing is based on individuals' resistance to the conclusion that their decision-making is flawed. Their thinking is frozen because they have relied on their intuition for years, they have achieved some professional success, and the idea that they are biased clashes with their awareness of their success. Bazerman and Moore hope that their book provides enough concrete evidence to unfreeze readers' notions that their decision-making processes do not require movement.

There are three critical steps to changing how one makes decisions: clarify the existence of specific judgmental deficiencies, explain the roots of these deficiencies, and reassure the decision-makers that these should not be taken as threats to self-esteem. Bazerman and Moore advise that when looking at data, evaluate how likely that data would be generated if the opposite of your working hypothesis were instead true. Also, look at an alternative hypothesis, and then examine confirming and disconfirming evidence for both hypotheses.

Having done the work to unfreeze and change, many people do not realize that they then refreeze judgmental practices. After improving one's approach to making decisions, one can then refreeze the new and improved process. Bazerman and Moore suggest that everyone continue to reexamine their decisions for bias for a long time.

Reason Analogically. People learn better from cases and experiences when they are able to take away an abstract form of the learning message. It is better to ask how two different exercises are related rather than simply examining the lessons of each of the two experiences.

Take an Outsider's View. People reason better when they take a meta or outsider view. Even if one's estimate of a project duration is accurate, it is best to remember that most projects take longer than forecasted, and then remember to apply that outsider point of view to the project.

Understand Biases in Others. People can adjust their forecasts of others based on understanding bias. Kahneman and Tversky (1982) suggest the following approach: select a comparison group (i.e., a group that has engaged in a similar project for which actual results are available), assess the distribution of the comparison group, incorporate intuitive estimation, assess the predicted results of the decision, and adjust the intuitive estimate. As an example, when Kahneman was part of a faculty group designing a new curriculum, the group estimated the project would take 18-30 months; however, when looking at comparison groups, the team leader identified that no similar groups at other universities had accomplished this task in less than seven years.

In conclusion, Bazerman and Moore are disturbed by the fact that most managers reward good results rather than good decisions. In so doing, they are likely to be rewarding behaviors (and decision-making practices) that may not work in the future.

Discussion and Implications

 Bazerman and Moore's book demonstrates that individuals are prone to an astonishing array of biases in how they evaluate probabilities and make decisions, even when they are experienced at the specific type of decision at hand, and even when the stakes are high enough to call for careful analysis and consideration. Massimo Piatelli-Palmarini's *Inevitable Illusions* (1994) covers some of the same ground and is more informal and fun to read.

The whole field of behavioral economics bias owes its origins to a multitude of experiments and articles written by the psychologists Daniel Kahneman and Amos Tversky in the 1970s at Stanford (work that earned Kahneman the 2002 Nobel Prize in Economics). Kahneman provides another less formal book covering this research, and the broad conclusions he has drawn from it, in his popular and well-written *Thinking, Fast and Slow* (2011). He describes how individuals engage in two types of thinking: *fast thinking* using association and metaphor to produce an instant reaction or assessment of reality (what Bazerman and Moore call System 1 thinking), and *slow thinking* which arrives at well-reasoned choices after a period of consideration (i.e., System 2 thinking). Biases arise because people tend to be sparing in applying slow-thinking resources, and so generally over-rely on fast-thinking reactions, thereby generating the biased decision-making observed in so many of these experiments. Kahneman's prescription is to consciously apply the effort of making decisions based on System 2 thinking, unless one has over 10,000 hours of training in a rapid-feedback environment to hone one's System 1 reactions in that particular realm.[3]

---

[3] Another way to engage in System 2 thinking is to process problems in a different language than one's native tongue. An interesting 2012 study by Keysar, Hayakawa, and An indicates

Kahneman's (2011) work appears to contradict those who have found examples where an expert's intuition leads quickly to a productive result, such as the firefighter who senses something wrong in a room and evacuates his team just before the floor collapses. Gary Klein developed the recognition-primed decision model, which applies to experts like firefighters and chessmasters who hone their intuitive skills. However, Kahneman and Klein (2009) worked together to reconcile these different views, and concluded that intuitions are likely to be skilled when an expert develops knowledge in an environment that is sufficiently regular to be predictable, combined with an opportunity to learn these regularities through prolonged practice. This distinction enables people to be more likely to trust the intuition of physicians, nurses, athletes, and firefighters who face complex but orderly situations. On the other hand, there is sufficient evidence to warn against trusting the intuition of anyone who makes long-term forecasts in an unpredictable environment, such as stock pickers and political scientists, as they do not get the feedback they need to distinguish skilled from lucky outcomes. Kahneman and Klein conclude, "intuition cannot be trusted in the absence of stable regularities in the environment" (p. 241).

The work in cognitive bias represented something of a revolution in economics. For decades, economics had assumed rational wealth maximization by individual agents, which allowed economists to model economic behavior mathematically based on agents' attempts to maximize their welfare subject to resource constraints. If some outlying agents were not rational, they were at least expected to represent minor noise that averaged to zero in the aggregate. Behavioral economists (like Kahneman and Tversky and subsequent researchers) showed that not only are economic decision-makers often not rational, but also the majority of people are irrational in exactly the same ways and directions, so that their deviations would not even cancel out in the aggregate. This research has had a serious impact on the acceptance of theories that depend on rational behavior, including the theory of efficient markets which has come under new criticism since the 2008 financial crash.

Behavioral research has also sparked economists to conduct laboratory experiments to observe—rather than assume—the actual behavior of individuals facing economic decisions. The field of experimental economics developed over the 1980s and 1990s in the wake of Kahneman and Tversky's work (a great resource is the 1997 *Handbook of Experimental Economics*, edited by Kagel and Roth). *Experimental economics* is distinct from behavioral economics both because not all experiments are psychological, and because behavioral economists use theory and field data in addition to experimental information. However, there is enough overlap to conclude that Kahneman and Tversky's career work may have sparked both genres. There is now an even newer field of

---

that, when a thought experiment is presented to people in a language they have studied but not mastered, biases from framing and loss aversion tend to disappear.

neuroeconomics, which combines methods from neuroscience, economics, and psychology to explain human decision-making. Camerer, Loewenstein, and Prelec (2005) and Glimcher, Camerer, and Poldrack (2008) are two of the several works summarizing the initial contributions and promise of this relatively new field.

Perhaps the most worrisome feature of cognitive bias is the difficulty of overcoming the challenges that most of us make in evaluating probabilities. Experts are not less susceptible—in fact, they appear more susceptible to at least some of these issues. Tversky (1995) describes how confidence appears to rise faster than actual subject knowledge: physicians who describe themselves as 90% confident in a pneumonia diagnosis (i.e., they assess a 90% statistical confidence interval) turn out to be accurate about 50% of the time. Coupled with the finding that people make different choices based on framing (i.e., descriptions of an operation in terms of the probability of survival versus the probability of death may evoke opposite responses), some medical schools have started incorporating training to at least make new doctors aware of these tendencies. The same processes have been found for other specialists, including equity analysts, airplane pilots, CEOs, and other people that we all rely on for their expertise. We know of at least one venture capital firm (Ulu Ventures of Palo Alto, managed by Clint Korver and Miriam Rivera) that engages a decision-making algorithm for investment in startups that is explicitly designed to follow the recommendations described above for minimizing obvious cognitive biases (see Korver 2012).

Failing to account for base rates is another recurring theme in the managerial realm: why are so many CEOs eager to play an acquisition game when 80% of mergers fail? It takes a lot of work and humility to avoid having one's confidence outpace one's learning in almost any field of endeavor. The key is to recognize that even if your decisions have made you relatively successful up to this point in your career, your own judgment can be noticeably improved by accepting that you fall prey to these biases and working to mitigate them, especially for the larger decisions in your job and life. Do the work to engage your System 2 thoughtful reasoning.

3. MARKETING

The concept of marketing has evolved, from finding buyers to differentiating products to creating customer loyalty. Since 1990, marketers have tended to view their role as collaborating to focus on the customer and improve competitive position. The first article that we review in this section (Webster 1992) argues that the changing role of marketing in practice should motivate a corresponding evolution in the academic study of marketing management. The next article (Jaworkski and Kohli 1990) explores what it means for a company to have a marketing orientation. The last article (Thaler 2008) shows how marketers exploit our cognitive biases to influence consumer behavior.

FREDERICK WEBSTER
"The Changing Role of Marketing in the Corporation" (1992), *Journal of Marketing.*

Thesis: Marketing is inseparable from strategy, and the rise of strategic alliances requires marketing to take on new responsibilities in defining what gets done inside and outside the firm in order to best meet customer needs.

Webster outlines the roots of changes in marketing management both as a body of knowledge and as it is practiced. The study of marketing began around 1910, looking at the processes by which farm products were brought to market as a set of social and economic processes. In 1948, the American Marketing Association began to define marketing functions as business activities, and this managerial approach evolved throughout the 1950s and 1960s. Drucker (1954) posited that the main purpose of any business is to create a satisfied customer.

Marketing gained analytical rigor, utilizing economic analysis to analyze demand and statistics to look for relationships in data. Early organizational pioneers in establishing professional marketing departments included customer-focused brands like Procter & Gamble, Colgate-Palmolive, General Foods, General Mills, and Gillette. Others put marketing professionals at the corporate staff level (e.g., GE, IBM, RCA). Throughout this period, large, hierarchical, integrated corporate structures were the dominant form of organization.

In the late 1970s and 1980s, the concept of the strategic business unit (SBU) gained favor, and corporations decentralized decision-making for many functions including marketing. More organizations downsized layers of corporate management. The trend was toward more flexible organizational forms emphasizing partnerships between firms (e.g., divisions, subsidiaries, joint ventures). Networks were based on relationship management rather than on market transactions. All of this had implications for marketing.

In the old competitive paradigm, activity is conducted as market-based transactions, with the job of marketing being to find buyers. In industrial markets, relationships were often adversarial. The next step on the continuum is the repeated, frequent purchase of goods and components, with each brand spending aggressively to win the customer's preference and repeat purchase. Marketing's role is then to guide product differentiation and create loyalty that will enable a higher price, which involves rudiments of trust and credibility. Industrial relationships become based on mutual dependence. This model of mutual dependence is illustrated by the decline of Ford (with its completely vertically integrated operation) and rise of GM (which depended heavily on its suppliers), and then the ascent of Japanese auto manufacturers who learned that quality does not just sell well but actually costs less. Other industrial firms (e.g., GE, IBM, DuPont) restructured around the concept of strategic customer partnerships. The Japanese concepts of *keiretsu* (a close relationship of manufacturers, suppliers, and contractors) spread to other countries.

In a strategic alliance, the partnership takes an entirely new form: collaborations among partners involving the commitment of capital, designed to improve a company's competitive position (Develin and Bleakley 1988). From this, Webster argues that strategic alliances are in fact a marketing phenomenon. Joint ventures are a form of strategic alliance, and networks are multifaceted organizational structures that result from multiple strategic alliances. For example, GM had a partnership with Toyota in the NUMMI automotive manufacturing joint venture (in Fremont, California), while at the same time GM has pursued partnerships with other auto manufacturers. Here, "marketing is the function responsible for keeping all of the partners focused on the customer and informed about competitor product offerings and changing customer needs and expectations" (p. 9). Through this process, firms become more specialized in their core activities.

Webster argues that the intellectual core of marketing management must expand beyond its microeconomic roots, with a shift from products and firms as the units of analysis to organizations and social processes. Marketing operates at the three distinct levels of corporate, business, and SBU (matching the levels of strategy), as well as at the functional and operating levels. Marketing also has three dimensions: culture (at the corporate and SBU level), strategy (at the SBU level), and tactics (at the operating level).

At the corporate level, the strategic problem is to define what business the company is in and to determine the mission, scope, shape, and structure of the firm. Scope and shape involve decisions about whether to enter into strategic alliances. At this level, marketing's role includes the following:

- Assess market attractiveness by analyzing customer needs and requirements as well as competitive offerings in the firm's potential markets.
- Promote customer orientation by advocating for the customer's point of view.
- Develop the firm's overall value proposition, reflecting its distinctive competence, and articulate that value externally and internally.

In network organizations, marketing helps design and negotiate strategic partnerships with vendors as well as customers.

At the SBU level, marketing and strategic planning may be blurred, with both addressing how to compete in the firm's chosen businesses. Outcomes of that planning are market segmentation, targeting, and positioning in target segments. In network organizations, marketers must decide which marketing functions (research, telemarketing, advertising, package design) will be purchased from partners, purchased from other sources, or performed internally.

At the operating level, marketers tend to act in the traditional territory of the four Ps: products, pricing, promotion, and place (distribution). Even here, Webster argues that "market forces compel companies to do a more thorough job of responding to customer needs and developing long-term customer relationships" (p. 12).

The well-defined distinctions between firms and markets, or between the company and its external environment, have disappeared (Badaracco 1991). Evolving organization forms create new definitions of marketing's role and responsibilities. Investment in information and information technology can help give firms and marketers an advantage in this landscape. Mass media advertising is becoming less effective, and targeted communications are becoming more important. Customer focus assisted by IT "will be the flexible bonds that hold the whole thing together" (p. 15).

BERNARD JAWORSKI and AJAY KOHLI
"Market Orientation: Antecedents and Consequences" (1993), *Journal of Marketing.*

Thesis: The market orientation of a business is an important determinant of its performance. Marketing orientation is facilitated by senior management's emphasis on responding to customer needs, higher interdepartmental connectedness and less conflict, compensation based on customer satisfaction, and decentralized decision-making.

Market orientation refers to the organization-wide generation of market intelligence, the dissemination of that intelligence across departments, and organization-wide responsiveness to it. The marketing concept was introduced in the 1950s but was lightly studied for the next forty years; some prior research suggests hypotheses to be tested. Jaworski and Kohli investigate two national samples to determine (a) the effect of certain factors on market orientation, (b) the hypothesized impact of market orientation on business performance, and (c) the role of environmental characteristics in moderating the relationship between market orientation and performance.

Jaworski and Kohli begin by discussing the antecedents to a company's development of market orientation. They present hypotheses regarding the behavior of top management, interdepartmental dynamics, organizational structure and systems, and measurement and reward systems.

- **Top management.** An organization must get clear signals from top management about the importance of being responsive to customer needs. The senior management's risk posture is also important: if senior managers accept occasional failures as being natural, junior managers will propose more new offerings in response to customer needs. The authors hypothesize that market intelligence, generation, intelligence dissemination, and the responsiveness of the organization will increase with greater top management emphasis on marketing orientation, and decrease with higher risk aversion by top management.

- **Interdepartmental dynamics.** Conflict inhibits communication, while connections facilitate interaction and the exchange of information. The authors hypothesize that the market intelligence dissemination and responsiveness of the organization will decrease with higher interdepartmental conflict, and increase with higher interdepartmental connectedness.

- **Organizational structure and systems.** The authors hypothesize that intelligence generation, dissemination, and response design will decrease while response implementation will increase when any of the following occur: greater formalization, greater centralization, or greater departmentalization.

- **Measurement and reward systems.** The authors hypothesize that market intelligence generation, intelligence dissemination, and organization responsiveness will increase with higher reliance on market-based factors for evaluating and rewarding managers.

Having discussed conditions affecting the development and implementation of market orientation, Jaworski and Kohli then consider the consequences of having a market orientation.

- **Business performance.** Several researchers have found a link between market-oriented companies and their business performance, including Lusch and Laczniak (1987) and Narver and Slater (1990). The authors hypothesize that the greater an organization's market orientation, the higher its business performance.

- **Employee commitment.** A market orientation offers psychological and social benefits to employees. The authors hypothesize that the greater the market orientation, the greater the esprit de corps and organizational commitment of employees in the organization.

- **Environmental factors.** Environmental factors can moderate the linkage between a market orientation and business performance. *Market turbulence* is the rate of change in the composition of customers and their preferences.

Competitive intensity reflects the number of choices customers have to satisfy their wants. *Technological turbulence* measures the rate of technological change. The authors hypothesize that the relationship between a market orientation and business performance will strengthen with greater market turbulence or greater competitive intensity, and weaken with greater technological turbulence.

Jaworski and Kohli tested their hypotheses on two samples. For the first sample, they collected data from marketing and nonmarketing executives within 27 business units in 13 member companies of the Marketing Science Institute, plus 229 business units in 102 companies in the Dun and Bradstreet Million Dollar Directory. Their second sample was generated from 230 members of the American Marketing Association.

Market orientation was measured by a 32-item scale (10 items related to intelligence generation, 8 to dissemination, and 14 to business unit responsiveness). Performance was measured both subjectively by respondents and objectively by the dollar share of the served market. Other variables were measured by respondent perceptions.

The hypotheses were broadly supported. In particular, they found the following:

- The emphasis placed on market orientation by top managers does impact the generation and dissemination of intelligence and the organization's responsiveness to that intelligence.

- Senior managers' risk aversion does depress responsiveness (though it does not appear to affect intelligence generation or dissemination).

- Interdepartmental conflict does reduce intelligence dissemination and responsiveness.

- Connectedness across departments promotes a market orientation.

- Reward systems are related to market orientation; in fact, the design of rewards has the strongest impact on market orientation of all the factors considered in the study.

- Centralization of decision-making serves as a barrier to market orientation.

- Formalization does not appear to be related to market orientation.

- Market orientation is significantly related to business performance as measured based on executive perception, but is not related to objective market share. It is possible that market share is not a good measure of performance (i.e., some companies pursue a focused strategy), or that there is a lag between market orientation and increased market share.

- There is evidence that market orientation positively impacts employees' organizational commitment and morale.

- The link between market orientation and performance is not found to depend on the moderating variables considered (market turbulence, competitive intensity, and technological turbulence).

Overall, Jaworski and Kohli conclude that "the market orientation of a business is an important determinant of its performance, regardless of the market turbulence, competitive intensity, or the technological turbulence of the environment in which it operates" (p. 64).

RICHARD THALER
"Mental Accounting and Consumer Choice" (2008), *Marketing Science*.

Thesis: Consumers' cognitively biased tendency to engage in mental accounting has implications for marketers seeking to influence consumer behavior.

Thaler reviews data on how individuals deviate from rational economic decision-making (see Section 2 of this chapter for an in-depth discussion of cognitive bias). Consumers often pay attention to sunk costs when they rationally should not, and often underweight opportunity costs relative to out-of-pocket costs. Consumers may be maximizing a value function called *transaction utility*, which is consistent with prospect theory, rather than maximizing expected utility as consistent with economic theory. People frame outcomes in inconsistent ways, for instance by preferring to think of their gains separately but their losses all together.

This behavior has implications for marketers. For example, the desire of consumers to segregate gains implies that a seller of a product with more than one dimension should work to have each dimension evaluated separately. Think of late-night television ads touting products with multiple uses (plus bonus items "if you call right now"). The same desire to segregate savings may fuel the popularity of rebates (which are economically less efficient than simply having a lower price). The desire to combine losses means that small add-ons to a larger purchase will encounter less resistance than selling the add-on as a separate transaction. Integrating losses with larger gains may explain why income taxes are resisted less when the bulk is deducted from each biweekly paycheck rather than being due in full in April.

Why do sellers of tickets allow scalping, rather than raising their prices to match demand? Scalpers exist when two conditions are present: prices are too low, and there is an ongoing relationship between the buyer and seller that would create ill will in the form of transaction disutility if the seller were to appropriate the value being claimed by scalpers. A seller in this circumstance will want to raise prices without generating ill will. Knowledge of cognitive biases suggests several ways to do so:

- Raise the reference price directly, or raise it indirectly by increasing the perceived cost (providing excessive luxury with the product). This can also be done by quoting a very high suggested retail price but offering deep discounting to generate positive transaction utility.

- Increase the minimum purchase required or tie the sale to another product (e.g., Super Bowl packages including ticket, airfare, and hotel; or instituting a three-night minimum around a one-night event).

- Try to obscure the price by selling in an unusual size or format (e.g., sell candy in movie theaters in unusually large boxes to mask its higher price).

Consumer use of budgeting rules also has implications for gift giving. Standard theory suggests the benefit of giving someone a gift of something they have already indicated they value by using. In practice, however, the giver often buys something the recipient would not buy for himself—particularly a luxury item. This behavior implies that goods priced at the high end of the market should be marketed as potential gifts, and that advertising should be targeted at the giver rather than the receiver. This finding may also explain why people at times prefer a gift in kind over a gift in cash (again violating microeconomic theory). Tupperware dealers compensate salespeople with gifts (primarily to female second-income-earners). This allows the saleswoman to segregate her earnings from family income, direct extra income toward luxuries, and increase her control over how this additional income is spent. The NFL used to have trouble getting players to attend the all-star game at the end of the season, but after moving the game to Hawaii and including free airfare for the players' wives or girlfriends, no-shows became rare.

Discussion and Implications

 The concept of marketing has evolved toward an emphasis on collaborating to focus on the customer (and thereby improve competitive position). This emphasis has motivated strategic alliances among different companies, as when GM partnered with Toyota in the NUMMI joint venture applying Japanese lean manufacturing practices in a U.S. plant. Like strategy, marketing now operates at the distinct levels of corporate, business, and SBU, and also at functional and operating levels. Similarly, mass advertising is becoming less effective and targeted communications more central. Webster makes a good case for researchers to keep up with practitioners.

Jaworski and Kohli build on their earlier article (Kohli and Jaworski 1990) that demonstrated the previous lack of agreement within the literature about the definition of marketing and its implementation (which hindered development of theory). The operational definition of marketing orientation in their 1990 article was picked up by others: *marketing orientation* refers to the generation, dissemination, and responsiveness of an organization to market intelligence. When a cola company assesses preferences through a taste test, it is generating intelligence. When it shares the results throughout the company, and alters its formula and advertising in response, it is reflecting a market orientation. Jaworski and Kohli also point out the overlap between such orientation and strategy, given that marketing orientation also provides a unifying focus for employee efforts. In addition, since a market orientation requires the commitment of resources, it may or may not be worth undertaking (particularly under conditions of limited competition).

In their 1993 article, Jaworski and Kohli refine and test the theory they developed in 1990. Narver and Slater (1990) found that market orientation is significantly related to business profitability. Jaworski and Kohli go further, exploring whether environmental factors impact that link, and identifying which factors facilitate or impede a market orientation, as well as illuminating the impact of market orientation on other measures (e.g., employee commitment and morale).

Building on the resource-based theory of strategy (see Chapter 1, Section 3), Day (1994) investigates how a firm can generate and sustain a marketing orientation. He cites the most distinctive features of such organizations: their mastery of market-sensing and customer-linking capabilities. According to his recommendations, any change program can help improve these capabilities in several ways:

- diagnose current capabilities;
- anticipate future needs for capabilities;
- redesign, from the bottom up, the underlying processes;
- ensure top-down direction and commitment;
- creatively use information technology; and
- continuously monitor progress.

Several other papers in the marketing literature emphasize the overlap between marketing and some of the other functions considered in this book. In a separate paper, Narver and Slater (1995) find overlap with organizational design, concluding that a market orientation provides the cultural foundation for organizational learning. Bergen, Dutta, and Walker (1992) find that agency theory from the finance literature has particular relevance for marketing management, as "marketing involves a wide array of agency relationships" (p. 1). They suggest that agency theory is useful in examining situations with goal conflict between principal and agents, environmental uncertainty, information asymmetries, and challenges in evaluating performance. They also suggest that many of the actions required to mitigate agency conflicts fit well with marketers' distinctive competencies.

Thaler's article shows how marketers exploit people's use of cognitive shortcuts. Floor mats for cars are generally available at Wal-Mart for $20, yet many people pay several hundred dollars for those mats to the auto dealer at the moment they purchase their car; Thaler's framework shows that auto dealers are exploiting people's documented tendency to exhibit less resistance to small add-ons when combined with a larger transaction. Many U.S. taxpayers have too much withheld from their paychecks, making an interest-free loan to the government until the following April so they can receive a tax refund. Here, the Internal Revenue Service is exploiting people's more general tendency to integrate losses with larger gains. Hotels often charge a high "rack rate" but advertise the discount from this inflated reference price, making people feel smart and effective for getting a good deal while in fact paying a high price for a hotel room.

When discussing <u>Machiavelli's</u> description of how leaders can most effectively manipulate their followers, we pointed out that his work may benefit followers more than leaders. Similarly, exploring how marketers can exploit an understanding of how consumers actually make purchase decisions may help consumers as much as it does marketers: such analysis can explicitly reveal the dollar price we pay by using transactions to feel better about ourselves, as opposed to achieving the economically most-efficient outcome.[4]

4. COMPLEX SYSTEMS

Most researchers in economics and management have utilized linear models that allow a logical progression from assumptions to theoretical conclusions (which can be taken as predictions to be compared to actual behavior). This approach has yielded productive results, but has created a focus on equilibrium situations where mathematical models yield discrete solutions. The use of models of complex adaptive systems allows researchers to explore phenomena that have to date been relatively ignored, and thus offers great promise for yielding an improved understanding of how people and systems actually behave. For those without a high level of technical training, Miller and Page's (2008) book offers glimpses of the phenomena that it is possible to capture with these complex systems tools.

---

[4] Thaler's article is a very specific application of work in consumer research. Academic readers may want to take note of Wells (1993), who offers a fairly scathing indictment of consumer research up to that point in time, and gives some constructive suggestions for how to advance this part of the academic discipline within marketing.

JOHN MILLER and SCOTT PAGE
Complex Adaptive Systems: An Introduction to Computational Models of Social Life (2007).

Thesis: A *complex and adaptive social system* consists of interdependent interacting agents whose micro-level behavior responds to the macro-level patterns those agents produce, resulting in a system that evolves over time. Computational modeling tools are well-suited to understanding such systems. A wide variety of social phenomena (e.g., political, financial, economic, and natural behaviors) appear to be better understood using the perspective of a complex adaptive social system.

Miller and Page discuss adaptive social systems composed of interacting agents, and the complexity that arises when the dependencies among the elements change the form of the system. Complex is different from complicated. Unlike complication, complexity is a deep property of a system: "A complex system dies when an element is removed, but complicated ones continue to live on, albeit slightly compromised" (p. 9). Complicated worlds are reducible, and it is relatively straightforward to model or build a complicated system (e.g., a car, watch, or skyscraper). In social worlds, the connections can lead to irreducible complexity; as "agent interactions become highly nonlinear, the system becomes difficult to decompose, and complexity ensues" (p. 10).

Complex systems also differ from complicated systems in their ability to evolve. Cars and watches are complicated, containing differentiated parts that play specific roles. Some parts are optional (e.g., the back seat), whereas other parts are essential (e.g., the timing belt), but none of the parts adapt. An economy is complex—when one firm fails, others adapt. This adaptability allows resilience, but at the cost that the system does not always run smoothly: economies have booms and crashes, whereas a watch either does or does not work.

Examples of Complex Systems

One representative example of a complex system is a model of the occurrence (or nonoccurrence) of a standing ovation at the end of a performance. Standing ovations may depend in a nonlinear way on the quality of the performance, seat location, relationships among those in the audience, and other factors. The fact that ovations may depend on where people sit and with whom is an example of the general observation that heterogeneity (e.g., differences among the actors or parts) is often a key driver in social worlds.

Another useful example is that of a hive or swarm of bees. In some social situations, differences cancel one another out (the behavior of a swarm of bees tracks the "average bee"). In some complex systems, differences interact with each other such that the resulting behavior deviates strongly from the average, which can lead to stability (bees' ability to regulate hive temperature relies on individual bees huddling together or spreading out at different temperatures, so that the heterogeneity in temperature response actually leads to maintaining a constant temperature). Hive behavior can also lead to instability (one bee tends to attack an invader when another does, which leads to a cascading response whereby all the bees attack a threat). The difference of response depends on feedback. With beehive temperature, for example, heterogeneity introduces a negative feedback loop whereby one bee's action makes action less likely by others, whereas with beehive defense there is a positive feedback loop whereby one bee's action makes action more likely by others. Economies exhibit similar feedback loops: negative feedback in markets produces stability and positive feedback creates bubbles.

Models of public policy illustrate how, in a complex adaptive social system, small differences in rules can lead to large differences in outcomes. If every town is identical, and votes on a policy issue, then the majority will prevail in each town. However, in more complex formulations, with multiple issues or different ways of choosing policy, Miller and Page find that the method of optimal decision-making depends on the initial circumstances.

- With a single town, social welfare is maximized by using democratic referenda to decide each policy issue (the next best level of welfare comes from two political parties competing directly, then from multiple parties with proportional representation, and then from multiple parties competing directly).
- With multiple towns in the system, the effectiveness of different choice mechanisms is completely reversed, and social welfare is now minimized by using democratic referenda.

The choice mechanisms that work best in the more complicated model have two properties:
- introducing noise into the system when local citizens' preferences are varying, and
- reducing this noise as the citizens become more similar.

Basically, good political mechanisms should deliver something that everyone in a district wants, but if there is a diversity of wants, a good mechanism will jump around the various options. Many social models have considered noise to a disruptive force, but in this complex choice model, noise is a means of moving toward desirable solutions.

The Value of Computational Modeling

Although many social phenomena are complex systems, social scientists have largely chosen not to examine complex systems. Qualitatively, researchers seek to understand complicated systems by reducing them to their constituent parts, understanding each part, and then summing up that understanding. Quantitatively, researchers tend to use mathematical models for many phenomena, as in economics. However, complex systems with interacting parts resist being reduced to a point where reduction offers insight, nor can they always be modeled in a mathematically tractable way. As a result, many social phenomena have simply not been studied in detail until recently. This lack of examination has been exacerbated by the fact that important questions are often hard to categorize into a specific field so may not be studied by experts in any one field.

The application of computational models can help understand complex adaptive social systems, because computer models are not restricted to studying problems suited to the use of convenient mathematical tools. Miller and Page encourage the use of these models.

> First, such tools are naturally suited to these problems, as they easily embrace systems characterized by dynamics, heterogeneity, and interacting components. Second, these tools are relatively new to the practice of social science, so we take this as an opportunity to help clarify their nature, to avoid misunderstandings, and generally to advance their use. Finally, given various trends in terms of the speed and ease of computation and diminishing returns with other tools, we feel that computation will become a predominant means by which to explore the world, and ultimately it will become a hallmark of twenty-first-century science. (p. 27)

The authors discuss the use of computational models as a tool for modeling social systems, providing a defense of such models and cataloguing and responding to various criticisms from those who advocate the use of more traditional tools (e.g., more precise but less flexible mathematical methods). They also point out that computational costs are declining, while traditional analytic methods may be reaching the point of diminishing marginal returns in their application to social phenomena. When using mathematical tools, researchers tend to assume that agents are either completely blind (and so they randomly search), completely knowledgeable, or exist in a smooth world with one optimal point. The complexity approach allows for landscapes in which elements interact in nonlinear ways, resulting in various maximums and minimums and creating a path-dependent world where early choices determine future possibilities (Page 2006). This approach has implications for innovation (where past discoveries form the basis of new technologies).

Miller and Page advise that studying complex systems will require new approaches, and recommend the following for researchers and practitioners:

- Find ways to separate complex systems from merely complicated systems.
- Determine how robust social systems are.
- Avoid extremes (in assumptions about the skill level of the agents).
- Explore the role of heterogeneity in systems (i.e., where do differences lead to unstable outcomes versus enhancing stability).

Much of the work discussed by the authors relaxes the assumptions of traditional models regarding how information is acquired, processed, and acted upon. Miller and Page consider models in which information is selectively acquired across restricted lines of communication, agents process information using narrow rules instead of precise logic, and possible actions are limited.

Characteristics of Complex Systems: Emergence and the Central Limit Theorem
One hallmark of complex systems has tended not to be fully appreciated: *emergence* describes how individual, localized behavior aggregates into global behavior that is not tightly connected to its origins. An observer standing close to a pixelated picture or television screen sees only small, individual pixels of different colors. As the observer moves farther away, at some point an image emerges. Each level of emergence can allow the observer to understand the larger system.

> Indeed, the boundaries of modern science rely on this property—for example, physics resolves into chemistry, which resolves into biology, which resolves into psychology, which resolves into economics, and so on. Each new science is able to exploit the emergence that is attained by the previous level. (p. 45)

The brain provides an example of emergence, as the interaction of simple neurons at the micro-level produces the very different phenomenon of consciousness at the macro-level.

Emergence theory and emergence models have already contributed to understanding social processes. Systems can locally adapt to a critical region in which the global properties of the system take on regular behavior. This approach can help explain social scaling phenomena like income distribution or firm size (as described in Axtell 2001). Within markets, it has been shown that models of self-organized systems with simple institutional rules (e.g., forcing new bids to be better than existing ones) results in predicting observed behavior such as predictable prices and trading patterns (as in Rust, Miller, and Palmer 1992, 1994; Gode and Sunder 1993). Emergence models also show how entities maintain their core functionality despite significant internal and external changes, which helps understand the robustness of markets, cultures, firms, and political parties.

In many merely complicated systems, outcomes appear to be characterized by the Central Limit Theorem, which shows that a large number of individual actors may create aggregate behavior which can then be described by a normal statistical distribution (i.e., a bell-shaped curve). In many complex systems, on the other hand, interactions may reinforce each other rather than cancel out, which can result in physical phenomena like earthquakes, floods, and fires or in social phenomena like riots, traffic jams, and stock market crashes. (Indeed, Miller and Page point to the failure of Long-Term Capital Management in 1998 as an example of an investment system governed by a fat-tailed distribution rather than a normal distribution.[5]) A defining feature for outcomes of any system is whether the system contains *negative feedback*, where changes are absorbed and behavior tends toward stability, or *positive feedback*, in which changes are amplified and outcomes are unstable.

Models of Complex Adaptive Social Systems

Miller and Page establish a basic framework for modeling interacting systems of agents, using the Noble Eightfold Path from Buddhism as a metaphor: view (information and connections), intention (goals), speech (communication among agents), action (interaction), livelihood (payoffs), effort (strategies and actions), mindfulness (cognition), and concentration (model focus and heterogeneity). With this framework, they build a model of forest fires,[6] which turns out to be quite similar to models for bank failures, the spread of viruses, and the flow of information. In fact, the ease of transforming one model to another suggests that all complex, adaptive social systems may be intimately connected in a fundamental sense.

Social systems are different from physical systems in that agents alter their behavior in response to anticipated outcomes. Adaptive systems have a tension between the benefits of achieving precise behavior (versus simpler approximations) and the risk of increased system fragility; Miller and Page posit

---

[5] Nassim Taleb (2010) provides a more recent and nuanced analysis of how the stock market may be a good example of a fat-tailed distribution (as a result of positive feedback), with the result of periodic financial shocks which come as a surprise to those who were expecting a normal distribution of outcomes.

[6] Consider a world in which trees grow along a ridge. Each spring there is a fixed probability g of a tree sprouting in an unoccupied spot. In the summer, lightning storms hit the ridge and each spot has a probability f of being struck. If a tree is struck, it burns down, and any tree burning takes with it all adjacent trees. Empty locations serve as fire breaks. Production is defined as the average number of trees standing at the end of the summer. If the forest ridge has 100 possible tree locations and the probability f of lightning is 2%, then production will peak for a growth rate g of 43%. This figure reflects the countervailing forces of the growth rate itself and the chance that lightning impacts contiguous stands of trees. There is a very dramatic change in production as growth rates are altered. There is also a critical value of g that results in the system going from a disconnected collection of trees to one in which all the trees are connected together (and burn together) as one.

that there will usually be a "bias toward emphasizing simple structures that resist chaos over more complicated ones that handle difficult situations" (p. 140). They expand their basic framework to allow for more elaborate agent dynamics, evolutionary models, and organizational dynamics.

- **Agent dynamics.** When there are two "types" of agent, each agent has a different strength of preference for living with other agents of the same type. In this model, the result will move toward the segregation of agents into two groups, even if most of the agents do not have a noticeable preference for grouping with their own type. This outcome is due to the phenomenon of "tipping," whereby the early movements of even a few agents can create incentives for other agents to move. Similar frameworks can be applied to modeling the decision of city-dwellers to go to the beach on the weekend, or to a particular bar—everyone wants to go so long as it is not overly crowded, and so agents have to predict what other agents will do in order to make their own decisions. The authors also explore the social dynamics of city formation, network behavior (including the concentration of criminal behavior), and avalanches.

- **Evolutionary models.** Agents adapt their behavior based on experience, allowing the application of computational methods to game theory. In these evolutionary models, it matters whether agents are playing a single game or multiple games, and different behavior is predicted if agents have limited cognitive capacity and face multiple games. Evolutionary models also have promise for yielding insights into the evolution of trust and cooperation, and even the development of alternative political institutions.

- **Organizational dynamics.** Models considering collections of agents that transform information into decisions can be used to explore organizational dynamics (i.e., the dynamics of groups of agents). According to these models, classes of organizations may be significantly constrained in their ability to solve all potential problems. Rather than solving whatever problems they confront, organizations may in fact solve whichever problems are easy for that group to handle. Organizations (groups of agents) may be productive on only a small subset of problems, making them more reactive than proactive.

Contributions of the Complex Systems Approach
Social sciences have used a variety of methodological tools: empirical research, natural and laboratory experiments, qualitative methods, mathematical and game theory, and computational models. These tools can be substitutes or complements for each other, and Miller and Page describe how the ideas behind complex adaptive social systems have already contributed to understanding social processes.

Important contributions have been made in a number of areas. In addition to emergence theory and concepts of nonlinear interaction, the complex systems approach has facilitated the new network theory and thus revealed properties of social connections and social capital. The complex systems approach has led to new models of adaptation and been applied to describing how political parties change their platforms and how agents learn in games. Finally, the complex systems approach has helped researchers understand how cooperation emerges (see Axelrod 1984; Miller 1988). Miller and Page provide a list of new frontiers in the social sciences identified and introduced by the complex adaptive social systems approach:

- between simple and strategic behavior,
- between pairs and infinities of agents,
- between equilibrium and chaos,
- between richness and rigor, and
- between anarchy and control.

Researchers have made some initial progress in understanding complexity. The stimulus for this progress is a recognition that there are deep commonalities—ones that do not respect the usual academic boundaries—across the various systems we observe in the world. (p. 230) Reaching across disciplines to understand these boundaries can enhance understanding of much of the social behavior in the real world.

Discussion and Implications

The academic study of complex, adaptive social systems remains on the fringes of social science, as does the use of computational models as a tool to study economic and political systems. However, in other disciplines—particularly epidemiology and climate studies—the flexibility of computational models has resulted in their supplanting mathematical models. It is true that in these other disciplines, the parts (viruses or atomic particles) exhibit more predictable behavior than do individuals, firms, and governments—making social systems more difficult to model at large scales. Nonetheless, we think that both the field and the tool hold great promise, as they allow us to explore phenomena that have been relatively unstudied. Work in economics has primarily focused on equilibrium situations where mathematical models yield solutions, while work in chaos theory explores systems in which small changes in initial conditions can yield large changes in outcomes. Complex systems stand apart from either of these traditions—complex systems can achieve equilibrium and can also produce large events, but most often they produce novel and unpredictable patterns.[7]

Some of the concepts from complex systems have already been popularized and applied to business contexts. For example, Malcolm Gladwell's 2002 book *The Tipping Point* describes "that magic moment when an idea, trend, or social behavior crosses a threshold, tips, and spreads like wildfire" (Amazon 2002, "Book description"). He shows a range of social phenomena (including the popularity of new products) that can be conceptualized and modeled like the spread of disease or information. Steven Johnson (2002) offers a book for the layperson that illustrates emergence using examples like when a colony of individually simple ants behaves in a collectively intelligent manner, or when the population density of a city promotes the spread of ideas. Clayton Christensen (2011) applies the core intuitions of complex systems to his model of product innovation in *The Innovator's Dilemma*. He shows how large companies tend to focus on incremental improvements to existing products (sustaining technologies), and fail to notice disruptive technologies that introduce completely superior performance in a new product which achieves the same goal as the earlier product in a new way.[8] These entirely new technologies may not compete initially against the traditional products in the broad market, but once they cross a tipping point threshold, they emerge rapidly. Such disruptive technologies can be thought of as fast evolution in a complex systems context.

Watts and Hasker (2006) describe a social experiment not unlike the standing ovation model described by Miller and Page. Researchers had one group of teenagers rate the quality of unknown songs, and invited them to download songs they liked. Another group heard the songs but also saw how many times each song had been downloaded by the first group. The researchers found a far greater inequality of outcomes for the group subject to social influence: popular songs were more popular, and unpopular songs less popular, than when each participant made decisions independently. In addition, the rankings of songs was unpredictable, and the strength of inequality and unpredictability increased with the strength of social influence feedback. Given the inherent difficulty in forecasting the sales of socially-consumed goods, Watts and Hasker suggest that marketing executives for such goods should increase

---

[7] Page (2010) characterizes complex systems as both between ordered and random (BOAR) and difficult to explain, engineer, or predict (DEEP). We appreciate his acronyms.

[8] Masnick (2009) has prepared a concise, two-minute video explaining the heart of the Innovator's Dilemma. If horse-and-buggy customers were asked what they wanted, they probably responded "faster horses." Buggy makers did not initially see newly-invented cars as a significant threat, because they misidentified their market as the product (buggies) rather than as the benefit to customers (transportation). When the technology behind the new product (e.g., cars) improves at a much faster rate than the old product (buggies), the provider of the old product fails quickly, unless that provider makes its own products obsolete before another company does.

the number of bets they make and decrease their size, and should direct the attention of a wide audience to the individuals who are already enthusiastic. Who could have forecast that the Angry Birds game for smartphones would be downloaded over one billion times in its first year? This research shows how demand for socially-consumed goods (i.e., music, films, video games, books, restaurant and bar spending, social networking website participation, venture funding for startup companies, etc.) exhibits randomness and path-dependence.[9]

How many of the interesting phenomena in the physical or social world can be reduced to constituent parts and modeled with linear tools? We venture that it is a small subset indeed. Reducing the scope of behaviors for analysis to this fractional subset reminds us of the joke about the drunk who looks for his lost keys under the streetlamp—not because that is where he lost his keys but rather because that is where the light is. These new models of complex adaptive systems can help us proceed into hitherto-unexplored dark areas to explain observed phenomena. We would even venture that much of what businesspeople refer to as "intuition" may simply reflect an understanding of nonlinear relationships in complex systems, and the decisions resulting from this intuition may be better understood with models geared for such systems.

In this section we have only scratched the surface of complex systems thinking, but think there is value simply in providing a new lens with which to view the world. Many actors may be viewed as single entities in one context, but as complex systems in another. For example, is a firm a single actor among several in an industry or an economy, or is it a complex system itself composed of many individual employees interacting with each other in an irreducible way? Perhaps in strategy we can take the former view, whereas in organizational culture we might more profitably take the latter. Complex systems thinking allows for different frames of reference, which we expect will prove useful for both scholars and practitioners.

Further Reading

If you're interested in reading more on the topics discussed in this chapter, here are some sources to get you started. We do not offer this as a comprehensive or exhaustive list, but rather have selected well-regarded or significant works that space did not permit us to include in the main discussion.

---

[9] By this logic, in order to maximize our own book sales, we probably should have written several small books instead of the one you are currently reading, and developed a way to broadcast the reaction of the first individuals who responded positively to each book.

1. Managing Nonprofits (and Businesses)

Heyman, Darian R. 2011. *Nonprofit Management 101: A Complete and Practical Guide for Leaders and Professionals.* New York: Jossey-Bass.

Renz, David and Robert Herman. 2010. *The Jossey-Bass Handbook of Non-Profit Leadership and Management,* 3rd edition. New York, Jossey-Bass.

Rothschild, Steve. 2012. *The Non Nonprofit: For-Profit Thinking for Nonprofit Success.* New York, Jossey-Bass.

2. Decision Making

Ariely, Dan. 2010. *Predictably Irrational: The Hidden Forces that Shape our Decisions.* New York, Harper Perennial.

Camerer, Colin. 2003. *Behavioral Game Theory: Experiments in Strategic Interaction.* Princeton, Princeton University Press.

Hammond, John, Ralph Keeney, and Howard Raiffa. 2002. Smart *Choices: A Practical Guide to Making Better Decisions.* New York, Crown Business.

Thaler, Richard and Cass Sunstein. 2009. *Nudge: Improving Decisions about Health, Wealth, and Happiness.* New York, Penguin Books.

3. Marketing

Jeffrey, Mark. 2010. *Data-Driven Marketing: The 15 Metrics Everyone in Marketing Should Know.* New York, Wiley.

Kotler, Philip and Kevin Keller. 2011. *Marketing Management,* 14th edition. New York, Prentice Hall.

Scott, David M. 2011. *The New Rules of Marketing & PR: How to Use Social Media, Online Video, Mobile Applications, Blogs, News Releases, and Viral Marketing to Reach Buyers Directly,* 3rd edition. New York, Wiley.

4. Complex Systems

Boccara, Nino. 2010. *Modeling Complex Systems,* 2nd edition. New York, Springer.

Chu, Dominique, Roger Strand, and Ragnar Fjelland. 2003. "Theories of Complexity." *Complexity* 8(3), 19–30.

Henshaw, Philip. 2010. "Complex Systems." *The Encyclopedia of Earth,* 22 November. http://www.eoearth.org/article/Complex_systems?topic=49492 (accessed 4 June 2012).

Johnson, Neil. 2009. *Simply Complexity: A Clear Guide to Complexity Theory.* London, Oneworld.

Mitchell, Melanie. 2011. *Complexity: A Guided Tour.* New York, Oxford University Press USA.

Solomon, Sorin and Bran Shir. 2003. "Complexity: A Science at 30." *Europhysics News* 34(2), 54–57.

WORKS CITED

Amazon. 2002. Book Description, *The Tipping Point: How Little Things Can Make a Big Difference* [book sale page], 7 January. http://www.amazon.com/The-Tipping-Point-Little-Difference/dp/0316346624/

Bazerman, Max and Don Moore. 2008. *Judgment in Managerial Decision Making.* New York, Wiley.

Bergen, Mark, Shantanu Dutta, and Orville Walker Jr. 1992. "Agency Relationships in Marketing: A Review of Implications and Applications of Agency and Related Theories." *Journal of Marketing* 56(3), 1–24.

Byrne, John and Lindsey Gerdes. 2005. "The Man Who Invented Management: Why Peter Drucker's Ideas Still Matter." *Business Week*, 28 November, 96–106.

Camerer, Colin, George Loewenstein, and Drazen Prelec. 2005. "Neuroeconomics: How Neuroscience Can Inform Economics." *Journal of Economic Literature* 43(1), 9–64.

Christensen, Clayton. 2011. *The Innovator's Dilemma: The Revolutionary Book that Will Change the Way You Do Business.* New York, HarperBusiness.

Day, George. 1994. "The Capabilities of Market-Driven Organizations." *Journal of Marketing* 58(4), 37–52.

Drucker, Peter. 1954. *The Practice of Management.* New York, HarperCollins.

Drucker, Peter. 2005. *Managing the Nonprofit Organization: Principles and Practices*, First Collins Business edition. New York, HarperCollins.

Drucker, Peter. 2007. *Innovation and Entrepreneurship*, 2nd revised edition. New York, Butterworth-Heinemann.

Gladwell, Malcolm. 2002. *The Tipping Point: How Little Things Can Make a Big Difference.* Boston, Back Bay Books.

Glimcher, Paul, Colin Camerer, Russell Poldrack, and Ernst Fehr. 2008. *Neuroeconomics: Decision Making and the Brain.* New York, Academic Press.

Jaworski, Bernard and Ajay Kohli. 1993. "Market Orientation: Antecedents and Consequences." *Journal of Marketing* 57(3), 53–70.

Johnson, Steven. 2002. *Emergence: The Connected Lives of Ants, Brains, Cities, and Software.* New York, Scribner.

Kagel, John and Alvin Roth (editors). 1997. *Handbook of Experimental Economics.* Princeton, Princeton University Press.

Kahneman, David. 2011. *Thinking, Fast and Slow.* New York, Farrar, Straus, and Geroux.

Kahneman, David and Gary Klein. 2009. "Conditions for Intuitive Expertise: A Failure to Disagree," *American Psychologist* 64, 515–526.

Keysar, Boaz, Sayuri Hayakawa, and Sun Gyu An. 2012. "The Foreign Language Effect: Thinking in a Foreign Tongue Reduces Decision Biases." *Psychological Science* 23(6), 661–668.

Kohli, Ajay and Bernard Jaworski. 1990. "Market Orientation: The Construct, Research Propositions, and Managerial Implications." *Journal of Marketing* 54(2), 1–18.

Korver, Clint. 2012. "Applying Decision Analysis to Venture Investing." *Kauffman Fellows Report* 3, 1–12. http://www.kauffmanfellows.org/images/documents/Journal_Vol3/ClintKorver_vol3.pdf.

Masnick, Mike. 2009. "Explaining the Innovator's Dilemma...In Two Minutes With a Whiteboard" [video]. *Say That Again, TechDirt* [blog]. http://www.techdirt.com/articles/20091116/2307256958.shtml (accessed 5 June 2012).

Miller, John and Scott Page. 2007. *Complex Adaptive Systems: An Introduction to Computational Models of Social Life*. Princeton, Princeton University Press.

Narver, John and Stanley Slater. 1990. "The Effect of a Market Orientation on Business Profitability." *Journal of Marketing* 54(4), 20–35.

Narver, John and Stanley Slater. 1995. "Market Orientation and the Learning Organization." *Journal of Marketing* 59(3), 63–74.

Page, Scott. 2010. *Diversity and Complexity*. Princeton, Princeton University Press.

Piatelli-Palmarini, Massimo. 1994. *Inevitable Illusions: How Mistakes of Reason Rule Our Minds*. New York, Wiley

Simon, Herbert. 1956. "Rational Choice and the Structure of the Environment." *Psychological Review* 63(2), 129–138.

Taleb, Nassim Nicholas. 2010. *The Black Swan: The Impact of the Highly Improbable*, 2nd edition. New York, Random House.

Thaler, Richard. 2008. "Mental Accounting and Consumer Choice." *Marketing Science* 27(1), 15–25 [1985].

Tversky, Amos. 1995. "The Psychology of Decision Making." *AIMR Conference Proceedings: Behavioral Finance and Decision Theory in Investment Management* 7, 2–6. doi: 10.2469/cp.v1995.n7.2

Watts, Duncan and Steve Hasker. 2006. "Marketing in an Unpredictable World." *Harvard Business Review* 11(September–October), 25–27.

Webster, Frederick. 1992. "The Changing Role of Marketing in the Corporation."*Journal of Marketing* 56(4), 1–17.

Wells, William. 1993. "Discovery-Oriented Consumer Research." *Journal of Consumer Research* 19(4), 489–504.

ABOUT THE AUTHORS

Dr. Eric Ball is currently Senior VP and Treasurer of Oracle Corporation in California and was named as one of the "100 Most Influential People in Finance" in 2011 by the editors of *CFO* and *Treasury & Risk Management* magazines. His team has raised over $20 billion in acquisition financing for Oracle since 2006. After studying at the University of Michigan and University of Rochester, Eric earned a Ph.D. in management from Claremont's Peter F. Drucker and Masatoshi Ito Graduate School of Management; his research in venture capital has been published in the *Review of Financial Studies*. Eric is also a Kauffman Fellow—a participant in a selective program to groom leaders of the venture capital industry. He has taught at Rochester, Rutgers, and USC's Marshall School of Business; has worked at Fortune 500 companies including AT&T, Avery Dennison, Cisco Systems, and Flextronics; and serves on multiple corporate and nonprofit boards. He lives in Menlo Park, CA with his wife, Sheryl Axline, and their two sons Spencer and Carter.

Dr. Joseph LiPuma has more than 25 years of business experience, much of it in information technology consulting in the United States, Europe, and the Middle East. He currently serves as associate professor and director of the international MBA program at EMLYON Business School in France. He has started businesses in the United States, United Kingdom, Italy, and Saudi Arabia and has held executive management and board-level roles at small- and medium-sized companies including Synetics Corporation, Tessera Enterprise Systems, and iXL. Joseph holds an MBA from SUNY Buffalo and a DBA in strategy and policy from Boston University; he has taught at both of these schools, as well as at Drexel University and St. Joseph's University. His research centers on international entrepreneurship, and he has been published in leading academic journals including the *International Entrepreneurship and Management Journal*, *Frontiers of Entrepreneurship Research*, *Journal of Business Research*, and *Small Business Economics*. He lives in Lyon, France with his wife, Mary Roark, and their two sons Lucca and Ercole.